Advertising

Copywriting

SEVENTH EDITION

Advertising Copywriting

Philip Ward Burton

NTC Business Books
a division of NTC/CONTEMPORARY PUBLISHING GROUP
Lincolnwood, Illinois USA

Library of Congress Cataloging-in-Publication Data

Burton, Philip Ward
   Advertising copywriting / Philip Ward Burton. -- 7th ed.
    p. cm.
   Includes index.
   1. Advertising copy. I. Title.
HF5825.B8 1996   96-21090
659.13′2 -- dc20   CIP

Acquisitions Editor: Lynn Mooney
Cover and Interior Design: Jeanette Wojityla
Production Manager: Margo Goia
Production Coordination: Denise Duffy-Fieldman
Compostition: Precision Typographers, Inc.

Published by NTC Business Books, a division of NTC Publishing Group.
© 1999, 1990 by NTC Publishing Group, 4255 West Touhy Avenue,
Lincolnwood (Chicago), Illinois 60646-1975 U.S.A.
All rights reserved. No part of this book may be reproduced, stored
in a retrieval system, or transmitted in any form or by any means,
electronic, mechanical, photocopying, recording or otherwise, without
the prior permission of the publisher.
Manufactured in the United States of America.

890 QB 0987654321

Contents

Contents   **vii**

Contents

Foreword

Philip Burton has the tough job. He has to keep track of the myriad changes of advertising since his previous edition. I have the easy job. I read them, ask myself, How does he do it? And then I let you know, He did it. He's made comprehensive changes in chapters covering advertising art, marketing, fashion, direct response, television, advertising law, and research. So you can stay up-to-date on all the important developments.

Some parts of this book should not change. They're as pertinent today as they were five years ago, and five years before that, and back to the First Edition, for which Leo Burnett wrote the Foreword. These, I must admit, are my favorite parts, for this is Burton at his best. As explanation, I offer up something I said five years ago. I'm glad to say it again.

Advertising Copywriting has always remained within arm's-reach of my typewriter. There's Mr. Roget. Mr. Webster. And Mr. Burton. These three gentlemen have kept me out of trouble for years. And although Mr. Webster and Mr. Roget never asked to write forewords for their books, Mr. Burton did. And of the three, he's the one I owe the most.

Through his book, I can relive my career, chapter by chapter. When I got my first job writing about the glamorous world of potato blight, I reread the pages on agricultural advertising. When I "moved up" to write about rebuilt washer transmissions, I reached for Burton's thinking on trade advertising. And when I finally walked into an agency that was doing 90 percent TV, I closed my office door and became an instant expert on television terms.

This is a college book that serves long, long after college. A book so broad that it gives a working knowledge of every aspect of copywriting. So focused that it gives details on structure and timing. A book that's as big as a 50-year campaign and as small as a 10-second spot.

I have carefully avoided calling *Advertising Copywriting* a textbook, though it is what I consider the most definitive text on copywriting. And it is certainly a book. To put those two words together implies that the reading is going to be tedious and stuffy. I referred to the "coffee factor" when I was in school. How many cups does it take to get through a chapter of a textbook?

Happily, here the answer is zero. Each chapter begins with a scenario of advertising people in action. It's involving. It's fun. It reads like a story. Like any great copywriter, Mr. Burton has you "hooked" before you know it. And he never lets you down. The facts are presented in a style that's lively and lucid. All in all, this book is just plain good reading.

The Sixth Edition has changed many ways from the Fifth. The chapters on television, research, fashion, law, and direct response advertising have undergone major revisions to keep the reader current. The illustrations, storyboards, and photos have all been updated, reflecting some of the best advertising out there.

The good news is that much of the book is unchanged. This spanking new Seventh Edition holds the same time-tested advertising principles that are found in my frayed and tired Fourth Edition. A solid foundation of learning provided by a man who knows how to teach. A man who knows how to turn students into professionals.

A man who introduced me to advertising. So hold the phone, Mr. Webster. Save the telex, Mr. Roget. This foreword belongs to Mr. Burton. You opened up new words. He opened up new worlds.

Mary Beth Reed
Vice-President and
Associate Creative Director
Leo Burnett, Inc.

Preface

Each new edition of a book must offer new material or it's pointless to buy the new edition. Let's start out, therefore, by mentioning some of the changes you'll find in the Seventh Edition of *Advertising Copywriting*.

Computers. It is amazing that in the short interval between the Sixth Edition and the Seventh Edition, computers have been able to effect such changes in advertising. Most affected are those working in advertising agency art departments, which have been transformed, one might say, into self-sufficient production houses. The computer has also significantly affected the way copywriters work with art directors.

Emphasis on campaigns. Because it has seemed important to recognize that in national advertising—and in some local advertising—creative people should be thinking in long-range terms, this new edition includes 20 examples of campaigns for products and services. These are scattered throughout the book so the point won't be overlooked. In each case, the reader sees how the campaign idea and look have been carried out in successive print advertisements or commercials. The point is that the creative person should learn to think beyond one advertisement. In the Seventh Edition there are examples of campaigns used in business, the professions, agriculture, and heavy industry both in print and the broadcast media.

Advertising Council. Even among many in advertising, the great work of the Advertising Council is not given its due, and this, of course, is even more true in the general public. Accordingly, Advertising Council advertisements are found throughout the book not only because of a strong belief that the work of the Council should be recognized but also because it's good creative work that offers instructive examples to anyone in copywriting.

Marketing and marketing planning. Attention is paid in these chapters to the emergence of the "baby boomers" as a market force in the aging population, the implications of the graying population in general, ethnic considerations generated by the explosion of non-English-speaking numbers, and ways to achieve and hold on to brand identity in a period of increased competition from lower-cost products that lack brand recognition.

Direct response. With direct response marketing enjoying a boom, increased attention is paid to it in the two chapters on the subject. One addition, for example, is a discussion of small-space advertising for the direct response marketer.

Fashion advertising. Increased attention is given in this chapter to the selling of clothing to the fashion-conscious male, and to the emergence of the "casual look" in clothing for men and women.

Chapter on advertising art. As said in the beginning of this preface, the computer has transformed art departments and the way copywriters interact with art directors. There are, consequently, many changes in this chapter.

Legal. It seems reasonably safe to say that no other book in advertising (unless it is a book wholly devoted to advertising and marketing law) does a more thorough treatment of the subject. This is largely due to a revamping based on numerous suggestions and comments offered by a specialist in the field who has a national reputation in the subject.

Illustrations. With a few exceptions here and there, the illustrations are new. The exceptions are illustrations that are especially appropriate and that are timeless in their message. You may notice that the captions for illustrations are far more than mere labels. In almost all cases they explain the illustration and the principle(s) that it exemplifies.

Beginnings and endings. To give the new edition a fresh look, all chapter beginnings and endings have been changed. And part of this new look is in the subheads, the vast majority of which have been changed and, it is hoped, improved.

Yes, there are some changes in every chapter, many major, but some chapters have been changed only slightly. Such chapters are concerned with unchanging fundamentals. For instance, human appeals haven't changed, nor will they. These human appeals are reflected in copy and artwork today, just as they were in the past. Accordingly, because these fundmentals don't change, you'll find that only slight modifications have been made in sections that discuss headlines, body copy, and illustration material.

Even in the chapter on advertising art—the most drastically changed chapter in the Seventh Edition—the changes are in the application of computer techniques, not in time-tested, appealing subject matter.

As one looks back at the advertising of yesteryear, the most noticeable differences in today's advertising are the superior printing and artwork. Also, current writing is more polished and is freer of copy that is blatantly dishonest or ludicrously exaggerated, as in the claim of a cigarette company that trumpeted, "Not a cough in a carload," or another that urged, "Reach for a Lucky instead of a sweet."

Despite the obvious refinements in today's illustrations and most copy, today's advertising is different but the same. What appealed to, and sold, prospects in the past continues to do so today. These timeless truths are evident in a number of chapters that have not been changed simply for the sake of change.

What was viable in the First Edition, and in succeeding editions, is viable in the Seventh Edition. When human nature changes, then advertising will change profoundly. Until then, in advertising and in this book, we stick with what we know reaches out to our audience.

Acknowledgments

Special thanks to:

Stephen R. Bergerson, J.D., of Kinney & Lange. When called upon to update the chapter on advertising law, Mr. Bergerson contributed so much that was new and needed that I was astounded and grateful. In the Seventh Edition his contribution has been even more extensive, and the result is a chapter that stands now as an invaluable guide to the subject. This has been, you might say, a pro bono contribution, because Mr. Bergerson did all of this work simply because he has devoted a lifetime to raising the legal standards and level of honesty in advertising. A practicing attorney and prolific writer, Mr. Bergerson has contributed mightily to the field and is a widely respected authority in laws pertinent to advertising, marketing, and communications.

Sam Bregande, Executive Creative Director, Latorra, Paul & McCann, Inc. Advertising, who made significant contributions to the chapter on advertising art. With his extensive background in creative management, writing, and production, he was able to introduce fresh viewpoints, especially in explaining the changes computers have made in advertising agency art departments.

Andrew J. Byrne, President, Andrew J. Byrne, Inc., for advice that strengthened the chapters on direct response. To give this advice, he drew upon a long and diversified background in direct marketing in the U.S. and a number of European countries. In addition to his years in important management positions, he is a prolific writer on the subject. Because Mr. Byrne has a deep background in phases of advertising other than direct response marketing, I have used some of his written thoughts in other chapters as well.

Scott Purvis, President of Gallup & Robinson, Inc. Mr. Purvis, who heads a leading and respected firm in advertising and marketing research, went over the Seventh Edition research chapter line by line, updating here and eliminating there. To do this personally, despite his important executive duties, calls for special recognition. Mr. Purvis takes a strong interest in raising the standards of advertising research, and the chapter reflects this concern.

Mary Beth Reed, Vice-President and Associate Creative Director, Leo Burnett, Inc. Her review of the two television chapters in the Sixth Edition was so helpful that I called upon her once again in the Seventh Edition. Her prize-winning work at the Burnett agency is almost totally involved with fashioning creative television commercials for important advertisers, and she brought to Burnett similar high-level experience with other leading advertising agencies. In reviewing material for the television chapters in the Seventh Edition, she updated and pruned, so that each chapter now has a fresh look in key areas. It is comforting to know that she has cast a critical eye on these two important chapters.

Eugene Sekeres, Professor, Youngstown State University, who furnished much current material on infomercials. This topic, which is of ever-growing importance, is one that has engaged his interest to such an extent that he was able to provide valuable guidance during the preparation of this new chapter.

And here are names of people and firms who have contributed in one way or another. It's depressing to contemplate what I might have done without their cooperation. Naturally, I'm deeply grateful to them: Arthritis Foundation; F. C. Baker, CMF&Z (a Young & Rubicam affiliate); Eric Ball, Goodyear Tire & Rubber, Inc.; Dave Ballard, Sew-Eurodrive; Stephen Bautista, Pagano, Schenck & Kay; Rick Binkley, Yellow Freight System; Black & Decker; Robert H. Bogacz, Creative Resources, Inc.; Gina Bowman, Target Base Marketing; Adam M. Bree, Outdoor Advertising Association of America; Ellen Brett, Pfizer, Inc.; Darryl Brown, Miller Brooks, Inc.; Joseph E. Brumley, The J. Peterman Company; Reed Bunzel, Radio Advertising Bureau; Allan Burns, Royal Products; Lourdes Caballero, Hartzell Fan, Inc.; Joseph Caminiti, Roper Starch Worldwide, Inc.; Heidi Christensen, Franklin Templeton Group; Courtney Claar, North American Watch Company; Mary Clemens, Trifid Corporation; Shari Clubine, Park Outdoor Advertising of New York; John Coll, Gardner Geary Coll & Young; R. Luther Conant, Conant Financial Services, Inc.; Bailey L. Condrey, Jr., American Plastics Council; Ellen Conn, Black & Decker Corporation; Judy Connatser, Neiman Marcus; Lynne Cook, Dentsply Inplant; Cynthia Corso, Ogilvy & Mather; M.P. Delaney, Bank of America; Maria L. Delton, Leo Burnett, Inc.; Kwame DeRoche, Eric

Mower & Associates, Inc.; Sal Devito, Devito/Verdi Advertising; Erica Epstein, New Era Optical Company; Amy Evans, Hallmark Cards, Inc.; Ray E. Evans, Farm Journal Publishing; Shane Farris, Radio Advertising Bureau; Vicki Franklin, University of Kentucky; Betty Fried, SAS Institute, Inc.; Leo Garfinkel, Lowe & Partners; James Girard, Fiske Brothers Refining Company; Ted Goeglein, Abelson-Taylor, Inc.; Robin C. Gorneau, Systems Y Computer Technology; Sally Gralla, Eden Foods, Inc.; JoAnn B. Greenup, Sew-Eurodrive; David Griffin, Young & Rubicam New York; Veronica M. Gutierrez, Trickle Up Program; Michelle G. Hanna, National Pork Producers Council; M. H. Hardiman, Brintons, Ltd.; Vincent J. Heindenreich, Bayer Corporation; Ann Higbee, Eric Mower & Associates, Inc.; Mark Higdon, Cranfill & Company; William G. Hillsman, North Woods Advertising; Kaki Hinton, Warner Lambert Company; Mark Homchick, Kawasaki Motors Corporation U.S.A.; Carol N. Holmelund, Parke-Davis; Jennifer Howe, Fairbanks Scales; Ken Howie, Morton Buildings, Inc.; Robert L. Ibsen, Den-Mat Corporation; Dan L. Imler, Tension Envelope Corporation; William Johnson, William Johnson Advertising, Inc.; Dominique B. Kahn, Lowe & Partners; Allen Kay, Korey Kay & Partners; Robert Koren, National Switchgear Systems, Inc.; Scott Krahn, Birdsall Voss & Kloppenburg; Susan Krause, Northwestern Mutual Life; Scott Langmack, Wilson Sporting Goods, Inc.; Sylvia Lauer, *Plant Engineering*; Victor Lipman, Massachusetts Mutual Life Insurance Company; Trey Little, Sunbelt Transformer; Terry Lohmann, Sandoz Gro, Inc.; Claudia Mancini, Educational Assistance, Inc.; Jo Mattern, *Fortune* Magazine; Joseph R. Miller, Air Hydraulics, Inc.; Yvonne Mink, Gardner Geary Coll & Young; Marilyn Mock, Copper Development Association; Patricia A. Murtaugh, L. L. Bean; John Nagy, Sive/Young & Rubicam Advertising Agency; Stephen Neale, Abelson Taylor, Inc.; H. Peete Petersen, Modern Application News; David Pritchard, Penn Advertising; Scott C. Purvis, Gallup & Robinson, Inc.; Phillips Ramsey, Phillips Ramsey Advertising; Mary Beth Reed, Leo Burnett, Inc.; Jay Rendon, Haggar Clothing Company; Dave Robinson, Graphic Persuasion, Inc.; Richard L. Rogers, Sr., Readex, Inc.; John Rose, Friedman & Rose; M.E. G. Roy, Coopers & Lybrand; Elizabeth A. Schama, Land Rover of North America; David W. Schmid, Dekalb Genetics Corporation; Mary Ann Schur, American Cyanamid Company; Steve Scott, Federal-Mogul Corporation; Eugene Sekeres, Youngstown State University; William C. Selover, USL Capital; Michael G. Snell, ICI Seeds; Eddie Snyder, Fitzgerald & Company; Harry Somerdyk, Business Week; Leo Spellman, Steinway & Sons; Ron Stanley, Phillips Petroleum Corporation; Tammy Stastny, Neogard Company; Charles H. Teeter, Anderson Consulting LLP; Rebecca L. Teets, Tucker Wayne/Luckie & Co.; Maria Tenaglia, The Advertising Council, Inc.; John W. Van Zanten, Optical Products, Corning Incorporated; C. Vasselin, Polaroid Corporation; Alexis B. Waters, American Physical Therapy Association; Vicki Wells, Oscar Mayer Company; Russell W. Whitacre, Oscar Mayer Company; Nancy J. Wiese, Xerox Corporation; Don C. Williams, Don C. Williams Advertising, Inc.; Jack D. Wolf, Targetbase Marketing; Peg Wright, Miller Brooks, Inc.; Matt Zarbaugh, The Richards Group.

Copywriting

What You Can Expect to Learn By Reading a Book about It

You'll find it's a *Yes* and *No* situation.

Yes—you can learn to distinguish good copy from bad copy. You will learn the dos and don'ts that can save you time and trouble on the job.

Yes—you can learn the terminology of the field of copywriting and of advertising.

Yes—you can learn what motivates people to buy and what types of appeals to use.

Yes—you can learn the technical requirements that are peculiar to the different media so that you can proceed confidently whether you're writing a 10-second television commercial, a 4-color magazine spread, or a 24-sheet outdoor poster.

Yes—you can learn the special requirements of the different forms of advertising, such as retail, mail order, industrial, professional, trade, and others.

Yes—you can learn what a copywriter must know about research and law and how a copywriter can write copy that is in keeping with the tenets of consumerism, yet can sell efficiently for the advertiser.

Yes—you can learn how a copywriter cooperates with, and learns from, artists and production people.

—but—

No—you cannot learn from a book the ability to come up with an inspirational idea that forms the basis of an outstanding campaign or a memorable, award-winning advertisement. Some people have a heaven-sent ability to think creatively and originally. They have this, book or no book. A copywriter can be trained, but there are some who are naturals. They are born with the ability to spark original ideas, just as there are artists, poets, and musicians whose talent shines through almost from birth.

No—you cannot learn from this, or any book, how to write first-draft copy speedily and under pressure. This skill is learned on the job and is developed from constant practice.

A book on copywriting can point you in the right direction. It can give you a helping hand in a course in advertising copywriting, and it can help you significantly during those first days on the job. It can help you even after you've had working experience, because all writers need to go back to the fundamentals occasionally.

There may be moments when you experience doubt and insecurity. Perhaps this book can help you get through such moments. If it does, it will have justified itself.

CHAPTER 1

Copywriting
An Exciting Blend of Creativity, Common Sense, and Hard Work

It's Saturday morning. No, you're not on the golf course or heading for the beach. You're at the office looking at the word processor monitor, as if by staring at it hard enough a brilliant creative idea might pop out. As a copywriter, you're always looking for that "big" idea, and you're used to working at odd hours and on occasional weekends. But you don't mind, because once you get your idea and your fingers start hitting the keys, you relish the challenge. You enjoy what you're doing, so who needs golf or the beach? Not you. Not all the time, anyway. You are a copywriter. You have a job that's actually fun, one that is a mixture of creativity, common sense, and hard work. You're willing to trade a few hours on the links or at the beach for the satisfying flow of ideas and words that wells up from inside of you.

For most workers on a factory assembly line, the hours go slowly as they repeat what they're doing, time after time, hour after hour. Clock watching is a way of life. Not so with copywriting. Each writing assignment is different, and each has its individual approach.

Most copywriters will tell you that the only clock watching occurs when they glance at their watches and exclaim, Ye gads, it's 5 o'clock already! As the saying goes, Time flies when you're having fun.

Of course, you don't *always* enjoy working overtime and on weekends (and there *can* be plenty of that), and there are some assignments you enjoy more than others. Also, if you're not a fast writer, the pressure of turning copy out in a hurry might make you jittery. Still, despite these qualifications, copywriting is a fulfilling, highly satisfying job.

You Need More than Mere Writing Ability

The duties of a copywriter, although practically unknown to most persons, do not discourage advertising aspirants. Persons who might, for example, question their ability to do satisfactory work in the research department or the media department of a company will apply very confidently for a copywriter's position. Without advertising knowledge or experience, applicants will try unhesitatingly to enter this tough, competitive field. When their applications are received indifferently or without too much serious consideration, the applicants are hurt and amazed.

Just what is there about copywriting that makes it seem easy and desirable? The answer is that there is almost 100 percent ignorance among nonadvertising folk of just what copywriters are supposed to do—and what they get paid for doing it. They have no comprehension of the hard work and supplementary knowledge that must accompany a copywriter's expected ability in writing.

Advertising managers, like newspaper editors, are continually squashing the hopes of applicants who have little else in their personal sales kit than an alleged flair for writing. Because of letter-writing ability or a succession of A's on high school or college themes, the youthful men and women of self-asserted literary merit feel that writing advertising or newspaper copy is merely an extension of the writing they have already done.

People think they can write because everyone has to write at one time or another. How many times have you looked at an advertisement and said to yourself, And they call that copywriting! Why didn't they do it this way? The world is filled with people who feel they could do a better job of writing advertisements than the persons who make their living as copywriters. Under the delusion that they "could do it better," the uninitiated approach the copywriting field eagerly and confidently.

Much More than Spewing Out Slogans

Most people in the general public have only the vaguest idea of a copywriter's work, and some of these ideas have been colored by exaggerations of motion pictures and trashy novels that "tell the truth" about the advertising business.

The idea that the usual copywriter is a glib "sloganeer," is very deep-rooted. A sizable portion of the public, including many businesspeople who should know better, think of copywriting in terms of writing clever slogans. Such persons, wanting to enter the advertising and the copywriting field, believe that they can "turn out slogans." The fact that "99 and-44/100% pure," "Say it with flowers," and others have become a part of the American vernacular has helped create the illusion that copywriting is basically slogan writing.

Newswriting versus Copywriting— Similarities and Differences

Reporting and copywriting demand ability, knowledge, and experience far beyond a surface facility in writing. Requirements for the two occupations are similar in some points. In both, for instance, it is vital to understand people and to use that understanding in the fashioning of lucid material.

A copywriter, like a reporter, must be analytical, observant, and thorough. Each has specialized knowledge for the work. Where, for example, the aspiring reporter might find it advantageous to obtain a background in political science and labor economics, the future copywriter might acquire a knowledge of sociology and mass psychology.

Before you sit down at the keyboard, you should have a background of business experience that enables you to write copy intelligently and competently. The knowledge of selling, of merchandise, or of general business procedure gained from this experience gives you confidence.

The copywriter adds another element to writing that is not present in the news story—the element of persuasion. Whereas the reporter gives the facts without embellishment, the copywriter, while also giving facts, must add words and sentences that will cause readers to take action.

A journalism school, granted normal intelligence and aptitude on the part of the student, can teach the student the newswriting formulas. Having mastered the rather stylized forms of newswriting, the intelligent journalism school graduate can do a creditable beginning job for most newspapers.

Copywriting is less precise than newswriting, and it is less amenable to "formula" writing. Take the writing of

Figure 1–1. Long-range institutional-advertisement campaign. Such advertising like this Phillips example has been described as appealing to the mind instead of the pocketbook. It is concerned with issues—often abstract—that are of concern to the public as a whole, not with the outright sale of a product. In following chapters you will find other *Phillips Petroleum Company* advertisements that exemplify the best in such advertising. Emphasis in this series of advertisements is on environmental concerns and the company's involvement with those concerns. Another term for this kind of advertising is "corporate" advertising.

crime stories. Reporters who have worked a police beat have developed a format for crime stories. Depending on their ability, they can work within this format, but they essentially follow a definite writing pattern. Their work is made easier and faster if they follow the pattern.

You have no such formula to help you in copywriting. You cannot use any mechanical style of writing as a crutch to make your job easier. Each advertisement is custom built to time or space requirements and to the product. Words must create a mood, an excitement, and a desire for the goods or services. A mere recital of facts is not enough. Copy must sell as well as tell. As anyone knows who has done face-to-face selling, persuading a reluctant prospect to a course of action can be difficult. Yet this is what the copywriter must do in advertisements.

To sum up, copywriting, like reporting, demands much more than facility with words. Whether it is more difficult to become a good copywriter than a good reporter is debatable, but there is no debating the assertion that copywriting calls for hard and extensive preparatory work.

If you want her to have a shot at reaching the stars, she needs to get her baby shots now.

Every child deserves the best opportunities life has to offer. Especially yours.

The odds of her becoming an astronaut and reaching the stars are out of this world. But the chances are more than 1 in 4 that your baby isn't protected against childhood diseases like polio, measles, chicken pox, tetanus and others.

So, even if you're sure your child is up to date and on schedule with her baby shots, ask your doctor at every visit. It couldn't hurt.

In fact, it could give her the chance to grow up to be whatever she wants to be. Even if it's something out of this world.

Even if you're sure, ask again.
1-800-232-2522

Figure 1–2. Public service advertisement. Some of the most interesting and most worthy advertising is supplied through the Advertising Council, drawing upon advertising agencies for free creative work, advertising media for donations of time and space, and corporate sponsors through the Association of National Advertisers. Hundreds of millions of dollars are spent on advertising that promotes a myriad of causes such as child abuse, fire prevention, recycling, etc. Because of the importance of the Advertising Council and its excellent advertising, examples of its public service advertising are found throughout this book.

Courtesy of the Advertising Council.

No Public Acclaim for Your Copy

Although copywriters may write top-flight copy and develop slogans, trade names, and descriptive phrases that become a part of the nation's idiom, they may never be identified with their work. Copywriters are anonymous. They are among the thousands who do their jobs day after day—efficiently and unknown. Here again the copywriter is removed from the class of the artiste.

Not for the copywriter is the acclaim of the byline newspaper reporter or of the motion picture scenario writer. If the only satisfaction you get out of writing is the glow you feel when people talk about your work, then copywriting will give you only limited satisfaction. The only people who will know what you have written are those who are associated with you in business. As a copywriter,

you are just another salesperson peddling merchandise and ideas.

Temperamental? You're in the Wrong Field

Purple drapes, a cathedral-like hush, and sweet violin music playing softly in the background—these were provided (the story goes) to create the right mood for one temperamental advertising agency copywriter in the fabulous 1920s.

During this period, when advertising billings were beginning to zoom, copywriters could do no wrong. If they wanted mood background, the indulgent advertisers let them have it. The copywriter was a favorite actor in a dizzy drama of lush profits.

Today's copywriters are less likely to be coddled than the copywriters who worked during the period from the end of World War I until the 1929 crash. At that time, copywriters were credited with the sensitivity of any other "artiste." They were littérateures who condescended to work at the prosaic job of selling soap, automobiles, and washing machines.

When the crash came, advertising emerged from the golden haze. The era of advertising research began. Advertising became a serious, painstaking business instead of a madcap adventure. Copywriters pulled down the purple drapes and looked out soberly upon the smoky city below. They were no longer artists with special temperamental rights, they were businesspeople.

Admittedly, not all copywriters have given up the idea that they are apart from the ordinary businesspeople. Generally, however, most of today's copywriters think of themselves as businesspeople—not artists.

Pay Scales for Copywriters Are Often Exaggerated

Salaries for copywriters are generally thought to be much higher than they are. Although top agency copywriters draw very high pay, many beginning copywriters start with salaries lower than those paid in less demanding jobs.

Skill, however, is rewarded as well in copywriting as it is in any other business activity. Some advertising agency copy chiefs, to illustrate, are paid huge salaries, but for every high-salaried person, there are hundreds of copywriters who earn modest salaries. The high salaries paid to relatively few copywriters have, unfortunately, been so widely publicized that the beginner has been led to believe that all copywriters are paid bountifully.

If you are able to check the salaries paid to copywriters in the different kinds of advertising activity—retail, agency, newspaper, business concerns, and radio—you will soon discover that such copywriters are paid no better and no worse than persons of comparable skill in most other fields of business activity. A few make the top-bracket figures—most make average salaries.

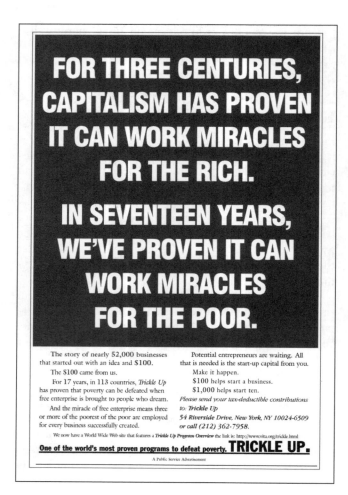

Figure 1–3. Advertisement that works for social good. Advertising has lent itself to many enterprises besides the selling of goods and services. Designed and written on a pro bono basis by McCann Erickson Worldwide, this advertisement carries an important and powerful message. Incidentally, the editorial format of this advertisement characteristically obtains high readership.

Rush! Rush! Rush!

Like the newspaper reporter, copywriters are hounded by deadlines. If they are nervous types, they will find the work taxing. Day after day, month after month, they will be hurried, always conscious of publishing or broadcasting dates. What field of advertising is most trying on the nerves of the copywriter? It is difficult to say.

The retail field, in which the artists, copywriters, and production people are just a step ahead of the publishing date, is full of worry for persons who like to do thoughtful, careful work. As one retail copywriter said, "There's an empty feeling in turning out copy this way. I'm always haunted by the consciousness that this hurried, rush-rush work is not my best work. I'd like to work in an agency where the deadlines are farther apart."

Retail copywriters typically sigh for the green fields of agency copywriting. Agency copywriters are envied. But

what is the situation with the agency copywriter? Is the job relatively easy? Actually, they voice almost exactly the same complaint heard from the retail copywriters. True, their deadlines are not usually daily deadlines, but agency copywriters are seemingly always behind the schedule. Then, there is always the unexpected presentation, the new account, or the quick revision. All these call for hurry-up writing dashed off to the accompaniment of the impatient jigging of the copy chiefs or clients waiting for the copywriter to get through.

Copywriting provides little quiet, leisurely writing. The copywriter is a businessperson who writes under hard-driving business conditions for other businesspeople who have no time for creative temperament. Copywriters must produce work—good work—quickly, or out they go.

Still, many successful copywriters feel that they do their very best work when under extreme pressure. Like athletes, you may often find inspiration when circumstances force you to do the "impossible." If you're the type who can enjoy being pushed, you will find the pressure stimulating.

Your Hours and Working Conditions May Be Odd

The drain on the copywriter's creative talent is considerable. Whereas a successful magazine writer might make a good living turning out a few articles or stories a year and have a chance to rest up between efforts, copywriters must turn out a quantity of good writing daily. Each day they search for new ways to write headlines, body copy, commercials, and direct-mail pieces.

If you, as a copywriter, are assigned miscellaneous accounts, you must adjust yourself rapidly to each new product. You are expected to give a fresh twist to your copy in order to satisfy the probing and skeptical examination by executives of the client company. Such quantity writing puts a great strain on your freshness and originality.

The working hours of copywriters are likely to be irregular. When an emergency arises (and emergencies are always arising), you are expected to stay on the job day and night until your part of the work is done. Overtime is a part of creative work. Then, too, as a conscientious copywriter, you are likely to take your work with you wherever you go.

As you walk down the street, you may see new uses for the products about which you write copy. You jot down the ideas before they escape you. At night, you squirm in your bed, musing over a new approach for a current campaign. Finally, unable to get back to sleep, you snap on the light, sketch the idea, and wait impatiently for morning so that you may give your sizzler the test of daylight examination.

The combination of irregular hours and work that creates nervous tension makes good health an important requisite for copywriters. Obviously, you don't need the muscles of a Samson, but if you can bounce out each day fresh and vigorous, all the better. Health and an ability to take each new assignment as it comes are important in the profession.

What Will You Like about the Job?

You've read about some of the negatives. What about the agreeable sides to the life of a copywriter? If you can stand the pace, you'll truly enjoy what you're doing. You may grumble, threaten to quit, or fight with the boss, but you know it would be difficult to find another job that you'd like as well.

The lure of the copywriter's job is a compound of various factors. Some of these factors mean more to one person than to another. You, for example, might experience a never-ending thrill in the creative side of the work. Seeing your copy in *Reader's Digest* or the *New Yorker* or your commercial over a national network—these moments are your bonus for the hours of word hammering.

Reading your words in print is a satisfaction whether they appear in a country weekly, a huge metropolitan daily, or a national magazine. Although much of the copywriter's work is mere common sense put into selling words, some efforts fall into the classification of sheer creativeness. Such work is a joy to perform; it is never routine and it is always satisfying.

Feeling Useful Is a Reward

Copywriters might derive satisfaction from the important part they have in the movement of goods. They realize that all the manufacturing skill and marketing genius behind a product are wasted unless their words convince the customers to buy the product. To these copywriters comes a sense of usefulness in the business picture, the feeling that they are "movers of goods."

This feeling of being useful is vital to the copywriter. Your work is better if you can feel that it is of service in the social and economic sense. Admittedly, the utility of many products is so questionable that you feel no glow in having written the copy that makes the goods move from the producer to the consumer.

On the other hand, if the product is beneficial to the user, you are gratified that you can inform users about the product and that you can cause them to buy it. One of your real pleasures is to see the sales curve rise as a result of a successful advertisement or series of advertisements. You soon discover that if your copy doesn't sell, it represents so much wasted effort. The successful copywriter and the sales department are never far apart.

If you feel that you are part of business, if you see your work as contributing to the marketing pattern, you are likely to be a better copywriter. You then see the marketing pattern as it is concerned with the product research and sales plans behind the goods advertised. You include in your working knapsack some knowledge of the manufacturing difficulties and even the legal aspects, such as the patent rights, trademark details, and regulations, affecting the distribution of the products about which you write.

Think of Yourself as a Merchant

You are aware, too, of the many things that happen after you have punched out copy. You know that untruths or careless wording may cause trouble with such groups as the Federal Trade Commission, the Better Business Bureau, or the Food and Drug Administration. Possibly, your words might cause consumer "kickback" which will make the sales department storm and ask angrily, "Who wrote this?"

Copy, you realize, is a sharp-edged business tool that is part of the marketing process involving you, salespeople, wholesalers, retailers, consumers, manufacturers, research people, and all others engaged in business. You have an obligation to all of these individuals and especially to the consumers, who, like you, are entitled to honest, competently written copy so that they may make the best possible use of their money when they purchase goods.

In a sense, you must also look upon yourself as a merchant who has goods to sell. Your words either take the place of salespeople or they make the salesperson's job more productive by acting as the door opener. They tell the truth about the goods, but they tell the truth persuasively—so much so that the reader is given a reason to buy. Again, you must, above all, become a part of the vital business of moving goods.

Get Out of That Chair and Mix with People

The feeling of being a "merchant" must be especially strong in the department store copywriter. True, some of these writers merely sit passively in their tiny advertising department offices. By preference, these "sitters" deal with goods—not with people, and not with the big, dynamic selling process of modern retailing. They become wrapped up in their task of writing words—countless words—about merchandise. Such copywriters are not businesspeople/writers. They have the writer's viewpoint only. It is not enough.

The good retail copywriter must be a part of the retail business. If you write newspaper advertisements for an aggressive department store, you have the privilege of learning merchandising in its most vigorous form. Some of the best copy in any business activity is turned out daily at such stores.

Do the men or women copywriters turning out these words learn to do so by spinning them out in their offices, far removed from the bargain hunters in the basement? No! These writers become a part of the business scene. They get out of their offices and into the store.

They talk to buyers. From them these writers can learn merchandising fashions, trade talk, prices, and customer likes and dislikes. The topnotch retail copywriters also learn the jobs of other people in the store. The salespeople, in direct contact with the customers, can provide much grist for copy.

A personal service shopper can be pumped for comments made by customers. In the retail trade, the learning of all the functions and services of a department store is known as acquiring the "whole store" viewpoint. The acquisition of such a viewpoint by you, the retail copywriter, is a part of your training as a businessperson and, hence, a better copywriter.

Copywriters Will Always Be Needed

If you have become a good copywriter, you will derive satisfaction from your standing in the business community and in the firm for which you work. Although it has been pointed out that good copywriters are not coddled as artists, they are definitely treated with respect as important working professionals.

If you are in an agency, you are one of a relatively small group of specialists. To picture this, assume that XYZ agency has lined up a new account through the work of its new-business person. The account executive who is to service the account has been approved. The agency's financial stability and business integrity have been found satisfactory by the client.

Despite the foregoing—the fast-talking and persuasive new-business person, the charming and efficient account executive, and the firm's unquestioned integrity—all these will mean nothing if the agency cannot, through you, furnish good selling copy. Copy is a last and very important link in the manufacturer—agency—consumer chain. As the welder of the link, you are an important person. The final responsibility is yours.

A retail copywriter has the same sort of prestige. The men and women who write the copy for Ohrbach's, Wanamaker's, Lord & Taylor's, and Bloomingdale's are solidly established in the business community. In addition to having developed the ability to write selling copy, they have stored in their brains valuable knowledge about products, merchandising, and other general business facts.

So long as advertising is used in the mass distribution of goods, there will be need for skilled copywriters, especially in retail advertising—the biggest field of all. Mediocrity in copywriting brings the usual reward of mediocrity. Skill in the profession enables you to name your ticket in the advertising world.

Conclusions to Consider

1. Copywriters are primarily business people. You're a writer. But never forget that you're also a businessperson.

Figure 1–4. Human interest approach. This ad, one in a series, stresses human interest allied with persuasive copy. Each advertisement uses the same headline and sells the company rather than an individual insurance policy. Strong illustrations such as this one make the advertisements stand out.

You're expected to know how to write, but you must remember that your writing is a tool of business, not a stepladder to literary prominence. If copywriting ability were easy to acquire, there would be no need for this book, for advertising copy courses, or for the slow apprentice system so often found in agencies and retail stores—nor would copywriters be paid so well. But copywriting is not easy to learn. It's an exacting craft that a very few learn easily and that the great majority learn through trial and error, perseverance, and instruction. Some never learn it.

2. Some copywriters can write any kind of copy. Some can't. It's sometimes hard to switch from one type of copy to another.

Competent copywriters can usually write all kinds of copy. For example, because they handle diversified accounts, agency copywriters often attain proficiency in almost every type and style of copy. The fact remains, however, that a person who has done nothing but radio or television copy has learned different techniques than the copy person who has created only magazine or newspaper copy. The retail writer who began in depart

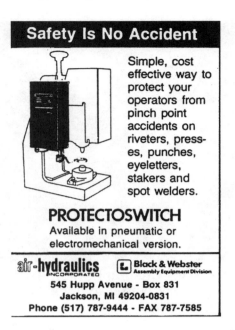

Figure 1–5. Small-space advertisement in industrial magazine. In heavy industry, great emphasis is placed on plant safety. This small-space advertisement hits the point and demonstrates an effective use of a small space. Not many advertising beginners envision themselves writing industrial advertising or small-space advertisements, but this is an important area of advertising.

ment store copywriting and has remained in it is in a little world of his or her own that has its own problems.

Even within the same field, there are pronounced differences. In Chicago, for example, Carson, Pirie, Scott & Company, the widely known department store, develops the "Carson" copy approach. Copy and art treatment are distinctive enough to identify advertisements as "Carson" advertisements, establishing the store's character and individuality unmistakably. The store's copy people, ever mindful of their great rival, Marshall Field & Company, strive constantly to be different from Field's advertising.

The same thing is true of nearly all big cities—big stores build up individuality through their copy and art treatment. Thus, a successful writer for one store may be so thoroughly indoctrinated into certain copy techniques that a job change would require conscious adaptation to the general approach used by the new store.

For example, look at mail-order and fashion copy. The first is stripped of nonsense. It's direct, detailed, and slugs the message home. The customer knows just how to order. He probably even knows how many seams were put in that pair of overalls about which he inquired. Fashion copy, on the other hand, is normally light, fluffy, and inclined to substitute atmosphere for facts. Perhaps each writer could take over the other's job. In a good many cases, however, it is doubtful that

such a switchover could be made without considerable flexibility on the part of the copywriter.

As a last warning on the point that certain adjustment is needed in order to switch from one kind of copy to another, think about the industrial material magazine advertising writer. Consider the technical knowledge needed to write industrial advertisements. Then, think again of your fashion writer or your average writer of consumer copy. The airy, nonsensical touch of the fashion copywriter would be out of place in a hard-selling advertisement for steam boilers. Some writers can do both types of copy. Others simply can't.

3. What are the requisites for copywriting other than writing ability? Personality, work experience, and education.

Quite a stress must be placed on the copywriter's personality. Of course, you can find some good copy people who shy from human contact. They're the exceptions. Unless you like people and share the usual enthusiasms, annoyances, and disappointments of most people, you are handicapped as a copywriter.

And, too, if you are overly sensitive to criticism of your work, you'll suffer as your fellow workers or bosses roughly and caustically criticize what you consider your choicest copy.

As for work experience, we depart from American tradition by suggesting that you try several jobs. Work experience is ideally composed of writing and selling, with an accent on diversity of experience. A sort of composite reporter-salesperson may have floated before your eyes as the ideal precopywriter. That's our ideal, too.

Although there are and have been successful copywriters with no more education than one might pick up from McGuffey's Fourth Grade Reader, education—especially college education—is an advantage to copywriters. Certain courses of study are more suited to a copywriting career than others, but this doesn't mean a copywriter can't profit from almost any course of study.

Advertising, newswriting, and such courses are directly applicable to a copy career, but courses in history, economic geography, or sociology might provide a background that could be very useful some day.

4. It's stupid not to be honest and ethical in everything you write.

Your conscience should guide you in your work, but if you're tempted to be untruthful or tend to exaggerate, remember that there are powerful forces ready to chastise you.

On one side, you have the law ready to pounce if you transgress. Knowing the points about which the Federal Trade Commission is very sensitive will help you avoid trouble with that body. On the other side are the consumers of your products. Their buying power is an effective inducement to honesty. Sooner or later, the cheat and fraud is discovered; when that happens, sales are lost.

When you are dealing with the public—the very young and the very old, the shrewd and the feeble-minded, the very poor and the very rich—your own conscience, also, should dictate honesty. In your person-to-person contacts, you wouldn't cheat anyone out of one cent, yet, through their copy, some of your fellow copywriters bilk thousands of people. It's a matter of extending your conscience beyond what you're writing and to visualize the undiscerning people who will buy your product because you tell them to. The saying "Let your conscience be your guide" can be most apropos in this instance—just be sure to put your conscience in order before you write copy.

5. An extra reward: Sometimes your copywriting job leads to other forms of creative writing.

Most copywriters find all the creative satisfaction and challenges they seek in the daily writing of good advertising. They don't *need* to do outside writing in order to satisfy their creative urges. They are fulfilled on the job, and that, they will tell you, is why they like their work so much.

If, on the other hand, your training in copywriting leads to other forms of writing, count this as an extra reward—a reward, as was said, that has been enjoyed by many copywriters.

One evidence of the right of advertising copywriting to be considered a legitimate example of writing art is in the number of writers of contemporary literature who began as advertising copywriters. The exactness, the economy of phrasing, and the requirement for subtle shadings in word meanings have given many copywriters the precise training they needed for their subsequent literary efforts.

It is not surprising then to discover how many well-known writers spent their early years behind a copywriter's desk. A few of these are Richard Powell, Cameron Hawley, Sinclair Lewis, and Sherwood Anderson. Many successful writers have, like Richard Powell and Cameron Hawley, produced best-selling novels or plays while they were still employed in advertising. These accomplishments are beyond most copywriters, who find all the creative challenge they need in turning out good copy day after day. It is not recommended that persons enter the copywriting field as a preparation for producing literary works. It is true, nonetheless, that numerous literary people have found such preparation valuable.

One agency head had this to say about copywriters who write outside of their copywriting jobs:

> Let 'em moonlight as poets, novelists, or freelance article writers. Just so they don't drain themselves so much creatively that they have nothing left for their copy jobs, I'm all for it. It's sort of a two-way street. Working in copy can make someone a better poet or novelist. And doing literary stuff can make copywriters better ad writers. All I ask is that they don't do these literary productions on company time.

1,214,361 Custom Combinations. Delivered in days.

So you need a helical-bevel drive with a 1:14,526 ratio? Or an adjustable-speed drive with some unusual configuration?

And you're having to wait, and wait, and wait?

At SEW-Eurodrive, we'll deliver most drives in days – not just "off-the-shelf" drives, but any one of over a million different custom configurations. Ratios from 40,000:1. Horsepower ranges from 1/4 to thousands. Torques from 300 lb-in right up to 8 million lb-in.

How can we do this? SEW has developed the most expansive modular program in the industry.

Tens of millions of dollars of interchangeable gears, shafts, housings, and motors. Components are stored in 5 major assembly plants across the US, ready to be custom assembled into any one of over 1.2 million combinations for the fastest delivery in the industry.

We can take it even a step further. Need a drive in a real hurry? Choose our "Rush" service, and we'll ship your custom drive within 2 working days!

Call us at **1-800-601-6195** to find out more about our modular program and our vast product line of speed reducers, motors, and electronic motor controllers. We'll get right back to you — our sales response time is pretty fast too.

SEW covers the country with 5 assembly plants & 58 technical sales offices.

SEW EURODRIVE

Figure 1–6a. Industrial advertising campaign. Advertising such as this requires not only writing skill but specialized knowledge. It is a far cry from consumer advertising for baby powder, clothing, and non-technical items. Copywriters with technical backgrounds, or inclinations, may be suited to industrial advertising. In this advertisement, and two others in this chapter, you see good writing, striking illustrations, and a strong industrial feeling. This first advertisement employs a number in the headline, a technique that attracts readership—especially true when your target-audience is composed of persons with technical and engineering backgrounds.

Good advice. Most copywriters, however, are so drained from their daily work that they have nothing left for outside writing. If you're the type who yearns for writing outside the job, then go to it—but as the agency head said, "Not on company time!"

You and the Computer

In those innocent, simpler times before the computer, the writing of copy was a fairly lonely task, a matter of the writer communing with a sheet of paper and a typewriter. Upon finishing the writing, the copywriter came blinking out of the copy cave to look for an art director, who then sent the copy out for typesetting. The copywriter didn't see it again until it had been proofread and appeared in galley form.

Figure 1–6b. Industrial advertising campaign. See Fig. 1–6a in this chapter for a discussion of the campaign. In this second advertisement of three, we have a clever play on words in the headline that talks of "uptime" in contrast to "downtime," a word used in industry to refer to a machine that for some reason is not functioning and thus is "down." Another point is the emphasis on the low maintenance of machinery because of the advertiser's product. Low maintenance means cost savings, the goal of every plant manager.

Figure 1–6c. Industrial advertising campaign. See Figures 1–6a and 1–6b in this chapter for discussion of this campaign. Once again, you will note the emphasis on cost savings and productivity achieved through use of the advertiser's product and the reference to "uptime" vs. "downtime."

Today, as will be noted in Chapter 5 on advertising art, the creative process is much more reciprocal between an art director and a copywriter. And this reciprocal aspect is enhanced by the use of computers. It can't be a one-sided relationship. In short, if the art director can work faster than once was possible and can store and recall information handily, the partnership suffers if the copywriter can't match the artist in speed, storage, and retrieval.

Accordingly, today's copywriter, in addition to utilizing the computer's word processing function, also uses the computer to store considerable amounts of text. If needed, this text can be sent to the art director as copy to be set immediately into advertisements, brochures, and other printed material. Concepts can also be stored for later use. For example, sample layouts might be prepared and stored for future discussions with the art director.

As part of the partnership, the copywriter should be familiar with the art director's computer techniques; this knowledge helps the writer mesh his use of the computer with that of the art director. This computer cooperation is reflected in the fact that copywriters are expected to be proficient in at least two or three word processing/drawing programs.

Because of computers in advertising agencies, more can be accomplished by fewer people in a shorter time. As a result, a copywriter may now be responsible for areas of the creative process that once were handled by other employees. Today, for example, copywriters have often become the primary proofreaders of copy.

Computers Can Make Your Job Easier—or Harder

Easier because: In the pre-computer era, the copy might have been handwritten and then typed. With each client revision, a new copy version would have to be typed, a tedious and time-consuming task. At times, all this handwriting, typing, and retyping tended to make a writer worry so much about avoiding mechanical mistakes that the quality of writing was affected.

Using the computer, the writer can now make changes easily. Each sentence can be evaluated as it is written and editing can be done instantly. More brevity and the elimination of mechanical distractions that diminish writing quality have resulted.

Harder because: As said previously, because of the computer, the copywriter has become the primary proofreader. Another result of the new technology is that the clients, who in the old days were worried about the expense of making copy changes, now feel free to make change after change at the computer-layout stage. They now have more time to make these changes. The copywriter may view the computer as a mixed blessing in this instance, because each time copy is changed, however slightly, the material must be proofed. Perhaps, for example, a margin was changed accidentally, a period or comma was deleted, or the leading was set incorrectly. Enter the copywriter. To be sure these mistakes don't slip through, the copywriter becomes a copyproofing "traffic cop," the

person who must check every change to make sure that all is as it should be. Formerly, a typesetter, as well as the copywriter, proofed the copy. Now it's likely to be the copywriter's sole responsibility.

Some of the old-timers in copywriting sigh as they think of how relatively simple life was before computers took over. Today, in order to work smoothly with their art director, copywriters are almost forced to improve their layout skills. As a result, copywriters are becoming increasingly comfortable with such aids as PageMaker, Photoshop, and Dimensions (a 3-D drawing program). Where once they might have lived and died with a manual typewriter or an IBM Selectric, the Macintosh is now so indispensable to copywriters that they can't imagine life without it.

Currently, of course, copywriters are getting their feet wet on the Internet and in designing Web sites. With all the complexities initiated by computers, the average copywriter of today finds a never-ending challenge in adapting to the new technology—an adaptation that's mandatory if he or she wants to keep up with computer-wise art colleagues.

CHAPTER 2

Who Can Say What "Copy" Is? There Is No One Answer

An **artist:** It's all those words that back up the artwork or photography I've supplied.

A print writer: It's the written message that conveys my ideas and gives full meaning to the artwork.

The printer: I look at copy as a term that includes everything that makes up what we call an "ad." So copy to me means words and artwork—all the material a reader sees when he looks at an ad.

A broadcast writer: Because we think visually and/or orally, copy is that part of a commercial that consists of words. Our job is to supply a backup for those words with sound effects, music, pictures, and human voices.

A critic: It's what I see or hear when I'm assaulted by hundreds of advertising messages daily—sometimes boring, sometimes informative, often intrusive. I just wish there wasn't so much of it.

A lawyer: Usually it's just words that involve us, although artwork gets into the act sometimes. Sometimes the words are accurate and truthful; sometimes they aren't. It's the latter that concern us—along with the FTC, FDA, and others.

While, as you see, definitions of copy vary, there's little argument about what copy *does*. It *sells*. Sometimes it's an idea, as in an advertisement passionately attacking the rolling back of affirmative action. Or it might sell a cause such as contributing to a fund for the blind. Its basic selling task is, of course, to promote goods and services. But whether it is frankly commercial or idealistic, copy is a conspicuous form of persuasion that convinces those who hear or see it to take some sort of action or to accept some sort of belief.

Selling in Advertisements May Be Subtle, but It Is Always There

Rarely is an advertisement found that does not have a sales motive somewhere behind its writing. True, as one looks at many advertisements, it is difficult to find any obvious sales message. For example, many advertisements that appear in print media or in broadcast media are written to build a feeling of goodwill, to strengthen public opinion, or to break down a possible negative public opinion. Such advertisements, often called "institutional advertisements," normally do not offer products or services for sale.

The copy, nevertheless, is *selling* copy. It is merely selling something different. If you are a salesperson and you invite a customer or a prospective customer to dinner, to play golf, or to see a ball game, you are engaged in a form of selling. Perhaps you aren't actually clinching your order—you might make no attempt to talk business—but you are selling your company or yourself, or both. The impression you create in the mind of your client is almost certain to have an important bearing upon the ultimate signing of the order.

So it is with advertising copy. In almost any type of advertisement you are asked to write, remember that you have something to sell to your readers. Otherwise, there would be little reason to spend thousands of dollars, or anything at all, for the space or time that will be used to deliver your message.

Can we agree that copy is merely salesmanship in print? Is that as far as the definition goes? No. It isn't half-defined—especially as far as you, the copywriter, are concerned.

Copy can be the voice of the advertiser, boasting about the product, shouting its merits in bald, unlovely terms, damning the competition or gaining attention through sheer weight of words, extravagant claims, or noise level.

Or copy can be the voice of a friend, a trusted adviser offering help to the consumer in purchasing problems—clear, arresting, interesting, and honest.

Copy can be the enthusiasm of salespeople, echoing their words, reflecting their pride in their products, opening doors for them, and easing their jobs. It can be your contribution to the merchant who knows what he wants to say but doesn't know how to say it. It can be a primer for the dealer, the jobber, and the distributor—a means of preconditioning their selling. Copy can be an instrument of better living, easier living, happier living. Through copy that stimulates mass sales, the whole economy of a field of enterprise may be improved

A Copywriter Is Concerned with All Elements in an Advertisement

To newspaper reporters, copy is simply the text of a story. This text is usually their sole responsibility. They needn't worry about headlines, subheads, typography, or illustrations.

Advertising copywriters consider everything that appears in an advertisement as copy. When you are asked to prepare copy for an advertisement, you are expected to write everything required for the complete advertisement. If you are asked, "Is the copy ready?" it is expected that you have completed headline, subheads, body text, captions, blurbs, signatures, and even copyright notices. To you, copy means every word appearing in your finished advertisement, depending upon its format.

In an informal working session, however, sometimes "copy" will mean nothing more than the headline, main body text, and possibly a subhead.

Copy's Elements

Occasionally you will find one advertisement that contains all the different elements of copy. This is rare. Normally, your advertisements will be made up of two or three of the common copy elements. There is certainly no rule of thumb by which you can predetermine exactly which elements you will use and which you will not need.

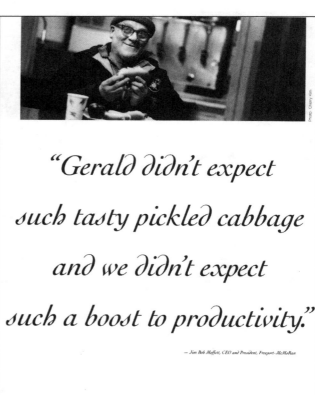

Figure 2–1. Public service advertisement.

Courtesy of the Advertising Council.

When preparing a campaign for a client or a prospective client, a copywriter may often need only two elements of the complete advertisement in order to convey the basic campaign idea or approach. These elements are the headline and the illustration.

A number of layouts may be prepared that show the client different headlines and illustrations. If the client approves the campaign idea, as demonstrated in these layouts, the copywriter will then supply the body copy for the advertisements, plus the subheads, captions, or other elements needed to complete the advertisements.

Main Headline

Any reader of news stories or magazine material is aware of headlines that use larger type than any of the material underneath. The reader often sees these headlines tied up with illustrations, the combination attracting maximum reader attention. In advertisements, you will use headlines in the same manner as the story editors.

Normally, the headline of an advertisement will present a selling idea or will serve to intrigue the prospective purchaser into a further and more exhaustive reading of the advertisement.

Headlines can and do fall into many varied patterns. It is not necessary, for instance, for a headline to be big.

Figure 2–2. Agri-business advertisement. There is almost a poetic feeling to this, which might come as a surprise to anyone who thinks advertising for agricultural products is basically routine. Note, too, the clever twist provided by the punch line at the bottom.

Some headlines—notably in newspaper advertisements—are set in very large type, and, in general, resemble regular newspaper headlines. Others, however, may be quite small in type size and qualify as headlines by their leading position in the advertisement.

Still another common form of headline is the blurb or balloon, in which a character is supposed to be speaking. Headlines do not even have to say anything. A company name, for instance, might be used as a headline. So might a familiar brand or signature. But practically all advertisements have headlines of one sort or another, the primary function of which is to immediately attract the attention of the reader.

Overline

In some instances, you'll see an advertisement that is topped by a combination that looks like the following:

Cut heating costs this winter.

(This is an overline. It is usually set in smaller type than the main headline that follows.)

A new MIDAS furnace control can slash fuel bills by 40%.

(This is the main headline.)

Figure 2–3. Industrial advertisement. At the top of this advertisement that appeared in *Plant Engineering,* aimed at industrial readers, you see a headline that is long and attention getting with its strong message and heavy type. Then to facilitate reading, the copy is broken up by subheads, a desirable technique when copy is long. Lastly, the double-meaning headline imparts a light touch to an otherwise serious approach.

As you see, the overline, often called a "lead-in," is placed over the main headline and is almost always in smaller type. In the foregoing example, the copywriter may have found that putting the two lines together would have forced the use of smaller type in order to fit the headline in the space. The attention-getting value of the headline would have been lessened in smaller type. Thus, the first line was made an overline. Then, big type could be used for the words required for the main headline.

Sometimes the overline can be used as an attention getter that says nothing specific, leaving the headline to do the convincing. To return to the headline mentioned in the foregoing example, the overline might be used to build curiosity, as in: "Here's an easy way to save money this winter." This would then be followed with the main headline that talks about slashing fuel bills.

Subheads

In writing an advertisement, you will often have some important facts that you wish to telegraph to your reader but that require more space than you care to use in the display of the headline. These facts might not be appealing as attention attracters.

When such information is displayed in type smaller than that of the headline yet larger than the body text of the advertisement, it is known as a "subhead." Subheads may be three or four lines of copy underneath the headline, or they may be display lines throughout the text or in other places in the advertisement.

In our nation of quick readers, who so often are more picture minded than print minded, the subhead serves an important function. It quickly tells the reader what is coming in the copy and enables them to judge whether they want to continue. In most advertisements, nothing is lost if the subhead causes readers to skip the following copy. Usually, the headline and illustration, plus the signature of the advertiser, have already enabled the readers to judge whether it is in their self-interest to read the body copy.

A subhead, on the other hand, will normally lure readers into the following copy. In the case of very long copy, it will break up type masses and make the advertisement look easier to read. This is especially true of advertisements that do not sell products but instead talk about the company or its point of view. These institutional, or "corporate," advertisements often obtain low readership. Well-written subheads can help make the advertisements look more interesting.

In some places, particularly in department store and other retail advertising operations, subheads are also known as "captions." This is not usually the case, however. As will be discussed shortly, caption normally has a meaning all its own.

Body Copy

Body copy, sometimes called "body text," is the main message of your advertisement. Your selling is done in the body copy. It is where you reason with the reader and show how persuasive you can be. Your body copy, if you structure your writing properly, is an extension of the idea conveyed initially by the headline and the illustration.

You have probably heard salespeople talk about "getting a foot in the door." Well, your headline is your foot. The body copy is the follow-through on that foot. Some advertisements actually have no body copy, from a technical standpoint. That is, they contain no major unit of type. Advertisements built around a comic-strip style, picture-and-caption advertisements, and others fall into this category. Because the entire story is told in these advertisements by other than the usual means, they will be discussed later as a highly specialized form of body copy.

Captions

Captions are the small units of type used with illustrations, coupons, and special offers. They are generally less important to the main selling points of the advertisement than

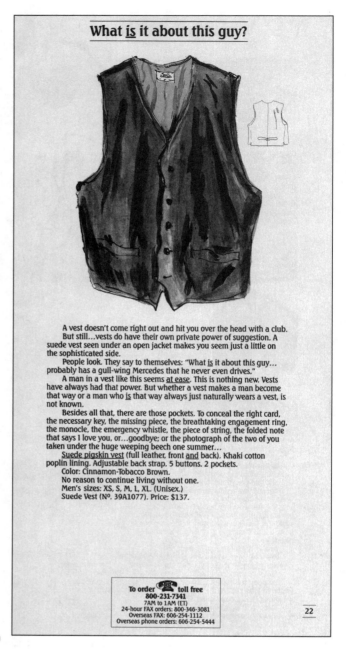

Figure 2–4. Direct response catalog advertisement. As you examine the copy on this page from a J. Peterman catalog, you will notice the easy, conversational style, the informality, and, above all, the readability for which this advertiser is renowned. This is very personal copy that doesn't, however, omit to include some selling details. You will find several other examples of J. Peterman advertising throughout the book.

Courtesy of The J. Peterman Company.

body copy and are usually set in type sizes smaller than the body text.

Now and then you will want to plan an entire advertisement in picture-and-caption style, presenting your sales point by illustrating them and explaining them at the same time, much the same way a magazine handles news stories. Here, of course, the caption assumes far greater importance and must be considered as body text.

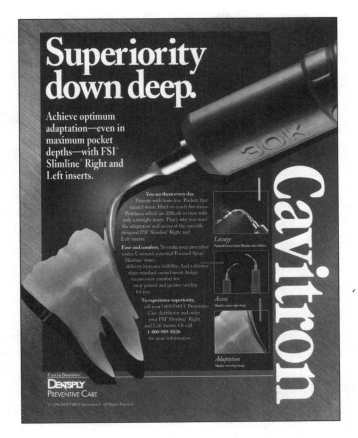

Figure 2–5. Professional advertisement. In this advertisement you notice immediately the technical language characteristic of advertising directed at the dental and medical professions. In this particular advertisement, we also have an illustration with great impact. No reader coming across this advertisement could fail to notice the striking illustration and powerful headline. To write an advertisement such as this requires a background, or training, of a technical nature. Not every copywriter can handle such an assignment.

Blurbs

A "blurb," or "balloon," is the advertising profession's term for copy set up so that it seems to be coming from the mouth of one of the characters illustrated in the advertisement. As with the caption, it is most often used to punch across some secondary feature in the story you are telling. Sometimes, however, it can constitute the complete body text, as in the comic-strip style.

Blurbs are often used as headlines. When so employed, they are not changed in any way except to be displayed in larger-sized type and placed at the head of the advertisement. In this case, they are still known as blurbs or balloons.

Boxes and Panels

You'll hear copywriters and artists referring regularly to "boxes" or "panels." These, as their names imply, are simply captions that obtain greater attention value by being placed in special display positions. A "box" is a caption around which a rule has been lined, singling it out from other copy.

```
CLIENT:  MOTEL 6
JOB:     :60 Radio
TITLE:   "Larry at the Bat"
TOM:     Hi Tom Bodett for Motel 6 with my "Ode to the
         Replacement Players."
         The outlook wasn't brilliant at Edna's Bar they sat.
         But hope was still alive, for there was Larry at the
         bat.
         The boys at Edna's cheered his name and called for
         even wagers,
         for Larry, once a regular, was now playing in the
         majors.
         He and his teammates played for love, not financial
         gain,
         so they stayed at Motel 6 for the lowest prices of
         any national chain.
         The room was clean and comfortable, so Larry was
         well-rested,
         and once the pitcher wheeled and threw he knew
         that he'd been bested.
         The ball soared ever skyward, and the crowd let
         out a cheer,
         then a plumber -turned-left fielder jumped and
         missed the sphere.
         Now everywhere hearts are happy, and everywhere
         children shout,
         and there's plenty of joy at Edna's too, for Larry
         had knocked one out.
         I'm Tom Bodett for Motel 6 and we'll leave the light
         on for you.
```

Figure 2–6. Radio commercial in verse. This commercial, part of a campaign for the advertiser, represents a variation from the usual approach. (See Fig. 19-1a in Chapter 19 for a discussion of the campaign.) Every copywriter likes occasionally to try something different as in this use of verse. Unless handled well, as it is here, versifying copy can sometimes be confusing or can obscure the sales message.

A "panel" is a solid rectangle of black or color in the center of which is the caption, either in white or "reverse" type or centered in white spaces. Boxes and panels are usually used in advertisements with such features as coupons, special offers, and contest rules. These elements will often be set apart from the rest of the advertisement by means of boxes and panels. Boxes should be used sparingly.

Slogans, Logotypes, and Signatures

At times you may write copy for a company that insists on the use of its slogan in every advertisement. Almost all advertisers logically demand that their company name be displayed in its familiar form. This display of the company name, seal, or trademark is called a "logotype" and is a common part of most advertisements. The term is often abbreviated in advertising jargon as "logo," "sig," or "sig cut." In addition, copyright notices are often required for legal reasons and must be included in all copy prepared for such advertisers.

An important point to remember is that *everything* that appears in print in an advertisement must appear on the copy sheets that the copywriter prepares. These sheets serve as a guide to the artist, typographers, and other production people who will be working on the advertisement after the copywriter has finished. If the copywriter leaves some element out of the copy, the whole advertisement may be delayed, resulting in a missed publication date.

One way to make sure of including the various elements is to set up the copy neatly and logically on the copy sheet by labeling the different elements on the side. Many copywriters are sloppy in their execution. An example of an ideal copy sheet is shown in Figure 2-1. If all copy sheets were handled in this manner, there would be fewer mistakes in production.

Broadcast Copy

The requirements for broadcast copy in radio and television will be discussed in more detail later. The same attention to form must be observed in writing radio commercials and in preparing material for television. In the latter, the writers must think in two dimensions: sight and sound. They encounter an entirely different vocabulary from that used for print. Because, in many advertising agencies, copywriters create broadcast commercials as well as print advertisements, they must be equally familiar with the terminology and form required in this kind of advertising.

Later, as you will see, much of what has been said in this chapter will apply to other forms of print such as leaflets, folders, and catalogs.

Copywriting: A Mixture of the Routine and Distinguished

Many copywriters are competent, but routine, writers. Still others are first-rate writers by any standard. Copywriting, if done well, is one of the most exacting forms of writing. It requires not only a command of the language but also an ability to coordinate persuasive, colorful writing with music, photography, artwork, printing, engraving, vocal intonations, and acting.

All this skill and coordination takes place within stern limitations of time or space. Copywriting thus requires the writer to be precise, clear, and persuasive in relatively few words as compared to most other forms of writing (always excepting poetry, of course). Furthermore, the good copywriter brings to the craft a knowledge of psychology, salesmanship, merchandising, marketing, and purchasing habits.

Like any writer, you try to make each piece of copy as perfect as possible, but "perfect" often means that what you have written has produced sales rather than memorable prose. Many of the best advertisements will never win writing awards, but they will make the cash registers sing.

Headline: Small boys, delivery men, plumbers, and husbands with dirty shoes—they're murder on floors.

Subhead: Protect the finish with Enduro Wax.

Copy: When you apply Enduro, you'll see gleaming floors immediately. And over the long run you'll have a scuff-proof finish that lasts and lasts. In

Caples on copy.

On headlines:
"Headlines make ads work. The best headlines appeal to people's self interest, or give news. Long headlines that say something outpull short headlines that say nothing. Remember that every headline has one job. It must stop your prospects with a believable promise. All messages have headlines. In TV, it's the start of the commercial. In radio, the first few words. In a letter, the first paragraph. Even a telephone call has a headline. Come up with a good headline, and you're almost sure to have a good ad. But even the greatest writer can't save an ad with a poor headline. You can't make an ad pull unless people stop to read your brilliant copy."

On word power:
"Simple words are powerful words. Even the best educated people don't resent simple words. But they're the only words many people understand. Write to your barber or mechanic or elevator operator. Remember, too, that every word is important. Sometimes you can change a word and increase the pulling power of the ad. Once I changed the word 'repair' to 'fix' and the ad pulled 20% more!"

On first drafts:
"Overwriting is the key. If you need a thousand words, write two thousand. Trim vigorously. Fact-packed messages carry a wallop. Don't be afraid of long copy. If your ad is interesting, people will be hungry for all the copy you can give them. If the ad is dull, short copy won't save it."

On directness:
"Get to the point. Direct writing outpulls cute writing by a big margin. Don't save your best benefit until last. Start with it, so you'll have a better chance of keeping your reader with you. Don't stop by just telling people the benefits your product offers. Tell them what they'll miss if they don't buy it. If you have an important point to make, make it three times: in the beginning, the middle, the end. At the end, ask for action. If people are interested enough to read your ad, they want to know what to do. Tell them."

On humor:
"Avoid it. What's funny to one person isn't to millions of others. Copy should sell, not just entertain. Remember there's not one funny line in the two most influential books ever written: the Bible and the Sears catalog."

On changing times:
"Times change. People don't. Words like 'free' and 'new' are as potent as ever. Ads that appeal to a reader's self interest still work. People may disagree about what self improvement is important, but we all want to improve ourselves. Ads that offer news still work. The subjects that are news change, but the human curiosity to know what's new doesn't. These appeals worked fifty years ago. They work today. They'll work fifty years hence."

Figure 2–7. This excerpted material from a 1978 *Wall Street Journal* advertisement contains basic advice by John Caples, famous copywriter. Every advertising writer—beginner or veteran—can profit from following these maxims.

fact, the finish is so hard that you'll probably never again need to pay out money for floor refinishing expenses.

Floor-wrecking crews of small boys? Bring 'em on.

Illustration: Pictures and captions.

1. Small boys jumping up and down on kitchen floor.

2. Delivery man dropping crate.

3. Plumber working at sink.

4. Husband coming in from the rain.

(Somewhere in layout is a can of Enduro Paste Wax prominently displayed.)

Sales versus Literary Excellence

In most copy you strive for sales, not literary recognition. Instead of concentrating on literary excellence, ‧you're thinking of the copy's suitability to the media used, the market for the product, and selling points. Often, "fine" writing would be incompatible with a nuts-and-bolts type of product, or service, being sold.

Yet, there are times when your copy can be almost poetic in its execution; at other times it will be prosaic and businesslike. The following examples were aimed carefully at their audiences. Each is executed well, but note the total difference in writing style.

Reclaim Camelot, and set it towering over a Hampton's beach. Or relocate Rome's Castel Sant' Angelo, from the Seven Hills it has guarded for 1800 years, to the sands of Fire Island or Malibu. Then, the fate of a sandcastle being what it is, watch it crumble.

"Safe upon the solid rock the ugly houses stand: Come and see my shining palace built upon the sand!"

Like Edna St. Vincent Millay, you may have noticed that reality is not always a preferred alternative. Certainly not when you are sitting on a beach, gazing across the water thinking…

About the office? Car repairs? What's for dinner? No. If you have read and pondered well the lessons of SANDCASTLES, you will be on the verge of a magical endeavor of will and imagination, a ceremony of inevitability.

In the following is another example of the more lyrical form of copywriting, writing that reaches for expression rather than a recital of product facts. The product is a necklace.

Intricate sculpture that dazzles like the night sky. Ablaze with fiery crystals. Accented by crystal teardrops that shatter the light into a thousand flames dancing to the beat of your every movement. Here at last is a necklace designed to put you in the spotlight.

Sultry, sophisticated. And very, very rich.

Contrast the following copy.

Balances heaviest, bulkiest loads with incredible ease! Can't tip or spill! Essential for every gardener or homeowner. Gets

THANKS TO PHILLIPS, WEARY TRAVELERS WILL ALWAYS HAVE A PLACE TO STOP AND REFUEL.

By donating a former plant site to the Cactus Playa Lake Project, Phillips Petroleum helped expand and protect the habitat of hundreds of thousands of migratory birds. The project resulted from the cooperative effort of Phillips, wildlife and conservation agencies and the community of Cactus, Texas. Now bald eagles, waterfowl and dozens of other bird species have a better place to rest along the Central Flyway. It's yet another example of what it means to be The Performance Company.

PHILLIPS PETROLEUM COMPANY 66

For a copy of our annual report, call 918-661-3700, write to: Phillips Annual Report, B-41, Adams Bldg., Bartlesville, OK 74004, or visit us at www.phillips66.com.

Figure 2–8. Long-range institutional-advertisement campaign. See Fig. 1–1 in Chapter 1 for a discussion of this campaign.

more done in less time with much less effort. Precise balance of this cart carries the load—NOT YOUR ARMS! So you avoid the back strain and heart-straining effort of an ordinary wheelbarrow or those small-wheeled inadequate carts. The Garden Way Cart rolls so easily, it practically seems self-propelled, even with very heavy loads. . .like manure. And its extra heavy duty construction makes it easy to carry up to 400 lbs. Many owners actually claim that their cart feels LIGHTER when fully loaded!

Writing Style Depends on the Situation

Regarding the preceding examples, the first two are ethereal and interpretive. They are concerned with mood instead of fact. The third is informative and uses common sense in its approach. Would you say the writing in the first two advertisements was better than that used in the third?

Ask that question of laypeople and they'd probably answer, "Yes." They would be impressed by the color of the words, the sensory appeal, the emotion. Advertising people, however, would say, "To each his own." They would mean that the third advertisement was just right for the product and the market. To attempt the approach of the first two advertisements in the third advertisement could be detrimental to sales.

It is possible that the copywriter who wrote the third advertisement devoted more time and thought to the copy than did the copywriter who turned out the first. The writing you do must be tailored with precise craftsmanship to fit the job at hand.

Judgment and Versatility Are Needed

Judgment and versatility are other attributes that stand high among the requirements of good copywriting. As an agency copywriter, you will be expected not only to pace your copy correctly but to write copy that differs in approach and feelings as radically as do the foregoing three examples.

It should be pointed out that some agencies and many retail establishments and mail-order houses consider the neophyte copywriter little more than a space filler. In other words, you may start to work for a company whose policy will not permit you to do much creative thinking on your own for some time.

During the preliminary phases of your training, you may be asked simply to write the body text, captions, or other parts of advertisements for which the major planning has already been done by others. No attempt is made here to determine whether this system is better or worse than that which calls for the beginner to jump into the business of thinking out entire advertising right from the start.

Both have produced, and are still producing, successful copywriters. It is somewhat a question of temperament. Some copywriters like to have their assignments blueprinted for them, while others find satisfaction in being their own copy architects.

The One and Only Way to Write Copy? There's No Such Animal

Give 10 copywriters an assignment. Give them all the same set of facts, put them in a room, and tell them to write a good advertisement. Chances are good that all of the ads will be different. They may all be good. They may all be bad. But almost certainly they will differ from one another.

Just when you've become comfortable with your own set of rules and principles, you will see a brilliant advertisement that thumbs its nose at those rules. That's because there are infinite ways to write copy. Sometimes those ways follow the rules; sometimes they don't.

As you'll discover from Gallup & Robinson research, the "rules" will work most of the time, but there is always that scintillating approach that doesn't follow the rules. This means that you should dare, at least occasionally, to depart from your comfortable ways of writing copy. If you have that strong inner feeling that a different approach is called for, try it!

So once more, let's all say together: *There is no one way to write copy.*

CHAPTER 3

The Copywriter Is an Important Member of the Marketing Team

Susan Springer started out writing copy for a small-town agency, got restless, and landed a job in a big-city agency. Ruefully, she soon realized that her small-agency experience hadn't given her any involvement with marketing. As she told a friend: "Wow! Suddenly, I have to talk pricing, distribution channels, market share, product analyses, sales projections—you name it." Susan learned in a hurry that her skill as a writer was valued, but only as it contributed to the agency's total marketing effort.

If Susan had taken marketing in a business school, she would very quickly have heard the term "marketing mix," and as a copywriter hopeful, she might have felt a sense of letdown to hear copywriting, if it was discussed at all, described as just one of the many elements of the "mix."

It's important for beginning copywriters to realize the place of copy and copywriters in the total picture—often minor, sometimes important, but never preeminent.

You and the Three Ps

You may never have much to do with the establishment of the basic sales strategy unless you happen to work on a new product promotion or with a product that needs a complete promotional overhauling. In either case, you might sit in on meetings during which the sales setup of the company is established or reorganized. However, you will do most of your creative work for organizations that have been operating profitably and whose sales strategy is well established.

Part of your job will consist of studying this policy. You will need to understand why it was established. Such understanding will be accomplished through a thorough examination of what might be termed "the Three Ps": the product, the prospects, and the purchases. To write effec-

tive copy, you must know your three Ps well. Whatever product you're writing about, consider it in the light of the following analysis.

P Is for Product

Does the Product Fill a Definite Need or Desire?

An automatic washing machine, for example, fills a definite need. It enables a person to wash the family's clothes cleaner, with less effort, in less time, and with less wear and tear on the clothes. If a person had been using a laundromat prior to the purchase of the automatic washing machine, such a machine will also save money. Thus, an automatic home laundry can fill five basic needs.

Perfume or shaving lotion, on the other hand, does not fill a specific need. It does fill a very strong natural desire felt by many people to be attractive. People use these products to fulfill a wish—to feel better groomed.

Then there are products that fall in between. For some, they fill a need. For others, they fill a desire. Such a product is the CB radio, which caused a buying wave in the mid-70s. Only a relative few in the population really *needed* CB radios, but millions *desired* them, and this latter group formed a vast market. A more recent example is compact disc players, which many *had* to have even though their cassette players were perfectly adequate.

Other products with this in-between status are cellular phones, snowmobiles, all-terrain vehicles (ATVs), mountain bikes, and digital cameras. These items are needed by few and desired by many.

Need, Not Novelty, Is the Key to Most Product Success

Almost all successful products fill either a need or a desire. Unfortunately, however, there is a continuous flow of products on the market that fill neither a need nor a desire. These products are usually spawned by "mad" inventors or by creators whose imagination is spent on fashioning the inventions—not in figuring out a real use for their creations.

Without seeking competent advice from persons experienced in marketing, they blindly rush into production "before someone steals the idea." Their reasoning, if it may be called that, seems to run something like this: "There's no product on the market like it! Therefore, it's bound to be a best seller!" They fail to see the reason that there is no similar product—*because there's no real need or desire for one*. An example of this type of "predoomed" product would be a left-handed shoehorn. Such a gadget might amuse you, but you wouldn't buy it. The marketer of such a product would soon run out of prospects because it fills neither a need nor a desire.

Just the same there is—and undoubtedly will continue to be—a constant flow of novelty products that—because they do not fill any lasting need or desire—can only hope to enjoy flash sales over a short period and then almost die out.

The objective is to whip up a desire for the product through its novelty. If it catches on, sales skyrocket; but they usually plummet a short time later, as illustrated by "soapless" soap bubbles, hula hoops, and pet rocks, which piled up sales for a brief time and then were seen no more.

Such products come and go. They are freaks and should not be likened to the normal, stable products that are your primary concern as an advertising person. Once it has been established that your product fills a valid need or desire, the next thing you will want to know is user satisfaction level.

Are Most Users Satisfied with the Product?

It is a fundamental of marketing that a product must live up to the buyers' expectations if it is to be a successful repeat-sale item.

Living up to expectations is probably even more important in the case of low-cost, nondurable products. Bread, hair oil, and soft drinks can't attain sustained success, no matter how sound your advertising may be, unless a good percentage of buyers constantly and quickly repeat their purchases when the initial purchase needs replacement.

In the case of the printing press, it is important to the continued success of the manufacturer that the product live up to its claims. Repeat orders for printing presses, however, would come at very long intervals. Few printers would make such a huge investment without first finding out from companies already owning similar presses whether they were satisfactory. Thus, the buyer of such an item would be satisfied in advance of purchase that the product was all right.

Regardless of the nature of a product, then, it must represent honest value if it is to obtain lasting success.

Does the Product Possess Any Exclusive Features of Benefit to the User?

The answer to this question is important. When your product does possess exclusive advantages over competition, it often will give you an advantage over the copywriters working on the competitive accounts—a knockout punch they don't have.

Crest toothpaste, with fluoride, is an example. It was a success from the start, vaulting into first place almost overnight. Polaroid's instant camera offered another exclusive benefit that made the copywriter's job easy. The remote control device introduced on Zenith television sets is still another product to which the public responded. The lesson? Give people a *meaningful* exclusive benefit and they'll buy.

Other "firsts" or product exclusives were the Ford convertible hardtop, Sanka coffee (caffeine removed), and the original mentholated cigarettes. Speaking of mentholated cigarettes, although you may not recall when they were first marketed, you certainly have been aware of the results of imitation. The first mentholated cigarettes were followed by a parade of new cigarettes featuring everything from dry ice to crème de menthe.

Many products have exclusive features. Unless, however, their advantages are rather obvious to prospective buyers, these exclusives may be difficult to write about and thus far less effective as selling tools. That a product differs from competitive ones does not mean, of course, that the difference necessarily will sell more merchandise. The differences must be a definite value of demonstrable importance to the buyer.

Be careful that you are not lulled by the glowing description you may get of a product from its maker. Human nature being what it is, almost any advertiser may be overly enthusiastic about what is offered, endowing the product with advantages that actually don't exist outside the imagination. Only your own close study of the product, independent laboratory tests, or large-scale sampling studies can give an unbiased comparison between two or more similar products, insofar as possible consumer reaction and your copy approach are concerned.

Such laboratory tests or samplings, though they may be fairly expensive, often prove to be excellent investments. If the product lives up to expectations, buyers will respond more readily to copy backed by impartial comparisons than to copy filled with unproved claims.

Figure 3–1a. Campaign advertisement. With women making up fifty percent of the work force and filling more and more managerial positions, this advertisement, one in a long-range series, recognizes the place and problems of working mothers. Three more ads from this campaign follow in this chapter and in Chapter 4. Notice how the campaign look is achieved through consistent visuals, headlines, body copy, and logotype placement.

Figure 3–1b. Campaign advertisement. See Figure 3–1a in this chapter for a discussion of the campaign.

For instance, the car that delivers greater *proved* mileage; the washing machine that has *proved* it uses less hot water; or the tire that has *proved* it lasts longer gives the advertisers powerful material for advertisements.

Is the Product or Service "Positioned" Correctly?

Positioning a product simply means that you and others concerned with product promotion examine that product to determine just what it is you are offering, what kind of people you are offering it to, and how you want these people to think of the product. Out of these three findings is born much of your creative strategy.

Few products are intended for everyone. In today's market segmentation, there are specific products for specific groups and subgroups. Advertising is directed to them. The same is true of services. A bank, for example, might position itself as the "young family" bank that aims at those who are buying homes and furnishings, taking loans, and are generally on the way up—and going into debt to get there.

In the same city, another bank is positioned as a "solid, conservative, business-oriented" institution. Its advertising and media choices (no radio stations featuring rock, country western, or bluegrass) zero in on the older, more affluent group. The stress in advertising is on the bank's understanding of the needs of business people and investors.

First, you determine what your product really is and what needs it will satisfy. After this, you position it in relation to your prospects. At that point, you can more surely find an advertising strategy that will convince the prospects that the product is suited to their needs and that it will answer their problems better than competing products.

This separation from the competition is vital. Thus, "positioning" can be thought of as a search for the product's proper identity in the marketplace.

One of the problems in positioning is that it is becoming increasingly difficult to change a consumer's mind about ideas that have been constantly reinforced over a long period. Thus, when you position your product as better than the outstanding leader in the field, whether the leader is in computers, airlines, or rental cars, the consumer resists your positioning of superiority.

Accordingly, your copy should not be obvious in trying to change the consumer's mind but should relate your client's position to that of the leader without making a frontal assault on the leader. If the leader has firmly implanted a reputation for unquestioned excellence in the field, a frontal attack will generate nothing but disbelief.

P Is for Prospects

When you have examined the foregoing product considerations, you will have explored only one area of the precopy approach. Now that you have familiarized yourself with the product, what about the people you hope will buy your goods instead of your competitor's? You must know these people equally well.

In many instances, you will know clearly who your best prospects are. In many other cases, what you may consider obvious may be wrong. You might think that men would be your best prospects for men's shirts. You may find that they are not. To your surprise, you may find that so many wives shop for their husbands, that women buy more men's shirts than men do.

Never ride a wild conclusion when determining who your best prospects are. Get the facts from actual sales studies.

Are Your Best Prospects Men or Women?

For maximum effectiveness, your copy must be aimed at your best prospects—not at just anyone. Certain copy approaches appeal especially to men, others to women. When you write to women, for example, your copy should be consistently directed only to women if it is going to be fully effective. If, as with cigarettes, both sexes are large buyers, your copy will be written to appeal to both.

When you're communicating with women, for example, your knowledge of certain feminine characteristics is helpful. Women pay attention to small details, tend to personalize more than men, and seem to have a more sharply developed sensory feeling when they are shopping. They buy, you might say, with their senses. This is apparent in their sensitivity to irritating noises in machinery. "Noiselessness" sells them.

As for male-directed copy, the writer must recognize the changing role of men, largely due to the fact that 50 percent of women are now in the working force. Males have become more domestic. In U.S. households, men are taking on many of the responsibilities and interests once almost entirely the province of women.

Men are now involved much more in family shopping, cooking, dishwashing, laundry work, vacuuming, and child care. In the past, copy people usually wrote copy for most household products with the 18–35-year-old feminine market wholly in mind. Now, such copy must reflect the more important role of the man in the selection of household goods and in the running of a household. Those caricatures of the bungling husband are less and less pertinent.

You decided to be
an organ and tissue donor.

But you didn't tell
your family.

Then you haven't really
decided to be a donor.

Right now, thousands of people are dying, waiting for transplants. If you've decided to be an organ and tissue donor, you must tell your family *now* so they can carry out your decision later. To learn more about donation and how to talk to your family call **1-800-355-SHARE**.

Organ & Tissue
DONATION
Share your life. Share your decision.

Ad Council A Public Service of
This Publication

Coalition On Donation

Figure 3–2. Public service advertisement. *Courtesy of the Advertising Council.*

To sum up: Decide whether your product will appeal to men, women, or to both men and women. Having determined this, key your writing to fit the group.

Are They Young, Middle Aged, or Old?

And why is a knowledge of age of value? As people grow older—as they proceed from grade school, to high school, to college, to business, to marriage, to family, to middle age, and possibly on to grandparenthood—both their needs and desires for products change. (Children are clearly your best potential customers for bubble gum, but they are your worst prospects for automobiles—the law and the family budget see to that.)

Young married couples buy the largest percentage of baby necessities, but they put up strong resistance to the cemetery lot salesperson. People over 35 years of age are fine prospects for home improvement products, but they would laugh if you tried to sell them boxing gloves or popsicles. So, birthdays are important—not only to the people themselves but also to the copywriters who can make money out of birthdays if they key their copy to the correct age.

Because of our aging population, with growing and significant numbers in the 65-and-older grouping, marketers and copywriters are taking a fresh look at what this market buys and how advertising should be written to them.

When you read about men and women as prospects, you learned that men are assuming a changing role in the household. Likewise, the "geriatric set," as it is somewhat condescendingly termed, has changed as well. Older people are in better health than in the past and lead longer, more vigorous lives. When you write advertising addressed to this group, you must recognize this change from the one-time sedentary retiree to the older person of today who, in many cases, plays tennis, cycles, skis, takes luxury vacation trips, and in general defies the stereotype of those who have reached the so-called golden years.

While you may continue to sell these people dentures and tonics for "tired blood," you will also sell them a host of products that would at one time have seemed out of place for this market. It's a market that has developed political power, buying power, and a group awareness. Unless you wish to alienate the market, you no longer write as if a 65-year-old's idea of the full life is to occupy a rocker on the front porch and watch the cars go by.

Like farmers, older consumers tend to be cynical about claims made in advertising. Over the years, they have had enough disappointment to become wary. Instead of trying to make them believe that you know all their problems and are deeply concerned about them, stick to stressing benefits when advertising to older consumers. They quickly see through superficial and obvious attempts to be caring and concerned.

In writing television commercials for the older market try to remember that hearing deteriorates with age. To allow for this, slow down the pace and use announcers whose enunciation is sharp. Vision, too, is affected by the years, which means you should be aware of the types of charts, graphs, and other visuals you use.

Language changes from generation to generation. Constant warnings are issued to advertisers of products aimed at the teenage market. You are told: "Don't use phrases that have gone out of favor. Be current." This concept applies to some degree to the older market, because this group is not likely to know or use hip language.

Figure 3–3. Advertisement with strong product identification. Emphasis on the product name is a must for identification. It is an art to repeat the name without having readers overly aware of the repetition. In this advertisement, the advertiser's name appears 14 times, but the name is worked in so well in the layout and copy that there is no annoyance factor. Like other DeKalb ads that appear elsewhere in the book, considerable ingenuity is displayed in devising interesting visuals.

Making a Difference—The Baby Boomers

In January 1996, the questions about the older market took a new turn, because it was then that the 176 million persons known as "baby boomers" (those born between 1946 and 1964) started turning 50. This is like no other older group—it is the best educated, most affluent, and the healthiest.

At one time, it was rare that older consumers were shown in advertisements. This has changed, with many sellers of products and services now using older persons in their advertising. These advertisers recognize that the baby boomer market controls enormous amounts of capital and that, because of their improved health, baby boomers will work beyond the conventional retirement age, very often on a part-time basis.

This is a group concerned with what they buy. Food, for example, will find acceptance in this market if labels show low-fat, low-sodium, and high-fiber content. In automobiles, safety and performance are musts.

One difference in the baby boomer millions is technology savvy. This generation was the first to be nurtured on television. Computers and electronic devices of all kinds were part of their growing-up years and will continue to influence their personal and business lives. In fact, because of technology, great numbers will do all, or a portion, of their work at home. The Internet and the World Wide Web are part of their vocabulary, and through cyberspace, they will become a force in politics and commerce.

Advertisers must expect more questioning from this generation, which was rebellious from the start. They will ask, for instance, how the advertiser's products mesh with environmental concerns. Involved in social issues themselves, baby boomers will demand such concern from corporations. In short, this 'older' market has differences from past older markets that advertisers must study with intense scrutiny.

Those differences show up in many ways. Reared on the Beatles and the Rolling Stones, baby boomers are not big band and Lawrence Welk enthusiasts. Their tastes in entertainment via motion pictures and television are shocking to previous generations.

Known as the "me" generation, the boomers insist on more time for leisurely pursuits, including more quality family time. And, because of later marriages and early divorce, their families are smaller.

Exercise equipment is big with the boomers, who early in life heard about aerobics and became the force behind the jogging craze. Exercycles, NordicTracks, rowing machines, and other such items find a ready market, along with expensive athletic shoes and ski equipment. Of course, if you have ski equipment, you're likely to take expensive trips to Aspen, Stowe, and other meccas for skiers. This is a far cry from past portraits of older people who were warned not to engage in vigorous exercise after reaching the ripe age of 35 or 40.

Are Your Best Prospects Rich, Poor, or Average?

Who, would you say, would be your best prospects if you were writing an advertisement for fur coats—women of wealth, women of average means, or working women? The answer to that question would depend on what kind of fur coats you were writing about! You would know that Park Avenue or Gold Coast women would be your best bets for ermine evening wraps. You would also know that the Park Avenue prospect would shudder at the low-priced, dyed-rabbit coat that a store clerk would go without lunches to buy. Clearly, sex, age, and income are important factors in the movement of many types of merchandise.

One warning: Income level isn't a sure guide to what people will buy. Education and taste must also be considered. Many skilled blue-collar workers (such as machinists, tool and die makers, pipefitters) make handsome annual incomes—more than many college teachers and other better-educated white-collar workers. This superior income, however, doesn't necessarily mean that the blue-collar worker will buy all of the same goods and services as the white-collar worker or respond to the same language and appeals. Once more, the copywriter is forced to study market characteristics carefully to gauge the proper writing approach.

Copywriters, and everyone else in marketing, will often be hazy when asked to define what is meant by such terms as rich, poor, and average. If you *are* hazy, then your copy may reflect your ignorance of the buying potential and expectations of the prospects to whom your copy is directed.

It is not easy, however, to obtain clear-cut explanations of the income classes because they shift constantly, especially in times of financial stress. Government sources provide the income levels of each income group. Because any figures provided in these sources might change markedly by the time the book is published, specific figures are not presented. As a copywriter, you can obtain these figures. In place of them, here are general observations that are pertinent.

- Those persons described as *affluent to rich* usually make up about 10 percent of the nation's households. Persons in this group tend to be middle aged or older.

- About 70 percent of the households fall into the middle-income group. This group takes in a wide range of incomes, from the lower middle-income to the upper middle-income persons. At the upper level of the middle-income group, individuals are likely to be middle aged. At the lower end of the group, individuals are younger.

- The *poor to poverty* level includes about 20 percent of U.S. households. In general, individuals in this group are older. This group has a substantial number of the retired, the unemployed, and elderly women living alone.

Where Do Most of Your Prospects Live?

If your product is burglary insurance, your best prospects would be among city dwellers, because statistics show that a huge percentage of burglaries occur in cities. Small-town people, on the other hand, would probably be more interested than urbanites in your copy story on home canning equipment. Farm families, logically, are your audience if you're writing about agricultural equipment.

Again, you may say, "But all of those things are obvious." You're right. Throughout this entire chapter, you have been given examples that would be obvious to any thinking person. Why? Because when you write copy, you tend to forget what was once so obvious to you. You forget the simple truths—the obvious thinking that makes your copy sell. You get so wrapped up in technique and the ultra refinements of the copywriter's art that you forget these obvious truths and facts that sell merchandise.

Accordingly, this section has not endeavored to be subtle. You have been told, "When writing to women, write exclusively to women." "When writing about a home canning product, write primarily to small town or country dwellers." If you learn these obvious stratagems early in your copy career—and remember them—you'll be a better copywriter.

To show how the obvious can be overlooked, wouldn't you think that it would be a waste of money for an advertiser to take large space in California newspapers to warn motorists to "Get Set Now for Winter's Sub-Zero Blasts!"? but one major advertiser did just that. The illustration showed Old Man Winter blowing an icy breath. It failed, however, to chill the sun-tanned spines of Californians.

The copy pushed antifreeze, tire chains, high-powered heaters, and other arctic equipment—all of which the average Californian has as much use for as for Florida oranges.

Remember where your prospect lives. Location has a direct bearing on lifestyle and often affects wants or needs.

What Are Your Prospects' Tastes in Reading, in TV, and in Radio?

If you have been able to determine the sex, age, income, and habitat of your prospects, you have covered some of the important points of their private lives. You will still want to know something about their preferences in reading, TV, and radio. What kinds of newspapers and magazines do they usually read? Do they read the *New York Times, Harper, Fortune,* and the *Wall Street Journal,* or do they read a tabloid newspaper, *Playboy,* and *Variety?*

Naturally, you can find out much about reading tastes by closely examining various publications read by your prospects. Another great help is the "Publisher's Editorial Profile" that heads each listing in the *Standard Rate and Data Service* magazine section. These profiles give you a strong clue as to the nature of the publication and the readers of that publication. To provide an example, here's a profile for the magazine *Family Circle.*

> *Family Circle* is edited for women who enjoy their role as family manager. Editorial is intended to fulfill women's needs for information, advice, tools and shortcuts by providing regular features on subjects such as health, diet, nutrition, careers, travel, children, food, entertaining, decorating, remodeling, fitness, beauty and fashion. Book-bonuses, mini-magazines, pull-out sections, and regional features address the active lifestyles of women today.

When they watch television, do they lean toward high drama, low comedy, sports, news, or sitcoms? In radio listening, are they likely to be hearing your commercials in the car driving home from work or at home doing the ironing?

In cross-section studies of potential consumers, the equal appeal of a product to different groups often necessitates diversified radio or television advertising.

This wide appeal is particularly true of products such as cereals, which are equally enjoyed by children and adults. A cereal television commercial written for use on a show produced for young children is not likely to have much selling appeal for viewers of an adult TV show.

How Much Do Your Prospects Already Know about the Product?

Are most of your best prospects already familiar with the products, just as most people are now familiar with home permanents, for instance? Or is it a new product, whose utility or other benefits must be clearly explained, just as VCRs originally had to be explained? How much potential buyers know about the product, and how well they know it, will definitely affect your copy.

Given either case, you will face certain difficulties when you begin your copy. If your product is well known, you either say the same thing over and over again hoping to sell through repetition, or you work for new ways to start your copy. If you use this latter technique, copy will "start" out of your inventiveness and your application of the P's. You'll strain to give an old story a new fascination in each advertisement.

On the other hand, your problem with a new product is that you can assume so little. You're not entirely sure of your prospects because you cannot tell by any previous sales record, as in the case of an already marketed product, how the consumers react to your product and copy mes-

Figure 3–4. Professional advertisement. In this advertisement aimed at dentists, we find the suffering point principle at work because it answers a common problem—that people don't have the time (or take the time) to brush their teeth after meals. This is featured strongly in the headlines and opening copy. *Courtesy of Warner-Lambert Company.*

sage. The reader will not know your product name, how it works, what it's made of, who makes it, and just what it will do for the buyer.

You must explain and sell, and you must do your best to gauge the readers' interest in a knowledge of the type of product you are advertising. If they are already acquainted with the type of product, for instance, it will make your copy job easier, even if your product is being put on the market for the first time.

It may mean that you will need to do less selling of the *need* for the product. Advertising of similar products may have given your type of product an acceptability to the general public. Thus, you may start off your copy confident that you don't need to stress the need for the product so much as the qualities of your product that make it superior to other similar ones on the market.

P Is for Purchases

You now have arrived at the point where you may think you have done enough analyzing. Perhaps you're eager to get your ideas down on paper—but wait just a minute. You may know a good deal about your product. You may know fairly well the people who should be your best prospects. There are still, however, some important points you haven't touched that affect the actual buying of the product.

Where Do Customers Buy the Product?

Early in their careers, copywriters must recognize that most people are *not* particularly anxious to buy the products for which they're writing copy. During World War II, when shortages existed, a single whisper from a salesperson to a friend could have sold a carload of nylon stockings. That's because there weren't enough nylons to go around.

Normally, there's more than enough of all commodities. There's plenty of your product and plenty of your competitors' products to go around. The public, under normal conditions, won't react to your selling message with a fraction of the mad greed they displayed for nylon stockings years ago.

Today it is not enough to sell people merely on the desirability of your product. You must be a sort of remote-control Pied Piper and lure them from their easy chairs right down to the store. You must make it as easy as possible for them to buy. Unless the product is one that is so well established that everyone knows where to buy it, you will want to identify where it is sold—whether at drugstores, hardware stores, grocery stores, or all three.

Never leave any question open because, unless you're selling diamond rings for a dollar, few people will be so anxious to purchase your product that they will be willing to go out and search for a place that handles it. Tell your readers or listeners where they can buy it—and be as specific as possible. Don't rely on such empty phrases as "sold by leading stores everywhere" or "get it at your nearest dealer."

The first of these statements possibly has some vague value as advertising. It may enhance the prestige of the product in the minds of a small percentage of prospects. Some people may reason, if they take the trouble, that if leading stores carry it, it must be good. But this type of statement is sometimes no more than an expression of wishful thinking on the part of the advertiser, and it often backfires to his disadvantage.

To illustrate, picture a man reading a shoe advertisement in a national magazine. The shoes look good to him, and he wants to buy a pair. The advertisement explains that he can get them "at better stores coast to coast." He concludes that Neiman Marcus carries this particular brand. Certainly, Neiman Marcus is a "better store," so he goes down to Neiman Marcus. He finds that Neiman Marcus doesn't carry the brand in which he's interested. What happens then? While in Neiman Marcus, he eyes a pair of shoes by a different maker and decides to buy them instead.

The copywriter who wrote the shoe advertisement that appealed to this man actually ended up making a sale for a competitive brand. Wouldn't it have been much wiser if this manufacturer had clearly listed the dealers in the classified section of the phone book and advised readers to "see the classified section of your phone book for name of your nearest dealer"? Or run in the advertisement a list of stores in the country that sell the shoes? Or provide a free "800" number?

Similarly, the phrase "get it at your nearest dealer" is meaningless if a prospect doesn't have any idea where the nearest dealer is. It may be seventy-five miles away for all the reader may know. You have to *tell* where to buy all but the most commonplace products. If your brand is available only at Safeway Stores, *say* so. If all good stores carry it, *say* so. If the name and address of the nearest dealer is obtained by calling a telephone number, *say* so. If the item can be ordered by mail, *say* so. In short, do everything in your power to make it easy for the prospect to buy.

Are the Purchases Primarily Seasonal or for Special Occasions?

Most products sell well all year round, but many are sold as seasonal items. You know that snow shovels, Christmas tree lights, and ice skates aren't bought in June, and you aren't surprised that lawn mowers, flower seeds, and sun shades sell poorly in winter.

But what about electric light bulbs? Do they sell equally well throughout the year? Offhand, if you didn't stop to analyze it, you might answer yes to that question. However, because it is dark earlier in winter—which means more use of electricity and more burned-out bulbs—sales are naturally greater during the winter months.

Similarly, you might reason that because people must know the time every day, watches wouldn't be subject to any sharp rises and falls in sales. But you would be wrong, because watches—and perfume, jewelry, and candy, to name but a few items—are largely bought as gifts for Christmas, graduations, birthdays, and wedding anniversaries. Thus, they are referred to as "special occasion" items.

Why is it important that you know whether the products for which you are writing copy sell more readily in one period than another or are bought primarily as gifts? The answer is: to help you avoid misdirecting your copy.

Suppose you are an agency copywriter and you are assigned to write copy on watches. The contact person, or account executive in charge of the account, is so familiar with the peculiarities of the market that he or she may take it for granted that you know the slant your copy should take. Without knowing that most people receive their watches as gifts, you might naturally assume that your primary objective would be to persuade readers to buy a watch for personal use. In actual practice, you would probably have much better results if you told them the watch would make a wonderful gift for a coming graduation.

If there's the slightest question in your mind as to whether a product falls into one of these specialized cat-

There are 30 different products from Amway in this photo. (The other 5000 or so wouldn't fit.)

Figure 3–5. Institutional advertisement. Here the company positions itself as concerned with protecting the environment, and one that produces products in surprising numbers and varieties. This contrasts with most advertisements that promote one specific product rather than the company as an entity.

egories, ask, don't guess, so that you can be sure you're aiming at the right market. Be humble and remember that although you might think candy bars sell in about the same volume every month of the year, actually they don't.

Is Purchase Premeditated or Impulsive?

Any major purchase, such as a car, washing machine, computer, refrigerator, or compact disc player, is usually made only after lengthy consideration. Before buying, people usually debate their actual need for a new stove. They ask themselves if, instead of buying a new sofa, they might not have their old sofa repaired. In the purchase of an automobile, there is usually a long deliberation regarding the family's ability to pay for a car.

Even after a decision has been made to buy the super-deluxe, buyers still take their time before actually making the purchase. Almost every major purchase is made slowly. The buyers shop around, comparing one VCR against several of its competitors.

Such sales are made only after the buyer has weighed the facts. Thus, they are termed "premeditated purchases" to differentiate them from what are known as "impulse

purchases." In this latter classification falls such merchandise as chewing gum, soft drinks, cigarettes, and any and all other goods that people normally buy without going through the long process of reasoning that precedes a planned purchase.

Typical impulse buyers are the persons who insert coins in Coke dispensers in a service station. They drive in to get gasoline, but when they see the Coca-Cola cooler, they decide to have a cool drink. This purchase is completely impulsive.

To show the extent of impulse buying, various researchers interested in grocery-buying habits have pointed out that more than 50 percent of women shoppers buy one-third of their groceries on impulse. The figure is even higher for men shoppers. Does your product come within this one-third group?

You should learn into which category a product falls if you hope to attain maximum effectiveness in your copy. You can be flippant and capricious—and deal in generalities—in an advertisement for a bubble bath. The technique changes when you're persuading a person to part with thousands of dollars for a Cadillac. This person wants facts, not foolishness; sincerity, not flippancy.

How Does the Price of Your Product Compare with Prices Charged by Competitors?

If buyers have a choice between two products of equal merit, the lower-priced product is almost always selected. Product loyalty vanishes in the face of lower prices. Should you doubt this, watch how the person making up a grocery list marks down for purchase those products that are on "special" that day.

Price, especially in times of economic distress, is an important factor in the selling of merchandise. You are handicapped if you don't know how the price of your product compares with the prices of competitive goods. If your price is appreciably higher, then you will want to explain, as convincingly as you can, why it's higher. If it's lower, you'll want to tell your readers or listeners that they not only can get good service from your product but also that they can save money by buying it rather than some other make.

Psychographics: A Copywriting Tool

For the marketing person, demographics (groupings by age, ethnic composition, income, etc.) are vital, and as you have read, they are also important to the copywriter. Psychographics, in contrast, are more useful to the copywriter than the marketing persons. Psychographics which are concerned with lifestyles, social roles, personality traits, and personal values, are more abstract than demographics and are thus of less use to the marketer in defining markets. On the contrary, the copywriter finds them useful in devising copy appeals.

Psychographic groupings are subject to variations, according to the authority to which you refer. Following is one such breakdown of groupings resulting from an extensive research project.[1]

Female groups
The Conformist
The Puritan
The Drudge
The Free Spender
The Natural, Contented Woman
The Indulger
The Striving Suburbanite
The Career Seeker

Male groups
The Quiet Family Man
The Traditionalist
The Ethical Highbrow
The Pleasure-oriented Man
The Achiever
The He-Man
The Sophisticated Man
The Discontented Man

Although the names of these groups give a clue as to the group characteristics, it is useful to a copywriter to obtain a full description of the traits of group members (or to fashion such a description from observation and experience). Here are descriptions of two of the foregoing groups that demonstrate the usefulness of psychographic analysis when one is writing copy.

The Career Seeker (Female)
These are women who are likely to reject the housewife role in favor of a career. They tend to feel liberated, like to cultivate their intellect, and want to feel important in life. They are impulsive buyers, spend money freely, and like attractive things.
   It is the best-educated group, with the highest socio-economic status; and although 83 percent of them are married, they have the lowest proportion of marrieds among them.

The He-Man
He is gregarious, likes action, seeks an exciting and dramatic life. Thinks of himself as capable and dominant. Tends to be more of a bachelor than a family man, even after marriage. Products he buys and brands preferred are likely to have a "self-expressive" value, especially a "Man of Action" dimension.
   Well educated, mainly of middle socio-economic status; the youngest of the male groups.

Values and Lifestyles Systems (VALS)

Coming after psychographics, VALS offers some similar ideas in its delineations of lifestyles. As devised by the Stanford Research Institute, VALS breaks the population into four groups and nine types. These groups and types are categorized not only by lifestyle but also by buying style.

---

[1] "Psychographics, A Study of Personality, Life-Styles, and Consumption Patterns." Newspaper Advertising Bureau Study. Sponsored by the Newsprint Information Committee, 1973.

One of the groups, for example, is made up of those persons described as "Need-Driven." One of the important types is named the "Achievers." (Look for a fuller description of the groups and types in the appendix and the chapter on research.)
   Many important corporations and advertising agencies have utilized VALS. In comparing VALS with psychographics, proponents say that VALS relates better to demographics and can be applied to a greater variety of products.

Know Your Market's Segments

Closely allied with positioning, which was discussed earlier, is segmentation that is involved with all three of the Ps. This term refers to breaking the total market into units of various types. As you will discover in reading the numerous articles and books on the subject, segmentation has many definitions and appears in many forms.
   Sometimes the segmentation breakdown is geographic. Regional magazines recognize this form of segmentation. Then there is Zip Code marketing, which can enable the marketer to zero in on certain areas and certain demographic groupings.
   For the copywriter, the demographic segmentations are more important. It is important to know that people of similar interests tend to cluster and that they tend to exhibit common buying habits and attitudes. Such people will likewise have similar goal-related characteristics.
   Another type of segmentation is by rate of usage of a product. Accordingly, the market may be broken down into heavy users of a product, light users, and potentially heavy or light users among those who are not presently users.
   Usage might have ethnic overtones. A number of studies about the consumption of rice have shown interesting variations according to racial and ethnic groups. Chinese in San Francisco—and this should come as no surprise—were heavy rice consumers. And so were the African-Americans in that city. In New York City, African-Americans, along with Puerto Ricans, were big consumers of rice. Cubans in Miami were heavy rice consumers, whereas in Los Angeles, leading rice consumers were Mexican-Americans and African-Americans.
   Market studies of ethnic and regional preferences are going on constantly for such products as mayonnaise and regular coffee that have shown extremely wide consumption levels from city to city.
   Other foods affected by ethnic groups include salsa, green chilies, and horseradish. Growth in the Hispanic and Asian population segments has spurred big growth in these foods. And when these ethnic groups adopt these foods, a ripple effect ensues, stimulating sales in the general population.
   These variations, of intense interest in the marketing and sales departments of the manufacturer, will ultimately be of concern to the copywriter who shapes an approach

Figure 3–6. Long-range institutional-advertisement campaign. See Figure 1–1 in Chapter 1 for a discussion of this campaign.

to what market research has revealed—especially if markets are developed on a section-by-section basis.

Still another segmentation breakdown is psychographic, referring to the lifestyles or personality characteristics of buyers within the segment. According to psychographics, the market might be described in such terms as: religion-obsessed, radical chic, buttoned-down-conservative, macho, white-Anglo-Saxon-Protestant, executive, militant, activist, women's lib, ski bum, hippie, or back-to-nature.

Some of these are easily defined and are thus easy to write to; others have blurred profiles that make it more difficult for the copywriter to write to them effectively.

Although segmentation is more directly pertinent to the marketing strategist than the copywriter, it is, nonetheless, one more factor in your search for understanding those complex, fascinating prospects to whom you address your copy messages. The more you understand such matters as positioning and segmentation, the more confident you can be in your writing. Some aspects of segmentation and positioning you already know through observation and experience; others you learn as you go along.

For instance, an example of segmentation in the sports field is provided by the Spalding company, which has divided tennis players into several types. A special racket has been designed for each type, such as those who play a

power game, a forcing game, a percentage game, and an anticipation game. A copywriter writing for such equipment is provided with much on which to base a copy approach.

Then, there is J.C. Penney, which bases its long-range planning on developing selected market segments but puts merchandising and promotional emphasis on young married couples whose income is above average because both are working.

Segmentation is possibly most obvious in the media. Except for the very general media (most of which have disappeared), media have by their nature, always segmented the market. Magazine titles reveal the segmentation—*Scientific American, Hot Rod, Golf Digest.* Today, media are segmenting their markets more than ever in order to serve the needs of special demographic groups. Direct mail, too, has always aimed at specific market segments, possibly more pronouncedly than any other medium.

Marketing to the Many Foreign Language Groups

Any observer of the American scene is certain to be struck by the explosive growth of Spanish-speaking persons from coast to coast. Put together the thousands from Cuba, Mexico, Puerto Rico, and other areas and you have a market of many millions who speak a language other than English at home.

Another very fast-growing segment of foreign language citizens comes from Korea, Vietnam, and China, along with many more from the Middle East. Increasingly, advertising agencies are called upon to supply advertisements in Hebrew, Farsi, Polish, and Russian, as well as in languages spoken by the other groups mentioned.

Ordinarily, you as a copywriter won't be involved in this foreign language problem (unless you're one of those rare persons equally at home in English and other languages), but you certainly must recognize this foreign language phenomenon when you consider predictions that up to 50 percent of the U.S. population may be more comfortable speaking some language other than English in the not-too-distant future.

Holding on to Brand Identity—A Growing Problem in Marketing

Walk down the aisles of any supermarket or discount drug store and you'll see dozens of "parity" products—products that are not nationally advertised but are competing with well-known brands that have advertised for years.

These parity, or generic, products are potent competitors because they are usually sold at lower prices and stress that they are just as good as advertised brands—and they often are.

What is the answer? First, branded products need more than ever to establish a personality, just as retail establishments do in distinguishing themselves from rivals that offer essentially the same merchandise and services. Second, a branded product must register in the shoppers' minds some powerful and obvious product superiority. Apple Computer has done this with its easy-to-use emphasis, and Saturn has succeeded with its outstanding job of stressing friendly, superior service.

Think about how many products on the market offer the same benefits (and often similar packaging). This is evident for an endless list of products, including toothpastes, pet foods, soups, and breads. Identity must be established by national advertisers. If they don't, their advertising will represent many wasted dollars and shopping will be dominated by price, with discounted prices being considered the norm.

CHAPTER 4

You're Saturated With Market Data. Time Now To Do Your Copy Planning

Allen Medford was surrounded by several mounds of paper. He looked worried. "How can I use all of this information?" he asked his office mate, Julie Henderson.

"That is a lot of data," agreed Julie. "Have you read it all?"

Allen noted. "It's the only thing I've read for days."

"There must be something useful in all that paper."

"That's the problem. It's all interesting. How do I select the best stuff for the campaign?"

"You know what they say, start with the copy platform."

"I know," moaned Allen. "But it would be so much easier if this product had only one distinctive feature or one benefit. Then I'd know what to write!"

For all copywriters, there's a *fact-gathering time* and a *thinking time*, during which you absorb facts, eliminate some as not pertinent, and then organize the facts that are usable. Then, you're ready for *writing time*, which requires you to plan how you're going to apply in your advertisement what you and your marketing partners have gathered.

Not so much a consideration of what a single advertisement might require, this chapter is more a description of the kind of thinking, planning, and writing needed for *campaign* thinking. In short, you're looking ahead to writing a series of advertisements with a common theme and a similar art and copy approach.

The importance of campaign thinking is evident when you consider that many campaigns run for years with no basic changes. Such campaigns were not dashed off by the writer but evolved from painstaking planning.

First, Dig Up Some of Your Own Data

If copywriters personally collected all the data needed for an analysis similar to the one presented, they would be taking too much time from the writing job. No copywriter would be expected to gather it. Much of the data may have been already well established by previous experience with the given product. Most of the rest of the information will come from research studies.

You can take an active part in this data collection by doing what has for many years been popularized as "The Hat Trick." That is, you should put on your hat and go out to do some firsthand research. Make a representative number of the interviews yourself. Ask questions—not among your own friends, but of the ordinary people on the street.

Talk to dealers and wholesalers. Talk to people who use your product and like it. Find out why they like it. Talk to people who have tried your product but now use something else. Find out why they didn't like your product. Do "The Hat Trick" often and thoroughly.

Your study of the basic strategy is not completed. You have done enough personal research to give you a good feel of the problem.

You now have what seem to be all the pertinent facts.

You have determined what seem to be your best selling points, you've identified what seem to be your best prospects, and you've come to a decision on how best to reach these prospects.

You are ready now to start building a good, sound advertising program that will sell more of your goods to more and more people.

Out of Your Planning Comes a Copy Platform

A dictionary definition of *strategy* is "employing plans toward a goal." A plan for advertising, if it involves a campaign, is almost always expressed in a written presentation. This plan, sometimes called a "copy platform," may take weeks, or even months, to work out. It can be very long but usually is short, a mere outline, in fact. Brevity is desirable. If the plan is very long, it is more difficult to use on a day-to-day basis. Also, it can be subject to more misinterpretation.

You may be certain that if a client and the advertising agency have developed a plan, or copy platform, through weeks or months of hard work, you will, if you're a copywriter, deviate from the plan at your peril. It is your guide until a new plan has been worked out.

Although creative plans, copy platforms, and enunciations of copy strategy differ, all have certain common points. Following are three examples: Creative Planning Guide, Creative Strategy, and Written Advertising Plan.

Any one of them will be useful in helping you determine the direction of your creative efforts, no matter what it is called.

Creative Planning Guide

1. Overall, what do we want to accomplish: Increased sales? Bigger share of market? Favorable opinion toward company or product? A change of public attitude toward company or product?
2. To whom are we addressing our message?
3. What do we have to offer that is unique? If we have nothing unique, what is our strongest selling point? Supporting points?
4. What media will carry our advertising?
5. How do we position our product (or service)?
6. What is the best creative strategy? Hard sell? Soft persuasion? Strong identification approach?

Creative Strategy

1. Objective—what the advertising should do
2. Target audience—who the consumer is
3. Key consumer benefit—why the consumer should buy your product
4. Support—a reason to believe in that benefit
5. Tone and manner—a statement of the product "personality"[1]

Written Advertising Plan

1. Statement of advertising objectives
2. Written advertising strategy
3. List of reasons for buying
4. Product positioning statement
5. Creative blueprint

Look for the Big Idea or Theme

Once the basic sales strategy for any product or service is established, the next step is to develop a *campaign* theme. This is the vehicle in which you deliver your selling points to the public. It's the central idea—the imaginative spark plug—that will give your advertisements continuity, recall value, and thus, extra selling power.

Your theme is the lifeline of your campaign, and as the copywriter, its development will largely be your responsibility. So take your time; make sure you develop a good theme. The success of the entire campaign may well hinge on the effectiveness of your theme.

Copywriters working the national level are almost always looking for big ideas or themes that can be repeated in many advertisements as part of the long-run campaign. Even on the local level, the copywriters for such organizations as banks and dairies will work mightily to come up with a strong campaign theme that will be used many times with effectiveness.

The writer who consistently presents campaign themes or ideas is the one who shoots ahead in advertising, not the one who thinks only in terms of "one-shotters." In the following material, you will be given some suggestions for utilizing certain basics from which powerful advertising themes spring.

It's Important to Develop a Long-Range Theme

You have already determined from your basic strategy planning *why* people might buy yours and similar products and *what* they want and expect for their money. Your first interest is to develop a theme that will, over a long period, influence a large number of people to want and buy your product instead of that of a competitor. To accomplish this, you want to appeal to their own selfish interests.

Another point about campaigns. Good ones should not be changed quickly unless your product itself is changed significantly or some other truly major change has occurred. Too often an advertiser using an outstanding campaign changes it to meet the challenge of competitive advertising. If the campaign is productive, its effective life span may be years.

Alas, an advertiser frequently tires of a campaign long before the public does or, as said, deserts the campaign in order to counter a campaign of a rival product. There are two ways to thwart this tendency by the advertiser: (1)

---

[1] Kenneth Roman and June Maas, *How to Advertise* (New York: St. Martin's Press, 1976), p. 3.

Figure 4–1a. Campaign advertisement. In this instance, the theme is that there is life beyond business hours. See Figure 3–1a in Chapter 3 for a discussion of this campaign and campaign technique.

Figure 4–1b. Campaign advertisement. This is one more advertisement in the advertiser's long-range campaign that is noteworthy for its realistic approach to the business scene. See Figure 3–1a in Chapter 3 for a discussion of the campaign and campaign technique.

Develop a long-range campaign theme that will result in advertisements that wear well; and (2) supply campaign advertisements that will utilize the theme in a fresh, engaging way in advertisement after advertisement.

These two stratagems are evident in such long-lasting campaigns as those for Volkswagen, Maytag, Marlboro, and Keebler. Maintain such quality in the advertisements you produce and the advertiser won't dare to change what has worked so well.

Consumer Drives and Your Copy

You may ask, "Aren't the basic human appeals used by a copywriter simply the means by which I can satisfy consumer drives?"

The question can neither be posed, nor answered, unless you understand "drives" to mean urgent, basic, or instinctual needs. Sometimes such drives may also be defined as culturally acquired concerns, interests, or longings.

Human beings do what they do because of certain stimuli. It's unlikely, however, that you will talk learnedly of drives and stimuli in your daily work. Instead, you will usually refer to basic human appeals, or simply "advertising appeals."

Nevertheless, each of us is motivated every day by psychological stimuli, either consciously or subconsciously. You hope, when you write, that your copy will trigger the stimuli that lead to buying action. To accomplish such action, you draw upon your understanding of human appeals.

When you write, you are not limited to the basic, or primary, appeals of hunger, thirst, and the sex drive, nor do you need to worry that some psychologists insist that all human appeals stem from fear, love, or hunger. The appeals you choose to use will be up to you, because lists of appeals are numerous, as are the varying opinions of psychologists. When trying to decide on a definitive list of basic human appeals, it is too limiting to utilize only the truly basic, or primary, appeals. On the other hand, some authorities offer lists of twenty-four or more such appeals. A copywriter will find such long lists unworkable.

It may be understood, therefore, that no one list of basic human appeals has been agreed upon by everyone. In this chapter, you are offered a list that is ample enough to be useful but brief enough for convenience. Each appeal is powerful enough to supply the desired stimuli, and each may be found in advertisements, some more than others, of course.

Figure 4–2. Public service advertisement. *Courtesy of the Advertising Council.*

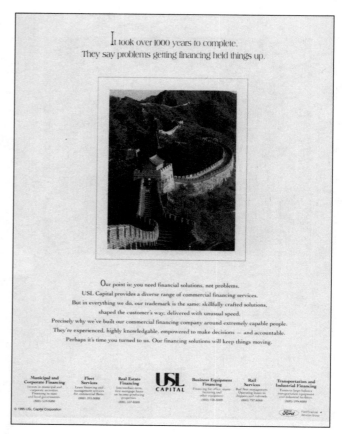

Figure 4–3a. Executive management advertising campaign. In this campaign (See Figure 4–3b and Figure 4–3c in this chapter) clever headlines and interesting illustrations make the advertisements stand out from more conventional business advertisements. The subtle humor in the headlines is appreciated by the sophisticated market at which the advertisements are aimed.

Many Advertisements Use More than One Basic Appeal

In studying these products and relating their sales stories to the basic appeals, you will again be aware that almost all of them employ multiple appeals. In many cases, one appeal can be made unmistakably dominant. Many advertisements, however, seem to put equal stress on two or more appeals.

A Goodyear tire advertisement might, through illustration and headline treatment, put over a smashing stress on fear. The copy will carry out this theme but will do so through a strong appeal to family love. The father will be urged to protect his wife and children against the hazards of a blowout. A copy section at the bottom of the advertisement emphasizes a strong third point—economy.

In many products you will find it possible to develop a theme that will intermingle appeals so that it is difficult to say just which is dominant. In one advertisement, for example, the headline reads, "How to be safe—and save 31¢ on our flashlight batteries." Which is stronger, the appeal to fear or to acquisitiveness?

Although it is difficult, and sometimes impossible, to develop a theme that falls unmistakably into one appeal

classification, it is best to try to come as close to this goal as possible. A "shotgun" theme that embraces several appeals may often fail to carry out your basic sales strategy by weakening the punch of your copy message.

All advertising, of course, is not built on such attention-catching themes. However, all advertising—even one-time insertions—should be built on a central theme that appeals to the prospect through one or more basic human interests. *The important thing to remember is to choose the appeal or appeals that will have the greatest interest for the greatest number of your prospects.*

Advertising Based on Human Appeals Has Built-in Power

Look over the following list carefully. Then test it. See if you can find advertisements that don't seem to use any of the listed appeals. Though rare, it is possible that this may happen. In short, this list of basic human appeals can serve as a reliable guide for your copy.

To repeat, you may be surprised how many advertise-

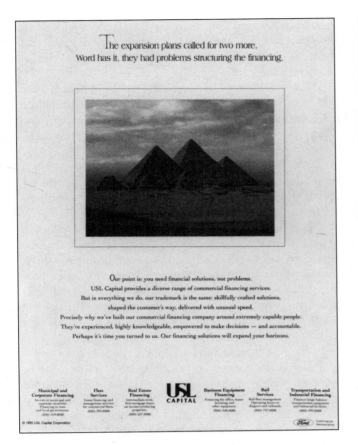

The expansion plans called for two more.
Word has it, they had problems structuring the financing.

Our point is: you need financial solutions, not problems.
USL Capital provides a diverse range of commercial financing services.
But in everything we do, our trademark is the same: skillfully crafted solutions,
shaped the customer's way, delivered with unusual speed.
Precisely why we've built our commercial financing company around extremely capable people.
They're experienced, highly knowledgeable, empowered to make decisions — and accountable.
Perhaps it's time you turned to us. Our financing solutions will expand your horizons.

Figure 4–3b. Executive management advertising campaign. See Figure 4–3a and Figure 4–3c for two more advertisements in this long-range campaign.

The original plans called for streets.
Rumor has it, they couldn't float the bonds.

Our point is: you need financial solutions, not problems.
USL Capital provides a diverse range of commercial financing services.
But in everything we do, our trademark is the same: skillfully crafted solutions,
shaped the customer's way, delivered with unusual speed.
Precisely why we've built our commercial financing company around extremely capable people.
They're experienced, highly knowledgeable, empowered to make decisions — and accountable.
Perhaps it's time you turned to us. Our financing solutions will launch your plans.

Figure 4–3c. Executive management advertising campaign. See Figure 4–3a and Figure 4–3b for two more advertisements in this long-range campaign.

ments include more than one of these basic appeals. Most often, one appeal will be given dominance, and this is the one stressed in the headline and illustration. Still, at times, you may deliberately choose to give equal weight to two appeals. An example of a two-appeal headline follows:

Insulate with Save-Heet—
it'll cut your heating bills
and give you greater comfort
this winter

Basic Human Appeals

Acquisitiveness. Desire for money, power, prestige, efficiency, material possessions
Comfort. Desire for physical comfort, rest, leisure, peace of mind
Convenience. Desire to eliminate work, to do tasks more easily
Curiosity. Desire for any kind of new experience
Egotism. Desire to be attractive, popular, praised
Family Affection, Togetherness, and Happy Home Life. Desire to do things as a family unit, to please members of the family, to help children in their growing years
Fear. Of pain, death, poverty, criticism; loss of possessions, beauty, popularity, and loved ones
Health. Desire for good health, longevity, youthful vigor
Hero Worship. Desire to be like people we admire
Kindness, Generosity, and Unselfishness. Desire to help others, our country, our church

Love and Sex. Desire for romantic love, normal sex life
Mental Stimulation. Desire to improve mind, to broaden mental horizons
Pleasure. Desire for fun, travel, entertainment, enjoyment in general
Sensory Appeals. Desire for any stimulus received through any of the five senses

To show how the foregoing may be used in developing advertising campaign themes, the table on pages 39-41 presents a list of familiar products whose advertising consistently reflects one or more of these basic appeals. You will recognize immediately the association between the appeal and the product sales story, even though, through the years, different words, slogans, and copy approaches have been used to express the idea.

S.I.C. Numbers: You Will Use Them If You Write Industrial Copy

When the industrial copywriters want to find out who will be reading their copy, demographics, psychographics, VALS, and lifestyles give way to Standard Industrial Classification (S.I.C.) numbers. You will find such numbers listed for the publications that appear in the "Industrial" section of *Standard Rate and Data Service*.

Use of the Standard Industrial Classification numbers is indispensable to anyone who wishes to know precisely the extent and character of the business market. It is especially useful to the advertiser who is deciding whether a certain business publication will reach more prospects than another.

Using a system of coding devised by the Division of Statistical Standards of the U.S. Bureau of the Budget, the S.I.C. assigns appropriate manufacturing industry code numbers to all industries in the entire field of business activity.

So important is the system that the federal government adopted it as a standard basis for the collection and presentation of statistics relating to the U.S. economy. Industrial data, gathered and reported by the federal government according to S.I.C. groups, include some of these important classifications.

1. Number of manufacturing plants in operation
2. Value of products shipped
3. Value added by manufacturer
4. Employment in the manufacturing industries
5. Hours worked and wages earned by manufacturing employees
6. Value of materials consumed
7. Expenditures for new plant and equipment
8. Value of fuels and electric energy consumed

Each division of industry—agriculture, manufacturing, transportation, finance, government, and others—is assigned an industry code based on its major activity. This is assigned according to the product or groups of products produced, handled, or serviced.

Under S.I.C., industries are classified by two-digit, three-digit, and four-digit classifications. The two-digit classifications are very broad in that they refer to industries as a whole. As the digit numbers grow larger, the industries in question are narrowed down to help the market refine specific prospects. Here is how the system works in the case of one type of market:

S.I.C. Number	Industry Definition
33	Primary metal industries
3311	Blast furnaces

Using the foregoing as an example, the advertiser who was content to get figures on the industry as a whole would use the two-digit classification. However, if the advertiser made components for blast furnaces, the two-digit classification would be too broad. Thus, the four-digit breakdown would be useful.

To give you further examples of how industry classifications become more precise as they go from two digits to four digits, examine the following listings

19 Ordnance and accessories
192 Ammunition, except for small arms
1921 Artillery ammunition
35 Machinery (except electrical)
351 Engines and turbines
3511 Steam engines and turbines

Advertisers find that many publishers will break down their circulation figures into three-digit subscribers so that the users of the publications can approach their marketing planning intelligently.

When publications put their listings in *Standard Rate and Data Service*, they not only break their circulation into S.I.C. industries but also show how many executives and what types of executives are being reached in each S.I.C. category.

An important side result of the standardization represented by the use of S.I.C. numbers in circulation breakdowns is the possibility it presents for the use of computers in media analysis.

While the uses of S.I.C. figures are almost limitless in marketing and advertising—such as coding consumer lists, laying out sales territories, and projecting samples—their special values to the advertiser-marketer are (a) helping determine which industries should be cultivated with special vigor because of the high sales potential; (b) helping select business publications for advertising schedules; and (c) giving the copywriters the target audience for their copy.

In the first case, an industrial marketer is helped greatly if he or she knows, for example, that 85 percent of inquiries resulting from an advertisement came from plants in S.I.C. 3555, printing trades machinery. Then again, if marketing information is needed, a mail questionnaire can be precoded by four-digit S.I.C. numbers before mailing. Returns will then enable the industrial marketer to classify products precisely.

As for the second case (selection of business publications), the circulation broken down by S.I.C. and by the number of executives reached in each classification gives the advertiser-marketers precise information on which to base media selection.

Third, copywriters will know not only the number of executives reached by the publications but also what kind of executives—plant operating engineers, safety engineers, plant managers, presidents, purchasing agents, and other management types—they reach. Having such information enables copywriters to focus their copy messages.

A Good Starting Point: See If Your Product or Service Has a Unique Selling Proposition

Some years ago, Rosser Reeves, a prominent advertising agency executive, stirred the advertising world with his book *Reality in Advertising*. In this book, Reeves made a number of powerful points that caused endless discussion in advertising circles. One of the most important phrases to come from that book was *unique selling proposition*, or *U.S.P.*

To paraphrase from the definition in the book, the U.S.P. is the proposition that each advertisement makes that is powerful, unique, and not offered by the competition. Sometimes the uniqueness lies in the product or in a

Figure 4–4. Business advertisement with 3-way power. A recipe for a successful advertisement is to make the three most important elements of the advertisement—illustration, headline, and body copy—work closely together, as they do in this advertisement. Note how the opening copy ties in immediately with the thrust of the headline. *Advertisement created by The Hughes Group in conjunction with TRIFID Corporation—St. Louis, MO.*

Figure 4–5. Agri-business advertisement with stress on environmental concerns. The agricultural community has an important role in environmental issues, a topic of much concern these days. There is an institutional flavor to this advertisement which, incidentally, was printed in a striking green, in keeping with its environmental message. *Copyright American Cyanamid Company. Reprinted with permission.*

claim that is made for the product. An example of the latter was Colgate's "Cleans your breath while it cleans your teeth."

What you must do in those minutes or hours before writing your copy is to look for the U.S.P. Sometimes it jumps right out at you. Consider the attributes of the following four products:

> **Product No. 1:** A power lawn mower that cuts tall grass evenly even when the grass is soaking wet.
> **Product No. 2:** Canned cream that tastes exactly like real cream.
> **Product No. 3:** An alarm clock that plays the Brahm's "Lullaby."
> **Product No. 4:** A magnesium tray that polishes silver without rubbing.

Can you *always* find a distinct U.S.P. in a product or service? No. If you're ingenious enough, however, you may be able to devise a unique claim, such as that mentioned for Colgate. But what if you can't seem to dig out any usable U.S.P.? In this situation, you might rely on the suffering points approach.

If a Product or Service Lacks a U.S.P., Look for Its Suffering Points

A suffering point is the need for the consumer that possession of the product will satisfy. Remember, people do not buy products, they buy uses of the product that will take care of some problems they have. A product may take care of a consumer's suffering points without having a U.S.P.

A product may start out offering a U.S.P. but then, when other products offer the same attributes, end up simply offering a suffering point. For example, after Teflon-coated frying pans became common, these products still answered a suffering point—the tendency of food to stick to frying pans.

Another suffering point, voiced by millions of nonprofessional painters, was the dripping of the paint and the habit of paint to run down the paintbrush when the brush was held above shoulder level. DuPont's Lucite answered this problem.

Look for the suffering points in every product you advertise and bring them up humanly and believably.

Figure 4–6. Long-range institutional-advertisement campaign. See Figure 1–1 in Chapter 1 for a discussion of this campaign.

Suffer with the reader. Sympathize. Let him or her know that you appreciate the problem, and then tell how your product solves that problem.

In the following, you will read a headline and a section of body copy for an electric knife sharpener. This material demonstrates the suffering point principle at work:

Headline: Don't let a dull carving knife spoil the effect of that perfect roast.

Subhead: Keep knives sharp always with a Keen-Edge electric sharpener.

Copy: Few sights are more trying than seeing your husband hacking the picture-perfect roast you just took out of the oven. You can avoid this sorry situation by making sure your carving knives are always sharp. Your Keen-Edge sharpener will see to that while, at the same time, it pampers your finest cutlery.

Twin aluminum oxide wheels—exclusive in this DeLuxe model—ensures scratchless sharpening while Keen-Edge's simple operation guarantees that the least mechanically minded person in your family can hone to razor sharpness any kind of knife you have. In the *kitchen*, paring, slicing, cutting chores are made easier, whether it's potatoes, tomatoes, or apples. And in the *dining room* your husband can do his stuff as a master carver whether you're serving turkey, Long Island duck, or Chateaubriand steak.

A quick inspection of the foregoing copy example shows that a number of suffering points have been answered:

• The hacking of a good-looking roast
• The scratching of fine cutlery in the sharpening process
• The difficulty of sharpening silver for an unskilled person

Point of Difference: A Powerful Attribute That Your Copy Should Stress

And then we come to the *point of difference*. While this would seem to be another way of saying U.S.P., it isn't necessarily. It may not be a U.S.P. that makes your product different from your competition's but merely a somewhat superior quality or product feature that makes it sharper, longer lasting, or cheaper to run. It could be a brighter picture tube or a more sensitive tuning device in the television set.

Because advertising is so very competitive, it makes sense to ask: "What do we have that is different? Is there a point of difference?"

If you hear the answer, "There *is* no point of difference," you may be excused if you feel a sinking sensation, because you now face a difficult job in making your product stand out.

If you are told that there is a difference and that the difference is important, you will probably stress the difference in the headline, opening copy, and the illustration. That difference might not be unique, as in a U.S.P., but it is enough to make your product stand out and to make it sensible for you to stress it.

If the difference is not very important, it simply becomes one of the selling points of the advertisement. If it's important enough to be considered a U.S.P. of the product, the copywriter will usually build the whole advertisement around it because, of course, the best point of difference is a U.S.P.

Examples of Basic Human Appeals at Work

Examine the following examples carefully. See how effectively the appeals have been flagged in the headlines. As you will notice, many of the headlines may not incorporate U.S.P., points of difference, or suffering points, but the use of a basic human appeal is powerful enough to make the headline stand out.

When later in this book you read the chapters on headlines, you might want to look over this listing again. You will get a lesson in headline writing simply by poring over these examples one by one.

Always Give Your Advertisements Three-Way Power

The most powerful type of advertisement slams a strong U.S.P. home to the reader by stressing it in headline, illustration, and opening copy. Yet, too often, we see advertisements that stress the most powerful point in headline and illustration but neglect it in the opening copy, or push it in headline and opening copy but let the illustration go off in another direction.

All advertisements should have three-way power—headline, illustration, and opening copy working together. What is astonishing is how many professional copywriters ignore this principle. Don't ever forget it! Give each advertisement you write three-way power.

Appeal	Headline of advertisement	Product or service	Advertiser
Acquisitiveness	How to enjoy your salary long after you've stopped working.	Personal finance planning	IDS Financial Services
	"I'm an easy guy to satisfy. I only want the best."	GMC truck	General Motors
	Your dream of owning a Jaguar just came a little closer to reality.	Jaguar automobile	Jaguar Cards, Inc.
good →	Life Insurance that helps you keep up with the Dow Joneses.	Variable appreciable life plan	Prudential Company
Comfort	Keep warmer in winter, cooler in summer, with money saving Window Quilt.	Insulating shades	Appropriate Technology Corporation
	Relaxation is a matter of perspective.	Caribbean cruises	Holland American Lines
	Think comfortable thoughts.	Shoes	Tretorn
good →	The Lane Recliner. Comfort to enjoy for a lifetime.	Easy chair	Action Industries
Convenience	All your beauty needs in one bottle.	Baby oil	Johnson & Johnson
	How to buy a gift from Cartier, when your plane leaves in 50 minutes from Kennedy.	*Package* magazine	Condé Nast Publications, Inc.
	First, there was the 2-minute egg. Now meet the 2-minute turkey.	Butterball turkey	Swift/Eckrich
	Introducing the gas self cleaning oven.	Gas oven	Modern Maid Company
Curiosity	A new world awaits you in a new travel magazine.	*Traveler* magazine	Condé Nast Publications, Inc.
	This is only the cover. . .you should see the rest.	Caribbean cruises	Windjammer Barefoot Cruises, Ltd.
	Get valuable information on collecting fine wines including *which* wines to buy and *how much* to pay.	Magazine	*Wine Spectator*
	Expand your natural horizons.	Books	Nature Book Society
Egotism *good* →	Small colleges can help you make it big.	College enrollment	Council of Independent Colleges
	The crystal is exclusive to us. The porcelain could be exclusive to you.	Baccarat crystal	Garrard Jewellers
	What does it take to be the best?	University enrollment	Hofstra University
	Exquisite. The diamonds, the classic designs and the woman who wears them.	Diamond jewelry	BEST Company Jewelers
Family Affection, Togetherness, and Happy Home Life	The family is more important than the family room.	Furniture	Ethan Allen Galleries
	Patent 2,823,421 has changed the way you look at your children.	Mylar® polyester film	DuPont
good →	Listen to your mother.	AT&T phone	Sears Roebuck and Company
	Family affair.	Vacationer's guide	Lee Island Coast

Appeal	Headline of advertisement	Product or service	Advertiser
	Listen to your mother.	AT&T phone	Sears Roebuck and Company
	Family affair.	Vacationer's guide	Lee Island Coast
Fear	Nuclear energy helps keep us from reliving a nightmare.	Booklet on energy independence	U.S. Committee for Energy Awareness
	Why be gray when you can be yourself?	Haircolor lotion	Loréal®
	One less thing to worry about.	Automobile	Hyundai
	"I don't intend to grow old gracefully. . .I intend to fight it every step of the way."	Cosmetic	Oil of Olay
Health	*good* → Fight cavities with a stick.	Sugarless gum	Warner-Lambert Company
	Now you can put your hay fever to sleep while you stay awake.	Anti-allergy product	Merrell Dow Pharmaceuticals, Inc.
	Finally: A sophisticated weapon in the war against plaque.	Plaque removal instrument	Dental Research Corporation
	Take control of your life.	Health center program	Palm-Aire Hotel & Spa
Hero Worship	Dennis Conner. Cardmember since 1983.	Charge card	American Express
	Give your favorite sports heroes a home.	Action posters	*Sports Illustrated*
	When Grandma Moses was in her 70s, she wanted to keep busy. So she took up painting.	Restaurant	Denny's
	The most unforgettable women in the world wear Revlon.	Complexion makeup	Revlon, Inc.
Kindness, Generosity, and Unselfishness	Commitment is supporting something you believe in.	Little League program	CNA Insurance
	For the cost of a morning coffee break, you can break the cycle of poverty for one small child.	Foster child sponsorship	Foster Parents Plan
	→ Animals wouldn't burn your home. Don't burn theirs.	Smokey the Bear	Advertising Council
	Four reasons why Upjohn's commitment to improving the quality of life is greater than ever.	Medicine	Upjohn
Love and Sex	Love at First Sight.	Sunglasses	Foster Grant
	"Laughter, Tears, Passion, Friendship, Love."	Diamonds	De Beer
	Romance on a Grand Scale.	Hotel	Grand Cypress Resort
	"I chose my crystal because of the way it came to life in candlelight. The same reason he chose me."	Crystal	Towle
Mental Stimulation	The New Encyclopaedia Britannica. . .it gives you something to talk about. And think about.	Books	Encyclopaedia Britannica, Inc.
	How to become a Straight-A Student.	Book	Publishers Choice
	European Travel & Life. A Wealth of Uncommon Knowledge.	Magazine	*European Travel & Life*
	With this sophisticated equipment, you can monitor the world for just cents a day.	Newspaper	*Christian Science Monitor*
Pleasure	Pleasure on a Grand Scale.	Hotel	Grand Cypress Resort
	Great Tennis! Great Fun!	Tennis camp	All American Sports
	The Greatest Adventure of a Lifetime could be 32¢ away.	Travel	Government of India Tourist Office
	→ When you're on top, you should enjoy the view.	Luxury apartment	Buckingham Towers

Appeal	Headline of advertisement	Product or service	Advertiser
Sensory Appeals	Fragrances for the mind, body, and soul.	Perfume	Princess Marcella Borghese
	A.1. makes stuffed peppers taste even peppier.	Steak sauce	Nabisco Brands
	Why buy a limp excuse for a pickle when you can crunch a Claussen pickle?	Pickles	Claussen Pickle Co.
	Turn an innocent salad into a sinful indulgence.	Salad dressing	Marie's Specialty Brands
	The taste is warm. The feeling is delicious.	Cognac	Courvoisier

CHAPTER 5

Advertising's Creative Duo— Art Director and Copywriter

Scowling, Alan Feeney tossed a copy sheet on Trent Bartel's desk. "Trent, here's the copy, such as it is, but I went dry when I tried to come up with an illustration idea." Alan's a good wordsmith who often has imaginative visual concepts, but when he's stuck, he counts on Trent to supply a visual that gives a punch to his copy. There's nothing quite like the working relationship of a copywriter and an art director who work together on ad after ad. Each sparks the other, and the result is a happy marriage of creative talents.

If a Picture Is Worth a Thousand Words, Why Bother Writing Copy?

From the time you were able to read, you've been aware of that well-worn saying about a picture being worth a thousand words. That would seem to relegate copy in an advertisement to a minor position. In truth, many times the visual in an advertisement does convey the whole message.[1] Copy may hardly seem necessary. Likewise, there are very successful advertisements that have no illustrations—just a headline and strong copy. However, the most effective advertisements usually combine a strong visual with a challenging headline and powerful copy. So, if you're asked the question: "Which is more important—the visual or the copy?" just smile tolerantly and reply that they are of equal importance and that the situation dictates the answer.

Poor visuals can doom advertisements no matter how good the copy. On the contrary, a brilliant series of visuals can ensure the selling success of a campaign for which the copy might be quite ordinary.

There is no sure way to determine whether the effectiveness of any piece of advertising is based on copy or art. One can very rarely stand by itself. Advertising graveyards are full of copywriters and art people who never learned the fundamental fact of teamwork.

It *is* teamwork—between you and your art associates— that will result in sound, selling advertisements that are properly executed for maximum impact upon readers. There is no room for the "I-can-do-it-alone" technique. If you learn quickly how to get along with your art people, you will have taken a major step toward your creative goal.

Be Glad—Not Mad—If Your Art Director-Partner Wants to Throw in Some Copy Ideas

It's not unknown for some copywriters to resent efforts by art directors to offer copy suggestions and even to supply some copy that they think might be an improvement on what you've written. Welcome such interest. If the suggested copy sharpens your copy, be delighted that you have such assistance. In this business of turning out advertising, you should take help wherever you can get it.

Most of the time, however, art directors are quite content to leave the writing wholly with you, but if you have

---

[1] Illustration and visual are used interchangeably, but "visual," which stands for either a photograph or artwork illustration, is more commonly used today.

an art director-partner who has a way with words, you're lucky. Incidentally, art directors may be especially apt with headline ideas because of the close tie-in of headlines with artwork. After all, the art director is eager to have a headline that does justice to the visual being furnished.

Competent art directors achieve great respect in advertising circles, as evidenced by how many of them are creative directors and even head of advertising agencies or department store advertising departments.

Intelligent Cooperation Is Your Role in Working with Art Directors

Cooperation is the key word, not dictation. You can certainly help your art director by supplying ideas, but *never forget that you are not an art director.* Go ahead, supply ideas. From you should emanate information about the elements important to the selling job. Once you've given this information, let the art director proceed.

A better layout will result if the art director's imagination is permitted to function freely without unwanted advice from you. The goal is to produce advertising of which you can both be proud—you of the thinking behind the advertisement and the power and clarity of the selling ideas, and the art director of the physical execution of these ideas.

Art directors will welcome suggestions from you, upon which they may improvise. In you, artists see art of another sort. Most of them will admit that they're glad they aren't faced with the responsibility of conceiving the original copy ideas. Artists are, after all, specialists in translating those ideas to layouts and illustrations, and they are much better at it than any copywriter or group of copywriters.

Regardless of the type of copy work you do, if your art associates realize that you consider the creation of advertising a job of close and friendly teamwork—if you can establish a method of joint operation with them—you will discover a richness in the routine of your daily work that many copywriters never find. Such richness will help produce good advertisements.

The success of your career as a copywriter depends in a large measure upon your knowledge of human psychology. Don't let that knowledge apply only to the people who read your advertisements. It will pay off fully in your dealings with your art directors.

You're Expected to Know a Lot about Writing—Not Art

It may be better for copywriters to know nothing at all about art than to know just enough to make them think they know a lot. Alexander Pope's "A little learning is a dangerous thing" applies very well here.

This is certainly true from the standpoint of economy of effort. Wherever you work—agency, department store, retail shop, direct-mail, or mail-order house—you will have available the services of men and women trained in making layouts and supervising artwork. They take your ideas and make attractive and compelling layouts from

them. If you, the copywriter, have a wide knowledge of art and layout, you will tend to spend time that should be spent in copywriting making rough layouts that will neither be used nor appreciated by the art directors. After all, no two artists will ever see a layout job in exactly the same way.

Instead, *write* your suggestions for illustrations; supply the other necessary elements, such as headlines and subheads; and then forget them until you have something done by a specialist to look at. If, after viewing the art director's work, you have suggestions to make—if you would prefer to see some slightly different style of handling and feel that your criticisms are justified for the good of the advertisement—then is the time to take them up.

By handling it that way, you will get along better with the art director and have more time for your own job. Also, copywriters' roughs often make lazy artists, as they are tempted merely to "dress up" copywriters' ideas instead of applying their specialized knowledge of layout to designing the advertisement as it should be designed.

Assuming that you have reasonably sensible taste, all you need to know about art is what you will normally learn working with and around art directors.

Most of your important relationships with the art department, wherever you work, will be concerned with print advertising. Many advertising agencies, however, maintain specially trained and talented art directors whose duties are entirely confined to television visualization. In no phase of creative advertising is a person expected to be so versatile and flexible as in the creating of television "storyboards." (Although concentration in this chapter is on the need for copywriter–artist cooperation in turning out good print advertising, the importance of TV creation must be mentioned here. A full discussion of this topic will be given in the television chapters.)

Computers are Kings in Art Departments

Numerous drastic changes in the way that copywriters and art directors perform their daily tasks have directly resulted from the introduction of computers in the art departments.

Behind these drastic changes are word processing programs, desktop publishing, and digital reproduction. Whether they are Macintosh- or PC-based graphic programs, the tools now available to the art director are powerful, flexible, and fast. Many of the traditional tools and functions of the past, along with the people needed to carry out those tasks, have been replaced. Consider some of these changes to see how deeply the art function has been affected:

Layouts. Today, the art director performs quickly the same tasks formerly reserved for the drafting tables (rarely seen these days) and traditional tools. Sizes, shapes, cutting and pasting, edits, photo retouching, and hundreds of other tasks are now executed by the computer. For layout purposes today, the key visuals are more likely to be artwork that exists within the computer memory. Otherwise, it is reference art (swipe) that is put through an electronic

Figure 5–1a. Agri-business campaign utilizing strong design element for continuity. Three advertisements in this campaign are shown in this chapter. This is the first, but you will see an unmistakable resemblance to the others because of that eye-arresting pie-design visual and the accompanying words in the upper-right. Target for the ad is the farm equipment dealer, as the fact-filled copy makes clear. Another factor to notice is the use of figures in all three headings, a technique shown by research to build readership. These advertisements provide still another example of the art director's influence in building family resemblance in campaign advertisements. *Reproduced with permission of Federal-Mogul Corporation.*

Figure 5–1b. Agri-business campaign utilizing strong design element for continuity. *Reproduced with permission of Federal-Mogul Corporation.*

Figure 5–1c. Agri-business campaign utilizing strong design element for continuity. *Reproduced with permission of Federal-Mogul Corporation.*

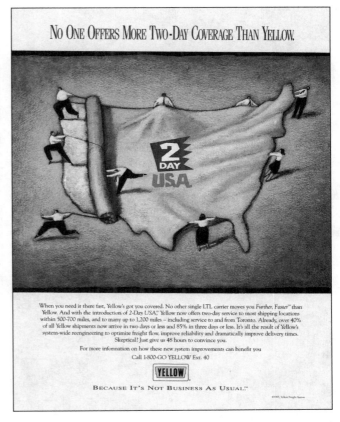

Figure 5–2a. Campaign advertisement with distinctive visual treatment. In this campaign we have a happy joining of the talents of an art director and a copywriter. Result? Smashing illustrations and strong, easy-to-read copy. And, above all, a campaign look that insures instant recognition for each advertisement in the campaign. All elements of the advertisements are set up consistently—headline on top, big illustration in striking color, copy given plenty of white space around it, and a logotype in color and given the same position in each advertisement. Look for two other advertisements in this campaign in this chapter.

Figure 5–2b. Campaign advertisement with distinctive visual treatment. Once again, the art treatment makes this campaign stand out and, in addition, each advertisement uses powerful copy to back up the visual approach.

Figure 5–2c. Campaign advertisement with distinctive visual treatment.

In America, you are not required to offer food to the hungry. Or shelter to the homeless. There is no ordinance forcing you to visit the lonely, or comfort the infirm. Nowhere in the Constitution does it say you have to provide clothing for the poor. In fact, one of the nicest things about living here in America is that you really don't have to do anything for anybody.

To the 80 million of you who volunteered time and money last year, thanks for all you've given. Imagine what more could do. Call 1-800-55-GIVE 5. It's what in the world you can do.

Figure 5–3. Public service advertisement. *Courtesy of the Advertising Council.*

digital scanner, resized, and ultimately placed in the layout.

Typography. What was once the job of a professional typesetter is now performed by art directors at their work stations. Currently, almost 100 percent of all layout type comes from libraries of fonts readily available on software. These are stored on the art director's computer, allowing him to choose and use type as needed. Lettering, once done slowly and laboriously by hand, is now referred to as "type treatment" and is computerized. Press-on type has also faded away.

Copyfitting, once a time-consuming task, is now done swiftly and accurately on the computer. Your art director can indicate on the layout just how much space is being allotted for body copy. Then, using simple commands, the art director's computer can give you a character or word count based on type size.

In the past, there was considerable concern about fitting copy accurately to space. Much rewriting was

required if the copy was a few words too short or too long. If the latter, you invited sarcastic comments from printers, who would disdainfully say, "Space isn't elastic. Write your copy to the space." Today, if you're over or under a few words, you can relax, because type size can be adjusted to the decimal point through the use of the computer.

Photography. Hail to desktop programs. Lightening, darkening, silhouetting, masking, cropping, enlarging, and special effects alterations no longer need to be subcontracted to photo lab technicians or retouch artists.

Mechanical. At one time, large advertising agencies employed an army of skilled mechanical artists to precisely align and assemble the elements of an advertisement for publication. Aided by the computer, this assignment now goes to the art director.

Types of Layouts[2]

An idea for a proposed print advertisement may be presented for client approval with a drawing called a "layout."

A layout, as its name implies, is the physical grouping of all the elements in an advertisement as originally conceived by the art director. There are several types of layouts: thumbnail sketches, roughs, finished, and comprehensives.

Thumbnail Sketches

The "thumbnail sketch" is the type of layout that has the least drawing detail. This is a very rough layout done in one-half or one-fourth size, or even smaller, by the art director, and it is normally used when several different ideas for a new campaign are being considered.

From the thumbnail sketches, it is possible for you and your art director to determine quickly whether an idea has possibilities. You may find, however, that the various units won't fit and that it would be a waste of time to prepare further, more detailed, layout attempts.

In this age of computerization, many young art directors tend to skip the thumbnail stage and go to concepting right on the computer. This can result in shortcutting a critical step in the conceptual process.

It is better to exhaust all of the layout possibilities with thumbnail sketches to arrive at the best possible solution; *then* execute your idea on the computer. Your own creative potential may well be harmed by lazily beginning and ending with the one solution you created on the screen. This warning applies to copywriters as well as art directors, because copywriters often experiment with thumbnails to get a feel for the layout approach.

---

2 In the following section, you will find four sets of "Before" and "After" advertisements. These will demonstrate that it is almost always possible to improve layouts by incorporating simple changes. Judicious use of white space is especially important in achieving more attractive advertisements. Also important is the arrangement of elements, which will make it easier for the shopper to read the advertisement.

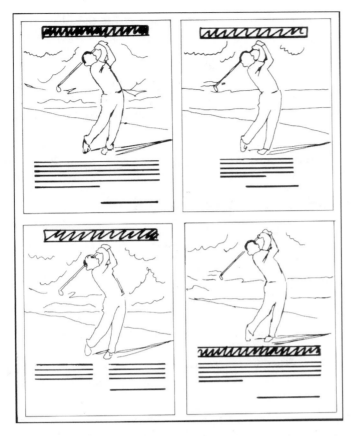

Figure 5–4. Thumbnail sketches. By executing thumbnails (and even a nonartist can do so), it is possible to experiment quickly with a number of different layout combinations. The art doesn't need to be expert because the purpose is to juggle elements until the best combination is achieved.

Figure 5–5. Rough layout. After the thumbnail (see Figure 5–4), the artist "roughs" up a layout that gives an idea of the finished concept. At this stage changes can be made inexpensively. If the client is sophisticated, he or she can visualize from a rough such as this. Some clients, however, like to work from more finished layouts.

Rough Layouts

When you have decided upon a headline, subheads, captions, and an illustrative suggestion for an advertisement, you will present the art director with this material, pointing out which selling points are to get the main emphasis and in what sequence the other elements of the advertisement should logically follow.

From this information, the art director will then arrange the advertisement in an orderly, balanced manner, roughing in your headlines and making a very rough sketch of your illustrative suggestion (or a different one, if it will work better).

This is called a "rough layout," or "visual," and from it you can determine whether the final job will focus proper attention on the right parts of your message and, in general, whether your idea is going to jell.

During your early years as a copywriter, you may be working under a copy chief or supervisor, with whom you will be required to clear your ideas before passing them on to members of the art department.

When the art director has made the rough layout, you will then discuss it with your superiors, and the three of you will decide whether it is okay to proceed or whether more roughs are needed. Possibly, especially if you are

working in an advertising agency, the rough layout or layouts will also be shown to others who are working on the account—contact people, account executives, and on some occasions, even representatives of the client's advertising department.

Finished and Comprehensive Layouts

Once the rough layout is approved by all those who are concerned with its formative stages, the art director is ready to do a "finished layout" or "comprehensive layout." Such layouts are more complete than "roughs." The client can obtain an accurate idea of what the printed advertisement will look like from the layout.

The "comprehensive" is a layout that carries the elements of the advertisement into a more refined stage. It serves two purposes: (1) to present the elements to the people who have the final say in approving them for publication; and (2) to solicit new business or to present an entirely new departure for an old campaign.

When advertisements are presented formally, all major elements in the advertisement appear, as nearly as possible, the way they will actually look in the printed advertisement. Because most of your clients will not possess the

Sweet Swinger

To play like a winner you have to look like one. In Sweet Swinger Golf Wear, you'll have the confident appearance of a professional—ready to challenge the most difficult courses.

Golf, Inc.

Figure 5–6. Comprehensive layout. All the elements are presented well enough in the comprehensive to furnish an excellent idea of the printed advertisement. Comprehensives require much art time and can be expensive. Usually, few changes will be made—preferably none.

trained imagination of you and your art director, they may be unable to visualize the published advertisement from a rough layout.

Comprehensive layouts are done with precision because of their use in presenting a new campaign idea or soliciting new business. They are usually "slick" enough to give a graphic idea of how the final job should look. When you ask an artist to make a comprehensive layout, the artist will very often ask you, "*How* comprehensive?"

In finished and comprehensive layouts, the standard procedure is to place type in the headlines, subheads, caption headings, and copy areas and to include a fairly accurate sketch of the illustration.

In some places, the rule is that you should spend your time writing body copy and captions while the layout is being made, so that your entire advertisement will be ready for study at the same time. You can than take up any final copy polishing while the finished or comprehensive layout is with the art department.

This "rule" depends, however, on the situation. As mentioned in a preceding chapter, you may, when presenting campaign ideas, merely write headlines and suggest ideas for the main illustrations. The body copy can be done later.

If, however, you know what you want to write and you have done the needed background thinking and investiga-

tion, you may prefer to write all the copy in the advertisement before you give it to the artist. If you do, the artist will know how much space is to be occupied by the copy and can do the layout accordingly.

Sometimes, when the layout technique for a campaign has already been determined, you will write the same amount of copy for every advertisement because the illustration size will be the same in every instance and the space for the copy will not vary from advertisement to advertisement.

✳ Steps in Print Production

After the layout and copy for your advertisement have been okayed by all of the necessary individuals, it is ready for production.

Production of any advertisement requires the following procedure:

1. The art director calls in a commercial freelance artist to make the final art (unless there is someone on the staff who can do the finished art). This usually requires a specialist in some phase of art, depending upon whether the illustration is to be a careful line drawing in ink, a painting, a cartoon, a photograph, or a wash drawing.

   Your art director could possibly do this artwork, but it is normally the job of a specialist, and in any event, the art director probably wouldn't have the time to do this in addition to other duties. It is the custom in many agency operations for the art director to farm out the actual artwork in this manner.

   Although some retail advertising departments also farm out this work, most have staff artists who do the final artwork. Except in rare cases, it is the function of the art director to supervise the creation of the final art. The director may ask your opinion on certain points, and you certainly are privileged to offer any suggestions you may have, but the responsibility for the job rests with the art department.

2. In most cases, art directors are also responsible for the direction of typesetting. As previously noted, almost all layout type is obtained from libraries of fonts available on software, ready to be loaded into the art director's computer. He can then choose the type style and typeset the copy.

3. Once the artwork is completed and approved and the copy is approved, the job passes to the printer. As previously stated, much of the work is produced by the art director on software or as black-and-white, camera-ready output.

Print Production: Know the Basics, But You Don't Need to Be an Authority

As in the case of art, you do not need to be an authority on production. Unless you feel that you're knowledgeable in thousands of typefaces and all of the complexities of the

Figure 5–7a. Before. Here is a layout that is well organized in the way it has grouped the two styles of furniture—Spanish and French. You will see, however, in the "After" version that an even more pleasing layout can be achieved. This example, and those in Figures 5–8, 5–9, and 5–13, courtesy of the Newspaper Advertising Bureau from *How to Make a Good Ad Better.*

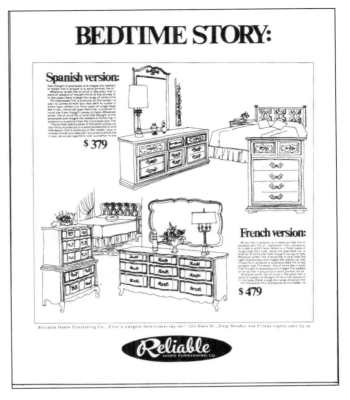

Figure 5–7b. After. As one change from the "Before" example, more white space is used giving the advertisement a pleasing, open look. Second, line art is used instead of halftones. Thus, details can be highlighted. Third, the new version has a clever headline that is set off for full impact. Fourth, there is less clutter with the elimination of the picture of the store, an element that adds nothing to the sales power of the advertisement. Most of all, this reworked layout demonstrates the role of white space in achieving attractive advertisements.

production processes, it is best to let the art department or production people take over. With or without a usable skill in production, you, as a copywriter, are still a valued commodity for your conceptual and strategic thinking and the crafted copy you turn out. These are the skills in your domain. If you know enough about production to work intelligently with your art director, that's usually enough, unless you're running a one-person operation that requires you to know every facet of the advertising operation.

Is it Risky to Use a Number of Typefaces in an Advertisement? Not Necessarily.

At one time, it was standard advice to resist using too many typefaces within the same advertisement. To some extent, this can still be good advice, but there has been a change in such thinking.

Since the early 1990s, there has been a so-called "type revolution" throughout the world of advertising and graphic design. The quest for advertising layouts with more impact has introduced a shift in typographic taste. The previous theory of limiting yourself to a small number of faces in an advertisement has been displaced.

Today, art directors freely mix and match typefaces, oversize and undersize words for emphasis, isolate words or phrases in boxes, set headlines in wavy or circular patterns (long a firm no-no), and even use a variety of colors.

In short, the rules have been shattered in this area of typographic freedom. If art directors choose to follow this new wave in typographic usage, they have the responsibility of doing so in good taste. You will see examples in this book that demonstrate the changing approach to typography. You will, however, see many illustrations that adhere to old practices. An art director should be guided by common sense when deciding whether to go new wave or stick with the traditional.

Guidelines for Typography

There are exceptions to every one of the following guidelines. In general, the rules of typography follow custom.

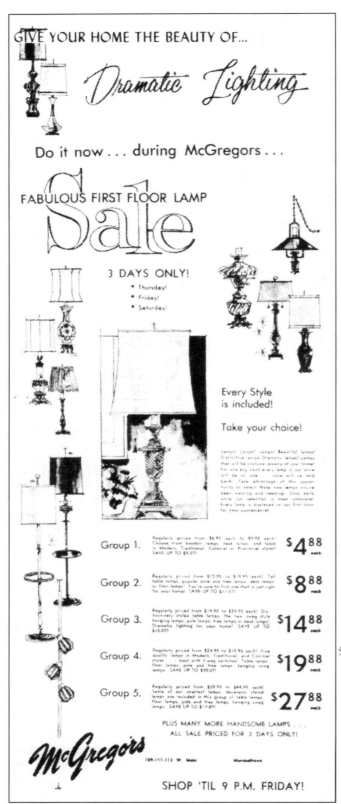

Figure 5–8a. Before. Every lamp in the store is on sale, a point not made clearly in the first layout. There is another problem with this layout that is solved in the following "After" version.

Figure 5–8b. After. There's no lack of clarity here. It's obvious that *every* lamp is on sale. It's more important to convey that point than to show a few styles. Likewise, the layout follows the principle of offering a dominant element. In the "Before" version there is nothing for the eye to focus on. In the new version we have more impact and excitement.

We find that what we are most accustomed to reading is what we read most comfortably and easily.

1. Body text should not be set in type smaller than 10-point. Some folks wear glasses.
2. A long copy block must be broken up! This is one rule that you will hardly ever want to break.
3. Avoid setting the body copy in reverse whenever possible. Reverse type will cut down readership.
4. If the paragraph leads are not indented, more leading is required between paragraphs.
5. Don't print the text over illustrations or design elements. It is a signal to the reader that the copy really isn't very important.
6. Use lowercase instead of caps in display lines. Lowercase is more legible.
7. When there are several copy elements, align them wherever possible. This is to avoid a cluttered, busy look to an ad.

8. Never run a picture without a caption. (Well, hardly ever.)
9. Try to run a cutline under every main illustration.
10. Don't be afraid of "widows"!
11. Use normal punctuation. Commas, semicolons, periods, and dashes serve a useful purpose in guiding the reader through your copy. Leaders (those nasty little dots. . .) usually are merely a crutch for the proper punctuation. In addition, they make copy look messy and uninviting.
12. Don't overdo the bangs. Exclamation points are often the refuge of the writer who can't think up exciting thoughts.
13. Keep your sentences short. They make copy look less formidable. They lend a feeling of urgency and conviction.
14. Use italics sparingly. Italics are good for occasional emphasis. A lot of italics in a piece of copy make it look paler and weaker, instead of adding impact.

Color: When to Use It

Sometimes you *can't* use color. Very small space units in magazines and newspapers don't qualify for color. Yet, these small advertisements often pull readership and sales very effectively. This is one answer to the question whether you "must" use color. Obviously, it is not an absolute requirement.

Still, research shows consistently that, all things being equal, color advertisements perform better than black-and-white advertisements. Common sense will tell you, for example, that the subject matter of an advertisement is important in making the color decision. Draperies, color film, floor covering, and food products are just a few of the categories that cry for color. These products are sold through color.

Advertisers whose products don't necessarily require color for selling effectiveness use color simply for added attention value.

Full color isn't always needed. Occasionally, instead of calling for a four-color treatment, you will do better to use one color in order to focus on an important element in the advertisement, such as a new lipstick shade.

In Layouts, Make a Hero Out of the Package

Although no one denies the importance of headlines, body copy, and illustrations, the most important single element in hundreds of advertisements is the package. If your product comes in a bottle, carton, package, or some other container, you and the artist should plan to make the package the "hero" in the layout. It should be big enough to have impact and should be placed for utmost prominence.

Consumers may forget your headlines when they're in the supermarket or drugstore, but they *must* remember the package. Package design is an art. Once that design has

been approved, the advertising must give it featured billing. This does not mean that you will very often ask that the package be the *only* illustration in the advertisement; in fact, readership studies reveal that this technique tends to obtain low attention. It *does* mean that in building the layout, the artist is ever conscious of the placement and prominence of the package. It is not an element to be inserted as an afterthought.

Such featuring of the package is vital in all media, including magazines, newspapers, outdoor, transit, and television. Even radio commercials use such phrases as "Look for it in the bright blue and white package on your grocer's shelves." If such an announcement has been preceded by strong featuring of the package in print advertisements, the radio commercial is thus enhanced.

When Should You Use Artwork Instead of Photography?

Photography is most often used in advertising illustration because of its realism. This is true whether you are concerned with consumer or business advertising. Thus, under normal circumstances, you will call for, or expect, photography for your advertising illustrations.

Still, artwork *is* used and may be suitable if:

- **Exaggeration is desirable,** as in the case of some high-fashion advertising in which the models have a fashionably elongated look never found in real life.
- **A schematic, or cross section, is wanted,** as may be the case in an industrial advertisement aimed at engineers.
- **A seasonal illustration is needed** in the off-season, such as a snow scene in the summer or a plowing scene in the harvest season.
- **It is difficult, or impossible, to find the right people as models for photography.** These might be current people or historical figures.
- **Speed is important.** It may take a long time to get the proper photographic shot, but a good artist can sketch what is needed quickly and on order.
- **Cartoon treatment is desired.** This treatment might be especially suitable for comic page advertising or for advertising to children.
- **Way-out mood or atmosphere is needed.** Horror, exclusiveness, or satire may often be conveyed more starkly or subtly through artwork.

Do You Do Rough Layouts? Try These Ideas

Here are some suggestions if you are a copywriter who works in small organizations—agencies, companies, or retail stores—that expect you to do rough layout work.

1. Make sure you supply a dominant element, something for the reader's eyes to focus upon and to attract his attention. This element will usually be the illustration,

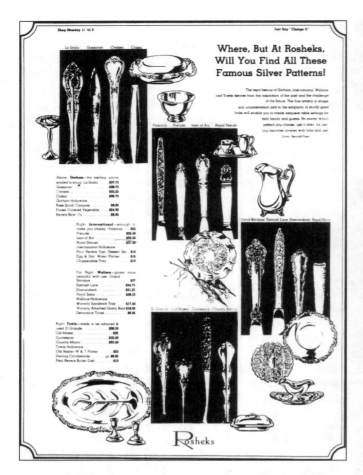

Figure 5–9a. Before. In this instance, the layout artist followed accustomed practice in displaying the product groupings in a reverse-C eyeflow pattern but notice in the "After" example, how the new layout has made reading the advertisement even simpler for the reader.

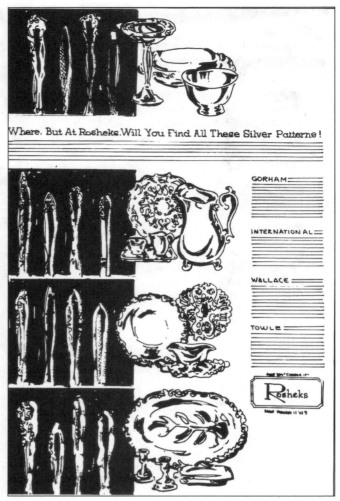

Figure 5–9b. After. Now we have an "easier" advertisement to read. Also, the re-do gives more space to the item, enabling the reader to examine the patterns more clearly. The headline, too, stretches across the advertisement creating more impact than the headline in the "Before" version, where it is tucked away in the upper corner for low visibility. In version "After," as pleasing as it is, it is possible that the reader might hesitate before deciding which copy block pertains to which of the four illustrations.

but sometimes it can be a big headline. Above all, avoid making layouts that have no impact because you've cluttered them with a number of different elements of equal size.

2. Make your headlines and illustrations competitive in size and character with other advertising. This suggestion is especially important when your advertisement is to be on a big newspaper page with advertisements that are equal in size, or even bigger.

   One way to tell whether your advertisement's elements *are* competitive is to mount your layout on a page with other display advertisements. Then, put the page on the floor or pin it up on a wall corkboard. You'll see quickly if you've made such elements as the headline, illustrations, logotype, or price figures big enough to compete.

   In most advertisements, make the logotype big enough, or distinctive enough, to stand out. Now and then, the mood of the advertisement or the nature of the product is such that the logo can be relatively small. Usually, however, it must be commanding enough to

ensure that readers know the advertiser, or the product, being advertised.

3. Keep copy elements such as headlines, subheads, and price figures out of illustration area. When such elements intrude into the illustration area, they distract from the illustration and give a cluttered feeling to the advertisement.

4. With some exceptions, don't play tricks with copy and headlines by putting them in circles, wavy lines, upside down, or in odd shapes. Whatever attention value you achieve will be offset by loss of readership and by the annoyance felt by many readers who find the message hard to read.

5. Favor the 3-to-5 proportion in layouts. From ancient times, artists have preferred the 3-to-5 proportion.

Figure 5–10. Imaginative visual for a farm product. The art director who composed this layout probably had other art directors muttering, "Why didn't I think of that?" Elsewhere in this book you will find other Dekalb advertisements—all marked by imaginative visuals and copy. They stand out in the agri-business field.

Figure 5–11. Offbeat illustration and headline followed by straight-line copy. This engaging and startling illustration insures strong and immediate attention for the advertisement as a whole, and is connected well with the following informative copy. *Reprinted with permission of Andersen Consulting.*

Except for unusual circumstances, they shun squarish shapes; long, narrow shapes; or wide, shallow shapes. A 6 inch by 10 inch advertisement exemplifies the 3-to-5 proportion. Furthermore, the 3-to-5 proportion fits nicely into the "pyramid" construction of newspaper pages. In fact, a wide, shallow advertisement may be rejected by newspapers because it is not suitable for the pyramid construction. Examine Figure 5–12 to see why this would be so.

How to Make Campaign Advertisements Stand Out

While, in national advertising you may, at times, devise advertisements that are not part of a campaign, most are part of a series that carry out a theme. This same theme may be used for a half year or a year, or it may go on indefinitely.

In order to identify advertisements in your campaign and make them stand out, you employ certain techniques in copy and art. In copy, each advertisement will feature a writing style, an individual use of words, a distinctive head-line approach, copy of a certain length, and possibly, the use of subheads or a slogan.

It is your art director, however, who will make the greatest contribution to the campaign resemblance in advertisement after advertisement. The two of you will collaborate in achieving this resemblance. This is truly a team effort, because there has to be complete agreement before you launch a long-term campaign. Here are some of the art elements to consider; note that these elements also involve typography.

1. If you use color, use similar colors in all advertisements. Type style should also be consistent. Don't change families of type.
2. Slogans and trademark characters (if either is used) should be in the same location and should be of the same size.
3. A distinctive logo (product or company name) should look exactly the same in every advertisement and usually should be in the same location. This is certainly one of the most important requirements for the campaign resemblance and product or company identification.

Figure 5–12. Industrial advertisement with dominant element. In industrial advertising you show your product big. It is the hero of the advertisement and, if you're addressing a technically-minded audience, you can cut away portions to show the insides. In this case, there was much to talk about, so rather than overload the body copy, the advertiser has used take-out lines to call attention to a number of important features.

Figure 5–13a. Before. Although this layout sets out the different elements in an orderly way, the theme of the advertisement—Beat the Tax—is somewhat lost.

4. A well-designed border can call immediate attention to a campaign advertisement, but this is usually more true if the campaign features advertisements of less than a page.
5. Headlines and illustrations that look alike mark the campaign advertisements instantly. This resemblance is created by using main headlines of the same length and type size, and illustrations of the same size and character. Character, in this instance, refers to the subject matter used and style of art or photography.
6. Copy blocks should be of the same size and usually, but not always, follow the same arrangement or placement.
7. The balance of the layout will be consistent once you have decided whether it should be formal or informal.

The result of the planning that you and your artist have done should be a series of advertisements that are so distinctive that readers will eventually be able to name the advertiser or product instantly without reading the body copy or even seeing the logotype. Most important, to repeat, is the incorporation of these various elements in

the same way until (and if) it is decided that it is time to create a new campaign.

Subject Matter That Pulls In Illustrations

Illustrations are as boundless as the imagination of artists. No one knows for certain what illustration will succeed or fail. Still, some subject matter of illustrations seems to have a consistent appeal. A few of the popular approaches are listed here:

- People pull better than things. Generally, an illustration featuring a person or persons—especially if something interesting is being done by the person or persons—will pull better readership than illustrations that feature an object such as the product, package, or something else that is inanimate.

  This suggestion isn't always pertinent in industrial advertising, however, because industrial readers may

Figure 5–13b. After. In this re-do, the "Beat the Tax" theme is dramatically highlighted in big type set in a reverse block. Furthermore, the whole layout has a cleaner, more open look. Because this is a once-a-year, important merchandising event, it is played up; but the individual items and prices are played down. Certainly, with the new layout treatment, no one will miss the theme.

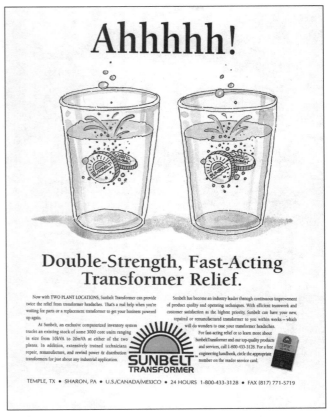

Figure 5–14. Industrial advertisement that uses artwork instead of photograph. Although it is generally felt that photography should be the choice in industrial illustrations, an occasional departure such as this makes for a refreshing change. Consequently, the advertisement stands out. Although the illustration may be whimsical, the following copy is straightforward and convincing.

well be more interested in an illustration of a piece of machinery or in a blueprint or schematic drawing.

- Babies, puppies, kittens, and animals in general have pulling power. Studies are available that tell which animals pull better than others. For example, because many people dislike cats, a cat isn't always the best choice to feature.
- Men tend to pay more attention to advertisements featuring men, and women are more attracted to advertisements featuring women. As you can imagine; there are numerous exceptions to this observation. Furthermore, as an observation, it is much more pertinent when the person in the illustration, regardless of the gender, is shown doing something interesting and/or relevant to the interests of the readers.
- Occasionally, an all-type advertisement works well. By the nature of the type and the editorial tone of the

advertisement, the type serves almost as an illustration. The all-type approach is used when an announcement of an important development or of a dramatic new product or service is needed. Because illustrations are so very important as attention-getters and for actual selling, it is generally better to use an illustration, but you may occasionally choose the all-type technique. If you do, make it look as much like surrounding editorial material as possible, with a big headline and news-type appearance.

- Celebrities pull well when featured in advertisements. Here again, it is necessary to qualify. Results are better if the celebrity can be connected in some way with the product or service advertised—such as a sports star and athletic equipment or a situation such as the one in the Volkswagen advertisement that showed a 7' 2" basketball star riding comfortably in the small car.

Just showing the celebrity isn't enough. The celebrity should be doing something interesting, relevant (to the reader), or both. Thus, if you had to choose between showing the product by itself or showing a celebrity by

Figure 5–15. Unusual illustration technique. In planning this advertisement, the art director had a problem—how to advertise seven items without crowding the page. The problem was solved in the ingenious method you see here.

Figure 5–16. All-type advertisement. Sometimes, when there is an important product development, the all-type advertisement creates a news flavor and importance that makes it possible to eliminate illustration. In this instance, the advertisement appeared in *Farm Journal* magazine. Its readers are more inclined than consumer readers to read long, illustration-less advertisements because they are seeking help and information in advertising. *Copyright © 1994 American Cyanamid Company. Reprinted with permission.*

himself or herself, in most cases you would choose the former, because the product should always be the "hero." The use of a celebrity should be employed only to enhance that product-as-hero status.

Want to Help Your Advertisements Stand Out? Use a Distinctive Logotype

When an advertisement does not carry the company's name, its "signature" is usually the product name. (With such family names as Campbell and Heinz, the product name is actually part of the company name. That is, the brand name, Heinz, is derived from the full firm name H. J. Heinz, Co.)

The style of type or lettering in which the name of a given company's product is displayed sometimes varies from one advertisement to another. Most often though it is given a distinctive design, and almost without exception, it is used in this particular style in every advertisement and in all other promotional material, including the actual product label.

When the product's name is thus treated, it is referred to formally as a "logotype" and informally as a "logo." Excellent

specimens of such logotypes are those for Sunkist, Hoover, Coca-Cola, Crest, and KFC to cite but a few.

Under most circumstances, it is preferable to use one consistent design in the logotypes. This makes for far greater recall value than when the style of type or lettering is frequently changed.

Creation of a logotype, being primarily a matter of design, is not the direct responsibility of the copywriter; nevertheless, you will often make suggestions and offer criticism of logotypes. A little knowledge of logotypes will enable you to tell whether the finished logotype is sufficiently simple, easy to read, and distinctive.

Since the logotype is of a distinctive style, and is ordinarily unlike the type in which the body text is set, it is rarely included within the actual copy block. Although you will not design the logotype or the signature, you may insist, for instance, that they be displayed in type that is big enough to be seen easily by readers.

Is this your idea
of a retirement plan?

There's an old saying which suggests that "A penny saved is a penny earned." We might also add that "The early bird gets the worm." At Farm Bureau Insurance, a qualified retirement plan is a wise, tax-deferred invest- ment for individuals who want to retire comfortably. It's a matter of planning. It's a matter of timing. And it's bigger than a Mason jar. Call today and let your local Farm Bureau Insurance agent help get you started on a retire- ment plan that is right for you.

Farm Bureau Insurance
For Retirement.

Figure 5–17. Layout using dominant-element. To insure attention for an advertisement, it is almost always desirable to have a dominant element in the visual on which the eye can focus. This is done well in this newspaper advertisement. Insurance advertisements are a challenge to art directors because illustrating a service is harder than illustrating a tangible product. *Courtesy Farm Bureau Insurance. Creative work by Cranfill & Company.*

Readership studies consistently show that many readers of print advertisements are unable to recall the name of the advertiser or the product. Quite often this is due to a silly delicacy on the part of the advertisers about display- ing their names in a type size that they think is vulgar.

The delicacy might trace back to an art department that is more concerned with artistic integrity than with such mundane considerations as registering company or prod- uct names.

Naturally, judgment must be used. An advertisement for Tiffany's, for example, will use restraint in the kind and size of type used for the logotype. For most advertisers and products, however, it is better to be conspicuous than to be delicate and unseen.

As the copywriter, you have a stake in this matter. You have the right to question the inconspicuous logotype or signature. Make your voice heard, or that low readership figure will be blamed on your copy and not on that diminutive logotype or signature.

A Few of the Art and Production Terms It Will Be Useful to Know

Although it is impossible to supply a full list of art and pro- duction terminology, here are a few of the terms that you may be using frequently, if not daily. These terms apply specifically to print advertising; you will need to learn another set of terms for television. For anyone seriously interested in the terminology of design and printing, there is a book—*Graphically Speaking*—that is a must.[3] Some of the terms that appear in the following list are included by permission of the author. Hundreds more terms are included in this excellent guide.

Bleed. Printed matter runs to the edge of the page. This creates an illusion of size and gives a natural appear- ance. It may add to cost—about 10 to 15 percent in some magazines. It is usually not available in regular press runs of newspapers.

Body type (or copy). Type size used in the body of an advertisement. The sizes range from 6 to 14 points. It is smaller than type used for headlines (called display type).

Broadside. A large printed sheet used as a circular and folded into a size that can be used for mailing. It differs from a folder in that its printed matter runs across the sheet, regardless of the fold.

CD-I (Compact Disc-Interactive). Used through a computer or television, the CD-I—a compact optical disc—displays type and plays visual and audio information, including items such as photographs, videos, sounds, and music. It can be randomly accessed, much like a comput- er's memory.

CD-ROM (Compact Disc, Read Only Memory). This plays audio and visual information, but unlike the CD-I, it can't be randomly accessed.

CEPS (Color Electronic Prepress System). This will include any combination of computers, scanners, printers, and other hardware and applicable software designed for a number of prepress activities, from image assembly to output for printing and proofing.

Clip Art. These are ready-to-use drawings that can be bought. They are used for unlimited reproduction and are free of copywriter restrictions. Storage can be on a com- puter disk or glossy camera-ready sheet.

Cloning. A computer process that duplicates a portion of an existing image.

CMYK. Abbreviation for the four process colors: Cyan, Magenta, Yellow, and Key (black).**Color Separation.** Division of images into four film halftones for platemaking and proofing in four-color process printing.

Column Inch. Advertisers use column inches to mea- sure the size of advertisements; they are charged for the number of column inches they use. A column inch is one inch deep and one column wide, regardless of the width of

3 *Graphically Speaking: An Illustrated Guide to the Working Language of Design and Printing.* By Mark Beach, Elk Ridge Publishing, Manzanita, OR. 97130. Produced in collaboration with Graphic Communications Association.

the column. A newspaper utilizing the SAU (Standard Advertising Unit) is typically 6 columns wide by 21 inches deep, for a total of 126 column inches to the page. Magazine advertisements are measured and priced in terms of page units such as a page, quarter page, half page, etc. Column inches would be used for magazine billing purposes only for very small advertisements.

Computer Graphics. Any images created by using a computer. Includes such items as illustrations, maps, and charts.

Contrasts. A difference in tonal values in an illustration or photograph that gives strong highlights or shadows.

Copyfit. Calculating the required font and point text space or editing text and typography to fit text into a layout.

Crop. To cut off or trim an illustration or photo to make it fit into a space.

DDCP (Direct Digital Color Proof). A color proof that is made without having to first make separation films. Typically, this is output on a laser printer.

Desktop Publishing (DTP). Using a personal computer to design and manipulate images, to originate type treatments, or to assemble pages for communication materials.

Display Type. Larger type, usually starting with 14 points, that is used for headlines, subheads, and other material that is to stand out.

DPI (Dots-per-inch). Used to measure resolution of input (scanners), display (monitors), and output devices such as laser printers and imagesetters.

Electronic Mechanical. A mechanical file in electronic file form.

EPS (Encapsulated PostScript File). A computer file that contains images and PostScript commands. Such files can be manipulated and enhanced without changing the contents of the files.

Free-Standing Insert (FSI). Loose insert between pages or sections of publications such as newspapers, magazines, or flyers.

Highlight. Light area in an illustration. This term is used frequently in photographic work and is understood to be the opposite of shadow.

Island Position. An advertisement entirely surrounded by editorial material is in this position. It is most often found in magazines.

Kern. A reduction of space between letters or characters. Kerning makes the characters appear to fit better together.

Laser Printer. Output device that uses a laser beam and xerography to reproduce images and type. It has a lower resolution than an imagesetter because dots are created on paper by toner rather than by chemical crystals.

Leading. The spacing between lines of type, or the distance between baselines of type. It varies by a point system, such as 2-point leading. If there is no leading, the type is described as "set solid."

Live area. The portion of a mechanical on which images and type will print. Crop marks appear outside the live area.

Lowercase. The small letters in a font of type as distinguished from capital letters.

Moiré. Unattractive patterns and screen tint patterns created in printing. Usually appearing on photos, these patterns result from improperly aligned screens.

Original Art. Original photographs or illustrations prepared by a photographer or artist for reproduction purposes.

Pica. In printing, a pica equals 12 typographical points, or 1/6 inch.

Point of Purchase Display (POP). Usually refers to retail store displays on a floor, shelf, counter, or other location where consumers can make purchases. Also called Point of Sale.

Progressive Proof. Press proof displaying each color of a four-color process job separately as well as the colors in combination.

RAM (Random Access Memory). Short-term computer memory used to hold, manage, and perform functions on files and applications currently in use.

Raster Image Processor (RIP). Translates page descriptions into rasters for output. Conversion of pages to rasters is often called "ripping" images due to the abbreviation RIP.

Retouch. To enhance or correct flaws in negatives, print, or film separations through techniques such as airbrushing, spotting, or softening.

Self-Mailer. A direct mail piece that can be mailed without an envelope.

Supplement. A separate newspaper section containing information on specially featured topics such as sports and entertainment.

Swipe. A collection of illustrated material filed by advertising artists. Such files may be filled with advertisements under headings such as "Babies," "Animals," or "Machinery." An artist can refer to the file for ideas. Ideas can be lifted in their entirety or be used as a point of departure. Collections like these are sometimes called "crib" files.

Tear Sheet. Page from a periodical that is sent to advertisers, authors, or artists as a notice of publication and evidence of satisfactory printing.

Track. Adjustment of space between all characters in a line, paragraph, or entire document by taking into account both sizes and optical traits of each character, unlike kerning. It is used to improve the legibility of a document.

TRUMATCH Swatching System. Used to specify CMYK color combinations to create as many as 2,000 colors. The colors are arranged by saturation, hue, and brightness.

Widow. A very short line carried over to the top of a newspaper column or magazine page. Sometimes a copywriter will be asked to rewrite a piece of copy in order to eliminate the widow.

WYSIWYG. (Pronounced "WIZ-E-WIG") Acronym for What You See Is What You Get. It is used to refer to the ability of a computer screen to reproduce what appears on the output device as closely as possible.

Comments by Three Art Directors on the Use of Computers in Their Work

The following are three tell-it-like-it-is observations by three very experienced art directors. Read what they say carefully. These comments can help you in your understanding and use of computers in advertising art.

Although computers have influenced many areas of advertising and marketing, nowhere has their impact been more noticeable than in art departments across the land. As you read what these art directors have to say, you will find that each is still learning computer application to some extent and that all three have found that computers are a powerful aid in the preparation of advertising.

Art Director No. 1: Works for a medium-sized advertising agency that specializes in design and is heavy in business-to-advertising.

The computer has given control of production to the designer, control that used to belong to vendors—typesetters, color separators, and retouchers.

This is both good and bad. It is good in that it gives to talented designers the power to be even more creative and detail oriented. It is bad in that it gives control to less talented or sloppy designers, and with that control comes responsibilities that used to belong to expert craftsmen in typesetting, color separation, stripping, and retouching. A bad designer has more power to create a bad design—aesthetically bad, illegible, and poorly thought out. A sloppy designer is more likely to miss or create typos, design flaws, bad color separations, and ink traps.

A comparison of the pre-computer design process with the current process reveals some of the strengths and the dangers of computer design.

Before computers: The designer hand-drew a layout with handlettered headlines, greeked text, and marker-rendered images. This could take hours, and color or typeface changes would require a whole new layout. When the copy was approved, the typewritten copy was specified for type style, size, line length, drop caps, etc., and was sent out to a typesetter who set the type, proofed it, and sent the galleys back to the designer. The designer then cut apart the type galleys, pasted it up with artwork on an artboard, marked it up with directions for color breaks, and sent it along with art and photos to the color separator. The color separator created films from the artboards and artwork, stripped it all together, and sent proofs to the designer to approve. Final films and proofs are then delivered to the printer.

Any changes made by the client during this process were time consuming and expensive. In the early stages, changes would require more hand-rendered comps. In the later stages, they would require additional typesetting and film-work.

With computers: The designer does layout on the computer. He or she can scan the images, import text, and *quickly* try different layouts, colors, typefaces, and sizes. When the copy is approved, it can be imported into the layout and finessed.

The client can see, even in early stages, a very tight, finished-looking comp. When the art and copy is approved, it is sent on disk to the separator (if color separations are needed) or directly to the printer.

Any changes made by the client during this process can be made fairly quickly. Color and layout changes would require a little computer work for the designer, and a color laser print could then be printed out to show to the client. Copy changes can be made and viewed in place right up to the moment the disk goes out to the printer/separator.

Due to the speed and ease with which copy changes can be made, clients are much more likely to make changes right up until the last minute.

Art Director No. 2: Works for a good-sized agency in Chicago that services a diversified list of consumer and business accounts.

My first brush with a computer in relation to design was in college (Herron School of Art), in 1984. It was a semester-long project that utilized a computer program to design a two-minute animated sequence. The reason the project stretched over an entire semester was because it took that length of time to access the program itself. The "mouse," which is now an indispensable command tool for every computer user, simply did not exist. All shapes and movements were input into the computer through the use of complicated, mathematical keyboard commands. At the time, many theories were floating about concerning the future of computers and their role in art direction, and the consensus was that they would one day change the industry. After working on the animation project, I couldn't believe it. The process was just too laborious.

In the early 1990s, I became fluent in QuarkXPress and Photoshop, two computer programs that have redefined my function as an art director. In other words, in less than a decade since I was fairly certain computers would perhaps have no role in art direction, computer technology has advanced to the point of user friendliness and has made a significant impact on my profession. This impact has been felt in a number of positive ways:

- Through the use of scanned images and typesetting capabilities, computers help to better communicate a creative's "vision" for an advertisement or marketing vehicle to an account executive or client.
- Revisions to layouts can be accomplished with incredible speed as compared to traditional pencil sketches or marker comps.
- Any array of mediums, from photography and rough marker comps to traditional or computer illustration, can be integrated and manipulated with a single computer.
- An art director gains more hands-on control of the multiple elements of a project.

The use of a computer is a day-to-day element of my job as an art director, and in many ways, it has indeed changed the industry. I wouldn't, however, go so far as to say they've revolutionized the profession of art direction. In the end, computers are extremely quick and capable tools that help art directors get closer to their vision and visualization of a concept. But the generation of the concept itself still lies exclusively within the mind and imagination of art directors themselves.

Art Director No. 3: Works for one of the world's largest advertising agencies as a senior art director.

I've been an art director for five years and have used a computer in my work ever since I started. Until recently, I worked mainly on TV, so I used the Mac to set tag lines or to create key frames of visual ideas/treatments that I had in my head but didn't have handy samples of. I never use the Mac when I'm concepting. I still use pen and paper. I use the Mac to flesh out or demonstrate concepts. It's strictly an executional tool for me.

I mentioned earlier that until recently, I worked mostly on TV. Well, my partner and I are now responsible for developing interactive material.

Right now we are working on the online aspect. Plans for my clients to have a presence on MicroSoft Network, America Online, and the Internet are being developed. We are currently determining just what that presence will be. This form of advertising lives only on computers. That's how we send it out, and that's how consumers see it. The medium will eventually support Quick Time movies, animation, and virtual reality features, but for now everything is static graphics.

My partner and I still concept about content in a traditional way, but as soon as we have a rough idea, we both attach ourselves to our Macs and go. I create "pages" for each subject we think up. I create a place for the text to live. I also create a lot of icons for buttons that take you to other areas. I'm also responsible for creating a consistent look for all the pages—there could be hundreds by the time we're through. Since whatever I create will live only on a computer screen, that is where I experiment and finally build everything. I suppose I could sketch out ideas with pen and paper, but if I've got an idea in my head, I'll know faster if it's going to work or not by just building it on the Mac.

I've got a great set of tools with which to do all this building. I have several software applications that I use together to achieve a final "look." I usually start out with Photoshop. As the name implies, I use it to manipulate photos or art work that I have scanned into the computer. This application lets me get everything I need into the computer at the size, color, and resolution I want. Once I've arranged the images the way I want them on the page in Photoshop, I take the file into Painter (my favorite application). Painter lets you draw and create using traditional fine arts techniques such as charcoal, watercolor, oils, pastels, etc. Everything finally comes together in Illustrator. Here, I piece together all of my images and set the type for the page. From here it's sent—via e-mail—to the online guys, who program it, make all my buttons work, and link it to other text links. The client also views and approves it via e-mail. I only print it out to keep track of what's been done.

Since we got this interactive assignment, I have been on my computer constantly. I love the work and it's a lot of fun, but I still like to get away from the machines and draw with a toxic marker on wood-based paper. Computers certainly help art directors, but they don't magically make you better.

CHAPTER 6

Headlines
They Attract, They Inform, and They Sell. It's Vital to Write Good Ones (Part A)

Amy Swanson sighed. All morning she'd whacked out headlines for a new model sports car. Not a winning headline in the bunch. Her boss, Marian Glassman, looked in. "Still at it? Give it a rest. Work on something else for a while and then try again." Glassman, an old pro, saw all of those crumpled sheets around Amy's desk and knew the problem. She had learned from painful experience that "keeper" headlines usually came after many tries. Like Amy, she didn't begrudge the time and effort because she agreed with the conventional wisdom that rates the headlines as the single most important element in an ad.

Most writers agonize over headlines. Rarely does the usable headline come quickly. It's write, write, and write, until suddenly that jewel of a headline appears. Writing a good headline is the hardest task of a copywriter. By comparison, body copy is relatively easy. Furthermore, the direction of the body copy is shaped by what is said in the headline and illustration. With only a small percentage of your audience reading as much as 50 percent of the body copy, you must make the headline count. If you do, you'll increase the number of body-copy readers.

Write for the Headline Skimmers

Jack Campbell is a nervous type. Although he boasts about his reading of magazines and newspapers, the truth is that he's a "skimmer" where advertisements are concerned. Unless advertisers can catch his attention with headlines and subheads, they can scratch Mr. Campbell as a prospect. A quick flick of his gaze is all they get for their carefully prepared advertisements.

Mrs. Campbell, although she runs the household and works at a parttime job, spends much more time on adver-

tising than does her husband. But with her double duties, she has no time to waste. The advertiser's task is to get busy Mrs. Campbell, and others like her, to hesitate before going on to the next advertisement.

In either situation, the advertiser relies on headlines to flag the reader and to create enough interest to force that pausing over the advertisement. The headline doesn't *convince* the reader, that comes later. It says in effect, "Here's something interesting," "Here's news," "Here's a useful item," "Here's something profitable for you," or "Here's an easy way to do something."

When you've written your headline, you've taken your first step toward the sale. It's a vital step, because if you fail to attract Mr. and Mrs. Campbell to your advertisement or your message, you're out of the action completely. You must get that initial attention and sparking of interest.

Winning Advertisements Combine Good Headlines with Good Illustrations

Arguments between copywriters and art directors about which does the better job of gaining the reader's atten-

To the birds, it matters very little that these boxes of recycled paper reflect a child's creativity and involvement.

But to the environmental education program that distributes these take-home nests, and Phillips Petroleum, who sponsors them, it matters a great deal.

Because as life unfolds inside these cardboard walls, so too does an enduring understanding and respect for the wonder of it all. Helping students realize a greater awareness and responsibility for the environment.

And confirming our belief that when you teach a child about nature, he learns facts about nature.

But bond a child with nature, and he learns to care.

PHILLIPS PETROLEUM COMPANY 66

Figure 6–1. Long-range institutional-advertisement campaign. See Figure 1–1a in Chapter 1 for a discussion of this campaign.

tion—the headline of the advertisement or the illustration—fail to settle the issue. Sometimes the illustration is the principal attention-getter; sometimes the headline wins.

Actually, you have only three ways of shouting "Stop and read" to your prospects:

• Headline alone
• Illustration alone
• A combination of both

You will find that—often enough to be called standard techniques—this last method will prove to be most logical. Headlines fall into certain categories or types. You will see how, in each type, the words and illustration are usually so closely allied that often neither the copywriter nor the art director could tell you which was the original thought.

Occasionally, the very first headline that rattles off your word processor will be what you use. Then again, you may work for hours to get the one you finally use. You will drop words, add words, change words, and shuffle words until the headline finally falls in place. Yet, you often end with the feeling that somewhere within you, an even better headline is crying for release.

Good Headlines Say: Hey! Pay Attention to Me!

For much of your creative time, you will be writing headlines that, in addition to attracting attention, must start to sell at once. You will often use the "sales appeals" of your product as attention-getting means. You must stop your audience by offering something they want, thus inviting their interest in further exposition of those appeals.

For example:

An Irish Stole to Keep You Warm

No literary talent was needed to fashion this headline, but it will interest anyone shopping for the product, and that counts more than high literary quality.

In contrast is this next headline for a hotel advertisement:

An exquisite escape from the humdrum

Here we have a different writing style that can be effective for hotels, restaurants, travel, fashion clothing, and a host of other products and services. This time the headline *does* have a literary air.

Most copywriters prefer writing unusual headlines, but they seldom get this chance. Day in and day out, your job will be much more prosaic than that. It will be a matter of stating the facts.

Headline writing varies a great deal with types of markets and types of media. The same techniques that are successful in one may not work well in others. Certain specialized principles apply to each of these fields: fashion, direct mail, catalog, trade and industrial, and retail newspaper advertising.

For the moment, consider only the agency copywriter who has a client with a product of national distribution, normal appeal, and reasonable price, and whose problem is to write headlines that will sell the product to the general public through magazine or national newspaper advertising.

Direct or Indirect Headlines: Which to Use?

In reviewing types of headlines that will be presented in the succeeding pages, keep in mind the differences between direct and indirect selling. *All* advertising headlines definitely fall into one of those two selling categories, regardless of which type of approach or appeal is used.

A "direct-selling" headline uses one or more of the primary sales features of your product to attract attention and influence sales. An "indirect-selling" headline merely stops the reader to get him to read past the heading.

The two previous examples illustrate the point:

An Irish Stole to Keep You Warm

This headline represents direct selling. An outstanding and desired feature gains immediate interest. The other headline:

An exquisite escape from the humdrum

sells a thought but offers nothing specific or direct.

You may ask, "when do you use a direct-selling approach, and when do you use an indirect one?" That depends almost entirely upon what you have to sell. If you can discover features in your product strong enough to arouse interest and stimulate sales response, then, by all means, headline them.

If you can attract your reader by telling him of the specific advantages your product has over others, you have a good chance to make an actual sale. The reader has enough interest in what you have to offer to read further. If, however, he must be caught by a nonselling device, you can't be sure that you won't lose him when you present your sales story.

As you review the types of headlines, note how many of them may be used directly or indirectly. Only in the "news" and in the "slogan, label, logotype" headlines will you find that either one or the other is a must. Those two, by their very nature, call for direct selling.

Headline Types

Everyone who writes about advertising will probably give you a list of headline types. You'll find one here. This list may be shorter than some and longer than others. It is not given as a definitive list but as a means of helping you visualize different types of headlines by their creation and function. If you just can't come up with a good headline—consult the list. It may suggest a new direction to try.

One point you should realize is that most headlines may fall into more than one classification. For example, the "stole" advertisement previously quoted can be classed as a news and direct benefit head, and the hotel headline can be classed as emotional or curiosity.

Except for a headline here and there that seems to defy classification, the following headline list covers headlines that you are likely to write. Sometimes a headline has no real meaning in itself because its meaning is clear only when the reader looks at the illustration.

News	Offbeat
Emotional	Curiosity
Direct benefit	Hornblowing
Directive	Slogan, label, and logotype

News

A news headline can be described as the workhorse of advertising because it's used so much; it should be used often, because readers are looking for new products, new features, new services, and new prices. In a sense, every advertisement contains news, but writers may elect to use headlines that aren't clearly news-type headlines for a variety of advertisements.

The true news headline is unmistakable. It presents a strong feature in a clear, brisk, no-nonsense manner. To be

Figure 6–2. Campaign advertisement. Instead of a headline, this advertisement uses a blurb at the top. It follows the general format of two other advertisements in the campaign (see Figure 9-1a and Figure 9-1b in Chapter 9). It is the introductory advertisement for a new product, but unlike the other two advertisements, it does not use a case history approach but, instead, stresses the announcement of the company's new product—and does so humorously.

sure that the readers are aware of the fact that news is being presented, the writer may use a word such as "new," or "introducing," or "announcing." (A danger here is that advertisement after advertisement in some magazines uses one or more of these words to the point of saturation. You might well aim at conveying the idea of new without using these words.)

A typical news headline follows:

Finally!
Ocean cruises for land lovers

By using the word "finally," the writer gave the headline a news flavor by conveying the development of a long-awaited event.

Rate the headlines you see in magazines and newspapers. Judge how quickly, clearly, and forcefully they give selling facts. Grade them on how well they attract attention and start the selling of the product or service. Also, notice whether they are believable—another must.

Be sure your product or service *deserves* a news headline. When you plan to use a news approach, determine quickly whether or not you really have a news story. Headlines announcing new features, sensational developments, unheard-of-low prices, or any of the other selling points must be backed up. You cannot afford to write a headline that will attract the attention of your readers because of its news value and then fail to gain conviction as you develop your later copy.

If you announce "a new amazingly low price," be sure that your price *is* amazingly low—not just lower than the highest-priced product in the same field, but low clear across the board.

Here, for example, are two news story headlines. Each offers a statistic or presents a different degree of that "believability."

**Doctors prove 2 out of 3 women
can have lovelier skin in just 14 days.**

Without question, the above headline is designed to attract the attention of a majority of women, young and old. It tells them something they wish to know, something that they'd like to believe, and it doesn't appear to be too impossible. Furthermore, it is a headline that can be backed up by factual evidence.

Now consider this statement:

**50% Faster!
200% Smoother!**

This is a headline about a razor—a product with which most men feel familiar. It is within reason to suppose that male readers of that headline will believe the "extra speed" promise. The nature of the razor seems to make that possible, even though the average man would have trouble believing that he could actually cut his shaving time in half.

It's doubtful, however, that the second part of that headline ever attracted anything more than a hearty laugh—200% smoother! In the first place, it's a quality that can hardly be measured. Secondly, the average man is a cynic when the percentage figures climb too high. "Shaves smoother" is a statement to be accepted. "Shaves 200% smoother" asks for disbelief. Be careful in your presentation of news. *It must be believed if it's going to sell!*

In writing news headlines, it is wise to be wary of words such as "amazing," "new," "sensational," "what you've been waiting for," and others. There is nothing wrong with using these words and phrases if they are true. Many copywriters, however, avoid them because they feel they have been overused—to such an extent that they have lost their selling value.

Where a product (or its characteristics) is in reality "amazing" or "sensational" news to the reader, it is a reasonable selling technique to say so.

The copywriter can back up "amazing" not only by stating factual evidence but also by presenting the testimony of several people who agree. The whole feeling of the headline is one of important news that is supported with dignity and credibility.

On the other hand, here is another news headline:

**New . . . A history-making advance in the
annals of electric clockmaking!**

This headline might have led you to expect a clock that ran by radar or played Brahms. But, on reading further, the "history-making" advance turned out to be a simple improvement in design.

This is a classic case of overselling, a gross misuse of the news headline. On the contrary, here are a few news headlines that are believable, as well as newsworthy:

New life for your financial future

**New pastry pockets
Turn ordinary stuff into hot stuff.**

**At last. A way to keep warm
no matter how cold it is.**

**Now, you can have extra crispy
hash browns in minutes**

Announcing the Barbizon Tower suites

**The new Spanish-language magazine
you can hear**

All of the foregoing avoided the use of words such as "amazing" and "sensational." None used exclamation points, and all had strong news value. None used subtlety, because you don't have to be subtle (in fact, you shouldn't be) when you must impart quickly some interesting news about a product or service.

Emotional

A common approach to headline writing is to appeal directly to the emotions of the reader. It could probably be argued that all selling—in headlines, in copy, and in artwork—does this in varying degrees.

Unlike the news headline, which is usually used only in making a direct sales presentation, the emotional headline can be either direct or indirect. The following two headlines illustrate this point.

**Beautiful lingerie—
you'll both enjoy the romance**
(direct)

But will he want a second date?
(indirect—for a mouth wash)

In one, though it makes use of strong emotional appeal, both visually and in the headline, a claim is advanced. In the other, the headline has no direct-selling virtues. It does have sales value in that it sets up a situation that, in itself, is representative of the campaign strategy. But as a headline, it sells only curiosity and attention value.

Both headlines capitalize on the reader's interest in anything that can be linked to personal problems.

Make the Campfire Right Before You Light

Smokey is counting on you to build a safe campfire.

1. Dig a small pit away from overhanging branches.
2. Circle the pit with rocks.
3. Clear a five-foot area around the pit down to the soil.
4. Keep a bucket of water and shovel nearby.
5. Stack extra wood upwind and away from the fire.
6. After lighting, do not discard match until it is cold.
7. Never leave a campfire unattended, even for a minute.

REMEMBER, ONLY YOU CAN PREVENT FOREST FIRES.

A Public Service of the USDA Forest Service and Your State Forester.

Figure 6–3. Public service advertisement. *Courtesy of the Advertising Council.*

Certainly love and pride are two strong emotions with which to lure the reader into further examination of the advertisements.

It will be obvious to you that certain products, or types of products, lend themselves particularly well to emotional approaches, and you will find that the emotional approach is used in their advertising. Your job is one of interpretation.

Almost all products used in the intimate daily lives of both men and women are well adapted to this type of approach. In the campaigns behind toothpaste, soap, perfume, hair tonic, shaving cream, deodorants, and similar items, you will find headlines that use emotional appeals.

If you are selling an automobile, a cigarette, or a typewriter, a straight emotional headline will be used less frequently.

Most of us are emotional about our health: frightened, joyful, worried, uncertain, or apprehensive. Thus, many emotional headlines have a health base, such as this unusual example:

Love can make your ears ring, your heart sick, leave you breathless, and wreck your health.

So can wisdom teeth.

Many headlines featuring emotional appeals represent statements from either real or imaginary people. It is easier for the reader to identify himself with a person of some resemblance to himself who is saying something familiar than with the impersonal words of an advertiser. Furthermore, your reader is much more ready to apply the sales psychology to himself if someone else is "guilty" than if you come right out and tell him he has terrible teeth or bad breath.

One of the most important points to remember in writing headlines with an emotional slant is that they must be realistic. Don't put words in the mouths of characters in your headline that your reader would not say himself. The more human and down-to-earth you can make your headlines, the more attention you will get and the more believable you will be. If you were the reader, what would *you* think of the following headlines?

It's Grape Nuts for me; they're crammed with nutritious goodness for me and my family.

I like Kool-Aid because it tantalizes my taste buds.

Every bite of Mrs. Jones's fudge is pure eating pleasure.

Looking at the foregoing headlines analytically, as you just have, you undoubtedly reject them. Yet, time after time, you see such statements in print or hear them delivered by characters on television or radio.

On the other hand, a testimonial-type headline of the emotional type can be very effective if it creates a sympathetic reaction in the readers, such as the following headline for a product aimed at elderly women:

Main head: "My brown aging spots were so embarrassing, I tried to hide my hands when people were around."
Subhead: And then she discovered Fade-Kreme.

It should not be assumed that all good headlines of an emotional approach must be testimonial types or purport to be the words of actual people. There are many ways to reach the reader's emotions—and most of them are good, provided they are based on sound psychology.

You have much more latitude in writing emotional headlines than is possible with the news approach. For example, no woman would actually believe that any lotion on her hands would render her sweetheart "helpless." Still, this headline attracts attention. It is not intended by the copywriter to be taken literally by readers, and they realize that. But they associate the exaggeration with the fact that hand lotion makes hands soft, and soft hands are appealing.

Certain types of emotional headline writing must be done with special care. Insurance, at least life insurance, represents one of the most common fields of advertising in which the emotional approach is used. Yet, because the subject is anything but frivolous, and because the invest-

Figure 6–4. Offbeat headline. If we may accept 'offbeat' to mean a departure from the usual, it certainly applies here in this advertisement for a farm product. The following straight-line copy provides informative, readable material. An interesting layout touch is the sorghum stalk in the middle pointing to the headline.

Figure 6–5. News-type headline followed by straight-line copy. This advertisement follows a good formula by making a close relationship between the illustration, headline and opening copy.

ment involved is more than the price of a bar of soap, great care must be taken to stick to the facts.

A few examples of emotional headlines demonstrate the many directions they can take:

Relive the romance of the Riviera

A gift for lovers

Beautiful memories aren't all you'll bring home

Carlos knows hunger and fear.
Help him find security and love.

Experience those enchanting childhood
years all over again

Don't suffer the anguish of
a blotchy complexion

Even industrial advertisements can use emotional headlines occasionally. An advertisement for a safety system might appeal to a plant manager's pride in cutting down-time caused by accidents. Another advertisement may use a head and illustration that stress how the adver-

tiser's farm machinery has made life better in a drought-stricken area of the Third World.

In many instances, only your headline (and possibly your illustration) will be emotional. The body copy might be quite factual. Emotion causes reaction. It's a stopper, an attention-getter. Once that attention has been obtained through the headline, its job is done. (Actually, it is quite difficult to maintain an emotional tone throughout an entire advertisement, at least if you're selling a product or service. This point is made later in the chapter on fashion writing, where it is explained that fashion advertisements frequently use emotion in headlines but may be literal and almost cold in the body copy.)

Direct Benefit

In general, a direct benefit headline is also a news headline, and it can often be called a hornblowing headline in that it trumpets some outstanding quality of the product or service. By definition, a direct benefit headline is a simple statement of the most important benefit offered by the product. For example:

Q-Vel® prevents nighttime leg cramps

When you have a strong benefit such as this, why be cute or clever or subtle? Why try to arouse curiosity? Your most powerful selling weapon is, in this instance, a straightforward statement of fact.

In today's ingredient-conscious world, the following direct benefit head carries a strong message for the reader. Set in big type, it commands heavy readership.

Wesson Oil is 100% Pure Vegetable Oil.
No chemicals.
No preservatives.
No coloring agents.

Two more observations can be made about this headline. One is the use of the product name. There are some advertising authorities who declare that *every* headline should carry the name of the product or advertiser. Although this statement is extreme, it is true that flagging readers with product or company name in headlines will result in higher identification for either the product or the advertiser. In fact, this result has been shown in figures gathered by the research group of Gallup & Robinson. Why be modest? Let readers know who is advertising. Names of well-known companies or products used in headlines attract immediate attention for advertisements, and even if your product isn't well known, putting it in headlines is a good way to eventually achieve recognition and identification.

The second observation is that the use of the subheads strengthened an already powerful and seemingly complete headline.

Beginning copywriters, thinking that they must always be clever, shun direct benefit headlines as unimaginative and dull. They forget that a strong benefit is never uninteresting to the reader, who reads advertisements for benefits, not for cleverness and entertainment, which are strictly by-products.

People in the car-buying mood will find it fascinating if you tell them directly in the headline that the car you're selling has front wheel drive that will provide better winter driving handling. There is nothing dull about this to anyone who drives in the snowbelt.

Suppose you have no special advantage over a competing product. Should you, as so many copywriters do, avoid the direct benefit headline in favor of pure cleverness? Definitely not. You can still use the direct benefit headline, but you will need to combine it with a twist, an interesting phrase, or a different way of expressing the benefit. In that way, you can satisfy your urge to be clever and simultaneously give the reader a strong reason to buy.

A way to simultaneously be clever and offer a direct benefit is to be clever (but obscure) in the main headline and to offer your direct benefit in the main subhead, as is demonstrated in the following:

Main headline: Farberware found that the best way to get something done is to go around in circles.

Main subhead: The Farberware Convection Oven. A cooler, cleaner, faster, and more economical way to cook.

Figure 6–6. Directive headline. Corn trash that lures various bugs (shown in the illustration) is the subject of this powerful headline. This headline, combined with a specific and attention-getting illustration, and hard-hitting copy, creates high impact for this agricultural advertisement. *Copyright American Cyanamid Company. Reprinted with permission.*

Another example of an interesting way to communicate a direct benefit is offered by an advertisement for a rich-looking but relatively inexpensive carpeting. The writer might have written a headline that said:

Here's carpeting that looks
expensive but costs little.

Although this headline would attract readers and sales, the copywriter preferred a headline that would express the benefit with more flair and imagination. The headline actually used was:

Bigelow's sculptured elegance for the woman
who likes to feel extravagant—but isn't.

Notice once again the use of the company (and product) name in the headline.

A third example of a direct benefit headline that uses the name of the product and incorporates an interesting—and in this case, humorous—twist is the following:

TASTER'S CHOICE® makes fresh coffee
in seconds.
Our competition is still boiling.

Other examples of direct benefit headlines include:

Gore-Tex® Fabrics
Keep you warm and dry
Regardless of what falls
Out of the sky

Speak a foreign language in 30 days
or your money back

100 pages of free advice for anyone
wishing to visit Alaska

Summing Up

- Tie headlines closely to illustrations and opening copy. Time after time, this connection is not made, and it is one of the most serious faults of copywriters, beginners and veterans alike.
- A direct headline is almost always preferable to an indirect headline. Example: "In a class by itself" versus "Nine reasons why (company name) can make your group insurance sales bigger and better."
- News headlines are consistent attention-getters, have impact, and are widely used, but be sure that what you are offering is newsworthy. What you call "news" *must* be news.
- Emotional headlines draw upon basic situations common to all of us—worries about money, safety, health, and getting along with others. All of these are powerful, considerations, but if you have to choose between a direct benefit headline that focuses upon the product versus an emotional headline that does not, skip the emotion and hit the benefit.
- There's no point in being cute, subtle, or overly clever if you are offering a product or service that has a strong benefit. Flag the reader with that benefit and avoid distracting cleverness or cuteness.
- Whenever feasible, use the name of the advertiser and/or product in your headline. This increases identifi-

cation and remembrance and carries an extra impact, particularly if the advertiser's name has strong recognition such as General Electric, Black & Decker, and General Motors.

Other Noteworthy Points

- As shown consistently in Gallup & Robinson research, using numbers in the headlines gets attention and readership. Examples: "How a 40-year-old man can retire in 15 years"; "Now. Save $15 on every grocery bill"; "Louie Clifford was the kind of newspaper editor who would have trimmed the Ten Commandments to seven and led with the one about the murder"; and "The army's new troop carrier costs $1.5 million. It can be destroyed by a $2 grenade." The last two headlines were used in advertisements for the *Reader's Digest*.
- In general, it is better not to capitalize all the words in a headline. Be content to limit capitals to the first letter of the first word. People are most comfortable with reading what they are accustomed to and they are not accustomed to seeing all those capitals. An exception to this suggestion would be putting the name of a product in all caps.
- Avoid writing headlines that require mental effort on the reader's part. Your words should make it clear instantly what the advertisement is about. Again, Gallup & Robinson research demonstrates that the failure of many headlines is due to this requirement for mental effort.
- David Ogilvy, one of the most-quoted advertising authorities, questions the habit of headline writers to put a period at the end of the headline. Readers spend a lifetime seeing headlines in newspapers and magazines that don't end with periods. This is what they're accustomed to, but they see advertisement after advertisement that departs from what might be viewed as the norm. It seems especially odd that periods should be used for headlines that so often are simply sentence fragments, not whole sentences.

CHAPTER 7

Headlines
They Attract, They Inform, and They Sell. It's Vital to Write Good Ones (Part B)

"**F**inally," Amy Swanson thought, "I think this last headline might do." She had written a news-type headline. Her choice made sense because the sports car was all new. Good old news headline. The old reliable. But she wasn't through yet. More headlines would have to be written for the total campaign. Mentally, she went over other kinds of heads. Maybe this would give her ideas for different approaches. Normally, she didn't bother classifying headlines. She just wrote them, and if they fell into a specific class, so be it. But when she had to whip out a number of headlines, it was useful to think of a specific type of head and try to tie it in with campaign objectives. "Let's see," she said to herself, "How about trying . . . or . . . ."

As indicated, Amy finally settled upon a news-type headline. But she might have tried a combination of headline types. Suppose the new sports car represented a dazzling breakthrough in design and/or performance. Then, her headline might have combined news with hornblowing—the latter because the car's maker is expressing pardonable pride in what has been achieved. The combination of news and direct benefit might also have been used because the car offers not only something new but also a benefit in superior performance and styling. In short, knowing the different types of headlines helps the writer when he or she is searching for headline approaches.

More Headline Types To Choose From

Directive

Salespeople know that prospects must be nudged to get them to act. A command or directive headline provides this nudge. Although retail advertisers use this type of headline frequently, national advertisers also make strong use of it because it imparts a vitality to headlines and because such headlines spur decision making.

Directive headlines alternate between outright commands and suggestions, with more of the latter being used. It is often difficult to identify that dividing point where a suggestion becomes a command. For example, the following might be called commands:

Learn French on your own

Don't let Lisa become a street child

In contrast, the following alternate between suggestion and outright command:

Before you crack, do this

**Moving? Make sure *Reader's Digest*
goes with you.**

**Go on, cut. You'll be brilliant.
Armstrong guarantees it.**

**Check the mirror. Have you been telling
yourself a little white lie?**

Whatever you call your directive headlines—command or suggestion—they seldom call for immediate action, but they *do* indicate that some action should be taken. When Greyhound tells you, *Next time take the bus and leave the driving to us,* the company is thinking of some future time. They do not envision hundreds of people leaping from their chairs and rushing down to the bus station. If immediate action *is* taken, it will more likely be from directive headlines in retail advertising than in national advertising. Retailers depend upon and expect quick response. The directive headline helps achieve this.

To demonstrate the popularity of the directive headline, here are some picked up in a quick perusal of two magazines:

Grace your home with beautiful books

Own the sword that crowned 25 kings

Exercise more with less

Stop burglary before it starts

Give up the single life

Don't just sit there. Do something!

Start each day with a smile

Try a little tenderness
(for meat)

Sail the ageless, cageless Amazon

Return to tradition

Don't buy a big tiller for a small job

Offbeat

Although most of the headlines you write will be based upon common sense and will, consequently, fall into the news, direct benefit, or directive types, you may find it desirable to occasionally try an offbeat headline.

When you do, you will, for a brief time, be that kind of copywriter shown in motion pictures or television. You will let your imagination run freely. For the moment, you will forget common sense. But first, what is offbeat? In advertising, it is used frequently to describe almost anything that defies easy definition.

Offbeat describes a headline that is unconventional and uses for its appeal something that may have no apparent relationship to the advertised product.

Usually, you will use the offbeat headline for a product that has few important competitive advantages. There may be nothing newsy about the product, nor can it be sold through emotion. Your offbeat headline will cause readers to linger long enough, you hope, to check out your illustration and body copy.

If you have a good story that can be told effectively through use of a straightforward headline, *don't* use an offbeat headline. Beginning copywriters with a yearning to be "creative" tend to use it too much.

Examples of offbeat headlines follow. As you look over these and other offbeat headlines, notice that sometimes the meaning is clear when you combine the headline with the illustration. In most cases, however, the reader must go into the body copy to fully understand the headline. If you *have* succeeded in making the reader delve into the body copy, you can consider your offbeat experiment a success.

Roads Scholar
(for a car that has an axle that "thinks for itself")

If you can't see the beauty of *Sporting News,* our new sales rep may have to adjust your eyesight
(Illustration shows scowling 280-pound NFL lineman.)

Rush hour traffic in New Zealand
(Illustration shows flock of sheep blocking a lonely New Zealand road.)

Hotline
(for an airline)

Wow. Wow. Wow.
(Each "Wow" is used with three different illustrations of a remodeled home.)

Curiosity

Anyone who is even moderately perceptive will notice that all of the foregoing examples of offbeat headlines arouse curiosity.

Offbeat headlines usually arouse reader curiosity about nothing in particular, or about nothing that is instantly obvious. Curiosity headlines, in contrast, arouse curiosity about the product or service they are advertising. For example:

**Hartman has an interesting angle on luggage
The right angle**
(Illustration shows luggage standing on end.)

"What is Hartman talking about?" would be your response to this headline-illustration combination. It is reasonable to suppose that you would read the copy to find out.

Another curiosity-arousing headline:

At Saab, This Is What We Call A Beautiful Car.
(Illustration shows a Saab that has been smashed in an accident.)

Like a good curiosity headline, this one offers the unexpected, such as the famous Volkswagen headline of years ago that simply said "Lemon." It would be a strong-willed reader who could resist reading the copy to discover why Saab finds beauty in a wrecked car. Remember: Give the reader something unexpected to ponder when you write a curiosity headline.

An effective device for writing a curiosity headline is to tell just enough of a story via a quotation to pique reader

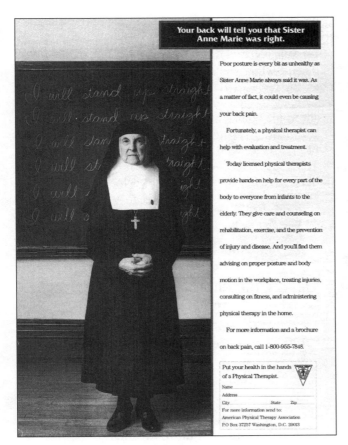

Figure 7–1. Curiosity headline combined with attention-getting illustration. Following this effective combination is straight-line copy of the reason-why type.

Figure 7–2. Curiosity-type headline. A number of aspects contribute to the power of this advertisement. Dominating is a colorful, breathtaking illustration. The headline impels readership and uses numbers, a technique shown through research to attract readership. And the following copy offers a number of very good reasons to buy this vehicle.

interest. An example is the headline for a Gulf Oil advertisement that was accompanied by an elaborate motion picture set of an old hotel building.

> **This is the set where they shot "Hello Dolly!"**
> **What you can't see is us pumping oil behind it.**

Both curiosity and offbeat headlines are methods of indirect selling, one a little less indirect than the other. Both should be used when the same general conditions prevail as far as the product's characteristics and appeals are concerned.

If you have any means of direct selling at your command—any logical, believable approach to the reader's interest through a straightforward presentation—*use it*. If you are selling an idea, an institution, or a product that fails to offer any attention-getting appeals, then it is good copywriting to examine the other means of approach.

Examples of curiosity headlines include:

> **It's headed for your face at 119 MPH.**
> **How does it feel?**
> *(Illustration shows a hockey goaltender*
> *at the net.)*

> **Your search for a perfect cup of coffee ended in**
> **Gayle, Sweden, more than 100 years ago.**

> **The Russians were here!**
> **The Russians were here!**

> **Some people don't even tell their**
> **best friend about us**

> **Discover a little bit of Europe**
> **on Madison at 69th**

> **Look what just came into bloom**

> **Could a cat that eats supermarket pet food**
> **take this test and land on its feet?**

Hornblowing

The research organization of Gallup & Robinson gives low marks to what they call "Brag and Boast" headlines. Furthermore, every beginning copywriter is told to go easy on superlatives and to avoid outright boasting. Yet, that same writer will see hundreds of such headlines in printed media. Why is this?

One answer, of course, is the natural pride felt by someone offering a product or service. All of us tend to boast a bit about ourselves, those we care for, or about our possessions. A maker of a product is no different. Furthermore, it might well be that the maker's product or service *is* superior in a significant way. Why shouldn't this superiority be called to the attention of prospects?

There are different shadings in the hornblowing headline. Some such headlines are outright boasts that have little grace or charm. They may simply trumpet:

Most luxurious

The finest ever built

Incomparable!

Other headlines may stress an honest pride of craftsmanship. Manufacturers *do* put much of themselves into the products they make, and those offering services try mightily to provide the best service that can be rendered. Here are some typical *pride of craftsmanship* headlines.

Oil of Olay. Amazing. And still ahead of its time.

For those who demand the best workmanship

Often imitated . . . never duplicated

When it looks this good—it's got to be Dansk

When this type of headline is used, the product *must* be superlative, and the body copy should make clear the reasons for the claimed superiority.

Many hornblowing headlines are based on claims of "the only," No. 1 status, or exclusivity. If such claims are true, the use of the hornblowing headline is not only sensible but almost mandatory in this competitive world. If you are No. 1, it's absurd not to let your prospects know this fact. Americans respect product leaders, reasoning that a product that is tops in its field must be good. Hertz has exploited its leadership for years, while Avis has done the best it can in building up the theme "We're No. 2, so we try harder." You can assume that Avis has deep yearnings to be No. 1 and that the minute the firm reached this level, the headlines on its advertisements would shout the message to the car-renting public.

Here are some headlines that stress *"the only," No. 1 status,* or *exclusivity:*

For buttery taste no margarine can match

There is no other store in the world like Hammacher Schlemmer. And no other catalog.

The world's most efficient peppermill.

The first dry dog food that's like a homemade meal.

One of the problems with using some of the foregoing headlines is that you may be called upon to defend your claim. When you say "only" or "No. 1," you are being specific, and when you're specific in a claim, you may be asked by the Federal Trade Commission, or some other legal body, to document your claim. Such action may result from complaints by outraged customers.

Advertisers who do not have No. 1 status or who do not want to exploit such status may still utilize powerful hornblowing headlines based on opinion. Anyone making a product or offering a service is usually entitled, without worry about legal action, to express a strong opinion about the worth of that product or service. The following are hornblowing headlines based on *opinion:*

You're not fully clean unless you're Zestfully clean

This new car will change the way you measure world-class luxury

Perhaps the most lavish catalogue of 18th-century reproductions ever published

The Ritz-Carlton has always been synonymous with culture

The kind of car Mercedes might have built if they were a little more frugal and a lot more inventive

Although legally the foregoing headlines are safe enough, the question is, Are they believable? This question of believability is a problem with hornblowing headlines in general, with the possible exception of the headlines that are obviously capable of proof, such as those that claim No. 1 standing or "only" status. Likewise, a hornblowing headline that says something specific, such as

14 ways better than a wheelbarrow. Easier and more enjoyable to use.

carries credibility that is lacking in headlines that the reader senses are backed by nothing specific. For example:

Everything the grand resort hotels used to be . . . we still are.

Molla. Something a little bit different— and a lot better.

Fashionberry. The true essence of elegance.

While, as you have seen, many hornblowing headlines serve a legitimate purpose, many are written because the copywriter didn't work hard enough to find a more creative and effective headline.

Boastfulness is one of the less-endearing qualities of human beings. It is no more desirable in advertisers. Now and then a hornblowing headline represents a part of a carefully worked out plan that fits well into marketing and sales strategy. In other cases, it represents the failure to discover a better way to accomplish your objectives. Therefore, before writing such a headline, you should ask yourself: Would another headline approach be better? If you can answer "no," then go ahead. Otherwise, keep working.

Slogan, Label, and Logotype

Sometimes your goal in an advertising campaign is to obtain a high recognition for the company name, the product name, or the advertiser's slogan. Many times, of course, this objective is achieved through an illustration of a product's package or container that shouts the name in big type and/or carries the slogan. Other times, the headline may offer the best way to get the recognition, and sometimes *both* the headline and illustration carry out this objective.

When copywriters use the slogan-label-logotype approach, they do so with one of two ideas in mind. They feel that the name of the product or company is, in itself, their most important attention-getting tool, *or* they are willing to sacrifice a potentially more intensive reading to pound home a name or an idea.

Name emphasis has been the goal of many famous and successful advertising campaigns. As a copywriter working for such accounts, your headline-writing chore is easy. You may simply head your advertisements:

The Burberry Look

Or if the product is a perfume, you simply write:

Chanel No. 5 Perfume

Then again, as the copywriter for a car or well-known store, your respective headlines consist of nothing more than:

Dodge Ram Wagon

or

Bonwit Teller

Just about as simple is the *label* headline used for a wine that reads:

Collector's Items

Although name emphasis and label headlines can be effective and are often seen, most copywriters would look for some other type of work if there were no more challenge to their creativity than the writing of such headlines.

What about the *slogan* headline? It can be effective for a long campaign if it is a strong slogan. Perhaps the headline began as a slogan placed at the bottom of the advertisement, but its strength became so apparent that it was upgraded to headline status, and there it stayed, possibly permanently. In other cases, a good headline was used briefly and then became a permanent slogan, used in every advertisement.

Sometimes the slogan headline is adaptable to products promoted through reminder advertising, such as Coca-Cola, Pepsi-Cola, candy bars, gum, cigarettes, and other items selling in volume across the counter and for low cost. Such products frequently have no demonstrable superiority over their competitors.

In other cases, this lack of competitive advantage may not be true, yet the slogan headline is used. Examples:

Lord & Taylor
The American Store

The Bold Look of Kohler

Long-time campaigns using a slogan as a headline are exemplified by:

A title on the door . . .
Rates a BIGELOW on the floor
(Advertisement for carpeting)

When you care enough to send the very best

A truly strong slogan is used not only in all print advertising as a headline but also as a theme line in the broadcast media. One use reinforces the other.

As a beginning copywriter, you probably will not decide the use of slogan-label-logotype headlines on your own. That decision may have been made long before you entered the scene. You simply carry out policy in most cases when such headlines are used.

Try for a Little "Twist" in Headlines to Make Them Jump off the Page

As you mature in copywriting, you will find that certain types of headlines are easier for you to write than others. You may never be a good creator of offbeat headlines because you just don't think that way.

Don't be discouraged. Many competent copywriters don't think that way either, but they may have strong talent for writing other types of headlines—powerful news presentations, for instance—or they may have an unerring feeling for emotional headlines that will reach out to the reader.

Although many headlines are of the straight news or direct benefit type that do not call for the offbeat type of thinking, you will go farther in this business if you can add the little twist, or the touch of cleverness, to such headlines to make them stand out on the page.

Otherwise, the world of copy would start to become a bit dull, with every copywriter churning out straight headlines that have nothing to distinguish them from all the other straight headlines.

As a copywriter, you would be pleased with yourself if you wrote a headline for a clock that reads:

Give her a clock like this and she'll have the time of her life.

Don't Put Your Baby's Health On The Line.

It's a thin line between having a healthy baby and a baby that's sick. Don't take the risk. If you're pregnant— or even think you are — getting prenatal care early is the most important step you can take. Call 1-800-311-2229. We'll put you in touch with the many services available to you. The call is free and it's completely confidential.

Get Prenatal Care Early • Call 1-800-311-2229 • Confidential

Take Care of Yourself So You Can Take Care of Your Baby.

Figure 7–3. Public service advertisement. *Courtesy of the Advertising Council.*

It's hard work to get the twist, the touch of cleverness, or the different approach in a headline. Sometimes you simply turn a familiar phrase around, as in the following headline written for a luxurious resort hotel:

Every view comes with a beautiful room

Sometimes you jar the readers out of their apathy with a headline, such as in this *New Yorker* advertisement for high-priced aluminum cookware:

If the price doesn't shock you, it could mean you're either very rich or very serious about cooking

There is a well-bred breeziness about the foregoing headline that is admirably suited to the readers of the *New Yorker*.

Or, if you work extra hard, you might create a headline that uses a humorous twist in headline and illustration that will evoke a smile (and attention) from every reader. Here's such a headline:

Can a chair this beautiful also be comfortable? Would a sleeping dog lie?
(The illustration of this advertisement shows a small dog sleeping comfortably in the chair.)

Despite the fact that creativity in headline writing is a quality admired and rewarded in advertising, such creativity isn't always allied with "cleverness." Straight thinking, clear writing, and a deep knowledge of what moves consumers are all important too.

Questions and Answers about Headlines

Get a group of young copywriters, or potential copywriters, together. They'll usually get around to questions on the headline, because headlines are more spectacular than most body copy. Furthermore, every advertising writer has been fed figures relating to the astounding percentage of readers who read nothing but headlines.

Here are the answers to some of the questions that beginners so often ask about headlines. Remember as you read the answers that no rules are given as inflexible—it is a matter of fitting the answer to the situation. You may consider the answers as observations rather than rules.

What About Question Headlines?

The question headline is very useful. It can get directly to the point that is in the reader's mind. In such cases, it serves as a lively opening to the discussion that answers the question.

Perhaps the suitability of the question headline hinges upon the ability of the question to draw the reader into the body copy for the answer. If the reader can answer the question without further reference to the advertisement, you'd better revise your question. Be especially careful with direct questions. This warning is doubly emphasized in radio and television commercials.

All of us have, at one time or another, sassed announcers when they asked directly, "Wouldn't you like to double your income?" Despite the fact that all of us do want to double our income, it is hard to resist saying "No" when the question is asked.

Keep that in mind when you write your question headline. Also, the question headline is often overused by beginning copywriters. Make sure that the question headline is the best device for putting over your copy message, and be sure to shape your question to get the answer you want.

One of the more annoying traits of good salespeople is that the questions they ask are phrased in such a way that you, as the prospect, must answer as they wish you to answer. A smart salesman won't ask, "Wouldn't you like some of these?" because such a question invites an interview-terminating "No!"

In advertising, follow the salesman's example. Avoid the direct question that elicits a "No" answer or, in some cases, a "Yes" answer. For example, suppose a woman were asked:

Have you had a lab test to see if you were pregnant?

Which one reads Arthritis Today?

It could be any one of these active, productive consumers. Readers of *Arthritis Today* are affected by arthritis, but it doesn't control their lives or their lifestyles. They are financially secure, giving them the time and the resources to travel, to invest and to enjoy a wide range of interests. *Arthritis Today* helps them control arthritis so they can get on with life. Let us tell you more about the readers of *Arthritis Today*. Give us a call at (404) 872-7100.

ARTHRITIS FOUNDATION®

Figure 7–4. Indirect question headline. Such headlines consistently pull good readership figures. This kind of question headline is generally preferred to a direct question which can be answered yes or no.

Whether she answers "Yes" or "No," you may be in trouble. Either answer might kill further interest in the advertisement. To avoid such a situation, provide the answer quickly, usually in a subhead placed in conjunction with the main head. Here's how the technique was handled in the headline just mentioned:

**Have you had a lab test to see if
you were pregnant?
With E.P.T. you use an identical test method
at home.**

Other direct questions that are followed by quick answers include:

**Like luscious brownies?
Try Kwik-Bake tonight.**

**Got something you can't glue?
Hold-Tite does the job in seconds.**

Most copywriters avoid the direct question. For example, an interesting example is the following:

**How smart is the new G.D. 2500 dishwasher?
Just ask it.**

**Hay fever plus a headache?
Now there's a special Allerest just for you.**

A well-designed question headline doesn't *have* to be answered with a subhead. Handled correctly, a good question headline is hard to resist, impelling the reader to read the copy for the answer. The following examples demonstrate:

**What does Lipton Noodles & Sauce do for
simple, everyday dishes?**

How would he feel if you looked younger?

**What's an easy way to make lunches
something scrumptious?**

If you were in their place, what would you do?

In short, use question headlines, but in general, avoid the direct question unless you provide the answer quickly. Also, don't overuse question headlines at the beginning of your copywriting career; such overuse is too often the mark of the beginner.

Can Short Headlines Do The Job?

This question would have been called silly a few years ago. The answer would have been, "Of course." That's because early advertising people felt that long headlines told too much of the story, and, in doing so, discouraged readers from going over the body copy. There are still people in advertising who believe that the headline should say just enough to entice the reader into the following copy and no more.

Evidence seems to be piling up, however, that long headlines often sell better than short ones. Following are a number of lengthy headlines that would have shocked the advertising experts of yesteryear. If you happen to be more comfortable with the short-headline philosophy, would you say that *these* headlines are wrong?

**At Last. A Lightweight Cordless Lawn Mower. It
Mows a Full-Size Lawn on One Two-Hour Charge.
No Noise. No Gasoline Smell. No Hassle with
Cords.**

**"There are hundreds of homes better than
mine but I love this one.
I like big wonderful rooms with a lot of wall
space.
Art is important to me.
I like mobiles and I like movement.
It brings a room to life."**

**Advertising with Val-Pak® won't make you the
darling of your agency's creative team,
but you just might get to be pretty darned popular
with the gang down in accounting**

**Presenting four reasons to buy an RCA DSS®
system.
And one reason to buy it right now**

**If your wife didn't like Sundays before
just wait 'til she gets a load of this**

Figure 7–5. Long headline advertisement. There are many good features in this industrial advertisement that ran in *Plant Engineering* magazine. First, there is a long, informative headline set in an attention-getting type, and a subhead that carries out the headline theme. In the copy the advertiser uses bullets to point up product features, a good technique to avoid cluttering up the body copy section. Finally, a strong logotype makes it clear what product is being advertised. In total, the ad follows good basic procedure by making a close connection between illustration, headline, and opening copy.

For everyone who's ever seen the NFL, NBA, or NHL on their screen.
These are the desktop models

Impeccable Precision Cleverly Disguised As An Ultra-Thin Watch That Gives You Goose Bumps As Well As The Time

If you begin to worry about the rule "Headlines must be brief," just remember this: Your prospects are assaulted by so much advertising that only those advertisements with big, informative, and catchy headlines and illustrations may have enough attention-getting quality to make readers pause and to partly sell them. Today's headlines do more preselling of the reader than was true in the past, when headlines had completed their mission if they had attracted the reader's attention.

Despite all the defense in this section of the long headline, it is normally desirable to write short, interesting headlines that say much in a few words. If you wish to use large type in headlines, you are forced to keep it brief unless you have a big-space advertisement.

There is a certain drama in the punchy one- or two-word headline—a memorable quality that is lacking in the very long headline. Volkswagen advertisements over the years specialized in such headlines, achieving an impact that caused them to be discussed, admired, and imitated.

Are Verbless Headlines Okay?

Hardly anything must *always* be done in copywriting. That is true of the use of verbs in headlines. Almost every authority in copywriting will tell you that it is usually better to use a verb in a headline. Others declare that every headline should have a verb, or at least an implied one. While there is no question that it is desirable to use verbs in headlines, many fine heads are verbless. Some of these good heads don't even employ a verb. For instance, consider this headline that was written for a fine bone china to emphasize its timeless quality:

Yesterday, today, and tomorrow

Sometimes the verb is clearly implied, such as in this head:

Lagerfield
A Fragrance for Men

On the contrary, the headline "Catamarans & Caviar" (for a luxury beach hotel in the Bahamas) tells its story graphically without even implying a verb, and because it is such a short head, the type size is attention getting. The same graphic quality is true of the following:

7 miles at sea . . . an island of pleasure
Martha's Vineyard

Out of the pages of history into the hearts of collectors

Verbs impart vigor. The verbless headlines just listed create atmosphere and provide descriptions, but they do not impart movement. That is their negative trait, although if you must choose between action and a particular suitability to the subject or situation, you may sometimes select a verbless headline.

Passivity is a characteristic of a headline such as "News about Nike." Compare that to "Nike makes news," "Here's news about Nike," or "Nike *is* news."

Still, because of its appropriateness with the illustration, the verbless headline often has its place, but if you follow expert opinion when writing headlines, you will *use a verb as often as you can.*

Can Directive Headlines Be Annoying?

From early childhood through adulthood, we're told to do this or do that. In the main, we accept such orders without thinking much about them. Added to the orders received in your personal lives are thousands of printed advertise-

Figure 7–6a. Industrial advertisement campaign using directive headlines. In this advertisement, we have headlines that reflect the power and vigor of heavy industry—no light, delicate type could fit the product, nor its message. *Reproduced with permission of Federal-Mogul Corporation. Advertising design by Randall Reno Design, Troy, Michigan.*

Figure 7–6b. Industrial advertising campaign using directive headlines. The sheer size of this second advertisement in the series commands the attention of industrial magazine readers. A directive headline is especially appropriate when conveyed in such a powerful type. *Reproduced with permission of Federal-Mogul Corporation. Advertising design by Randall Reno Design, Troy, Michigan.*

ments and radio/television commercials ordering, suggesting, and directing us to:

- Don't ever be late to work again.
- Watch your diet for better health.
- Get top mileage from your motor oil.

Orders get under anyone's skin after a while. On the other hand, the average reader is inclined to move only after prodding. What do the copywriters do when they consider that readers may resent an order but won't make a buying move unless they are given some sort of push? The answer is that the copywriter must pitch the headline in the right "tone."

All through life you have probably found that if one person asks you to do something, you will do it willingly, whereas you may resent a request from another person to do exactly the same thing. Perhaps it was the latter's tone of voice—the *way* of asking—that caused your resentment. It is your way of phrasing that causes success or failure in your directive headlines.

You will usually do better to suggest than to command. The words "stop" or "don't" often sound unpleasant to the reader. From childhood to the grave, someone is using

those words. If you start your headline with them, the reader may react instinctively against your product.

Also, be careful not to offend the reader by assuming in your directive headline that he or she is doing something foolish. Headlines of this type would be: "Don't waste your money" or "Don't be careless with your child's health."

On the contrary, the following directive headline will not annoy anyone, but it *does* add vitality to the headline.

Hear the Bose® difference.
Then make your call

There are two directives in this short headline, but it is unlikely that readers will react negatively, because there's a big difference between ordering something to be done and merely suggesting it.

When and How Should I Use Quotation Headlines?

The quotation headline is often a pleasant variant of the straight headline. When you remember that dialogue

Figure 7–6c. Industrial advertising campaign using directive headlines. This third advertisement in the series follows the formula of the others in presenting big, powerful headlines, competitive copy and an overall feeling of vigor and strength. *Reproduced with permission of Federal-Mogul Corporation. Advertising design by Randall Reno Design, Troy, Michigan.*

enlivens almost any book, you can see how quotation headlines can be useful in advertisements.

A headline using a quotation has human interest and it often enables the advertiser to make a product claim more believable. A quotation headline has an element of story-telling about it. Most of us like a story, so when we read

"We took a few steps into this dark cave, and then it happened . . ."

this headline for a flashlight is pretty hard to resist. What *happened* in the cave? Any normal reader will want to find out. The quotation headline is especially suitable for creating suspense and curiosity.

"Testimonial" copy is, of course, the most logical vehicle for the quotation headline. Too many of the persons pictured in advertisements seem unreal. The quotation headline can humanize them.

In view of the foregoing, what possible objection can be made to a quotation headline? When it is used by experienced copywriters, there will usually be no objections because it will be used with discretion.

Beginning copywriters, on the contrary, will be inclined to overuse such headlines. Not being able to write effec-

tive straight headlines easily, they constantly make people in advertisements do the talking. Because the quotation headline is especially desirable as a change from the conventional headline, the copywriter robs it of its freshness by using it too often.

It has been observed in college copywriting classes that, left to their own devices, the young copywriters would rarely write anything but question or quotation headlines. Such headlines are easy to write, and that's that.

Sometimes a quotation headline is followed by a body copy that continues quoting the person delivering the headline. Perhaps all the body copy is a quotation, or just the opening paragraph, or all but the last paragraph.

Some examples of quotation headlines follow. The first three use a quotation only in the headline, not the body copy. The other headlines continue the quotation wholly or partly in the body copy.

Quotation headlines that are not followed by quotation in the body copy:

"The earth abounds with luxuries but precious few are musts."

"I had this throbbing right on top of my head. Then I took Anacin."

"They told me not to drink the water. I think I'm going to need The Specialist."

Quotation headlines followed by quoted body copy:

"I stay here because of Otto and Teleplan."

"Switching to Hershey's Cocoa made my devil's food cake richer and more chocolaty."
(The paragraph that followed continued the quotation.)

"At Gulf we're working on a way to light lights, cook meals, and heat homes with energy stored in water."
(The long body copy that followed continued the quotation except for a closing paragraph.)

How about it? Is it desirable to continue the quotation from the headline into the body copy? In general, it is better to let the quotation headline suffice. That is, do not have the person delivering the headline also deliver the whole copy message. Occasionally, such a technique works very well, but on the whole, it is difficult to keep such advertisements believable. A single, short statement, as expressed in a quotation headline, is about all you can expect a person to say about a product or service. When such a person also provides copy for an entire advertisement, he or she tends to sound like a copywriter. The message sounds contrived and phony.

On the other hand, a short opening paragraph tied in with, and continuing, the quotation can be believable and effective. This is illustrated by the following example:

Headline   (delivered by a smiling woman in a home setting): "My husband would want the house to take care of me. Now it gives me money every month."

Opening copy: "My husband always said, Melinda, the money we put in this house is like money in the bank. It will be there to take care of you when you need it."

If the writer had continued the quotation through the entire copy, the woman, inevitably, would have sounded like a salesperson and her believability would have vanished.

Incidentally, this is an example of the quasi testimonial mentioned later in Chapter 9. Quotation headlines are used quite often in quasi testimonials because doing so eliminates the problem of finding actual users of a product or service who might deliver a testimonial. If such quasi testimonials are written naturally and in low key, they carry much impact.

Are Hanging Headlines Usually a No-No?

A hanging headline is the type of headline that is not complete unless the reader reads the first words in the body text. An example would be:

Headline: What company . . .

Body text: . . . makes the solar-powered electric shaver?

When you examine the example, you see that the headline doesn't make sense unless the reader immediately reads the first words in the body copy. Likewise, the body text beginning doesn't mean too much if the reader hasn't read the headline.

Inevitably, readers fail to follow neat paths in their reading. Some will start with the headline and skip to the logotype. Others will start with the first line of body text, look at the illustration, and then glance at the bottom of the advertisement. It is difficult to predict just how the reader will read your advertisement.

If you have used a hanging headline, therefore, you may lose much force in your advertisement. Headline readers may look at the meaningless fragments you have written and not bother to find the first line of body text to complete the headline's meaning. They may be irritated if they start the body text and find that they must backtrack to the headline to find out what you're talking about.

Even if you lay out your advertisement scientifically, using every possible device to lure the reader from the headline to the first line of body text, you will often fail. This situation is made even worse in layouts that widely separate the head and body text with illustrations and other elements.

Generally, therefore, it is sounder practice to avoid hanging headlines. Unless your headline and body copy are completely independent of each other for meaning,

and unless each will make sense by itself, you would be wise to avoid hanging headlines.

This advice about hanging headlines is aimed directly at the beginning copywriter; the experienced writer simply isn't going to use the technique. If you examine hundreds of advertisements, you may not find one example of a hanging headline. Yet, initial advertisements turned in by beginners will almost always include one or two hanging headlines.

Clever Headlines Are Fine, but Only If They Sell and/or Are Clear

A problem with cleverness is that the clever headline is often obscure. In addition to being difficult for the reader to interpret, it may have no sell and lack a direct benefit.

However, there is need for cleverness in advertising, a quality that might make your headline stand out from others. A clever or uniquely different headline may draw more attention to your advertisement.

What can you do to use that clever and/or different headline and still make the headline a selling vehicle? One answer is to put the clever (or different) words in big type to draw immediate attention to the advertisement. Then, in order to do the selling, use a main subhead that gets specific and sells directly. An example of this technique is demonstrated in the following:

BAFFLE THE BURGLE

Our Shur-Alert alarm system stops thieves cold

"Baffle the Burgle" has little meaning to the reader and offers no discernible benefit, but the phrase is a good attention-getter. In combination with the strong subhead, it becomes a strong headline.

Of course, you can be clever with one-liners, such as the headline:

Our China tour will have you climbing the wall.

or the head for a bargain-priced dictionary that read:

The price of looking it up just went down.

Cleverness, as long as it is relevant, is almost always desirable in advertising.

Think About These Points Before You Accept That Headline You've Just Written

1. If in doubt, use a strong news headline with an appealing benefit. This is an all-powerful combination. Look for the news value in your product and find its most appealing benefit. Join them in a strong headline that can still, if you're clever, provide a twist that sets it apart from other headlines. Remember: News and benefits are always good and always in style.

2. See that the headline is important *looking*. This is a matter of type size and/or type style. Check with your art colleagues on this point. Make your wishes known, or you may end up with an anemic-looking headline.

3. Be sure your *clever* headline is truly clever and not baffling. Cleverness defeats itself if you, or a tight little group of insiders, are the only ones who understand your headline. Prefer clarity to cleverness unless, of course, you can devise a clever head that's also clear.

4. Try to write a headline in such a way that the readers know at a glance what your big point is, what benefit you're offering, or simply what you're advertising. In short, hook them quickly. This can sometimes be done simply by being specific. Instead of "fast," say "in less than 2 minutes."

5. Be sure your headline appeals to the reader's self-interest more than your own. Too many headlines are company or product oriented—not reader oriented.

6. Decide whether you should include the name of the product or the name of the advertiser in the headline. There's no rule that says you must do either, but often you'll get better products or advertiser identification if you do. Do not, however, force the name into a headline that may be clever or forceful in its own right (and might be more effective without the inclusion of the product or advertiser name).

7. Consider giving your headline an editorial look instead of an advertising look. This "look" may result from the content of the headline, or from the kind of type that is used.

8. If you have a particular segment of your market in mind, one that is large enough to be worth promoting, aim the headline directly at this segment. If you know your target, let them know from your headline that you're talking directly to them.

9. As previously suggested, question the overuse of capital letters in headlines, such as:

MILDER THAN SOAP

or

Milder Than Soap

Readers favor printed messages that give them what they're used to seeing. Accordingly, why not write the foregoing heading like this:

Milder than soap

If you do, you're following the advice of the readability experts, who frown on capitals, italics, and other artificial forms.

Even after considering these nine points, there is one more action to take: Ask yourself (and answer honestly) in a loud voice:

**IS THIS THE MOST INTERESTING
HEADLINE I CAN POSSIBLY WRITE?**

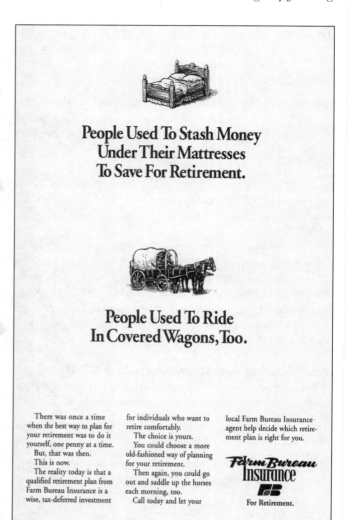

Figure 7–7. Newspaper campaign using balanced headlines. *Courtesy of Farm Bureau Insurance. Creative work by Cranfill & Company.*

If you can't say "Yes" to this question, try again. Too many writers are lazy. They settle for what comes easily. Most good writing comes hard. Scratch out that headline you were willing to use and try once more. And, if necessary, try again, and again, and again.

You May Want to Use Unusual Words in Your Headlines Occasionally

A good headline writer isn't afraid to experiment. Often, that means daring to use words not usually seen at the top of advertisements. For instance, a recent advertisement for an off-road vehicle shows a rugged looking, mountain man type. Above him is the following headline:

**No phone. No razor.
No one who cares if you stink**

"Stink" might jar some readers, but no one will overlook it. While his word is within the boundaries of acceptable usage, it's easy to step over the boundary into the area of bad taste in an effort to be daring.

An advertisement for a book on proper writing and speaking used the headline "It isn't hard to speak good English." Results were just fair, but when the headline was changed to "It ain't hard to speak good English," sales soared.

Another instance of the difference an unusual headline word can make is illustrated in the change of the headline "When doctors don't feel well, here is what they do" to "When doctors feel rotten, here is what they do." Results improved dramatically because of the use of "rotten," a word seldom, if ever, seen in headlines.

David Ogilvy, a blazer of new trails in the advertising world and a devotee of advertising that uses unusual approaches and words, once put the word "cognoscenti" in a headline on the assumption that it would be appreciated by those who knew what it meant. Others, he reasoned, would not only be reaching for the dictionary but would also be flattered, as they would consider the use of the word to be a tribute to their intelligence.

Of course, as you consider the use of striking headline words, you must think about where the headline will appear. A *New Yorker* reader may accept the unusual word with urbanity and appreciation, but that same word might be inappropriate for a Sunday supplement audience.

CHAPTER 8

Body Copy
Where Buyer Convincing Takes Place (Part A)

"Okay. Let's say I buy your idea that only about 10 percent of the readers read as much as half of the body copy. I _still_ say that most of the sale stems from all of those words under the head." Having said that with some heat, Walt Brierly looked aggressively at Bill Levenson, an account executive with whom he sparred regularly. "Take it easy, Walt. Sure, you _have_ to have body copy, but my clients, and I agree with them in general, believe that the _real_ selling takes place _before_ the body copy—in the headline and illustration. So, let's cut down on the words and put our big push on heads and illustrations."

Conversations such as this one between Walt and Bill have been heard since the birth of modern advertising. Of course, there are times when the "keep it short" advocates are right. How much copy is really needed to sell gum, a soft drink, or shoelaces? For such products, a strong head, short copy, and a big, product-identifying logotype are sufficient.

But the picture changes when the product is expensive and complex, as in the case of electronic devices, computers, and cameras. For these products, the head and illustration arouse strong interest, but hard-hitting informative copy does the selling. Body copy is, and will always be, a primary selling force for products that need product details explained.

Interest Them with Your Headline; Convince Them with Your Body Copy

Look upon the headline as the piquant sauce whose enticing aroma arouses your salivary glands. Now you're interested in the meat and potatoes that follow. Body copy is the main course of the copywriting meal. Headlines, illustrations, subheads, captions, slogans, and logotypes are important elements in the meal. Your sales-clinching argument, however, must be done in the body copy. It is here that you present your facts or your reasons-to-buy material.

In some advertisements, the chief objective is merely to identify. Where this is the case, headlines, illustrations, and logotypes carry the advertising burden. Advertising for perfumes, soft drinks, sugar, and salt usually falls in this category. As a rule, body copy plays a minor role in promoting these products.

Should selling be required, however, body copy assumes a major role. Although an illustration of a new car model can certainly create interest, prospective buyers usually need more than an attractive picture to get them into the dealer's showroom. They need to know what is under the hood, what improvements have been made, what kind of mileage to expect, whether power steering is offered, and so forth.

Your body copy does the same sort of persuasive work for a host of other products. In a television commercial, "body copy" is normally a powerful combination of video and audio, although sometimes all of the selling can be done by video, or by video with a minor contribution by audio.

Body Copy Follows Pattern Set by the Headline and Illustration

Copy direction and the type of copy will be set by the direction of the headline and illustration. Once you have decided upon a good headline and illustrative device, the selection of the body copy style will not require much planning. For example, if you use a direct selling, factual headline, your body text will usually be most effective if it, too, is factual. Make it back up your headline claims *immediately.*

As an example, read the following headline and opening body copy:

How to enhance your exterior environment

Send for our Small Building Catalog and discover easy-to-assemble garden houses, storage spaces, cabanas, and much more. There's an architect-designed small building for every use.

Likewise, if you employ an offbeat or a curiosity element in your headline and/or illustration, your body copy should explain the connection before you get into your selling arguments.

Setting the direction of your body copy requires common sense. Logic will show you that effective body copy must, in the main, follow the pattern established by the headline and illustration.

Be Able to Write Any Type of Copy

You are going to discover—if you are like most copywriters—that you write one or more types of copy better than you do others. The question then arises: Should you attempt to make yourself a specialist? Should you try to limit your writing to those types of copy you do best? The answer is "No."

No matter what kind of copywriting you get into—agency, retail, mail order, or direct mail—you will find that your daily routine may call for all types of copy. The products you will be asked to sell will not lend themselves to one specific style of copy or headline-illustration-copy treatment.

If you try to specialize, you may have more fun writing what you do write, but you'll soon be writing strictly for fun and no longer for cash. There are few places for a "one-shot" copywriter in the nation's big advertising operations today.

To be more sure of your future, you should be versatile. Naturally, the advertisements decorating your sample book will demonstrate the type of copy you write best. Your seniors in the business will certainly recognize your skill in handling certain types of work and will make that recognition evident in the assignments they give you. Just the same, become proficient in writing keyed to all the various categories.

Be Believable

One of the most common errors made by copy people is that of overselling. When you create an advertisement, you have two objectives: 1) to wrest the attention of your readers from whatever else they may be thinking about, and 2) to persuade them into some sort of action or belief.

Your job is highly competitive, as you are bidding not only for a sale of your product against the editorial material of the magazine or newspaper but also against the ingenuity and skill of other trained and imaginative copywriters. In this competitive situation, it is easy for copywriters to be foolishly enthusiastic in making claims that simply cannot stand up. They are often encouraged in such extravagances by clients, who may take a somewhat inflated view of their own product's attributes.

In almost every one of the major copy categories, you can find examples of flagrant violations of good taste and sound selling principles. Copy that is intended to represent the endorsement of someone, real or imaginary, is a particular offender.

However, claims for a product seem somewhat less bombastic if they appear to be made by a user of the product rather than by its manufacturer. Thus, a testimonial often seems more believable and sincere than a straight claim of a manufacturer, but when overselling occurs in a testimonial, it is more noticeable than when it occurs in the straight claim of a manufacturer. The cry of "phony" rings out in such cases. Regardless of the technique, overselling must be shunned.

Don't Promise More for the Product than It Can Deliver

If you are writing advertisements for a soft drink, for example, be certain that what you say about that soft drink is recognizable to people when they try it. Straight-line copy simply cannot promise more than the product offers. It must do more than produce a consumer, it must produce a satisfied consumer, or it fails to accomplish the job for which it was intended. If you say of your soft drink—

Once you taste the completely new and different flavor of Gulpo, all other drinks will seem flat and insipid.

—you are guilty of the worst kind of overselling. Your own experience, common sense, and practical analysis of what's in that beverage will tell you that the public will not get that kind of reaction from a bottle of Gulpo. If consumers have been led to suppose that Gulpo has some magical qualities of life and sparkle that other beverages don't have, the disappointment will be sharp when they find that Gulpo is just another soft drink.

You will make your first sale, but you will have left the people with the feeling of having been deceived. Thus, your repeat sales will suffer. You have sacrificed the good attributes your product has to offer for an extravagant claim that can't be backed up. A more modest claim might have led the way to repeat business.

Don't Be Guilty of Glib "Advertising" Talk

Because advertising writers are so prone to exaggeration, hyperbole, and unbelievable statements, you have a special problem in writing strong copy that *will* be believed.

To illustrate the kind of unbelievable, exaggerated statements that cause the general public to say too often, "That's just 'advertising' talk," here are a few lines culled from national and local advertising. This list could have been expanded by hundreds of examples, but the point is made clearly after you read but a few examples:

**The only way to get anywhere
is with a new** *(name of car)*.

**Victory employees are
the most courteous anywhere.**

**The purchase of a mobile home at
Oakridge is the smartest investment
a couple can make.**

(Name of car) **makes any trip more fun.**

Every meal's a feast when you serve 7-Up.

Biggest little treat in all the land.

**This beer is the most enjoyable companion for
any time and any occasion.**

**Chewing Doublemint gum doubles the
pleasure of everything you do.**

Nothing tastes as good as a cold Ballantine beer.

**Quality takes a back seat these days unless
you shop at Acme.**

None of those statements could stand close inspection. None are illegal, but none are credible to any thinking person. When advertisement after advertisement uses such flagrantly unbelievable, unprovable assertions, it is no wonder that so many people look upon advertising practitioners as a bunch of glib "con" artists. You would do well to look over this list of statements occasionally to remind yourself to keep *your* copy believable.

Beware the "Alka-Seltzer Complex"

Many copywriters suffer from what is called the "Alka-Seltzer complex." That is, they are sometimes inclined to project "immediacy" into their copy that the product cannot substantiate. Alka-Seltzer, or any of the effervescent

salts, can be sold on the basis of the immediacy with which they act to help relieve unpleasant ailments, such as headaches of certain types, gas on the stomach, and indigestion.

To use the same sort of appeal for bacon, cigarettes, beer, or ballpoint pens would seem to make little sense, yet a glance through any magazine will bring to light plenty of examples in which copywriters have done just that.

**At the first captivating taste you'll recognize
this beer as tops in master brewing.**

**Even the aroma of this marvelous bacon
convinces you instantly of its quality.**

**Just a few words written with this precision
instrument will prove to you that it's the *peak
of pen craftsmanship*.**

Do you think any of those statements are true? You may fancy yourself as an expert on beer, but could you recognize any beer as "tops in master brewing" with one taste? Of course not. So why lead your consumers to thinking they're going to get a beer so outstandingly different that they'll be able to do so?

Anyone who happened to be in the market for a new pen might be impressed with "precision instrument" and "peak of pen craftsmanship," but do you believe that these abstract boasts could be proved by a few scrawled words on a piece of paper? Doesn't the pen's leakproof quality, or shape, appearance, or capacity have anything to do with such claims?

Don't be a "baloney artist," as copywriters many times are called. Far too many copywriters—men and women who have turned their typewriters into tripewriters—have already sacrificed believability and sincerity for the one unit sales that exaggerated selling can and will bring.

When you write copy, make sure that it is straight in *honesty* and in *presentation of product points*. Your job is to build a sales curve of steady customers, and the only way to do that is to advertise your product for its merits alone.

Believable copy is not difficult to write if you keep straight-line "selling" in mind. Sell, with the words you choose, in exactly the same direct, uncomplicated and sincere manner you would use if you were selling in person.

Naturally, you should use care in the selection of the right phraseology—observe the rules you learned long ago that make writing smooth flowing and smooth sounding—but remember, in all good copy, the overall aim is simplicity.

It Ain't Smart to Use Bad Grammar

English teachers have been noteworthy for their disdain for the lack of observance of the rules of grammar shown in advertising copywriting. Some of their criticism has been justified, because not all copywriters are good writers and a large number certainly are not grammarians.

People in advertising are among the severest critics of the bad grammar of copywriters. In the trade press, they complain constantly about such advertising phrases as:

Nobody doesn't like Sara Lee

You never smiled so good

We better be better

I could care less

When you gotta have one, you gotta have one

Me and my R.C.

"'cause they make me look like I'm not wearin' nothin'." (*model talking about her pantyhose*)

I only smoke Facts

Because of often deliberate misuse of the language, the advertising business is on the defensive. Critics from many segments of our society deplore the liberties that are taken in printed and broadcast advertising messages.

A common defense is that the offending words and phrases are used not because the writers are ignorant but because this kind of writing will be more effective and more memorable. Others in advertising assert that English is a flexible, ever changing language and that advertising writing reflects those changes more quickly than other forms of writing. Furthermore, they say, the object of advertising is to communicate quickly with a vast audience; and if unorthodox words and phrases can accomplish this goal, they should be used.

A strong argument is that advertising is written as people talk, but even granting that this is true, critics counter that the advertising writers shouldn't write as if their audience were composed mostly of dropouts. For instance, even a copywriter employing "talk" language should not write "less calories" instead of "fewer calories."

Probably no one has summed up the write-as-you-talk point so well as T.S. Eliot in his observation: "If we spoke as we write, we should find no one to listen, and if we wrote as we speak, we should find no one to read."

The fact is that printed advertising simply creates the *illusion* of spoken communication. To test this, listen carefully to people when they talk. Such speech, put into print, will be a mishmash of single words, chopped-up phrases, and incomplete sentences. There will be no form, grace, logic, and continuity.

No one will deny that a thorough knowledge of the fundamentals of grammar and sentence structure is helpful to a copywriter. Yet you will find that sometimes a piece of copy will sound better and more sincere if it does not *quite* meet the standards of perfect prose.

Remember that most of the people reading your advertisements do not sport Phi Beta Kappa keys. Give them simple talk, not fancy language. But one caution is needed here: Usually, you should not violate good grammatical usage. Your readers will soon see through your attempt to write "on their level."

"Usually" was used two sentences ago because occasionally an outstanding successful advertisement has resulted from the deliberate breaking of a grammatical rule.

Despite these successful violations, most copywriters observe the rules of writing and grammar without being pedantic. Most good copywriting has a conversational tone. Although such easy, informal writing might offend the purists and the authors of social science textbooks, it is admirably suited to advertising that communicates with a mass audience composed of people who vary greatly in educational background.

Your writing style in advertising should be interesting, yet simple. It should be straightforward, yet subtle. You should abhor dull writing above all else.

Ways to an Easy-to-Read Writing Style

One writer had the following words to say about achieving interest through observance of a number of writing niceties. His hard-boiled, commonsense suggestions should be read very carefully.

What do I mean by writing style?

Just this. The simple sentence starts with a subject. Then the simple sentence has a verb. Then the simple sentence has an object. The simple sentence ends with a period. The simple sentence gets boring as hell after you've read three or four of them. And you just did!

Let's try again. By hanging a phrase out in front of the subject, you can add extra thought, and more interest to a sentence. And by starting sentences with a "non-th" word ("th" words are the, then, there, etc.), you make your copy flow more smoothly . . . read more easily. Of course, ending a sentence with a question mark helps, too, doesn't it?

If you're the copy-writer, become the copy-reader. Read what you write with a red pencil in your hand. Be brutal. Cut out meaningless words and useless phrases. Combine some sentences and eliminate others. Give the reader a long flowing sentence that combines several thoughts and presents facts which are of average importance. Then use a shorter sentence to quicken the pace for the reader.

And then . . . hit him in the eye! Shock him. It's amazing how short sentences can catch people. They stir the imagination. They create desire. And produce positive action.

Of course, there's more to good writing than varying the length of your sentence. Vary the length of your paragraphs, too.

Like this.

Simple, isn't it?[1]

Free-flowing, easy-to-read copy will be more effective than writing that is self-consciously stiff and precise—whether you're selling cologne, corn plasters—or even a book on English grammar.

---

1 *Copy Service Newsletter,* International Newspaper Promotion Association, February 1973, p. 7.

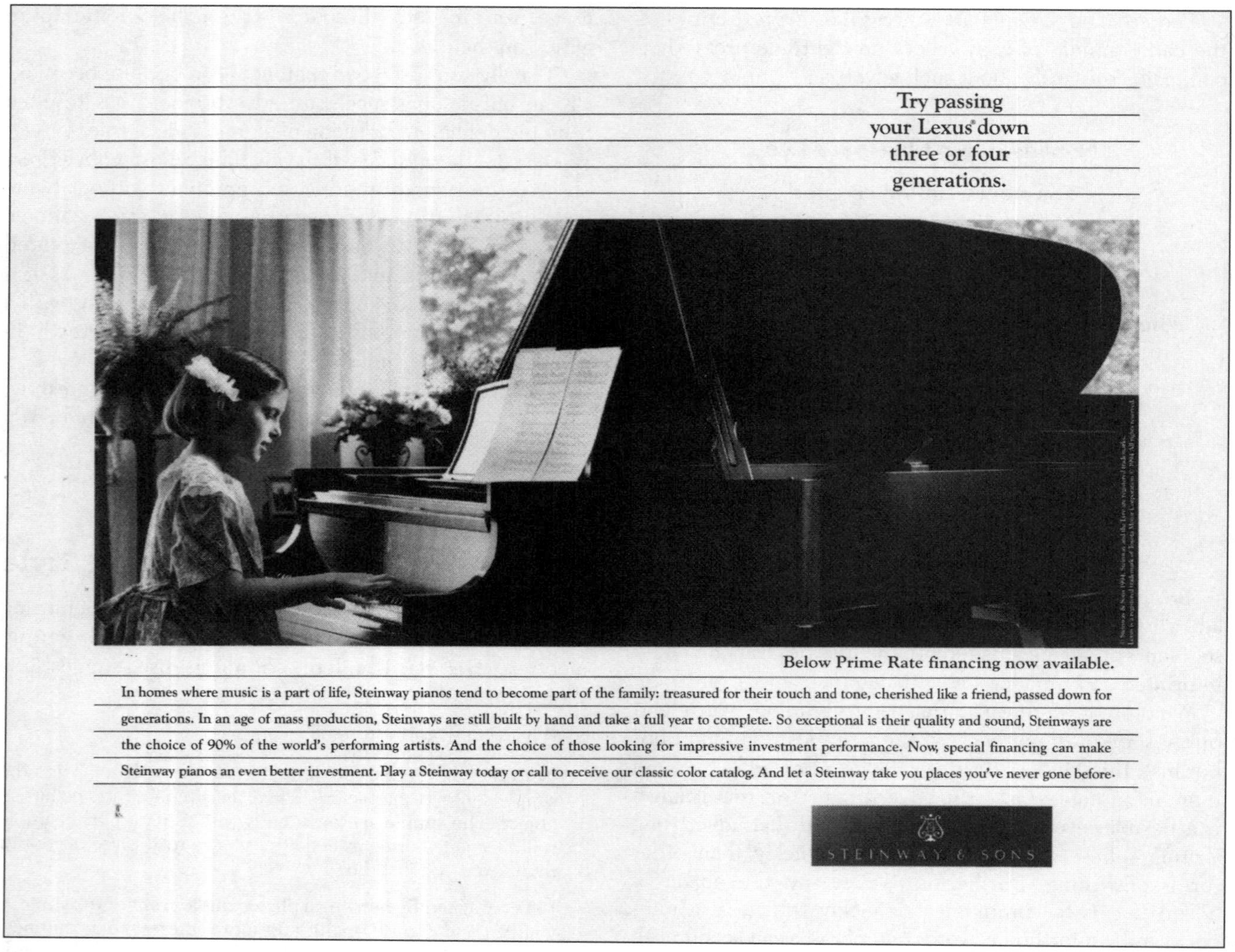

**Try passing
your Lexus® down
three or four
generations.**

Below Prime Rate financing now available.

In homes where music is a part of life, Steinway pianos tend to become part of the family: treasured for their touch and tone, cherished like a friend, passed down for generations. In an age of mass production, Steinways are still built by hand and take a full year to complete. So exceptional is their quality and sound, Steinways are the choice of 90% of the world's performing artists. And the choice of those looking for impressive investment performance. Now, special financing can make Steinway pianos an even better investment. Play a Steinway today or call to receive our classic color catalog. And let a Steinway take you places you've never gone before.

STEINWAY & SONS

Figure 8–1. Prestige advertisement combining the emotional and practical. A strong emotional appeal is generated with the picture of the young girl at the keyboard. This is enhanced by the opening copy with its emphasis on the family. Since the purchase of a Steinway is a formidable investment, there is also copy about financing. A clever touch is furnished in the line at the top that indirectly calls attention to the lasting value of a Steinway piano. In almost every advertisement for this exceptional product, there is a mention of the piano's use by an overwhelming number of performing artists.

Types of Body Copy

Once again, a list is given to you, this time of body copy types. It's a short list because body copy can be categorized rather well in six types. Each type has its own advantages and difficulties. You decide which will do best in helping you reach your sales objectives and copy platform objectives.

- **Straight-line copy.** The body text begins immediately to develop the headline and/or illustration idea in direct selling of the product, using its sales points in the order of their importance.
- **Narrative copy.** The establishment of a story or specific situation which, by its nature, will logically lead into a discussion of a product's selling points.
- **"Institutional" advertising.** The copy sells an idea, point of view, service, or company instead of presenting the selling features.
- **Dialogue and monologue copy.** The characters illustrated in your advertisement do the selling in their own words (testimonials, quasi testimonials, comic strip, and continuity panel).
- **Picture-and-caption copy.** Your story is told by a series of illustrations and captions rather than by use of a copy block alone.
- **Offbeat copy.** Unclassified effects in which the selling power depends upon humor, poetry, foreign words, great exaggeration, gags, and other devices.

You will be able to discover more than one type of copy in many advertisements. Pictures and captions, for

Figure 8–2. Long-range institutional-advertisement campaign. See Chapter 1 for a discussion of this campaign.

instance, are very often used as an amplification of the selling ideas, although the main block of copy is straight line and factual. The same is true of all other classifications.

Although occasionally you may find some advertisement that defies classification, the six preceding listings can almost always be used for classification purposes. To check this out, all advertisements in a copy of *Woman's Day* (published at the time this new edition was being prepared) were examined carefully. Each advertisement was classified.

The classifications were as follows:

Straight-line	86
Narrative	1
Institutional	1
Dialogue/monologue	0
Picture/caption	5
Offbeat	7
Combination	2
	102[2]

Notice the great dominance of the straight-line copy style. It would be surprising *not* to find such dominance. Every examination of an entire issue of a publication reveals the same utilization of straight-line copy, but this will vary somewhat from magazine to magazine. The *New Yorker,* for example, while being dominated by straight-

Figure 8–3a. Executive-management campaign using straight-line copy. When you have something important to tell business readers, straight-line copy without any gimmicks is always a good choice. In this chapter you will find two other advertisements in this series. Each has an interesting illustration to go along with the informative and helpful copy.

line advertisements, will have more narrative, dialogue, and institutional advertisements than will women's service magazines such as *Woman's Day* and *Family Circle.*

For Consistent Results, Use Straight-Line Copy

Straight-line, or factual, copy is copy that proceeds in a straight and orderly manner from beginning to end. It does not waste words but starts immediately to sell the product on its own merits directly following the headline. Such copy is naturally the most used type because, in a majority of cases, magazine or newspaper space is bought for just one purpose—*to tell people about something for sale.* That space costs money—a lot of money.

From the standpoint of getting satisfaction for your advertising dollar, straight-line copy is like a white shirt—correct for any affair—whereas testimonial copy, picture-and-caption copy, and the other forms of copy are not always suitable for every purpose. This does not mean that straight-line copy is ideal for all advertisements. It simply means that straight-line copy can be used for any

---

[2] This total does not include the many small advertisements in the back of the magazine, almost all of which were straight line.

Figure 8–3b. Executive-management campaign using straight-line copy. In addition to straight-line copy that presents the sales story with admirable clarity and persuasiveness, this advertisement also has an appealing illustration. Unfortunately, the full impact of the visual can't be conveyed in the black and white reproduction in this book. In the magazine version, the gaudily colored parrot stands out in eye-catching contrast to the black and white penguins.

approach, whereas the other types have more specialized functions.

Especially good if your product has an advantage. The style or type of copy you write for advertisements must follow the pattern and pace established by your headline and illustration, which are, in turn, paced by the theme idea of your campaign. If you are selling a product that has certain competitive advantages over other similar products, lends itself to interesting uses, or does something unusual (glows in the dark, for instance!), the chances are that your theme idea will capitalize upon those facts in its plan. Your headline will flag the reader's attention with the most appealing and interesting facts.

The body copy of your advertisement must maintain the momentum already established. All body copy—regardless of product medium, or market—must be written to keep alive the interest that the headline and illustration have created. Nowhere is this of more immediate importance than in the straight-line type of copy. Straight-line copy will almost always follow a headline (and possi-

Figure 8–3c. Executive-management campaign using straight-line copy. In this computer-driven age, the illustration going along with the advertisement's straight-line copy will strike a responsive chord with business readers.

bly a subhead) that has used a product feature to gain the reader's attention.

Body copy must not fail to maintain the interest, and yet it cannot logically confine itself to one feature if the product has more than one. This type of copy must be a rapid-fire form of selling—starting with one idea or one sales point and quickly putting others across. The most important fact to remember in writing straight-line copy is this: *Most often, if you have something to say to your readers that you have reason to believe will interest them, it pays to say it at once.*

In the following example, notice how quickly and directly an advertiser's body copy carries out the benefit described in the overline and headline.

Overline: Shocked by the new furniture prices? We'll help you recover!

Headline: REUPHOLSTERY

Opening copy: For a lot less than it costs to buy new furniture, you can restore the furniture you already own to its original, beautiful condition. Or give it a new look. Custom upholstery can save you 25%–50% off the cost of comparable new furniture—which can mean hundreds of dollars in savings.

Headline:	As a hostess, you want to be *sure* the meat is tender.
Subhead:	Tender-ite, the electronic tenderizer makes it happen—and in only five minutes.
Copy:	What a blow at your dinner party to find that the gorgeous roast you're serving is tough. If you had popped it in Tender-ite's pressure pan, you'd be smiling instead of worrying.
	Tender-ite makes the toughest meat tender and does it every time. One less item for a fastidious hostess to worry about. Here's how Tender-ite works. (Etc.)

Example A. Straight-line copy. The main headline is followed directly by the opening copy. Notice that the main headline is written chiefly to get attention. It does not mention the product, nor is it selling directly. Thus, the burden of selling and product identification is carried by the subhead.

The foregoing example of straight-line copy shows how an advertiser with a strong product advantage stresses that advantage immediately. There is no wind-up. There is no attempt to be cute, different, or clever.

The advertiser knows that nothing will engage the attention of the reader more firmly than to show the product in the illustration and then use the body copy to let the readers know what they are seeing.

Picture-and-Caption Copy

In an earlier chapter, *caption* was defined as being a small unit of type employed descriptively in connection with illustrations and other parts of an advertisement. When such captions are the principal means of telling a copy story, the advertisement is said to be a picture-and-caption advertisement. Reference is made here only to advertisements in which the captions are the sole selling copy.

No rule will tell you precisely when to plan advertisements of a picture-and-caption style. That can depend on the type of product you are advertising, the type of sales features the product has to offer, and the physical space for the story, as well as other factors.

One point to remember is that picture-and-caption advertisements lend themselves much better to sizable space than to small space. Magazine quarter-pages usually don't allow enough room to produce top-quality illustrations in series, together with headline, subhead, caption, and logotype.

Even in half-pages, the problem may be difficult unless your captions are so brief as to be almost classified as subheads. You will find that if you try to put more than one or two illustrations in the space of one-half pages or less (still speaking of magazines), you will tend to be cramped for room to give adequate display to your copy or to say all the things you wish to say. In addition, unless you plan to illustrate something very simple, the illustrations will suffer by being reduced too much.

As a generalization, caption copy goes best in advertisements where you have a page or more to tell your story. There will be advertisers who go ahead and defy the principle by using less than page units for picture-and-caption

Headline:	We <u>PROMISE</u> . . .
Subhead:	If you get one of our PRESSURE-PAN electronic meat tenderizers, no one in your home will ever be served a tough piece of meat.
Copy:	You'll admit that's quite a promise when you think how tough meat can be at times. But PRESSURE-PAN can make the toughest meat tender in five minutes. That's for uncooked meat. If you find that meat you've cooked is <u>still</u> tough, PRESSURE-PAN will make it tender in even less time.
	How is this possible? It's really very simple. (Etc.)

Example B. Example of straight-line copy that follows up the headline directly. This is retail copy. The illustration showed the product in full detail.

advertisements. Despite this, you would probably do better to plan most of your picture-and-caption advertisements in page sizes—it will be less strain on the ingenuity of your layout people.

The type of product you are advertising may influence your use of caption copy. If you are working out a campaign for an automobile, for example, you'll agree that the reader is likely to be more interested in the looks of the car and more attracted to your advertisement if the predominant portion of it is given over to a large illustration showing the beauty of the car rather than a series of illustrations and captions concerning its brakes, mileage, upholstery, and driveshaft.

Shoes provide another good example of products that do not lend themselves particularly well to picture-and-caption advertising. The points of interest to the reader in shoe advertising are primarily style, price, and name. Because illustrations of these features would be dull, the use of picture-and-caption copy is eliminated.

Use interesting material. Before you plan to break down the selling points of your product into pictures and captions, be very sure (a) that those selling points will be of personal interest, pictorially, to most of your readers; and (b) that the captions you write for the illustrations back up the promise of the illustrations.

Some time ago, the manufacturers of a new type of automotive lubricant inaugurated a series of picture-and-caption advertisements in which the features of this lubricant were highlighted. Illustrations, dramatic and interesting, pictured what happened inside your car when the product went to work. Captions backed up the illustrations with hard-selling copy.

The public response to this campaign was sluggish and disappointing. Finally, aid was solicited from one of the nation's top advertising people. He had no quarrel with the pictures and thought the copy was well written and strong. "But," he said, "people just aren't interested in the mechanics of what goes on inside their cars."

The reason for this, of course, is that the average person doesn't know enough about motors to understand anything even vaguely technical. The advertising expert wrote

Figure 8–4. Campaign advertisement for an association.
It's an axiom that if you're selling a food product, include a recipe to give your product appetite appeal. In this advertisement the Potato Board has followed the formula admirably. In representing the potato growers, the Potato Board has added another touch by identifying at the bottom of the advertisement four different kinds of potatoes, useful information for shoppers. Two more advertisements in this campaign appear in Chapter 9.

a headline that stated, "Cuts Your Repair Costs in Half!" used a block of straight-line copy telling how, and the lubricant immediately became a sensational seller.

If you are going to use pictures and captions, be positive that the pictures reflect the self-interest of the readers, or your finest copy in the captions will not sell.

Research people will tell you that, generally speaking, advertisements of a picture-and-caption style will get more thorough reading of the copy than will advertisements that contain a big block of body text. This may be true, because people are interested in pictures and will read short captions.

It is, however, true only if the advertisements you are comparing are both good advertisements. An all-type advertisement with a good headline, for instance, will usually get better reading than a picture-and-caption advertisement with a poor headline and dull, unimaginative pictures.

Easier to write captions than straight-line copy. You will find it easier, usually, to write captions for picture-and-caption advertisements than to write straight-line copy. The reason is clear. In straight-line copy, you must develop your story in a strong, orderly progression of

Figure 8–5. Public service advertisement. *Courtesy of the Advertising Council.*

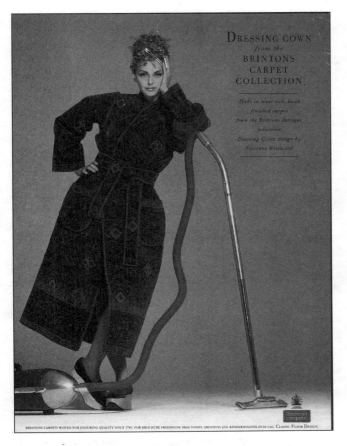

Figure 8–6. Offbeat approach for a carpet manufacturer. It took considerable creative daring to apply a high fashion look to carpeting. See Chapter 12 for two other advertisements in this campaign.

Figure 8–7. Advertisement using straight-line copy that capitalizes on a current trend. "Organic" has become a buzzword in nutrition circles, and this advertisement zeroes in on the subject. Technically, it is well laid out, leading the reader through the copy with subheads. In keeping with good procedure for food advertising it provides strong appetite appeal in the illustrations.

ideas, but you have no such problem with caption copy. Once you have selected the specific sales points to be illustrated, your job is to sell each point by itself. You don't have the "transitional" type of writing that carries you easily from one point to another as in straight-line copy.

One of the great weaknesses of beginning writers is that their copy lacks flow and transition. They fail to make their ideas and sentences connect. If the pictures in picture-and-caption copy have been arranged in a logical sequence, the transition is assured. The writer merely writes the captions independently, as dictated by the pictures.

An example would be a versatile garden and lawn tool that performs many tasks. Suppose that in analyzing its functions, you discover that this tool does the following:

Trims hedges	Shapes bushes
Edges walks	Mulches leaves
Prunes trees	Destroys crabgrass
Cuts grass	Cuts branches
Mows weeds	

Now, you devise a headline that stresses the versatility of the unit and points out that it can do nine lawn and garden tasks. You then call for illustrations that will demonstrate each of these nine functions. You arrange the illustrations in a sensible order and write each caption without any reference to the preceding and following caption.

Your advertisement is tied together by the headline that tells of the overall function of the unit—to perform many lawn and garden tasks. From then on, if you have arranged the pictures logically, your advertisement will be a smooth, flowing production.

Major and minor captions. In planning picture-and-caption advertisements, evaluate first the nature of the claims you want to make in selling your product. If you discover a single particularly outstanding feature that distinguishes your product from the competition and you are sure that this feature will be important to prospects, discard the picture-and-caption idea in favor of a smashing presentation of that certain feature. (You can always illustrate other features in minor roles, but a good strong block of straight-line body copy can do the best job of selling *one* specific feature.)

The picture-and-caption technique is best adapted to products with multiple sales features, no single one of which is outstandingly potent.

It is possible, of course, to use picture-and-caption copy and still gain major emphasis on one point in a series of product advantages. The emphasis is gained by displaying the major illustration in larger size than the other illustrations and by running the lead caption in larger size type.

Such treatment may be considered as almost a combination of straight-line copy if it does not confine itself to selling the one feature involved in the picture and if it presents a complete story. It must be considered a caption, regardless of the length of copy and what size type it appears in, if it does not stand by itself as a complete and all-inclusive sales story.

Too many ideas in captions can hurt. Avoid covering too many ideas in captions. If you are using a picture-and-caption technique, be sure that your caption completely covers the illustration to which it is keyed and does not wander off into selling other features that have no bearing upon what is illustrated.

Every extra idea that you insert in your individual captions should have a direct relationship to the main point you're trying to get across in that specific caption. Also, each idea should maintain the connection with the main selling ideas written in the headline. Use this technique to prevent your advertisements from being disconnected and incoherent.

If you have hooked the prospects into reading each caption solely on the basis of what they see in the picture, don't lose them by failing to give them a direct and powerful sell on what they are interested in in the first place (through the overall theme set by the headline).

Lead-in lines and headings. If you had enough space to work with, every caption would have a headline that highlighted what it was going to say. Rarely can you afford, however, to give that much space to minor headlines. Copywriters, therefore, use three means of gaining immediate attention to key words and phrases. One of these techniques should be used in the writing of every caption.

- You may display a word or two as lead-in, running it in heavier, slightly larger type.
- You may simply have the first few words of your caption set in boldface type or color (if color is used).
- You may number captions to help increase readership.

All of these devices help the advertisement from two standpoints. They serve to gain just that much more sell, in case the reader looks at the illustration but fails to go on to the copy, and mechanically speaking, they help dress up the page.

When you write your captions, keep this lead-in idea in mind. Put down your most interesting words first, thus giving them the added strength of the extra weight or color.

Narrative Copy

Your job becomes much broader when you are following a format that requires narrative copy. Your writing problem is no longer one that can be solved with a clear, straightforward, well-organized summary of your product's sales features. You must also create a "preface," a prologue to your selling story, that is not only calculated to select the proper reading audience but that also fits into the overall sales plans of the product you're selling.

Figure 8–8. Institutional farm advertisement. Because of its story-telling approach, this advertising should obtain good readership in *Farm Journal* magazine. No attempt is made to sell a specific product or service, but rather to stress the advertiser's assistance in an emergency situation. *Copyright © American Cyanamid Company. Reprinted with permission.*

Take, for example, an advertisement for a $1000 wristwatch designed especially for men. Copywriters may reason that $1000 watches are not very often sold by simply pointing out how pretty they are or how well they run. They also know that few people who would be reading their advertisements in a popular weekly magazine would actually be live prospects for such an expensive watch, regardless of what superlatives they could think of.

Neither do they consider as prospects the women who want to give a watch to their husbands or sweethearts. Accordingly, straight-line copy is out. So is testimonial copy, because while Mr. America possibly will wear jeans because a theatrical figure does, he will not be likely to spend $1000 for a watch because anybody does.

No, the problem here is to write an advertisement that will hand-pick those men and women from the millions who read it who could afford a $1000 watch and to offer them a subtle enough sales message to make them wish to do so.

The entire selling power of this copy lies in its ability to cause a small group of people to act. By adroit writing alone, this copywriter appeals to the good taste of the successful executive, the ego of the semi-successful executive, the wishful thinking of the newly rich, and the desire of many people to make an impression upon others.

Narrative copy is enjoyable to write. Product selling, narrative style, is usually more fun for copywriters than any other type of copywriting because it allows a freedom from the rules and regulations that sometimes inhibit copywriters doing straight selling copy. For instance, few people will disagree with the fact that insurance is best sold to a person who is "in the mood" to buy insurance. You can scarcely get a person in the mood to take on another policy by reciting a series of facts and figures, unless they are sensationally interesting.

You may, however, start someone thinking about insurance needs by painting a word-picture of some of the unpleasant events that could happen if that person did not have enough insurance.

By using (a) an illustration of sufficient strength and human interest that he can easily associate with himself or his own family, and (b) a poignant story that also could well be his own, you can precondition someone to listen to your offer much more receptively than you could if you started by saying, "Look, I have an insurance policy here that . . ."

It's fun to let your imagination wander into such writing, away from the fetters of product features, laboratory reports, scientific tests, advertisers' dos and don'ts, and other qualifying factors that regulate much of a copywriter's daily work. Narrative copy gives you a chance to write a "story."

Figure 8–9. Straight-line copy. For pure salesmanship it is always safe to draw upon straight-line copy that gives product facts directly and understandably. Although this advertisement was directed to the farm market, with slight adjustment it could find buyers in other fields as well as in the general public.

Narrative copy in product selling does not, however, require such unusual products as $1000 watches. You will find that narrative structure, although it may be used effectively for almost any kind of product, is best adapted to products that can be sold on a highly emotional basis. Insurance, deodorants, toothpaste, jewelry, cosmetics, clothing, antiseptics, and similar articles or services may be described in their most appealing light when you can dramatize the results they produce.

Narrative copy is usually not short. If you are writing an advertisement in straight-line style, be as brief as possible while still giving adequate emphasis to all the sales points you wish to make. If you have only one thing to say and you can say it in three words, then three words is all the copy you should write.

However, if you are preparing a piece of narrative copy, you can't very well confine it to a few words or sentences, although your copy may be every bit as or even more powerful from a sales angle than a terse, telegraphed message.

Don't waste time worrying about whether copy should be long or short. When you have convinced yourself and your associates that the approach is right, tailor the copy to do the job, regardless of the number of words you use.

Make your narrative copy sell. Narrative copy, then, is fun for copywriters to write. It is a challenge to creative imagination. It is a fine way to establish a good selling situation—sometimes.

Be very sure that the story you tell in your narrative has a quick and easy transition to your selling message, and be sure your selling message *sells hard*. Don't waste space telling a story that does not give a powerful springboard into the sales arguments that you wish your reader to hear. Once you make that transition, leave the characters of your playlet to themselves. Get back on the straight line to show how your product is needed to overcome the problems you have presented.

Here's a chance to get emotion in your copy. Because narrative copy doesn't utilize a straight recital of facts, there is a chance for the copywriter to employ emotion to draw people to the advertising message. To do so is to answer those critics (within the advertising field) who say that print advertisements and commercials stressing product attributes simply bore the audience.

Emotion is too often discarded by noncreative advertising people—product managers and/or account executives—who feel safer with strictly factual and formula writing. Yet, everyone knows that many, possibly most, buyer decisions are made wholly or partly for emotional reasons.

Advertisers of motorcycles, for instance, have made purchasers feel that buyers of motorcycles are buying not just a piece of machinery but a way of life, an unharnessing of the free, adventuresome spirit.

Figure 8–10. Straight-line copy. An intriguing headline is followed immediately with words that tie in with the headline and illustration—one more example of an advertisement that makes all three parts work together for sales effectiveness. Because of the nature of the prestige product, this is not a hard-sell advertisement; it will, however, appeal strongly to the type of buyer it seeks.

Figure 8–11. Association advertisement. With its interesting headline and graphically specific illustration, this advertisement gets immediate attention from industrial readers. Both in the illustration and in the technical copy there is emphasis on cost savings, a point always on the minds of management. To back up the savings claim, the copy provides full proof. Putting actual figures in the illustration is a sure attention-getting device that research has shown conclusively works well in headlines, too.

Eastman Kodak sells the emotional rewards of recording baby's first step and then following that baby through the growing-up years.

The telephone company, likewise, stresses an emotional theme: the joys of keeping in touch with family members through long-distance telephone calls.

A good aspect for the writer who uses emotion is that, because there are so many emotions to draw upon—sorrow, pathos, melancholy, pride, joy, anger, satisfaction, humor—a great deal of variety is possible.

Many copy people find emotional copy hard to write. A bad aspect of emotional writing is that many writers can't execute it well. Instead of sadness, they produce mawkishness. Instead of justified indignation, they express waspishness. Instead of humor, they produce silliness. Humor, especially, is an emotional tool that only the rare writer should attempt, and yet the attempts continue because successful use of humor in broadcast and print pays enormous dividends in attention and sales.

Emotion is especially useful when a product or service offers no distinct advantage. The skillful use of emotion

will create your point of difference because your product or service cannot.

One prominent creative person has listed the times when it is useful to incorporate emotion into copy. They are:

• When I have absolutely nothing of importance to say
• To add importance to something of relative insignificance
• To add interest when there is nothing new to say
• To heighten the drama and importance of significant messages
• To create a difference when our benefit is generic
• To create a common denominator in appealing to a diverse audience
• To suggest superiority when it cannot be proved
• To provide continuity between diverse messages
• To help preserve and improve a client's image while at the same time selling his product[3]

---

[3] Hal Riney, "Emotion in Advertising," *Viewpoint* (New York: Ogilvy & Mather, 1981) Vol. 1. (Booklet)

Information Is What Readers Want from Advertising. Give It to Them

Although you have just read that emotional and narrative copy can be successful despite being long on interest but short on facts, most advertising is based on giving information that enables readers to make buying decisions. If this information is written clearly and interestingly and offers benefits such as solutions to problems, you're on your way to making a sale. Put yourself in the position of canny prospects. Anticipate the questions they might ask in a sales interview and give them answers in your copy. Here are some questions those prospects will ask:

- What exactly does your product do for me?
- Why do I need it? And why do I need it *now*?
- What makes your product any better than your competitor's product?
- What is the price? (There may be situations, such as in many national advertisements, where prices aren't given.)
- How do I know I wouldn't pay less for a competitive product?
- Have other people been happy with it? Prove it.
- How do I know that the value of your product is worth the money I will pay for it?
- Do I get my money back if I don't like it? (Direct response advertising with its liberal return policy makes money-back guarantees a key factor in its advertising.)
- Is it easy to order? Easy to pay for? (This is another key element of direct response advertising.)
- How do I know your company is trustworthy?

If you happen to be a short-copy enthusiast, you may wonder how your short copy can answer all the foregoing questions. It can't. Long copy is needed. In Chapter 9 you will find a discussion of the power of, and need for, long copy.

Your Aim Should Be Primarily to Sell—Not to Entertain or Win Creative Awards

Undeniably, there's gratification and a heady satisfaction if your advertisement or commercial wins one of the numerous awards bestowed so freely these days. Unfortunately, however, many of these awards are based on entertainment, or shock value, rather than on whether the winning award paid off in sales.

In widely quoted comments in the press, David Ogilvy touched upon these two points—entertaining advertising and the pursuit of awards—in a speech in 1991 before a meeting of the Association of National Advertisers. Speaking bluntly, Mr. Ogilvy said:

> "I am worried about the kind of advertising that is in fashion today. Too much of it is pretentious nonsense, highbrow, and incomprehensible. Copywriters and art directors aren't trying to sell their clients' products. They are trying to sell *themselves*. They regard advertising as entertainment, or an art form. I look on them with contempt."

Zeroing in on awards, Mr. Ogilvy hit a familiar theme but expressed it so pungently that award-givers, and award-winners, must have winced as they heard the following from one of copywriting's most renowned authorities:

> "We sell or else. If I could persuade the lunatics to give up their pursuit of awards, I would die happy. . .If you spend your advertising budget *entertaining* the customer, you are a bloody fool. Housewives don't buy a new detergent because the manufacturer told a joke on television last night. They buy it because it promised a benefit."

Although one cannot dispute the premise that the *chief* purpose of advertising is to sell, there have been many instances where entertaining print or broadcast advertising has rung up sales while pleasing readers and viewers. This is especially true in outdoor and transit advertising, as you will see when you observe the examples in Chapter 18 that discusses out-of-the-home advertising.

Final Note on Putting the Sell in Your Copy

Some of the passion for entertaining at the expense of selling has emanated from overseas—from England, in particular. Speaking on this issue, Andrew J. Byrne, direct marketing executive, referred to a survey of 50 United Kingdom company marketing executives who were asked about advertising and advertising agencies. Conclusions:

- Almost 80 percent thought advertising's key function was to accomplish tasks other than selling.
- None of them gave the ability to sell products in print as an important skill for an advertising agency to possess.

Three more comments from Mr. Byrne's discussion bear on the key role in advertising of selling. A head of one of London's top advertising agencies referred to the results of the foregoing survey: "It matters a great deal if advertising is thought to have no commercial effect. Because if it doesn't, then what the hell is anybody spending money on it for?"

A market research executive has said: "All too often, advertising research reveals that someone has yielded to the temptation to write copy and make layouts that are clever, or smart, or different and, in so doing, has lost sight of the simple objective of nearly all advertising—to sell. Forgotten is the fact that the best means ever devised to sell anything is to tell potential buyers what the merchandise can do for them—simply telling it clearly and completely."

In Mr. Byrne's discussion, he refers to Richard H. Stanfield, author of the *Advertising Manager's Handbook*, who had this to say about advertising designed not to sell but to win awards and praise:

> "Much of this advertising is superficially intriguing. But upon closer inspection, it becomes apparent that the wild layouts and 'way out' copy have nothing to do with the product. And they are unrelated to the advertiser's marketing objectives."

> "The creativity cult has forgotten, ignored, or perhaps never knew. . .that the name of the game is selling more of the product at a profit and reducing the cost of selling."

CHAPTER 9

Body Copy
Where Buyer Convincing Takes Place (Part B)

Jim Lundy and Kathy Weiss were sharing a pizza in the Kwik Pizzeria down the block from the agency office. Jim was speaking between bites. "Kathy, maybe you can help me with a question that always bugs me."

"Sure, what's up?"

"What do I say about how long copy should be? Time after time, I get asked this question when I'm talking to beginners."

"I don't think that's so tough. Just tell them that. . ."

Sometimes a copywriter will be given a layout and will be told to fill in the space allotted for copy. In these instances, copy space dictates copy length.

Other times, copywriters, keeping in mind the headlines and illustration they're planning, are free to write copy whatever length they think is needed to sell the product or service. They know, for instance, that research has shown that long copy *will* be read if the product needs hard selling and it is written well.

So, copy length is determined by the situation and product. There is no ideal or fixed length. Basically, you should write what you estimate will sell the product or service. Sometimes short. Sometimes long.

Testimonials: They Work If They're Believable

Time after time you've seen advertisements claiming that the product or service they're promoting is the best. "But," you say to yourself, "they can't *all* be the best," and another cynic has emerged. Advertising believability is rarely high and is quite often low. Consider those supposedly unrehearsed interviews you hear or see in print and broad-cast advertising. They are the source of much of the skepticism about advertisement's believability. Testimonials wrung out of the interviewees too often sound forced, hollow, and unnatural.

An example of the kind of testimonial that occasions incredulity is the quasi testimonial (described on pages 99-101) for More cigarettes. The illustration shows a glamorous-looking young woman reclining in a chair. She is holding a package of More cigarettes in one hand and a cigarette in the other. The headline reads:

More Never settle for less.

Underneath, there is a quote from the young woman:

"Me and My MORE.
We've turned a few heads, I admit.
My MORE is longer. Smoother.
And we both have such great taste.
I guess it shows."

Contrast this statement with the two following quotes, which were overheard as this book was being written. The speakers were people who didn't know that their words were being jotted down:

"Ever use that Fantastik? You just put it on smudges or fingerprints. It's terrific. It's one of the few products that lives up to its advertising claim. It does exactly what it says it's going to do."

In another instance:

Person A: "This floor *does* look better."
Person B: "Yeah! It's *shining*."

When an advertisement features a person who is talking about a product—usually praising it and telling how it worked—you may have a smashing success, or you may arouse cynical disbelief.

In the successful advertisement, you will undoubtedly have a strong, *believable* statement delivered by a person whose credibility is unquestioned.

If your advertisement generates disbelief, you may have (a) a statement that doesn't ring true because it makes a salesperson out of the person delivering it; (b) a statement delivered in artificial or unnatural language (where a homemaker talks like a Ph.D. in chemistry about a cleansing cream, a household detergent, or a cold remedy); or (c) a statement that seems to have been written by a professional copywriter.

Monologue and Dialogue Copy

Included in monologue and dialogue copy are true testimonials, quasi testimonials, comic strip, and continuity panels. This is a copy in which you let others—real people, imaginary people, or cartoon characters—do your selling for you. It can be down-to-earth or whimsical.

Testimonials, when judiciously handled, have proved their ability to produce outstanding results. The trick is to write testimonial headlines so that the message retains its selling power and, at the same time, is natural sounding when placed in the mouths of human beings. The same problem is of constant concern to copywriters when they carry the testimonial type of advertising into the body copy.

If you use personalized selling in your headline, it does not mean that your copy must *continue* with personalized selling. Very often you will want to use a testimonial headline from some well-known person as a means of attracting attention and then develop your own sales message in straight-line copy, captions, or other copy approaches.

Often, however, you will wish to make more monologue or dialogue copy than is possible to put into a headline. You may do this by letting your featured character do the complete selling job through the entire advertisement (a dangerous procedure) or by including additional endorsing remarks in captions.

You will be called upon to write three different types of copy for personalized advertisements: (a) true testimonials, in which you prepare statements for real people to "say"; (b) quasi testimonials, in which you illustrate, by photography or artwork, supposedly real persons but do not identify them by name; and (c) comic strip and continuity panel advertisements, copy for blurbs, or balloons where the testimonial-givers are obviously fictitious.

True Testimonials

Many testimonials are delivered by celebrities, and even more are presented by ordinary people—housewives, business men and women, farmers, and a host of other types. Let's consider the celebrity testimonial first.

Fact: The longer the testimonial statement, the more danger of incredulity. You must start off fast in testimonials because your audience is influenced by the name and picture of the celebrity in their first exposure to the advertisement. In fact, the stopping value of a celebrity testimonial is in the person's name, not necessarily in what he or she says.

After the first statement is cleared, however, and the reader settles down to what purports to be sincere talk about the product by the testimonial-giver, *plain talk is necessary*. Movie stars, lion tamers, baseball heroes, or ballerinas shouldn't be presented as experts on nutrition, engineering, or economics.

It is possible that thousands of American readers will buy a certain product because a famous persons says that he or she likes it. Readers can also be urged—in straight-line copy—to use the product on the reasonable assumption that it will help them (ingredients and other factors that make it a quality product may be discussed, for instance). However, the moment you attempt to put such selling into the mouth of a celebrity, you are injecting a phony note into something that might otherwise be easily believable and salable. There is a huge difference between the following two statements when you are asked to believe that a screen personality said them spontaneously about a well-known soap:

I think Blank soap is just *wonderful!* It seems to leave my skin extra soft and smooth. I never use any other brand but Blank soap.

That is believable, but who could seriously believe that a person would normally speak in the words of this second testimonial:

Blank soap is the perfect soap. That cottonseed oil in it keeps my skin soft and smooth. None of us in Hollywood would think of using any other soap.

Notice the difference in those testimonials. In one, the person speaking does not make any claims other than having a very strong liking for a brand of soap and giving her own personal reactions to using it. That is enough to gain power from the name of the celebrity as far as influencing the public is concerned.

Avoid Words That Make "Experts" Out of Testimonial-Givers

With its reference to cottonseed oil and the use of the product by all of Hollywood, the second of the foregoing testimonials has gone too far for credibility. The endorser is claiming more than she could possibly be expected to know. She asserts that the cottonseed oil in the soap is what keeps her skin smooth and soft, yet so far as the public is concerned, she would have no understanding of the action or effect of any of the ingredients, even assuming she knew what they were. After all, she's a name star, not a dermatologist. Furthermore, she makes a completely unbelievable claim concerning the soap-using habits of her Hollywood colleagues. There is a big difference between saying that you prefer a certain product and crediting everyone else with the same sentiments.

If you are writing a testimonial for use in cereal advertising, it is logical to have your endorser say that the product has "finer flavor," is "crisper," or "stays fresh longer," or even makes a general claim about its being "good for you." It is not logical to have the endorser refer to the actual nutritive qualities of the cereal, such as claiming that its wholesomeness comes from "niacin and Vitamin B_1" or that children will thrive on it because it has a high protein content.[1]

Testimonials for candy can indicate a natural preference for its "delicious goodness" and its "nutty, crispy, crunchy, chocolaty, chewy, delicate, or otherwise luscious flavor," but they are on thin ice if they present normal citizens talking about "dextrose" or "food energy."

A testimonial for a whiskey advertiser demonstrates the folly of putting "expert" words in the mouth of the endorser:

"I tried it and it's true."

"(Product name) true bourbon taste comes from the finest grains, long, lazy years of aging in charred oak barrels and the priceless know-how of *(name of distiller).* It's a true value."

It is very easy to let yourself drift into such errors in writing testimonial copy because you know more about the products you are advertising than does the general public. If you are responsible for writing advertisements for men's clothing, for example, you know how those clothes are made, what percentage of wool they contain, how they are styled and tailored, and other features that only someone close to the operation could know.

If one of your friends asked you, "What's so good about these clothes?" you would undoubtedly answer with a rundown of the features that most impress you. If the same question were asked of a man who had been wearing one of the suits, he would probably reply, "It fits well," "I get lots of compliments," or "I like the style and the price."

This kind of simple, believable talk is used in the following headline and copy for a washer. The illustration is of a mother with her husband and two children:

Headline:	"A working mother's best friend is her Maytag," writes Mrs. Lang.
Subhead:	Between her family and her job, who has the time to wait around for repairmen?
Opening copy:	"Thank you for making a washer a working housewife and mother can count on," writes Mrs. Nancy Lang, Hampton Bays, New York.
	"Eleven years ago, I purchased a Maytag. It wasn't till just this past spring that it needed its first repair."

Simple, short, and believable. Keep those words in mind for testimonial copy. For example, consider the conversation overheard of a man talking to his wife about a new type of cracker: "These things stay crisp. They don't seem to lose their crispness no matter what the humidity is." That's "real people" talk, not the nonsense that causes so much disbelief in advertising.

Here are a couple of suggestions to help you avoid causing your endorsers to talk too expansively and/or technically in testimonial copy:

1. Associate the copy you are writing with some real person with whom you are familiar and ask yourself what he or she would say about the product if giving an endorsement. Remember that this person does not know much about the product beyond having a high regard for its qualities in general. If you can easily imagine your friend saying what you'd like to have the advertisement say, then the chances are that you have created a good, believable testimonial statement.

   If you can have this friend actually make a statement to you, or even read aloud what you have written, you'll be aided even more.

2. Test your copy on somebody not in the advertising business, preferably a person who already uses the product you are advertising. Let this person read the statement and tell you whether he or she would make such a remark. In this way, you can be sure that you are not, because of your knowledge of your product, putting words into the mouths of real people—words that sound strained, insincere, or too expert.

Be sure testimonials are honest. Testimonials should be used to gain the name of some prominent person *only if that person actually uses the product regularly and subscribes wholeheartedly to the opinions you wish to convey.*

The Federal Trade Commission, the various advertising organizations, and other groups interested in better advertising frown upon the practice of writing testimonial statements without regard for the identity of the endorser and then paying someone a large sum of money for the use of the name and for signing the statement.

You may look foolish and dishonest if one of these operations backfires, as they often have, and it is learned that your prize endorser actually uses some rival product. Know your endorsers. Talk to them, if possible, and get their own honest appraisal of your product before you

---

[1] Here and there, however, an exception might be made for persons who conscientiously read the information on packages that describe vitamin content, saturated fat, cholesterol, sodium, and other items of concern to wary shoppers.

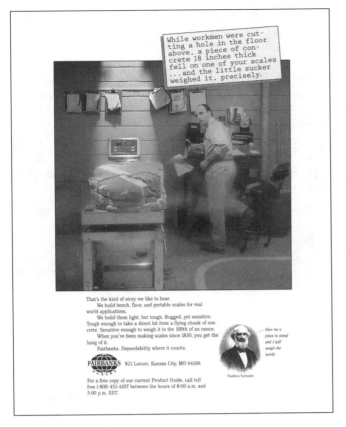

Figure 9–1a. Campaign advertisement using testimonial. The situation pictured here is based upon an actual incident. This ad and two others appearing in this book have a "campaign look." This creates curiosity and insures instant recognition of the advertising among other industrial advertisements in *Plant Engineering* magazine.

Figure 9–1b. Campaign advertisement using case history approach. Like the advertisement in Figure 9–1a, this advertisement is based upon an actual incident which, in this instance, has humorous overtones. Instead of an insert at the top of the advertisement, this one uses a blurb. It serves as a headline.

write anything. You'll come up with better-selling copy and save yourself some embarrassment.

You will often be responsible for writing the testimonial statements that your endorsers sign. Just remember to make all testimonial statements sound like normal people talking. On rare occasions, endorsers insist upon making their own claim and refuse to sign anything else.

Quasi Testimonials

In planning an advertising campaign, you and your associates may decide that the story may be told most effectively in the first person, testimonial style. However, for one of many reasons, you may not wish to use the statements of actual personalities. The increased costs of paying for testimonials may be one reason. Availability of well-known people who might be interested in endorsing the particular product may be another. The most common reason for discarding the true testimonial approach is simply that the product does not lend itself particularly well to the endorsement of a celebrity.

In this case, you may decide to use the quasi-testimonial approach. In the quasi testimonial, you have a copy

approach, and also the sort of product (or service) that might be sold by an unidentified person as well as by an identified person.

For example, you might have what appears to be an endorsement of a certain type of retirement insurance and an insurance company by a man of late middle age. The headline and practically all of the body copy are of testimonial character, with the selling story handled in the first person singular.

Yet nowhere is this man identified. He is used solely as a *type* with whom every man of 55 can conceivably associate himself. It would be worthless to use the endorsement of a well-known person here, since most readers would not believe that any celebrity could or would retire on the modest retirement income mentioned.

Secondly, most people who have retired would be reluctant to publish the facts concerning their income from an annuity or elsewhere. Therefore, to gain the added human interest of the personalized copy, those responsible for this advertisement decided to write it just as if it were to be a signed testimonial but to use a photograph of a professional model rather than that of a real endorser.

An interesting slant to this advertisement is that the headline is written with a "you" approach to capture the personal interest of every reader, while the body text is entirely within the testimonial pattern.

If the copywriter had used a headline "How I retired at 55," he would have sacrificed readership from those men who might automatically say to themselves, "Well, maybe he could do it, but I'll never be able to retire." The "you" approach flags interest; the testimonial technique provides believability.

This type of copy is one of the most frequently used and most successful tools of copywriters. Just remember, though, that you must keep such copy material simple and believable.

An example of a quasi-testimonial approach is offered in an advertisement that shows a very masculine man holding up a partially eaten drumstick and wearing a chef's hat. He is saying:

"The only thing ZIPLOC can't protect food from is me."

In the following copy, he talks about the many virtues of ZIPLOC® brand storage bags.

You might even wish to use a whimsical type of quasi testimonial in which the lines are delivered by an animal—a bird, a fish, or some other creature. An example is an advertisement for Kitty Litter® brand showing a cat in the illustration "saying" the words (in headline form):

"Doesn't anyone care about the odor in my cat box?"

An example of an unnatural type of quasi testimonial is demonstrated in an advertisement featuring a sultry-looking young woman who says:

"I'm absolutely bare. My face doesn't have a stitch on.

And it looks and feels better than ever.

Because before I put anything on, I clean and moisturize with nothing but (product name). And (product name) nothing is really something.

Hypo-allergenic and fragrance free.

Then I dress up my face with (product name) fresh, natural-looking foundation.

(Product name). Everything you want. And nothing you don't."

Make quasi testimonials natural and factually correct. You will have more latitude in writing statements for imaginary people than for real ones. In the first place, you eliminate all worry that the endorsers might not really believe what they say or are not actual boosters of your product.

Secondly, and this is especially true when the illustration of the "endorser" is shown in a painting or a drawing rather than a photograph, the public has become familiar enough with the quasi testimonial to understand its motives.

People will not be so critical of the statement of imaginary characters in advertising as they are of those supposedly said by real people. However, don't let this comment lead you astray. The difference is very, very slight, and you will be wise to treat the copy in quasi testimonials exactly as you would if you were writing a quotation for a real individual. Keep it natural. Keep it simple. Don't try to sell.

In the following example of a quasi testimonial, the illustration showed a glamorous, curvaceous model drinking a nonalcoholic beverage through a straw. The headline and copy were:

Headline: (*Product name*) has got the taste that keeps me lookin' good."

Copy: (*Product name*) Mix, you keep me lookin' good. 'Cause there are only 2 slender calories in every glass. I just add water and stir up something delicious. Becasue (*Company name*) blends choice teas with natural lemon flavor, then presweetens to taste . . . M-m-m-m. (*Product name*) Mix, you've got the taste that keeps me lookin' good . . . from top to bottom."

It is highly unlikely that any real person would deliver such a perfect sales pitch in language that is obviously that of a copywriter, not that of a typical product user. Thus, the credibility of the copy message is low. Even the headline sounds contrived. The fault isn't with the quasi-testimonial technique but the way it has been handled. Again, be *natural*.

Personalized copy can sometimes get so far afield that the foregoing rules don't apply. If you are preparing advertisements for a dog food, you may want to show a talking dog and let him do your selling for you. You may use an illustration of a baby for a soap or talcum advertisement, putting grownups' words in the baby's mouth.

If you look through magazines and newspapers long enough, you can find examples of almost every conceivable kind of object brought to life for advertising purposes—railroad trains, cats, clocks, fish and fowl, vacuum cleaners, and hundreds of others. These advertisements represent an imaginative use of personalized copy in which the copywriter is working more for the humorous and attention-getting value of the unusual.

There are some advantages to using nonpeople spokesmen: (a) they are memorable; (b) they don't die, get old, or get into situations that result in bad publicity, and they don't ask for more money; (c) they are less likely to wear out their welcome than a person; (d) they can be used in print and broadcast copy (as can people, for that matter); (e) they create a "fun" feeling that extends to the company using them.

As a possible disadvantage, it is incongruous to have a humorous, fun-type character delivering an earnest, factual copy message. Real people can do better in this respect.

Fish, birds and animals have become famous spokesmen for their brands. Because of the humorous way they do their selling, full attention will be given the sales message, in contrast to the half attention that is given to so many commercials.

Despite the fun-and-games approach used in commercials delivered by nonhumans, copywriters must remember that, even though the statements may be delivered in an unrealistic atmosphere, such as the bottom of the sea, they cannot have a cat or a tuna making claims that aren't literally true.

In short, as a consumer, you don't have to believe that the message is coming from the ocean depths, but you have every right to believe that whatever a fish says about a product is as true as what the president of the company might say.

To sum up this particular point, when writing for human beings, make their statements and language realistic. When writing for cats, dogs, fish, and so on, don't worry about realism but *do* make certain that product claims are wholly true. Also, don't get *too* cute in your writing.

Institutional (Corporate) Advertising

Even more common than narrative copy is the type of copy called "institutional." Because you are not trying to sell a specific product or service, institutional copy is, in many cases, narrative in style.

At one time, defining institutional advertising as "all advertising that attempts to sell the company instead of its product or service" seemed to satisfy advertising people. In recent years, however, the definition has seemed too narrow.

Thus, we now have "idea" advertising, "corporate" advertising, "public relations" advertising, and "management" advertising. While each of these designations has merit, the term "institutional advertising" is still the term most commonly used to describe advertising that does not sell the goods or services of a corporation.

One criticism of the term, of course, is that a considerable amount of advertising that is called institutional advertising is conducted in behalf of hotels, hospitals, and other organizations that fall under the heading "institutions." In this chapter, we are *not* referring to this type of advertising.

Reasons for Using Institutional Advertising

Before copywriters begin to write an institutional advertisement, they must have a clear idea of what it is they are trying to accomplish. In the usual product advertisement their objective is relatively clear and simple—they are trying to sell the product. Objectives in institutional advertising are not so clear-cut and are often quite subtle. Ordinarily, however, those objectives will fall into one of the three following designations:

1. To create confidence in the company that will help sell its products and to make the company's stock appealing to investors. This confidence may be required because:

Figure 9–2. Case history approach. Closely allied with testimonial advertising is advertising that describes successful the application of a product or service. This advertisement in *Business Week* magazine describes such a success to readers of the magazine.

a. The company makes so many products that the institutional campaign serves as a sort of umbrella. Thus, if confidence is engendered, it is not so vital that the public remember individual selling points for each of the products.

   Instead, if the institutional campaign has done its job, public reaction will be: "I don't know much about this product, but if it's made by the ABC Company, it must be good." Such thinking is especially valuable when quick buying decisions must be made by supermarket or drugstore shoppers.

b. The company makes the kind of product that will never be bought if the consumer doesn't have strong faith in the reliability, integrity, and skill of the maker. Pharmaceuticals, such as remedies and medicines, require consumer belief. Squibb, Lederle, and Eli Lilly are advertisers whose great growth has largely developed because of the public trust they have enjoyed through the years.

2. To explain the company management's stand about such pressing matters as a labor dispute, a bad product, or a drastic price rise. Such advertisements have a public

relations flavor and very often are tied in with news releases published at the same time. Sometimes they are signed by top officials of the company, although they have been written by the copywriter.

Exceeding care must be exercised in the writing of such "policy" advertisements because they are scrutinized closely not only by the company's advertising department but also by top management, by the company's public relations agency, and by the corporation lawyers.

3. To express the company's philosophy about government, politics, or other aspects of society. Enlightened management executives in a corporation feel keenly the need to speak out on the pressing issues of the day, such as ecology, the drug problem, education, and drunk driving. Advertisements are often used to give voice to these feelings. Once again, critics will be looking over your work to be certain that it expresses accurately what management intends to convey.

Institutional advertisements that are done well often obtain good readership, such as a Phillips Petroleum advertisement that won a *Fortune* magazine award for the advertisement receiving the most response from their readers.

Ron Stanley, director of corporate advertising for Phillips Petroleum, made this comment about the campaign:

"Phillips has a long tradition of good corporate citizenship. We believe in doing our part to help improve the quality of life wherever we operate and in providing innovative products that benefit society. And we try to reflect that in our advertising.

"The most recent emphasis in our advertising is the importance of corporate partnerships with other public and private organizations to accomplish things that might not be possible otherwise, such as environmental education programs or habitat preservation projects."

Institutional Advertising Can Help Make Your Message Stand Out

Think about all of the print advertisement and broadcast commercials that have been seen and/or heard in your household and elsewhere this past week. Now try to recall five of them. It's hard to do, because these advertisements pass through your mind so quickly.

What has probably driven more companies into institutional advertising than any other factor has been the increasing difficulty of impressing advertising messages for individual products on the minds of prospective buyers. The profusion of brands, coupled with the similar profusion of advertising messages, has made it increasingly difficult for advertisers to register their selling points. Research of print and broadcast advertising has revealed a dismaying lack of product-point registration and, equally as alarming, poor identification of the advertisers paying for the advertising.

Interesting institutional advertising, which is designed not to sell but to create a favorable feeling for the advertisers and any product they promote, has been viewed as a possible way out of the "too many products, too many advertising messages" impasse. Accordingly, copywriters writing institutional advertising face a stern challenge in their writing task.

Give extra long and careful study to the subject about which you are to write. If you are going to sell your firm to the public on the basis of its ability to help develop a jet engine, be very sure that what you write about that jet engine makes sense not only to people you think don't know but also to jet experts. If you are going after readership with the story of an antibiotic, get your information from unimpeachable sources.

There is no room for extravagant claims in institutional advertising. If you lose believability, you lose everything. Be sure of what you're writing before you start to write, and check it after you've finished with the same unimpeachable sources.

What Kind of Advertisers Use Institutional Advertising?

In this type of copy, the nature of the firm or product you are advertising has a lot to do with the selection of the style of the format and, therefore, the body copy style. Institutional copy is used mainly by four kinds of advertisers:

1. By organizations such as drug firms that serve the public's vital needs. Institutional advertising lends itself very well to building goodwill and prestige.
2. By companies whose products require precise engineering or research, such as the oil companies or the automotive industry. Thus, an advertisement based on "creative imagination" sells General Motors' ability and ingenuity rather than the separate merits of the individual GM cars. These advantages are advertised in other campaigns planned individually for each car.
3. By advertisers who, because they make a great many products themselves or because they are discouraged by the difficulty of fighting for recognition against the myriad of advertising products, decide to strive for company-name registration as a form of advertising umbrella.
4. By "association" advertising or advertising paid for by a group of independent operators in the same industry. Thus, the fruit growers of California advertise Sunkist rather than their own names, the Washington State Apple Association advertises the merits of the big red beauties grown in Washington, and the National Association of Life Insurance Underwriters uses copy that sells "life insurance" rather than the services of any particular insurance company.

This category of institutional copy often promotes sales of a certain type of product. A beer advertisement run by the U.S. Brewer's Foundation, even though it cannot describe the good features of any brand of beer in competitive beer selling, can sell beer in straight-line copy and sell it competitively against other beverages.

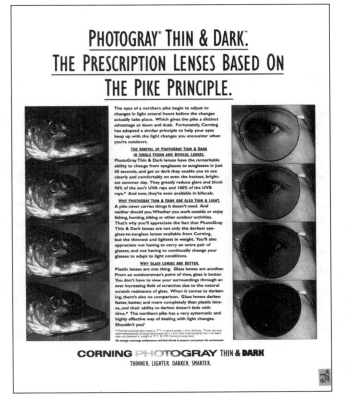

Figure 9–3. Long copy advertisement. If the subject and writing are interesting, long copy is desirable, as in this instance. Striking and unusual illustrations tie directly to the theme of the advertisement, as does the headline. In fashioning this advertisement, the planners wisely broke up the type mass with strong subheads. Although there are times when short copy will do, this is not one of them.

Figure 9–4. Campaign advertisement. Because this advertisement is consistent in the general construction of the layout and copy it will be instantly recognizable as part of the Eden campaign.

Focus on What the Reader Will Want to Know

Downplay the "we"—stress the "you." Beware of the outstanding peril of institutional copy. That peril is the tendency to write in terms of the company and not in terms of the readers' interests. Writers, especially beginners, get so wrapped up in the traditions of the company, in its astounding (to them) manufacturing processes, in the details of its operations, that they completely forget the reader. The copy becomes chestpounding in its boasting, and the "you" approach is entirely replaced by the "we."

Such copy often results from the urging of a self-satisfied executive of the advertiser's company who finds it difficult to believe that the success story can fail to be as fascinating to the readers of the advertisement as it is to him. Remember then—keep in mind your reader's interest and never let your reader become subordinated by the urge to stress "us" and "our" and "we."

A poem, deriding institutional advertising, appeared in the magazine *Advertising & Selling* some years ago. This irreverent verse, after pointing out that the advertiser may be interested in the factory and the company history but that no one else is, ended with the following almost bitter admonition:

So tell me quick and tell me true
   (Or else, my love, to hell with you!)
Less—How this product came to be!
   More—What the damn thing does for me!

Memorize these words and they may keep you from going the way of a good many copywriters when they tap out institutional copy on their typewriters or word processors.

Picture some typical readers of an institutional advertisement. They turn the page, and there is your creation. It has no product that will make their lives easier or more pleasant or more profitable. There are no prices to arouse their interest or selling features to compare with other products.

In short, your advertisement is likely to be viewed as a big fat nothing that offers not one reason for their taking the time to read it. If it follows the lead of too many institutional advertisements, it is likely to be dull, self-centered, stuffy, overly long, and full of "we" and "our" and the board-of-directors language.

You have a vital obligation to be interesting because you won't be read if you're not. Institutional advertising is characteristically at the bottom in readership figures.

To get readership, pull out all the stops. Entertain, shock, amuse, fascinate, be unusual and even bizarre. Grab attention with your headline and reinforce it with a different, exciting illustration.

Except for unusual situations, forget dignified prose. Be human. Write relaxed, conversational copy. Concentrate on the "people" approach. Reduce the awesome corporation to a person—possibly a person who works for it, or a person it serves. The telephone company has done this for years. AT&T is a monstrous corporation in size, but the advertising for this company has consistently focused on people over the years with each advertisement usually spotlighting one person. The corporation is thus reduced to dimensions that the readers or viewers can understand and to which they can relate.

To repeat, from the writing standpoint, your most vital single job is to be *interesting*. Then, and only then, will you force readership of your institutional advertisement—an advertisement most readers would rather "not read" than "read."

Offbeat Copy: Anything Goes

If the discussion on offbeat headlines is not fresh in your mind, it might be wise to review it briefly, since the term "offbeat" is also used for body copy for which it is difficult to find a better term. Any copy not falling into one or another of the foregoing categories may be termed "offbeat" copy. You are familiar with advertisements written as limericks, jingles, or formal poems. Those are offbeat. So are advertisements in which the copy is set to music, written in pig Latin, or set upside down and sideways.

These offbeat advertisements are rare because, despite the type of headline treatment you use or the unusual bizarre illustration you and your associates may plan, the body copy is usually a place for sober selling. And you can't get much selling out of an advertisement written backwards.

Offbeat copy is used in those instances where you have no need for telling a straight, hard-selling story and you wish to gain added attention and continued interest in an already interesting situation. You aren't shown any fundamentals of writing offbeat copy because there aren't any. At any rate, you won't have many occasions to worry about it.

Some More Things to Think About When You Write Body Copy

Before getting into additional aspects of body copy, ponder once again the importance of simplicity, honesty, and sincerity in all of the copy you write. Then, remember that if you have the ability to write well, the desire to write, and have a full knowledge of your product or service, you'll need to do little thinking about which copy type to use.

The style of your copy will be the style that will appeal to the greatest number of prospects and that will cause them to act. This style can be any one of the types described in the two chapters on body copy.

Make Word Pictures and Get Readers into Those Pictures

Too much copy is impersonal because there is no use of the "suffering points" mentioned earlier. Body copy should involve readers by picturing situations they have encountered. Consider the breakable thermos. Anyone who has used one has heard that dread tinkle when the thermos falls off a table, rolls off a bench, falls out of the car, drops from a picnic table, or is knocked over on a table. In your copy, bring in those happenings. If you happen to be selling an *unbreakable* thermos describe those happenings in your copy. Don't just talk about the steel construction. Show what that steel construction means in terms of solving everyday problems.

Let's say that you're selling a cordless, battery-powered lawn mower. What pictures are evoked? There's the tangle of the cord on the conventional electric lawn mower that catches on every bush and wraps itself in a snakelike fashion around the feet of the user.

Another picture comes to mind if you're selling against the gasoline-powered mower—the glares of the neighbors disturbed by the racket made by the mower. A contrast could be illustrated by showing the relative serenity of a Sunday morning created by a homeowner who is using an electric lawn mower.

Think in everyday pictures as you spin out your body copy because, through such pictures, you create empathy, involvement, and sales.

The following "picture" copy gives the reader a picture in the headline, illustration, and body copy.

Headline: How can a man only 5'7" clean the snow off his roof?

Subhead: He can use our 19' Sno-Go snow puller—that's how.

Copy: Each blizzard piles snow on your roof-line. And then a thaw, followed by a freeze, builds ice. After this, water backs up under the shingles. Result? Ruined ceilings and wallpaper spotted and wrinkled by seeping water.

If you have a Sno-Go puller, you can stand on the ground and clean off the snow before it turns to ice. You see, Sno-Go has a lightweight 19' pole that lets you reach way up on the roof with the toboggan-shaped shovel. It beats doing the job from a slippery, swaying ladder.

Another reason for clearing off that snow is to avoid the hazard of ice sliding off the roof—ice that can injure people and wreck shrubs, shutters, and outside lighting fixtures.

But, you might ask, what do I do with a 19' pole when spring arrives? That's easy. Sno-Go comes in three sections. In a minute you can take the unit apart and store it. By the way, the poles and shovel are rustproof as well as durable.

ON ANY GIVEN DAY, YOU'LL FIND COUPLES AT THE PARK ENJOYING THE BENEFITS OF ULTRACLEAN PROPANE.

Sometimes you have to drag yourself out of the den to get some fresh air. So to help keep the air clean, a growing number of vehicles have been using alternative fuels from Phillips Petroleum like UltraClean® Propane.

They burn cleaner, leaving more room in the air for other things. Like air, for instance. To all of us at Phillips, that's what it means to be The Performance Company.

PHILLIPS PETROLEUM COMPANY 66

For an annual report on Phillips' health, environmental and safety performance, write to: HES Report, 16 A1 PB, Bartlesville, OK 74004.

Figure 9–5. Semi-institutional advertisement. Although this advertisement promotes a company product, the advertisement as a whole has a distinctly institutional flavor. This is enhanced by the engaging illustration that fits in with the company's advertising emphasis on environmental issues.

| | Better look into this handy item before the first big snowfall. Only $16.95. |
| **Illustra-tion:** | Short man using Sno-Go snow puller to remove snow from roof-line of a two-story house. Snow is deep on the roof. |

There Is Danger Ahead If You Do Humorous Advertising Badly

Some very good advertising people find themselves in opposite corners about the use of humor in advertising. Those who like it point to the attention-getting power of humor and the fact that if humor is done well, it provides the basis for a long campaign.

On the contrary, the sales message *can* get lost in humorous copy. It's easy to become so involved in the humorous story line that the product is subordinated to the humor, and poor sales and/or poor identification may result.

Furthermore, humor can kill you in the marketplace if it is poorly done. Bad humorous advertising has a short life and an ability to irritate enormously, much to the detriment of the company and its product. A poorly done humorous campaign is less likely to enrage the print audience than the radio and television audience. The wear-out factor is especially quick in the latter.

However, there have been numerous successes chalked up to humor on television (and also radio), especially with the under-35 market that has been reared on television. These successful campaigns using humor, such as Maytag, go on for years, entertaining and selling millions.

Television has an advantage over print in the use of humor because of its ability to convey humor through voice intonations, bodily movements, and changing facial expressions. Gag humor, however, is less successful than humor based on human interest situations to which people can relate.

The biggest problem in the use of humor, apart from trying to judge how long to use it before you've worn out your welcome, is to judge how many people will like and respond to your particular type of humor. What makes one person laugh may disgust another person.

The moral here is that a humorous approach should be tried out on many persons before the campaign is launched. Two objectives should be sought: (1) to determine how well the sales message, or product identification, comes through; and (2) to determine how well the mass audience is likely to respond to the humor.

Humor is great if it works, but it can be a disaster if it doesn't. Use it with caution.

Public Service Advertising Gives You a Chance to Be Proud of What You Write

Public service advertising promotes causes such as the ones that are the subject of so many notable advertisements furnished by the Advertising Council in behalf of education, participation in politics, conservation, and innumerable other topics related to public benefit. In this period of public protest and consumer advocacy, such advertising has been seen more and more, even though advertisements of this type touch the average copywriter very little.

If you do have a chance to fashion such advertisements, consider yourself lucky. You have an opportunity to use advertising as a useful social tool and to write body copy that gives you a chance for more intelligent writing than you find in much of the product copy you do.

There is no formula writing here. Usually, you will be writing from the heart, although if your advertisement is concerned with economic issues, it must be very rational indeed. Your copy will center around the reader's sense of fair play, justice, and goodwill toward those less fortunate. You may wish to arouse the reader's awareness of the need to protect those less fortunate, the environment, or the political and economic traditions that have made us strong.

Such advertising, like institutional advertising, answers no selfish interests of the reader. It can be passed over very easily unless, as in institutional advertising, you (a) use strong attention-getting headlines; (b) use ample, but not overly long, body copy; and (c) are, above all, *interesting* in headline, body copy, and illustration.

Last, avoid reproving the readers too much. Don't be accusatory. Refrain from making the readers feel ashamed of themselves. It's easy to cause resentment in such campaigns. Assume that the readers have done well in their contributions to causes. Your advertisement should lift them to new levels in their contribution to whatever worthy cause you're promoting.

If You Don't Have a U.S.P., It's Time to Be Creative

Applicants for copywriting jobs are sometimes asked to write advertisements for products that have no product advantage. The reasoning is that building copy around a unique selling proposition (U.S.P.) is relatively easy but that true creativity comes hard when you must achieve an interesting and selling approach for a product that doesn't stand out from the crowd. In today's crowded marketplace, products with a U.S.P. or strong product difference are becoming fewer.

It is a fact that many products simply do not have a U.S.P. and are greatly similar to others in the market. For example, soaps, coffees, soft drinks, cigarettes, gasolines, and many other products have become indistinguishable in the public's mind. If you are writing for such a product, your challenge is to make your product stand out by the way you promote it.

An advertising agency that has been unusually successful in achieving such recognition is Leo Burnett, which has produced memorable and long-lasting campaigns for Marlboro, Virginia Slims, Maytag, United Airlines, Green Giant, Pillsbury, and Keebler.

Let's examine some of them to see how the agency's creative teams made the product or service a prominent part of the American scene:

- A real-life spokesman is used (the lonely Maytag man)
- A trademark character is invented (the Pillsbury Doughboy)
- Memorable music is applied (United Airlines)
- A symbol is used (the Marlboro Man)
- A lovable animated character carries the message (the Keebler elves, the Jolly Green Giant and his lovable companion, Sprout)

These are just a few of the ways to create recognition for products. Creativity is the ability to sit in front of your word processor and let ideas evolve to make that just-one-of-a-mob product stand out like a beacon light.

Sometimes your success will be the evolving of something as outlandish as the gone but not forgotten Mr. Whipple and "Don't squeeze the Charmin." It helps, of course, to have your success assured because of the sheer weight of advertising put behind the product, as in the case of Charmin. The Mr. Whipple character may have annoyed a portion of the television audience, but as a whole, the campaign sold the product in a very competitive field and against products quite similar to Charmin. This is another instance of selling a product that has no scintillating advantage.

Selling products without an advantage? Rise to the

Figure 9–6. Association advertising. Advertisements such as this speak on behalf of an industry and are closely allied to institutional advertising. In keeping with good practice for food advertising, there is strong appetite appeal in the presentation.

challenge. How you do so will help peg you as a real prize or as just another ordinary creative person.

Organize—Then Write

Unfortunately, some writers write first and think afterwards. A good writer organizes first. A careful review of the selling points is made for straight-line advertisements or, for products without selling points or specific advantages, the general theme is carefully worked out.

You have probably already gone through much of this operation in the original planning of your advertisement. You have selected the most outstanding feature your product has to offer and have worked out a clear, forceful headline built around that feature. Your opening copy should also be aimed at the feature. *Immediate follow-through on the headline* is nearly always vital to top-notch copy. Whether your copy actually fulfills its function and maintains interest and selling power depends largely upon how you carry on from there.

Practicing copywriters have various methods of organizing their thinking before writing, depending upon their temperament and manner of working. Some simply close the office door and think. They keep the different angles of their sales story in mind until they develop a clear picture of how it should unfold. Others write a preliminary piece of copy with little attention to sequence, point of order, or emphasis, and then, when they decide what they want, they rewrite in order to obtain sufficient continuity and strength in the sections lacking those qualities.

Neither of these methods is ideal for producing the best in copy. One places too much burden on the copywriter's memory; the other often causes a stilted style of writing. Nothing seems to work as well as a simple checklist of selling points. To see how you may compile such a list, look at an actual advertisement and see what steps the copywriter might have taken in writing it.

Notice that the advertisement will usually follow a list of the points of importance. As a result, it has continuity and a simplicity that makes it easy to read and understand. It gives primary emphasis on the sales ideas the copywriter wished to feature, yet one point leads to another in logical progression.

Making a list of what you want to tell the reader before you write a word of copy seems like a great deal of extra work, but it will result in clarity and continuity. After you have worked out your campaign and written a number of advertisements within its pattern, the listmaking will be less important, since experience with a given product and a given sales approach will so familiarize you with what you have to say that reminders won't always be needed. In most cases, once you have established your list, you need never change it, unless:

- Product is improved.
- Audience aim is changed. You might have started out with a homeowner campaign and then decided to advertise to carpenters through business papers.
- You decide upon an entirely different approach.

Especially for your first attempts at *straight-line* copy, close reference to your checklist is an excellent means of keeping your copy on a straight line. It is a system used successfully and continuously by some of the nation's most experienced copywriters.

Brainstorming Sometimes Supplies Ideas

Occasionally, a group can do what an individual cannot in generating ideas. This is the time for brainstorming, a process in which a few persons sitting in a room spark each other by supplying ideas in rapid succession.

The participants may sit in a circle. Each member supplies an idea in regular turns. In order to encourage a free flow of ideas, no criticism is offered. Thus, many of the ideas may be wild and wholly unusable, but sometimes the wildest idea might spark a brilliant, usable idea.

Often an idea will appear that seems to have merit, so the group may supply ideas that build up this idea until the group leader halts the buildup. Usually, a brainstorming session will be limited to an hour. Above all, no negative thinking is permitted. Otherwise, participants will be inhibited and idea generation is slowed. Criticism takes place *after* the brainstorming session.

Before the session, the participants should determine what the problem is and, if they are sparking ideas for selling a product, they should be thoroughly knowledgeable about the product.

Although brainstorming can result in some good ideas, most of the ideas so produced are usually worthless. Furthermore, to go over the ideas (usually taped) is time consuming, especially when so little usable material may result. Still, the procedure occasionally provides a campaign idea when ordinary methods have failed. Also, there is a creative excitement engendered by such a group effort that is stimulating and enjoyable for jaded creative people.

Editorial-Type Copy Captures Readers

Occasionally, you'll notice advertisements that look like the surrounding editorial material. As an unsuspecting reader, you may have begun reading some of these advertisements and then realized suddenly that you were *not* reading an *article* in the newspaper or magazine. To help you differentiate between articles and advertisements that look like articles, publishers will put "Advertisement Advertisement Advertisement" at the top of such advertisements or put a small "Adv." at the bottom.

Despite the warnings, such advertisements obtain good readership because they have the editorial look. The secret is to be consistent. Be editorial throughout—in headline, body copy, and illustration. Avoid the hybrid of part editorial and part advertising. Usually, the one departure from the wholly editorial approach is the use of the logo. Even this can be sacrificed on rare occasions.

Sometimes you eliminate the illustration. If the "advertorial" advertisement is small, for example, there is little point in jamming an illustration into the space, especially if you destroy the editorial look by doing so.

In other cases, you may cut the illustration because you're announcing an important new product breakthrough or a new service to be offered. The use of the usual illustration will detract from the news article feeling.

Your writing should have the news flavor throughout. In making your important announcement, write like a newsperson instead of like an advertising copywriter.

For instance, because "editorial" style advertisements are often lengthy, break up your copy with punchy subheads and make your main headline bold in size and newsy in flavor. The total advertisement should look important.

Although some magazines prohibit such a technique, some "Advertisement Advertisement Advertisement" types of advertisements adopt the type style, kind of headlines, and writing style found in the magazine. In short, the reader can hardly detect the difference between your advertisement and the magazine's editorial material. This makes it imperative that your advertising material is interesting and important enough that readers won't feel tricked when they realize that they're reading an advertisement rather than one of the publication's features.

Comic Strip and Continuity-Panel Copy

Although there is little chance that you will write comic strip or continuity-panel copy, the practice of making advertisements resemble comic strips or editorial cartoons is widespread and successful. Researchers have provided considerable evidence that such formats for advertisements often gain greater attention from readers, especially in newspapers, than those designed in a more conventional format.

There is not much variation between the comic strip and the continuity-panel advertisement. Both are normally planned to tell a story that stresses the selling features of a product. Both usually involve a character or group of characters whose actions present a problem to be solved. The problem is then solved through the purchase of the product being advertised.

Both types feature copy displayed in blurbs or balloons, and in many cases, this copy accomplishes the entire job of telling the story, reaching the happy ending, and selling the product. Often, however, either a straight-line copy block or selling caption under each panel is used in addition to the balloons.

Newspaper comic strip advertisements should be designed to resemble, as closely as conditions permit, an editorial comic strip. If possible, they should be of the same size and horizontal shape and carry a heading and title just as regular comic strips do.

Continuity-panel advertisements may use a horizontal or vertical arrangement of panels that tell a type of story similar to that of the comic strips, but they often carry a headline, a large illustration, and a logotype.

In many advertisements you will see a series of comic strip and continuity-panel advertisements of various kinds. Note that there is no set pattern for their construction. Some use the last panel for a display of the product and a straight-line copy story, while others depend on the payoff of the blurb continuity to carry all the sell.

All these points about this style of advertising are mentioned because your job requires a greater amount of creative ingenuity in both comic strip and continuity advertisements than is needed in many other forms of advertisement writing.

Since success of panel advertisements depends upon a logical, believable story, you must plan the illustrations and the action before you write your copy. In creating most other advertisements, you can often count on plenty of help from your art associates to get a good illustrative device; your main task will be the writing of headlines, subheads, and body copy. In the strip or continuity-panel advertisement, you'll have to go way beyond that. Your job here can almost be likened to that of a movie scenario writer rather than a copywriter, although it is actually a twofold proposition, since in addition to artistic creation, you are trying to sell something.

The Newspaper Advertiser Bureau, Inc., has made these suggestions to copywriters interested in improving

Figure 9–7. Public service advertisement. *Courtesy of the Advertising Council.*

their copy for comic strip advertisements. The following is a discussion and enlargement of some of their suggestions:

- **Follow editorial style.** If you are writing a comic strip advertisement, make it look as much as possible like a real comic strip. Do not include panels that look like little advertisements. Do not vary the size of the panels. Remember that you are trying to hook readership on the basis of public familiarity with and liking for comic strips. You will not obtain this bonus readership if your advertisement doesn't look like a comic strip.
- **Keep your first panel interesting—humorous or action-packed.** By doing so, you gain impetus in leading your reader along into the next panel and through to the conclusion. You will sometimes see examples of comic strip advertisements that beg for further reading and that do not offer enough excitement about what is coming to lure maximum readership.
- **Change focus.** Comic strip artists and writers have discovered that it attracts attention to mix up long and short shots of characters in the strip. The same technique is true of comic strip advertisements.
- **Keep blurb copy short.** If you can't set up your situation, develop it and sell the product in short, natural-sounding blurbs; don't try to use the comic strip style. You will repel the reader if you jam your blurbs with long, involved copy in order to establish your story. Your characters are supposed to be speaking, and the things they say must be things anyone would say in similar circumstances. If they aren't, you will lose selling power.

Most of the foregoing comments on comic strip copy are also applicable to continuity-panel copy, except, of course, for the requirement of staying within the physical confines of the comic strip format. Continuity panels are used when it is felt that the comic strip technique is desirable but for one reason or another—usually space limitations—the true size and shape of the comic strip cannot be followed.

For instance, continuity panels will be used in magazines because readers of magazines are not accustomed to seeing comic strips in them; also, magazines do not sell space the size and shape required for comic strips. The continuity panel is also often used in newspapers when a space larger than the standard comic strip is considered necessary.

Both of these types of advertising depend, for their maximum effectiveness, upon their ability to lure readership rather than to compel it. The closer they can be designed and written to resemble the editorial features after which they are patterned, the better chance they have of succeeding.

Your Copy Must Be Acceptable to an Increasingly Moralistic and Legalistic Audience

In today's consumerist climate, it isn't enough merely to write copy that is legal; it must also be socially responsible. Corporations and the advertising they issue are being held accountable by aggressive consumers and by the numerous federal and state consumer bureaus. Your copy must recognize the responsibilities of business in today's changing and contentious world or you and your client may find that you have become targets.

What are the consumer attitudes toward business and hence toward advertising that affect how you write your copy? Some of these attitudes are expressed in the anti-business gripes that follow. These were written at a time when all of our institutions (especially business) were under fire. They are still pertinent, because large segments of our society continue to distrust business.

Common Complaints That Have Given Business an Image Problem

1. Business is obsessed with the bottom line. This is demonstrated by its heartless downsizing and the consequent loss of thousands of jobs.
2. Business expects loyalty from its employees—a loyalty that too often is one-sided.
3. Despite criticism, there is still much planned obsolescence that lowers the value of recently purchased products.
4. Bloated executive salaries and bonuses often are given at times when employees are denied wage increases or are even given wage cuts.
5. Business is not sensitive to environmental concerns about pollution or destruction of forests and wetlands.
6. Great amounts of money are spent on advertising by business to blow up superficial, meaningless attributes of the products advertised.
7. Many feel that business has little interest in improving relations with minorities unless there is a big profit to be gained.
8. Too many businesses sponsor television programs that are in poor taste. High ratings, not the worth of the shows, determine what programs will carry the advertising.
9. Products made by U.S. manufacturers are too often of poor quality as compared to foreign-made products.
10. Business is perceived as being reluctant to get involved in important social issues.

Obviously, most businesses and business people are not guilty of most or any of these transgressions, but those that are at fault throw a shadow on the entire business community. Furthermore, in recent years, business has taken forward steps in such matters as minority hiring, protecting the environment, and improving the quality of manufactured products, from automobiles to household appliances.

Still, as a socially aware copywriter, it's important to be aware of these consumer sensitivities when you write about certain products or services.

Beware of Careless Words That Arouse Group Sensitivities

In the 1960s, Volkswagen ran an advertisement that showed a "Beetle" with a dented fender. The headline copy and opening were as follows:

Headline: Sooner or later your wife will drive home one of the best reasons for owning a Volkswagen

Opening copy: Women are soft and gentle, but they hit things.

The rest of the copy continued the theme of feminine driving incompetence and pointed out that, because Volkswagens were inexpensive to repair, husbands could be tolerant of their wives' errant driving habits.

Today, this sort of condescending advertisement would result in a storm of complaints from women who, justifiably, resent being portrayed as helpless or incompetent as a group.

Allied with consumerism is the heightened sensitivity of so many groups in the United States these days. Copywriters careless with words will sooner or later offend one of these groups. Women, especially, have developed a new advocacy and are quick to resent words or situations that seem to demean them or their status.

While it is impossible to list all of the words and phrases that might be described as sexist, a common charge, here are a few that seem particularly offensive to women who read advertising.

- Lady, instead of woman. The former is considered by some feminists as connoting affected, artificial, overly nice persons. Girls, instead of women, spurs similar wrath. Gals is even worse.
- "Man-sized job" seems to imply a task beyond feminine abilities
- Chairman, instead of chairperson
- Housewife, instead of homemaker
- Salesman, instead of salesperson

Women are annoyed by advertising that implies that the chief concern of all women is running a home and fails to recognize the importance of women in industry, politics, and other facets of American life. Depicting women as being wholly dependent upon men is another sore point.

Although women now make up 50 percent of the work force, too many copywriters are writing as if stay-at-home housewives were the majority group. These same writers too often fail to show the working women in responsible, executive roles (although there has been a slight improvement in this respect). An oft-voiced complaint is that copy and illustrations in advertisements and commercials depict women as sex objects, household drudges, or mental lightweights. A critical assessment of advertising for household products provides justification for the complaints.

Copywriters will find that it is not easy to write without offending the special-interest audience. Constant awareness of the problem is the only answer. Therefore, as a copywriter in this modern world, you must have a keen knowledge of the social currents and cross currents because your lack of knowledge and vigilance can cost your clients goodwill and sales.

Overall, Consumerism Has Had a Good Effect on Copy

You should be grateful for the critical, skeptical looks given copy these days. Writing copy in today's climate is more than writing copy that is pure in a legal sense.

In addition, you must be credible. You must avoid the careless statement, the almost dishonest claim, or the claim not backed by proof, even though the claim is technically correct. In the category of the careless statement was the claim of milk producers using a slogan "everybody needs milk." The slogan was changed when doctors protested, saying that some people are allergic to milk. Legal objectives were not raised to the slogan, but it was changed nonetheless because of the concern of the medical profession.

Watchful for the consumerist's baleful glance, you try to eliminate simplistic portrayals of your product as the answer to all domestic problems. You're conscious of the need for copy that is not offensive but is in good taste and is defensible legally. You try to write copy that is useful because it helps the consumer arrive at a rational buying decision.

Figure 9–8a. Campaign advertisement for an association. See Chapter 8 for comments on this Potato Board advertisement.

With all this good stemming from consumerism, how can the movement be bad for copy? The answer is simple enough. Rather than take a chance with strong claims and aggressive advertising, the copywriter may play it safe with innocuous copy or silly copy. Humor is substituted for information and challengeable claims. Copy becomes blank and boring, or if not boring, it relies on cleverness for cleverness' sake.

Sometimes it is easier to go institutional in advertisements rather than to dig up hard facts about the product. Accordingly, as a substitute for "selling" advertisements, we find a myriad of campaigns that boast of the advertiser's contributions to the solving of world problems—anything from environmental concerns, to economic panaceas, to population control. These are "safe" campaigns, though unfortunately even they must be executed with exceeding care or risk being criticized for oversimplifying complex issues.

The demands of consumerism are not outrageous. You are asked merely to write about your products in a way that you would approve if you were a consumer instead of a copywriter. With this in mind, you should approach each copy assignment with two viewpoints, the copywriter's and the consumer's. You will omit the latter at your peril.

Figure 9–8b. Campaign advertisement for an association. See Chapter 8 for comments on this Potato Board advertisement.

To Start an Argument, Say the Words "Comparative Advertising"

When you buy a product in a retail store, you're accustomed to having the salesperson show you competing brands. If you buy a toaster, for example, you check such points as the pop-up feature, controls for light/medium/dark, the appearance of the unit, and so on. Or, if you're interested in a General Electric refrigerator, the salesperson will tell you what features this brand offers that make it superior to the Amana, the Coldspot, Westinghouse, and other brands. You take such comparisons for granted when you buy an item in a store. Indeed, you would not feel very intelligent if you did not insist on these comparisons.

Despite the acceptance of product comparisons in the shopping situation, the use of comparative advertising has become one of the most controversial issues in the field of marketing. On one side, it is considered a beneficial development by many in the consumerism movement and the FTC looks indulgently upon it. As long as there is no clear-cut deception or unfairness and advertisers can substantiate their claims, the FTC is not likely to take action because of the Commission's feeling that product comparisons serve a useful consumer function.

Within the field, however, advertising people either revile it or praise it. As for consumers, some don't know what to think, although many feel that it isn't cricket to name competitors in an advertisement. Furthermore, as comparative advertising is used increasingly, consumers seem to find it more difficult to make judgements when they are assailed by so many contradictory claims.

Differing Viewpoints

Some say comparative advertising increases brand identification, but others disagree. Some say print is a better vehicle for comparative advertising than television because the latter, it is asserted, cannot make valid comparisons in 30-second commercials. Some say that the comparative technique helps consumers make rational buying decisions; others declare that comparative advertising reduces the credibility of advertising. Some say that comparative advertising gives free advertising to competitors; others point to strong recall of such advertising by consumers.

If you write such copy, you should see that it is done sensibly and honestly. To aid you in doing so, you would do well to follow the guidelines of the American Association of Advertising Agencies. If you follow these guidelines, there is a reasonable chance that your copy will gain the approval of consumerists, lawyers, and even most present critics of comparative advertising. The following guidelines have been widely printed in the advertising press:

Guidelines for Using Comparative Advertising

1. The intent and connotation of the ad should be to inform and never to discredit or unfairly attack competitors or competing products or services.
2. When a competitive product is named, it should be one that exists in the marketplace as significant competition.
3. The competition should be fairly and properly identified but never in a manner or tone of voice that degrades the competitive product or service.
4. The advertising should compare related or similar properties or ingredients of the product, dimension to dimension, feature to feature.
5. The identification should be for honest comparison purposes and not simply to upgrade by association.
6. If a competitive test is conducted, it should be done by an objective testing source, preferably an independent one, so that there will be no doubt as to the veracity of the test.
7. In all cases, the test should be supportive of all claims made in the advertising that are based on the test.
8. The advertising should never use partial results or stress insignificant differences to cause the consumer to draw an improper conclusion.
9. The property being compared should be significant in terms of value or usefulness of the product to the consumer.

10. Comparatives delivered through the use of testimonials should not imply that the testimonial is more than one individual's thought unless that individual represents a sample of the majority viewpoint.

NBC has placed particular emphasis on the need for care in price comparisons, an issue that worries many in marketing.

1. Comparisons of retail pricing may raise special problems that would tend to mislead rather than enlighten viewers. For certain classifications of product, retail prices may be extremely volatile, may be fixed by the retailer rather than the product advertiser, and may differ not only from outlet to outlet but from week to week within the same outlet.

   Where these circumstances might apply, NBC will accept commercials containing price comparisons only on a clear showing that the comparative claims accurately, fairly, and substantially reflect the actual price differentials at retail outlets throughout the broadcast area, and that these price differentials are not likely to change during the period the commercial is broadcast.
2. When a commercial claim involves market relationships, other than price, which are subject to fluctuation (such as but not limited to, sales position or exclusivity), the substantiation for the claim will be considered valid only as long as the market conditions on which the claim is based continue to prevail.
3. Whenever necessary, NBC may require substantiation to be updated from time to time.

First in a series of discussions in the M/A/R/C Symposium.

A Candid Discussion About Database Marketing.

Q: What is the difference between database marketing and traditional direct marketing?

A: Database marketing is the next evolution of direct marketing. The primary difference is the ability to communicate more precisely with different market segments and incorporate the consumer response back into the database. Once the response information becomes part of the file it can be used for segmentation purposes in creating the next direct marketing program. The advances in the data processing industry over the last 10 years have made storing of large amounts of information about prospects and customers much more affordable. The real magic is in the analysis of the data and its application to a particular marketing problem.

Q: I currently employ targeting tactics in my media buys. How will this be different in a database marketing environment?

A: It'll give you the ability to communicate more precisely with identified market segments. Analysis of promotion responders can yield strategic marketing direction.

So, the collective intelligence of the database improves with use. By appending the database with additional information from previous promotions or database overlays, targeting can be refined to much higher levels. Each new promotion or database overlay added to your consumer database provides more marketing variables to segment market niches that have a higher propensity to respond to your offer.

Q: What kind of marketing applications should be considered for database marketing?

A: Categories which have a high degree of switching, are mature, or have well-defined niches are excellent candidates. Examples of programs which work well in a database strategy are competitive and continuity promotion programs, frequent traveler and shopper programs, sales lead generation and business-to-business direct marketing programs.

Q: If you had to describe the biggest difference between M/A/R/C Database Marketing and others, what would it be?

A: There is a big difference between just collecting information and knowing what to do with it. The most important difference is our ability to leverage over 25 years of marketing and consumer research experience to design, develop and implement marketing programs that best suit your needs. It becomes a matter of knowing what to ask, and then knowing what to do with the answers. Database marketing allows you strategy in as many or as few markets as you choose. With M/A/R/C Database Marketing, pre-emptive planning will become the norm because you will have quantified knowledge of the category consumer base.

Q: Isn't database marketing going to make an already expensive advertising vehicle even more so?

A: The true benefit of database marketing is that is optimizes each marketing program that you run. As mass media costs rise and response to these programs gets harder to quantify, the need for measurable marketing solutions increases. The ability to fine tune your targeting, so you only reach those prospects which have a high probability of responding, can dramatically reduce your costs while improving your volume. M/A/R/C can provide a turnkey test of database marketing with your brand or service for less than $100,000.

Q: I know M/A/R/C has a great reputation in custom research, but I imagine you use a service bureau for database management. Don't you?

A: No. Most direct marketing agencies do use a service bureau. M/A/R/C is unique. Information has long been our business and our state-of-the-art computer capabilities enable us to do everything in-house. We think it is the only way to offer clients a formula for success where one plus one equals four.

M/A/R/C has a long history of proactive client service. We have been dedicated for the past two decades to working with clients to understand and create the best product or service mix to sell in changing market conditions. This expertise and dedication to service are carried forward into our newest service, database marketing. When you think about it, an integrated system customized to meet your individual needs—a system that's capable of revolutionizing your marketing strategy—is a powerful concept.

Q: OK. You've got my attention. How do I find out more about M/A/R/C Database Marketing?

A: Call Ken Orton at 1-800-527-2680 or return the coupon.

❑ *Yes, I want to arrange an interview to find out how effective M/A/R/C Database Marketing can be for my company.*
❑ *I'm interested, but before we meet, call me at my office.*

Name ____________

Company ________ *Title* ________

Address ____________

City ________ *State* ____ *Zip* ________

Figure 9–9. Editorial-type advertisement. Many successes have been rung up for advertisements that looked more like editorial material than like advertising. The question-and-answer format is especially well-adapted to editorial-type advertisements. *Courtesy of Targetbase Marketing.*

There Are No Big Differences in the Copy You Write for Newspapers and Magazines

You will not find separate chapters in this book on the writing of newspaper and magazine advertisements because the material on appeals, headlines, and body copy applies fundamentally to both. Newspaper and magazine readers respond to the same basic appeals. As for writing approach, many advertisers use similar advertisements in newspapers and magazines and certainly utilize the same campaign approach in each.

If, however, you make certain assumptions about the magazine reader, you may, in the light of those assumptions, write copy somewhat differently for magazines and newspapers.

You might make the following assumptions: (1) Magazine readers tend to be somewhat better educated and of a higher income level; (2) Magazine readers read in a more leisurely fashion over a longer period of time; and (3) During this period, magazine readers will pick up and put down the magazine a number of times. (This is in contrast with newspaper readers who read quickly and tend to finish their reading at one sitting.)

What implications are there for you in these assumptions? One, of course, is that the language level in newspaper copy may sometimes be a trifle lower then for magazines, especially selective magazines aimed at an obviously upper-level audience.

Headlines in newspapers can be more direct and localized, and the following body copy should likewise be direct and localized. The body copy may tend to be brisker and more telegraphic than magazine copy. Because newspaper readers go through the publication so speedily, it is wise to break up long copy with subheads in order to hold their attention.

However, copywriters usually do not need to make a sharp distinction between the way they write for newspapers or magazines. By and large, the rules for writing headlines and body copy apply to both. This is especially true of mass circulation magazines and newspapers. Differences will become pronounced only when the advertisements are to be placed in publications appealing to high-level audiences.

Whether for newspapers or magazines, advertising's highest awards go to writers who consistently create fresh writing that stands out from conventional approaches. Few writers are capable of such sustained freshness, and even fewer can spark campaign ideas that can be used year after year.

Figure 9–10. Professional advertisement. No type of copy requires more care in getting facts right than advertising to the medical field. Consumer techniques for attracting readership give way to specifics. Every claim is documented to help busy doctors decide whether the product can live up to its claims. Most such advertisements are accompanied by densely set type that summarizes every fact that needs to be known about the product and its application. © *1995 Pfizer, Inc.*

Keep these two objectives in mind: (a) Write fresh, different copy; and (b) Write copy that will, in the words of the Leo Burnett advertising agency, incorporate the "power of the enduring idea" for longtime campaigns.

Seven Tips for Making Your Body Copy More Effective

Here are a few suggestions, some more important than others, that you can use when you're at the word processor. They are concerned more with actual writing than with strategy and bigger issues of body copy.

- Start with the reader, not the advertiser or product. Beginning writers tend to become so full of facts about the advertiser and the product that they neglect the reader. If you've begun your copy with the product, rewrite it. Talk to the reader first.
- Use the singular you. Avoid the "all you readers" approach. Talk to the individual in order to achieve a personal, intimate style.
- Write transitionally. A mark of the professional writer is the way the copy hangs together. You achieve this by connecting ideas, sentences, and paragraphs. Learn to use bridging words for writing flow and cohesion. What are bridging words (or phrases)? Here are a few: "moreover," "furthermore," "too," "also," "in addition," "to continue," "and," "but," "otherwise," "of course," "as for," "thus," "above all," "while," "although," "accordingly," "or," "lastly," "to start," "another," "then," and "if, however."
- Use an occasional underline. An underlined word can sometimes convey powerful emphasis, such as: "This is the

only product that gives you . . ." Don't overuse the underline, but employ it when it gives force to your writing.
- Use contractions freely. Advertising copy is usually informal and conveys a conversational feeling. Contractions are used constantly in conversation.
- Go easy on "so" endings. Beginning writers tend to end most print advertisements and practically all commercials with "so" phrases such as "So don't forget," "So be sure to see this product," "So next time you're shopping." The use of "so" in such instances isn't a major offense, but it is grossly overused. Furthermore, when the readers or listener hears "so," he knows the advertiser is winding up the message and tends to tune out what follows the word.
- End almost all advertising copy with an urge to action. By urging action, you supply a climax to what you have written and perhaps move the viewer or reader to do something. Don't let your copy trail off without making a suggestion of some kind, such as "buy," "try," "see," "look at," "drop in," "find out," "don't wait," "do it today," "learn," "discover," or "examine." Too often copywriters end their copy with vapid, cute phrases instead of using a positive, action-inducing ending.

Long Headlines Work. So Does Long Copy

In the chapters on headlines, you saw many examples of long headlines. You saw that they can be interesting, powerful, and effective. They refuted the now passé rule that all headlines should be short—the shorter the better.

What is true of long headlines is likewise true of long copy. Yet, there are still many in advertising who firmly believe that copy should be short "because people don't read long copy." These short-copy advocates seem to ignore figures that indicate that people *do* read long copy if the subject matter warrants it and the writing is interesting.

Below are some long-copy research results that appeared in the book *Over 125 Ways To Improve Advertising Results* by Andrew J. Byrne. First, Byrne cites results from a seven-year study of 72 retailers. In this study, it was found that the more information a retail advertisement provides, the more successful it will be. To determine this, the study related the number of merchandise facts in each advertisement to the success of the advertisement. The results of the study are summarized in the following table:

Number of Merchandise Facts	Success Ratio
4 or more	44.2%
5 or more	49.6%
6 or more	57.7%
7 or more	60.0%
8 or more	66.7%

In the preceding table, it is assumed that as advertisements added more merchandising facts, more copy was needed, resulting in a long-copy advertisement. Conceivably, however, an advertisement with fewer facts could have used more copy to explain each one, thus using more total copy than an advertisement that wrote short copy for each fact. In such a case, it might be asked whether it was long copy or simply the inclusion of more facts that brought success.

Long copy is no stranger to national advertising. Full-page advertisements with heavy copy have been around a long time in automobile advertising. In this computer age, long copy is the norm for such products as Micro Router, BSD Berkeley Software Design, Galacticom, and others. Examine almost any national magazine and you will find long-copy advertisements.

In Byrne's list of long copy examples, he offers a classic example of successful use that occurred some years ago when the investment firm Merrill Lynch ran a 6000 word advertisement in the *New York Times*. Especially noteworthy is the fact that an offer for additional information, buried deep in the copy, drew 5000 requests. No coupon was used.

Of course, not every advertiser will use long copy. In general, it is not favored for low cost, simple products of mass consumption, such as soft drinks, gum, and candy. Other products, such as perfume, while not inexpensive, also tend toward short copy, as do advertisers for high priced watches and high-fashion clothing.

What, then, are the products that warrant long copy? Largely, they are what might be called "decision" products.

Characteristics of "decision" products include the following:

- They tend to be expensive.
- They are often technical, as in computers, electronics, robotics, photographic equipment, and high-tech products.
- They are products that require demonstration, such as jeeps, ATVs, and some cooking equipment.
- They are products new to the market that must be introduced and explained.
- They may be products whose function or value cannot be easily conveyed by an illustration.

Another advertising category that almost invariably uses long copy is corporate, or institutional, advertising. In this case, no product is involved. As explained previously, such advertising requires special effort because, unlike product advertising that may be read eagerly for information, institutional advertising offers nothing to the reader but an idea. Therefore, that idea must be written so interestingly that it makes up for the fact that it satisfies no selfish interest of the readers.

Techniques to Make Long-Copy Advertising Easy to Read

- Break it up with subheads.
- Put it in picture-caption form.
- Use short words, short sentences, and short paragraphs.
- Space liberally between lines.
- Give advertisements an open look by using white space judiciously.

CHAPTER 10

Copywriting's Odd Jobs Are Interesting, Challenging, and Call for a Varied Background

Let's take a peek at what some copywriters are doing today:

Sally Richards: Preparing a publicity piece for a client's new cold remedy.

Chuck Senderal: Writing a speech to be delivered by the president of the big department store where he works.

Marge Sims: Making a big list of names for her client's new packaged soup.

Jack Northrup: For the first time in his copywriting career, Jack's been asked to write a slogan. It's for a new type of all-purpose household cleaner.

This is just a brief sampling of the wide range of assignments that might land on your desk. So you see, being a copywriter can entail much more than simply churning out ads day after day.

Assignments classified as "extras" are the frosting on the writing cake. Almost any copywriter will welcome a chance to vary the daily routine of writing print or broadcast advertising. A copywriter, for example, who has brought to his copywriting job a background in newswriting will enjoy putting that background to work in writing a publicity story. And the copywriter composing a speech calls upon a background of rhetoric, the art of public speaking.

That "Odd Job" of Yours Could Be Your Most Important in a Day's Work

Copywriters turning out a client publicity story, for example, may discover that clients are sometimes more impressed by a five-inch publicity story in the newspaper than by a full-page advertisement running in the same issue. They may learn to their chagrin that the same clients will overlook the truly excellent creative work in an advertisement if something about the company's signature dis-

pleases them. Thus, these "little jobs" that a copywriter does, or supervises, are very frequently "big" when viewed through the eyes of a critical client.

Let's look over some of these miscellaneous activities that you may do but which may not be mentioned as part of your regular duties in a formal job description.

- Providing the dialogue for executives taking part in a closed-circuit sales meeting.
- Writing the copy for window or interior displays for stores.
- Preparing a feature magazine article about a client's business that will appear in a national magazine and will be signed by a top executive of the client company.
- Writing copy for a company's bulletin board.
- Preparing speeches for various client executives or for the members of the advertising staff.
- Organizing and writing a taped interview in which the client or possibly someone in the advertising agency, such as the agency president, will take part.
- Helping out the account executive by writing a presentation to be given at a client meeting. This will describe

creative, media, and marketing plans for the forthcoming six months or a year.

- Writing copy for sales portfolios. Contained in these may be sales talks, examples of advertising and display aids, and a boost for the advertising support.
- Putting together comments, talks, or remarks to be made by agency or client personnel at regional or national sales or dealer meetings.
- Inspiring dealers or salespeople with pep letters, urgent bulletins, or telegrams.
- Writing the sales portion of package copy (the legal material will be furnished by lawyers).
- Preparing booklets, or even short books, that concern the client's products, history, or personnel.
- Turning out promotional pieces for the advertising agency that can be left with prospective clients.
- Writing a client's company newsletter, preparing articles for it, or acting as its editor.

You're More Valuable If You Can Write Good Publicity Stories

At one time, publicity was mostly handled by public relations concerns, which turned out publicity as part of their overall job of providing public relations assignments for clients. Offering publicity, however, has expanded into a big-time activity that is now being performed by publicity departments of advertising agencies, by publicity departments of corporations, by individual practitioners, and, of course, by the aforementioned public relations concerns. These public relations companies often work in close cooperation with advertising agencies or with corporations.

From time to time, you may well be called to write publicity stories to be released to newspapers, magazines, and trade papers. Publicity stories are run free by publications, but only if they are newsworthy and if the editor happens to have some space to spare at the time.

Because publicity releases will not be published unless they meet accepted editorial standards, you must write them as straight news stories, avoiding the jargon of the advertising business and any attempt at high pressure selling. Don't, above all, attempt to make publicity stories into thinly disguised advertisements.

What kind of situations produce publicity stories of real news value? Here are some:

- An executive of a company makes a speech of some importance.
- A company builds a new plant or wins a safety award.
- An executive is promoted.
- An employee of long standing retires.
- An employee wins a big national contest.
- A company makes an important change in a product that is well-known nationally, regionally, or locally.
- A company announces the introduction of a product totally different from anything on the market.
- An employee wins a big suggestion-box award.

Figure 10–1. Sales promotion and publicity take many forms. This hot dog-shaped vehicle carries Oscar Mayer's message into all areas of the U.S. Piloted by recent college graduates, called Hotdoggers, six vehicles crisscross the nation generating publicity and media attention wherever they appear. About 800 young people apply each year to drive a Wienermobile. Since 1936, Wienermobiles have been a conspicuous feature of the American landscape and play an important role in Oscar Mayer's promotional and marketing plans.

All of these are legitimate news stories. Don't lose sight of that word "legitimate," because any publicity story without real news value is doomed to end in the editorial wastebasket. Do you really know what "news" is? Editors may disagree with your definition of the word. They may refuse to run an item you think is the story of the century.

What is important to you, or to your client, may be wholly unimportant to editors because they feel your "news" will not interest enough of their readers. A newspaper editor may refuse a story that a trade magazine editor will accept and vice versa. Each story, then, must contain news of consequence to the readers of the publication in which you'd like your story to run.

Knowing just what constitutes news is the whole crux of successful placement of publicity material. One test, of course, is to ask yourself this question: Would I (or anyone) have any interest in this story if I didn't already have a personal stake in it?

Techniques You Can Follow

The writing of publicity copy, sometimes disparagingly called "puff" copy, requires a sound knowledge of news procedure. After you have determined that your story has real news value, you must prepare it in accepted news style. It should be ready to insert in the news columns as you have written it.

If it is a general release going to a great many newspapers, you may send out one version of the story, since in most cases there will be no duplicate readership. The papers may or may not rewrite your copy; it makes little difference here.

Say, however, that you are sending a story of interest to the grocery trade and that you send the same version of the story to three magazines. All these magazines may have high duplication of readership. If the readers read

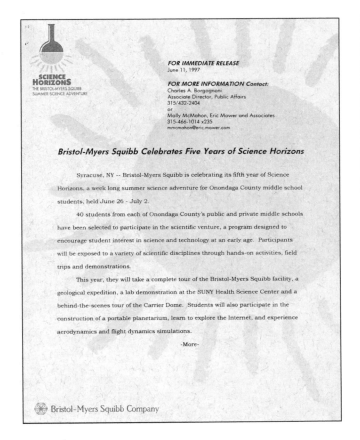

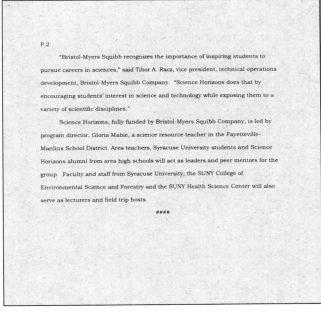

Figure 10–2. Corporate publicity release. There is close adherence to the 5-W's (who-what-where-when-why) formula in this straight publicity release. It is the kind of release in constant use by corporate America and may be written within the company, by an outside public relations firm, or by the corporation's advertising agency.

the same story in the same words in all the magazines, they will be bored and disgusted. Furthermore, the editors will be resentful when they discover that you were too lazy to write the story differently for each of the publications.

To be able to write the same story in three different versions and make each version interesting will test your ability in news writing. If you have done some reporting, you won't have much trouble. If you haven't, a publicity release may cause you some anxious moments. The principal things to keep in mind are:

- Follow the usual news style of putting essential facts early in the story in all but obvious feature stories. One way to accomplish this is to use the well-known 5-Ws approach; that is, tell who, what, when, where, and why early in your story.
- Remember that, because of makeup requirements, a story may be cut to fit a space; the space won't be stretched to fit the story. Write your copy so that it can be cut at the end of any paragraph and still make sense (all the more reason for getting important material early in the story!).
- Make paragraphs, sentences, and words short, and write so that it will be easy for the copy desk to dig out a headline for the story. In other words, say something significant and say it quickly.
- Don't worry too much about style rules, but if in doubt, use a "down" style for newspaper stories since most newspapers are inclined toward that style. A "down" style uses a minimum of capitals; an "up" style newspa-

per capitalizes heavily. The *Associated Press Stylebook* offers a handy guide for style rules to follow.

- If possible, get a picture to send along with the story and write a snappy caption for the picture (8 X 10 glossy prints are best).
- Avoid too many references to your company or client. If you can put over your idea without any direct mention of your product name or company, all the better. If not, tread very easily. Many editors will throw a story out as soon as company or product is mentioned.
- If your story has an interest for a special section of the newspaper, such as finance or automotive, send it to the editor of that section.
- Be accurate. If your facts aren't correct, your first story will be your last. Don't kill your chance for future publicity stories.

Here's an extra note about the 5-Ws approach previously mentioned. If you're wondering what elements might properly go under each of the Ws for a publicity release, here are a few ideas for you. These are, of course, only a few of the many points you might consider.

- WHO are the people involved in the story?
 Names
 Titles
 Departments
 Interesting history or accomplishments
 Newcomers or old-timers
 Quotes from important people involved

- WHAT has happened?
  Is this the first time?
  Is it a major event in the field?
  Is there anything different about it?
  Does what happened fill a long-felt need?
- WHEN did it happen?
  Has it already happened?
  Is it taking place over a period of time?
  (How long is the period?)
  Is it yet to happen?
  Exact date (and time, if necessary)?
- WHERE did it happen?
  At the workplace?
  It is local, or did it happen at a number of places simultaneously?
- WHY is it happening?
  What is the story behind the event?

An Interesting Challenge: The Feature Article

The foregoing material has stressed the writing of straight news publicity material. You may, however, be occasionally asked to write a feature story. Normally, this will be a longer piece suitable for publication in a newspaper or magazine. If the latter, very often you will write it for the signature of an executive in your client's company, possibly the president.

When doing a feature style, you forget the 5-Ws approach for the lead. In fact, whether for a newspaper or a magazine, the feature story resembles magazine articles in writing style and general structure.

Especially important and distinctive is the feature lead. This may stress human interest, an oddity, an historical event—anything that is interesting enough to capture quick attention.

Throughout the feature story, you should maintain this magazine style, but you should also manage to incorporate hard news value. Quite often, if the piece you are writing is a magazine feature, it may be quite acceptable to refer frequently to your company, personnel, and products because your feature is being sent to a publication that serves the client's field.

Thus, if your client is a bank, the article in *Banking* magazine could discuss the inner workings of your client's bank. There is no need, as in the straight news release, to hold back the references to the client.

It is especially desirable when placing feature stories to accompany the material with good photos and lively captions. In fact, the magazine will often request photographs or illustrative material.

As a copywriter in a small or medium-sized agency or in a company advertising department, you may be expected to do both news and feature publicity stories. If, however, you work for an agency or company big enough to have a separate public relations department, such work will normally be assigned to that department.

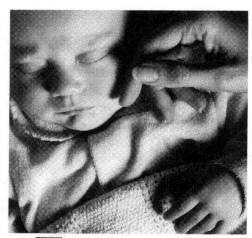

THE ABILITY TO STOP CHILD ABUSE
IS FINALLY AT OUR FINGERTIPS.

Now there's a way you truly can help stop child abuse. By simply lending your support to a new kind of prevention program. A program that teaches new parents how to deal with the stresses that lead to abuse. One that interrupts the cycle of abuse before it can begin. We're already achieving unprecedented results, but we need your help where you live. Call 1-800-CHILDREN. And learn how close at hand the solution to child abuse really is.

THE MORE YOU HELP THE LESS THEY HURT.

1 - 8 0 0 - C H I L D R E N

National Committee to Prevent Child Abuse

Figure 10–3. Public service advertisement. *Courtesy of the Advertising Council.*

Counteracting Bad Publicity

With some companies driven into bankruptcy or actually out of business because of huge settlements resulting from class-action suits, bad publicity has become a matter of grave concern in the business world.

In recent years, our increasingly litigious society has produced a new challenge for those who write publicity. This is the need to write good publicity to counteract bad publicity. Some years ago, as an example, Rely Tampons were blamed for the deaths of some users. Inevitably, lawsuits ensued, resulting in a great deal of unfavorable publicity.

The question then arises: Should the product company combat this with advertising or with publicity? Both have been used and both have worked.

Sometimes a product can become an innocent victim. For example, Tylenol suffered sales drops when poison was put into product containers by some demented person. Through adroit use of advertising and publicity, the makers eventually overcame lowered sales and adverse reaction, but not before the company suffered considerable financial and emotional trauma.

Another interesting instance was the widespread whispering campaign that associated Procter & Gamble with Satanic symbolism because of its man-in-the-moon trademark.[1] At first, because the accusation was so patently absurd, the company ignored it. Eventually, however, with thousands of letters pouring in and the subject being taken up in television shows, the company acted vigorously through advertising, public and legal action to answer its tormentors.

Often, of course, these parlous situations are more than the ordinary copywriter can handle and require the services of skilled public relations practitioners and upper-echelon advertising people. Somewhere along the route, however, the copywriter may become involved.

Sweepstakes and Contests

Sweepstakes can be tremendously effective sales stimulators. Many advertisers run sweepstakes year after year. (Although the more commonly used sweepstakes are stressed here, the points given apply equally to contests.)

If you should ever be assigned to write a sweepstakes advertisement, there are several points you will want to know. For instance, there are two schools of thought on the subject of such advertising. One camp believes that a fair part of the advertisement should be devoted to the regular copy story on the product itself. The second group is convinced that the entire advertisement should be used to sell the sweepstakes—the sweepstakes being the "product," in such an instance.

The first school reasons that because every reader isn't going to enter the sweepstakes, you should make an effort to sell the product on its own merits. Straight product copy is necessary to sell that "undecided" segment of the audience. The people who question their chances of winning must be persuaded that they have nothing to lose by entering, that they will get their full money's worth for what they spend in buying the product even if they don't happen to win a prize.

The second school reasons that more entries are obtained when the entire space is given over to selling the sweepstakes. The inclusion of straight product copy, they feel, divides the reader's interest because it presents two separate thoughts to be considered, just is if two different products were being advertised in the same advertisement.

Regardless of which of the two foregoing patterns your sweepstakes advertisements take, here are some copy points worth remembering:

- Most readers think in terms of winning the first prize, so play up your major prize; stress it. Use a big headline to do so.
- Generally speaking, a long list of secondary prizes has been found to be more effective than a small group, even though the total cash value in each case is the same. If you have an impressive list of such prizes, don't merely say "50 prizes." Instead, give that fact extra appeal by saying "50 chances to win!"
- Spotlight total retail cash value of all prizes if this is an impressive sum.
- "Win" is a magic word, so headline it.
- In a subhead, drive home how easy it is to win.
- In your copy, quickly communicate how easy it is to enter the sweepstakes.
- If you are writing contest copy, give examples of jingles, sentences, and puzzle solutions that might be typical of prizewinning entries.
- List rules simply and clearly, leaving unanswered no question that might come to a reader's mind. Always include the specific date on which the sweepstakes entries close.
- Be sure to tell readers that they may enter as often as they wish (if this is the case).
- Urge readers to enter "NOW."
- Warn that offers are void where prohibited by law.
- Make clear that all prizes will be awarded and that a list of winners will be mailed upon request.

Package Copy

No layman can possibly imagine the effort devoted to packaging by every packaged-goods manufacturer, but *you* will if you are assigned to write package copy. Every bit of package space is taken up with illustrations, directions for use, legal requirements, ingredients—*and* selling copy. The latter is your chief responsibility, but you may be involved with the other factors, too.

Writing package copy is no easy job, especially since you can count on everyone looking over your shoulder to

[1] In 1995, the rumors gained strength once again. Calls to the company increased from an average of 22 a day to approximately 200 a day. Procter & Gamble, attributing the increased concern to rumors spread by a competitor, sued. In addition, mass mailings were sent to areas from which most of the calls were coming.

criticize, to make suggestions, and to reject what you've done. Your critics will be anyone from brand managers to account executives, lawyers, creative people, and the sales staff.

Because copy on product packages is infrequently changed, this is an assignment you will be given only on rare occasions.

The following is a checklist of some of the more important elements of package copy. Some are "musts" for all packages, while others are included only under certain conditions.

- *Brand name.* This, obviously, is a "must." It's the headline of your copy.
- *Nature of product.* Let buyer know what the product is, whether it is coffee, cheese, or a mattress.
- *Specific nature of product.* If product is tea, give the exact type—green, black, Ceylon, or India. If coffee, tell what kind of grind—drip or regular. If aspirin, indicate how many grains are contained in each tablet.
- *Uses of product.* If use of the product isn't obvious, give its use clearly. For example, although you might presume that everyone would know that Betty Crocker is used for cake mix, the manufacturer doesn't take this for granted. In letters almost as big and bold as the product name itself, you'll find the words "cake mix."

    If the product has multiple uses, give these other uses. The Cascade package, as an example, points out that Cascade can be used for washing dishes, aluminum, and silver.

    A package containing a food product ordinarily consumed as a result of further preparation will often carry recipes. Your purpose in listing multiple uses of recipes is to induce the consumer to "run through" a package of the product quickly, thus hastening the repeat purchase.
- *Sales claims.* If the product has some definite sales point highlight it. To illustrate, Comet "bleaches out stains"; it's Crest toothpaste "with Tartar Control"; and Beautiflor wax "cleans as it waxes."
- *Directions.* If special directions must be given for use of product, state them clearly and simply, avoiding all scientific or technical terms and any words that might not be immediately understood by a person of limited education.
- *"Family" products.* If the manufacturer makes other allied products, call the buyer's attention to them. For example, every box of Kellogg's corn flakes mentions that Kellogg also makes other cereals.
- *Premium offers.* If premiums or contests are being offered by the manufacturer of the product—and this policy will continue long enough to justify its mention on the package—it's sound strategy to include this information, provided the package offers you enough space.
- *Ingredients.* Food and drug products are required by law to state their composition on the package. Copy of this nature, however, is usually prepared by a lawyer, so it is of but passing interest to you.
- *Nutrition information per serving.* This information, required by the U.S. Food and Drug Administration (FDA), is another legal requirement. Under a heading of *Nutrition Facts,* information is listed about the product's calories, cholesterol, fat, fiber, sodium, and other elements. With so many people concerned about nutrition and health today, *Nutrition Facts* is one of the most important elements in packaging. Thousands of shoppers select or reject products based on what they see included under this heading.

Probably the best advice anyone can give you regarding package copy is to "make your package a good advertisement." That's what it is or should be. Don't clutter it with words at the sacrifice of good design, but don't keep your product's good points a secret either. When a person picks up a can of peas to inspect it, *sell* those peas with the copy you've written.

Many supermarkets offer "storecasting," which, in conjunction with packaging, gives shoppers one more last-minute nudge. The intercom "storecast" mentions the product and then the shopper sees the package—a powerful combination of sight and sound.

Brand Names and Trademarks

Work long enough in copywriting, you will eventually be asked to supply a list of proposed new names for a product or service. As you can surmise, this is not a frequent assignment, but it's a refreshing change from the usual work. It can be, however, somewhat discouraging. As you will discover, many good names are already being used and are protected by law. Thus, your initial list of 200 names may not have any winners. Furthermore, when you compare your list with those supplied by your fellow workers, it's deflating to see how many names are duplicated. It's hard to come up with different, original names.

Product names are commonly known in business as "brand names" or "trademarks." Brand names, as we shall refer to them, are not necessarily registered as trademarks. They may become so, however, once they have been used on goods shipped in interstate or foreign commerce, and provided they violate no governmental restrictions applying to trademarks. Pictorial representations may also be registered as trademarks.

As a result of a 1995 ruling of the U.S. Supreme Court, even a single color can now be trademarked by an advertiser. Heretofore, only colors combined with shapes, words, or other colors were protectable. See Chapter 23 for a full discussion of what may, or may not be protectable under trademark law.

Because a new product must be highly developed prior to its introduction into retail channels, its naming is an assignment met more often by those copywriters who work in agencies or for a manufacturer than by writers in the retail field. Developing a brand name is only an occasional assignment at most, but it is one whose importance cannot be overemphasized.

On the brand name rests much responsibility for distinguishing one product or family of products from any and all others; the brand name must make a given product (or line) stand out above the mass of competitive goods or services. In the soap field, for instance, any new name must compete with Ivory, Dial, and the numerous other soaps now being manufactured.

Usually, you will not be charged with the full responsibility of creating a new brand name. You will be asked to create a list of as many suitable names as you can think of. Other people in your organization will be asked to do the same thing.

The advertiser's employees, as well as those of the agency—from top brass to office clerks—may contribute ideas. Sometimes, as an incentive, a bonus will be rewarded to the person who offers the name finally selected. The selection of a brand name is so important that getting a good one is worth almost any effort.

A Good Name Should be Long Lasting

Even products and services of exceptional merit have little chance of survival, much less marked success, if they are burdened with unappealing, inappropriate, or hard-to-pronounce brand names.

Changing a brand name once a product has been put on the market and advertised is a costly and involved procedure. It necessitates writing off as a loss the advertising expenditures made prior to such a change. Satisfied users, accustomed to calling for the product under the abandoned name, must be made aware of the change. Thus, if you start with a name, you must usually continue with it.

The firm establishment of a distinctive brand name protects the consumer and producer alike. In the "cracker barrel" days, great grandmother had to ask for products in terms applicable to all merchandise of similar nature—the good as well as the bad. (Many types of meats, fruits, cheeses, and vegetables must still be called for by their generic names.)

When great-grandmother needed oatmeal, she could only ask for "oatmeal" by the name and *hope* that it would be satisfactory—not full of chaff, vermin, or other foreign matter. Today, grandmother can ask for Quaker Oats and *know* that the quality is high—that every subsequent purchase will meet the same high standard. Such repeat purchases are vital.

Advice To Follow When You're Making Up a Name

There are many guideposts to follow in the selection of a good brand name. There are, nevertheless, numerous brand names now known in every corner of the world that violate many of the suggestions you will be given here. As exceptions come to mind, remember that they have, for the large part, been constantly advertised over many years. It has taken millions of repetitions and millions of dollars to win for them the eminence that they enjoy today.

Make it distinctive. Since a brand name's first function is to *identify* one product from others, it should be, above all things, distinctive. It should be different, preferably different from all other products but certainly entirely different from the brand name of any product which might be considered even remotely competitive.

To be distinctive does not necessarily mean that a brand name must be clever or tricky. The name Perdue is simple and ungarnished. Yet, because it is an uncommon surname, it is distinctive. Many other family names, on the other hand, lack such distinction.

When submitting suggestions for brand names, be careful to avoid names similar to those of established products. In the early days of brand names, some brand names almost identical to established ones were intentionally chosen. The purpose, of course, was to attempt to capitalize on the established product's reputation and to try to capture a portion of a competitor's sales by confusing the public.

Actually, such sharp practice has almost invariably harmed rather than helped the imitator. The similarity in names, in fact, usually confused the public so much that upon reading the newcomer's advertising, people assumed the advertisements were boosting the established product rather than the new one. Purchases were thus made automatically for the well-known brand, defeating the imitator's purpose and causing the advertising to lose a large degree of its effectiveness.

Not only is it dishonest and poor business to trade on an established leader's name, but costly lawsuits for infringement are almost certain to be instituted. Every possible precaution should be taken to learn whether a proposed brand name has been previously registered by someone else as a trademark. Such preliminary checks may be made by contacting any one of the various trade mark services found in many large cities.

One such trademark service is the Trademark Bureau of the Diamond International Corporation, New York. This company, for a small fee, will check files to see if your proposed trademark has been used before. The file is the largest independently owned collection in the country.

It must be noted that, while such organizations make fairly comprehensive searches, their findings are not an absolute guarantee that the name is not already in use. This can be officially determined only after the U.S. Patent and Trademark Office has passed on the application for trademark; and even a federal registration is subject to challenge by someone who has made prior use of the mark. The files of the trademark search organizations, however, include U.S. Patent and Trademark Office trademarks almost as soon as they are recorded by that agency.

Make it easy to remember. A brand name should be easy to remember. If the name is not memorable, it will take longer and be more expensive to win widespread public recognition. A few examples of brand names that are extremely easy to remember are Duz, Seven-Up, and Jif.

The ease with which a person can remember a brand name is of great importance. To illustrate, imagine that a person goes into a drugstore for a hair tonic. The night before, he read about a certain brand and was impressed by the benefits it promised him, but now that he is in the store, he can't quite recall the product's name.

It's right on the tip of his tongue, but he can't remember it. As a result, Vitalis or Wildroot gets the sale, a sale actually created by a competitor's advertising.

It's unfortunate, but true, that if people have to think to recall the name of your product, they will buy a competitive brand bearing a name that comes to mind automatically.

Make it pronounceable. Still another very important consideration regarding brand names is that they should be easy to pronounce by consumers and by announcers in the broadcast media. As the makers of Baume Bengué Analgesique (now simply Ben-Gay) learned, the general public is reluctant to ask for a product whose name it finds difficult to pronounce.

There is a very sound psychological reason for this. All of us fear ridicule. Consequently, we resist putting ourselves in a position where we might appear ridiculous, even in front of a completely impersonal clerk whom we may never see again.

A customer might well hesitate to ask a druggist for Hexylresorcinol, a name only a scientist might be expected to pronounce with any facility. Recognizing this, the makers of this product wisely give it an additional name— S. T. 37—which a child could easily remember.

If you had never heard the name Sal Hepatica pronounced, there's a possibility that you might have trouble pronouncing it. Constant advertising, however, has familiarized a huge section of the population with its correct pronunciation. Still, Sal Hepatica may well be losing sales it could make if its name were easier for all people to pronounce.

A somewhat similar example is Campho Phenique, which is easy enough to handle if you have heard it, but think of the trouble it might give the poorly educated or those who speak English as a second language.

An exception to this rule about ease of pronunciation is the naming of perfumes, such as Yves Saint Laurent, cosmetics, high fashion clothing, and a number of luxury items, such as Cristal d'arques. Many advertisers of such products feel that the use of foreign, scientific, or other difficult words provides a certain aura that enhances the names. Difficult names such as these are sometimes provided with pronunciation instructions.

Despite some successes for products with difficult names, it is best to use simple names. Selling products is hard enough. You simply add to your problems by providing names that the public cannot pronounce or remember. Remember, too, that a product may be advertised in the broadcast media. The name may be hard to visualize or hard for the announcers to handle.

See that it has pleasant associations. The fourth "must" in the selection of a good brand name is associations. Unpleasant associations should be avoided. For example, the initials DT might seem an acceptable name for a coffee made by a man named Daniel Thompson. Here is something short, distinctive, easy to remember, and easy to pronounce. In seeing the name of the product in print, or in hearing it mentioned on the air, however, many would instantly think of drunkenness, not coffee. Others might possibly think of DDT, the insecticide. In either instance, unappetizing mental pictures would be created, instead of the pleasant thoughts that should be associated with the product.

"Balloon" would obviously be a very poor name for a girdle, for another example, even though it might be made of balloon silk.

Avoid dating your brand name. Unless you are trying purposely to establish a product as being of old-fashioned vintage—obviously the case in the selection of Old Spice as a name for a line of toiletries—brand names that too closely ally a product with a certain era are best avoided. For instance, although "23 Skiddoo" might have been a "stopper" as a name for a mosquito repellent in grandmother's day, the term is now almost meaningless because it is out of vogue.

If a catfood named "Hepcat" had been introduced in the 1940s, it might have enjoyed success for some time, but as jitterbugging went the way of the bunny-hop and the Charleston, the term would have lost its meaning. The danger of becoming passé is always present in any name adopted to take advantage of a current craze. When the craze is over, your name then becomes unintelligible or old hat.

Types of Brand Names

One of the most frequent objectives in the creation of brand names today is to make the name suggestive of some property or benefit of the product. An example is Plax. You can surmise from the name FilterQueen that this vacuum cleaner filters the air. It is a benefit in which you can easily see the merit, and the product's name blares forth the virtue. Mum and Ban are two other examples of suggestive names.

Suggestive names are of special advantage during that period when a new product is fighting to win wide recognition. This is particularly true if the product is one that is entirely new or one that has definite properties or benefits exclusively its own.

Once the product has become firmly established, however, the full significance of its name is often lost. Illustrative of this is the fact that when you refer to the brand name Frigidaire, you aren't actively conscious of the fact that you are, in essence, saying "air that is frigid." At least you aren't if you are like most people. The same principle is true with other such well-known brand names as Beautyrest, Kissproof, and Eveready.

Numbers and initials. Many famous brand names are built on numbers or initials, or both. For example, 3-in-1, S.T. 37, PM, ABC, and ZBT. These are easy to pronounce, and, because of their brevity, they allow for a proportionately larger logotype, both in advertisements and on the packages itself, than do brand names that are longer. But again, they are often difficult to obtain as one's own exclusive property.

Geographical or patriotic names. Columbia, Liberty, American, Hartford, Waltham, and Palm Beach are foremost examples of brand names in this group. Such names have been popular in the past, but because they lack true distinctiveness in most instances and are not subject to exclusive proprietorship, they are not considered among the best for new products.

Coined names. Another rich source of brand names is tapped through coining words. Coined brand names may be divided into three types:

1. Those devised by uniting various components of the company name to form a single word. Exemplifying this are Nabisco (*NA*tional *BIS*cuit *Co*.), Alcoa (*Al*uminum *Co*rporation of America), and Duco (*Du* Pont *Co*.) Such contractions or abbreviations, if easy to spell, pronounce, and remember, often make excellent brand names that have the added advantage of calling to mind the full name of the product. Armco (*American Rolling Mill Co*.) and Texaco (The *Texas Co*.) are contractions that proved so successful that the companies eventually changed their corporate titles and now are known legally by what once were just their brand names.
2. Those such as Tenderleaf, Treet, Perma-Lift, Holeproof, Palmolive, and Rem. These are created in several ways:
   a. They may be shortened versions of common words, as is Rem (for "remedy").
   b. They may be phonetic spellings, such as Kool and Duz.
   c. They may be created by combining two or more words, or parts thereof, employing either orthodox spelling or simplified variations. For example, Spam (from "spiced ham"), Pepsodent, Car-Nu, and Noxzema. Among these are many of those brand names that spotlight some benefit or property of the product. No-fade and Pye-Quick promise definite benefits, while Bromo-Seltzer and Pepto-Bismol are semiscientific descriptions of properties of the products.
3. Those brand names that are out-and-out inventions, such as Keds, Kodak, Dic-a-Doo, and Drax.

Coined names are today among the most popular brand names. Good ones have numerous advantages. They are distinctive. They have high recognition value, are easy to pronounce, easy to remember, and are timeless in their durability. Full legal protection may usually be obtained for them, making them the exclusive property of a single company or individual.

Some names such as Cellophane, Linoleum, Aspirin, Kerosene, and Shredded Wheat have become so firmly associated with a product that they have become generic—that is, part of the language. When this happens, the company loses the exclusive right to the name. Call it the penalty for having a really excellent name. The only protection is constant watchfulness by the advertiser.

One of the most determined corporations in the protecting of its trademark is the Coca-Cola Company. This organization reminds others constantly that when they refer to Coca-Cola in its abbreviated form, they will keep the meaning "clear" if the shorter version "Coke" is spelled with a capital C. This, the company explains in its advertising, will help protect a "valuable trademark." The Coca-Cola Company recognizes the peril confronting its trademarked abbreviation; editors and others are constantly reminded that the word *Coke* is the trademarked property of the Coca-Cola company and not merely a convenient and generic term for a general class of soft drink.

Even though the true meaning of suggestive names may after a time no longer consciously register in the minds of customers, their value in the initial stages of a product's development can be considerable. So long as the benefit or promise contained in the brand name is both important and believable, it is difficult to see how it can be other than an asset in promoting sales.

General designation of quality. Excel, Royal, Ideal, Perfection, Acme, Hi-Grade, Apex, Superior, A-1, and so forth, are included among those brand names that may be said to give general designation of the quality of the product. These are not the best of names. They are not distinctive.

Among the many brands emblazoned with the name Acme, to name but a few, we find Acme pencils, Acme paint, Acme oil burners, carbon paper, card cases, fire extinguishers, snap fasteners, shower curtains, scissors, wire, stepladders, thermostats, tables, chair seats, and gasoline. And that list could be enlarged with ease.

Another point against such general descriptions is that constant usage has caused the average person to become oblivious to their literal definitions. Third, the claims to superiority implied by such names are so lofty as to lack credibility. In addition, being common words of the public domain, it is almost impossible to protect such names adequately.

Family names. More numerous perhaps than those in any other one classification are products named after the founder or owner of the company marketing them. Among those most advertised currently are Parker, Heinz, Borden, Westinghouse, Pabst, and Remington.

There are three reasons that it is often wise to avoid family names: (1) Often a family name lacks distinctiveness; (2) The name may be difficult to spell or pronounce, such as is Ghirardelli, the name of a large West Coast chocolate producer; and (3) Family names are hard to protect. Any person of the same name can enter business in direct competition with you and use the name you both possess. Sometimes, if another person's so doing will obviously cause damage to your business, the courts will rule against this practice. In the past, however, a number of unscrupulous firms have deliberately hired people having the same names as leading competitors. Giving these people the title (in name only) of head of the firm, they were thus able to use their competitor's name as their own brand name and still argue that they were technically within the law.

Fictional, historical, and heroic names. Robert Burns, Chesterfield, Victor, Admiral, De Soto, Pontiac, Maxwell House, Aunt Jemima, and Bo Peep all fall into this category. There is nothing wrong with such names so long as they fulfill the requirements of distinctiveness (which Admiral certainly lacks), ease of recall, ease of pronunciation, and pleasant associations. They are, however, difficult to protect.

When you choose such a name, care must be taken to make your selection from those characters, events, or places whose durability has been firmly established. If you select the name of some person, place, or event of recent prominence, you may find in the years to come that such fame will have passed.

Group sensitivities, previously discussed, must be considered also in such names. Sambo food establishments ran into trouble with African-Americans, who felt the name was demeaning.

Animals, minerals, vegetables. Among the first examples of brand names in this classification that come to mind are Camel, Caterpillar, Blue Boar, Walnut, White Owl, and Swansdown. Again, some such names lack distinction and, in some cases, are difficult to spell, pronounce, or protect. One virtue, however, is that they usually have more pictorial interest—much more, for instance, than brand names based on the name of the company founder.

Familiar objects. Names based on common objects generally are not as distinctive as some others. In that respect, they are like brand names in group number one—Hi-Grade, Acme, and Ideal. For example, in addition to Arrow shirts, we have Arrow mucilage, Arrow shovels, Arrow desks, Arrow golf balls, and Arrow needles, to mention but a handful.

Names such as Diamond, Anchor, Star, and so forth are similarly duplicated on products of almost every conceivable variety. These names usually do, however, have the advantage, like the animal/mineral/vegetable group, of being translated easily into a pictorial form that increases

the recognition value of the name. Nevertheless, they are best avoided.

Trade Characters and Pictorial Trademarks

Trade personalities or symbols such as Aunt Jemima, the Pontiac Indian head, and the Fisher Body coach are often employed to give an extra and continuous recognition value to a company's advertising. When such characters or symbols are also affixed to the product or package (as are all of those just mentioned), the advertising and the product itself become closely identified. Application to the product or package, where practicable, helps to create instantaneous recognition in the minds of consumers when their eyes alight on the product on the shelf of a store, on the hood of an automobile, or on a gasoline pump in a service station.

Moreover, many products are actually requested by a description of the pictorial trademark on the package rather than by name. That is, a customer might ask for "the cocoa with the lady on it" instead of saying "Baker's Cocoa."

The actual designing of suitable trade characters or symbols is plainly a job that requires the talents of an artist. But more often than not, these illustrative devices are based on ideas sparked by copywriters. Here are a few dos and don'ts for you to remember if you are ever confronted with an assignment of this nature.

Review the requisites of brand names that are also applicable to things pictorial. That is, an illustrated trademark should be: (1) simple, yet distinctive; (2) easy to remember; and (3) subject to legal protection.

You should *avoid* unpleasant associations and current fashions (which might appear ludicrous ten years hence).

If the subject is something the passage of time might make obsolete, it should be avoided. An example is the use of the radiator design of an automobile. Because these designs are changed periodically, any trademark showing one would necessarily also have to be changed from time to time, appreciably reducing its recognition value.

Trademark and Copyright Symbols

As a copywriter, you may wonder at times about when to use certain symbols in connection with your brand name or trademark. The symbols ®, ™, ℠, and © appear in countless advertisements, and the best advice is not to use them unless the lawyers insist on your doing so. Consumers are confused enough by all the various abbreviations encountered in daily life without having to wade through more clutter in advertisements.

Still, you should know what the symbols represent and when they might be used. An ® included in your advertisement means that the trademark is registered in the U.S. Patent and Trademark Office and a certificate has been issued by the Commissioner. You can own a brand name without using the ®, but it can help warn off others who might wish to use it, perhaps not realizing its proprietary nature.

The ™ is used for a trademark that has not yet been registered; an application may be pending. A similar situation is encountered with the use of ᔆᴹ, which stands for service mark. The symbol ™ is for merchandise of any kind, while ᔆᴹ, which is seen very little, is for services, such as insurance, transportation, broadcasting, and so on.

The symbol © stands for copyright, but this symbol has no legal meaning when used by itself. If you are going through the process of copyrighting, which means you're trying to protect the entire content of your advertisement, you will have to use a notice that includes the © and the name of the copyright owner as well as the year the advertisement was first published.

The best advice is to use these symbols as little as legally possible. They simply get in the way of easy reading by the consumer. However, be *sure* to use them if the advertiser insists, because there are many situations in which they can be vitally important.

You May Never Be Asked to Write a Slogan

Long before you began working, your client may have been using a slogan that will continue to be used. A good slogan, once established, has the permanence of a national monument. An example is "99 and ⁴⁴/100% pure." Occasionally, however, you may be asked to write a slogan for a new product.

Many slogans are accidents. They start out as headlines and then become slogans. Others begin as campaign themes, such as:

Promise her anything but give her Arpège.

You might write a deft phrase that pops out of the middle of your copy and begs for recognition as a slogan. You weren't deliberately writing a slogan; it just happened. If you think that you have a good slogan, see if it meets these criteria:

Does it make a specific claim or promise a believable benefit? Such a slogan is:

"Dove doesn't dry like soap/because Dove isn't soap"

This specific promise for people who suffer from dry skin is a powerful sales tool when repeated. A direct promise of this type is more potent than mere cleverness, an attribute most people associate with slogans.

Strong promise is contained in this slogan aimed at arthritis sufferers:

Bufferin: For the pain and inflammation of arthritis.

Clearly, there is no cleverness but lots of sales power there. A slogan for a charge card says:

VISA: It's everywhere you want to be

These few words express a strong benefit in easy-to-remember words, as does this dog food slogan:

"All the appeal of a homemade meal"

Does it contain a command to action, a direct appeal to buy? This type of slogan has merit because it has vitality. Likewise, it involves the reader directly in the action. Placed at the bottom of the advertisement, it ends the advertisement with an urge to action, always a desirable technique. Examples include:

Get back into life with Depend

American Express: Don't leave home without it.

EconoLodge: Spend a night, not a fortune.

Does it create a favorable identification or image for your product, service, or company? Some slogans that answer this third question are:

Bayer: The wonder drug that works wonders.

Mercury. The shape you want to be in.

AT&T The right choice.

America's favorite store K-Mart. The saving place.

Certain writing attributes of slogans appear in the examples that have been offered here. For instance, most have a strong sense of the vernacular, of a conversational style that is breezy, informal, and offhand. A slogan talks "people" language. It is rarely literary in tone and it almost never uses a word that will make anyone reach for a dictionary.

It is rare, too, to find a long slogan. To be memorable, a slogan must almost always be brief. A world of copy strength can be packed into a few words, as "It's toasted" and "It floats" will testify.

A further aid to memorability is the use of rhyme and alliteration. "Be sure with Pure" is more likely to be remembered than "Be certain with Pure," although the meaning is the same for both. If you used alliteration by writing "Pick Planters Peanuts," you'd achieve more memorability than if you wrote "Choose Planters Peanuts."

In local advertising, a rhyming slogan repeated year after year can't be overlooked. It becomes a part of the local scene. It's mystifying why more local advertisers don't utilize this sure aid to memorability. Such rhyming slogans don't require cleverness, just repetition, such as the local dealer who is heard several times a day telling radio listeners that:

Sam Dell

Will serve you well

It's highly desirable to inject cleverness into a slogan if you can retain sales power while doing so. Yet, thousands of slogans have been effective without cleverness, just as millions of advertisements have been effective without slogans. Furthermore, effective slogans often are rather ordinary examples of writing; they're effective simply because of heavy use, not because they have any notable literary quality.

Premium Offers

At one time, magazines and newspapers were replete with advertisements containing premium offers of everything from sailboats to clothing items. Such offers were made not only by manufacturers of products but also by banks eager for new depositors. Premium specialists started up companies of their own or held important positions in corporations and advertising agencies.

While premium deals haven't vanished completely, they are no longer the vital force in marketing that they once were. Still, should you be asked to write copy for advertisements containing premium offers, it is sensible for you to employ certain techniques in what you write.

First, what is a premium? It is an item that product buyers get at a greatly reduced price for sending in some evidence of purchase and a specified amount of cash. Evidence of purchase is usually in the form of a label or box top, but a purchase receipt might be used also.

An example of a premium offer run in the summer (premiums are often seasonal) was a Wheat Thins offer of a picnic basket. "This $25 basket can be obtained by sending in $9.95 plus proof of purchase." Like most premium offers, this is a bargain for the purchaser.

A premium is sometimes related to the product being sold, such as the premium offer of a serving tray with the purchase of a Butterball turkey. Many times, however, there is no close relationship between product and premium.

While you will probably be more concerned with the writing of premium advertising for newspapers and magazines, you may also write package copy featuring premium offers. Packages have been important vehicles for premium promotions, especially for very youthful prospects.

Here are some suggestions for premium offers:

- If the premium is physically attractive or interesting looking, give it a good illustration.
- Highlight the cash retail value of the premium if it is sufficiently high or if there is a substantial gap between the amount to be sent in and the actual value of the item.
- Sell the premium. Dramatize it. Make it appealing. If you don't, the advertiser may end up with a warehouse of unwanted premiums, the end result of which will be an unhappy advertiser.
- Include a statement of a time limit for the offer.
- Urge readers to take up the offer quickly. It's vital that they act at once; if they delay, you may lose them.

Premium Offers—A Summation

We may (as the expression goes) be "beating a dead horse" in this discussion of premiums. A diligent look through publications and the backs of packages yielded only one premium offer. At one time, premium advertisements and package offers were common. Meanwhile, in the hunt for premium offers, the search revealed an impressive number of sweepstakes, contests, and coupon offers. It is in those areas that the action lies.

Still, this section on premium offers is being included because, if competition becomes even fiercer than today, premiums may make a comeback.

CHAPTER 11

If You Do Copy for Local Businesses, You're in Close Touch with Your Market

Judy Katz laughs when she hears someone talk enviously about "bankers' hours." It's 7:30 a.m. Since arriving well before that, she's been going over the copy and layout for a home loan ad. It's the quiet time for her since First Merchant's doors don't open until 10.

Another early bird down the street is Joe Gaston, the promotion manager at Acme Motors. He's out on the lot looking over a just-arrived shipment of minivans. At the moment, he's deciding how to apportion his ad budget between newspapers, radio, and the Pennysaver.

A couple of miles away from the downtown section, Glenn Worley is getting a fact sheet ready for pickup by the local agency that prepares ads for his mall jewelry shop. With three jewelry shops fighting for the business of mall shoppers, Glenn is giving much thought to the message he wants to convey.

Local businesses are the commercial heart of com- munities across the land. Their advertising is seldom glamorous, but it is a vital force in the movement of goods and services—from dignified banks to tanning salons—and from snooty, high-fashion boutiques to martial arts store fronts. There's something for everyone on the local business scene, and because the response is so fast, that gives copywriters a chance to see their copy at work.

"Local" Advertising Is an All-Inclusive Term

Local advertising is often inaccurately called "retail" advertising, a term not broad enough to embrace advertising for such businesses as health clubs, auto repair shops, hotels, racquetball clubs, warehouses, and others. Local advertising is an all-inclusive term; retail advertising is not.

Whatever term is used, this advertising is fast-paced, at the point of sale, and significant in the numbers of people and dollars it involves. Workers in local advertising enjoy satisfactions that are denied the writer of national adver-

tising: (1) to see an advertisement prepared on Wednesday in print on Thursday; and (2) to learn on Thursday how successful their Wednesday creative efforts have been. No other phase of advertising permits the writers to deal so directly with their merchandise and their customers or to learn so quickly how effective their approach and methods have been.

In this chapter, the emphasis is on department store advertising because it provides the most diversified picture of such copywriting. Most of the principles can also be applied to other forms of local selling.

Retail copywriters usually turn out more copy at a faster pace than the usual agency copywriters working on national advertisements. Furthermore, the power of their copy is checked immediately by sales results, whereas the copy written by national copywriters is seldom measured by the sales results obtained by one advertisement.

When local copywriters type out selling copy for a $250 microwave oven or cross-country skis at $115-$270 they know just how many units were sold by the advertisement. If many, they have quick gratification. If few, they're depressed, despite the fact that some other factors may be responsible for the poor sales figures. Thus, local copywriting is exhilarating, demanding, satisfying, and exhausting. Above all, it's exciting because it's where the action is, at the consumer buying level.

Unfortunately, much local advertising is poorly done. An examination of advertisements in newspapers (with the exception of first-class establishments in big cities) reveals a depressing picture. Too often, the copy is prepared by persons in the establishments who have had no training in advertising or by newspaper space salespeople who do the copy because they are expected to write copy as part of their overall selling duties. It is obvious from their copy that many space salespeople should concentrate on their selling and leave the writing to better qualified persons.

 ## Common Faults in Some Local Advertising

The inexpert approach in advertising on the local level often results in these common faults:

1. Telegraphic copy that has no flow or character.
2. Label headlines that don't lure readers into reading the body copy.
3. Impersonal writing that doesn't reach out and involve the reader.
4. Little, or no, use of suffering points to give solid reasons for buying.
5. Product-oriented copy instead of people-oriented copy.
6. Too much mere listing of product or sales points.
7. No localization of the copy that takes advantage of the shared experiences of the advertiser and the customers.
8. Overall dullness of the copy—a lack of sparkle, imagination, and use of colorful, persuasive words.

The principles of good copywriting can be applied by these advertisers and, in the case of banks, are often applied exceedingly well. This excellence is largely due to the fact that most bank advertising is prepared by advertising agency copywriters. This is also likely to be true of large dairies, hotels, car dealers, and other local enterprises that invest substantially in advertising. Still, there is much local advertising that is not done well.

In the material immediately following, you'll find suggestions for the actual writing of local advertising.

Four Questions and Answers

Who's the Customer for This Item?

Obviously, if it's a very high-priced pair of shoes, you appeal first to the person who can afford to pay that price. That consideration is going to govern your entire approach. Your advertisement is dignified. Your appeal must be to pride and a desire to wear the best of everything.

If the shoe is a moderately priced item, you know it will have general appeal to all people. If it's a sale item, you know again that it will have general appeal, but now you concentrate on the price feature. Meanwhile, you will be determining whether it's the type of shoe worn by young college students or dignified bankers. Perhaps your market is the rugged outdoor type, or possibly the shoe is the type fashion-conscious people wear.

What Personal Benefits Does the Item Offer?

This is part of, yet different from, the actual description of the merchandise qualities. The shoe is described as "soft and pliable." These are qualities, but you must translate these words into copy that is meaningful to the people who wear the shoes.

Saying "soft and pliable" doesn't mean as much to Mr. Smith as saying that the shoe will allow his feet to bend properly, thus easing foot fatigue. Saying that the leather is durable is not the same as reminding the prospective customer that the shoes will take all sorts of rough treatment and bad weather and that they will last a long time.

Saying that the shoes are handsome is not as strong as saying that they're the latest thing out of *Gentlemen's Quarterly* or that they'll really make his wardrobe stylishly complete.

The idea of benefits is tied up with the idea of knowing who your customers are and what they expect to get out of the merchandise you want them to buy. Translate the buyer's facts into personal benefits that your reader wants—foot comfort, value for money, prestige, and admiration.

How Do I Draw Attention to the Advertising?

This is most vital, particularly in a newspaper, where your advertisement—whether it's a full page or two columns by six inches—is competing vigorously for the attention of the man or woman who paid money to read the news stories in the paper.

Remember, most of your readers did not pay their money to read advertisements, although a considerable number may have. Since many people are interested in news, not advertisements, your advertisement itself must be news if you want to interest such readers.

You must get those factual benefits up where they can be seen. You can stop readers with benefits and with advertising headlines—just as news headlines catch the readers' eyes and cause them to stop.

Layout and illustration will stop them, too—but merely stopping the readers is not enough. Well-chosen words in the body copy, captions, or subheads must instantly tell the story of your merchandise and get readers to recognize that this merchandise is what they've been looking for, that this merchandise fills a need they have, and that this merchandise is what they're going to buy.

Your headline, in this instance, has stopped the readers and has caused them to read in the body text why they should buy these particular shoes. However, that's not enough. As far as you are concerned, these shoes are for sale at one place and one place alone. You must convince the customers not only that they should buy these shoes but also that they should buy them at *your* store.

What Do I Do to Be Sure That Readers Know Who Is Advertising?

In identifying themselves, some stores merely put the sig or store name logotype at the top of the advertisement and let it go at that. You will usually make your advertisement more effective if you also mention the store in a subhead or lead-in line and refer to the store as often as you can in your body copy.

This matter of identification is vital in all local advertising in this day of "famous brands," competitors on every street in town may be carrying the same brands. Without proper identification of your store as the place to buy, you're often merely running an advertisement to help your competitor sell his merchandise.

Your main points then are:

1. Determine who your prospective customer is.
2. Present the appeals of your merchandise in the form of direct benefits.
3. Present those appeals to attract and hold the reader's attention.
4. Identify the store so that it will be linked immediately with the benefits to be obtained.

Generating the urge to buy the product advertised —to stimulate the reader into coming to your store to buy your goods—must be the ultimate end of your copy.

Learn How Local and National Advertising Differ

Although no one will deny that all copy—national, local, radio, direct mail, newspaper, and magazine—has certain basic similarities, it is also true that local copy has some characteristics that set it apart. A local copywriter, especially one who has been familiar with the national field, should be aware of these characteristics. You will find the characteristics in varying degrees in copy for small, medium, or large stores.

Imagine that you have had some experience with other types of copywriting but that you have decided to try local copywriting. At that moment, you are seated across the desk from the advertising manager of the department store for which you are going to work.

Knowing your background in other types of copy, the manager is discussing local advertising. You realize that he is very diplomatically indicating to you that although you were competent in other forms of copywriting, it doesn't follow that you can automatically write local copy. He is giving you the same briefing he would give anybody else entering copywriting.

It isn't your writing the advertising manager is concerned about; he's aware that you're a good technician. Rather, he's anxious for you to understand the basic con-

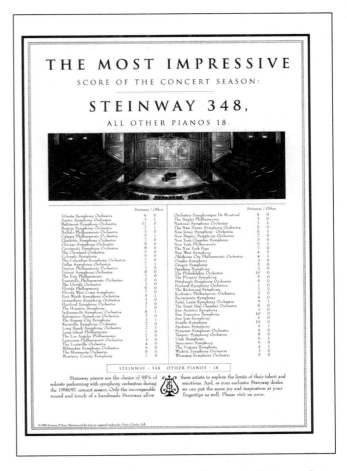

Figure 11–1a. Local campaign for a prestige product. Steinway pianos, the ultimate expression of the piano-maker's art, cannot depend solely upon their national advertising in upscale magazines such as the *New Yorker*. They must also support their dealers with promotional advertisements such as this that maintain the same high level of their national advertisements. Steinway-authorized dealers reflect the Steinway aura and advertising sponsored by them on the local level must also have that aura.

cepts of the local approach—some of the important differences between the writing you have been doing and the kind you'll do in local business.

A methodical person, the advertising manager ticks off points for you. He says, "We're glad to have you with us. Also, I'm glad that we have a few minutes now to talk about this local business. I'm well aware of your background. I know you can write, so we'll forget that.

"What I do want to make sure of is that you get something of the local picture before you type a word of copy. Some of the things I'm going to tell you may be obvious, but they bear repeating because their very obviousness often causes them to be overlooked, even by those of us who have grown up in local advertising.

"First of all, and I'm not sure that I wouldn't list this as the one and only point I'll make: *A store is part of the community.* A big part. You people who write the copy share the same community with your readers. You swelter in the

The Sooner You Trade Your Piano For A Steinway, The Sooner You'll Appreciate The Difference.

The day you trade your piano for a Steinway, the differences will be immediately obvious. When you touch the keys, you'll experience the same incomparable sound and touch that make today's Steinways the choice of 9 out of 10 performing artists.

And, as years go by, you'll discover another reason to appreciate your decision. Steinway pianos actually *increase* in value. History has shown that the new Steinway you buy today could be worth *3 to 4 times* its original purchase price 25 years from now.

Get A Generous Trade-In Allowance On Your Piano.

Invest a little time to visit us soon. We'll give you a copy of the "Steinway Investment" brochure. And right now, we can offer you a lot more than you might imagine when you trade your old piano toward a new Steinway.

AUTHORIZED STEINWAY DEALER

Figure 11–1b. Local campaign for a prestige product. In this strongly competitive advertisement the copy touches upon a point often stressed in automobile advertising—resale value, along with trade-in allowance.

STEINWAY

What kind of school would turn down free pianos and buy 61 new Steinways?

Carnegie-Mellon enjoys a reputation that attracts gifted music students from around the world. So, when a large piano manufacturer offered their pianos at no charge, Carnegie-Mellon said "No thank you." They invested in 61 new Steinways instead. Only the handmade artistry of Steinway pianos creates the famous touch and tone that allow players to reach the limits of their abilities. And that same experience can be shared by every player, from the youngest beginners to the world's leading concert artists. So we invite you to visit us soon and play our selection of Steinways. You'll hear for yourself why the country's leading music schools refuse to lower their admission standards.

AUTHORIZED STEINWAY DEALER

© Steinway & Sons, 1991. Steinway and the Lyre are registered trademarks.

Figure 11–1c. Local campaign for a prestige product. This advertisement uses an effective curiosity-type headline, accompanied by interesting copy and a strong action ending.

same heat and get nipped by the same frost. You enjoy the same football team, and the current crime wave is a mutual worry.

"The financial ups and downs of your city and country are of acute concern to all of you. The business is, except in the case of some very large stores, 100 percent local. You will feel this fact in all the copy you write. Let's see how this affects your thinking."

The advertising manager then makes the following points. He tells you that three facts must be recognized in local advertising:

Urge to "Buy Now" Is Stronger

There is immediacy in most local copy. Stores depend upon turnover of stock. The best kind of stock is the kind that is "here today and gone tomorrow." Local copy, for the most part, should be slightly breathless and urgent. You should generally push for the quick sale.

In local advertising, you expect a quick response to your copy and you must get it. Thus, your copy should always be prodding the customer, sometimes subtly and sometimes with all the subtlety of a meat axe. Get the readers to come to the store; get them to telephone; get them to put their money down for a quick purchase.

Phrases such as "Come in today," "Buy while they last," "See them today," or "Get yours now while quantities last" are important in local advertising. Sometimes you push people more delicately, but almost always there is some sort of urge to action—*immediate* action. This urge is much more pointed than in national advertising, which usually doesn't expect or need such immediacy of purchase on the part of the reader.

Readers Are More Price Conscious

People who read local advertising want to know the price of merchandise. They have become accustomed in national advertising to price-less copy, but in much of local copy, price is all important. Consciousness of cost creeps into all your copy. It weaves a web around the customers until they ask themselves, "Can I afford not to spend my money?" When you think of price in local copy, you don't think of price figures. Instead, you look upon your entire advertisement as building justification for the moment when the customers dig into their pockets and say, "I'll take that."

There are very few stores that aren't price-conscious down to the last word in the last line of copy. Big stores, little stores, exclusive stores, and bargain stores—all of them use prices as the wedge for sales.

When you finish a piece of local copy you should get in the habit of looking it over and asking yourself whether your words would make you buy if you were the ordinary reader—to whom dollars are keenly important. You have few chances in local copy to forget that all the words you write simply act as background music for that all-important tag line, which reads, "Only $00.00 while they last."

Developing of Store Personality Is a Must

Taken as a whole, you probably don't look much different from the people around you. You have the usual number of limbs, eyes, and ears. Compare yourself with the next-door neighbor. Based upon appearance, there isn't much to choose between you, yet you may have many more friends. Credit your personality.

Likewise, you can credit successful stores with personality. Development of the personality of your store is a constant copywriting job. The ability to write "personality" copy is something you acquire on the job. You don't learn it the first day. It comes after you have studied your store's advertising; after you have got the feel of the place; after you have talked to other store employees; and after you have been around a while.

Those saucy Bloomingdale's advertisements, those dignified productions of Lord & Taylor's, those sales-producers of Dayton Hudson—they reflect personality. *Personality in your advertising is what makes people come in to see your merchandise instead of going to your competitor's store to see the same merchandise.*

The basis of store personality is found in many things—friendliness, bargain prices, service, dependability, long establishment in the community, size of operation, or perhaps a combination of some, or all, of these. Remember that most stores can match goods with their competitors these days. If all you have to offer is merchandise, you may fall behind competitors who have found a personality and let it shine through their advertisements.

Personality marks you as different from your competitor. Downtown streets are lined with famous stores, each striving to be different from its neighbor. Saks is different from Bonwit Teller. Bergdorf Goodman differs from B. Altman's, Neiman-Marcus is different from Bloomingdale's, and no one would mistake a Lord & Taylor advertisement as one from Ohrbach's. Each store works hard to be different, especially from its closest rival. A celebrated rivalry exists between Marshall Field's and Carson Pirie Scott & Company in Chicago. Although both stores use effective selling copy, many little differences exist that enable the reader to recognize a Field's advertisement from one out of the Carson copy department.

Personality comes also from the creative technique—from the borders you use, the twist on words, the art treatment, the typography, and the repetition of certain copy points or phrases, such as the well-known "It's Smart To Be Thrifty" of Macy's.

Companies engaged in national advertising develop personality in their campaign themes, but unlike retail stores, they are not usually forced into doing so. The normal store has certain natural rivals who sell the same kind of goods at the same prices to the same type of customer.

Rivalry between these stores is very personal. It is a matter of frantic interest to them that the stores themselves and their advertising reflect an individual personality that makes the customer differentiate one store from the other.

When you work in a store, you may find that your toughest assignment is to capture your store's special personality in your copy. It's tough, because the personality is made up of so many little things. Be sensitive to those little things and be observant, and one day you'll find that you have pinned down the elusive spirit that spells your store to the customers. If you don't capture this spirit, you'd better move on.

Use Specific Words in Local Copy

Your language in a local advertisement walks a tightrope. Normally, local copy goes out to secure the sale, but this hard-smacking sales copy must be clothed in friendly, good-neighbor talk because of the personal relationship of the store to its customers.

The specific words are the ones that sell. If you're selling moderately priced items like hats, then "Prices cut in half" punches harder than "Huge savings." Perhaps the line "Save $5 to $10" may sell the best of the three because it gets even more specific.

A salesperson is specific in talking to a customer—you

can be, too. Naturally, there is some difference between printed sales messages and those spoken by the person behind the counter. The clerk can be more specific, more pointed, and more down to earth because he or she is not held down by the space limitations of a newspaper page.

Just the same, your copy will be more effective if you talk in the specific language of the salesperson rather than in the words of a copywriter reaching for the well turned phrase and the empty adjective.

Write Enough to Make the Sale

In local copy, as in other types of copy, you will be faced with the problem of how much copy to write. As in other copy, your solution is obvious: write enough copy to do the sales job.

For instance, suppose you are writing an advertisement that is describing several items. You have decided to use a main copy block and several subsidiary copy blocks that will serve as captions for the multiple items being advertised. You'll defeat your advertisement if, in an attempt to describe in detail all the sales points for all the items in the advertisement, you jam too much copy into the main copy block.

In short, here is a case where you would be writing too much copy. You would do a better sales job if you made one overall sales point that covered all the items in an interesting way, thus luring the reader into the specific selling copy in the captions. In such a case, the main copy block might be more effective if it had six lines of copy than if it had twenty.

Judging the right amount of copy is the mark of the skilled, experienced copywriter. As the young copywriter soon finds out, it is often easier to write a page advertisement than a one-column, three-inch advertisement. Most people have more trouble "compressing" than "expressing."

You may find it particularly hard, at times, to keep from writing too much copy. Suppose, for example, that you have a really sensational promotion—really "hot" merchandise. The natural tendency is to write your head off. You and your buyers get excited. You load yourself with so many interesting facts that you could write a campaign for the product.

Sadly, however, you realize that all these facts and all this enthusiasm are going to be earthbound by the fact that you have just one advertisement in which to do your sales job.

In such a case, don't lose your momentum. Go ahead and write your head off, and then start the sifting process. Get rid of the fluff. Get rid of the long-winded explanations that attempt to make clear this remarkable value. Tell the story straight, like a newspaper reporter.

Knowing when to stop in the writing of copy is especially difficult in the writing of institutional copy. Such copy, in which you explain store policy, pricing, service, and other facets of store operation, can easily become too

long. You can get so wrapped up in the store that you forget the customer. Institutional copy can be fascinating copy, but if you write too much, it can easily be the dullest copy for readers, because you may take many words to talk about something in which they are not basically interested.

Follow Up Your Copy to See What Happened

A good copywriter rarely can sit in an office and write about merchandise two floors below and not have personal contact with the merchandise. That's why you should school yourself to follow the entire process from start to finish—from the buying of the merchandise, if possible, to the investigation of the effectiveness of the advertisement you wrote.

If you can possibly find the time, you should get to the selling department after your advertisement has run. Find out the reaction. If a crowd of shoppers flocks in at the opening bell and rushes to the department using your advertisement, you have a good idea that your copy was effective.

Later, again granting that you have time, check with the buyer and the salespeople to find out what they've sold. At the end of the day, ask again, and keep a record of the dollar volume and the advertised items sold off your advertisement. Some stores will actually require that you attach a form listing these results to a tearsheet of the advertisement. You then turn this in to the advertising manager.

Whether or not your boss requires it, make it your business to keep in touch with your advertisements all the way through. If an advertisement doesn't click, find out why. If you ask the buyers, they'll more than likely tell you why it was a poor advertisement.

Buyers might tell you, for instance, that the item is one that is usually bought by the husband and wife together. They might show you rather pointedly that your advertisement is slanted too much to one side—that you failed to recognize that both parties share in buying responsibility.

Perhaps you'll say the merchandise wasn't salable. Puzzle out the trouble. You might even rewrite the copy. Some copywriters have actually rewritten advertisements, asked that they be run again with the new slant, and hit the jackpot on the second running.

You May Use Outside Help

Copywriters in a local organization do not have to depend on their brains alone for ideas. In small stores, especially, where the copywriter may be a person with a thousand jobs, outside material may be a lifesaver.

Agencies, manufacturers' advertising departments, newspapers, and magazines—everybody wants your store to work cooperatively in promoting their products.

Magazines will give you tie-in promotional material complete with copy and illustrations for use in your newspaper advertisement. Agencies and company advertising departments will send you brochures full of information, glossy prints, TV scripts and tapes, radio spots, and copy ideas—and they're all yours to use or discard.

How much you will use depends upon several factors. The most important factor is the soundness of the ideas offered to you. Sometimes these outside sources forget that they are operating in local advertising. They seem to overlook the fact that on the local level, when you talk with your chin right up against your customer's, you must be direct and careful in your use of ideas, often even more careful than in national advertising.

For instance, a national campaign on girdles and "designer" shoes may be built around the distinctiveness of a certain brand—the exclusiveness of its makers. Played up in a good color art treatment, such a story may be interesting and effective and may do much to keep the firm's name connected with prestige and dignity.

On the local level, your customer is primarily interested in how those shoes will go with other outfits, and what that girdle will do for her particular figure. Out go the fancy words, and tricky, cute expressions, and vague references. Your language is direct. Chances are that in all the material provided you'll find something on which to hang your "direct" advertisement—something about the variety of sizes, prices, shapes, and so on and that will be your springboard.

Direct Response Copy Can Also Be Part of Your Job

You'll find that most local organizations think largely in terms of newspaper advertising. Buyers will talk about a "spread" in their favorite evening paper. Most of the store's budget will be spent in newspapers because the store can see what it's doing and can depend on reaching a healthy circulation guaranteed by the newspaper. Because it's a proved medium, you'll find that most of your time will be spent writing newspaper advertisements.

In larger stores, you'll find much use of direct response advertising. Some stores have had great success with this. Many have built big orders with simple postcards or bill inserts sent out to inform charge customers that a certain item will be offered. With no other advertising of certain items, some stores have found selling departments jammed with customers who responded to mailing pieces. Stores have also enjoyed great success in response to mailers that invited the customers to phone or mail in coupon orders.

You should understand the basic differences between direct response and newspaper copy. Though the selling purpose may be the same, your direct response piece may necessarily lack the forcefulness of illustration that your newspaper advertisement could command.

Size alone can make a big difference. A full newspaper page, for instance, has the wallop of a pile driver—a wallop that direct response can hardly match. Since newspapers have this impact advantage, your words, whether in letters, postcards, or inserts, must be even more carefully chosen.

Remember that although the newspaper itself had some attraction for the customer (in its news value), your insert comes entirely uninvited into the home. In fact, the letterhead or store name itself may be enough to cause it to be thrown away without being read.

Be just as specific as you can. Avoid being cute. Make your letter friendly, newsy, and interesting. Get out what you have to say as quickly as you can, catching the reader's eye and imagination with a fact that is of personal interest to him. Avoid printing letters upside down or employing other such tricks. Devices of that sort only irritate and confuse.

Much material can be obtained from the manufacturer of the goods you advertise—a fact of great value to the small store. Almost all companies produce mailing inserts for their local outlets to use.

Some are given to the store free, while others can be bought on a cooperative basis. Be sure the store name is imprinted on any mailing piece you buy from a national source, and avoid mailing pieces that lack a local, personal flavor. After all, your purpose is not so much to sell the national brand but to sell the national brand in your store.

Direct response for stores may require you to write much in addition to letters. You may do copy for postcards, illustrated invitations to fashion shows, announcements, and college booklets. You'll usually find an interesting variety of challenges.

Local Radio Commercials

Writing for local radio is so similar to writing for national radio that there is no need to detail how to write radio copy for a store. The suggestions found in the radio chapter will apply to local radio writing.

One caution might be observed, however. You might remember that, as in the case of local newspaper advertising, you will do well to capture the local flavor in your radio commercials. You can be a shade friendlier and more intimate. The very fact that you are mentioning a local store in your copy immediately establishes a rapport difficult for the national advertiser to match.

Notice how the following radio commercial stresses the local advantages such as the strong emphasis on price, the reputation of the advertiser, and the push on "act now." Also, the writing style is more chatty and breezy than the usual national commercial.

Wow! Here's an offer from Johnson's Jewelers that'll knock your hat off or, better yet, get you to visit Johnson's today to take advantage of a tremendous bargain. You see, Johnson's is starting its *remount* days today. This means that you can bring in your old diamond jewelry and then, while you watch, one of Johnson's experts will reset the stones in 14K yellow, or

CLIENT: CNY Regional Transportation Authority
JOB: :60 Radio
TITLE: "All Things Relative"
WOMAN: My grandmother is old school. She loves to call and tell me what's wrong with my life. Last time it was, **"Laura, your job always has you in a rush. Rush here. Rush there. You've got to slow down!"** Gram' I said, I don't rush anymore. I started taking Centro to work—I just get on the bus, relax, get there on time—and I even save money. She says, **"Save money—from one who lives from paycheck to paycheck."** I said, "Gram', Centro is just 75 cents each way. No parking. No gas. I save alot by taking the bus. **"The bus!"** she said. **"And who do you ride with, strangers?** Gram' I said, trying not to lose it, Centro riders are mostly women. Although yesterday, a nice man said hello to me. Why did I tell her that? She said, **"meet a man without an introduction? That's not ladylike. (Pause) Are you going to see him?"** Is he nice?" I said, <u>nice</u> talkin' to you, too, Gram, love ya' bye.
ANNCR: Take the work out of getting to work. Ride Centro. It's getting around.

Figure 11–2a. Local radio commercial campaign. Using a personal monologue to deliver a 60-second commercial can be tricky. Too often the technique backfires because the content is unnatural and forced. Also, the person delivering the commercial sounds more like a salesperson than a real-life person. In this example, the writer has avoided the problems by creating situations to which listeners can relate. And for a close, the announcer comes in with an action ending that would have been unrealistic if the monologist had given it. In short, this is a plausible, listenable commercial.

white gold, settings. The price for this includes sizing, setting, polishing, and ultrasonic cleaning. All this for prices starting as low as forty dollars. Now, you know Johnson's reputation in this area for quick, reliable work and for unexcelled low prices. Get in on this latest chance to save money. And hear this—Johnson's will *give* you a genuine diamond worth twenty-five dollars just for keeping your appointment. Phone for your appointment now at 677-8888. That's 677-8888. Remember, this is a once-a-year opportunity from Johnson's. Grab it!

Another local radio commercial is given below. Note how the writer begins and ends with the stress on locality. Once more, price—the big local advantage—is emphasized throughout, as is a strong push for action.

People in Greene County have become used to great savings from the Vision Center in the Greene County Mall, but wait'll you hear this. Vision Center will pay you *ten dollars* to wear Bausch and Lomb Softlens contact lenses. That's right. You'll get a ten dollar rebate for wearing Bausch and Lomb Softlens contact lenses for thirty days. Here's how it works. Come in for our complete eye care package. This includes a thorough eye examination, fitting fees, the B & L lenses, followup care,

CLIENT: CNY Regional Transportation Authority
JOB: :60 Radio
TITLE: "Everyday Adventure"
WOMAN: Everyday is an adventure for me. Sometimes getting to work is a job in itself. <u>Yesterday</u> I get up, shower, dress, feed the cat, feed myself, get ready to leave, and lose my keys—so, I go through every room in the house only to find them right in my pocket. Then I slam my coat in the car door. Then I start the car and see that I have to stop for gas. Then I see it snowed 6 inches so I have to shovel. Thirty minutes later I'm sliding down the expressway, get stuck behind an accident, so I tune into the traffic report, why I don't know, 'cause the man in the helicopter tells me to avoid the expressway and I already know that. Twenty minutes later, I'm looking for a parking lot with any space left—then I find a space in the only parking lot left. Now I'm 5 blocks from work and 55 minutes late. So I make a mad dash, slip on some ice and down I go—<u>that</u> was yesterday. So <u>today</u>, I started taking the bus. Now for just 75 cents, Centro gets me to work and back with no hassles. I save money, and my sanity. So, everything I just told you about my everyday adventures?—never mind.
ANNCR: Take the work out of getting to work. Ride Centro. It's getting around.

Figure 11–2b. Local radio commercial campaign.

and a complete care kit. Then, if you wear your Softlens contact lenses for thirty days, we'll give you a ten dollar rebate off the $99.95 price. You get the whole eye care package for the astoundingly low price of $89.95. Come see us today—right opposite the fountain in the beautiful Greene County Mall. That's the Vision Center where we care for your eyes *and* your budget.

If a department store is a heavy user of local radio, it may air numerous spots. Short commercials will be mixed in with regular-length commercials, especially when some special event is being featured. The following short commercial is typical:

Dress up that porch or patio, and do it at bargain prices during Steuart's summer clearance sale. Prices that were $120 to $450 are now $59 to $219. Select from wrought iron or aluminum in chairs, loveseats, cocktail and end tables. Limited quantities means you'd better come to Steuart's *today* to take your pick of summer furniture bargains. Nine to five every day in Steuart's second floor furniture department.

Even though short, such a commercial should include item descriptions, prices, store hours, and the department in which the item is sold.

Local commercials are usually quite enthusiastic and fairly hard-driving. How much pressure is exerted depends upon the nature of the account and the kind of radio station airing the material. A used-car dealer, a price-cutting supermarket, or a discount house are usually pushy

CLIENT: CNY Regional Transportation Authority
JOB: :60 Radio
TITLE: "Sooo Convenient"
WOMAN: My girlfriend Marsha just <u>loves</u> winter—her relatives have been in Syracuse since the Ice Age. Anyway, she also thinks that driving to work is <u>sooo convenient!</u> Oh, really?—169 inches of snow last year, 192 inches the year before, and this year even more—driving to work is <u>sooo convenient!</u> There's nothing like the old slush in your face through the crack in your window at 55 miles an hour for a morning wake-up. Or, how about fishtailing on the expressway while watching your entire life pass before you in a split second. Then suddenly, you're facing the car that was behind you—now that's my idea of a <u>convenient</u> ten minute drive to work. And if I do arrive, I look forward to the safety of an isolated rooftop parking lot. Now to me, <u>convenience</u> is riding Centro to work. Centro stops close to just about every office building downtown. I get to work on time, and back home for just 75 cents each way—and that's <u>sooo convenient!</u>
ANNCR: Take the work out of getting to work. Ride Centro. It's getting around.

Figure 11–2c. Local radio commercial campaign.

ANNCR: It's Monday and you're a business person—got lots of things to think about. Will the new sales clerk show up?...Did the bookkeeper remember to mail the checks to get your discount period?...Will the new order of merchandise be delivered to you this time instead of Aashhtuhhbuuhla? Yeah, there are lots of things you have to worry about because you're a business person. Oh yeah, since it's Monday, remember you gotta get your newspaper ad ready for the local paper. Yep, you know how it works. The local paper rep shows up and says..."got cher ad ready?"..."Whatta ya wanna run this week?"...Oh, isn't that great? You pay them—you lay out the ad! Well, my harried businessperson, at **(station)** we write the ad and produce the ad. Heck, we'll even buy time on the other stations and make dubs for you. And listen to this...we'll deliver every "copy" of the ad you buy on **(station)**. Uh huh! You can look out back of our building anytime and never see your paid ads just layin' around after being brought back. On the other hand, when you look out back of the local paper's location, you can see lots of your paid ads sort of layin' around. Did you get a refund for every undelivered ad?...Just thought we'd ask. If you're tired of doing all your own ad work and having only about half of it get delivered, then try **(station)**. Call 555-5555.

Figure 11–3. Competitive local commercial. In every community where radio stations and newspapers compete for the local advertiser's dollars, each medium fights for those dollars. This straight commercial reflects the competition. *Courtesy of the Radio Advertising Bureau.*

in their approach. The talk may be fast and the selling quite forceful, especially if the commercials are aired on a rock station that features super-glib announcers who maintain a mad pace all day long.

On the other hand, hotels, banks, and insurance agents are normally low key. You'll slow the pace and avoid any sense of pressure. This doesn't mean that you won't incorporate the urge to act or that you won't write enthusiastic copy. How you judge the dividing line between high pressure and permissible enthusiasm is something you'll learn with experience. Sometimes, the advertisers you're writing for will tell you when you've stepped over the line.

Still another factor that influences how you write local radio commercials is the announcer. Sometimes, of course, you don't know who will be announcing what you write. If you do, you should write for the style of that announcer. Some are better at hard-sell commercials with fast-paced deliveries. Others are sincere, slower-talking persons. Some will deliver humor deftly; others have a heavy touch unsuited for humor.

In a local market, you soon become acquainted with all local announcers. Study them. Capitalize on their strengths; avoid their weaknesses. If you supervise taping sessions where announcers are doing commercials you've written, talk to the announcers. Find out what they like and don't like. Get their suggestions. You'll discover that they have strong opinions about writers of the commer-

cials they deliver. As professionals, announcers have much to tell you that will make you a better radio writer.

What's the likelihood of your writing local radio commercials? If you're working for an advertising agency handling local accounts such as banks or department stores, you may do a lot, because banks and department stores hire agencies for such writing. Conversely, if you're working for the bank or the department store, you'll usually have no chance to write radio commercials.

If you're working for smaller organizations such as hardware stores, shoe stores, or independent drugstores, you'll find that such writing is often handled by the radio stations that have copywriters for the small budget advertisers. Copywriters in these stations crank out volumes of commercials, often of unimpressive quality.

For Local TV Commercials, Keep an Eye on the Budget

Naturally, every local enterprise is fascinated by the thought of using television advertising, but the majority of such enterprises simply cannot afford to be on the air frequently enough, or long enough, to make an impression on the market.

Unless they're in a big-city market, those who can afford the medium rarely use the expensive commercials that are customary with national advertisers. No fancy animation. No expensive live-action commercials using big name stars and exotic location shots.

Local copywriters create television within the framework of a limited production budget. Occasionally, they may call for live studio shots or open-end syndicated materials. Also, co-op commercials may be supplied by the advertisers. These supply information about advertisers' products but allow cut-ins for local identification.

You'll depend upon your local television stations' production facilities for talent and mechanical equipment. You may draw upon their stock shot collection and their musical library, and if you happen to shoot any live-action studio material, you may use station announcers.

Great improvements continue in videotape, however, with the present use of smaller, more versatile and flexible cameras, and stations of almost any size are prepared to offer videotape facilities. Such facilities bring down costs, thus making possible more use of local television advertising. Furthermore, optical effects, now possible with videotape, are available to local advertisers.

On the other local level, in bank advertising especially, the copywriter may make heavy use of bank personnel as presenters. Presidents, tellers, vice-presidents, and other personnel may appear before the camera. Customers or well-known local personalities may also be used to speak in behalf of the bank. If these presenters are not amateurish, they can be effective. Their use ensures a local flavor that is desirable. Videotape, with its instant playback, gives the production people a chance to go over the announcement enough times with the amateur talent to ultimately come out with a commercial that looks reasonably professional.

In the case of big-budget banks and department stores, the advertising money allowed for television may be sufficient to permit the use of a first class production house. Accordingly, if you're writing for such an advertiser, you can call for the sort of production used by national advertisers. Normally, however, you'll be using creative procedures that hold down costs, which are always very much on the mind of local television users.

Here are some suggestions for the writer of modestly priced local commercials:

- A commercial should star the product or service, use the camera skillfully, and avoid the use of high-priced talent.
- Use a good voice—male or female—for voiceover presentation, even though the general rule is that on-camera voice is more effective.
- Develop a distinctive logo.
- If several commercials are to be used, produce them all at one session to cut production costs.
- Use music in public domain.
- Shoot in 16mm instead of 35mm.

- Hold down editing or use no editing in videotaped commercials.
- Use actual advertisements for artwork, as is often done on local shows in which commercials are presented live by station announcers.
- Where appropriate, use suitable stock shots such as crowd scenes, historical moments, personalities, nature scenes.

What you have read in the material under the heading of local television advertising has been slanted toward the cost-cutting aspect of television commercial writing. Later in this book, there are two chapters on television advertising that cover most of what you need to know. While those chapters zero in on national advertising, most of the principles also apply to local television commercial writing.

The big difference is that you are severely restricted by how much your commercials will cost when you are writing for local advertisers. While budget and cost is a factor on the national level, the national advertiser is thinking in tens of thousands of dollars while you (or the local advertiser) may be thinking in hundreds of dollars. This has quite an influence on your approach.

You Do a Lot of Talking Before You Write That Local Advertisement

Now to get down to the actual procedure of writing an advertisement. Suppose the buyer of women's shoes has an advertisement on her schedule and that she's supposed to have her "buyer's copy" up to you by a certain date (you usually will work anywhere from six to fourteen days ahead of publication date).

Ultimately, after the buyer has sent her material through her own merchandise manager and then through the advertising manager, you and the other staff members will discuss this advertisement, along with others, when you confer about advertisements about to be put into work.

Some stores may have such discussions for each advertisement. Others may simply determine a general treatment for a group or series of advertisements and leave it up to the copywriter to develop copy for individual advertisements according to this overall plan. General copy meetings in such stores may be called only for special promotions.

During your meeting, suggestions for treatment may come from any advertising person at the copy meeting, including any of the copywriters, the advertising manager, the art director, and the production manager. Perhaps it may be decided that the advertisement is to be hard selling and that it will emphasize the variety of styles.

You and the art director will discuss the tie-in of illustration and copy. You'll agree that the illustration should feature many shoe styles. You are to write captions for the numerous shoes pictured. After much discussion, you leave the meeting with a rough idea of the copy and art approach. You're ready to go to work.

An Important Stop: The Art Department

At this point, one of your most important jobs is telling the art department what sort of layout treatment the advertisement requires. You discuss the merchandise being advertised, suggest the type and the number of sketches, and tell what your headlines and subheads will be. You may even prepare a rough layout or thumbnail sketch of the advertisement. This last item will be even more vital in a smaller store, where the copywriter may be called on to turn in a complete "visual" of the advertisement.

The instructions to the art department are not the final word, of course, since the layout must be approved by the advertising manager before any finished art can be started.

The ideal way to tell the art department exactly what you have in mind is to write every word that you want to have in the advertisement. The layout person then knows how much of a copy block you need, how many and how long the display lines must be, how many items you will have in a listing of merchandise, how many figures must be illustrated, and so on.

By providing the actual copy, you are assured that the layout you get from the art department will be much closer to your wishes than if you had merely turned in some vague directions about "large copy block required," "big display head," or "generous copy space."

If you were the artist, what would "generous" mean to you? Just as you need complete information from your buyer in order to describe the merchandise, the layout people need complete information in order to turn out the right layout for the merchandise.

Remember, however, that many stores do their artwork before the copywriter goes to work. In such stores, you would write copy that would fit the character of the artwork and would fit into the space that wasn't taken up by the illustration. As a copywriter, it is much more satisfactory to work in the situation where you, rather than the illustrator, control the makeup of the advertisement.

Unfortunately, there are probably more stores in which the art treatment comes first. You might as well realize this right now and be prepared to adjust yourself to playing second fiddle to the art department if you happen to land in a store that gives the art people principal authority in the construction of advertisement.

At this point, the layout is made and approved; the art now needs to be prepared. In this case, the shoes were photographed in the photographer's studio after the buyer had delivered them to the studio. If you can, it's desirable for you to be around when your merchandise is being photographed or sketched. You might be able to make useful suggestions.

A Lot of Your Copy May End Up in the Wastebasket

While all this art activity is going on, you're supposed to be writing the copy. In large departments, you'll be given a

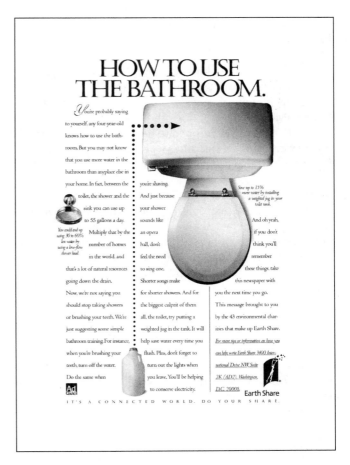

Figure 11–4. Public service advertisement. *Courtesy of the Advertising Council.*

copy of the layout as it was actually approved, and the headlines, copy space, and listings will be represented properly.

Perhaps you may have some simple adjustments to make. You may need to cut your copy slightly or change your headline somewhat. The important thing is that this layout is no stranger to you. Most of your planned thinking has been done.

Sometimes, of course, your original ideas may be thrown out completely and you will have to start from scratch when you receive the final layout. Now assume that this is the case with the advertisement in question. You had what you thought was a fine idea, but someone along the line—the advertising manager or sectional manager, or perhaps both—caused your fine idea to be dropped into the wastebasket. Now you see the fresh layout in front of you. You're really starting all over again because a new slant has been thrown at you.

Dig into That Buyer's Copy and Talk to the Buyer Again

Pick up the buyer's copy—the sheets containing all of the information that the shoe buyer had to offer. First ask yourself: What am I selling? No, the answer isn't shoes alone, because everybody sells shoes. What's the idea behind this advertisement? What's the story behind all the illegible writing on the buyer's sheet?

Dig down into the buyer's copy. Digest what was given to you. Call her up or go see her. Ask to see the shoes. Ask to see any manufacturer's data on the product or any promotional material. Why does she want to advertise these shoes? How does she happen to have this merchandise? Is it a new brand, a special price, a new idea? *Get all the facts before you sit down to write.*

A Magic Moment: You Write Final Copy

Although you may have all the information you need, you might, as a newly minted copywriter, want to make a checklist that will put down those facts in order of importance and in the order you will present them. Then, when you write, you can refer to the list to keep yourself on track. Such a checklist is useful for broadcast copy, direct mail, or newspaper copy.

Obviously, if you're under great pressure, you'll be in too much of a hurry to operate with a checklist. You'll simply start writing. But if you have time, try the checklist.

When you take all the preliminary steps discussed—the talk with the art department, the talk with the buyer, the rechecking of product facts, and the making of a checklist—you'll find that the copy will usually not cause you much trouble because you've prepared so well. Good copy is harder to achieve when you dash into it.

There's been no discussion of headlines, because most stores seem to be content to write label headlines that simply identify the merchandise. Creative headline writing is not common for most retail advertisements, but if you can persuade your superiors to let you try creative, selling headlines, both you and the store will profit.

Another Challenge: The Multi-Item Advertisement

Up to this point, the stress has been on how to write single-item advertisements, but a department store with many items to sell frequently features a number of items in one advertisement.

For clarity, the multi-item advertisement is described here as an advertisement containing three or four strongly related products. The omnibus advertisement, taking up a larger space of possibly a page or two pages, will include numerous items, far more than the multi-item advertisement.

When you write a *multi-item,* follow certain procedures for top results: (1) Write a strong selling headline that expresses the commonality of the products; you might also use a strong main subhead immediately under the main headline; (2) Write an opening copy block that sells the items as a whole and sets the tone for the entire advertisement; (3) Write strong selling subheads for each of the copy blocks that sell the individual items. These subheads will carry the reader through the advertisement; and (4) Write the copy blocks and, in them, sell the big points for each item. Each copy block will contain information about the department selling the item.

Layout is important in the multi-item advertisement. Work with the artist in the judicious placing of elements—prices, product labels, and others.

As for the *omnibus* advertisement, supply a headline that ties the advertisement together. Unlike the multi-item headline, this one won't have a close relationship to every product because you'll usually have a hodge-podge of product types in an omnibus advertisement.

If time and space permit, write selling subheads for each product section. Try to avoid the impersonal, telegraphic writing so often characteristic of item copy in omnibus advertisements.

In some ads, some of the items can be related to other products, as in the case of ski equipment, golf equipment, men's apparel, and others. Make the connection in such cases.

Perhaps your omnibus advertisement carries the headline WINTER CLEARANCE SALE. In such a case, all the products will be cold-weather-related, even if they're not closely related to each other. Thus, you'll have a common theme of cold weather and low prices, even with greatly different products.

Good Copy Will Help You Stand Out in a Crowd

You're a vital part of the selling process in a big department store, but you may sometimes feel insignificant as you contemplate that big superstructure over you—all those buyers, managers, and others who see, supervise, and criticize your work.

A department store is a subtle, vital organism that is composed of many parts. You find immediately that you must learn those parts and how to fit your skills and efforts into this complicated structure of which you've become one of the smaller parts.

Always, however, you have the ultimate comfort. Your words are going to be visible on those newspaper pages or in the direct response pieces. If they're clever, bouncy, persuasive, elegant, *selling* words, they'll be noticed. And if you turn them out day after day, you can be assured that, no matter how massive the retail structure, you're going to get recognition and an escape from anonymity.

You Have Three Bosses

You have three bosses in retail advertising—your advertising boss, the buyer who buys the merchandise, and the salesperson who stands behind the counter selling the goods about which you're writing. If the salesperson works on a bonus or percentage basis, his or her very living may depend upon the skill with which you do your job—that increases your importance, too. Local copy can't be written without a close relationship between the copywriter and the store personnel inside and outside the advertising department.

In the following material, you will find a description of

some of the activity going on about you in a typical department store. You will also find details about the work of those people who are so important to you, such as the advertising manager, the buyer, and the comparison shopper.

Who Are the Key People in the Department Store?

To get an idea of the extent of your copywriting duties, examine the organization of a large department store. Keep in mind, too, that despite differences stemming from the type and size of the store, the advertising budget, and the size of the advertising department, the situation is basically the same in all local establishments.

Advertising managers. Advertising managers oversee the entire advertising operation and plan future campaigns on a top-management level. In direct contact with the store manager, they translate management's wishes into actual printed or spoken advertising. Many times they are merely "yes" management. Other times, they may come up with fine ideas to sell to management.

Advertising managers usually make up the entire month's advertising schedule in advance. They might even plan two or three months ahead. All advertising goes through their hands for final approval, whether it's a newspaper advertisement, a television or radio commercial, or a mailing insert. They control all personnel in the advertising department, including you.

Section chiefs. Large department stores often employ section chiefs or divisional advertising managers to head the various copy sections, such as homewares, men's furnishings, downstairs store, fashions, and others. These people are responsible for the actual planning within their divisions. They work with buyers and their merchandise managers, check advertisements as they are written by copywriters, and consult with the art department on layout suggestions and art treatment. In effect, they are the advertising managers for a group of "clients" within a division of the store.

Merchandise managers. Each major division within the store has a merchandise manager who may control as many as thirty buyers. Such managers are responsible for buyers' buying plans and their spending and sales figures. In an advertising sense, the merchandise manager's job is to allocate money from a monthly budget to the various departments in his or her division. Merchandise managers also turn in a tentative monthly schedule to the advertising manager that is used to make up the entire store's schedule for the coming period.

Merchandise managers pass on individual advertisements for their departments and see that buyers provide full information to the copywriters preparing the advertising.

Buyers. These men and women go into the market to buy the goods about which you write. Some of them gladly cooperate with the writers who must turn out selling copy about their goods. They provide "buyer's copy" to tell the writer about merchandise.

The buyers can give the copywriter every chance to see, feel, try, and test the goods. They are, in a sense, the copywriter's clients. You will respect their wishes as long as they result in good advertising.

Regrettably, a good many buyers give copywriters the poorest kind of cooperation. They must be begged for information. Not seeming to care about the copywriter's side, they give information only about the obvious things such as colors, sizes, and prices.

Your job will require you to dig for more than these bare facts. You may desperately hound the buyers for more help than the scanty facts they give you in their buyer's copy. Though some buyers will be a real help to you, rely on your own effort and ingenuity to get facts for writing your copy.

Buyers have their own problems to worry about, and copywriting is not among them. If they give you complete information—fine. If they don't, get it yourself.

Comparison shoppers. Almost all large stores maintain a comparison shopping department to check the truthfulness of statements made in the store's advertisements, to determine whether quantities of merchandise on hand warrant advertising, to act as liaison between the buyer and the advertising department, and to shop in other stores in the community for comparable values and comparative store activity. "Comparison" usually has the final word on all advertising, especially on descriptions that may go counter to policies of the store and trade principles as laid down by the Better Business Bureau.

In addition to being in contact with the buyers, section managers, and the others mentioned during the advertising day, you will also work closely with the *art director*, who is responsible for layouts, finished art, and photographs; the *production manager*, who marks the type, handles the proofs, enters corrections, and sends all material to the newspapers; and the *clerk*, who controls the flow of merchandise that is sent up for sketching or photography.

As you can see, a great many people contribute to the preparation of every advertisement, from the warehouseperson who hauled furniture for a camera shot to the clerk who checked copy for accuracy. The combined activity is slanted toward one end—to create advertisements that sell!

You May Wear Many Hats As a Small-Store Copywriter

Upon graduation from college, an advertising major began work with a small store as a copywriter. She reported that, sure enough, she *did* write copy, but she also did all of the layouts, planned the monthly advertising schedules, gave the space orders to the newspapers, and worked with the store manager in determining the advertising budget. This "copywriter" also filled in as a salesclerk at busy times, put up window displays, and, when time was heavy on her hands, talked on fashion trends to local women's groups.

Although all small or medium-sized stores might not expect so much from their young copywriters, you may well find, if you work for a small establishment, that writing copy is just one of your activities.

Be prepared to be a copywriter, advertising manager, production chief, media buyer, and display manager rolled up into one very busy person. In such a position, you will often not write much original copy. A good portion of your writing will consist of revising, shortening, or lengthening the "canned" copy that accompanies the material from the manufacturer of the goods you are advertising.

Many small stores depend upon art services and proofbooks to provide them with layout and copy ideas. Also, small stores very often let their newspapers do copy-layout work for them. If you land in a store like that, you won't find much challenge to your copywriting ability. In other stores, however, you may write much copy, since you will wish to key your advertisements to the local situation. You may use outside material, but just as an occasional help.

One thing you can almost be certain of: In a small store, you will usually find that there is not enough copywriting to fill all your working hours. This means that you will fill out the rest of the time doing practically anything that comes along.

Do You Sell the Store or Sell Items?

For most department stores, the answer will be quick—items, of course. When you depend upon day to day revenue from the sale of goods, you stress item selling. Aggressive stores that stress low prices and almost constant sales scorn institutional advertising as a luxury they can't afford.

There are stores at a higher level that rarely, if ever, run storewide sales and sell quality and prestige rather than low prices. You will occasionally find such an establishment that concentrates on the institutional approach. It has developed such an aura of exclusiveness that the store never offers a grab bag of items; instead, it features only a few items of the kind that reflect the exclusivity of the establishment.

Some well-known stores include institutional copy in every advertisement they run, but this copy is included only in part of the advertisement, with the bulk of the advertisement being used to sell items. In the institutional section, shoppers are reminded constantly of the unique attributes of the store. Thus, personality is developed. Such a store might occasionally run an entire advertisement of the institutional type to remind readers of the unique assortment of products offered by the store and of its unrelenting stress on quality, service, and fair prices.

Except for the promotional-type stores described in the first paragraph, the majority of bigger stores that aim to develop a personality should combine item selling *and* institutional. The problem is: How much of each?

One big department store answered the question in a novel way. Once a week, a copywriter from the advertising agency handling the radio portion of their advertising was given freedom to roam the store in search of interesting—sometimes bizarre—products and services. This person might, for example, write about a kitchen-of-tomorrow exhibit, a hemstitching service buried back on the seventh floor, the store's elegant tearoom, or an art service.

These unique radio commercials were developed not to generate sales but to present a fascinating picture of the diversity of the store's offerings. In short, this was purely institutional copy that contributed to the personality image of the store. These commercials ran one day each week. On other days, radio commercials were devoted to the low-key item selling favored by this upper-level establishment.

CHAPTER 12

You Toss Out the "Rules" When You Write Fashion Copy

After a couple of years as an agency copywriter, Kathy Simmons found that nuts-and-bolts copy wasn't for her. When she applied for a job as a writer for a smart boutique, she told the manager: "I like the excitement of the fashion field. The way the products and even the language change so fast that you have a constant challenge to simply keep up with the trends."

After a few weeks on the job, she found even more challenge than she had expected in learning a new way to write. The relatively prosaic words she used in her agency ads just didn't fit the high-powered, emotion-charged world of high fashion. She loved the change.

Kathy found a new mindset in her new job. Where previously she had written for an astounding variety of products, many of them intended for the male market, almost all of her writing now was for the female market, mostly for women's clothes and a few other items such as perfumes, cosmetics, and accessories.

Now she was being paid to think as a *woman*, while in her agency work it was often the opposite. A man can write fashion advertising, and indeed, some famous fashion designers are men, but a woman writing about fashion has the advantage of feeling and instinct that few men can achieve.

There's Excitement in the Terms and Names of the World of Fashion

Just as sports enthusiasts can rattle off the names of basketball, baseball, football, and tennis stars, so will you, soon after entering the fashion field, learn quickly to identify the Who's Who of fashion.

Fashion designers such as Armani, Joseph Abboud, Ralph Lauren, Calvin Klein, Liz Claiborne, Gianni Versace, Adrienne Vittadini, Donna Karan, Escada, Isaac Mizrahi, and Christian Dior will become your "idols." You'll quickly feel at home in the fashion centers of B. Altman, Nordstrom, Bergdorf Goodman, Bonwit Teller, Neiman Marcus, Givenchy, Saks, the Gap, and others. You'll become acquainted with the fashions displayed in many catalogs, including J. Crew, Neiman Marcus, and many, many others. And, of course, the magazines of fashion—*Vogue, Town & Country, Glamour, Harper's Bazaar,* and *Mademoiselle*—will be a mainstay in your reading.

Suddenly, you will be using a different language. You and poets will have much in common in the way you twist the language into interesting and sometimes zany shapes. Like the poets, you'll employ imagery and mood. "Poetic license" lets poets explore unconventional writing bypaths; likewise, we indulge the fashion copywriter. Forget the rules that once guided you in selling the usual goods and services. You're now in a new creative world where often the bizarre works better than the humdrum.

Fanciful Language, Yes, But Don't Leave Out the Facts

Warning. Perhaps what has been said thus far might cause you to think that fashion writing is all mood and odd language. Not so. Although fashion often calls for a flip or mod language, you'll find that facts are important, too. Readers don't *always* base buying decisions on fluff.

Furthermore, you'll discover that in the bulk of fashion advertisements, words are less important than illustration, the latter almost always photographs. Any casual reading of publications such as *Vogue* will demonstrate that readers are obviously more interested in *seeing* clothes than in reading about them. Copy is found most frequently in cosmetic and shampoo advertisements.

Still, despite the subordination of copy to illustration in fashion advertising, there is a place for copy that sparkles and titillates the reader and helps create the fashion mood.

What other copywriting world inspires such prose as the following from one of the fashion magazines?

> Night hybrid in bloom,
> botanically inspired.
> A bejeweled bud
> gathers double ripples
> of this yellow chiffon
> jersey struck with
> shimmering dew drops.

You can't learn such copywriting in school or by writers for more prosaic products. It is developed from a long exposure to and deep love of fashion and from a knowledge of words that trigger response.

Most fashion copy, however, is not so totally fanciful as the example just given. Most is written partly in the language expected of fashion advertising and partly in practical, reasons-to-buy language, as shown in the following:

> You're going to love 'The Fuzz." It just might be the world's softest tunic. Also could be the world's most comfortable fashion-thing. You'll believe it when you touch it. Feels like whipped cream. Soft because of the blend: lambswool, angora, and nylon. Soft because of the cut: full, flowy sleeves, shirt-tail bottom, seven-button neckline you can open as wide as you want to. Soft because of the color: foamy heather gray. You'll wear it at the office, on country weekends, maybe even (with a bright sash and slim pants) to dinner parties. In other words, you shouldn't try to live without this tip-top tunic by Vesna Bricelj for Overture.

Added power is given to the foregoing copy by its very pronounced involvement of the reader in picturing the various uses for the product.

Below are two more examples of the fashion writer's ability to depart from the humdrum with saucy, offbeat words and phrases; they are informal, sharply descriptive, and like nothing you'll see in other types of advertising.

> It's in. It's now. It's easy on the eye. Not to mention the lips, cheeks and nails. A lighter look. Relax. Kick back. In softer shades of pale. Come-hither Fawn. Gentle pink nude. Oh, all are very subtle. But no, not shy, not frail. Never EVER underestimate the power of a pale.
> pixie dust

Figure 12–1. Prestige advertisement with a high fashion flair. Some companies offering products of superior quality and reputation find it unnecessary to use full copy in their advertisements. Striking illustrations are sufficient. This is especially true of such products as high-quality watches, perfumes, jewelry, and high-style clothing.

> For instant de-wallflowering, try a night of sparkly makeup and stardust-sprinkled hair. Brush on a blush of soft, barely iridescent pink, then dust face with slightly silvery powder.

First, You Must Define Fashion

What is fashion copywriting, and how can you learn to write it successfully? Like all other types of copy, it has its tricks. Also, before you can learn to write fashion copy, you must first learn what fashion is.

Perhaps you'd better start by thinking of fashion in two ways: (1) as exemplified in high fashion periodicals and in advertisements for exclusive stores, and (2) as exemplified in volume selling in department and moderate-price stores. When you have thought about these two divisions of fashion, you will be ready to absorb a few dos and don'ts of fashion writing.

You have probably already surmised that fashion is a capricious commodity. What is and what is not fashion almost defies analysis. Every few years, some scholar comes out of research activities to write a new and learned treatise proving that fashions stem from wars and the general economy of a country.

In the broad, overall view, the researcher is probably right. However, in view of fashion's inherent ephemeral quality and because the motives and causes underlying changes in fashion are as subject to change as the fashions themselves, it is of no great importance to pin it down, dissect it, and catalog its component parts.

Consider what happened to fashion after World Wars I and II. When women began bobbing their hair after the first war, it was supposedly to assert equality with men by looking more boyish. It was even argued that since women had shared the hardship of war as Red Cross workers, nurses, and so forth, they intended to share the rewards.

Ostensibly, the generalization to be drawn from this example is that women express their emancipation after a war through more masculine fashions, but this analysis does not work out. Many thousands of women also served in World War II. Again, when the war was over, they swarmed to have their hair cut shorter. This time, however, the motive was changed. They clipped it off not to look more boyish but to achieve a fluffy, feminine look.

The war had made fashion static: it imposed regulations, prescribed tailored suits, and demanded practical, mannish clothes. The outburst of the new, the curved, and the longer-skirted silhouette, as well as of the short coiffures, was an expression not for equality but against the deadly regimentation of war.

More recently our culture has been swept up in the feminism movement; we have entered the era of the working woman. This is a time of independence and great gains for women in politics, business, and science. Such dynamism affects and influences fashion.

Selling Fashion Is More Natural for a Woman

The approach in fashion is so personal that many feel that it takes a female copywriter to sell to another woman. A man can understand how important it is to a woman to wear a skirt three inches longer (or three inches shorter) than last season, but he's at a distinct disadvantage in having to guess how she *feels* in it. A woman knows. She sells the feel of fashion—of low waists or high waists, flared skirts or straight skirts—almost before she sells the specific merchandise.

Fashion moves in cycles. If you aspire to a top job in fashion copy, you'll need to read as much as possible about the clothes of all periods. While you're at it, you'll also profit from exposure to the humanities, history, literature, and the economics of the world. Writing fashion advertising is less inspiration than it is a comprehensive knowledge of what made the world turn in Cleopatra's time and what keeps it spinning today.

Fashion is emotion. You must live with it. It is your job to begin where the photograph or illustration leaves off. Your work is good when you give the reader the feel of fashion, when you make a coming event inviting by letting your reader know how it will feel to appear in an original by Yves Saint Laurent.

Keeping Up with Fashion Is a Full-Time Task

Keeping up with fashion is both your joy and despair. One moment, it's the peasant look, at prices far beyond the "peasant's" ability to pay. Gone is the tunic over pants and the graceful drape of chiffon. Suddenly, the sumptuous look takes over in place of the simple chiffon or jersey dress. "Importance" has become the word.

Because the dress must look important, the swing may be to new fabrics. For originals, the price is important, too, at $950 (less, of course, for copies). Understated elegance is out, and the change can occur at a dizzying pace. For example, one high fashion store, less than two weeks after a Paris showing by a renowned designer, presented the new style in New York. Eight dresses at $500 were sold the first day, and the store continued to sell the new fashion at the same brisk pace.

Positive fashion images can be created by important events such as a change in the White House or a royal wedding in England, two events that caused one designer to declare that the future fashion image would be rich, warm, and gala. Looking ahead, the designer saw clothes as young, sometimes very sophisticated, and rather stately.

At the same time, other designers were envisioning clothes as more softly feminine than in recent years, with flowing skirts, ruffled dresses, and an opulent theme. But who really knows what can happen two years ahead? Fashion runs from season to season, with dramatic changes possible between seasons.

Unless your antennae are quivering ceaselessly, significant changes may catch you unawares. When they occur, you need to call upon new words and to evoke new moods. Meanwhile, amidst all the newly coined elegance, you may still be selling designer jeans with a fashion flair and at prices unmistakably in the fashion range.

Fashion Designers Experiment Constantly

Nothing demonstrates the mercurial nature of the fashion cycle better than the lightning adoption in 1987 of daring new styles that featured, above all, knee-revealing short skirts. Seemingly, there was almost a rebellion against the "success" look, the conservative approach to dressing adopted by women intent on career advancement.

Suddenly, women's fashions were more feminine, sometimes outrageously so, with skirts high above the knees, bubble dresses, and flounced and ruffled styles. At the time, surprised suppliers made such statements as "It swept the country overnight" and "It was a change." That's what fashion is all about: change.

Even *within* change there is change, as demonstrated by the combination of stretch fabrics and short skirt lengths. One designer, for example, alternated short skirts with snug, long pants, making it hard for the observer to judge whether a woman should be in trousers or a miniskirt.

Experimentation is what fashion change is all about. When radical new styles appear, it is the result of experimenting both by the designers and by the women who wear the styles. These are the bolder spirits. Still, as in the 1987 switch to shorter skirts, there are many who will not change. Thus, the writer of fashion advertising will be writing to a considerable number of women who simply don't want to expose their knees and who know that because of maturity or body build, or both, they would look ridiculous in the extreme new styles. Then, too, what might be worn socially is rejected for office wear. Above-the-knee skirts find little acceptance by the working woman.

Sooner or later, the fashion pendulum will swing the other way again. With this change there will be a change in fashion writing once more. Volatility is the very essence of fashion. As a fashion writer, you anticipate change, welcome it, and adjust to it. These dizzy swings to and fro make your job ever interesting and ever challenging.

So much for fashion in general. We now identify the distinctions between high fashion advertising and volume-fashion copy.

Changes in Fashion Often Stem from Advertising

High-style fashion writing can be fairly formal, as on the pages of *Vogue,* or *Harper's Bazaar* or in the advertisements of Marshall Field's; informal, as in *Mademoiselle;* or formal *or* informal, as in the top fashion advertisements of Lord & Taylor. Whichever it is, this copy is authoritative; it sets the fashion.

From these editorial pages and advertisements spring the words and phrases that articulate the fashion. Through the years, the words associated with fashion have been as essential to the fashions themselves as the very fabrics from which they are cut. For instance, consider the Gibson Girl shirt, the hobble skirt, the swing skirt, and the D'Orsay pump.

High fashion copy is designed primarily *to sell the idea of the coat of the moment, rather than a specific coat in stock.* The importance of this objective must not be underestimated. Writing for this type of advertisement is an exacting job.

From time to time, newspapers and magazines carry striking examples of superb advertisements. Quite a number, by their originality and daring, have started whole new circles of advertising thought. In New York, for example, such establishments as Lord & Taylor and Bloomingdale's run newspaper advertisements written by copywriters who have distinguished themselves by being able to put down on paper just a few carefully chosen words. These writers are masters of the art of saying a lot by writing little. It isn't easy. Years of apprenticeship and hard work are necessary before a writer can hope to achieve this skill.

Nothing has been said here about the fashion artists as important members of the creative team. In many eyes, they are more important than copywriters in inducing sales. Fruitless and unending arguments can be held on this point since words and illustration must ultimately work together. Each can enhance the other.

Make no mistake, however. Recognize that illustration, as important as it is in other forms of advertising, is still more important in fashion advertising in conveying mood and authenticity. Fashion artists are usually superior artists. Such artists will provide you with a strong creative challenge—to do as well with words as they do with art. The test is whether the art embellishes the copy or vice versa; or does each match the other perfectly?

A study of high fashion advertisements will reveal these characteristics:

- They are directed toward people who set the pace.
- Their appeal is prestige.
- They speak with authority (usually written in third person).
- They strive toward mood and illusion.
- Their concern with details, if any, is secondary.
- They contrive to make the readers feel they are influencing fashion rather then being influenced by it.
- The copy is usually brief and is always enhanced by dramatic artwork and distinctive typefaces.
- The words themselves are highly dramatic and descriptive.

Notwithstanding the fact that good high fashion advertising has these characteristics, there is a regrettable amount of high fashion advertising appearing in magazines and newspapers that does not measure up. One criticism is the sameness in the sleek illustrations and the copy's artificial sheen—the bright, insincere patter that has confused shallowness with sophistication.

There is the tendency, too, for fashion advertisers to fall in love with prettiness. Advertisements are judged as pretty or not pretty regardless of whether or not they have ideas or selling arguments. The advertisements—copy and art—show and talk about merchandise but make no real attempt to sell it.

Selling in Volume but Keeping the Fashion Mood

Whereas high fashion advertising is designed to set the pace, volume-fashion advertising is directed to selling the people who must keep the pace. The student looking forward to a career in advertising will very likely start here. This does not mean that volume-fashion advertising is easy, nor does it imply that the techniques involved are less exacting.

It does mean that there are more opportunities in this phase of advertising, because this is the category into which most advertising falls. The stores and agencies engaged in promotional work to move stocks of merchandise are in the thousands. In contrast, the smart shops and periodicals whose concern is high fashion are relatively few.

You must realize that a flair for writing is not enough for writing fashion advertising that sells. You need to understand selling techniques, adaptations of style, and human

Sir Edward H.

A man in a tweed suit can't be flummoxed or rushed. Departs slowly but arrives on time. Cogitates, muses, affects long pauses, but answers with stunning clarity. You could listen to him forever. In fact, you have.

The former PM gives a 2-hour lecture without notes. Chides Mrs. Thatcher, berates Mr. Major; displays his European Identity Card, wears his tweed suit.

During the Q&A he's magnanimous. Gives me the name of his Bond Street tailor. Luckily, I bought an amount of tweed when greenbacks were at par with sterling.

Now I've had it replicated for one-fourth of the original price. Don't ask how. That would be insider information. Let's just say between a certain Dublin mill and my Louisville tailor, we've worked it out.

The Former Prime Minister's Tweed Suit. Never out of favour.

Jacket: Single-breasted. 100% Irish tweed. 3 dark horn buttons. Notched collar. Welt flap pockets. 2 back vents. Men's even sizes: 38 through 48, Regular; 40 through 48, Long.

Pants: Lined to the knee. 100% Irish tweed. Pleated front. 6 belt loops. Welt back pockets. Seams are serged, pressed open and flat. Men's even sizes: 30 through 46. Free hemming (max. 36") or cuffing (max. 34").

Color: Sable, Brown, and Charcoal Tweed.

Tweed Country Suit. Jacket, Regular (Nº. 39A2689); Long (Nº. 39A2690). Price: $360. Pants (Nº. 39A2548). Price: $176. You'll save enough for the wine at Quaglino's.

67

Wide-Legged Wool Pants (M1995).

I've seen the report from Intelligence and I must say that you are to be congratulated.

Women now hold 53% of all professional jobs and 45% of managerial positions. The percentage of top executive slots occupied by women has gone up nearly seven-fold since 1975. Younger women who work full time earn 98% of what their male peers do. (Figures on comparative Maalox consumption aren't available.)

This is good, very good. But let's not be complacent.

I am issuing our best-selling Reckless Wide-Legged Pants in soft, drapey, mid-weight <u>wool</u>. They still make any figure seem longer, lankier, elegant. But wool is more at home in the corridors of power, more substantial, and not exactly "reckless"; "intrepid" is more like it.

I expect you to make great strides in them.

Intrepid Wide-Legged Wool Pants (Nº. 39A2597), lined in acetate, with zip fly, on-seam side pockets, and inverted box pleats. Price: $147.

Women's sizes: 4 through 16.

Colors: Sage Plaid or Camel Herringbone Stripe. Please specify.

To order ☎ toll free
800-231-7341
7AM to 1AM (ET)
24-hour FAX orders: 800-346-3081
Overseas FAX: 606-254-1112
Overseas phone orders: 606-254-5444

9

Figure 12–2a. Direct response catalog advertisement. In the lofty copy of this J. Peterman catalog page you'll find references to British Prime Ministers and Bond Street tailors, all shedding glamour and prestige on the product for sale. Nothing crass here. Every word is calculated to arouse the male prospect's interest in the garment displayed. Many practical details are included to make the purchase seem sensible.

Figure 12–2b. Direct response catalog advertisement. J. Peterman is aiming this copy very definitely at women holding positions in executive suites. It fits in, also, with the more casual wear now seen in business offices, but words such as "elegant" hit the fashion note. Above all, the copy conveys flattery for women who have made good in a hitherto man's world.

nature, and above all, you must have an intimate knowledge of the people who buy and wear the clothes about which you are writing—the people who do the volume buying upon which all stores depend.

In one sense, your knowledge of people's buying habits, their whims, and their enthusiasms is more important than your writing skill. If you don't have the former, you're just another writer spinning out glib, bright patter that fails to convince and thus fails to sell.

Although there are vast differences in the markets and in the writing techniques used, a fashion writer and an industrial writer have a lot in common. Each must have an intense personal interest in his specialized field and must be able to turn out copy precisely geared to that field.

As mentioned earlier, you must, above all, be breathlessly intrigued with fashion change and fashion detail. In the illustrative part of your advertisement, it must be important to you how a glove stops at the wrist and where the flower is pinned on the dress. It is easy to be wrong in these details. Likewise, it is exceedingly difficult to recover the confidence of the reader who looks over your advertisement and finds that you, seemingly, have less interest in these details than he or she does.

This sense of fashion leadership is demonstrated in the following copy that stresses the offering of a fashion exclusive originated by a famous designer:

Another Lord & Taylor *exclusive*
Andrea Pfister's
black satin Pierrot pump
glistens with enchantment.

Ours alone, dazzled by a golden sequined orb in a gilt-edged Pierrot cocarde, the evening pump is transformed into pure magic. On the little Louis heel we love. $220.00

The writer engaged in volume-fashion advertising must correlate three factors: selling techniques, human nature, and forceful style.

Effective volume selling, like other forms of selling, is based on six rather commonly accepted objectives: to attract attention, to hold interest, to create desire, to overcome obstacles, to stir to action, and to give satisfaction and pleasant reaction for money spent.

Write More to the Individual than to a Group

As any student of adolescent behavior knows, youngsters and teenagers are strongly influenced by group pressures in what they wear and what they do. If the grungy look is in, then that's what the teen will adopt.

As we evolve out of the teenage cycle, we tend to continue to think in group terms to some extent but more in individual terms than we did in the formative years. Certainly, the person to whom you address your fashion advertising has group desires such as the need for recognition, security, new experience, excitement, and love.

Granting all that, we still must think of the person to whom we write as an individual with his or her own set of problems, wants, and desires. If you want your copy to sell, you show your reader how to dress attractively, but you must also be aware of the concern with a budget and the determination to keep healthy.

Your job is to sell this person fashions. Dozens of considerations and economies are pulling against you. Hundreds of commodities are competing with your dress jacket for this reader's attention, and to make your selling job tougher, a dozen stores are competing with you to sell that same $255 dress.

If your advertisement is successful, you will attract that reader, persuade him or her, and bring that person into your store to buy the dress jacket you describe. You will have found a way to say it better. You will have convinced your reader.

A successful advertisement involves good writing plus a

Figure 12–3. Well-written catalog page. Many fashion advertisers are content to let their illustrations carry the entire selling burden. In this instance, however, the fine illustration is accompanied by colorful, effective copy.

point of view that enables your copy to begin where the reader is.

Volume-Fashion Advertising Has Its Own Set of Requirements

- Tells more of the details, such as width of seams, fabric, colors, and sizes. A woman may be looking for a dress or coat in pink wool. She reads carefully, but nothing is said about color—or about the fabric. Remember, you do not necessarily detract from the atmosphere of "style" by supplying information about the color and fabric of the merchandise.

- Gives more stress to price. While you should certainly be aware that price gains more prominence as it drops lower and lower, watch out for basing fashion copy wholly on an economy appeal. "Now—a woolen suit for $59.98" probably will not appeal. Women prefer not to identify themselves with $59.98, even if that's all they have to spend.

Although interesting style is pretty much a personal matter, there are, nevertheless, some precepts and rules that cannot be ignored. Since copywriting is a craft—like building a bench or cobbling a shoe—you should think in very clear terms of problem solution. Every block of copy, whether it pertains to mink or walking shoes, has a message to convey. You decide what is to be said and why, and you must say it exactly the way it should be said.

You must do justice to the fashion in terms suitable to the age, tastes, and ways of life of your audience. The medium and the audience set the slant for the copy. An advertisement scheduled for *Seventeen* must be written to dovetail with its readers' way of speaking or thinking. This is not the way of speaking or thinking used by a woman who reads *Vogue* or *Harper's Bazaar*. The fashion writer knows to whom the eyes peering at the page belong.

You must have facility with words, a sharp ear attuned to the turn of a phrase, and the perception to recognize gestures and attitudes of readers. If you're good, you visualize the reader before you attempt to reach him or her with your copy.

You Use Different Appeals in Volume-Fashion Advertising

The appeals used in volume-fashion advertising are significantly different from the specialized appeals used in high fashion advertising. In the case of women's fashions, the message is toward the woman who must keep the pace. A volume advertisement does the following:

- Helps a woman to feel that she is buying and wearing the new smart style, that she is *keeping* pace.
- Assures her that she is well dressed (not because she is imitating but because she has the good judgment to recognize "smart fashion").
- Recognizes that she may be a working woman whose attire must be appropriate for her personal and her professional life.
- Emphasizes what is new about the dress being advertised and shows her why it will be becoming to her.
- Indicates that her standard of dressing is parallel to "best dressed" through the merchandising or designing abilities of your store—her store. (Note: It's always a good idea to sell the store or the label in addition to the merchandise. In the long run, if the merchandise is good, it will add to sales by making the manufacturer's line, or that store, a habit with the woman.)
- Connotes fashion in terms of her activities.
- Answers her implied questions on wearing qualities, washability, and so forth.

A noticeable difference in volume-fashion advertising is the amount of copy used. True high fashion advertisements may use little or no copy, depending upon illustrations, mostly photographs, to carry the message. In volume-fashion advertising, copy plays a more important role. There is more selling and less reliance on the illustration to supply a reason for buying.

Want to Write Interestingly? Follow These Ideas

Here are some dos and don'ts on interesting writing style. You will do well to remember them.

- *Do* … make your caption sound smooth and unstilted.
- *Do* … use an active verb instead of a descriptive adjective for description whenever possible. Verbs make a caption stronger and give it movement. NOT: The black skirt has circular bands around it. BUT: Black ribbon bands encircle the skirt.
- *Do* … keep your sentences simple, whether long or short. Be careful to ensure that your modifiers fall as close as possible to what they modify.
- *Do* … avoid last year's phrases. Catch phrases of the day can be effective, but bear in mind whether you are writing for a daily newspaper or a periodical. The smart phrase that's on everyone's lips now is likely to become completely passé in the long interim between writing and publication of a periodical.
- *Do* … be light and gay and humorous, if you can be. Don't try to be if you can't.
- *Do* … digest thoroughly all information on merchandise (study the photograph or layout intensively if you can't see the merchandise yourself) before you put your pencil on paper. You can't write interestingly if you don't write knowingly.
- *Don't* … use a tired simile. It's even more soporific than the tired adjective. Don't say "crisp as lettuce," "sleek as a seal," or "striped like Joseph's coat." Say "bright, like a fire-engine," "fresh as a four-year old's cheeks,"and "gala as the evening that starts with an orchid."
- *Don't* … rely on a clutter of lush adjectives. When you do use adjectives, make them as specific and fresh as possible. Embellishments like "pretty," "marvelous," "charming," "wonderful," "divine" don't really accomplish anything. On the other hand, "Paillette floral designs," "dropped-torso bodice," "supple, glove-tanned cowhide," and "pin of patinated brass" all give you a definite picture and a definite association. These adjectives have feeling.
- *Don't* … imitate someone else's style. Read other people's advertisements for the ideas they contain, but when you have an advertisement to write on the same dress, write in your own way. Be fresh.

By this point in the chapter you have come to realize that the fashion copywriter must be as subtle as a glance behind a veil and as direct as a salesclerk in Macy's basement; as factual as a catalog sheet and as imaginative as a mystery writer.

Fashion writers must have a strong love for fashion, for glittering, human, persuasive words, and most of all, for ideas, around which they wrap the words with precision and that mysterious quality called "flair." Possessed of all these qualities, they may survive, and even thrive, in the demanding, volatile field that is fashion copywriting.

You Have a Different Set of Guidelines When Writing to Fashion-Conscious Men

At one time, men smiled indulgently at women's concern with fashion, cosmetics, and other feminine enthusiasms.

The woman's world was far from the world of clean-shaven males who wore dark suits, sober ties, and short, neatly clipped hair.

In the last decade, however, men have burst into the fashion scene. We shrug as they daub themselves with colognes and perfumes and apply makeup. Clothing and personal grooming ideas are dictated by *Playboy, Esquire, Gentlemen's Quarterly,* and the many men's magazines that have caused much of the departure from male conservatism in dress and personal habits.

How can you, a fashion writer, create advertising for this newly emerged male butterfly? First, you must understand that you are addressing three markets.

One is the *still* conservative, young-man-on-the-move market. Your target is the young executive whose clothes have a quiet distinction suitable for the appearance of the investment broker in the boardroom, for the account executive who must present a campaign at a client meeting, and for the young lawyer in a prestigious Boston law firm. This man's well-groomed hair may be slightly longer than in the past, but he is much the same in dress as he always has been.

Copy for this market is subdued and deferential. It recognizes the importance of the impression that the reader's attire must make on his associates. The stress is not so much on what is new as it is on what is appropriate. This man doesn't want to be innovative in dress, he wants to be quietly—and possibly expensively—correct.

The second group is the swinging market. This is the machismo male who revels in his virility and attractiveness to females. Copy directed at him, whether for musk oil scents or contoured slacks, has sexual overtones. Sometimes, the copy can poke fun at the image. Fun or not, this male target is moved by self-gratification and a desire to impress the women he meets. He has a self-image that is largely created by the clothes he wears, the hairstyling he adopts, and the cologne he splashes on himself. The *Playboy* reader, typical of this market, is highly conscious of styles, innovative, eager to try the new, and blanches if described as not in the know.

In writing to this market of males, you pull out all the stops. Your words are bolder and more colorful to match the styles, and you cater to the fantasies and self-image of these men who have broken the shackles that inhibited men's styles for so many years.

Finally, the third group is the casual market. This group includes men who dress to please themselves, not others. Clothes selection is easygoing, with the accent on comfort: open collars, sport shirts, denims, slacks with sport coats, slacks with sweaters or denim jackets, and loafers.

This market is more complex than it seems. For instance, allied with the casual look is the "country" look, which embraces a number of fashion permutations, such as the pairing of rustic Harris tweeds with country tartans or suede elbow patches on a plaid sports jacket.

Likewise, the "preppy" look, a self-consciously youthful look, has been a part of the casual scene for some time. Warm-up suits for jogging and other sports are now part of

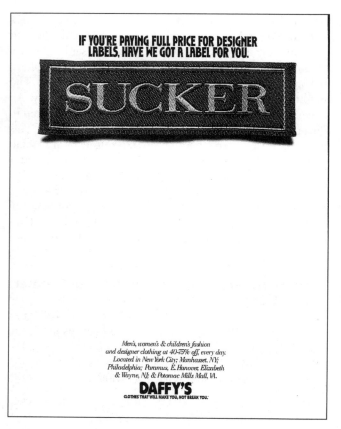

Figure 12–4. Offbeat transit advertising. An irreverent treatment of designer clothes is taken in this transit advertising that represents a distinct departure from conventional fashion advertising. Obviously, this humorous approach will get the attention of price shoppers. *Courtesy Devito/Verdi Advertising.*

the casual look and are worn quite often at nonathletic times by men and women.

Copy matches the mood of the casual man. You recognize his easygoing lifestyle, his interest in sports, and his desire to be individual in his dress. He likes to put combinations together to suit himself. You "suggest" to this person: you don't tell him that he *must* dress according to a fixed or prescribed mode.

Carrying the casual look to an extreme were trendy overalls with designer labels and selling for around $200. This is but one more example of the unpredictability of the fashion world. The wearing of such garments fits in somewhat with the "grungy" look popularized by teens and preteens.

Designer Clothes Are Important in Men's Fashions, Too

Today's fashion-conscious male pays a price for his fancies. For example, T-shirts bearing designer names like Armani, Dolce & Gabana, or Joseph Abboud sell for as much as $70, and two-pleat trousers from Armani sell at $230. Sports coats and jackets with designer names attached easily range from $595 to more than $600. Though not quite so chic and lacking the designer label, comparable coats

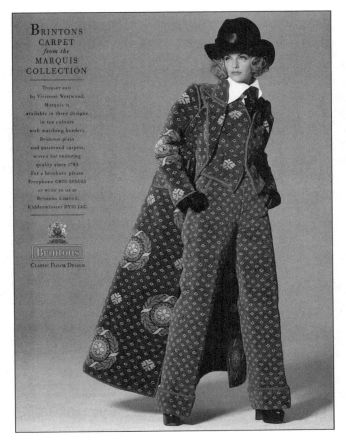

Figure 12–5a. High fashion application for an unusual product. This British carpet manufacturer has captured the high-fashion look for a model wearing a garment made of the company's carpeting. It's a highly creative and fashion-sensitive approach to the selling of carpeting.

Figure 12–5b. Imaginative ad for carpeting. This highly creative campaign is a decided departure from conventional carpet advertising and fits nicely into the high-fashion category.

sell for sums in the $80 to $90 range at the Gap, Banana Republic, and J. Crew.

While men's fashions will never change as rapidly as women's, the fashion writer must be aware of the changes or be left behind. Take, for instance, the matter of buttons. For years, two buttons dominated. Today, there are double-breasted suits and suits with one, two, three, four, five buttons. The ubiquitous Armani stresses the three-button suit.

Careful selection of style and fabric carries assurance to the male shopper that what he buys will not go out of style in a season and may, unlike women's clothes, be acceptable for years. This idea of the relative durability of men's fashions is captured in Ralph Lauren's Polo Chino fabric, which is described in an advertisement as a classic open to modern interpretation.

What to Wear on the Job Is an Important Question

For working men and women, the question is *how* casual? This question has been significant since industry instituted "dress down" days on which workers were permitted to dress informally. Most often the dress down day

has been Friday. For men, this often means going without a tie or wearing what have been termed "soft" suits. Usually, however, men who meet clients or customers are more likely to dress conventionally. As an alternative to dress shirts, the suited male will often wear polo shirts or turtlenecks with his soft suit.

Dressing Down

As reported in a news item in the Chicago Tribune on July 20, 1995, the focus in many workplaces now is on comfort and casual wear. Quoting *Working Woman* magazine, the article includes a list of clothes for the casual, well-dressed woman. Some of the clothes and fabrics deemed acceptable included the following: denim or chambray shirt; thin sweater or heavy T-shirt; cardigan; linen or cotton shirt; short skirt; khaki or navy twill pants; pleated trousers; three button, unstructured blazer; vest; and stacked-heel loafers.

Recognizing the trend toward the casual look was an advertisement for Macy's in *Vogue* magazine. On one page of a two-page spread were the words:

LOOK. IT'S SIMPLE.
WHAT YOU WEAR ON SATURDAY WORKS FOR YOU
ON MONDAY.
YEAH. CASUAL WORKS.
WHAT A CONCEPT.

"Corporate Casual" Takes Hold

Nowhere has the mercurial character of fashion been more apparent than in the nationwide swing to what is called "corporate casual." Some of the many corporations approving casual dressing are such household names as Ford, IBM, General Electric, General Motors, Clorox, and Chrysler.

While corporations consider casual dressing a morale booster, they expect that casual doesn't mean messy. Jeans, for instance, are acceptable, but only if they are clean and unfrayed.

A copywriter who hasn't kept up with this casual trend isn't doing his or her job. This is one more example of the importance of the fashion writer's need to constantly study the field in order to be ahead of the trends.

Be Alert to News Events (and People) That Affect Fashion Trends

Big news events that center around national figures—presidents, heroes, rock stars, and television celebrities—affect what men will wear and thus affect fashion writing.

An illustration of this was shown by what happened when President-elect Carter announced that he would be wearing jeans at the White House.

The story was headlined in all print media and was given full treatment in broadcast media. Denim manufacturers, already worked to capacity, anticipated an avalanche of additional sales once the White House became the locale of scores of photographers snapping pictures of a denim-clad President of the United States.

Denim, already a phenomenon for its acceptance by both sexes and its use for all occasions, was thus given a further boost up the ladder of total acceptability.

Then, along came a U.S.A. Olympic team garbed in Western style, followed by Ronald Reagan, a horseback-riding President who popularized jelly beans and a Western look. Cowboy hats appeared everywhere, and numbers of urban males looked as if they had just ridden in from the Bar-X ranch, complete with sombreros, high-heeled boots, and other items of Western living. Meanwhile, back at the White House ranch, Nancy Reagan was encouraging a dressier mood for women than had been seen during the Carters' White House occupancy.

Still later, Lt. Col. Oliver North burst on the television scene in 1987. Immediately, there was a national rush for "Ollie" T-shirts and "Ollie" haircuts. Had he been wearing a civilian suit instead of a Marine uniform, the men of the nation would soon have been dressed the same way—another example of the exasperating, yet fascinating, capriciousness of the fashion scene.

Fashion-wise, the Bush presidency had little impact, but this changed when the Clintons took over. Casual attire was the norm, and Hillary Clinton's clothes and hairstyling were the topics of endless discussions. As usual, the style was adopted across the land. During the O.J. Simpson trial, women viewers watched intently the hairstyling changes of Marcia Clark, the much-photographed prosecutor. One more instance of current events influencing fashion.

An alert fashion writer also keeps an eye on the entertainment industry, which so often initiates a new look. Rap video also had its effect, influencing the younger set to adopt the aforementioned grungy look with oversize pants and shirts and baseball caps worn backwards.

The "European" Look Invades the U.S. Fashion Scene

To these other types, we might add the avant garde male clothing purchasers who welcome the European look. Thus, we have the tweedy look of the British designers and the bold colors from France. Italian men's fashions, in contrast to the French boldness, tend toward simplicity expressed in toned-down, quiet elegance—elegance for which the fashionably dressed male pays handsomely. In European-style suits, slimmer cuts and double vents are likely to prevail.

Despite the invasion by the purveyors of men's fashions from the Common Market, the three previously listed men's groupings still hold true. In European styles, however, the distinctions tend to blur, with a subtle crossing-over of styles; for instance, the casual combines with the business and the swinging blends with the casual.

Fashion swings in men's clothes are less likely to gyrate as wildly as those in women's fashions. Still, the writer for men's fashions must keep an eye on fashions in the United States and around the world.

CHAPTER 13

Direct Response
A Quick Test of Your Message's Effectiveness (Part A)

A t this very moment, people across the country are riffling through catalogs from Lands' End, Norm Thompson, Eddie Bauer, and hundreds of others, or they're selecting offers on TV or from magazines.

There's Gwen Shelton, for instance, who's putting down her credit card number for an order of embossed stationery from a Walter Drake catalog.

And twice a year, Joe Ganley, an eager eater, dials an 800 number to order succulent Vidalia onions from the Georgia grower.

People of all types, incomes, and tastes yield to the fascination of direct response offers. This fascination has made direct response the fastest growing segment of advertising and marketing—a field for <u>you</u> if you yearn to see your words bring direct results.

Catalogs? You groan as even more arrive each day. Sadly, you toss many unread into the wastebasket. It's a grim race for survival for those who send them out. Those who *do* survive do so because they offer appealing products; because they sell those products with warm, intimate, persuasive copy; and because their copy instills a sense of urgency that impels readers to call the 800 number or to fill out the order form. Every copywriter who is not in the direct response field should make an intense study of those catalogs that continue to thrive in this unbelievably competitive field.

The survival of companies sending catalogs depends not only on having appealing products and prices but also on having good mailing lists of people who are potential customers. Furthermore, catalogs aren't sent out haphazardly, they are primarily sent to people who have bought products in the past. These people are evaluated in terms of how recently they've bought, how frequently they buy, and the dollar amount of their purchases.

Defining "Direct Response"

This term isn't mysterious, but it is often considered synonymous with direct mail. Actually, direct mail comes under the umbrella of direct response when it seeks business directly. Also under that umbrella are the broadcast media, magazines, newspapers, and catalogs. In short, if you're inviting someone to respond to an offer, you are engaged in direct response, regardless of the media vehicle you choose. Remember, however, that much direct mail does not seek direct action and therefore does not fall under the direct response umbrella.

In defining direct response, it is necessary to mention the testing component that is vital to this activity. This testing is one of the biggest differences between direct response advertising and other forms of advertising. There's a certain amount of "let's hope it works" in other forms of advertising. In direct response, however, everything is tested, including the media selection, the headlines, the size of the advertisements, the time used, and the major benefit of the product or service. After the initial testing has been done and the advertising has appeared, the results of the advertisement are measured and analyzed. If the results are not good, the elements are examined to discover which of the elements might be at fault. New testing will be done to see if a change in the elements will bring improvement.

As a Writer of Direct Response, Think of Yourself as a One-Person Sales Force

Thousands of hopeful people running small businesses seek sales through direct response for a staggering variety of goods. Sadly, many do not succeed. Perhaps their products are not right for the market or the times. Their advertising often has no magic pulling power because the writers simply don't know how to do an entire selling job through advertising.

To balance these failures, there are many successes. Currently, direct response buying is reaching new peaks. There are many reasons for this. Costs for transportation and for fuel continue to rise, making trips to stores more expensive. More and more women are working and have less time to shop. Last, buying by direct response has achieved a general acceptance, and this acceptance becomes even greater as the variety of purchases through direct response increases.

In addition to a complete range of conventional goods, direct response business now includes many luxury items and even food, including meats, poultry, and gourmet items that are mailed packed in dry ice.

If *you* write copy for any of these items, you do the complete sales job through words and illustrations alone. This means that those words capture interest, spur want or desire, overcome objections, and persuade the prospect to sign the order. In such selling, you have no alternative. There is no sales force to carry the burden. *You* are the sales force. If you don't create sales, you're a failure and your business fails; or, if you're working for someone, that person goes out of business.

This direct responsibility for results is not necessarily the curse it may seem to be, because such selling produces such a prompt reaction—or lack of it—that you have an almost instant measure both of the effectiveness of your idea and of the success of your message. If they've proved "pretty good," you may be able to inject into your next message just the right touch needed to make it produce excellent results.

If your first message has proved to be "not so hot," you know that you need to try another version of your idea or even a new idea. You may then, through analysis of the results of the first message, be able to spot the exact flaw.

A writer may "figure out" why results are not satisfactory, but as previously mentioned, testing is the better way to find out what to do. For example, this could be the time to use an A/B split-run test (see Page 279 in Chapter 22) to test one version of a headline or appeal against another. A superior headline, for instance, might pull three to five more responses.

What and How You Write Are Important but Product and Prospects Are Even More So

Of course, you can't ignore the possibility that a poor reaction to a piece of direct response selling and the accuracy of any analysis you may make of that reaction may depend somewhat on two other factors not basically a part of the advertising sales effort: "product" and "prospects." If the product is poor or if the prospects are not reasonably well defined (and therefore not reached), reaction is fairly certain to be discouraging.

The single most important factor in success is the product. You *must* have a product people want. A poor product will hurt you more than poor copy in attaining results. Superb copy, on the other hand, can't sell a poor product.

Although only a genius, or a very lucky person, can be right all the time in picking products that will be successful sellers, here are a few questions to ask yourself when evaluating a product's potential:

• Does it have an exciting newness?
• Is there a real need for the product?
• Will *most* of your prospects find the product appealing?
• Is the product right for the market in terms of price, market's general taste, and way of living?

Direct Response Sells Services, Too

Because of the nature of the selling method, the product offered is usually some item of merchandise. However, a service may be sold by the direct response method. For example, a personal income-tax computing service, a manuscript criticism/correction service for amateur writers, and a direct response copywriting service (on a fee basis) for small businesses that have no advertising agency or creative personnel of their own can all be sold by direct response. Normally, such a small percentage of direct response selling is of services—and so much is of tangible goods—that throughout this discussion the terms "product," "item," and "merchandise," will be used to designate anything sold by direct response.

What Media Are Being Used Has a Big Effect on How and What You Write

As in all advertising, in addition to knowing everything possible about product and prospects, you need the answer to one other major question before beginning to write your direct response sales message: How—through what medium—am I going to tell my prospects about my product? The medium used affects not only the physical requirements of your message—its length, its layout, its illustration, its space for and location of headline, and so forth—but also the handling of your message.

This handling may include the approach your copy takes, the use of attention-getting words and copy devices,

The Vermont Country Store®

Brass Electric Candles Give Festive Glow To Holiday Windows

We never liked those plastic electric candles for holiday windows. They topple over at the slightest vibration and look less than elegant. These, standing 9″ tall with bulb (included), are solid brass electric candles that tastefully light up your home with a festive holiday glow. And, they don't topple over! Each has 5' cord with in-line switch. $5.95 each. *SPECIAL:* Set of 4, $20.00. Set of 8, $36.00 *postpaid.*

Please Ship Postage Paid	100% Guarantee
___ #16353 Brass Electric Candles	$ 5.95
___ SPECIAL: Set 4 Candles	$20.00
___ SPECIAL: Set 8 Candles	$36.00

Payment: ☐ Check ☐ VISA ☐ MC

Card No. _____

Exp. Date: _____ 4% Tax Vt. Shipments

FOR RUSH SERVICE CALL (802) 362-2400

NAME _____

ADDRESS _____

CITY _____

STATE _____ ZIP _____

THE VERMONT COUNTRY STORE®
715 Main St., Weston, VT 05161
☐ SEND FREE CATALOG

Figure 13–1. Effective small space advertisement. In this example, the copy uses the "suffering point" principle by mentioning a common failing of window candles—that they fall over easily. At the top, the headline sets a holiday note for a product sold chiefly at the Christmas season. According to the advertiser, this advertisement pulled very well, but magazine advertising for such a product normally would not bring the sales generated through catalog offerings.

the relative emphasis of appeals, and the inclusion (or exclusion) of other copy elements.

Although television has become a significant factor in direct response selling, along with the telephone, the average person often equates the term with catalogs. This person has become conscious of a host of catalogs that offer almost any item or service the human mind can conceive. Some of these catalogs have achieved steadily increasing recognition.

Consider the widely varied offerings of the following catalogs, which have become household names that are often as familiar to us as our newspapers and big circulation magazines: L. L. Bean, Norm Thompson, Carroll Reed, Lands' End, Eddie Bauer, Orvis, The Sharper Image, Herrington's, J. Crew, Lillian Vernon, Talbot's, Williams-Sonoma, and Hold Everything. In a smaller group are those catalogs offering unusual and/or luxury items; these include The Horchow Collection, Williams-Sonoma, Levenger's, Smith & Hawken, J. Peterman, Hammacher Schlemmer, and Gumps.

Newspapers and Magazines Target Almost Every Market Segment

As already stated, when talking about direct response, your average person thinks immediately about catalogs. But newspapers and magazines, especially the latter, reach into all levels of society to pull in massive dollar amounts for direct response.

In the magazine field, typical publications in which appropriate items are successfully offered for sale include many that on first thought might not be considered good direct response media at all, including upwardly targeted consumer specialty magazines in the home furnishings and fashion fields. *Town & Country, Better Homes and Gardens, Vogue,* and *Glamour* customarily devote special shopping sections to advertisements, for instance. The advertising columns of general magazines occasionally carry successful direct response offerings, usually in small-space advertisements because of the high rates of wide circulation publications.

Even executive management magazines offer opportunities for direct response marketers. *Business Week,* for example, has two pages of small direct response advertisements that appear under the heading, "Business Week Market Place." Interestingly, a current issue of "Market Place" contains an advertisement with a headline that reads: "Reach Millions With America's #1 Direct Response Radio Program."

Also, in the back of women's service magazines such as *Family Circle* and *Woman's Day,* direct response advertising is represented by many small advertisements for a variety of products and services.

Somewhat more commonly associated with the direct response selling of specialty types of merchandise are those magazines appealing to certain classifiable economic, occupational, avocational, and/or social segments of the population. Typical examples of these might be:

- Movies, romance, adventure, and detective magazines appealing mostly to the people of modest education and income.
- Farming and livestock publications such as *Farm Journal.*
- Comics and the children's and youth magazines.
- Sports and body-building publications and outdoors periodicals.
- Hobby publications such as those concerning home mechanics, amateur photography, arts, and antiques.
- The lower income and/or small town and rural magazines such as *Grit.*
- Publications appealing to specific racial groups, such as *Ebony.*
- Magazines whose paid advertising columns are composed largely of direct response offers—and whose readers over the years have come to regard them as "marketing places."

In addition to their prestige and selectivity, magazines offer color to enhance direct response items. A writer, however, used to the long-copy possibilities of direct response brochures, leaflets, and booklets, will find that writing must be tighter in magazine advertising.

At one time, direct response advertisers shunned newspapers because color either was not offered or was poor. Now, with newspapers jammed with inserts printed on good paper stock and offering excellent color, business has picked up. Thus, despite the handicap of a comparatively short life, newspapers offer many opportunities for successful direct response advertising, especially in comic sections, Sunday magazine pages, and Sunday supplements. Comic page advertisements have been important in reaching the youth market with box top premium offers, whereas Sunday magazines appeal to a wide audience and offer a variety of products and services.

Friendly Cousins: Direct Mail and Direct Response

As previously mentioned, when the average person hears the term "direct response," advertising catalogs pop into the mind. A somewhat similar reaction occurs with direct mail. Most people think immediately of letters. While letters do make up the biggest portion of direct mail, the medium takes many other forms. Keep in mind, too, that the direct mail discussed in this chapter is looking for sales and for response, so it has a legitimate place in the direct response category. Thus, we are talking specifically about *direct-mail selling.*

Direct-mail pieces may take many forms, some of the more common ones being leaflets, circulars, return post cards (today usually with postage payment guaranteed by the vendor), letters, broadsides, booklets, brochures, and envelope stuffers.

These may be sent in reply to a paid (or unpaid) response to some other advertising. Often they go out as individual mailings. At other times, they are grouped with similar pieces making other offers and are sent out to mailing lists either maintained by the merchandiser or rented

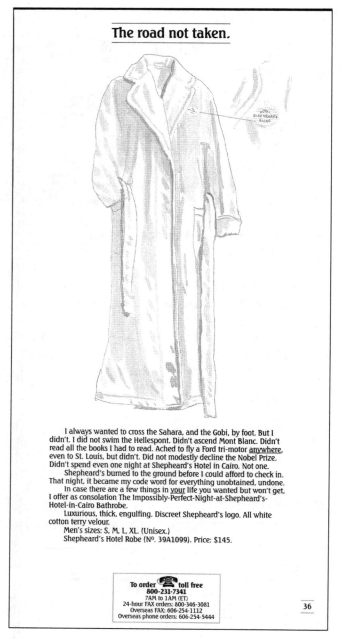

Figure 13–2. Direct response catalog advertisement. The engaging story-telling copy used in J. Peterman catalogs has stirred considerable attention because of its literary style and content. Despite the seeming nonchalant approach, there is considerable sales power on each page of the J. Peterman catalog.

or bought from a mailing list service or another advertiser. Often, too, they are used as enclosures, perhaps with a department store's monthly statement to its charge account customers or with other purchases being sent from the store or from a firm.

Television: Effective but Expensive for Direct Response Advertising

Any steady television viewer must be aware that commercials with direct response offers have been increasing, a

AT&T

Dear Business Person:

    At first you tell yourself, "One phone's as dependable as the next. Besides, look at the money I'll save." But when you catch your phone deceiving you call after call, when you're forced to resort to a phone booth . . .

    That's when you need good, old reliable AT&T -- and the **MERLIN®** Communications System. The **MERLIN** System is a perfect combination of old-fashioned service and sophisticated technology. And it's designed expressly for a small business like yours.

    Consider a system so dependable it memorizes your most important numbers for fast one-touch dialing, redials your last busy number, sets up conference calls, provides an intercom, pages -- even grows as your business grows.

    And a system so flexible it can be customized to meet the needs of each employee -- with the flick of a switch.

    Above all, think of the peace of mind you'll have with a system from AT&T. One that offers everything from a neighborhood office to a support staff of specialists ready to help in any way, at any time.

    Plus, the **MERLIN** System is more affordable than you think -- with payment plans to meet your budget -- including low monthly rental rates, low purchase prices and financing options.

    Come back to phones you can trust. Come back to AT&T. You'll wonder why you ever left.

    For more information on how the **MERLIN** System can help you run your business better, complete and send the enclosed reply card or call our Small Business Specialists today.

              Sincerely,

              Susan Stoll

              Susan Stoll
              Sales Manager

P.S. Send for your free brochure <u>today</u> and find out how the **MERLIN** System can help your small business.

Figure 13–3a. Direct response letter. Such letters develop a strong selling message and then end with a call for quick action. Two other examples of direct response material for this company are included in this chapter.

Figure 13–3b. Direct response mailing piece. This unit gives full buying information on one side, and on the other side is a reply card that is obtained by cutting around the dotted lines.

somewhat annoying development given the high-pressure character of many such commercials. Television offers the almost-perfect medium for the direct response advertiser because viewers can see the product, can watch it demonstrated in action, can hear the product (such as an album), and can be persuaded by the enthusiastic voice of the announcer. And, very importantly, a vast audience may be exposed to the television commercial.

On the negative side, there is the cost, which is so high that disaster looms if the product and the advertising aren't appealing enough to draw heavy response. It is little wonder that so much pressure is applied in writing commercials. Also, in contrast to print media, the message, once given, is gone; there is no page to read and reread and no coupon to study and to fill out.

If you write direct response advertising, you find out quickly that the usual offer simply cannot be made in television's standard unit, the 30-second commercial. In fact, you're hard put to do an offer justice in a 60-second commercial. Thus, you may find yourself working with longer units. Very often these units are not available, another handicap for the direct response advertiser, and of course, such a long commercial is discouragingly expensive.

To be able to justify the cost of a 120-second commercial, the item *must* be timely and of wide, certain appeal,

and it should be announced by a trusted figure, such as a famous football player whose sincerity and character were admirably suited for promoting insurance plans in a series of commercials.

A writer of television direct response commercials should, before writing, understand what objectives are sought by the advertiser paying for these commercials. Obviously, many such commercials seek quick, direct sales. Other commercials are more long range. Some, as in the case of insurance plans and policies previously cited, try to build up a prospect list by getting viewers to send or phone for more information. Other commercials simply support advertising appearing in other media such as magazines, newspapers, and direct mail.

Home shopping by television gives the direct response advertiser a huge audience for his messages. More than a half-dozen cable channels now sell, nonstop, a limitless array of goods. Presenters demonstrate the goods forcefully, as anyone who has watched the shopping networks will testify. Considerable pressure is exerted through a push on "buy now," "this offer won't be repeated," and similar phrases. To lure viewers, these channels offer attractive discounts on the merchandise they push.

Radio: Not Perfect, but a Bargain for Direct Response

Radio advertising has produced good, and sometimes outstanding, direct response success stories because of the persuasiveness of good announcers, especially of local announcers known and trusted by radio listeners. Listener loyalty is a significant factor in local advertising.

Radio has other pleasing qualities for the direct response advertiser. It is low in cost and it can be produced far more simply than almost any other medium. It can also be produced quickly, an important factor to the advertiser with a hot, timely item that should be put before prospects while the appeal is the greatest. And radio can give the advertiser same-day delivery.

It takes little perception, however, to see that radio has serious handicaps when used in direct response advertising. Among these are no visualization of the product, no coupon, and the transitory character of the message.

By the time an announcer has tried to describe in words what the product or service is and has then attempted precise and repeated ordering instructions, time will have run out. Thus, except for cost, radio direct response advertising suffers from the same handicaps as television advertising and adds some handicaps of its own.

Vary Your Approach Sharply for Different Media

If the same product were to be advertised in magazines as different as *Town and Country* and *Grit,* your copy would differ not only because your prospects were of a different economic and social status but also because your advertising, to be effective in the medium in which it appears, must conform to the makeup of that type of medium. An advertisement planned, designed, and written for *Grit* will frequently look out of place if used in the *New Yorker,* and vice versa. With few exceptions, an advertisement that is out of its element will not produce successful results.

Assume, similarly, that the same product was being sold by radio or television direct response to different groups of prospects in the same general area. Not only would your programs differ but also your time of broadcast and the stations used. Your copy, likewise, would probably be geared to each group, despite the fact that the basic appeal to each group might be almost the same.

For the moment assume that you are writing commercials for a large retailer of tapes, records, and CDs located in a medium-size midwestern city. The retailer handles a complete line of records, tapes, and disks from all the major recording companies; it does a large direct response business, but it sells at regular retail prices (including postage, however).

It has been decided to push three types of records—classical music, jazz, and country/western. This means that three distinct markets must be reached, perhaps at three different times of the day or week. Depending upon the coverage and listening patterns of your local radio stations, you may use more than one of them to reach your markets.

Your programs will be similar in that all of them will feature recordings (naturally!). Your commercials will also be similar, and yet they will vary widely. Your basic appeal to all three markets is almost certain to hinge on one idea: the convenience of getting any recordings you want without the bother of going to a store. Yet, just as you will vary your programs to appeal to lovers of symphony, to youthful addicts of popular tunes, and to bluegrass devotees, so must you vary the appeal in your commercials to suit the varying situations of your audiences:

- *To the rural audience:* "Shop from your fireside; no need for a special trip to town. And avoid disappointment; our stocks are always complete."

Figure 13–4. Direct response envelope with outside message. Such messages on the envelope build curiosity to see what's inside. In advertising parlance such message carrying envelopes are sometimes called "flashes."

- *To the teenagers:* "Just drop us a note (or fill in an order blank) between classes or in the evening; don't miss that important class meeting, play rehearsal, or basketball game just to come downtown (or into town)."
- *To the serious listener:* "A new concert's just as near as your desk (or your phone—if charge accounts are permitted or C.O.D. deliveries encouraged); avoid a long bus ride, traffic jam, and parking worries downtown."

To everyone, of course, goes the general story of "same-day" service, quality products at standard prices including packing and mailing costs, satisfaction or your money back, and perhaps some sort of a premium with each order of so many dollars.

Most likely, you will write even such "standard" parts of the commercials in a different style and in different words for each audience. If you do, then you've adapted your copy to your media, and other factors being favorable, you should have a set of successful direct response commercials.

Writing for Direct Response Advertising: General Suggestions

Assume that your product is one that can be sold to your prospects and that the medium selected is an effective one for reaching the prospects at low cost. The next question is how to induce those prospects to make purchases. What are you going to do to make the potential customer order?

Figure 13–5. Direct response in the farm field. In keeping with other Dekalb advertisements that you will see in this book, this ad uses a clever headline and illustration. In this one, the company invites orders for its various products numbered on what is called a "menu." Each is described on the back of the advertisement page.

The results depend on how effectively you present the merchandise.

Think like a Retail Merchant

Since you are the salesperson, compare your job with the selling process of the owner of a small specialty shop. First, the shop owner creates an inviting window display to attract the casual shopper or passerby into the store. Assume that the shopper does go in. The shop owner gives the shopper a closeup view of the merchandise; he opens it up or takes it apart, giving a sales talk point by point. He answers the customer's questions and meets all objections. Finally, as the customer is about convinced to buy, he presents his final sales point—the clincher—an irresistible reason for not postponing the purchase. Then, ideally, the customer says, "I'll take it" and lays the cash on the counter.

That's the ideal sale and it is exactly what you hope to do with your direct response offering. Your show window that stops your prospect is your display (in type and illustration) or the opening words of your commercial. Your copy (and detailed views, if any) comprise your closeup of the product and your sales talk.

Next, because you're not face-to-face with the prospect, you have to anticipate what his questions and objections are most likely to be and work the answers into your sales talk (keeping them in a positive vein, of course).

Then, you weave in your clincher—*why it's important or necessary to order now*—frequently a matter of limited supply, a special price for a short time, or perhaps a premium for promptness. To this point, you've pretty well paralleled the retail sales procedure.

At this point, your retail customer would say, "Wrap it up" and dig into his wallet. You'd take his money and hand him the change and his parcel. It's not that simple in direct selling since the customer—the prospect—still has one more step to take on his own. He has to make out his order (perhaps getting out paper, envelope, and a stamp), probably write a check (or quite possibly go to a bank or post office to buy a money order), and then mail the order to your firm.

Not only do you have to make these extra steps simple and easy as possible, but you must also make your whole offer seem so attractive that the customer won't mind the extra work.

The extra attraction you must weave into your copy is difficult to define, but it might be explained by saying that you should write in a somewhat "higher key" so that your copy reads or is heard at a higher pitch. Perhaps some of this is the result of your urge to immediate action. This feeling, nevertheless, is often an integral part of the entire advertisement. Perhaps a careful look at each element of the direct sale will show what's required to give the entire advertisement its high pitch.

Your Headlines Are Show Windows

Headlines are the "show windows"—attention-getters—of your shop. Windows pull prospects into the shop from the sidewalk. Headlines pull prospects into the copy. In this instance, your headline material may be described as any display-size type appearing in the advertisement.

Considered alone, this physical handling (layout) of the headline material imparts a large measure of its high pitch—its aura of urgency. Direct headlines are frequently written in a more exciting style than for usual consumer advertising. They may be *exhortative*, such as:

Save on Farm Income Taxes before April 15th

Look Taller Instantly

Make Beaded SEQUIN Lapel Pins—Easy at Home

Now! Be Stunning in a Rainstorm

Remove Any Stump

Treasure Your Baby's Tooth

Each one is a command to action as well as an appeal to some need or desire.

Others, by brevity alone—a sort of terse *index* quality—impart a feeling of urgency:

Delphinium

New Miracle Wall Cleaner

Feet Hurt?

Gardenia Plants

Orchard Fresh Holly (*for Christmas*)

Wristwatch—Military Style

A third headline type, somewhere between exhortative and index for forcefulness, is the *exclamatory* headline. This is an excited, enthusiastic headline well suited to direct response advertising that creates a sense of urgency and merchandising excitement. Some examples include:

Dazzling duo in solid brass. $19.95 for 2!

Gift of the year. Only $12.95.

World famous tomato sauce now available after 76 years

Not every direct response headline *must* fall into the exhortative, index, or exclamatory types. There *are* other types, and combinations of types, but these are the most common. Some index headings include a selling word or two; others include none, except possibly by inference. Display lines in other advertisements rely primarily on exclamatory sentences or phrases for their excitement.

Two Bushels of Ripe Tomatoes from One Vine

3 Crochet Beauties Easy to Make

Lifetime Knife Cuts Anything

The Oriental Symbol of Power

At Home, Your Own Manufacturing Business

Price Pulls Prospects

Because the majority of people who shop by direct response do so for a real, or imagined, price advantage, a quoted price in the headline is usually your chief attention-getter. Price, as you can see in the following headlines, is a powerful element in the exhortative approach.

Develop your Kodak film for 39¢.

Bathe your body in pure silk. Le Tee $21.

Put an alarm, a stopwatch, and a calculator on your wrist for just $89.

Try our $16 alternative to the $24 button-down.

Remove hair permanently. $19.95.

Even index headlines, not considered so forceful as exhortative headlines, develop much more power when combined, as they often are, with price. Here are some examples:

4 new craft catalogs 25¢.

Pecans! Only $19.95 delivered.

Figure 13–6a. Direct response teaser campaign. Stirring fan excitement before the opening of the hockey season, this advertisement, one in a series, is designed to persuade readers to part with substantial sums for 20-pack, 10-pack or 6-pack of tickets. Each ad includes an order blank like the one at the bottom of this figure. Because fans pay to see their sports heroes in action, the advertisement series features three players and interesting material about each. As each advertisement in the series is published, fans' interest increases for the upcoming season.

Homemaker's garbage disposal wrench $7.99.

Solid brass piano lamp. Only $24.95.

Religious collection 30¢.

Like the exhortative and index headlines, the exclamatory headline can use or not use price, and like the others, it's a stronger headline when it *can* use price. Some examples include:

You'll never get a better offer. 5 pieces, $9.95.

Each magnificent panel is only $3.00.

Imagine this handsome crystal pendant for only $1.50!

You Can Imply Price

An attractive price directly in a headline always attracts attention, but occasionally you may want to suggest that the prospect is getting a good price without stating it directly. If so, you imply a good price or a good saving. Examples:

The quality alternative to high-cost inflatables.

Sew it together and *save!*

Shoes! At direct-from-the-factory-to-you prices!

In these examples, you see price implied in the direct-from-the-factory point, the do-it-yourself-and-save appeal, and the appeal of a lower-cost alternative.

Catalogs and Direct Mail: Readers Are Interested

Most of the examples you've read of direct response advertising have been from publication advertising, but just about all of them would be suitable for direct-mail pieces or catalogs. These latter two have an advantage, however. In the case of the direct-mail pieces, readers are not dividing their attention, as they do in reading publications, between many competing advertisements and editorial matter. In the case of catalogs, interest is already assumed, or the readers wouldn't be opening the catalog in the first place.

In such cases, unless price, or perhaps something essentially emotional, is your basic appeal, you will probably use material for your major display that tells some pertinent fact about your product, or identifies it categorically, and includes at least a mention of one or two of its features.

If you do copy for catalogs issued by the smaller organizations, you'll probably find yourself writing exhortative and exclamatory headlines that are just as forceful as any used in publications direct response advertising. As the long usage indicates, this approach is effective for the prospects of these catalogs.

There has been a trend in recent years for catalog copy to take a quieter tone, especially in the catalogs published by the giant mail-order houses. Index headings have increased. Where they are not used, the headlines resemble the kind of writing used by national advertisers in newspaper advertisements. Here are some catalog headlines that demonstrate the more subdued, clipped style:

Top carrier saves space; more comfort inside your car.

Flexible shafts—many tools in one.

Wash your window while you drive.

Much warmer—double-woven wool fleece overcoats.

Fine bags *can* be low priced.

You Can Assume Catalog Readers Are Definitely Prospects

Although you work hard to attract the attention of catalog readers, you can assume that they are more truly prospects than the casual readers of magazine advertisements. Catalog readers may already be customers, or they may want to be. The fact that they are reading the catalog is evidence of this.

Furthermore, they are usually in a buying mood—at least for a certain type of product. When they turn to that item, then what you've said in your display headings about the product focuses their attention more sharply on it or its features. But if your display fails to interest them, they may turn to your competitor's catalog.or decide to go to a store to shop.

Although lacking competition for attention, you still have competition for the order. What you say in your headlines (or in major subheads if the main heading is essentially the index type) and in your other display lines may well affect the prospect's interest and, in turn, influence his decision to purchase from you.

Direct Approach Is Usually Best in Direct Response Advertising

Almost all direct response display copy is direct and to the point. You tell something immediately about the product or the results of its use or application. Consider, for example, the following:

Develop a torso the girls will admire!

Quick-drying, one-coat flat oil paint—one coat looks like two!

You can communicate the same information less directly. For example:

The girls never even used to look twice at me on the beach.

You wouldn't think one coat of paint could make such a difference in a room!

However, you would never write a headline for a direct response muscle-building course that says, "I'd Rather Stay Home with a Book," or for one-coat wall paint that reads, "I Never Enjoyed Entertaining the Smiths until Tonight." You certainly wouldn't use these as major display lines for direct response selling. They *aren't* direct response selling. They may represent a technique suitable for a campaign in which you hope to build up an impression over a period of time, but a direct response sale, nine times out of ten, is an *immediate sale*—often even an impulse sale.

As you rough out your first draft of copy, the first caption you write may be just as indirect as the last two examples. If so, you'll find yourself hastening almost automatically to add a second display line that tells something much more meaty about your product or the *direct* advantages of its use. Next, you discover that you can either eliminate the first line entirely or at least incorporate its basic idea merely as a minor lead-in element of the second line. It will then be likely that you've written a display line that's a real stopper; you've set up a "show window" that brings the prospect right into your "store."

Radio Direct Response Has Show Windows, Too

If your commercial is used on a very distinctive program, you have a sort of built-in show window. But many commercials are not written for any particular program, and certainly not for a distinctive program. You must, accordingly, *create* a show window. This can sometimes be done with music and sound effects or with an unusual voice. Most of the time, however, you'll create your own show window with attention-getting, arresting words and phrases. You may use the direct approach previously mentioned as effective in catalog advertising. Examples of the direct approach include:

Joggers—here's a tip for better performance.

Gardeners—now you can haul big loads without effort.

Collectors—learn how to spot genuine values every time.

For a less direct approach, there are many phrases that can be used:

Here's good news ...

At last, there's an answer to ...

Everyone's a winner when he ...

If you want a new experience, try...

Getting in a rut? Here's how to get out.

There's a surefire way to ...

The first words in a radio message are important because the average radio listeners are paying only partial attention, or no attention, to the commercials. You need to pull them out of their indifference. Jar them to wakefulness with a statement that makes it clear that it might be profitable to listen to what the announcer is saying.

Ways to Hold the Attention of Listeners

As in print, you want the show window of your commercial to do more than merely arouse attention. You want it to inspire interest as well—listener interest sufficient to hold attention throughout your message. So, immediately following your stopper phrase or sentences, you write into your next sentence or sentences, some idea or thought that will be of interest to the largest group of prospects among your listeners.

This opening thought is the "display" of your commercial. See how these sample opening lines, all of them from successful direct response commercials, are written to hold the attention of the greatest number of potential prospects for the offers that follow:

Friends, the selection you just heard, and *any others* you hear on the _____ *(an evening-long program with several co-*

sponsors), can be bought from _____'s CDs-by-Mail. It's the new, easy way for you to buy the compact disks you want. ...

Ladies ... Here's how you can easily win a complete five-piece bedroom set, a portable electric Singer Sewing Machine, and 101 additional valuable prizes ... *(quilt-patch bundle offer, a contest entry blank accompanying each bundle ordered)*

Folks, due to a very special purchase, the makers of the national advertised _____ combination cigarette case and lighter ... for a limited time only ... will send you a remarkable three-dollar-ninety-five-cent value ... at the rock bottom bargain price of only *one*-dollar-ninety-eight!

Wouldn't you be thrilled to win a new minivan or equivalent in cash, just by taking part in a simple, interesting game? ... *(contest sponsored by rural magazine; each contest entry to be accompanied by $1 for magazine subscription order)*

Say, what musical instrument do you think is the easiest and quickest to learn to play? *(harmonica offer)*

An extra display line—an additional attention-getter—may be inserted occasionally in the middle of your commercials just in case interest in your message lags a bit after the first excitement has subsided. This is akin to a prominent subhead or second display line. About a third of the way through the commercial for the cigarette case/lighter combination, for example, we find, "But that's just the *first* half of this sensational offer! Second, you will receive the world's smallest ballpoint pen, complete with key chain!" Here, the advertiser has reserved part of his offering for use as a midway "headline."

You will write headlines and subheads into your radio direct response selling for the same reason that you would decorate the show window of your specialty shop. And you'd set up supplementary displays inside to attract and hold your prospect's attention and interest until he hears your complete message and decides to make the purchase.

These are not passive headlines and subheads. They're active, vigorous messages that inform, excite, move to action, and literally pull the listeners along. The subhead comes into its own in mail-order and direct mail.

Unlike so much of non-direct-response magazine and newspaper advertising that uses no subheads, the direct response advertising—no matter what the medium—uses subheads generously. Long copy will never put your prospect to sleep if it's broken up with lively subheads.

Ordering Instructions: A Big Problem on Direct Response Radio

Examine the ordering page for any catalog and note its detailed instructions about how to pay, what to add for shipping and handling, what color and sizes are wanted, and so forth. Now think of yourself writing a direct response radio commercial.

You've been told again and again to end almost any kind of advertising with a call for action. Usually, this amounts to no more than a suggestion that something be done, such as looking for the item, inspecting it, or calling for more information.

How much detail can you include when giving ordering instructions in radio? Very little. This limitation, along with radio's lack of a product visual, accounts for radio advertising not being a high choice for most direct response advertisers.

What happens if you attempt to give full ordering instructions in your radio commercial? With an eye on your word count, you must sacrifice words that otherwise could be devoted to product sell and description.

There is no truly satisfactory answer to this dilemma. Usually, you are better off *not* attempting *full* instructions. Keep them to a minimum and, on local radio, urge customers to phone the establishment offering the product or services; on the national level, give an 800 number that consumers can call for complete instructions. In short, radio can typically do only part of the job of supplying instructions.

Follow-Ups and Your Part in Them

After inquiry is made, follow-up mailings should go out as soon as possible. Studies show that each day of delay causes a lower inquiry-to-sale conversion rate. After this first follow-up, the next one will typically be made in about two weeks. Continued follow-ups will then go on for as long as they are profitable.

Consider the explosion in the use of 800 numbers. When a prospect uses the number, you may become involved in these telemarketing phone calls. When the call comes in for information, every effort is usually made to convert that desire for information into an order. As the writer, you may well be called upon to write a reply script for the person who is talking to the prospect who has used the 800 number. In a sense, that script is another form of follow-up.

A phone script can be a real challenge. Unlike a one-way communication, as in radio or television commercials, you're writing a conversation in which you anticipate certain questions and answer them appropriately.

In doing this, the script should be written as people speak, not in the same way as copy that is created to be read. In such writing, you put yourself in the mind of the person on the other end of the line and think about how he or she is mentally "seeing" the words that you're speaking. Take the word "complement" as an example. First, not everyone understands the meaning of this word when they see it in print. This misunderstanding becomes even more acute when they hear the word over the phone and confuse it with "compliment," a word they are more likely to know. This topic of word confusion is considered again in Chapter 19 on radio advertising.

Furthermore, any communication delivered over the phone—or elsewhere for that matter—should always think in the prospect's terms. An example is the claim that "our rates are extremely affordable." This is a subjective judgment. What is affordable to the speaker might not be affordable to the person on the other end of the phone. A change to "our rates are modest" might be better.

Likewise, consider such insurance jargon as "lump-sum payout." Why not change to "single payment"? Each business activity has its own jargon or set of pet phrases. Avoid such talk over the phone and over the air. As a writer of over-the-telephone scripts, try for utmost clarity in every word you put down.

CHAPTER 14

Direct Response
A Quick Test of Your Message's Effectiveness (Part B)

"Writing direct response copy's like fishing," said Fred Currie to his luncheon companion as they gnawed on crisp bagels at their favorite bistro. "Look," he continued, "in fishing, the bait you use is everything. If you toss out the wrong bait for the wrong fish, you don't get a nibble. The same thing is true with direct response—what you offer is vital. That offer must be right for your market—no rap CDs to classical purists."

Having washed down a big mouthful, Fred said, "And timing is just about as important. A canny angler knows that certain fish hit the lures, or ignore them, in certain seasons or even at certain times of the day.

"Everyone in direct response," he concluded, "times offers to months or seasons."

"But," his companion asked, "where does <u>writing</u> come into this fishing analogy?" Fred replied: "A fly fisherman uses a delicate touch in flicking out a Royal Coachman. It's an art that brings fish to the surface, just as skillful writing in direct response makes the offer irresistible. End of analogy."

You Don't Hold Back in Direct Response

Unlike most other forms of advertising, you go all out in direct response advertising. You often write explosive headlines. You write full copy in which you tell your whole story (not like a 30-second TV commercial) and then you ask for the order. If you fail to get that order, your efforts are wasted—unlike much national advertising, which reminds, identifies, or builds prestige and image, not orders. When you do that *complete* job, you're like a worker on an auto assembly line who turns out an entire vehicle, not just a part. You feel good about yourself.

Because you're not constrained by time restrictions, as in a 30-second television commercial or a small-space print advertisement, this kind of advertising can be more fun. In addition, you can reach in your writing grab bag for colorful words and phrases and even little stories about the products or services you're selling. A glance at any J. Peterman catalog demonstrates the creative freedom enjoyed by the direct response writer. And it's obvious that the Lands' End writers enjoy what they're doing, too.

Let's Talk About Catalogs

In the early days, the word "catalog" meant Sears Roebuck and Montgomery Ward to millions of Americans. Today, more than 10,000 catalogs flood the mails; selling anything from flashlights to his-and-her airplanes. Many more hard-selling catalogs are unleashed in the Christmas season by such big retailers as Bloomingdale's, Neiman Marcus, and Marshall Field's. Surprisingly, even the Metropolitan Museum of Art issues more than a million catalogs each year.

Just as in advertising in other media, your appeal in catalog copy is based on the product's ability to satisfy the desires of your prospects. One difference, however, is that catalog copy is "tell-all" copy. This means that you imagine all the ways in which your item can answer the wants or desires of your prospects, and then you include as many of these ways as possible in your message. Your hope is that you will thus interest the majority of your potential customers.

As previously mentioned, few advertisements in general media such as newspapers, magazines, or television offer an opportunity for tell-all copy, but then such advertisements are not usually expected to do the entire selling task. Tell-all copy requires space; it relies on a willingness on the part of readers to read a long copy message. Catalog readers have that willingness. Furthermore, they will read a message in print much smaller than that used in the usual general media advertisement.

Although the emphasis in these chapters is on consumers reached by direct response advertising, it would be a mistake not to mention the selling of products business-to-business using catalogs and mailings. This is a huge activity that involves selling such items as office supplies, business and technical books, safety products, computer-related products, business gifts, and an endless array of other items.

Chapters 16 and 17 discuss ways to write to the business, professional, and farm fields. Most of what is said in those chapters applies to the kind of writing that is used in business-to-business direct response advertising in catalogs and mailings. This means, in general, factual, no-nonsense writing that avoids the gimmicks, flamboyant techniques, cute phrases, and overly personal writing seen in consumer advertising. Some such catalogs would be viewed as dull by consumer standards, but if they sell the products, so be it.

While most business magazine advertisements these days use 800 numbers, they are not usually classed in the direct response category because their primary aim is not to develop mail order sales but simply to provide more information.

Three Broad Suggestions for Writing Catalog Copy

First, hard-sell is the norm in catalog copy. Soft-sell is rare. Those pages, or those square inches of space, are expected to produce sales. Woe to you if they don't.

Second, there are vast differences in catalog copy, from the somewhat unemotional copy of J. Crew, L. L. Bean, and Hammacher Schlemmer to the bouncy, irrepressible copy of Lands' End. Thus, you might be a sensation when writing for one type of catalog and a failure when writing for another.

Third, the word "clarity" assumes a new meaning when you write catalog copy. Because your reader is going to make a buying decision based on your writing, you must write words that simply cannot be misinterpreted. When you deal with people in large numbers, you learn that they have a sort of twisted genius in their ability to misread what seems to be clear writing. Our task is to reduce those misinterpretations significantly; you'll never eliminate them totally.

Fit Copy Style to the Catalog's Readers

Tell-all copy can be dull if you simply give every product fact without embellishment. You've been told that direct response copy is *complete* copy. This is true no matter who your prospects are. But the style in which you convey all those product points makes the difference between sparkle and dullness. Just what *is* style? It's the mood, impression, or character of the copy that varies from company to company and from writer to writer.

One way for you to understand this matter of fitting style to prospects, and hence to the advertiser, is for you to closely examine examples of catalog advertising as executed by two outstanding catalog advertisers: L. L. Bean and Lands' End. What makes these examples especially valuable for your analysis is that the styles are radically different, yet each is highly effective.

In the following example from the L. L. Bean catalog you see sincere, straightforward copy—the direct, uncomplicated talk of one outdoorsman to another. As you read, you may ask: "But where's the excitement? Those are index headlines. What about highlighting major selling points? And what about those small pictures?"

The answer is that this copy is written for a specialty catalog for hunters and outdoorsmen. Here's one case, admittedly a rather exceptional one, where, because of the limited appeal of the class of merchandise, the field of prospects is limited, too. Almost everyone reading this catalog reads nearly every listing on practically every page. Because this catalog enjoys this unique advantage, its manner of obtaining attention and maintaining interest in itself and in its offerings is not as apparent as in other publications.

Another advantage that eliminates the need for any specifically stated claims of quality or value is the reputation of the firm and the integrity behind the name L. L. Bean, which has become synonymous over a period of years with a good buy at a fair price.

These are things not easy to acquire, and lucky is the catalog copywriter in such a situation. Of course, it should also be noted that this firm does not seem to be overly anxious to expand its list of prospects greatly. Therein, perhaps, lies part of the reason for the seeming lack of the more aggressive selling that is usually considered normal for any merchandising house.

Despite its nonflamboyant style, the copy sells hard. There is a simple directness that is persuasive and disarming.

Notice, too, the clear-cut, simple explanations that tell all. There is conviction in these words—much more than most "hard-hitting" copy would achieve in pages of superlatives. This is intelligent copy. Much of it has been written by people who have tried most of the products in the fields and woods. For these specialized products, offered through this unique medium, to this definite group of prospects, this copy is appropriate.

Longer Squall Parka
has weather protection
built into every cozy
nook and cranny.
Now in eight great colors!

Figure 14–1. Direct response catalog advertising. As you see, Lands' End copy employs an easy-to-read style. Notice, also, the attention to product details. Full buying information is provided. *Courtesy Lands' End, Inc.*

An oddity of the L. L. Bean copy is that it seems to appeal equally to the backwoodsman and to the sophisticated city dweller who escapes to the woods for weekends. In fact, the L. L. Bean company has been the subject of many admiring comments in the *New Yorker* magazine and runs advertising—advertising written in the same simple style found in the company's catalogs—steadily in that urbane publication.

Now, to demonstrate a contrast to the L. L. Bean style, review the Lands' End copy. Examine the examples closely. This Wisconsin organization writes advertisements that carry out the principles for successful catalog copy.

Elements of Direct Response Copy as Shown in Lands' End Catalogs

- Tell-all copy that answers every question a prospect might have.
- Challenging and different main headlines.
- Strong main subheads that amplify the main headline (not used in *every* advertisement).
- Occasional use of strong selling subheads that lead the reader through long copy.
- Personal writing that is breezy and conversational and reaches out in a warm, friendly manner.
- Vivid, interesting writing that is never humdrum and is always *enthusiastic*.

- Clear ordering instructions and a no-questions-asked return policy.

Now that you've seen these contrasting styles, you may be puzzled. Do the index, or label, headlines of L. L. Bean contrast unfavorably with the power-packed, more interesting headlines of Lands' End?

Many catalog authorities would say they do, but once more we get back to this piece of advice: Fit your style to the catalog's prospects. L. L. Bean's customers like and respond to the index headlines, just as they respond to the less colorful copy underneath those headlines.

In both cases, however, the writers pack the beginning and middle of the copy with the most important facts and information and then follow with material that could be cut, if necessary. This technique is somewhat reminiscent of the newswriter who puts the who-what-when-where-why in the lead and writes the rest of his story so that it can be cut at any point without making the story an incomplete unit.

Last, as is the case with all successful catalog advertisers, both companies have made the writing of ordering instructions a precise art. These instructions, given in a separate section of the catalog, are detailed, clear, and reassuring to persons inexperienced in direct response advertising.

How to Write Direct Response Copy for Magazines

Most of what has been said about writing for catalogs applies to magazines. Obviously, the tell-all principle cannot be applied so literally because of space limitations and the fact that type size in magazine advertisements is bigger than in catalog advertisements.

As in catalogs, the copy is written to appeal to as many prospects as possible without scattering the message so broadly that it hits no one. Unless the publication itself is limited in circulation to one class of people, your display will have to do the job of attracting the attention and arousing the interest of the particular field of prospects to whom you are writing.

Despite having been warned that tell-all copy is not quite as comprehensive in magazines as it is in catalogs, don't be afraid to write long copy when doing a magazine advertisement.

Long-copy direct response advertisements very often outpull short-copy advertisements, but follow these suggestions if you want your long copy to be successful: (1) Use facts and figures; (2) Avoid general statements; (3) Write interestingly; and (4) Break up long copy passages with strong, selling subheads. (Persons writing magazine advertising too often forget to insert those subheads.)

Next, we come to *proof.* Even more than in catalog copy, it is necessary to provide proof of your claims to convince readers and to get them to act. A catalog can offer introductory pages to build its stature and reliability and, thus, the reader's confidence in the products it describes.

Figure 14–2. Direct response magazine advertisement. This informal headline and conversational copy are typical of Lands' End's successful advertising. *Courtesy Lands' End, Inc.*

Furthermore, after the catalog has been issued for a number of years, it achieves such a reputation for integrity that people know that the products advertised in the catalog will live up to the claims that are made. Proof is still supplied, but in catalog advertising it is, in a sense, simply added insurance.

Your magazine advertisement, in contrast, must supply proof of claims as a vital ingredient, especially if the advertiser is not well known or the product is new, unusual, expensive, or complicated. Here's how to present that proof.

Eight Ways to Support Claims in Magazine Advertising

1. *Testimonials or favorable statements.* A straightforward testimonial delivered by a credible user in a credible way is fine proof. The more specific, the better. Even if you only have a favorable statement, you'll convince the doubters. If you have the space, you might include several such statements from users.

2. *Performance of product under demanding (seemingly impossible) conditions.* Let's say your product is a steel storage box that safeguards valuable documents in the home. Two pictures, perhaps three, show the results of a home fire that consumed everything but the box. The box is opened after the fire. Behold, the contents are unscathed. You don't need many words if you have such pictures. Without the pictures, a strongly worded account can *still* supply proof of your fireproofing claims.

3. *Performance of product under controlled conditions.* Although laboratory tests are sometimes viewed with cynicism, if the tests are genuine and the laboratory is respected, they still convince many persons. Certainly, if the laboratory test is honest, it constitutes genuine proof.

4. *Figures and facts given by authorities.* Authorities are everywhere: doctors and dentists in the professions; scientists and engineers in the technical world; and athletes and coaches in the sports field. Your copy should make it clear that these individuals are voicing opinions not only as experts but, most importantly, as *disinterested* experts who have nothing to gain from their opinions. Such opinions are enough proof for many of your readers.

5. *Official recognition.* Your company's hybrid seed corn or animal feed won the gold medal at the state fair, or your flour won the bake-off at a home crafts show. Because the product won out over many rival products, you have proof of its superior qualities.

6. *Details of materials, ingredients, workmanship or design.* Unless you're careful, this approach can be boring. If written interestingly and enthusiastically, you may be supplying all the proof needed. A sportsman will devour details of the workmanship in a deep-sea fishing reel. A homemaker reads with interest the information about the design of a new food processor that prepares vegetables or meat. Many products—from clothes to garden carts, or stopwatches to reducing remedies—cannot be sold without giving details.

7. *History, reputation, or background of supplier.* You're almost forced to supply this information occasionally. Although many will already be acquainted with the firm, there are always new prospects who must learn.

    Sometimes, the history is the story of the founder of the firm, especially in the case of a picturesque individual such as L. L. Bean who, at the beginning of his operation, was said to have personally tried out every outdoor item offered by the firm.

    Whatever route you take, individual or impersonal, at some point you will build up the supplier as proof that the goods you describe have an honorable heritage.

8. *Money-back guarantee.* Although this has been abused, and sometimes mocked, it is still regarded as proof that the advertiser has confidence in the product offered.

    Some companies have not made it very easy to "get your money back if not completely satisfied," but nevertheless, most buyers are comforted by the presence of the phrase.

    When a firm achieves a towering reputation, it may not be so necessary for you to hammer this money-back assurance, but always use it for a little-known firm, especially if the product is the type about which readers might be skeptical.

Ask for the Order and Make It Urgent

You've read elsewhere in this book (and you'll read it again and again) how important it is to ask for the order. The super salesperson is the one who is a good "closer," the kind of person who, with vigor and persuasiveness, gets the prospect to sign the order to say, "Yes, I'll take it."

Be a "closer" in all of your direct response advertising. In magazine advertisements there are certain procedures you can follow. Asking for the order is handled more forcefully in direct response copy than in most other advertising (where you merely ask for some future action, perhaps no more than inviting the reader to visit a store to see the advertised product).

You're actually asking for action *now* or *today* in direct response advertising. You're asking the reader to get out a checkbook, to phone an order, or to give a credit card number. You're asking for buying action that very minute. Usually, your action suggestion is at, or near, the bottom of the copy, but you can make action suggestions throughout the text material and save the biggest push for the end.

Ways to Get Ordering Action in Direct Response Advertising[1]

Describe special nature of offer

If the offer *is* special, that fact should be made clear immediately. Normally, the special nature of the offer will be associated closely with the bargain the product or service represents. An example:

> Our burglar-proof system, used by thousands of businesses, has just been modified for home use. This means that you can now enjoy complete protection in your home—professional protection at a price you didn't think was possible.

Caution that price will go up or show savings because price has come down

A canny direct response person never forgets that the overwhelming reason for such shopping is to get a good product at a money-saving price. This can work two ways: (1) You do the prospect a favor by giving a warning of an imminent price hike, or (2) You reverse this by offering a reduced price because the firm made a good deal in its buying and is now passing on the saving, one that may never occur again. Some examples:

Warning of price hike:

- 14K gold chains $10 until Aug. 31.
- You'll never see such a low price again.
- This low price good only until May 1.
- Order today before the price goes up.
- This bargain price is going-going-GONE by Sept. 30.

Introducing the softest, coziest, most comfortable clothes we've ever offered.

Figure 14–3. Direct response catalog advertising.

Offering of reduced price:

> You may wonder why we offer these religious artifacts at even lower prices than last year. The reason is simple. Two months ago our buyer located a veritable treasurehouse of these artifacts. He bought the lot at huge savings, which we can now pass on to you. Savings such as you'll never see again.

Warn that there's a limit to time or supply

Prospective purchasers can get almost panicky when they learn that only a limited supply of a product is available or that they might miss out on a bargain by not acting quickly. This "limited time" or "limited supply" approach is one of your most powerful weapons in direct response copy. It's especially suitable to magazines because catalog copy seldom talks of limited supply. That's not the way catalog houses do business. Some examples:

- Offer expires Oct. 31.
- Limit 1 per customer.
- Limited time only!
- Limited one to a family.
- Offer good while they last.

---

[1] Obviously, some of these suggestions can be used in other media, too.

Figure 14–4. Direct response catalog page. No catalog is better known than the one L. L. Bean has been issuing for years—a catalog famed for its honesty and down-to-earth style. Over time the company has widened the line but it still features outdoor equipment for hunting and fishing enthusiasts without fancy headlines or flamboyant copy. Index headlines and simple copy are suited to the tastes of loyal L. L. Bean customers. With L. L. Bean you get what you see, and that accounts for the great success of this company that has become an American institution. *Reproduced by permission of L. L. Bean.*

Use action-inducing words

From the beginning to the end of direct response copy, strong, exciting, and moving words should be used. This is not calm, reflective prose. You must push to action people who find it easier *not* to act. Some examples.

- Rush name and address.
- Order this exciting new catalog now.
- Don't delay. Why miss out on even one day's fun?
- Act *now!*

Stress benefit of acting quickly

Delay is fatal. A prospect who puts off an ordering decision is too often a lost prospect. Give this person a reward for quick action and you may turn that word "prospect" into "customer." Some examples:

- Order now and save $2.
- Orders received by Oct. 1 earn this low $15 price.
- Earn a bonus for answering before May 31.

Offer money-back guarantee

Just as the money-back guarantee is proof of your confidence in your product, so it is the final convincing argument for quick action on the part of the prospect. It can erase the last, lingering doubt. Sometimes the guarantee is headlined, but normally it's placed at the bottom of the copy. An example:

You be the judge. If this unit isn't what you expected it to be in your 30-day trial period, return it undamaged for a no-questions-asked refund.

Use a coupon and urge reader to act upon it

Every readership study shows that coupons increase advertising readership. They also increase the number of sales and inquiries that you may expect. Unless you're very tight for space, you should stress the coupon in the copy, usually in the vicinity of the coupon. In the coupon itself, you should make the offer sound exciting and present the filling out of the coupon quickly as an absolute-must action. Some examples:

- For your peace of mind, fill out and mail this coupon today.
- Rush coupon now while this great offer lasts.
- To be sure to receive your free catalog, mail coupon now. It will open a new, exciting world.

You'll read elsewhere in this book about the construction of coupons, but the point is so important that some repetition is called for. Tips to remember: (1) Call attention to the coupon in some way, such as by using a distinctive border, tinting the writing area, or employing an attractive type style; (2) If the advertisement is in a business magazine, ask for the respondent's title and firm name; (3) Use generous spacing between lines so respondents don't need to squeeze their writing; and (4) Make lines long enough for name and address. Most of all, be sure that there's room for the city name because of the great variation in such names.

Direct Response Copy for Department Stores

If you write copy that is aimed at persuading department store customers to order by mail or phone, you'll find yourself providing full information. Bill enclosures are a common vehicle for such copy. Here are two examples:

Outstanding Value …
Wonderful Wool Sweaters for men $50 each
Two-ply French zephyr worsted … that's tops in wool! These handsome sweaters are firmly knit, and sized generously. Knit tapes at neck and shoulders reinforce the seams they allow to

stretch. Lightweight, warm, in colors for fall: tan, maize, blue, gray, or green. Small (38), medium (42), and large (46).

Blue, pink, or white wool for your little lamb! Baby blankets $19.95 each.

Keep baby warm in his transfers from bath to bed with this soft blanket. It's made in a lovely weave that is exclusive with our baby-pampering department! It has a deep fringe that actually will not tangle, thanks to an entirely new finish. Big enough for a crib ... 40 by 48 inches.

Notice how many more factual details are included in these pieces of selling copy than would normally appear in a department store's newspaper advertisement for the same merchandise. Yet the facts are not just listed. Their importance is emphasized and their meaning is expanded by an occasional, well-chosen word or phrase that does more than merely tell the reader something—it sells him on the merits of the item. The sweater is not "all wool," it's "worsted,"—"Two-ply French zephyr worsted" at that.

Yet the copy doesn't leave it to your knowledge or imagination to make even this categorized description of the material suffice. It doesn't dare, because the store knows that among its many customers are some who aren't acquainted with this type of wool or who may not get the full implication of its quality by merely reading even this impressive description. It says in so many words that two-ply French zephyr worsted is "tops in wool!"

What's more, it recognizes that two common faults of sweaters are unwanted snugness and a tendency to stretch out of shape, especially around the neck and across the shoulders. Thus, next to the size listings at the end of the copy, it tells you that these sweaters are "sized generously," yet "firmly knit" and "knit tapes at neck and shoulders reinforce the seams they allow to stretch." These are now good, positive, product selling points specifically included to answer possible questions and objections by the store's prospects.

So, too, with the baby blanket. The copywriter knows that some of the more experienced shoppers among the prospects may shy away from a fringed baby blanket. The necessarily frequent launderings may do things to fringe that make it unattractive, but this blanket definitely has fringe, as the illustrations show.

Does the copy ignore that possible objection? It does not. It turns the objection into an advantage: "deep fringe that actually will not tangle, thanks to an entirely new finish." The fringe becomes another selling point.

Ordering Instructions for Printed Direct Response Advertising

Magazine, newspaper, catalog, and department store advertisers all face the problem of making ordering instructions so clear and simple that the prospect overcomes a natural reluctance to bother with the inconvenience of ordering by mail. To many persons, any mail communication is a dreaded chore. Following are some of

Figure 14–5. Direct response catalog page. Notice the full details that answer every question of potential buyers. *Reproduced by permission of L. L. Bean.*

the specifics you'll need to know about setting up the ordering process for mail response.[2]

How do you make ordering simple, easy, or even inviting? There is no single way applicable to all direct response selling, but listed below are the three principal methods of encouraging or inviting the order by mail:

- An order blank (perhaps with an addressed, postage-guaranteed envelope).
- A return postcard (always self-addressed and usually, today, with postage guaranteed) and coupons.
- Advertisements without coupons that contain mere statements of ordering requirements and mailing address.

Obviously, the first two are definitely *ordering aids*. They remove some of the burden imposed upon the purchaser by the fact that he can't just hand you his money and carry off his purchase. The third relieves the purchaser of none of the effort required to place an order. Which method should you use? The major consideration is your medium. Catalogs, for example, usually include an order blank, perhaps several, to encourage frequent ordering. Direct mail-order offerings frequently have a return postcard enclosed. The coupon is commonly part of a direct response advertisement in a publication. Ordering infor-

---

[2] Use of toll-free numbers is discussed separately.

mation alone is usually used in printed advertisements too small to accommodate coupons and in radio commercials. Each of these methods will be discussed in detail in the following sections.

Order Blanks

Order blanks usually are the most elaborate of the methods used to invite orders. Because they normally accompany catalogs, more than one type of item may be—and usually is—ordered on one blank. This means that often different kinds of information may be required for each item: color; pattern; finish; initials (for monograms); width; length; size; model; price each, per pair, or per set; and so on.

General merchandise houses have many regular customers ordering several times a season or year; thus, they must keep up-to-date information on customers' addresses.

Because they sell on several different sets of terms—cash, time-payment accounts, open accounts, and credit cards are the most common—the payment method must be recorded on the order blank. Spaces are provided for such details.

A choice of shipment methods must be provided on the blank. Then, allowance must be made for catalog numbers, quantity ordered, name and shipping weight of each item, and, as required, totals on the weights, prices, postage, and taxes.

Coupons and Return Postcards

Coupons and postcards are similar to each other, although the customary difference in their sizes may at first mask the resemblance. A study of their mutual requirements will show their similarity.

Very frequently both return postcards and coupons include some inducement for prompt reply, often in addition to any such urge previously incorporated into the accompanying advertisement. One of the most common is some variation of the magic word "free":

Free Examination Postcard

Free 10-Day Trial Coupon!

Free Sample

Free Catalog

Don't Wait—Send Coupon Today for Approval Offer

Good for Both Free

As a rule, these inducements are in some sort of display type—quite often in a "reverse" panel—but sometimes they may be set in relatively small type, especially in small coupons. Other typical incentives for ordering include variations of the common "Mail This Coupon Today!" and others a little more original, like:

Clip This Coupon—Mail Today

Order with This Handy Coupon

We Accept Your Invitation

Mail This Card to Secure Your Copy

Complete Crochet Library—Only 10¢ a Book

Get the Facts by Mail

Mail Opportunity Coupon for Quick Action

Phone—Wire—Use Coupon

This Certificate Saves You $3

All of these, of course, besides urging prompt action, call attention to the coupon (or card). To accomplish a similar purpose, an arrow or eye-directing device is sometimes incorporated into the advertising layout, although nowadays many layout artists tend to scorn such "corny" treatment. They prefer to accomplish the same result more subtly by designing the entire piece to lead the eye "naturally" through the steps of the selling process, ending logically with the final step—the action-inducing coupon.

Another feature that most return postcards and advertisement coupons share is the inclusion of some sort of statement to make them more personal, as if the purchaser had written them himself. The one with which you are undoubtedly most familiar is "Please send me ...," or any of its close relatives, followed by a brief restatement of the offer made in the mailing piece or advertisement, again usually phrased in the first person.

Offer a Choice of Ways to Pay

Common also to both return postcard and coupon order forms is not merely a restatement of the price but a provision for stating the method of payment chosen. Even where no choice is offered, this is included as a precaution against any misunderstanding by the purchaser.

The following illustrations of typical wordings (most of them self-explanatory as to the terms offered) will show you how such statements may be handled:

❏ Charge My Account; ❏ Find Check or M.O. Enclosed. Please include 3% sales tax on orders in (*state*).

❏ Money Order or check; ❏ Charge My Account. (Please do not send currency or stamps.)

Check for _____ enclosed. No. C.O.D.'s
Check ❏ I am enclosing $_____. Ship Postpaid.
One ❏ Ship C.O.D. I'll pay postman $_____ plus postage.

Please send me the books checked, at 25¢ each. Enclose _____.

Mail (*Title of book set*) on 7 days' free trial. If O.K. I will remit $1 in 7 days and $1 monthly until $6 is paid. Otherwise I will return them. No obligation unless I am satisfied.

Within ten days I will either return the books and owe nothing, or send you $1.50 and the $2.00 a month for three months until the special price of $7.50, plus postage, is paid.

❑ Check here if you send the full price of $7.50 with this card. We will pay the postage. Same return privilege and refund if you're not satisfied.

Enclosed is 25¢ (in coin) and the top of a package or sack of your _____. Please send me one of _____.

Total enclosed	Or please charge to my
$_____	account
Bank #____ ____ ____	• Visa
	• MasterCard
Account No. _____	Expiration date_____

Many cards and coupons offer return privileges "without obligation," or perhaps a "free trial" offer, restated in the body of the card or coupon, to make sure the purchaser understands that his signature does not obligate him finally and irrevocably to buy.

Other Details, Such As Keying and Addressing

All return postcards and coupons include the name and address of the seller. The cards, of course, always have them printed on the address side of the card and sometimes repeat them on the order side for the prestige they may lend the offer. The coupons include them primarily to ensure that the purchaser has an accurate address for use on the envelope in which he sends the coupon.

One other use is to test the response to the publication in which an advertisement appears or the returns on each of several mailing lists the seller may be renting. This may be done by "keying" the address. Frequently, this key is a fictitious "department" designation.

For instance, suppose you are running the same advertisement in the magazines *Farm Journal* and *Successful Farming* and want to test their relative effectiveness in securing orders. You make the coupon the same in both publications except for the department in the address, which you would most likely designate as "Dept. FJ" and "Dept. SF," respectively.

As for the customer's name and address, illegibility is such a problem that you'll probably use the common request, "Please print." The form and space you provide for the purchaser's address may vary with the classes or groups of people who are expected to respond.

If they are city folks, for example, you'll most likely ask for *street and number* (and perhaps *apartment number*) *city, state, and zip.* In addition, you may want other information about the purchaser.

• Mr., Mrs., Miss, Ms.? (One to circle).
• Date of birth? (Often omitted).
• Own a car? What make? What model? What year?
• Homeowner or renter?
• Carry insurance? On self? On house? On car? Other?

Perhaps you need credit references such as a bank, names of two business houses where credit has been established, or names of two businesspeople. In any case,

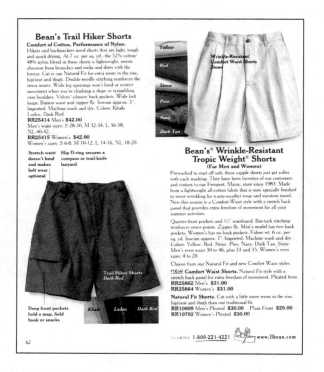

Figure 14–6. Direct response catalog page. *Reproduced by permission of L. L. Bean.*

your card or coupon will have to provide space for any of these additional pieces of information.

One word of caution: *Give your purchaser enough space to fill in the information most important to you— usually name and address.* You'll find it wiser and more profitable to forego some information in order to give the respondent room in which to write out name and address. If a customer's name and address is "Humphrey Stanislavski, Oklahoma City, OK," but you have provided barely enough space for a customer to write "Ned Hay, Erie, PA," then you'll get no reply. Give *plenty* of room for the city name.

Finally, your "miniature order blank" may have to provide spaces for information essential to proper filling of the order, particularly if any choice is involved or if alternate selections are offered.

Advertisements without Coupons: What to Do

What about the advertisement that doesn't have enough room for a coupon?

You might as well accept the fact that you won't get as many replies from couponless advertisements as you will from those in which you include coupons. You may say, "I don't have room for a coupon, and I don't have enough money to increase the size of my advertisement sufficiently to include a coupon, but I still have to run an advertisement for my mail-order offering. What do I do then?"

First, you can include adequate ordering information as a part of your advertisement's copy so that it brings in a

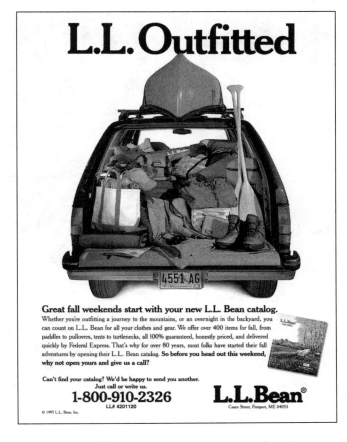

Figure 14–7. Direct response magazine advertisement. *New Yorker* readers have been good customers of L. L. Bean over the years and are accustomed to seeing advertisements such as this in their magazine. As you see, there is a cutting down on the detail seen in catalog pages, but the stress is still on items for outdoor living and the copy continues to be simple, but persuasive. *Reproduced by permission of L. L. Bean.*

L.L. Bean® Freeport, Maine 04033-0001

ORDER TOLL FREE 1-800-221-4221
CUSTOMER SERVICE 1-800-341-4341

This Order Form is printed on recycled paper.

Name and address of person placing order.
(Please verify your mailing address and make corrections below.)
Order Date: __/__/__

Gift Order or Ship To: (Use only if different from address at left)
Name
Address Apt. No.
City State Zip
Gift ☐ Address for This Shipment Only ☐ Permanent Change of Address ☐
Gift Card Message
Delivery Phone ( )

Phone: Day ( ) ______ **Evening** ( ) ______

First Line is Example Only

Page	Item No.	Description	Style (Petite, Regular, Tall, Pleated, Plain)	Color	Size (Neck, Waist, Garment)	Sleeve length/ Inseam	Qty.	Monogramming (if offered) See Reverse Side for Style choices Characters	Style	Price Each	Total
89	WH10310	All Cotton Dress Chino	Plain	Tan	36	30	2	William	BL	$37.50	$75.00

Please place a check beside the catalogs you would like to receive
☐ **WA11320 Fall Hunting Catalog** (Avail. 7/95) FREE
☐ **WA15240 Fall Home & Camp Catalog** (Avail. 9/95) FREE
☐ **WA11335 Winter Sporting Catalog** (Avail. 10/95) FREE

Method of Payment
Check/Money Order ☐ Gift Certificate(s) ☐ AMOUNT ENCLOSED $ ______
American Express ☐ MasterCard ☐ Visa ☐ Optima ☐ DiscoverCard ☐
Account Number
MO. YR. / Expiration Date
Signature ______
Orders are accepted and processed by L.L. Bean, Freeport, Maine.
F.O.B. shipping point Freeport, Maine.

FedEx. Federal Express

MERCHANDISE TOTAL ______
Total monogramming charges (see product description for cost) ______
6% sales tax on merchandise delivered in Maine ______
Regular FedEx shipping: $4.50 per U.S. delivery address (For delivery in 2 to 4 business days) $4.50
Please add $4.50 per each additional U.S. delivery address ______
FedEx Standard Overnight Service Add $6.00 for delivery in **2 business days** per contiguous U.S. address* ______
Any additional freight charges ______
International shipping (See shipping information on back) **Surface, Air or FedEx—Please circle one** ______
TOTAL ______

34819
34820

*For FedEx delivery to Alaska and Hawaii, please see shipping information on back.

Figure 14–8. Catalog order form. This simple form can serve as a model of its type. On the back of the form is added information about getting the best fit for clothing, additional ordering information and the return policy. *Reproduced by permission of L. L. Bean.*

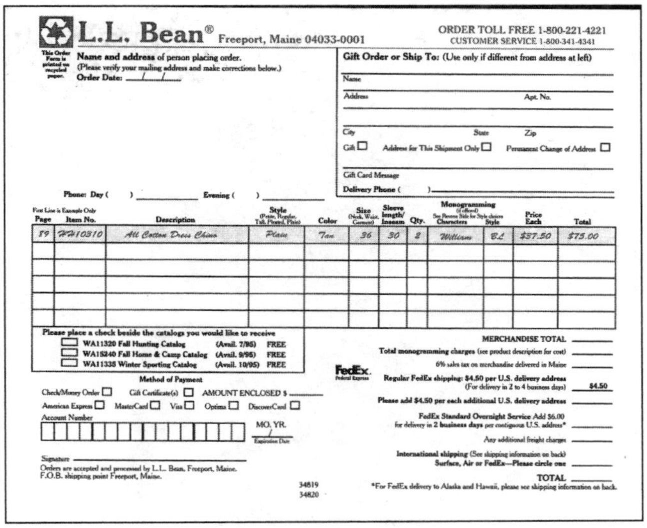

profitable number of orders. Second, you can state the ordering requirements simply. Third, be certain that the requirements are reduced to the basic necessities, and include only truly essential elements. Fourth, you can sometimes use the page margin as a place to put ordering information.

If There's No Coupon, How Do You Ask for Payment?

If you read carefully the quotations from postcards and coupons presented a few paragraphs back, you'll recall that even with these ordering devices, some merchandisers have avoided the need for a remittance with the order. Of course, this is relatively simple for a department store that is selling to its charge account customers or is making C.O.D. sales locally, allowing its truck drivers to collect for the merchandise at the time of delivery. But the requirement for cash, money order, or check with the order is being omitted by more and more nonlocal advertisers who have neither charge customers nor any delivery system of their own.

Credit card purchases through such reputable issuers as VISA, MasterCard, Diners Club, or American Express are welcomed more and more by mail-order advertisers. The credit card holder is asked to give the card number and the expiration date. This request can fit easily into the coupon-less advertisement.

Along with the invitation to buy through the credit card is the invitation to phone in the order through a toll-free 800 number. Usually, you'll ask the prospect to give his credit card number when the call is made, or you may warn that *only* prospects with credit cards should use the 800 number.

Once popular with advertisers, the C.O.D. payment is almost invisible these days. In fact, many firms include the phrase, "No C.O.D.'s please." Credit cards have done much to replace the C.O.D. method of payment, which was used chiefly for bigger purchasers.

"Bill me later" is a phrase found in some advertisements, especially when the advertiser is pushing hard for the sale and is willing to chance a number of nonpayments. Book clubs and record clubs also use time-payment plans that require the purchaser to pay each time a book or record selection is received.

Can You Use Tell-All in a Radio Commercial?

The answer is that you don't. Even a person buying an item in a retail store would seldom have each feature pointed out before deciding to make the purchase. In radio, although you include important details, you won't include *every* point. Suppose, for example, that you were writing the commercial to follow the interest-arousing

Figure 14–9. Direct response catalog advertisement. In addition to using the usual very different and very interesting copy style, this example demonstrates another characteristic of many J. Peterman listings—a reference to contemporary happenings and people, as you will see in the opening copy. Notice, however, that many down-to-earth details are included to help prospects make a buying decision. So it isn't *all* whimsy.

Figure 14–10. Direct response advertisement. Look carefully at this advertisement. It sold more than 5,000 of the item in a 6-week period. In that time it ran several times in the *Wall Street Journal, New York Times,* and *USA Today.*

Radio is not the ideal tell-all medium. Instead, it's used most effectively to put across one point emphatically. Listeners simply cannot absorb a number of points made over the air, even though they give the commercial full attention.

Despite the fact that it seems that the tray commercial was jammed with selling points, one big point was made and repeated—that the listeners owning the tray could clean silver easily.

Sometimes you may make an offer on radio that consists of many points, no one of which you expect to register strongly with your listeners. Your purpose is simply to make prospects aware that your product or service has an amazing number of fine attributes for the money you're asking. Although such a technique will work, it is still best to write radio commercials that register one idea overwhelmingly.

If you're typical you'll probably agree that cleaning silver is one of the most dreaded household tasks. Still, if you want to show off that fine silver of yours you have to *clean* it, so what's the answer? Here it is—the Ezy-Kleen magnesium silver-cleaning tray. Now, at *last*, you can clean silver without all that

lead-in for the silver-cleaning tray below. How best can you (in one minute or less) tell your prospects the features most likely to induce them to purchase? What would they want to know about the product? First, forget you're a copywriter. Instead, you are all of the listeners to the station carrying the tray offer. You're attracted by and interested in the announcer's opening lines, but even so, you may be overwhelmed by all the details.

hand-rubbing and those messy cleaning solutions. Here's how the Ezy-Kleen tray method works. Put tarnished silver in the tray, cover with hot water and detergent, and let it soak for twenty minutes. Take it out, rinse and dry. You'll find your silver sparkling clean. You see, while it's in the tray the detergent working with the magnesium coating of the tray cleans silver gently but with such effectiveness that it shines like new when you take it out of the water. No wonder Ezy-Kleen carries the Good Housekeeping Seal and is endorsed by leading silver manufacturers. But this tray, that lasts a lifetime, does more than just clean flatware. It's big enough to hold and clean bowls, platters and other sizable silver items. You've seen Ezy-Kleen advertised in *Woman's Day, Good Housekeeping* and other top women's magazines and now, while supplies last, you can buy it only at Barkliss Brothers in our downtown store. To get *your* Ezy-Kleen send $22.50 to our silverware department, or phone 338-9999. That's 338-9999. This is being offered only to our radio listeners. Get your order in now for Ezy-Kleen, the magnesium silver-cleaning tray—*only* at Barkliss.

You Show Them in Television; It's Better Than Just Telling

Television, of course, goes beyond radio in its ability to show merchandise to talk about it, and, often even more important, to *demonstrate* it. Your selling principles for copywriting are not changed but merely enhanced by television.

Because the product can be shown in actual use, including all views of it and demonstrations of its performance, the possibilities of television go beyond even illustrations in print. Different models, patterns, styles, and color selections may be shown, too. In fact, the scope of direct response selling by television is unlimited when the possibilities of showing products being modeled or otherwise in use and presenting a full range of styles and colors are considered.

Direct response selling will be adapted to suit the medium and the selling advantages it offers, but direct response selling principles will not—and cannot—be eliminated. Nor will the fundamental sales psychology be altered. Television's biggest asset as a sales-maker lies in its illustrative advantages, its ability to enhance verbal description, not replace it.

Added Tips for Direct Response Television

Believability, of course, is a goal of all advertising, regardless of what medium is being used. If you are used to writing print direct response, you may be shocked on occasion by what happens to believability in television commercials. That's because the announcer's style and manner of delivery can make such a difference. What is desirable enthusiasm in print can become pitchman pressure in television. Repetition that is acceptable in print copy can, if not handled well, become inexpressibly boring and/or irritating in television commercials.

If your announcer comes on too strong in your commercial, believability suffers. Believability in television is based on two elements: (1) Believable words and claims. These are *your* contributions; (2) Believable delivery of those words and claims. This is out of your control unless you can persuade your bosses to let you participate in the choice of announcers and contribute your ideas of interpretation at taping sessions. No one knows better than you how you want your lines delivered. But if you don't get the chance to express your opinions, an insincere or glib delivery can turn off your audience. So do everything you can to be a part of the production sessions.

Uncomplicated commercials, whether for radio or television, should be your goal. What is uncomplicated? An uncomplicated commercial limits the number of ideas it is presenting and speaks in language understandable by all levels of your audience. It is a commercial with a message that can be picked up even by the inattentive viewer (and you can count on most of your viewers to be inattentive).

Use *supers* freely. Supers (for superimposition) are printed words appearing on the screen that repeat an important point being made at the same time in the audio. When your audience reads a message at the same time it's hearing it, you put the point over strongly.

Ask for *orders* positively and don't hesitate to be repetitive. Ordering directions should be given at least twice. And the closing panel in which all the instructions for ordering—such as telephone number for call, method of payment, and description of the offer—appear should remain on-screen long enough to give the viewer a chance to write down what is needed to order.

Joe and Sally Fiske are sitting in the living room watching television. Suddenly, a friendly sounding voice is trying to sell a product on the screen. Now, as a writer, how do you keep Joe from instantly pressing the "mute" button on the remote control? You'd better be sure you've made that "friendly sounding voice" forceful enough to hold their attention for the message.

Above all, you want to persuade Joe or Sally to pick up a pencil and write down the 800 number. Otherwise, zap goes the commercial. As said earlier, your announcer must avoid being too aggressive, but he must, nonetheless, create a sense of urgency so that the Fiskes will pick up that pencil.

To create that urgency, you fill your copy with action words and then hope that the announcer knows how to deliver them forcefully. Your good copy can be enhanced by such factors as the announcer's tone of voice, emphasis, and rate of delivery.

There's a Big Payoff for Small-Space Advertisements If You Write Them Well

You may feel a bit deflated if your first direct response copy assignment is the writing of a one-inch or two-inch advertisement. Don't be upset. You'll find it a challenge. You'll learn quickly that it's an art to describe, persuade, and ask for the order in thirty words or less. Each word is important, so you learn not to write useless words. You cut, compress, and cut again.

You agonize over the headline, which, because of space limitations, must be short. You'll often use an index headline, but if you have enough room, you might try an exclamatory or an exhortative headline.

Opening the copy fast with your most important benefit or appeal is more important than ever because your space is so small that there's not much left when you've written the opening. What *is* left will usually consist of a vigorous push for action, again brief.

Notice the admirable compression in the following one-inch advertisement that, despite its brevity, avoids the dull, telegraphic style that characterizes the writing of many small advertisements.

> **Vibrant Violet Bouquet.** Plant a little blooming color in your kitchen when you hang this POTHOLDER by the stove! Also, Daffodil, Zinnia, Pansies, Hyacinth, Daisy, Perfect Pinks, and a crochet basket to hold them all in! Patterns, $2 ea. All 8, $7.98. Kits, $5.98 ea. All 8, $39.95. All ppd. Annie's Attic, F138 Rte. 2, Box 212b, Big Sandy, TX 75755.

(Illustration of the POTHOLDER just above the copy)

You're advised to write effective advertising, but particularly in the case of small-space advertisements, what you want is the most *cost-effective* advertisements possible—advertisements that obtain the greatest return in sales from the money invested.

To illustrate the point, it has been found over and over that in terms of percentage of inquiries (and, by implication, sales), units such as one-quarter, one-third, and one-half pages, and even smaller units, can pull better than full-page units. Daniel Starch, Gallup & Robinson, and other research firms have found such results.

Let's go back to the very small advertisements. It's a struggle for the writer to write copy complete enough to sell well in a one-inch space. "Oh," the writer says, "if only I had two inches, or even (sigh) three inches." That's the writer's problem. Now, we'll look at this from the *advertiser's* perspective.

Like the writer, the advertiser, too, would like the three-inch advertisement in a specific publication, but there are two other publications similar to that publication in circulation, pull, and cost. For illustration, assume that each of the three publications has a circulation of about 600,000. Should the advertiser simply run a three-inch advertisement in just one publication and omit the other two, or run three one-inch advertisements using all three publications?

Based on experience, the advertiser decides on the three one-inch advertisements, reasoning that these advertisements will be reaching 1,800,000 prospects instead of the 600,000 prospects reached by the single three-inch advertisement.

Don't scoff at small-space advertisements. In general, several small space advertisements will bring in more business than a single large advertisement in one publication. A single large advertisement may generate more impact and prestige, but several smaller ones will generate more exposure and sales.

Tips for Writing Your Small-Space Advertisement

When writing a small-space advertisement, your first task is to do a character count to find out *exactly* how much you can write. Set your margins to accommodate the number of characters per line. In your first draft, keep your eyes on those margins but write freely. You'll probably go over your allotment of characters.

Now comes the hard part. You'll need to cut some of those words. Try to weed out some of the articles, such as "a," "an," and "the." Keep the verbs for liveliness. If you must use adjectives, include the most engaging, colorful ones you can think of. Replace ordinary words with vibrant, attention-getting words.

Something that will give you a proper respect for a small space advertisement is to count the number of words you've written. Then, divide the total cost of the space by the number of words. Let's say you have written 60 words and the space cost is $1800. In this case, each word costs $30. When you value words this way, you become obsessed about not wasting a single word; you make them all count.

While being careful to write within your space, don't forget to make the offer enticing. An example of this principle at work is supplied by the enormous success of Lillian Vernon, who placed a small advertisement in *Seventeen* magazine in 1951 offering purses and belts. Her "enticing offer" was free personalization of each purchase with the customer's initials. The result? Orders totalling $32,000.

This initial success was followed three years later with the publication of a 16-page catalog that was mailed to 125,000 customers, who had been attracted to preceding advertisements. In 1995, the Lillian Vernon corporation, which started in 1951 with a $2000 investment, had a database of 17.6 million names and sales of 222 million dollars. A story of starting small and ending big.

CHAPTER 15

You Like Intimacy in Your Copy? Try Direct Mail

"**A**ll my life I've enjoyed writing letters, and now I get paid for doing it. I <u>love</u> it," said Susan Jacobs, talking excitedly about her new job to her mother.

Susan is a person-to-person type both in conversation and in writing. She shines in one-on-one contacts, and that's what direct mail is all about—writing to one person in a direct, "I'm-talking-only-to-you" way. What a chance to be personal, whimsical, persuasive, and wholly intimate in your copy. No advertising medium offers you a better chance for truly personal selling.

A public speaker talking to a large audience is well advised to look at the crowd, pick out a face, and talk to that face. Perhaps this connection allows the speaker to imbue a talk with more personal feeling than when he or she is merely addressing a mass of faces.

In a similar fashion, smart writers of advertisements for big-circulation magazines will try this same technique of zeroing in on an imaginary single person. As a direct mail writer, you don't need to *imagine* a person on the other end of the words being written because you *are* writing to that single person, so your words genuinely convey a personal, intimate feeling, something that is difficult for that national magazine writer to achieve.

What Is Direct-Mail Advertising?

Direct-mail advertising conveys your message personally and individually to a selected group of prospects or customers with whom you want to do business or whose goodwill you want to establish or maintain. This is a truly "direct" medium, usually conveyed entirely by "mail," as opposed to direct response, which may use radio, television, and publication advertising in soliciting mail business.

Some direct-mail pieces are also distributed in other ways. A folder, for example, devised primarily as a mailing piece to accompany a department store's monthly charge account statements, may also be used as a pickup piece in a suitable spot in the store—probably in the department whose merchandise or service it publicizes.

This kind of promotion is sometimes called direct advertising and is considered the same as direct-mail advertising. In this discussion, it will be assumed that you are writing to relatively sharply defined groups—in other words, you are creating direct-mail advertising.

Remember: Write to One—Not Everyone

As a direct mail writer, your writing could take any number of directions. You could be

- a broker calling attention to a hot stock offering.
- a worker for a public broadcast station asking for financial support.
- a banker selling your low-cost credit card.
- a dedicated volunteer asking for a tax-deductible donation to the Red Cross.
- a department-store copywriter announcing a big 24-hour sale.

In each case, you're asking for someone to give money, and you'll be more successful in these requests if you use a personal, friendly, one-on-one style. It's actually fun to write like this—to think of one person on the receiving end of your message.

Certainly, there's satisfaction in writing copy for advertising that will reach millions on TV or in magazines, but can you ever *really* get personal with millions of people?

Direct mail has become an almost universal medium because of this personal quality. Of the millions of businesses, relatively few advertise on the air, in national magazines, or in any medium other than their local newspaper. Almost every firm, however, uses direct-mail advertising.

Reasons for Using Direct Mail

At one time the Direct Mail Advertising Association issued a list of 49 ways that direct-mail advertising could be used as a part of modern merchandising methods. Although many variations in these applications have been made, a listing of some of the most common basic uses will give you an idea of the scope of this medium and how greatly you would have to vary your writing to meet the requirements of some of these uses. These uses include:

- To sell goods or services by mail. (Although this use does not necessarily anticipate return orders by mail, its purpose is primarily the same as "direct mail-order," covered in the last chapter.)
- To reach all customers regularly with merchandise offers, thereby keeping accounts active.
- To support salespeople and pave the way for them, thus backing their selling efforts and economizing on their time (and on the prospects' time and patience) when they are actually making sales calls.
- To bring in orders between salespeople's calls or from territories not covered by salespeople (or, in consumer selling, areas not serviced through retail outlets) or to open up new territories.
- To broadcast mailings to and request inquiries from a large group of prospects. Names thus obtained are passed on to dealers, jobbers, or salespeople for solicitation, or are further contacted by additional direct mail. Since requests are from definite prospects, getting names this way saves the expense of indiscriminate distribution of catalogs.
- To provide news and information about the firm or its products. This might include "education" of stockholders on company products, services, and policies—either from a public relations point of view, an encouragement of their patronage, or perhaps to stimulate their word-of-mouth advertising.
- To tie-in with trade or consumer publication advertising or to sell dealers on trade paper or consumer advertising programs. Such selling stimulates their cooperative efforts.
- To stimulate dealer sales by consumer mailings—perhaps by suggesting a visit to the prospect's "nearest dealer." Jobber sales may also be spurred by mailing to dealers.

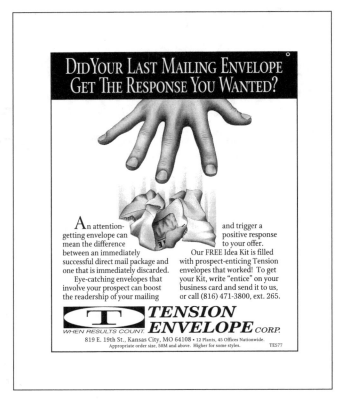

Figure 15–1. Advertisement stressing importance of envelopes in direct mail. Directed toward readers of *Advertising Age* magazine, this small-space advertisement emphasizes one more point to consider in obtaining results from direct mail.

- To induce a dealer's own customers or prospects to visit his store (or a manufacturer's customers his showroom) to see some special goods described or illustrated.
- To overcome adverse market tendencies or competition threatening the established customer. The quick publicizing of a revised price list might fall into this class.
- To pretest, on a limited scale, contemplated offers or presentations against each other by using different lists or splitting a single list.
- To stimulate sales or to increase acceptance of the firm's merchandise or services through enclosures in all outgoing envelopes (with dividend checks or financial statements to stockholders, for example).
- To request information from prospects to determine their needs. The information will be used as a basis for further mailings or a salesperson's solicitation. The items will be specifically suited to prospects' requirements.

In this incomplete list, you have a range of jobs that call for many different types of copy treatment. However, they all offer you one advantage—that of knowing the needs and wants of the prospects to whom you are writing. Because of the selective nature of direct mail, you write more surely to the prospect's interest than in general media such as newspapers, radio, and TV.

One prestigious retail clothing chain, for example, mails advance announcements of its seasonal traveling merchandise displays to charge customers and former cash customers. Because this is a very well-defined group of prospects that is already aware of the company's reputation, styles, and values, the headline of one announcement reads merely:

(Company name) Clothes for Spring and Summer

This is almost a pure index-type headline, with institutional and prestige overtones. Contrast this with another headline—this one on the cover of a nonmail-order catalog for a chain of retail auto supply stores. This appeal is based primarily on price, but it does include some assurance of quality:

SAVE 25% to 50% from List Price on GUARANTEED REPLACEMENT AUTO PARTS

This headline is aimed unmistakably at a large—almost universal—but yet quite definite class of prospects (automobile owners) to induce them to visit the local store of the chain where the products listed may be purchased.

You Ask for Action but Not the Order

Unlike mail-order selling, direct-mail advertising, except in the case of direct mail-order selling, does not attempt to do the entire selling job, right down to and including asking for the order. Rather, any one piece of direct-mail advertising is generally intended to accomplish only one step in the completion of the sale.

Referring to the list of common uses of direct mail, you will find that, while direct mail usually suggests some sort of action—perhaps only passively, as in showing willingness to listen to a salesman when he calls—it may actually be used merely to implant a certain idea in the mind of the recipient that calls for no action (for the present, at least) by him. Because direct-mail advertising is usually intended to further the sale and because it is not intended to complete the sale by itself, the copy you write must be keyed to the purpose for which the mailing is intended—but it *must not go beyond that purpose.*

There is another reason, however, for not telling all in many direct-mail pieces, even though they may be a single mailing rather than part of a series or campaign. Imagine that you are writing a "one-shot" direct-mail piece for the women's coat department of a retail store. You are announcing to your store's charge customers, in advance of your general newspaper advertisement, the arrival of a special group of luxuriously fur-trimmed cloth coats, and you are urging the customers' advance inspection of these models.

Your Objective Is to Get the Prospect into a Specific Department

Your purpose is to get customers into the department. Do you tell them, then, all about the coat? Do you list all of

Figure 15–2. Sales letter. The writer has made the letter physically inviting by using:

- A short opening paragraph
- Indented material to break up the type mass
- Paragraphs of different lengths
- No paragraph that is more than eight lines
- A short closing paragraph that asks for action

the colors available and every kind of fur in the group? Do you illustrate every style? You do not! If you list certain specific styles, you're sure to cause some prospects to shun the offer because they have other styles in mind.

Of course, there are some things you will want to tell your prospects such as sizes. There's no point in making the size 12 or size 44 customer angry at you for wasting the time it takes to come downtown when your size range begins with 14 and ends at 40. In most cases, you'll also list the range of prices, for much the same reason. If your buyer is a smart merchandiser, the group should include at least one model that can be priced at a comparatively low figure, perhaps because of a lesser amount of fur used (although probably not a cheaper fur) on a coat that, because of its styling or material, seems otherwise to "belong" with the more expensive models.

Thus, instead of having to admit to a limited price range of $375 to $449.50, you may be able to claim that "these exclusive creations begin at the tiny price of $225, while you'll hardly believe we could sell the most luxurious models for their modest price of only $449.50."

Jay R. Bearley
2810 N. Garden Street
South Haven, Michigan 49090

Dear Mr. Bearley:

Thank you very much for your letter of June 3 in which you ask for a leaflet and the name of a local dealer for Kwik-Aire, our portable electric air compressor. You will find the leaflet enclosed. Your dealer is:

Donald S. Ashcraft
Ashcraft Auto Supply Store
811 Fairfax Avenue Phone: 342-8791
South Haven

As you will notice when you read the leaflet, our Kwik-Aire compressor works from the cigarette lighter of your car. Just plug it in-attach to the valve of your tire and in seconds the tire will be inflated without effort on your part. It works equally well on tires for cars, trucks, campers, and bicycles.

You'll find Kwik-Aire handy for items other than tires too. For instance, use it to inflate beach balls, basketballs, air mattresses and inflatable furniture. This compact unit that fits snugly into your car trunk can be used around the car, home, cabin, the beach, or recreational vehicles.

It's important to keep tires inflated properly to make them last. Kwik-Aire is ready to use day or night. No need to depend upon service stations being open.

Your complete Kwik-Aire kit includes:

. Air compressor unit.
. 10 feet of electric cord.
. Nozzle adapter for inflatable objects.
. 3 feet of neoprene hose.
. Plastic carrying case.

After you've considered these facts and have looked over the leaflet, we'd suggest that you see Mr. Ashcraft to see a Kwik-Aire first hand. Mr. Ashcraft, who has handled our products for 10 years, has a supply of Kwik-Aires in stock. He'll be glad to demonstrate one of the units and to answer any questions.

With summer driving about to get into full swing, be prepared. Get a versatile Kwik-Aire. It can help you in many ways.

Yours very truly,

Joseph L. Beveridge
Sales Department

J3/a
Inc.

Figure 15-3. Follow-up to lead generated by advertising. One of the shameful areas of American industry is the lack of follow-up to inquiries generated by advertisements.

In such letters the most important task is to get the prospect and dealer together. Thus, as shown, the dealer's name leads off the letter, and at the end of the letter the prospect is urged to see the dealer.

The center of the letter sells the product by calling attention to important sales points that appear in the leaflet enclosed with the letter. With this sales talk, added to the leaflet and the advertisement that prompted the inquiry, the prospect should be very much aware of the advantages of the product.

Each Mailing Should Be Complete but Tell Just Enough to Keep the Prospect Interested

In all direct-mail advertising that contemplates an eventual sale, tell enough to interest the prospect—and to keep him interested until you have the opportunity to complete the sale. But don't tell "your all" or you may never have the chance to make that sale. This strategy applies as well to a series of related, progressive-step mailings as it does to a single mailing. Don't weaken your next mailing by telling its story before the strategic time. This rule applies even when your anticipated sale, following a direct-mail campaign, will be requested by mail as well—a direct-mail order.

When you don't follow this strategy—when you rob your following mailings of their impact by anticipating their parts of the sales story early in the campaign—your

That's the ideal sale. It's exactly what you hope to do with your direct response offering. Your show window that stops your prospect is your display (in type and illustration) or the opening words of your commercial. Your copy (and detailed views, if any) comprise your closeup of the product and your salestalk.

Next, because you're not face-to-face with the prospect, you have to anticipate what his questions and objections are most likely to be and work the answers into your sales talk (keeping them in a positive vein, of course) as you write.

Then you weave in your clincher—*why it's important or necessary to order now*—frequently a matter of limited supply, a special price for a short time, or perhaps a premium for promptness. So far you've pretty well paralleled the retail sales procedure.

At this point your retail customer would say. "Wrap it up" and dig into his wallet. You'd take his money and hand him the change and his parcel. It's not that simple in direct selling since the customer—the prospect—still has one more step to take on his own. He has to make out his order (perhaps getting out paper, envelope, and a stamp), probably write a check (or quite possibly go to a bank or post office to buy a money order), and then mail the order to your firm.

Not only do you have to make these extra steps simple and easy as possible, but you must also make your whole offer seem so attractive that the customer doesn't mind the extra work.

The extra attraction you must weave into your copy is difficult to define but might be explained by saying that you write in a somewhat "higher key" so that your copy reads or is heard at a higher pitch. Perhaps some of this is the result of your urge to immediate action. This feeling, nevertheless, is often an integral part of the entire advertisement. Perhaps a careful look at each element of the direct sale will show what's required to give the entire advertisement its high pitch. Begin with the headline.

Your Headlines Are Show Windows

Headlines are the "show windows"—attention-getters—of your shop. Windows pull prospects in from the sidewalk to the shop's inside. Headlines pull prospects into your copy. Your headline material in this instance may be described as any display-size type wherever it appears in the advertisement.

Considered alone, this physical handling (layout) of the headline material imparts a large measure of its high pitch—its aura of urgency. Direct headlines are frequently written in a more exciting style than for usual consumer advertising. They may be *exhortative*:

Save on Farm Income Taxes before April 15th
Look Taller Instantly
Make Beaded SEQUIN Lapel Pins—Easy at Home
Now! Be Stunning in a Rainstorm
Remove Any Stump

Treasure Your Baby's Tooth

Each one is a command to action as well as an appeal to some need or desire.

Others, by brevity alone—a sort of terse *index* quality—impart a feeling of urgency:

Delphinium
New Miracle Wall Cleaner
Feet Hurt?
Gardenia Plants
Orchard Fresh Holly *(for Christmas)*
Wristwatch—Military Style

A third headline type, somewhere between exhortative and index for forcefulness, is the *exclamatory* headline. This is an excited, enthusiastic headline well suited to direct response advertising that creates a sense of urgency and merchandising excitement. Some examples:

Dazzling duo in solid brass. $19.95 for 2!
Gift of the year. Only $12.95.
World famous tomato sauce now available after 76 years

Not every direct response headline *must* fall into the exhortative, index, or exclamatory types. There *are* other types, and combinations of types, but these are the most common. Some index headings actually use a selling word or two; others none, except possibly by inference. Display lines in other advertisements rely for their excitement primarily on exclamatory sentences or phrases:

Two Bushels of Ripe Tomatoes from One Vine
3 Crochet Beauties Easy to Make
Lifetime Knife Cuts Anything

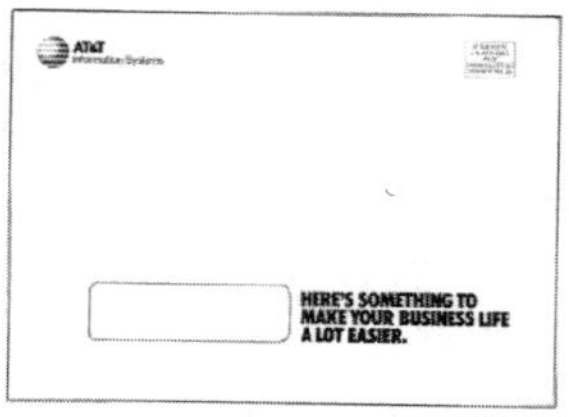

HERE'S SOMETHING TO MAKE YOUR BUSINESS LIFE A LOT EASIER.

Figure 12-4. Direct response envelope with outside message. Such messages on the envelope build curiosity to see what's inside. In advertising parlance such message carrying envelopes are sometimes called "flashes."

Figure 15-4. Sales letter to the dealer urging follow-up of a lead generated by advertising. Another weak spot in the advertising-selling chain is the lack of follow-up by dealers who have been sent sales leads. It is up to the advertiser to push dealers into follow-up action.

The letter has three functions: (1) To give the lead. (2) To sell the dealer on the company's advertising and promotion that generated the lead and may well generate more leads. (3) To resell the product.

prospects either become confused by the size and scope of the early bombardment or become tired and bored with the succession of old stuff that comes in subsequent mailings. In either case, you have almost certainly lost the sale.

One caution you should remember, however, in applying this strategy: In any direct-mail campaign—despite the fact that one major impression is all you can expect to get across in any one mailing—each mailing should be complete in itself. It should not be dependent either upon earlier pieces or pieces yet to come. Even though you cannot tell all of a multipart story in a single mailing, you must adequately stress the feature chosen for emphasis in that mailing. Know exactly what purpose you want each piece to accomplish, then write your copy to achieve that purpose—and nothing more.

Here's How You Make Your Copy Effective

As in any other type of copy you're concerned with, start out powerfully. Continue the momentum generated by the opening in the body of your writing (letters, folders, or mailers), and end positively.

Start out powerfully by:
- Offering a benefit in the first paragraph and/or headline.
- Playing up this benefit in the following paragraph to emphasize its importance.

Continue the momentum by:
- Explaining in detail the attributes of the products, or service, and how these attributes will be of value to the prospect. This explanation must be preceded by your learning everything about the product, especially what makes it different or superior to rival products.
- Offering proof that the product is what you say it is and will do what you say it will. Proof can be in the form of performance tests, laboratory findings, surveys, endorsements, testimonials, or a report that shows how well the product is selling.
- Building the stature of the advertiser for integrity, reliability, and longtime contributions.
- Using, in folders and other long-copy vehicles, attention-getting, strong-selling subheads. Make them so strong and so clear that the prospect will know broadly what you want him to know if he reads nothing but the main head and subheads.

End positively by:
- Repeating what benefit the prospect will derive if he gets the product or service and pointing out the melancholy consequences of not getting it.
- Urging immediate action, such as buying, trying, inquiring, seeing, or some other sort of follow-up.

Some Ways to Make Sure That What You Write Brings Good Results

Remember the previous stress placed on the personal character of direct mail? In general, use a simple, personal, conversational writing style. Avoid fancy words and sentences. (You may wish to ignore the very simple, very personal style for certain audiences that are used to technical language and suspicious of excessive familiarity. Such audiences might be composed of doctors, engineers, and other professionals.)

For direct mail, don't be afraid to repeat the name of the product. Repeat it enough to drive it home. You'll be surprised how often you can repeat the name without offense; that is, if you're clever enough.

You'll probably use a number of illustrations in folders and other long-copy pieces. Accompany each of these with strong, interesting captions. Write these captions so that the quick-glance reader will be given a quick, clear explanation of the illustration.

Make Your Material Attractive and Easy to Read

Certainly, what you say is important. Unfortunately, if your material is physically unattractive, your prospects may never read what you say. Make your letter or folder appear so attractive and easy to read that you won't lose your prospects before they find out what you have to offer. Much material received in the mails *looks* so difficult that a prospect's initial glance is the only glance given it.

Because direct mail appears in so many forms, it is not possible to discuss them all. Thus, only two of the more common forms will be covered here: the letter and the folder. Following are some ways to make them more physically attractive and, by doing so, to make more certain that they will be given more than one quick glance.

Letters

There are general rules that apply to sales letters. There are many variations possible, but what you read here, if applied, can help you avoid mistakes in the physical construction of your direct-mail letters. For this discussion, we will assume that we are talking about one-page letters and that we are using a block form in which the type is flush left with no indentations for paragraphs.

Short opening paragraph. Don't smother your reader with the first paragraph. Limit it to a maximum of four lines.

No paragraph longer than eight lines. When a paragraph is longer than eight lines, the sales points tend to become buried. Furthermore, the sight of long paragraphs has a depressing effect—the kind of feeling that they had when they were faced with long, laborious paragraphs in school textbooks—on readers. A textbook writer can get away with this because the student has to read a textbook; a prospect does not have to read a sales letter.

Paragraph length varied. A letter with all paragraphs the same length looks dull and monotonous. This observation applies whether the paragraphs are all long or all short. It is easy to vary paragraph length, so do it. Occasionally, you might want to use a paragraph of a single line or just several words. This will make your letter more interesting.

Type masses broken up. Why daunt the reader with a whole page of solid, unbroken type? One way to open up the letter is to use the occasional one-line paragraph already mentioned. Another effective method is to set off important material by indenting it and giving it space above and below. As an example, suppose you want to give a name and address in the letter. The preceding line might read:

When you're in Parkersburg be sure to visit:

> John G. Smelzer
> Smelzer Pottery Company
> 18 W. Elizabeth Street

The centering of the name and address creates a pleasing open effect in the letter and focuses the reader's attention on the information.

Laurence P. Grailing, Jr.
929 Ms. Piskor Drive
Tacoma, Washington 98422

Dear Mr. Grailing:

In a world where fulfilling obligations is often not done, you are to be congratulated for the conscientious way you have paid off your mortgage loan. We deeply
appreciate your consistent observance of due dates. In the 15 years we have
held the mortgage there has not been <u>one</u> missed date.

Naturally, your credit rating with Peoples National is at the highest level.

Too often people such as yourself obtain no recognition for quietly and steadily
paying off a debt. We'd like to extend such recognition by inviting you to utilize
any of the various services this bank can offer. Because of the credit rating I
spoke of above, you are automatically qualified for any type of loan, such as:

        Home improvement loans.
        Boat loans.
        Mortgage loans. (should you ever require another one)
        Personal loans.
        Consolidation loans (where we lend you money to pay off all debts
                            so that you have just one loan to settle).
        Auto loans (our rates are lower that those of the finance companies)

Should you require any such loans please let us know. Our loan officers will be
delighted to talk to you and to give you speedy no-nonsense service devoid of
red tape. After all, you <u>are</u> a very special customer of ours.

I hope, too, that you'll avail yourself of many of the other services of a full service bank including our various types of checking and savings plans as well as
the expert guidance of our trust department.

In your next visit to the bank I <u>do</u> hope that you come see me in order that I
may personally congratulate you for the honorable and businesslike way you
have fulfilled your mortgage loan requirements. My desk is immediately to the
left as you enter. It will be a pleasure to meet you.

                                    Sincerely,
                                    L.L. Linveil
                            Mortgage Loan Officer
                                  Peoples National

LLL/r

Figure 15–5. Letter to present customer. Present customers
are often a company's *best* customers. A pat-on-the-back type of
letter such as this will help an advertiser hold on to a customer
and sell him additional services. An alert advertiser will be on the
lookout for such opportunities.

You can use the same technique to call attention to several selling points. Suppose you are selling a word processor. You'll use an introductory line and then list the points
in this manner:

Some of the features you'll like about this word processor
besides its low price include:

1. Dual use as a typewriter *and* word processor
2. Full-size monitor
3. Easy-to-install ribbon cassette
4. Utility disk containing help files, thesaurus, spreadsheet,
   database templates, and a tutorial
5. Spell-right dictionary, auto spell, and word alert
6. Punctuation check

By centering material in this way and giving it space at
top and bottom, you spotlight your important material for
sure reader attention. Furthermore, you open up the letter with white space.

Short closing paragraph. You've said what you needed
to say, so end quickly. Three or four lines should be sufficient to end any letter.

Folders

One of the most frequently used mailing pieces is the four-
or-six-page folder that fits as an insert into a No. 10 envelope. Folders are also used as counter pieces in establishments such as hardware stores, drugstores, plumbing
shops, and banks. Considering the folder page by page,
here are some suggestions for physical attractiveness.

Page 1. Use a physically strong headline to catch the
reader's attention. An attractive illustration accompanied
by a short copy block is desirable. Save the long copy for
the inside pages. In many cases, it is desirable to use some
technique to create enough curiosity to impel the reader
to turn to the inside pages. Your headline might do this.
For example:

See the 10 ways this superb tool can save you time and money.

You may frequently wish to use curiosity-developing
words at the bottom of page 1 that make the reader want
to see the contents of pages 2 and 3. For instance, your
bottom line might say:

See inside if you want a more carefree, more colorful
home …

Sometimes, you may wish to use an arrow at the bottom. The arrow, pointing to the inside, could follow the
line that says:

Turn the page to learn how you can cut your fuel bills.

Also, three dots (…) can serve as a pointer that literally
forces readers to turn from page 1 to pages 2 and 3.

Here are some additional examples of copy lines used
on the cover pages of folders that almost force the reader
to turn the page by building up curiosity about the benefits to be obtained from looking inside the folder:

Here's an
important device
that can lower
your heating and air
conditioning bills
substantially!

How to get the most out of your painting effort.

If you don't know beans about boilers but you think your
heating system needs a new one …

Now … the incredible watch—
so incredibly water tight
it actually comes to you
packed in water!
And that's only one of the
extra features of this
amazing watch.

See how this planning guide can assure you a better financial
future.

How to give the most for
your money this year.

How to enjoy a marvelous vacation
and save money too …

Because we care, here is an
important message to you, one
of our many valuable shareholders.
Please take your time and
read it carefully …

Pages 2 and 3. Treat these pages as one. By so doing, you can use a strong headline that spreads across the two pages and you can use a big, dominant illustration that takes up part of each page. This combination of strong head and illustration will draw the reader's gaze and create a vitality that would be missing if each page were treated separately.

In order to create excitement for these pages, use selling subheads liberally over the copy blocks. If small illustrations are used, in addition to the dominant illustration, give each a caption. Use these techniques to carry the reader through the pages and infuse the section with vigor.

Page 4 (back page). Sometimes advertisers leave this space blank. This is a grievous mistake since the back page of folders receives good readership. Treat the back page pretty much as you do the front page, with an omission, of course, of any urging to turn the page.

The back page is sometimes a good place to put a guarantee, a special offer, or a listing of important points. Make it just as attractive as the front page since often readers look first at the first page, flip the folder over to the back page, and then, if sufficiently interested, turn to the inside pages. Make the back page worth looking at.

By all means, include the usual elements on your back page such as a headline, possibly subheads, and an illustration. In short, make it a *working* page.

Follow-Up Letters Are Vital

One of the greatest tragedies of American industry is the lack of follow-up. A prospect writes to a company about a product or sends in a coupon, but no answer is received. Or the answer arrives so long after the inquiry that the prospect is no longer interested or has bought a competing product.

Not only do many companies fail to follow up consumer inquiries adequately, they also fail to follow sales leads with their dealers. If a sales lead has been derived from advertising, it should be given to the dealer immediately. He should be made aware of the advertising backing that produced the lead because dealers need constant reminding of the power of advertising supplied by their manufacturing sources.

Often, too, the follow-up letter provides the manufacturer-supplier with a chance to resell his product and to provide the dealer with selling words and phrases that he can use on prospects who come into his store. This reselling is often needed because the dealers who carry many, many lines, can't possibly have in-depth knowledge of all of those lines.

This sales letter to the dealer is very much like an advertisement he might see in his trade magazine because it emphasizes the 3Ps of product, promotion, and profit. The chief objective of this letter is to get the dealer and the prospect together so that a sale can be made. Its secondary objective is to resell the advertising backing and the product.

Figure 15-4 illustrates a letter that follows a sales lead, sells the dealer, and strongly urges action that may result in a personal sales talk. Without such follow-up, the company has wasted money in conducting an expensive advertising campaign.

Put a Message on the Envelope If You Want More Prospects to Read the Letter Inside

Many a letter would be tossed unopened and unread into the wastebasket if not for an irresistible message on the envelope, a fact that alert direct mailers have recognized. The message, or invitation, on the envelope has become standard procedure these days. Thus, prospects are invited to "Look inside for the greatest bargain you've ever seen."

To make the message on the envelope even more exciting and curiosity provoking, many of today's envelopes have windows that let you take a peek at the treasures within. The following is an example of a selling envelope used by a chemical company. Within a box on the front of the big envelope is the message:

Would you like
to use only one
herbicide for all
your crops?
See inside …

A front-of-the-envelope message from a book company interests prospects with this message:

(Please don't tell your friends)

We have a special offer for you:
choose 4 books for $1 each with
no obligation to buy anymore.

See how two other envelope messages use different promises—direct benefits in the first, and new information in the second—to get you to open the mailing.

Learn how the revolutionary TROY-BILT® Chipper/Vac™

REDUCES & RECYCLES LEAVES, LIMBS
& YARD DEBRIS AS YOU WALK!

Another attention-getting envelope message follows. Undoubtedly, it caused many who received the communication to open the envelope.

WARNING

THIS MATERIAL MAY SHOCK YOU AND MAY COMPLETELY CHANGE THE WAY YOU SPEND MONEY. OPEN IF YOU ARE PREPARED TO TAKE ACTION.

Still another development in envelope messages (called "teasers" or "flashes") is the use of the *back* of the envelope. Troy-Bilt® has made good use of such space, as the following material demonstrates.

Making full use of the envelope, here is the message Troy-Bilt® used on the *back* of its envelope:

FREE CATALOG OFFER INSIDE!
Discover a whole new way to clean up and beautify your yard—as you walk!

See the ALL NEW LINE-UP of TROY-BILT® Chipper/Vacs!

Much of the type in this back-of-the envelope message was in attention-getting color (yellow and red) and was set in big type.

Try These Three Ways to Get Better Results from Your Direct-Mail Advertising

Entire books have been written on direct-mail advertising techniques. In this chapter, you have read some of the highlights. To sum up matters, three basic suggestions—suggestions that apply to all direct-mail users—follow.

Use the YOU Point of View

Look at any magazine or newspaper or listen to an evening of television commercials with the eye and ear of the consumer, the prospect. Which advertisements or commercials have the most appeal? Ten-to-one they're those that say "you."

In mail-order selling, using the "you" viewpoint is vital because it is your only contact with the prospect, your only chance to present your product so that he or she will want to make a purchase.

What is the best way to inspire that favorable thought? By shouting "I," "me," "mine," "we," "us," or "our"? By yelling "the biggest," "the best,""the oldest," "the newest"? Or simply by saying or implying "you" and "your"?

It is not important to tell your prospect that your firm is, for example, the oldest or the largest in your field. Our firm's age or size might give your prospect confidence in either the integrity of your house or the dependability of your other selling claims. But even such a claim can be phrased in "you" language: "Your assurance of a quality product is _____ Company's fifty-three years of building Dinguses for over 81 percent of the Whatsis Industry." That's written from the reader's—not the seller's—point of view, a requisite of good selling copy.

Be Truthful and Believable

You may think it superfluous to stress "truth in advertising" any more in the creation of direct-mail selling than in that of other types of advertising. You need only to think of the success of the great mail-order merchandising houses, such as L. L. Bean or Lands' End as ample proof of the fact that truthfulness pays, and pays well. A close relative of truth is believability. Some mail offers actually seem to ignore both of these qualities, depending upon startling,

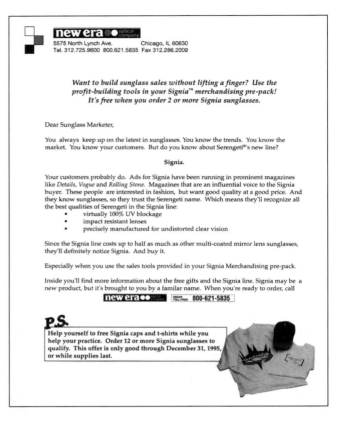

Figure 15–6. Direct mail letter addressed to the trade. In this example the writer has put a headline at the top, a good way to force the reading of the body of the letter. Additionally, it is well-spaced for easy reading because of the good use of white space. At the bottom there is a strong call for action.

even fantastic, claims for both their attention value and selling impact. These may trap the gullible once, perhaps twice, but no business lasts long when its sales depend upon such a weak foundation.

In some instances, you may be able to make an advertising claim in all truth that lacks believability. If so, don't make it, because your prospects will believe you are not telling the truth anyway. Don't make it, that is, unless, as soon as you do, you back it up with believable proof that can remove any taint of even suspected untruth.

This is particularly true of a new product and its advertising, which the buying public always examines with critical suspicion, if not outright distrust. Because your product will often be new to your potential customer, you must be particularly careful to create an aura of truthfulness and believability when selling by mail.

Some firms even follow the practice—and successfully, too—of underselling their products on the proved theory that the customer who finds his purchase superior to its claims will be an eager repeat customer, the ideal situation for any merchandiser who plans to stay in business. At any rate, avoid exaggeration.

Statements needn't be weak or unenthusiastic. You can state a simple fact in a way that comes out strong. Stick to

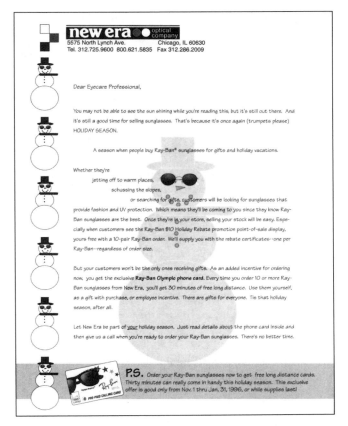

Figure 15–7. Direct mail letter addressed to the trade. There is a strong use of visuals in this letter, a cheerful note in keeping with the holiday season theme of the letter. Throughout there is strong sell with the use of prices, dealer incentives, offers of point-of-sale displays, and suggestions for selling the store's customers. Climaxing all this is heavy stress on ordering that takes up a considerable portion of the letter.

the truth, avoid exaggeration, and make your claims believable.

Keep Old Customers Sold

One of the most important points to remember is that the backbone of any permanent success in selling is the retention of the goodwill and the business of old customers. Much of the responsibility for keeping old customers as satisfied current customers is the province not of the advertising copywriter but of direct salespeople, sales and credit correspondents, and others. Nevertheless, the firm's advertising also has a share of the job to do in ensuring that the needs and wants of the old customers are not sacrificed in the attempt to win new customers.

Advertising also frequently plays a big part in the maintenance of friendly relations between seller and customer. During periods of raw material shortages, transportation delays, and other difficulties—even labor troubles—advertising, of every sort, including both mail order and direct mail, can and does help out in the big job of explaining the situation to customers and retaining their business.

Many firms, both retail and industrial, have adopted the practice of periodically sending purely goodwill direct-mail letters to their entire list of customers. These are sent annually at the New Year or at other appropriate intervals and times, thanking each customer for his business, hoping for uninterrupted "friendship," possibly pledging increased service and improved products, and perhaps requesting ideas for still better fulfillment of the customer's needs.

Sometimes a simple mailing such as this will make customers realize that here indeed is a firm interested in them and worthy of their continued business.

A Checklist to Insure More Profitable Mailings

This 21-point checklist was devised by Andrew J. Byrne, one of the nation's leading authorities in direct response and direct-mail marketing. Mr. Byrne has been involved in the field for many years in the U.S., Europe, and Mexico.

This checklist is included here for use by anyone in direct-mail marketing who wants to take a last look before sending out a mailing. Mailings are expensive, and here's one more way to make sure that they're worth the expense. You may find that the checklist repeats some of the content of the chapter; such reinforcement can only prove beneficial.

1. Create your mailings to provide information to genuine prospects (and not to "readers"). Prospects need and want information to help make a buying decision. Give it to them. Answer every reasonable question they might have. That means you're going to be lengthy.

2. Don't let anyone tell you your copy is too long. Or that no one will read it all. Your concern is not with the 98 out of 100 people who won't respond, anyway. It's with the one or two of 100 who can be persuaded to buy what you're selling.

   Long copy works. It works because it's complete, not because it's long. You're parting someone with his money. That requires information and persuasion. It's not done with a brief message.

3. Listen well to Don Kanter, vice-president, Stone & Adler, Inc. Don says, "Copywriters think their job is to write copy. That's equivalent to a salesperson saying, 'My job is to talk.' The job is not to talk. The job is to sell. Selling is the end result; writing is the means we use to reach that end."

4. Be wary of using advertising people who tell you how "creative" they are, or what fine writers they are, or how people admire the advertising they create. Don't even be impressed by an award that's been won, or by technical expertise. Rather, ask for samples of their advertising that got action by mail. That's your criter-ia. Never equate "creativeness" with "effectiveness."

5. Don't trust people's opinions of your mail advertising. If it's unusual, clever, cute or funny, they'll like it. But the objective of your advertising is not to amuse or entertain. It's to inform, to persuade, to sell. That kind of advertising never wins a popularity contest. Only a sales contest.

6. People read advertising mail to find out what's new, to get information of interest or benefit, to save money, or for ideas to help them do their job better. Is that what the reader finds in your mailings?

7. In your copy, don't get carried away with your newest product feature. It's important to you and perhaps gives you a competitive edge. But the reader also wants and needs information on the basic benefits your product offers. So don't underplay the regular benefits in your enthusiasm to describe your special new feature.

8. Don't think all you have to do is talk about your product and its advantages over competition. You must also document the need for it. Use case studies, case histories and official figures. Give specific examples of how your product solves the reader's problem.

9. Don't just say it, prove it! Everyone makes claims. But, your statements are believed only if proved to be true. So, support them with facts and figures. Use testimonials and case histories. Offer guarantees. Your product features can be proof of the benefits you promise. Remember that words like "quality," "value," "service," and "dependability" aren't proof of anything.

10. Test, test, test. Let's say a sale results from one out of 100 people receiving a particular mailing—a 1 percent return. Now, let's say a test gives you information that leads to a sale of one of the 99 who didn't buy. Bam! You've improved results by 100 percent and cut your advertising cost-per-sale in half! (But when you test, make certain you test an area with potential for a dramatic increase in results.)

11. The brochure is not your salesman. The letter is. So sell with it. It's never a "cover" letter. Because your brochure costs so much more, you think it's more important. Wrong! The letter is far more important. (I'm talking about the type of letter you should be using.)

    Put into the letter those great sales points buried in the brochure. Don't be afraid of three or four pages.

12. Relax. Be natural. Forget all those "our's" and "we's." (You're not really that pompous.) But use as many "you's" as you can. Remember that your letter is one person talking to another person. It's not a speech. If it reads just like your brochure, it's a lousy letter.

Don't let the writer think it's immodest to use "I" and "me." Those little pronouns help make it a personal communication. Again, one person talking to one other person.

13. Use short words, short sentences, short paragraphs. They communicate best. But don't try to sell with a short sales story or a short letter. A short letter can get sales leads, but not sales decisions.

14. Make your copy look easy to read. That's another reason for the short words, short sentences and short paragraphs. Try an opening paragraph that's one short sentence. On every new paragraph, indent the first word five spaces. Use wide margins. Underline key words and phrases. Use subheadings to break up a lot of copy. Save all the "easy-to-read" mailings you get. Use their techniques in your mailings.

15. Never set your letter in a typeface other than a typewriter face. (Consider having an excellent typist actually type out the letter.) The more your letter looks like an actual letter, the better it will work. (Don't be "done in" by an art director who doesn't understand this.)

16. Be direct. Come to the point fast. The "point" is the main benefit you offer the reader. You're direct when you answer the reader's unspoken questions, "What's the deal?" "What's in it for me?" Again, when you do that, you tell him the main benefit he gets. Nothing is more important!

    It is said that most letters are improved by eliminating the first paragraph. I've seen some that were improved by eliminating the first four paragraphs.

17. Use a good checklist to make certain you cover all key points. Don't fail to make an important point just because you made it in a previous mailing. Say it again!

18. Don't ever throw out a successful "old" mailing to start using a "new" one unless the new letter has outpulled the old one in a split-run test. Granted, you and your salesmen are sick-to-death of the old one, but not your prospects. "New" and "different" does not necessarily mean "better."

19. Use a P.S. Use a strong one. Use it to restate your most important point, or, for a testimonial, or, to give a reason to act now.

20. Do everything you can to get action! Can you offer a free look? A time limit? Money-back guarantee? An easy payment plan? Billing to a bank card, American Express, Diner's Club or Carte Blanche?

21. End your letter by telling the reader exactly what he should do, when he should do it, how he should do it, and what he stands to lose if he doesn't do it.

CHAPTER 16

No-Nonsense Advertising for People Engaged in Professions, Business, and Agriculture (Part A)

Norma Olney, who majored in biology, has found her calling writing copy for ads that appear in medical journals. As a senior writer, she is planning campaign strategy for a major pharmaceutical account with Gil Flannery, the account exec who handles several such accounts.

"Norma, as you know, our client has made a major breakthrough in developing a salve for the treatment of psoriasis. In addition to news-type ads in general books such as the <u>AMA Journal</u> and the <u>New England Journal of Medicine</u>, we'll go heavy in the dermatology mags. Now here's what I'm thinking, and I hope you'll go along. Suppose we ... "

Professional advertising in the health field is a serious occupation. Your advertising is going to be scrutinized by doctors, hospital administrators, and others who will be upset by the slightest suggestion of inaccuracy.

Those who write copy for such a critical audience are likely, as did Norma, to have a background in biology, chemistry, and other scientific subjects that enable them to survive in this demanding field. There's no place for the superficial writer in professional advertising.

Business Advertising Is Big but Unknown by the General Public

Despite the fact that there are far more business magazines than consumer magazines, few in the general public ever see such magazines, let alone read them. While the usual person can readily discuss *Time* or *Newsweek*, a blank look will greet you if you mention *Plant Engineering*, a strong magazine in the industrial field.

Professional advertising is a far cry from the general consumer advertising that appears in television, newspapers, and big circulation magazines. Consumer advertising that sells furniture, jewelry, gasoline, milk, perfume, airline trips, stock offerings, and a myriad of other personal products and services is a vital concern of many copywriters. Business advertising, however, is the chief and often only concern of great numbers of copywriters, especially copywriters in advertising agencies and in the advertising departments of large manufacturing firms. Furthermore, many copypeople write both consumer and business advertising.

Business advertising is often called "business paper" advertising. This is too narrow a term, because business advertising includes trade, industrial, and professional advertising. Don't look for such advertising in general magazines, newspapers, outdoor posters, radio, or television. Instead it appears almost exclusively in business publications, a term preferred to "business paper."

Nearly every field of enterprise is served by one or more publications, a magazine or newspaper that is published periodically and contains news and information of special interest to those in the industry represented.

Thus, *Drug Topics* is an expertly managed and edited magazine, that is circulated to pharmacists. *Metal Forming* is a magazine of the industrial type; *Progressive Grocer* is one of the many magazines of the trade type that serves the grocery field. *WWD* goes to the clothing industry, and *American Funeral Director* is read by most of the country's morticians.

There Are Several Types of Business Advertising

Because you can write acceptable copy for one class of business-publication advertising doesn't mean that you can do so for another class. For instance, you may be comfortable writing to physicians about a new pharmaceutical product, but you may be decidedly *uncomfortable* if you're told to write about a capacitor that will be featured in a magazine advertisement read by electrical engineers.

What you learn very quickly is that business advertising embraces a vast array of products and services and that much of it is exceedingly technical and complex. What will give you a sense of quick humility is knowing that the people reading your copy are, in the main, experts, specialists in their fields, who are quite ready to find flaws in what you have written.

As you read the following brief descriptions of three of the chief types of business advertising, you may be struck by (1) how different they are from each other, and (2) how odd it is to call advertising addressed to professional people such as doctors and dentists "business advertising." This is not so odd when you realize that such advertising generates much business in surgical equipment, pharmaceuticals, dental equipment, and numerous other products. Thus, it is professional advertising and business advertising at the same time.

Trade Advertising. The advertisements in business publications of the trade type are designed to gain the selling and merchandising support of the dealers who offer your product for resale.

When you write this kind of copy, remember to follow the 3Ps formula: product, promotion, and profit. Emphasis on one, two, or all three of these elements is characteristic of all trade advertising.

Industrial advertising. Advertisements appearing in business magazines of the industrial type enable one industry to advertise to another industry usually about items, such as a punch press, that can be used for helping production. In contrast to trade advertising, industrial advertising is not concerned with the factor of resale.

Professional advertising. Professional advertising, which appears in such publications as *Journal of the American Medical Association* and *Journal of the American Dental Association,* is aimed at professional people who can use your product and recommend the use of your product to others.

In addition to doctors and dentists, professional advertising is addressed to other professionals, such as architects, lawyers, and teachers.

To avoid confusion, we will use the term "business advertising" to refer only to that kind of advertising that

Figure 16–1. Unusual industrial advertisement. The use of artwork instead of photography makes this advertisement stand out because most industrial advertisements use photographs for illustrations. In addition to the attention-getting headline and illustration, the advertisement presents factual, informative copy.

appears in business publications—trade, industrial, or professional. Direct response house organs, films, and specialized presentations—all aimed at the trade—will be eliminated in this discussion.

For the time being, so will "collateral"—all the display or point-of-sale materials, training manuals, merchandising presentations, and portfolios that copywriters are called upon to produce and that usually come under the heading of "trade."

Business Advertising Is Important but Supplementary

Business advertising is essentially a supplementary selling force that strengthens and meshes with the merchandising and selling program of the advertiser.

Here are some facts to remember about business advertising.

- Business-publication space rates are low compared with consumer media. Thus, some copywriters may consider business advertising unimportant. Some agencies don't consider it worthwhile to hire competent writers skilled in business copy because space commissions aren't high enough. Yet there are notable exceptions to this. One large agency, for example, has a vice president in charge of their business-publication operation.

- Some advertisers and agencies feel that consumer advertisements alone can do the job and that specially designed advertising to trade or industry is not necessary. Such thinking can lead to unsound and wasteful advertising, especially in trade advertising.

Retailers can switch customers from one product to another. They can favor one product by displaying it at eye level on the shelves and putting others down low where people have to stoop to get them. Consumer advertising can and should be supported with a good, heavy program for the trade in most cases.

At Times, Trade and Consumer Advertising Are Similar

Sometimes trade advertising and consumer advertising aren't much different. In *Progressive Grocer,* for example, you will find many advertisements offering products used by the dealers themselves, such as paper bags, twine, and business machines. This, of course, is consumer advertising even though it appears in trade publications. The magazine's primary interest to them, however, is in its offering of a product or service as a source of profit, because these people are in business to make money—to earn a livelihood.

The beautiful new color of a transparent comb, for example, may be advertised in the *Ladies Home Journal* in terms of its vividness, glowing good looks, and newness. Advertising for the same comb in the trade papers that reach drug and department stores would also tell of the new color idea, but it would interpret this new look in terms of why more people will want and buy the comb; how well it is advertised to create a demand; and how store tests showed sales went up quickly when it was displayed.

And the advertisement might end, "If you haven't seen them … if your salesperson hasn't been around and told you the mighty pretty profit story we've got to tell, let us know—but quick. Better write or call right now."

There is no fancy writing there, just a straight appeal for action. But don't misunderstand. Trade advertisements can be dramatic and interesting and you can employ all the basic essentials of effective copywriting already mentioned in previous chapters.

Trade advertising, as previously said, is generally confined to products or services handled by wholesalers or retailers for resale. Some exceptions might be the advertising of flour and baker's supplies in bakery trade publications read by wholesale and retail bakers. Another exception is the advertising of certain equipment such as meat cases, frozen food cases, and paper bags in grocery and meat trade papers. These products, while not purchased for resale, can very properly be advertised in trade papers as a type of consumer advertising.

Products advertised to the trade are often nationally advertised through magazines, newspapers, radio, and TV. When this is true, you may often be called upon to tell the trade the story of these consumer advertising programs so that dealers will know and appreciate the promotional help the manufacturer is giving through the national consumer campaign.

Be Vigorous and Enthusiastic in Trade Advertisements

"Clever" slogans or gimmicks alone in small space will rarely pay off as trade advertising techniques. Such thoughts as "Beans by Glick Always Click," run time after time in trade advertisements with the assumption that "we're doing a job with the trade," do not offer retailers any reason for featuring Glick's beans.

Tell the trade how it can make money with Glick's beans—how repeat sales steadily grow—or how to display the product more successfully. Tell the retailers that store tests have revealed above-normal turnover and shelf velocity. Isn't that what good sharp salespersons would ordinarily tell dealers? They certainly wouldn't come in time after time just chanting "Beans by Glick Always Click."

Use as much space as possible. Only then can you give a certain amount of prestige and importance to the product. You need that space for fair readership and for a complete sales talk.

Many advertisers and agencies will turn out poorly produced business advertisements on the grounds that "the budget won't stand better stuff." This is faulty thinking when you have something important to say or when the time is critical (such as during the announcement of a new product, a price slash, and so forth). Get in there and pitch for more color, better art, or more space in your business advertising.

Trade advertisements will usually require more copy than consumer advertisements since you will be much more concerned with explanatory material. Also, your profit-minded readers are more willing to read long technical material if they see value in what you say.

Enthusiasm—the enthusiasm any good salesperson feels and expresses when talking to a prospect—is a priceless element of trade advertising. Such enthusiasm should be evident in every line of your copy because it carries conviction. Your enthusiastic ideas will be expressed in language that will generally be lower level than that used in industrial or professional advertising, but they will usually be expressed more forcefully and more colorfully.

The Message from Your Trade Ad Will Be Used in Sales Talks

Your whole week's wash done in 30 minutes…while you shop!

This headline was obviously written for an automatic washer. Assume that it is the headline of an advertisement in a campaign ready to break in national consumer publications. Support for this consumer advertising will be pro-

Figure 16–2. Industrial advertisement with stress on safety. Safety is constantly on the minds of those engaged in heavy industry. In this advertisement appearing in *Modern Machine Shop*, the emphasis is on the elimination of oil and mist. A large number of safety problems are of concern that, as the ad points out, affect health, morale, and productivity.

Figure 16–3. Unusual executive-management advertisement. White space is used artfully in this advertisement that is also noteworthy for its use of rich colors in red, blue and light green. It stands out among other advertisements in the magazine. *Reprinted courtesy of Polaroid Corporation.*

vided through a special campaign to reach the trade. Electric appliance stores, department stores, and a few special outlets will be the trade in this case.

The people who run these stores handle automatic washers for resale. To them, the only value of the claim "Your whole week's wash done in 30 minutes … while you shop" lies in the fact that this is a powerful weapon to use in their sales talks. It helps them sell more "X" washers.

Consider the foregoing heading. The thought expressed in it will probably be the basis for other consumer advertisements and will be used to merchandise that advertising to the trade. The people who handle the "X" washer—and prospective new dealers—will thus be informed that a comprehensive and effective national advertising campaign is starting; that it will reach people and prospects in every locality; and that, naturally, it will stimulate interest in the washer and bring people into their stores for more information or a demonstration.

Highlight National Advertising Support

An orthodox treatment might start out this way. The first advertisement is a double spread, uses some color, and employs the type of news headline mentioned in the chapter on headlines.

> Most powerful consumer advertising ever … To help you ring up record sales on "X" washers.

Subhead: New, surefire, full-page color advertisements run in 5 leading magazines—aimed to reach more than 65% of prospects in your own neighborhood!

Second subhead: All through the year, these advertisements will appear in *Ladies Home Journal, Family Circle, Better Homes & Gardens.*

The illustrations might show a few typical advertisements, as large as possible; small covers of the magazine mentioned; and, possibly, a small chart illustrating how 65 percent (figure used only for example) of prospects are reached by this advertising, for the average dealer.

The copy would explain why the consumer advertisements should be effective, why people are interested in saving time and in being able to do other tasks while clothes are being washed. All copy would be written from the dealer's side—how all this advertising is aimed to work for him; how it brings people into the store; and how it actually pays off at his cash register. Such an advertisement might logically ask for action at the end, like this:

> Continuous advertising support in your own neighborhood is only one reason why the "X" franchise is such a money-maker for dealers. A franchise might be available for you. A special Profit Table that shows sales and profit potentials for your own locality is yours on request. Get yours—and other facts and figures you should have. Better do it now ... before your competitor's request arrives first.

Notice that the headlines in this advertisement are quite long. The headlines and the subheads, however, certainly tell the story, and that's a good practice, because two kinds of readers see trade advertisements: Quick readers who seldom read more than the heads and subheads, and Thorough readers (a small group) who will read anything and everything having to do with their business. If you can get your fairly complete story into your headings, chances are you'll get high readership from both classes of readers.

The headlines contain some "you" element and mention the name of the product. The whole tone of the advertisement is on the "you"—directed straight to the dealer—and that is an essential in trade advertising, because the writer must explain everything the advertiser does in terms of benefits, profits, help, and so forth that the dealer-reader can expect from the product or service being advertised.

Bring National Advertising Support Down to the Local Level

Assuming that the national advertising is the most important message the "X" company has for dealers, the next trade advertisement in the series could well treat the "local" effect of all the advertising the "X" company does—including the new campaign. The heading for such an advertisement might be:

> New "X" washer advertising "talks to"
> nearly 7 out of every 10 people
> Right in your neighborhood.

The whole advertisement might use the "believe it or not" technique, and with several illustrations and a little copy for each, show how the advertising works for every dealer in his own area. This "local advertising" versus "national advertising" question is important since the local readership of national advertising is the only interest any dealer has in it. Boasting that yours is the biggest national advertising campaign ever to hit the magazines will leave the dealers cold unless you can show them the effect this campaign will have on their own customers. The question in any alert dealer's mind is, "What does this advertising do for me?"

The next several advertisements in the trade series could dramatize store tests and store experiences of progressive dealers with the "X" washers. Advertisements would explain how the consumer advertising brought in prospects and

Figure 16–4. Executive-management advertisement. Global matters are very much on executive minds these days as this advertisement with its eye-stopping illustration demonstrates.

how, with a few little display ideas of the dealer, sales of the "X" washer rose to a new high level. The purpose here, of course, is to persuade dealers reading about these experiences to think that they can do as well.

Stress What's New and Furnish Proof

Time of the year, specific problems that arise at times, and new company policies—all these and more affect trade advertising. The nature of these special conditions often dictates what the advertisements will say.

Suppose, for instance, users had experienced considerable difficulty with the Swirler—a patented clothes agitator of the "X" machine. Dealers were getting too many complaints; machines were returned; sales dropped ominously. One effective solution would be to eliminate the Swirler and introduce a new agitator of proven trouble-free operation. It would be big and important news for the trade to know:

> Revolutionary new clothes agitator of "X" washer eliminates service headaches!

The copy would explain how a "torture treatment," equal to five years' normal use, was set up in an independent laboratory and that five machines out of every one

Figure 16–5. Association advertisement. A challenging headline and strong copy effectively convey the plastic industry's story.

hundred going through the factory were put through this test. Attention would be focused on the "trouble-free new agitator" that would certainly overcome most of the previous difficulty. The same theme would be used by salespeople making their calls.

Suppose the washer action of the "X" washer is "oscillatory," while other washers use the "reciprocating" action. If it could be proved in unbiased tests that oscillatory washers were far superior, tests could be set up in noted laboratories, and the results of the tests would make the basis of a series of advertisements. Here's one such headline:

Oscillatory action of "X" washer
Outperforms reciprocating 3 to 1
in actual tests

You'd have to be prepared for controversy and you'd need to be very sure of your facts, but if the advertiser were strong enough, he could settle the argument positively. He might possibly devise an action that combined the advantages of both—if they were equal to varying respects—and, so to speak, work both ends. The heading in such a case might be:

Advantages of both oscillatory and reciprocating actions
Combined in radical new oscil-rep action of "X" washer

To the trade, that's big news. And as mentioned before, you've got to know the trade and know what interests dealers.

Build Heavy Promotion for Dealers and Salespeople

Your whole week's wash done in 30 minutes … while you shop!

Building around this theme line, you will create a package or a packaged promotion that will include point-of-display pieces, gimmicks, results of store tests, direct mail, and newspaper art for dealers' use. Also, you'll include a portfolio for the salespeople who call on dealers. The portfolio explains the whole deal. Added to the foregoing, you will also promote the package to the trade through regular trade publications.

Assume the Swirler is an ingenious and exclusive agitator of the "X" machine and is the main reason why clothes wash so quickly and get so clean. Also, the Swirler is one important part of the automatic operation that permits people to leave the machine while it goes on with its washing. You'll then dramatize the Swirler in every way, bring it into all your promotion and advertising, and introduce a catchy theme that will be the core of your promotion. The Swirler is your U.S.P.

You may decide to use the traffic light idea, which is quite suitable for this example. The slogan or keynote will be

Stop Washing
Go Swirling

In the consumer advertising, headlines would continue on the timesaving and leisure theme, as exemplified by the headline "Your whole week's wash done in 30 minutes." Copy would explain how this was possible, heavily promoting the Swirler.

Somewhere in the main illustration or in an illustration of the washer or Swirler, you might show a gaily waving banner with traffic light effects and the theme words, "*Stop* Washing … *Go* Swirling." Already you can see how this device can be carried through all promotion and advertising, including magazines, outdoor, newspapers, direct response, display material, trade, and even radio, where sound tricks would take the place of the signal lights.

Here's the promotional material that you could logically include in your package and that you will promote in your trade advertising (to be explained later on).

- A series of newspaper ads and radio and TV commercials for the dealer's use, built on the "stop and go" idea.
- A series of three to six direct-mail pieces for dealers to send to selected prospects, built on same idea.
- Several large display pieces using the red "stop" and green "go" traffic light idea, possibly plus one life-size cut-out figure of a traffic policeman with a red and green light above him (flashing on and off alternately) for use in store window or inside store next to "X" washer or washers on display.
- A series of "how to display the 'X' washer" suggestions. This would consist of several illustrations of putting

Figure 16–6. Trade advertisement that features heavy advertising support backing the company's products.

washer on elevated floor platform, placing certain display material around it, casting colored light from a baby spotlight on it in store or window, and other similar ideas.

Then, using the same red and green traffic light technique, all this material or pictures of it will be arranged in logical order in a salesperson's portfolio, titled

Stop Washing ...
Go Swirling

What to Stress in Trade Magazine Advertisements

With all this material ready to help the dealers and with the attention-getting red and green traffic light treatment, we now have:

- A packaged promotion—complete and available for the dealers to help them capitalize more effectively on the power of the consumer advertising.
- A gimmick—in the red and green lights and the slogan, which will provide immediate identity in all collateral and trade advertising.

First, the trade advertising could announce the big consumer campaign already mentioned, bringing in the slogan and the traffic light idea in a subordinate way. In every trade advertisement—sometimes large, sometimes small—this plug would always be made: "*Stop* Washing ... *Go* Swirling." Use of this phrase would provide a note of recognition when the salesperson called with the same device and wording on the front of his portfolio.

The second advertisement in the trade series might be a big play on the central theme of "*Stop* Washing ... *Go* Swirling" that explains how this catchy little selling phrase will work on the minds of people to wear down sales resistance and excite curiosity. Copy would still devote some words to the big advertising support.

The following advertisements might run in this order:

1. Big splash on all the material available to help dealers sell more "X" machines.
2. Reproductions of telegrams from dealers telling how well the new advertising is working for them.
3. Straight appeal to dealers to "see what's in the big black book the 'X' salesperson has ready to show you." This refers to the portfolio, and the copy would hint of the "money magic" that the book brings to readers.
4. Series of advertisements built on store tests that show how successful dealers used all the material available on "X" machines and how well sales are going. In other words, success stories.

Sell Dealers and Salespeople on Value of Advertising and Promotion

You've probably noticed that the store tests are mentioned many times. Unbiased store tests are convincing to dealers. First, no dealer can overlook such data when they have to do with his bread and butter. Second, not many advertisers are willing to go to the expense and trouble of making the tests (and results may not be suitable for publication). When such test results do appear, they constitute material that is far from common.

All the advertisements mentioned as suitable for this series—whether based on store tests or not—would, of course, always end with a strong urge to the dealer to "write or telephone us to get the full facts," or something along that line.

It should be mentioned that when the entire campaign was approved and the first samples of all the advertisements and materials were finally available, everything was timed in order that the whole plan could be presented to the sales organization at its convention, so the salespeople could sally forth into their respective territories filled with the fire and fervor of their cause. It's just as important to sell the sales force on your advertising and promotion as it is to sell the dealers or "the trade."

Try Institutional Copy If Company Makes Many Products

Most trade advertising tries to sell a product or service in a very direct way. Some advertisers, however, cannot always do this. Consider Hotpoint, which markets many products sold through the appliance trade.

If every Hotpoint product division decided to use an aggressive advertising campaign in trade magazines, a competitive free-for-all would ensue. In the case of such multiproduct advertisers, it is sensible to use an institutional theme. Here, for example, the name "Hotpoint" is promoted and each product is introduced as a member of the Hotpoint family of quality appliances. The selling-theme idea may be expressed as the "quality of Hotpoint."

Merchandising the national advertising and selling the dealer on promotional assistance and institutional advertising are not, of course, the only means of using trade-paper space. Hundreds of different ideas, plans, deals, promotions, and "packages" are offered to the retailers through trade campaigns. The subject matter of your trade advertising will be dependent upon the nature of the most important message you must convey to the trade who will resell your product.

Thus, if you are marketing a brand new product through a company with no national prestige or name, perhaps the most important single thing for you to accomplish in trade advertising is to build confidence in your company and in its financial background among the dealers. If you are introducing a new automobile, you may wish to inspire such confidence and backing by running trade advertising on your personnel and their experience in manufacturing, designing, and selling cars.

Trade advertising, as you have examined it here, is good for one major result: to gain the selling support of retail merchants. In order to do this, your trade campaigns must offer something to the dealers that will make them want to feature and sell your product.

Underlying everything, of course, is their desire to make a profit.

Still other advertisements will put the stress on the handsome display units offered to dealers. These units provide an attractive means of displaying the manufacturer's line, a very important consideration to dealers who have limited space and a pride in the appearance of their stores. Accordingly, you will find many trade advertisements that stress display opportunities or that feature packaging.

Do You Push Product, Advertising, or Both?

Copywriters are so product oriented that they almost automatically think in terms of product first, and yet this can be a mistake in some trade advertisements.

Let's assume that you are selling a product without any special distinction and that there is no new product feature to exploit in the advertising. Still, the product is a steady seller in retail outlets and must be advertised to maintain its competitive position. Assume, too, that the product has an outstanding promotion behind it that includes big circulation consumer magazines, television, radio, and newspapers.

Clearly, the promotional backing should be headlined and the bulk of the copy should concern the support the

Figure 16–7. Trade advertisement that points up the product's number one selling position and the advertising support behind the product.

dealer can expect. The product can simply be mentioned at the top of the advertisement, but the promotion is the point on which you concentrate.

Consider the situation of a new product that has appealing sales features and a strong promotional support behind it. In this case, the headline and possibly an opening subhead can stress the product *and* the excellent advertising support. The first impression the dealer gets is that the company is offering a hot new product and is backing it with equally hot advertising. You can then follow the headline by talking first about the product, or you can start with the promotion. Either is suitable.

Consider the situation in which General Electric is introducing a new microwave oven, a proven seller. When the advertiser has a name as powerful as General Electric, any product it introduces is big news in itself. In this case, stress the product and then bring in the advertising support strongly.

As you can see, there are various ways to handle this question of product or promotion. The point is that promotion can be as important as the product and should sometimes be stressed first and harder than the product.

Advertising backing should be sold specifically, enthusiastically, and with conviction. Too often, dealers aren't aware of

Figure 16–8. Executive-management advertisement. Appearing in *Fortune* magazine, this advertisement reflects the importance today of global markets.

the extent of the support; they should be told. Furthermore, because many dealers resent the amount their suppliers spend on national advertising, trade advertising should make it clear to them just how much such advertising can help them. Dealers must be sold over and over again on the value of promotion, and even company salespeople need such reminding because they, too, frequently fail to realize the power of a good advertising campaign.

Following is a suggested checklist that you can use after you have written an advertisement to appear in a trade magazine. See if your layout and copy embody most of these points:

Layout
Overall impression of excitement, liveliness, and vitality.
Liberal use of subheads.
Strong illustration of product in sufficient size to sell it.
Physical presentation of headline is big and bold.

Copy
Strong, exciting headline. Has specific benefit and/or promise.
Strong sell for product with sufficient details supplied.
Strong sell of promotional backing with sufficient details supplied.
Use of dealer language.
Use of material that will appeal to dealer, such as reference to display qualities of product, turnover, experience of other dealers, profit to be made, and customer appeal.
Use of strong selling subheads to lead reader through advertisement.

Overall employment of the 3 Ps (profit, product, and promotion).
Overall feeling of excitement and enthusiasm.
Copy about advertising backing brings advertising down to local level.
Copy *sells*—doesn't just *tell*.

An Important Backup: Trade Collateral

Closely associated with trade advertising is the writing and production of what is called "collateral." Under this term are included all of the special pieces of advertising used by the advertiser's own sales force and by the retail merchant in product selling.

Such things as special mailing pieces addressed to the trade, portfolios containing promotional aids for the sales force, store display material, and other miscellaneous advertising tools are called "collateral." Their creation represents an important and voluminous part of almost every copywriter's duties.

Much material is normally supplied to the product manufacturer's salespeople to aid them in soliciting business from the trade. If you are an agency copywriter, you prepare a considerable amount of this material on behalf of your clients. Preparation of such items will occupy an even greater part of your time if you are writing copy for an advertiser in the advertising department.

Sales Portfolio Performs a Three-way Function
Perhaps the most usable collateral piece regularly supplied to a sales force is the "salesperson's portfolio," or "sales manual."

These portfolios do a threefold job:

1. They show the dealers that advertising is being put behind the product, both nationally and locally; what display material is available to dealers for their stores; and how the combination works in preselling the product for the dealers.
2. They arouse enthusiasm for the product and its potentialities in the dealer's mind and generate the same emotions among the salespeople for their own advertising and merchandising promotion.
3. They offer the salesperson a complete graphic checklist to follow in giving the dealer a sales talk.

There are two important points to remember in writing a sales portfolio. One is to *write simply*. Much of the value that the sales force will derive from your portfolio will come while they are in routine conversations with their retailer customers. If you can write interesting, punchy, and informal copy in the portfolios you prepare, the salespeople will often find themselves picking up these expressions and using them in their daily calls. Use the kind of talk that salespeople would be likely to use.

To give yourself a working background in this trade talk, you should spend some time on the road with a salesperson, go on calls, and listen to what is said to the dealers. If you are working in the advertising department of a manufacturing house, you will find that such trips are considered standard procedure. If you are a copywriter with an advertising agency, you may find trips more difficult to arrange, since the agency will want to keep you busy writing. Advertising executives, though, will recognize the value of such extracurricular experience for copywriters.

A second point in writing sales portfolios is to *keep them brief.* Imagine yourself as a busy, impatient dealer who reluctantly agrees to take the time to look over the portfolio. Imagine yourself as the harried sales representative who goes over the portfolio with the dealer. Most dealers must be persuaded to give sales representatives time to put on a presentation of the advertising and display plans described in a portfolio. Prepare material so that it can be read and understood in a quick reading.

Here's What Goes into a Sales Portfolio

A lot of consultation will occur between the agency, company, and copywriter about the portfolio's content. Content can vary from portfolio to portfolio and changes in marketing and advertising strategies can affect it. Still, there are certain basics and certain materials standard to most portfolios. Here are some of the inclusions:

- A cover, with an illustration of interest, that tells what the portfolio is all about. If you are giving salespeople a manual covering their firm's spring and summer advertising, say so. Headlines of general interest to dealers and salespeople may be used if desired, but they are not necessary to the effectiveness of good sales portfolios. Usually, however, a breezy headline, such as "Even MORE Sales Power for YOU This Spring!" is a common device used to generate interest in the ensuing material.
- A section devoted to the planned advertising campaign. In this part of your portfolio you will show either reprints of the advertisement, which may be slipped into a "pocket" or flap in the pages, printed right on the pages themselves, or "tipped in"—glued along one edge and inserted in the manual.

  Normally, you will discover that the pocket method is best for advertisers who have a heavy and complete schedule of advertisements, since it enables the salesperson to carry more advertisements conveniently. It is also much less expensive than printing or tipping.

  In addition to showing the advertisements in your portfolio, you will want to give a complete schedule of where and when those advertisements will appear and how many readers they will reach. You will also want to point out to the dealers, if the campaign you show is national, that much of the national circulation is right in their town, even in their own neighborhood, so that the advertisements usually function partly as local advertising.

  If the operation is of a type that supplies complimentary advertising to dealers for their own local use, you will include a page or two in your portfolio to show

Figure 16–9. Trade advertisement putting stress on advertising support behind the product.

reprints and tell how to get them.

The same is true of all phases of the advertising program. Show the whole business: posters, car cards, TV and radio programs, spot announcements, and any other national or local advertising effort that is being put behind the product.

- A section devoted to merchandising. In this part of your manual you will illustrate the store and window display material that is available to the dealer and tell how to order it. You will point out how this material is designed to "tie in" with the national advertising theme in order to provide recognition and recall value and to give the final impetus to the buyer at the point of purchase.
- A windup page or pages where you can ask for the dealers' support, emphasizing that featuring your product means more sales for the dealers and is evidence of their sound business judgment.

You're Involved with Store Display Material, Too

Many copywriters make the mistake of giving too little attention to the creation of store display material. Because much of such creation is an art problem—simply adapting advertisements or parts of advertisements and simplifying

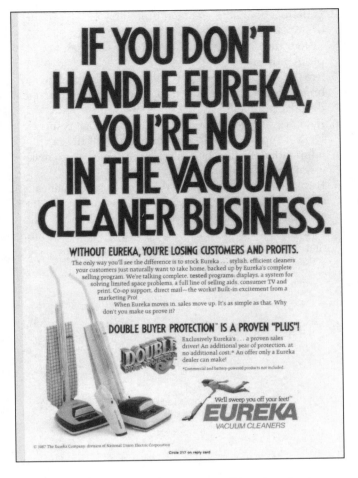

Figure 16–10. Trade advertisement featuring the importance of the product.

them to different proportions—you can easily take the attitude that it does not require much thought on your part. Many sales are lost daily because copywriters did not understand the nature of the display piece they were building and made an error that caused their work to be wasted.

For example, suppose you are copywriter on a chocolate pudding account. You do a good job of writing and directing an advertising campaign based upon the simple idea of large heads of happy, cute children just about to take a bite of Yummy chocolate pudding. A headline may tell the special good things the pudding has to offer. Following the headline is short copy and, at the bottom, a picture of the package and a logotype displaying the brand name. The campaign is fine. Everyone likes it. In the magazines or newspapers, it's sure to get lots of attention.

Now the pudding manufacturer wants you to make up a counter display card for grocery stores.

You whip up a counter card, perhaps 12 inches by 14 inches, that is almost an exact duplicate of your advertisement. That makes good sense, you say to yourself. A cute kid eating the product will be a sure-fire hit with shopping mothers.

The big hope for counter cards is that they are used together with a counter display of the product: card in the middle, packages around it. Where is the product identifi-

cation on your counter card when this happens? It is down at the bottom of the card, completely obscured by other merchandise. It's still a cute picture—still has that important appeal to mothers—but nobody has any idea what you are advertising.

That sort of mistake stems from a too hasty examination of what kind of collateral material you are asked to prepare and an inadequate study of how it is to be used.

When you've devised an effective display, you've helped the salesperson where it counts the most: at the point of sale. If your display piece is faulty, you make the sales job more difficult. Help the salesperson with consistently good displays.

Help Company Salespeople Help the Dealers

In addition to portfolios and displays, you will be called upon to write items designed to aid salespeople in making their rounds. These materials include circulars, merchandising folders, sales letters, and postcards. All of these items will usually contain highlights of one or more of the basic elements of your sales portfolio—advertising or merchandising.

The function of these sales aids is to arouse interest among the dealers to give display prominence to the product you are advertising, to push it because they are convinced that your advertising is helping them do business.

You will also probably write items to help the salespeople directly, such as sound slide films, skits, and other dramatic presentations to be used in sales meetings and sales rallies. By associating with the staff of the sales department, by cultivating their friendship and understanding, you can build information on sales problems that will help you throughout your career.

Some Questions to Ask Yourself About That Trade Advertisement You've Just Written

About the headline

1. Does it make clear what you're selling?
2. Does it sound exciting and enthusiastic?
3. Does it call attention to one or more of the 3Ps (product, promotion, and profit)?
4. Does it offer a strong benefit?
5. Is it powerful enough to stop the reader?

About the copy

1. Does it provide a strong sell for the product and provide the important product details?
2. If national advertising support is furnished, is the support sold strongly and are specific details of the advertising supplied?
3. Have you supplied information that will appeal to the dealer, such as display material provided, turnover possibilities, experience of other dealers who have handled the product, product's appeal to customers, co-op plans offered, and pre-selling of product as a result of supplier's advertising?

4. Have you used strong *selling* subheads—not mere labels—to lead the dealer through the copy?
5. Does your copy stress the 3Ps sufficiently (product, promotion, and profit)?
6. If the supplier supplies local advertising, have you emphasized this strongly?
7. Do you really *sell* the product or merely *tell* about it?
8. Do you really *sell* the advertising support or merely *tell* about it?
9. Have you created a strong sense of excitement and enthusiasm throughout the copy?

About the layout

1. Does it create an overall impression of excitement, liveliness, and vitality?
2. Are the headlines big, bold, and attention getting?

3. Is there a dominant element, preferably of the product or display of the product, in the layout?
4. Is your logo big enough and distinctive enough to supply identification?
5. Are the subheads strong enough, physically speaking, to break up the type mass and to lead the reader through the advertisement?
6. If you've supplied a coupon, is it correct in all respects? Does it supply enough room to write all of the needed information? Is the coupon set off in some way to make it stand out?
7. Has the layout been executed so that it is mechanically correct? (This includes use of a typeface that fits the character of the product, use of a tasteful border, judicious use of white space, setting copy lines in a width that invites reading, and arrangement of elements to avoid a cluttered look.)

CHAPTER 17

No-Nonsense Advertising for People Engaged in Professions, Business, and Agriculture (Part B)

Almost all advertising majors interested in copywriting envision themselves writing consumer copy for such familiar items as cosmetics, soaps, cereals, and clothes.

"It came as a shock," said Anne Swenson in a letter to her advertising prof, "to find that my first assignment was an ad for steam turbines. And after that, it was an ad for industrial pumps, and still later, I wrote an ad to appear in Hardware Age for a line of do-it-yourself tools."

There's a great big world out there, unknown to the average person, of heavy industry, top management, and retail merchants. There are hundreds of publications that serve these industries, and there are many agencies and copywriters to turn out specialized ads for them.

"I found out in a hurry," said Anne, "that I had to learn a new vocabulary for each of my audiences. I wrote copy aimed at plant operating engineers, heads of Fortune 500 companies, owners of small drugstores, small dairy farmers, and big-time agribusinessmen. What a challenge and what fun!"

It's a common experience for writers such as Anne to find, after their initial shock, that they feel good about themselves when they write business advertising. There's a substance to it that is often lacking in certain types of consumer advertising.

At the end of a working day, they can feel that they've been helpful to those engaged in the important world of business. That hydraulics engineer, for example, appreciated being informed of an exciting development in industrial pumps. And the retail merchant welcomed news about a product that will draw customers and increase sales.

Job Satisfaction and Challenge Are High in These Four Fields of Business Advertising

Think about the sharp and demanding people you'll be addressing in your advertisements aimed at the *professional, industrial, agricultural,* and *executive-management* fields—doctors, dentists, architects, lawyers, engineers, managers of huge manufacturing plants, superintendents, efficiency experts, farmers of all types, owners of giant agribusinesses, suppliers of farm equipment, ceo's and presidents of worldwide corporations, business owners who make decisions affecting thousands of workers, and other executives at all levels.

In general, these are well-educated men and women who are in the habit of making every moment count. They have no time for advertising that offers no benefit, but they welcome advertising that does. When writing to the people in these four fields, you'll usually pitch your approach at a higher level than that used for the readers of trade publications described in the preceding chapter.

While the term "professional" covers architects, lawyers, teachers, and others; our emphasis in this chapter is on the medical field, although much of what is said also applies to the dental field.

Writing for the Medical Profession Is a Special Challenge

Copywriters assigned to agricultural or industrial accounts can, if they are observant and industrious, learn the problems and language of these fields; it is more difficult to achieve similar success in the medical field. However, there are nonmedical copywriters who write medical or dental copy. Just as industrial writers profit from having a technical bent, so the medical writer profits from a scientific bent. An especially good prospect for such work would be a person who took pre-med in college or who dropped out of medical school. Some advice for copywriters in the professional field (especially in the writing of copy for advertising appearing in medical magazines) is offered in the paragraphs that follow.

Medical Advertising Suggestions

Use the specialized language of the medical profession. Look over this excerpt from a medical magazine advertisement.

> Most patients with sustained hypertension have normal cardiac output and an elevated total peripheral vascular resistance. Reducing cardiac output, as beta blockers do, lowers blood pressure but does not seem to correct the primary abnormality—increased peripheral resistance.

This example is relatively simple compared to the writing in many medical advertisements, but it demonstrates the language level expected of medical writers. Readers of medical magazines have learned a different vocabulary; it is your obligation to learn it and to use it until it becomes your language, too.

Advertising of pharmaceuticals is especially demanding of the writer who lacks thorough grounding in chemistry and biology, as the following excerpt demonstrates:

> Warnings: BEFORE CEPHALEXIN THERAPY IS INSTITUTED, CAREFUL INQUIRY SHOULD BE MADE CONCERNING PREVIOUS HYPERSENSITIVITY REACTIONS TO CEPHALOSPORINS AND PENICILLIN. CEPHALOSPORIN C DERIVATIVES SHOULD BE GIVEN CAUTIOUSLY TO PENICILLIN-SENSITIVE PATIENTS.
>
> SERIOUS ACUTE HYPERSENSITIVITY REACTIONS MAY REQUIRE EPINEPHRINE AND OTHER EMERGENCY MEASURES.

Avoid overly personal language. As in industrial advertising, the "you" approach should be avoided. When doctors read advertising in medical journals, they expect to be addressed in a professional manner. Don't write like an advertising copywriter. Medical people, whose writings and talks have been twisted and misrepresented by promoters of products, are distrustful of advertising people. Thus, they dislike "ad-dy" advertising but will accept advertising written in the style of one doctor addressing another.

Although few advertisements in medical magazines use consumer language or consumer approaches, an advertiser will occasionally choose a more "consumerish"

approach. If handled well, this approach will be welcomed by the readers as a change, but it must be viewed as a variation, not as standard procedure. One such departure was used by a respected pharmaceutical company in the following manner:

Illustration:	Portraits of Francis Bacon, Oliver Cromwell, Louis XIV, Carolus Linnaeus, and Thomas Gray.
Headline:	The touch of Louis XIV, it was said, would cure gout. But he was one of many famous men who had gout.
Opening copy:	Gout has had its share of wondrous "cures." In fact, in the early eighteenth century, many French physicians believed that a touch of the hand of Louis XIV would cure gout. Louis, however, was unable to cure his own case of gout. And that must have led to some embarrassing moments at medical meetings of the day!

Use scientific evidence. Persons dealing in matters of life and death eschew the casual approach. They want proof that is presented by recognized authorities and backed by careful investigation. Little wonder then that you must constantly draw upon evidence to back any claims you make—and woe to you if the "evidence" is not supported by proven facts.

Because readers of medical journals are not going to accept unsupported statements about results obtained by the advertiser's product, medical advertising is replete with the kind of support supplied in the following:

> Typical of the results obtained against these troublemakers: In a recent study of patients with acute, nonobstructed lower urinary tract infections caused by these organisms, Gantrisin therapy produced sterile urine in 9 out of 10 patients.

This supporting statement was backed by a table from the study and a statement about where the reader could obtain the complete findings of the study.

Scientific evidence is usually in the form of research conducted by doctors and sponsored by reputable pharmaceutical houses such as Bristol Laboratories, Sharp & Dohme, and Eli Lilly. Before a new product is accepted, many research studies may have to be made, a process that may take years.

A whole advertisement may be taken up with a description of a study that includes both the positive aspects of the product and—just as important—its limitations, given in the form of warnings about its use.

In this legalistic period of class-action lawsuits, advertisers and those who write their advertisements must pore over every word and every punctuation mark. The specter of a lawsuit that may cost millions, or even billions, is always in the back of their minds. No copy is more agonizingly prepared and scrutinized than the copy appearing in medical publications.

Recognize their desire to keep up in their profession. One of the trials of the professional person—doctor, dentist, lawyer, architect, teacher—is that new developments occur so rapidly that it is almost impossible to keep up. Thus, the

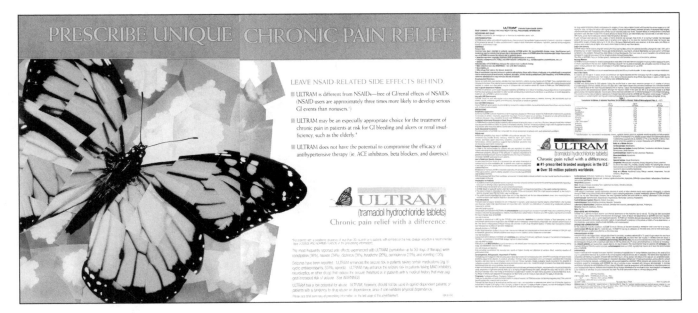

Figure 17–1. Professional Advertisement. In addition to this advertisement, a full page of prescribing information accompanied the advertisement. It is not included here. *Reprinted courtesy of the Warner-Lambert Company.*

doctor is constantly attending medical meetings, reading scientific journals, and exchanging viewpoints with other doctors to keep abreast of the latest advances.

Your copy should recognize this need to be informed. If you have new features, stress them. If yours is a real breakthrough that will make the reader a better professional person, stress it so that it won't be overlooked.

This compulsion to keep up with changes is illustrated admirably in the following excerpt from an advertisement for medical reports that appeared in a medical journal.

Headline:	Announcing a stimulating new educational alternative for AAFP members.
Subhead:	ER Reports gains AAFP approval! Now family physicians can stay up-to-the-minute and earn 30 AAFP prescribed credits a year.
Opening copy:	Good news for busy physicians. This year you have a practical and provocative alternative for meeting your CME requirement. Thanks to recent approval by the AAFP's Continuing Education Committee, ER Reports gives you one of the few sources of AAFP prescribed credit in a convenient journal form.

Any conscientious physician never stops learning or educating himself or herself. Medical school graduation is just the first step in a lifetime educational process. You will do well to consider your advertising in that context. Advertising is a part of what the doctor needs to know. He reads the advertising, along with the editorial content of medical journals, to keep his head above the flood of new developments in the field. In short, you are instructing the physicians in something that they may not know about your product.

Recognize the reader as a user or recommender. Doctors and dentists especially, among professional people, may be viewed in two ways: (1) as persons who will use the advertised product, such as a dentist's drill or a surgical instrument, in conducting their profession, or (2) as persons who will recommend the product's use to patients. A drying lotion for acne, elastic stockings for varicose veins, and a mild soap for bathing babies fall into this category. Ivory Soap, as an example, advertised for many years in medical journals because a doctor's endorsement is so powerful with the new mother anxious to give her baby the best care.

If your chief objective is to give physicians enough information about a product to enable them to recommend its use, your copy will probably include such phrases or headlines as:

Effective Therapy You Can Safely Recommend

After *your* counseling on the safety issue, she may decide that her best option is the *(name of product)*

Give your patients a break from ordinary antacids

When you write a good medical advertisement you are preparing the way for a call by "detail" men or women. These are highly trained sales representatives who call upon doctors (and dentists) to do just what your advertising attempts. They tell the doctors about new developments and, in a low-key way, suggest the use of the product by the doctor.

If you have written your copy well, the detail person's call will be more successful because you've already planted the important product points in the doctor's mind. You will not do your detail person a service, however, if your copy consists of column after column of tightly packed small type that makes your advertisement look like a section from a difficult-to-read medical textbook. Even eager-to-learn doctors are daunted by such advertisements.

Figure 17–2. Farm Advertisement. This advertisement combines several elements of effective advertising: A long powerful headline, a believable testimonial, and an appealing illustration that is especially good in farm advertising in its emphasis on the family factor in running a farm.

Figure 17–3. Agricultural advertisement with appetite appeal. In this advertisement aimed at a specialized market of beekeepers, we find strong reason-why copy, allied with an illustration with inviting appetite appeal. *American Bee Journal* carried this attractive advertisement that is a cut above a great many advertisements in agricultural magazines.

You'll pave the way for your detail person more effectively by at least occasionally cutting down the excessive columns of backup laboratory proof in favor of an open-looking advertisement with copy that both the busy doctor and the detail person can read and understand more easily and more quickly.

The Healthcare Industry: A Vigorous Cousin to the Medical Field

Closely allied to the medical profession is the healthcare industry, one of the fastest growing segments of American business. This explosive growth has opened new opportunities for copywriters who possess the proper training and background. Because so much of the healthcare business is allied with pharmaceuticals, copywriters working for such companies or their advertising agencies have ideally had strong schooling in chemistry and biology.

The combined factors of an aging population and an increased awareness of health concerns in all age groups are responsible for the heavy amount of professional advertising focused on medicine and healthcare. This focus should continue for many years.

As this new edition is being written, there is evidence of healthcare's promising future. The opening of a 280 mil-

lion dollar healthcare research center by the Procter & Gamble Company, an industry leader, exemplifies this growth opportunity. This center will concentrate on research relating to over-the-counter and prescription pharmaceuticals. Projections indicate $9 billion in sales by the year 2010 for this area of the company's business.

Industrial Advertising

Although you may be a star in writing consumer copy, you may feel like a beginner again if you switch to industry copy. Lacking the feel for technical copy, you're not at home writing to engineers, technicians, factory managers, chemists, electronics experts, and others who make up the industrial market.

Consider *your* background and abilities. Now read this description of the reading material found in an industrial magazine listed in *Standard Rate & Data Service.* Do you think you're qualified to write advertisements to the readers of this publication? Do you have the background, or more important, the *inclination* to do this work?

Serves those in such fields of experimental mechanics as stress analysis by strain gages, photoelasticity and brittle coatings—fatigue and vibration studies—impact—instrumentation. Feature sections include papers of experimental investigating methods and evaluation of new techniques and instruments, behavior of structures under test and analysis, and solutions to production problems.

Or this publication, edited for:

Mechanical, electrical, and nuclear engineers in the total power market—utilities, process and manufacturing industries, service complexes, plus the consulting engineering firms working in the power technology; they are responsible for the design, construction, operating, and maintenance of equipment and systems involved in power generation plus the process, control and supply of energy in its many forms—electricity, steam, water, compressed air/gases, and so forth.

Just Because You Can Write Good Consumer Copy Doesn't Mean You Can Do Equally Well in Writing Industrial Copy

Good writers usually learn quickly what they must know in order to write about most consumer products. There is no way, however, that they can learn quickly what they need to know about such products as industrial pumps or giant turbines. They can't bluff. They can't dazzle hydraulic engineers or electrical engineers with cute selling phrases.

Before they write, they must study the products, see them operate, and talk to the plant people, the salespeople, and the advertising manager. They must study the specification sheets and engineering catalogs. When they thoroughly know the equipment, its uses, and its applications, *then* they might be prepared to write in the language of their hard-boiled market. No glib consumer approach will work here.

Now and then someone in the advertising field will assert that there's little difference in the writing demands of consumer and industrial advertising. Contrarily, if you talk to people who have written both, you'll hear many times how an industrial advertisement appearing in an industrial publication that charges $6,000 a page took more creative time and downright hard thinking than a consumer advertisement in the *Reader's Digest,* which currently charges more than $160,000 for a 4-color page, or a 30-second television commercial that costs $400,000 for time charges and many more thousands for production.

Any writer in the consumer field has, on occasion, rattled off radio commercials or print advertisements in a few minutes, especially if this person has been working on an account for a long time and is thoroughly familiar with the background and general style desired.

In contrast, it's just about impossible to dash off an industrial advertisement. Every word is weighed and every fact is checked for accuracy and acceptability by an extremely critical audience. Furthermore, the vocabulary is usually specialized, extensive, and technical.

Some copywriters *do* work well in both fields, but they are the exception. Most writers concentrate in one or the other. It is more likely that a good industrial writer can adapt well to consumer copy than that a good consumer writer can switch successfully to industrial advertising.

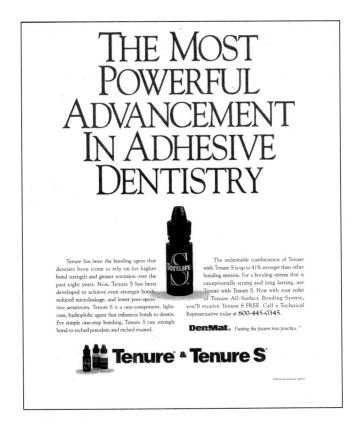

Figure 17–4. Professional advertisement. A very strong headline combined with persuasive and readable copy make this a good example of professional advertising. Because a new product is being introduced, there is a strong news flavor throughout.

What do you need to make it as an industrial advertising copywriter? Most of all, you should couple a reasonably good writing ability with an affinity for technical material or an education in technical or engineering curricula. Engineering school dropouts are often the types who adapt well to industrial advertising; they have the necessary vocabulary and ease in technical matters.

Tips for Writing Industrial Copy

Make your approach much less informal. The "you" approach, so loved by the consumer-product writer, is usually out of place in industrial advertising. You don't cozy up to a vice president of manufacturing, a plant manager, or a safety engineer. They don't use the products you sell; they consider their purchase for use in plant operations.

Then, if they like what they read, they may ask someone else to "look into it" or to "specify" it. Because there is no personal use involved, you have little or no chance for the "you" approach or for informal, personal language.

Don't use hard sell. You don't push industrial readers. You don't high-pressure them. You don't urge action as you do with consumers or trade-advertisement readers. The industrial purchase is likely to be large. A committee may be appointed to decide whether your product should be used plantwide. Perhaps the purchase will be in hundreds of thousands of units.

Possibly six months to a year will pass before the purchasing agent is told to put through the order. In that time, there may have been competitive bidding, demonstrations, tests, and presentations.

Against this background, you would look absurd if you were to use the consumer-copy exhortations of "order now," "act quickly," and "don't delay." Industrial buyers simply aren't the impulsive types; they aren't swayed by such urgency.

As a rule, avoid the light touch. You may occasionally invest industrial advertising with humor or a lighthearted, consumer-type approach—but rarely. Your readers aren't poring over industrial advertisements to be amused or entertained. Your product might reduce accidents, increase production, cut down pollution, or improve morale.

These are not lighthearted goals. They are approached in a serious manner, and you call upon the vocabulary of the readers to tell them what your product will do for their plant or the products they produce. That vocabulary will be down-to-earth, specialized, and often difficult; it is not carefree or (usually) even cheerful. This kind of writing comes hard to consumer-product copywriters who, to this point, have prided themselves on the "easy, conversational touch."

When you're writing to engineers, purchasing agents, and other industrial realists, you give facts, not frills. Although businesswriting principles in general apply to industrial-publication copy, some specifics are explained in the following material.

Get into your story quickly. Although interested readers of industrial advertising are willing to read long copy, they are not willing to waste time guessing what the copywriter has in mind. Many of your readers go through mountains of reading matter each day. Although your copy should be complete, it shouldn't be leisurely. Let the reader know immediately through headline, illustration, and the first copy block what you're talking about.

Getting into your story quickly means that your headlines are specific, and research shows conclusively that specific headlines get better readership. For example, here are three headlines for the same product. As the headline becomes more specific, it becomes more effective in attracting and holding readers:

Headline 1: The production boosters

Headline 2: Get more working time out of that router

Headline 3: Three reasons why Superior routers can cut downtime as much as 70% over your yearly production schedule

Push long-range savings more than long-range costs. Your competitor's metal tubing may cost 40 cents a foot but last only half as long as yours. At 60 cents a foot, your tubing would, consequently, be a better buy. Remember

that purchasing agents are buying greater productivity for the firm; that means they are interested in saving manpower and materials. Thus, long-lasting materials and equipment are almost always their first interest.

Connected with the same idea is the industrial buyer's continual interest in machines that will require little maintenance. Little maintenance translates to little cost and, over the years, long-range savings.

Write copy with an individual reader in mind. In many advertisements you'll be writing to management in general. Preferably, however, you should direct your copy with a specific person (called a "buying influence" in the industry) in mind, such as the engineer, the plant architect, the maintenance supervisor, or the head of operations. Direct your message to that person's interests. Use the person's language.

Using the "language" means being aware of not only the words but also the daily concerns of the person. What are the concerns and motivations of industrial management? Here are some concerns that would be appropriate if you were selling a floor absorbent that reduces slipping accidents on factory floors:

- To reduce insurance rates
- To boost worker morale
- To maintain production levels
- To lower accident rates
- To make the plant known as a good place to work

Here's how you apply these ideas in tough factory language:

"A worker who slips as he walks down a line of melting pots can be in for a bad burn—and you're in for a session on workmen's compensation regulations."

Another example:

"If your factory had a high accident rate last year because of skids and falls on stained or soaked floors, then you should think about using a floor absorbent as part of your company's regular safety equipment this year. And when you think of floor absorbent, think No-Slip. Better yet, specify it."

Another:

"Risks belong upstairs—not on the ground floor. Business management necessarily involves calculated risks, but when it comes to slippery floors on the manufacturing line, play it safe."

As for language, use words and terms of the field, such as "specify," "man-hours," "downtime," "men on the line," "OSHA regulations," and "union stewards." If you don't know the language, learn it—and do so before you write your first industrial advertisement.

An example of a down-to-earth industrial headline that achieves the right tone by using appropriate language is this quotation headline, supposedly said by a rugged-looking worker sitting astride a steel beam in a building under construction:

"If the guy who specifies bar grating had to make the field modifications, he'd specify something better!"

Use a strong news slant. Purchasing agents and others who read industrial advertising are constantly asking, "What's new?" Industrial readers are on the prowl for information that will help them or their firm do a better job. Your new product, or the new use for your product, should be presented in a fresh, lively, news style.

An example of the news approach in an industrial headline:

Diablo introduces the first printer that runs on four wheels

Another example:

Head:	A bright new engineering achievement moves air management into a new technological age
Subhead:	Newex. The all-new spun aluminum fan line from Greenheck.

Give complete information. Talk about your servicing facilities, the construction of the item being sold, the lasting qualities, and the type of work for which it is best suited. Tell why your product gives better performance. Why is the material in your product superior?

Remember this also: Your advertisement may be clipped and filed. It may be dragged out later to be placed next to a competitive advertisement. The copy that does the most complete job may get the sale. Industrial advertising, unlike much consumer advertising, is often referred to long after the advertising has run. Make your copy worth going back to. The typical industrial-paper reader doesn't shy away from long text—as long as it has something to say.

Although industrial copy should be thorough, the reader of such copy is like anyone else in not liking dull, lifeless catalog-type copy. If your material is better suited to a specifications sheet or parts catalog, save it for those uses.

Recognize a problem—then show how your product can help solve it. The readers of industrial advertising are beset with problems; abrasives don't hold up; V-belts break; the accident rate is too high; or perhaps production is falling. If your advertisement suggests a way out of their troubles, they'll read it like a novel.

An example of the problem-solving approach is afforded by the following headlines and a portion of the body copy of an industrial advertisement:

Headline:	Pittsburgh Paints Solves Downtime Problems
Subhead:	PROBLEM: Avoid costly production interruptions when repainting
Subhead:	SOLUTION: PPG Fast Dry Alkyd Industrial Enamels

Figure 17–5. Industrial advertisement using testimonial. There are a number of aspects of this advertisement that make it a good example: (1) An attention-getting quotation headline. (2) The use of real people on the job. (3) Quoted material in the body copy interspersed with hard-hitting straight copy. To put all of this copy in quotes would be unrealistic. The combination approach is effective.

Copy:	PPG Fast Dry Alkyd Industrial Enamels have a tough, brilliant, high-gloss finish that's dry to the touch in about 15 minutes and to handle in 30 minutes. This compares to normal alkyd paint drying time of 6 to 8 hours ...

Catch interest with case histories. The usual industrial buyer moves cautiously. Industrial advertising is largely directed to those who buy in big quantities. Successful use of your product by another business makes absorbing reading for persons going over your advertisement. Perhaps, in addition to selling them, you are helping sell management on buying your product. Your case history of successful use of your product may often be the only sales argument that carries weight.

One difficulty with the case-history approach is that the "history" used may be so narrow in application that many of your readers won't find what you say applicable to their situation. This problem isn't acute if you are using a verti-

```
CLIENT: Mobil Chemical
JOB:    :60 Radio
TITLE:  "Insects"
ANNCR:  If you could hear the insects that eat
        your corn, you'd start using Mocap
        nematicide-insecticide as soon as possi-
        ble. If you could hear rootworms (SFX:
        ROARING) ... wireworms (SFX:
        SCREECHING) ... nematodes (SFX: HISS-
        ING) ... and black cutworms (SFX:
        CRUNCHING). If you could hear the
        worms robbing you of 40 bushels of corn
        or more per acre. . . If you could hear
        the cutworms cutting your good, healthy
        stalks off at the base... (SFX: TIMBER
        FALLING) . . . .If only you could hear
        it... (SILENCE). But you can't. So you
        may be sitting back using no insecticide
        at all. Hoping the worms don't do too
        much damage this year. Or maybe you're
        using an insecticide that doesn't protect
        against all four of these deadly pests. We
        repeat: if you could hear the rootworms,
        wireworms, nematodes and black cut-
        worms, you'd be using Mocap--the only
        insecticide in America that protects
        against all four. Because you're in busi-
        ness to save corn. And so is Mocap.
        Mocap. Get it. (ROAR) And save the
        corn.
```

Figure 17–6. Clio-winning radio commercial. High drama is created here through outstanding sound effects that will rivet the attention of the farmer-listener—or that of any other listener. *Writer: Mike Hughes, Agency: Martin Agency, Richmond, Virginia.*

cal magazine (one that concentrates on a single industry, such as a magazine directed toward manufacturers and users of industrial pumps). In such a case, almost anything that can be said about industrial pumps will interest the majority of the readers.

On the other hand, if your advertisement appears in a horizontal magazine aimed at a wide cross section of industries, your case history may be of limited interest unless you make it clear that the kind of technical expertness applied in your case history would also be useful in other applications.

An example of the case-history approach written in such a way that readers will interpret the results broadly is shown in this excerpt from the body copy of an advertisement for an energy-saving ventilation system. This well-illustrated advertisement supplies *two* short case histories for added effectiveness.

No. 1

It's bad enough that the cost of energy is going through the roof, but the Chelo Brothers of Rhode Island discovered that their energy itself was going up the exhaust flue and through the roof. They installed a Seco Wash Ventilation System. The energy they're saving will pay for the system in about 3 years.

No. 2

In a United Airlines Flight Kitchen where as many as 20,000 meals per day will be prepared, both energy efficiency and almost nonstop operation are key requirements. With A Seco Wash Ventilation System they not only save thousands of dollars on energy but countless man-hours, too.

Use important-looking, reader-interest headlines. Industrial advertising deals with heavy industry and with big purchases. It is addressed to hard-driving decision makers engaged in important work. Make your headlines reflect the character of the industrial people and their jobs both in typography (no delicate script types) and in content.

Hit hard and specifically in attention-commanding headlines. A good example is the following headline that offers a benefit sure to appeal to step-saving, cost-cutting industrial-magazine readers. Not only is this headline very long (but specific enough to arouse quick interest), it also uses a price figure. Inclusion of price is rare in industrial copy, especially in headlines. If it is possible to mention price, however, it will increase readership.

Main headline: MicRIcon Rewrites
the law of
Cost and Effect

Subhead: It's a complete 3-mode process control system with automatic or on-demand printout logging for under $5,000!

Two more long headlines follow. Both are admirably direct, unlike many industrial advertisement headlines.

Microcomputer Hero

Intel's new 8051 packs more processing ingredients onto a single chip than ever before. And serves it up with total development support.

Designing a control system with 15 relays or more?

Specify this rugged General Numeric programmable controller that speeds up system design and gives you more flexibility for less money.

Think of readers' interests when selecting illustrations for industrial advertisements. You won't often be the one to determine the nature of an illustration to be used, but if you are, ask that the product be shown in use, if possible. Much of industrial advertising is concerned with equipment and machinery that often look dull when not in action. "Action" in such cases normally means that you will show a person, or persons, using the equipment or operating the machinery.

There are, on the other hand, occasions when a person shown in an industrial advertisement is a distraction. Unless the presence of a machine operator contributes to the understanding of the working of the machine, the industrial reader may prefer to look over the details of the equipment minus any human element. The operator is superfluous.

Figure 17–7. Humorous executive-management advertisement. Occasionally, humor may be found in business advertisements that usually take a serious approach. This example, appearing in *Business Week* magazine around tax time commands attention and a smile. It stands out, also, because it uses artwork instead of the usual photograph.

Big-space, dominant-illustration advertisements pull good readership from industrial readers. Because of their technical bent, however, not all of these illustrations are interesting in the consumer sense of the word. An engineer will find strong interest in a cross section of a machine, in a schematic drawing, and in a blueprint. Graphs and charts are a form of industrial language easily understood by industrial readers. They sometimes pull better than so-called interesting illustrations.

In calling for illustrations, always remember that the industrial-magazine reader is most often technically oriented. This reader's taste in illustration material is, accordingly, different from that of readers of consumer advertisements. Occasionally, successful industrial illustrations will have a consumer flavor, but most such illustrations are suited to the vocational bent of the industrial reader.

Coupons sometimes play a role in industrial layouts. When you prepare such a coupon, you will ask for a respondent's name and company affiliation. Too often,

however, the person's title is not requested. This causes trouble, because coupons come back to the advertiser's sales department and are then distributed to salespeople according to sales territories.

Such salespeople customarily find that only a few buying influences in any given plant are accessible to them. By asking for the title of a coupon respondent, you may provide a sales representative with a big list of buying influences upon which to call. Unless the title is given in the coupon, the sales department won't know whether the respondent is a purchasing agent, a company president, or an engineer; accordingly, the salesperson will not know just how to follow up the lead generated by the coupon. To repeat: *Always* ask for the title of any respondent to a coupon.

In addition to coupons, there are other, more popular ways to elicit responses from the readers of your industrial advertisements. One method is the inclusion of an 800 number. Fax numbers are also widely used. Another method of generating reader response is the Reader Service card. At the bottom of industrial advertisements, you will find words like these: "For information, circle 532."

Think in Management Terms When Writing Industrial Copy

Never forget that you're writing to a management person who is often engineering-trained. Well-educated in business as well as in technical matters, ambitious, and mature, this person is likely to be skeptical of advertising claims but will read advertising for news of products and techniques.

This person has pride in running a tight shop, and this pride is reflected in concerns about rising production curves and about safety as it affects production. What are management concerns? A few include union relations, insurance costs, problems with OSHA (Occupational Safety and Health Act), worker morale, and the perception by even higher management that the manager is doing a good job.

If industrial copywriters want to catch interest, they use terms that people in industrial plants use. They may refer to dust, fumes, mists, hot metal, flying particles, harsh light, or dangerous heat levels. Reference to familiar equipment—bench grinders, metal shavers, lathes, saws, and high-speed drills—will also catch attention.

You begin to see from what has been said in this summing up that you get very specific in industrial copy. Fancy writing is out. Direct, almost hard-boiled, writing is in. Think of yourself as being on the factory floor and casting your experienced management eye on what is going on around you. You see a problem. Now, as the copywriter, you write copy that points out how that problem can be solved with your product or service. If you do your work well, you're going to help management do a better job, and that is the primary goal in industrial advertising. The following checklist shows you how you can attain that goal.

Agricultural Advertising (or Agribusiness or Agrimarketing Advertising)

Unless you've lived or worked on a farm, you face a handicap—not an *impossible* handicap, but a severe one—in writing farm copy. And even if you *have* an agricultural background, you still have some handicaps to overcome. Your experiences as a hog raiser in Iowa, for example, mean little when you're communicating with a Southern cotton grower. Even those working the same crops have their differences, as a Minnesota farmer and an Arkansas farmer can tell you. Individual farmers know their soil and climatic conditions better than anyone else. Because of this, they are most responsive to advertising that seems to be aware of their particular problems.

What You Should Know about Agricultural Life

Apart from the actual business of writing to the farmer, what are some aspects of agricultural life you should know?

How farmers get information. Advertising is only one way of communicating with the farmer, an assiduous information seeker. Much of what a farmer needs to know about new products, methods, and equipment is obtained from state fairs, farm shows, agricultural schools, and word of mouth with other farmers, county agents, company salesmen, and farm dealers. It is especially important to farm marketers to get the farmer to talk to their dealers.

As for advertising media, farm magazines and farm radio are generally rated as the most important in communicating with the farm market. Approximately 50 percent of the farm advertising budget is invested in farm magazines. Following these two are outdoor advertising, television, and direct mail. Direct mail is becoming more important because farmers with specialized crops sometimes are so few in number that it is unprofitable to publish a magazine to reach them.

The farm market is sharply segmented. The extent of segmentation in agriculture is evident in the more than 200 farm magazines and in the many regional and specialized editions published in the field. Some magazines, catering to the regional and agricultural differences, offer as many as 300 different versions of their publications to meet the needs of readers.

To serve the segmented markets, many of the magazines are vertical, such as *Guernsey Breeders' Journal, Grass & Grain, The Sunflower,* and *The Sugar Producer.* In addition to segmentation by agricultural interest, there is segmentation by geographical region, as illustrated by *New England Farmer* or *Tennessee Farmer.*

To cover general farming news and developments, there are a number of strong horizontal publications, including *Successful Farming, Farm Journal,* and *Progressive Farmer.* These publications are useful to farmers who shift from crop to crop as prices vary and to those such as hog raisers, who must also raise grain to feed their hogs. A horizontal magazine can also appeal to the dairy farmer, who puts the herd out on part of his acreage and then raises corn, wheat, dry beans, oats, barley, and hay on the remainder of the acreage. Such readers are well served by the broad scope of the horizontal publication.

"Helpful" is a key word. Farmers help each other. They share with each other. They tell neighbors about products that work for them. Word-of-mouth communication is important for fertilizers, seeds, and tractors. Such help, when it is needed, has been called "country manners." Companies serving agriculture, such as John Deere for tractors, Pioneer for seeds, Monsanto for pesticides and herbicides, and Ford for trucks, are compared in terms of their helpfulness.

A majority of the nation's farms and ranches are run by individuals who, in the main, do not have full-time help. This means that products and machines do the work once supplied by full-time help. Thus, farmers need all the help they can get from whatever source.

Understanding the farmer. Farmers are individualists who are still strongly dependent upon others, whether the "others" are the banks that carry their loans, the farm machinery companies that defer payments, or the government that subsidizes them. Despite such help, they feel isolated, put upon by nature, the government, and the unrelenting laws of supply and demand that determine the prices they can obtain for what they produce.

You must realize the wide gulf between the agribusinessmen farmers, whose acreage is vast and equipment investment enormous, and the small farmer eking out a bare living from a few acres. These considerations affect the nature of your advertising.

Compare the medium-size farmer in the Midwest with a modest number of feedlot cattle to the big-scale Western rancher with 5,000 grazing cattle. For the first, you'd probably show the familiar red barn and nearby corn field in your illustration. For the latter, you'd show open plains and many cattle grazing.

Problems vary markedly from farm to farm. Dairymen have little in common with citrus growers. A truck farmer faces a different situation than the Dakota wheat grower. All, however, are classed as farmers.

Understanding the farmer calls for an understanding of the role of women on the farm, too. As farms have become more businesslike, women farmers have taken an increasingly important role in farm management and financial decisions. Women farmers are now, very often, owners or partners in a complex operation.

Figure 17–8. Agri-business advertisement that emphasizes research. Claims are meaningless to farmers unless backed by proof such as offered in this advertisement that appeared in *Farm Journal* magazine. Initial attention is obtained through the use of the dramatic, but relevant, illustration.

Specific Tips in Writing to the Agricultural Field

Despite all the differences in those who make a living from agriculture, there are some general principles you can observe in writing to them. Several are highlighted below.

Watch your language. Today's farmers have, to a large degree, received specialized instruction in agricultural school. Even those who lack this formal instruction have learned about antibiotics, animal husbandry, and the fine points of difference in hybrid seed corn on the job. You can use a level of language, therefore, that is much above that used some years ago. Be careful, however, that you don't write like a city person trying to talk to a farmer.

Use farm language and don't slip. If you do, your copy will be discredited. Remember, too, that although the farmer can be addressed in language more sophisticated than was once advisable, there are farmers who are not college educated. Avoid literary flavor and too much urbanity.

As an example of down-to-earth language, here is the headline for a chain saw:

"Three busted saws in the barn aren't worth a lick when I've got fence to build."

Though not elegant language, it is expressive, and it conveys a sense of realistic earthiness. In contrast is the following section of copy, aimed at a somewhat higher level, that also conveys a sense of on-the-farm language.

Gives instant, on-the-spot moisture readings so you can zero in on the optimum level of moisture for ensiling and harvesting. (Monitor moisture levels of forages and grains every hour if need be.)

To demonstrate how far the modern farmer is from his relatively unsophisticated predecessor of some years ago, here are a few phrases from an advertisement addressed to hog raisers. They demonstrate the technical and scientific bent of today's agriculturalist:

- Confinement research
- Artificial insemination
- Liquid feeding
- Feeder pig specifications

Give them proof. Agricultural people have traditionally been skeptical. Alone much of the time and given to introspective thinking, they are cynical about salespeople and their claims. This is also true of their attitude about advertising.

Testimonials and case histories, accordingly, are useful in agricultural copy if they relate to the reader's particular interest—hogs, corn, soybeans, dairy herd management, and so forth—if they pertain to the reader's geographic area.

Research has become a buzzword in agriculture, as this excerpt from a seed corn advertisement shows:

Results: In this area, this field-tested yield and standability performer averaged $45.30 more profit per acre than 3780; $17.40 more than 3901.

It was no accident. No one has a stronger commitment to seed corn research than we do.

With some agricultural operations becoming so big that they should properly be called "agribusinesses," your copy should stress information, facts, and research. Consider, for instance, a feed company in North Carolina that raises and markets 60 million broilers yearly. This organization owns three farms in Indiana simply to keep the broilers supplied with corn. In addition, the company owns breeder flocks, hatcheries, and processing plants. It even has a substantial interest in a supermarket chain, which functions as an outlet for the sale of the broilers.

The management of such an organization consists of businessmen-agriculturalists. They want proof that what you are selling will help them in the operation of their big business.

In general, proof can also be supplied by certain methods. You can show a product in use. If it is a fertilizer, for example, have the farmer put the fertilizer in a hopper or spread it on a field. You can also show the results of using the product, such as a lush corn field, that resulted from the use of a fertilizer or seed or herbicide. You can describe or demonstrate how to cut labor costs and increase production or yield. Illustrations of equipment and possibly charts, graphs, or tables might do this.

Instill a management feel (in some instances). This suggestion is made if your product or service is designed for the truly big agricultural establishment where the top people are business managers as much as agricultural people. They are buying big-ticket items such as combines, tractors, silos, and other equipment, not to mention fertilizer, seed, and less spectacular, but still expensive, items. Talk to them like management executives.

Obviously, because there are still many small farms, you must pick your situations and products when using management approaches. Nevertheless, the word "management" comes up constantly in agricultural advertising: herd management, crop management, and breeding management. A headline for the latter, for instance, reads:

> Your veterinarian's total breeding management program can help ensure successful results with Lutalyse.

Suffer with them. With some justification, farmers feel that the forces of nature, government, and economics are against them. Let them know that you're on their side and that you know their problems. This can be done subtly, of course.

In an earlier chapter, you were advised to use the suffering-points principle in writing copy. Basically, tell how the use of your product will answer a problem. Farmers have a multitude of problems, including how to dry hay in a hurry; how to hold down bugs and weeds; how to get seeds to germinate even in a cold, wet spring; and how to combat diseases in farm animals. Make the farmer aware that you understand such problems and give him solutions.

Here Are Some Ideas to Use If You Write Executive-Management Advertising

Products and services appearing in executive-management publications reflect the broad responsibilities of the readers, embracing such widely varying items as computers and calculators, financial services, security guard protection, high-speed building elevators, business insurance, corporate jets, and export banking.

We're concerned here especially with the high-level readers of business publications such as *Fortune, The Wall Street Journal, U.S. News, Business Week,* and the business section of the *New York Times.* Included in this readership are the readers of institutional magazines in the hotel or hospital fields and readers of industrial magazines aimed at management in heavy industry.

Horizontal publications such as *Fortune* include a substantial number of personal products in their advertising pages. Mostly, these are luxury products such as high-priced automobiles, watches, liquor, cameras, and other accompaniments of good living.

Gear Your Advertising to the Executive Suite

High-level, urbane language is much more evident in executive-management magazines than in any other business magazines. The men or women in the executive suite are likely to be sophisticated, well educated, and cosmopolitan. Today, they are likely to be global in their thinking. They may be in Japan one week and in Germany for a trade fair the following week.

Recognition of this multinational character of the readers of executive-management publications is quite evident in this small section of copy:

> The American International Group of companies has more pins in more parts of the world with more people offering more kinds of insurance than practically any other commercial insurance organization.
>
> So if your company has a lot of branches around the world, you have to go to a lot of insurance companies around the world to cover each one of them.

As for "urbanity," the writing in many management publications, like so many of the readers of such publications, is relaxed, polished, and very much at ease. This fact is evident in this fragment of copy from an advertisement for a Swiss bank:

> **Incredibly Swiss**
>
> If we were to have a national animal, it would very likely be a St. Bernard. We just simply cannot think of another beast so incredibly *Swiss.*
>
> Originally bred by monks in the 17th century on the summits of the Great and Little St. Bernard passes, the quiet, friendly, and dependable animal became famous for rescuing lost travelers.
>
> It's not that all Swiss are quiet and friendly, but most of us have a thing about being *dependable.*
>
> And we're quite Swiss in this respect at Credit Suisse. For us *dependability* is one of the most basic requirements in business today.

Dullness is the unforgivable sin in the writing of management copy. Although the readers engage in important work, they have a tolerant attitude toward whimsy in the advertising as long as that whimsy is accompanied by material useful to decision makers. For instance, consider this headline by a computer manufacturer.

Bugs, Burps, Glitches, and Other Computer Demons

And then there is the following headline, which is not whimsical but is certainly not dull in the way it addresses itself to management:

Need Business-To-Business Marketing Research?

Determining the competitive position of your brand, product, division or company? Pin-pointing the buying influences for your product? Describing the right target audience? Measuring the size of your market? Developing a new product? Evaluating the effectiveness of your advertising?

Call McGraw-Hill Research

McGraw-Hill Research has a variety of methodologies and techniques that have helped many companies take better advantage of their marketing opportunities. Our closeness to the business-to-business marketplace enables us to provide actionable research for your marketing decisions at an affordable price.

Put McGraw-Hill Research to work for you.

For a quote or proposal call Joseph T. Collins, Manager Marketing Research at (212) 512-3264. Or write him at McGraw-Hill Research, 1221 Avenue of the Americas, New York, NY 10020

If it's a marketing research problem, we probably pioneered the solution.

Figure 17–9. Executive-management advertisement that points up the importance of research in company operations.

You can't control
labor costs.
You can't control
material costs.
You can't control
fuel costs.
But you can control
your bottom line.

Recognition of the exalted lifestyle lived by the upper echelon of corporate management is ever present in horizontal business publications. There is a deference and subtle flattery of those beings who tread the thick carpeting in quiet executive suites. Advertisements for corporate jets that whisk two or three executives swiftly from New York to London and for luxurious foreign hotels that invite their business provide a vision of a life only a relatively few persons may experience. The copy must achieve the right tone—respectful but not fawning. The following headline for a corporate jet embodies this vision:

> With the amount of fuel it takes to fly the aircraft on the left from New York to London, you can fly the aircraft on the right from New York to London. Then Amsterdam, Brussels, Frankfort, and Munich.

While management people are concerned with ecology and the impact of industry on the environment, they are also concerned with such less broad-gauge management matters as profit-and-loss statements, plant safety, and stockholder attitude and satisfaction. Thus, they are always receptive to advertising that tells them crisply, and sometimes entertainingly, about products and services that will result in a better-run business.

Aim your language level at people who appreciate the nuances of good writing. The discussion to this point has centered around the very top management, but you might, in the case of many products and services, be aiming at ambitious middle-management people who have heavy responsibilities but not the final word in very top-level decision making.

If you are consciously aiming at the middle-management executives, your copy may tend to include more facts and figures that the readers can use to arrive at a decision. Advertisements intended for the very top management may, in contrast, be broader and less detailed. The purpose may be to interest the occupants of the executive suites enough to cause them to send a memo down a couple of floors asking a lesser executive "to look into this."

A headline can make it quite unmistakable whether you are aiming at middle or upper management. The following headline, for example, is clearly directed toward middle management:

> Introducing the Xerox 820. You tell us what you do, we'll tell you what it is.

Another:

> The 30-minute file fiasco vs. the 30-second file find

In contrast, here is a head that is unmistakably directed at top management:

> Why shouldn't boards of directors expect something more from accounting firms?

Business Is Beset with Problems That Present an Ever-Changing Challenge to the Copywriter

Every field of business faces ever-mounting problems. It is the executive-management area, however, that is confronted by the biggest worries, as the environmental activists point the finger at industry pollution and depletion of natural resources. Meanwhile, business keeps a wary eye on the aggressive resurgence of labor unions. Where once American business was the unquestioned world leader, that leadership is challenged today from all parts of the globe—Japan, Taiwan, China, the European Common Market, and elsewhere. Criticism is coming from all sides because of the moving of plant operations out of the U.S. to profit from lower labor costs. "Downsizing" has become a reproachful word, as drastic cuts are made in the work force due to mergers and the movement of plants out of the country. The explosion of expensive technology has given many industries the option to either adapt or die.

Most copywriters are not movers and shakers in these cosmic changes, but they must keep abreast of what is happening and how it affects the lives of their customers, and their copy must reflect their knowledge.

Problems in the medical and agricultural fields, while not as diverse as in the executive-management area, give the copywriter in those fields considerable concern. In the medical field, primary concerns include the ever-rising costs, worries about malpractice and class-action suits, and uncertainty about government regulations. The continuing flight of the small farmers, the possible loss of government subsidies, and escalating costs of farm machinery and supplies are of great concern in agriculture.

CHAPTER 18

Like Short Copy? Try Outdoor and Transit Advertising

"**H**ey, Ike! Ever see that great outdoor poster for convertibles that Ford did?" Shaking his head as he looked at his young assistant, Willie Wristen said, "Guess not. Before your time."

"So what about it?"

"Well, when I do copy for outdoor boards, or even for transit cards, for that matter, I keep that Ford poster in mind. It had all of the elements I want in a great poster."

"Short and to the point?"

"That, naturally, and much more. For one thing, it had a memorable line of just six words: 'The only convertible that outsells Ford.' Instant humor, product name featured, and an outstanding illustration tie-in."

"What <u>was</u> the illustration?"

"A baby buggy. I still smile when I think about it. And I still admire Ford for having the nerve and imagination not to show the car. Use this poster as a model. Fewer than seven words, an offbeat message and illustration, and simple words that used humor for a quick reaction."

Welcome to the world of outdoor advertising, Ike, a world where brevity is king and the ability to come up with a memorable phrase and illustration marks you as truly creative. No other medium gives you a sterner test because no other medium asks you to do so much with so little.

A Poet and a Writer of Outdoor Advertising Share Common Abilities

What Ike was discovering is that a poet and a writer of good outdoor advertising share some common abilities. Each is able to convey a powerful message and strong emotion in the fewest possible words.

You may never discover these truths because the average copywriter has few, if any, requests to write outdoor copy. If that chance comes your way, welcome it, because there is little in advertising that offers such a creative challenge. This is true of both outdoor and transit copy if the writer, not content with mediocre copy, tries for a creative twist that will make the copy effective, memorable, and different.

In recent times, outdoor and transit advertising have had problems: the former with environmentalists and many limiting laws, the latter because of the reduced use of inside cards on many transit systems. Yet, each survives because each offers a way to reach out-of-home prospects as they travel to buying centers. Each, while seldom a principal medium, serves as a powerful backup to major campaigns in print and broadcast. Then, on the local level, outdoor advertising may be the only medium usable by the motel, hotel, or eating place that wishes to sell itself to persons traveling through the area.

Figure 18–1. Humorous traveling display. This campaign reversed an eleven-year decline in bus ridership. The Twin Cities (St. Paul and Minneapolis) were the only major metropolitan area in the U.S. to post an increase in bus ridership during the year the campaign was initiated. *Courtesy Kauffman Stewart/Minneapolis. Creative director: Bill Hillsman; copywriter: Charlie Callahan; art director: Damon Lacey.*

Outdoor Advertising

Posters and Painted Bulletins

Posters called billboards by the general public are in standardized sizes. If you're assigned to outdoor advertising, you'll write copy mostly for 36-sheet, 30-sheet, 24-sheet, or 8-sheet posters. These sheets are heavy paper stock and are printed by lithography or silk screen.

In a striking departure from the conventional horizontal posters, the latest development in outdoor advertising has been the emergence of square posters. These large units are being used experimentally by the Leo Burnett advertising agency for one of its brands. See Figure 18-2 for a smaller version of a poster that, while not so square, is distinctly different from the usual horizontal outdoor poster. Proponents of square posters think that packaged goods will find them appealing because they are the same shape as many product packages.

Other developments in the hard-pressed outdoor advertising industry include the option of adding digital message signboards to existing posters. Another innovation, still in the planning stage, is to bring moving laser images to posters. Other hi-tech improvements include computerized painting that results in high resolution. This development has improved reproduction so markedly that fashion advertisers such as Calvin Klein are using outdoor advertising in greater numbers.

You may also occasionally write for painted bulletins. Painted bulletins, usually larger and more expensive than posters, are now generally standardized around the country and are becoming much more popular than in the past. Unlike posters, painted bulletins are bought and produced in individual units. They are usually left unchanged for longer periods than posters, which are most often changed monthly. With painted bulletins, the copy message and illustration are painted directly on a metal surface. The reproduction quality is less consistent than that of posters. In a number of larger markets, painted bulletins are rotated to different locations to vary the advertising message in various sections of the market area.

Painted bulletins have never had the quality of outdoor posters that use lithographed sheets. However, Superflex, a vinyl-coated fabric introduced by Gannett Outdoor Group that can be painted by computer, makes possible painted bulletins with magazine-quality reproduction that will not fade for two years. Because most painted bulletins are customarily repainted two or three times a year, the long life offered by Superflex has strong appeal.

Only Reputable Companies Are Engaged in "Standard" Outdoor Advertising

"Outdoor advertising," as the term is ordinarily used in the advertising business, is intended to apply only to those companies[1] engaged in standard outdoor advertising; that is, it applies to the companies represented by the standard,

---

1 Known in the trade as "plant owners."

Figure 18–2. Subway transit card. Persons riding daily on subways, buses and trains welcome interesting cards to pass the time. An interesting card will obtain intensive readership because there is a long exposure to the message.

well-maintained poster boards; the neat, regularly painted bulletins; and "well-groomed" units. It does not apply to those groups responsible for the torn and tattered circus, theatrical, and election posters, which continue to proclaim their wares months after their advertising usefulness has passed, or the rusty metal signs and crude homemade signs seen decorating fences, buildings, and roadside pastures.

Reasons to Use Outdoor Advertising

People, generally, like to read outdoor advertising because it *relieves the tedium* of the long journey or the daily commuting trip. This, of course, does not mean that people see and read every sign they pass, nor does it mean that the same results would be obtained everywhere. It does, however, indicate that outdoor offers you a huge potential audience for your message—if you make it appealing enough to arouse the public's interest.

Outdoor advertising *offers continuity.* Your message will remain at the same location for a full thirty-day period and may be backing up a copy idea that other advertisements have established. Since most people travel and retravel the same route every day on their way to and from their work or shopping, you are able to hammer home your message to the same group of people day after day after day.

You can *obtain repetition* because an outdoor poster showing will usually be displayed simultaneously on a number of boards along major traffic arteries. As people travel down such roads, they will often see (and read) the same poster several times before reaching their destinations. This constant repetition has a cumulative effect much like that that makes a song a hit. When a tune is introduced, it usually elicits little response; but as you hear it played again and again, you find yourself unconsciously humming or whistling it as you go through the day. The repetition, not the song alone, has made a deep impression; the same is true with the frequent viewing of the same outdoor posters.

Outdoor advertising *permits you to use color* at relatively low cost. Because newspapers and magazines will not accept color advertisements except in large-size space, many publication advertisers who would like to use color cannot afford to do so. An outdoor advertiser, on the other hand, can easily afford to use color, even though the total advertising may consist of only a single painted wall sign.

Outdoor showings of any magnitude *greatly impress dealers* stocking the advertised product. Day after day, they are constantly reminded of the advertising the manufacturer is putting behind the product in order to help dealers sell more of it.

Outdoor advertising is *often the only medium that can successfully reach an advertiser's best prospects.* The hotel signs a person sees when approaching almost every city in an automobile are a good example. They are the only economical and effective means the hotel has for reaching motorists who plan to spend the night in the city.

Keep Them Simple

What you put on that poster must rivet the attention of pedestrians ambling down the street, drivers rolling along in their cars or trucks, and bus passengers peering out of the windows. To get that attention, your posters must offer a good idea, preferably a *striking* idea. Also, the idea should be clever, although, admittedly, great numbers of posters are devoid of any spark. They are ordinary and even dull.

Let's assume you succeed in supplying a clever and/or striking idea. Your poster will still be a failure if you don't keep it *simple*—simple in execution and simple for the reader to grasp quickly.

Simplicity is very evident whenever effective posters are studied. You will find simplicity mentioned often as an important attribute of effective posters. There are, however, some situations in which it is possible to be more subtle in your copy situation—for instance, in a sign on a crowded city street. Such a sign could be read by walkers or slow-moving drivers. Where reading must be done more quickly, however, it is best to use a simple message.

Unfortunately, there is no set formula to follow that will enable you to hit on prizewinning poster ideas regularly. Such ideas are elusive to even the best creative people.

A pair of quotations might be helpful here as the first

Figure 18–3. Humorous outdoor poster. In addition to supplying ideas for purchasing through the illustration of many items, this outdoor poster commands immediate attention through the use of an unusual word in the headline. *Courtesy of Fitzgerald & Company.*

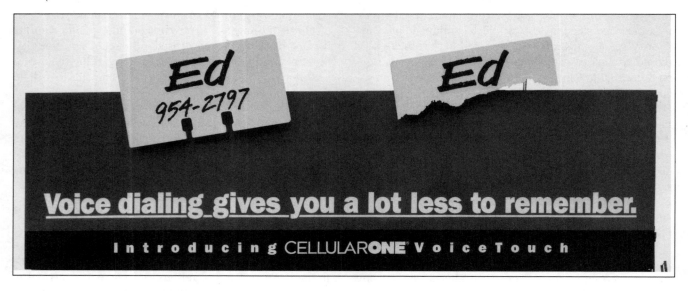

Figure 18–4. Humorous outdoor poster introducing a new product. *Courtesy of Herring Newman Company.*

guides for your poster-winning efforts. Both are from the pen of the famous nineteenth-century editor and theologian Tryon Edwards:

Have something to say; say it, and stop when you're done.

Never be so brief as to be obscure.

Or, as another man of note once said:

"The surest way to be dull is to try to say it all."

Having achieved your selling idea, it is important in glance-read poster copy to concentrate attention on your one idea. Don't try to make two, three, or four copy points. Be satisfied to slam one point at the readers. If it's tires, it

may be safety; gasoline, mileage; bread, taste; soft drinks, refreshment; automobiles, beauty.

Each of the foregoing products has other appeals, but they should not be used in combination. *Stick to one idea.*

The Copy Is Usually Brief

Remember, your message must be telegraphic—so concise, yet so clear, that people will get it the instant their eyes hit the board. If the panel is visible at 250 feet and the motorist is going thirty-five miles an hour, you have *five seconds* to register,

One study of poster advertising examined 500 posters to see how many words of copy were used in each. The analysis broke down as follows:

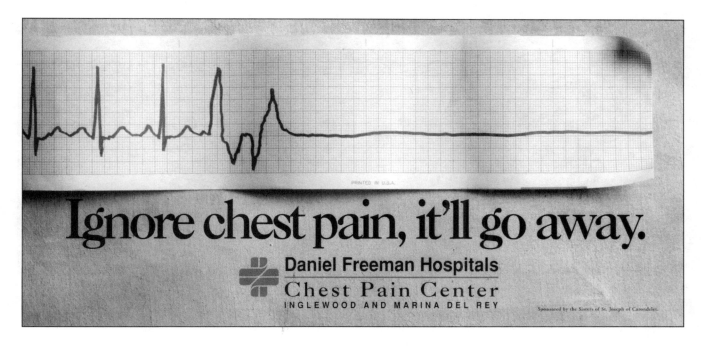

Figure 18–5. Grimly graphic outdoor poster. Reminders like this posted along well-traveled routes can do much to spur needed action. *Courtesy of William Johnson Advertising.*

Number of Posters	Percent
Without words	3.5
With one word	3.1
With two words	9.8
With three words	16.5
With four words	21.2
With five words	16.1
With six words	11.3

Such brevity was admirably illustrated by a Volkswagen poster that used a simple illustration of the automobile and four words of copy. Those four words were:

Buy low. Sell high.

Like everything else in copy, however, the length of poster copy is not to be established through fixed rules. Although it is obvious that keeping your poster copy short normally makes good sense, it is possible to find examples that use longer messages.

Readability and comprehension—not inflexible rules that limit your imagination and originality—should guide you in determining length of poster copy.

For example, suppose you know that your poster showing is going to be concentrated in areas of heavy pedestrian traffic. Under such a circumstance, when the viewer has more time to absorb the message, you can certainly exceed the four words used in the Volkswagen poster.

Volkswagen, incidentally, has used a poster technique in its print advertising; that is, it has used a simple illustration; a brief, clever headline; and a minimum of body copy. Volkswagen print advertisements, like posters, put over a clear message with the illustration-headline combi-

nation. The body copy is helpful but not absolutely necessary.

The Morton Salt Company, which has had many prize winning posters, used a short, simple, but hard-selling line for an extended period:

If it's worth its salt, it's worth Morton's.

This line was illustrated by luscious vegetables, melons, fruits, and other food items commonly improved by the addition of salt.

Standard Oil of Indiana once won a poster competition with a poster that had just one word on it: TOPS! It was illustrated only with the cap worn by the Standard filling station operator.

You don't have to be brilliant, but often it helps a great deal to make your poster stand out from a highway lined with less imaginative efforts.

Above all, whether you elect to be cute or whether your product and problem call for straight selling, keep your outdoor advertising simple, short, and interesting.

You'll see a number of posters in this chapter's illustrations. Study them. See how in every case the copywriter and art director worked together to create a fast, memorable impression.

Poster Elements

Although the number of copy and layout elements varies according to the complexity of a poster, the following is a list of the elements normally included. Not all five will be found in every outdoor poster, as in the case of the Volkswagen poster previously described.

Figure 18–6. Humorous outdoor poster. Humor is always a good technique to use for quick attention in outdoor advertising. *Courtesy of Gardner, Geary, Coll & Young, Inc.*

Figure 18–7. Award-winning non-English outdoor poster. In case you can't read the message on this poster, the English translation is: "Stop. Take Stresstabs." Humor is humor whether in the U.S. or abroad. *Courtesy of Friedman & Rose.*

- Product name
- Principal illustration
- Short copy to back illustration
- Package
- Headline (often a clever and/or selling phrase)

Other elements might have been included, but these five are found most often. To keep the list simple, elements such as trademarks, company name, and price were not included.

In many cases, the package may well be the principal illustration. A headline may be a slogan, or it can constitute the "short copy to back up the illustration." In brief, the elements can be juggled around as demanded by the institution, the campaign, or the product itself.

The elements are clear-cut. It is your use of them that results in effective or ineffective posters. Since simplicity is so important to quick reading, attain simplicity by avoiding the mixing of too many elements in one poster.

The fact that there are five elements in the foregoing

Figure 18–8. Humorous outdoor poster. *Courtesy Phillips-Ramsey Advertising.*

list does not mean that you must use them all. Remember: *Strive for simplicity by limiting the number of ideas and elements.*

Start by Putting Your Many Ideas in Thumbnail Form

When you receive a request for "one" outdoor poster design, do not be misled by the use of the singular. In order to create a Grade A poster, you may have to hatch a dozen or more ideas and have several rough, thumbnail layouts of each sketched out on tissue by an art associate.

After these numerous rough tissue layouts are assembled, you and the other persons working on the account will give them a going-over—discussing and appraising each in detail and eliminating many. The ideas or designs that survive this first session will be revised and polished and again be subjected to the close scrutiny of all concerned.

Posters are usually either (1) direct adaptations of advertisements, using the same headlines and illustrations used in magazines or newspapers; (2) semidirect adaptations, in which the theme idea is followed but specially created headlines and/or illustrations are used; or (3) presentations that are completely different from the advertiser's publication or radio copy. In the last type, no attempt is made to tie in with the campaign theme. New ideas are used, but usually a certain family resemblance is maintained.

Outdoor is an ideal medium for publicizing trade-names, trade characters, package identifications, slogans, or any idea that may be quickly stated with perfect clarity. Because it permits the use of color at relatively low cost, it affords an excellent means for putting over appetite appeal. A bowl of corn flakes and strawberries looks like wood shavings and licorice drops when reproduced in black and white. But give it color and it will look irresistibly tempting.

Although outdoor advertising is a true mass medium, usually aimed at the total public, there are exceptions in which the copy message is aimed at a relatively selective

group. A farm feed or hybrid seed poster advertisement along a road traveled by farmers is an example. Another is a motel poster aimed at that portion of motorists who are looking for overnight accommodations. An extreme example of "selective" outdoor advertising is the poster displayed in the Detroit area that read:

O.K. Show it on TV. But sell it in magazines.

This message was aimed at a tiny number of high-ranking executives in Detroit-area auto firms who might have some say in the selection of media for advertising campaigns. Outdoor advertising was used because it was felt that the targets of the campaign were too busy to listen to long media presentations.

Your Outdoor Poster Is Primarily Reminder Advertising

As you have already been told, outstanding outdoor advertising requires a high degree of creativity, largely because you must do so much despite the limited amount of space for words and illustration, the need for terse yet clever copy, and the requirement for product or package identification.

The chief function of poster advertising is to serve as a buying reminder to people who are, or will soon be, in a position to buy. You are often going after what is called the "impulse sale" when you write poster copy. Since you haven't the time or space to persuade people to buy your product, you have to assume that they have already been sold by some other form of advertising; your job is to remind them of your brand in a bright, memorable, and attention-getting way.

Products such as beer, soft drinks, gasoline, cigarettes, and candy are naturals for poster advertising. Your prospects are in an automobile and they are going to stop within minutes. Chances are good that they will purchase one or more of these items, or similar ones, when they do stop.

It must be equally obvious to you why hotels advertise so extensively on outdoor signs—also, restaurants, taverns,

Figure 18–9. Award-winning transit advertising. Informal language and humor are effective ingredients in bus advertising. They get smiles and attention. *Courtesy of Devito/Verdi Advertising.*

and other public services. They want to remind the immediate prospect of what they have to offer.

It is often said that the outdoor poster that advertises a grocery store product is a giant point-of-sale display. Food retailers know that a poster placed on a main traffic location near their store will serve as a quick reminder to shoppers who may very well be on their way to buy from them. These locations, near shopping centers and village business sections, are considered ideal by advertisers whose products sell through food stores.

You'll see much automobile advertising on outdoor boards. While an automobile is neither an impulse purchase nor an immediate-action type of product, remember that a large percentage of the people who see a car displayed on an outdoor poster are driving cars that are at least one year old. They cannot help being influenced by a sales message showing a beautiful new car. These impressions will multiply to help make the eventual sale. What better time to sell the product than when it is actually being used by the prospective customers?

Use Emotion—Humor, Pathos, and Excitement—to Evoke a Quick Response

Provided you adhere to the number one rule of simplicity, both in illustration and message, you can use cuteness, or cleverness, and the more of either the better. If you're bright enough to make your poster tell an entertaining story while it punches home a copy message and product identification, you have probably succeeded in creating a good poster. Remember, however, that you have to get the whole story told in five seconds or less.

Because the poster message must be read and understood so quickly, the use of emotional appeals—especially humor and pathos—is especially effective in outdoor advertising. Emotional copy elicits what might be called a "gut" reaction—a quick response that requires no considered thought or pondering.

Well-done humor is superb in getting viewer reaction and instant response, such as the outdoor poster for Fischer Hams that showed a very nervous turkey looking appealingly at the outdoor audience and imploring viewers to serve Fischer hams for Thanksgiving.

Cleverness and humor were also combined in a memorable campaign for a West Coast exterminator company that put the following startling message on a 48-foot outdoor structure:

There are no termites in Spokane.

One week later, a huge chunk had been taken out of the sign as if a giant termite had bitten it off. A few days later,

Figure 18–10. Humorous use of telephone booth poster. Outdoor advertising appears everywhere these days—telephone booths, bus shelters, kiosks, and on all the more conventional outdoor media. *Courtesy of Korey Kay & Partners, N.Y., and client, Comedy Central.*

another chunk was gone. The procedure continued until, at the end of the four months, only the advertiser's name was left.

Pathos and indignation also score well in outdoor advertising, especially for public service campaigns devised by the Advertising Council in such campaigns as those against racial prejudice, drunk driving, or child abuse.

Summing Up

To sum up, you might keep the following in mind when you write and design posters.

1. Be satisfied, generally, to put over one idea in a poster.
2. Use as few elements as possible and make those elements count.
3. Be brief, but don't be brief for brevity's sake. If your copy needs to be longer in order to do the job more effectively, then make it longer.
4. Don't be subtle in most posters. Make your poster simple and easy to understand at a glance.
5. If you're promoting a packaged product, you can increase package recognition by featuring the package on your posters.

6. Use positive suggestion. Although you won't use this technique in all posters, many posters will be stronger if you suggest something upon which the reader can act.
7. Above all, try for a twist—a clever, attention-getting (often humorous) phrase that ties in with an equally clever, attention-getting illustration idea. Actually, the phrase and the illustration are one. Your object is to make the viewer react quickly—smile, frown, get angry, feel pity, or make a resolution. Force the viewer to single out your message from all the competing influences around the poster. Use of emotion might help you get the attention you want.

Transit Advertising

Inside Cards

Inside transit cards come in different sizes and shapes, although most are proportioned about the same as 30-sheet or 24-sheet outdoor posters. The greater number of cards are in the side positions,. Popular sizes in these positions are 11 x 28 inch and 11 x 14 inch, although much longer cards are often used. You might also prepare copy for cards placed at either end of a transit vehicle. In this discussion, however, emphasis is on the side cards.

Some copywriters prepare all transit cards exactly as they do outdoor posters. This is a mistake. If they would compare transit cards and outdoor posters, they would see that, except for their shape, there is little similarity. Thinking of transit cards as "baby billboards" has caused many copywriters to write poor transit cards. They are not posters and should not be treated as such.

It is often mistakenly thought that it is necessary for an inside transit card, like a poster, to get its message over in the flickering of an eyelid. The thought is not sound. Your transit card is traveling right along with your audience, whereas the poster must be read quickly as the automobile whizzes by. The transit card and the reader are relatively stationary. The people you are interested in reaching don't rush by your transit card at a gallop. They sit or stand near it for a long time, twenty-seven minutes per one-way trip on the average. If you have caught their eye and if you have interested them sufficiently to make them want to do so, readers can linger over your copy. Accordingly, you don't have to limit your copy to five or six words, or even fifty or sixty for that matter. One important restraining element on the number of words is the requirement that the message be readable three seats ahead of or behind the card.

Transit cards can be designed to be real "traveling salespeople"—selling advertisements that can, by themselves, put over a sale instead of being mere reminders.

Design Cards for Easy Reading by Nearby Passengers

As you write a transit card, recall that you are not expecting to reach everyone in the car at one time. Passengers aren't going to stretch, crane, and twist to read your copy.

The only people you will usually reach at any single moment are those passengers standing or sitting close to where the card is posted. This is why it is not essential to keep copy brief or to use kingsize type. If a person can read your poster from six to eight feet away, the readability is acceptable. A good way to test readability quickly is to place the poster on the ground at your feet. If you can read it easily, the card will probably be readable for riders.

Another point to remember about transit cards is that they sometimes curve. Also, the bottom of the card, rather than the top, is closer to the reader's eyes and is, therefore, usually easier to read. That's why you find some transit card headlines at the bottom. Because of curvature, the upper inch or so of the card often is practically flat against the roof of the car or bus. If you put any of your copy story in this top area, make it a subordinate line, not your real selling message.

Regarding inside transit cards, remember that you may make them "miniature posters" if this format will convey your message more effectively, but do not consider such practice as standard. These days the poster often takes one technique and the transit card another.

Outside Cards

In recent years, there has been a decrease in the use of inside transit cards and a veritable stampede to the outside cards displayed on the ends and sides of buses. Advertisers using the outside cards obtain readership from pedestrians, motorists, and even from people in homes along the bus route. Today, about 90 percent of transit advertising expenditures are assigned to outside cards.

In a sense, the outside cards are a form of traveling outdoor advertising that carries the advertiser's message into all parts of the town. For the copywriter, the outside cards constitute a strong creative challenge since the length of the sales message must be severely limited. Truly, in the case of outside transit cards, the copywriter must consider them closer to outdoor advertising than to the transit advertising represented by inside transit cards.

To write the copy for such cards, the copywriter should, therefore, follow exactly the same suggestions that were made for writing outdoor advertising: brevity, a single compelling idea, few elements, and simplicity.

An example of this is the traveling display on the side of a city bus that showed three luscious ice cream sundaes with the message:

Ice cream
makes everyday
a Sundae

One clever outside transit advertisement displayed a small jar of a popular mustard along with these words:

We've graced the tables of Queens
Not to mention the other four boroughs.

Any resident of New York City would chuckle at the double meaning of this advertisement.

Figure 18–11. Humorous use of telephone booth poster. *Courtesy of Lowe & Partners.*

Another form of outside card is the station poster that greets subway and train riders before they step inside the cars. These are treated like outdoor posters except that they are vertical instead of horizontal. Somewhat more copy may be written for these posters than for 24-sheet posters because reading time is longer both by people standing on platforms and by people reading the posters when the transit vehicle is discharging and picking up passengers.

Anxious to avail themselves of every opportunity to reach the outside market, advertisers have made increasing use of signs on telephone booths, examples of which are shown in illustrations in this chapter. Kiosks, too, are included in such outside advertising. Another fast-growing advertising segment is "shelter" advertising, which consists of 4" x 6" signs placed on bus stop shelters. The Shelter Advertising Association currently lists 26,000 such units in the U.S.

Techniques for Producing Effective Transit Advertising—Inside or Outside

Although it has been pointed out that inside transit cards are not small posters, there are some techniques that might transfer from one medium to the other.

1. As in posters, transit cards will usually be more effective if one sales point is made. An attempt to make more than one point will usually dilute your message.

2. Although reading time is greater for your copy in transit cards, they, like posters, should not have too many elements if they are to be efficient and readable.

3. A transit card can use more copy than a poster, but don't go wild. Brevity is still desirable for most cards. The use of a little white space will be helpful sometimes in giving your card a favorable contrast to the crowded cards next to yours.

4. Simplicity is another quality shared by posters and transit cards. Because you can use more copy, you may indulge in more subtlety in transit cards, but don't overplay it. The average rider is usually better sold by a simple message.

5. The featuring of the package, of course, is desirable in transit cards as well as posters—especially since your card may be the last advertising contact with someone who is about to start a shopping tour.

6. Positive suggestion is a part of transit card copy, too. As in poster copy, it is not used in every advertisement, but in the right advertisements, it becomes a forceful, selling technique.

Thus, in summarizing the essential differences in handling posters and cards, you find that:

- Unorthodox layout tricks are often used in transit card designing—placing of the headline at the bottom of the advertisement, for instance, and allowing for the curved surface.

- More latitude is possible in writing transit card copy since average reading time of transit cards is about twenty-seven minutes, contrasted with five to ten seconds for posters. The end result is longer copy and an opportunity for more subtle copy.

Brevity Is a Key Word in Transit Advertising

It seems fitting in a chapter where so much emphasis has been placed on the need for calculated brevity to draw upon powerful outside sources to stress the point.

Shakespeare, for example, wrote that

Men of few words are the best men

and

Brevity is the soul of wit.

While Shakespeare didn't have outdoor advertising in mind, your outdoor illustration *is* powerful, and accompanied by a *few* carefully chosen words, it can be even more powerful.

Lastly, we have pertinent advice from Ecclesiastes: "Therefore, let thy words be few."

Cleverness Is Another Key Word

Travel down the streets and highways. Gaze at outdoor and transit advertising, both outside and inside, and what you find is advertising that, as a whole, is ordinary. It's not bad, just ordinary.

Suddenly, you see an outdoor poster, card, or traveling display that reaches out and pulls on your emotions. It makes you smile, or it pulls at your heartstrings.

If you're a writer, strive for the offbeat, for the poster or card that stands out in refreshing contrast to all of those ordinary productions. Be clever. Try for the twist or the play on words. Use an illustration that is dazzling in its impact. Originality and freshness are at a premium in this medium. There's no place where words and illustrations work in better harmony than in transit and outdoor advertising.

Any writer who wants to make it in this demanding field should study the annual catalog published by the Outdoor Advertising Association of America, which contains the Obie awards given to the creators of the year's most noteworthy transit and outdoor advertising. The illustrations in this chapter include a few of these award-winning creations.

CHAPTER 19

If You're There, So Is Radio Advertising

Steve Swerenski sat at a bar in South Boston half-listening to the radio broadcast of the final innings of a Red Sox game. Suddenly, he came to full attention and yelled to his companion, "Listen up, Milt. That's my commercial you're hearing."

This was a common experience for Steve. As a busy commercial writer for a Boston agency, he'd heard his commercials at the beach, in his kitchen, on his car radio, and in a dozen other places.

Talk about ubiquity. Steve, like all of us, has grown up expecting radio to pour out its messages wherever he happened to be. And, as Steve has learned, radio commercials sell a lot of goods and services to truckers on the road, farmers in dairy barns, and housewives busy in their kitchens. Radio is truly <u>everywhere</u>.

When television advertising broke like a bombshell on the advertising scene, gloomy predictions were rife about the sadly diminished role of radio advertising. Today, radio advertising thrives. With certain audiences and at certain times of the day, it even outdraws television advertising.

Radio is a flexible, relatively uncomplicated medium. And oh, so omnipresent. It reaches people where television cannot, and if you want to talk dollars, radio advertising is one of the great bargains in the world of advertising.

Furthermore, from your perspective as a copywriter, you may well find that you like radio writing for its relative simplicity. Radio lacks the artwork and mechanical production of print advertisements, and it has none of the problems, as in television, of camera work and casting.

Usually, you can turn out your radio material faster than print or television advertising. Let's say you're doing a commercial for a product or service you've worked on many times. If you're a facile writer, there's no reason you shouldn't be able to create a straight commercial in min-

utes. Humorous and two-voice commercials can take longer to create, of course.

Speaking of speed, there's an immediacy in radio that is appealing. That commercial you whipped out quickly can, if the circumstances call for it, be on the air instantly.

Perhaps best of all, there's an easy, friendly, and personal quality to radio writing that makes it more fun to do and less of a strain than most other forms of advertising selling.

Before You Begin to Write That Radio Commercial, Think of Yourself as a Listener

To understand how to write radio advertising, think of yourself and others as radio listeners. You have probably listened to radio in kitchens, bathrooms, bedrooms, basements, automobiles, boats, restaurants, banks, service stations, airline terminals, and doctors' offices. And while you listened to radio, you may have been milking a cow, ironing, knitting, cooking, studying, working under a car, writing a letter, eating, driving a tractor, operating a payloader or a truck, cleaning house, painting the siding, doing woodworking, playing bridge, dusting, fishing, sitting in a ski lodge, or passing time in a hospital bed.

Radio has become the medium that reaches people while they are doing something (other than purposefully listening to radio). Radio, as the industry reminds advertisers, reaches the audience anywhere and everywhere, no matter what that audience is doing.

Awareness that the radio audience is not immobile and attentive has caused radio writers to change their writing formats. Where once the typical radio listeners tuned in to program after program and listened carefully to all of them, they are now restless, dial-changing listeners for whom radio is a background to other activities. Their attention must be captured, and every device must be used to hold that attention.

Because of the flighty, inattentive listeners, radio commercials have become increasingly entertaining. In the effort to entertain, much humor is used. The hope, often vain, is that the humorous approach will hold the audience as effectively as the surrounding program material. Also, music is used to capture attention or to create moods.

Yet, despite the increased use of various attention-getting and mood-creating techniques, radio commercials have become simpler. Good radio writers know that in this era of half-listening radio audiences, it is vital to give the listener just one principal idea to carry away. They know, too, that details should be kept to a minimum.

If You Do It Right You Can Make Listeners "See" with Their Ears

Although many commercials do not call for descriptive writing, the ones that do will make you realize that the greatest handicap you face in selling by the spoken word is the inability to illustrate your product. This difficulty overshadows the restrictions of writing against time and the dependence upon the imaginations of your listeners. The lack of illustrative possibilities makes commercial writing a confining form of sales writing. You must be like the storytellers of ancient times who, through ballads and skillfully told tales, made their listeners see the wonders of other lands and other peoples.

You will envy the fashion copywriter, who can call for a gorgeous illustration, tag a short line of copy to the art, and be off to the next assignment. If you wrote a radio commercial for the same garment, you would describe the style and the cut, and you'd use all of your cunning to make the listener imagine how she would look in the dress, hat, or coat.

The need for visualization in radio greatly influences your commercial writing, since you must choose selling points that can be described readily and convincingly to listeners. You can no longer depend upon artwork or photographs to help you capture and hold the attention and interest of your prospects. If, for instance, you are describ-

ing the sales features of a ham on the air, you are missing your most potent sales howitzer—the strongest, most compelling attraction of any ham advertising—a colorful photograph of a big, ready-to-eat, luscious ham. Your job is to make those listening to your commercial see that ham—make them smell it, taste it, and want it—through your words alone.

If you are asked to prepare radio commercials for an automobile, you can't refer to the sleek, new compact parked alongside your copy in the magazine pages. You don't have that help. You must, solely by the deft use of description, put your audience in the driver's seat of that car and make them see its handsome lines and feel its lively response and ease of handling.

Description is vital in many radio commercials. Perhaps you aren't an agency writer concerned with cars and hams and nationally advertised brands. Maybe your job is to turn out radio announcements by the hundreds for use on local stations to bring people into your department store to buy shoes, clothes, radios, washing machines, and toys.

To those listening as they bustle about their homes, you must do more than offer generalities about your store's service, charming decor, or pleasant salespeople. To stir their interest enough to get them out of the home and into the shopping center or downtown area, you must create desire for the articles you're selling. You must make those articles appealing. And you must do it completely with words. Unlike print advertising, you can't depend upon the artist to do your selling job—possibly 75 percent of the selling. In your copy, you can't write: "As you can see from the illustration, this carpeting will fit nicely into any background." In radio, you draw your own illustration with words.

1.

EDNA:	Hi, Sally. What are you doing?
SALLY:	Making ice cream with my new Ezy-Mix ice-cream maker I got at Kitchenaire's store adjacent to Hawkeye Center.
EDNA:	Making ice cream? That's hard work.
SALLY:	Not with my new Ezy-Mix ice-cream maker. A few turns of the handle and I have a quart of flavorsome ice cream. And I can make it without using electricity, ice, or salt.
EDNA:	The Ezy-Mix ice-cream maker must cost a fortune.
SALLY:	That's the best part. It's only $39.95 at Kitchenaire's friendly store.

2.

| SMALL BOY: | Let's see now. Mom said this Ezy-Mix ice-cream maker can make super ice cream. She said it's not like the old days when it was hard to make homemade ice cream. All I have to do is turn this little handle a few times and I get all kinds of ice cream and any flavor I want. Mom says it's better than the old days because the Ezy-Mix doesn't use electricity, |

salt, or ice. And she says it's easy to clean, too. Mom's always talking about how hard things are to clean like my sweatsocks. But she says Ezy-Mix cleans like a whiz. When I grow up, I'm going to have my very own Ezy-Mix.

Figure 19–1. Commerical 1 demonstrates the straight man–stooge approach wherein Edna is a stooge who asks the right questions and supplies the right reactions. Sally plays it straight and ends up sounding like a salesperson instead of the real-life person she's supposed to be.

Commercial 2 makes the little boy unbelievably precocious. How many little boys of your acquaintance can deliver such a sales spiel? Give such a character a sentence or two and then let someone else do the sales presentation.

3.

(SFX background noises of court scene under speaking)
(Judicial-sounding voice): And I hereby sentence you to make the ice cream.
(Utterly distraught voice): Oh, no Judge, Not *that!*
ANNCR (Amused tone): True enough, making ice cream has been the equivalent of a sentence to hard labor, but now we have Kwik-Freeze, the ice-cream maker that turns out a quart of ice cream with a few easy turns of a crank—and doesn't require salt, ice, or electricity. Now, anyone in your family can make ice cream. Pick up a Kwik-Freeze ice-cream maker today at Kitchenaire, next to Hawkeye Center. Only $39.95.

Figure 19–2. Humorous commercial that sets the stage with two voices and then has the announcer come in to do the selling.

An Artist Has the Advantage, but Good Descriptive Writing Can Make You Competitive

As effective as they can be in enhancing a commercial, good sound effects and music cannot substitute for even ordinary artwork. The real picture beats the word-picture for putting over product detail quickly and surely. Still, the good radio writer tries to come close to art in the use of descriptive words. It's a difficult challenge, because writing good description isn't easy, whether in the writing of books, articles, or radio commercials.

The following excerpt is a radio commercial for a paint company. Paint is a colorful product. It must be seen. Television and colorful magazine advertisements are powerful media for selling any product as visual as paint. Yet notice how the radio writer can, through descriptive words, help the reader "see" the different colors of paint.

It's fall. It's beautiful. It's colorful. It's also time to paint your home before winter comes. At Every-Hue Paint Company we'll give you colors to fit the fall season and your moods. Reds like the scarlet maple leaves. Blues like soft October skies. Brilliant yellows like goldenrod waving in windswept fields. If your mood is gloomy in anticipation of the winter ahead, we have blacks as deep as cold, starless fall nights. But, why be gloomy? Every-Hue has whites to lift your spirits— chaste whites as pure and unspoiled as the snows to come. Paint to suit your mood, your home, and the season—paint with Every-Hue paints.

Obviously, not *all* radio commercials require great descriptive powers. Neither do all of them demand writing perfection. The appearance of some products does not need description. Why describe an aspirin tablet, a cigarette, or a tube of toothpaste?

Many radio commercials belong to the "see-how-many-times-you-can-get-the-public-to-listen-to-it" school, where the main object is to pound away with your product's name and perhaps one sale idea or buying reminder. Others, such as those for cosmetics and food products, require explanations of what the product can do for you. A third huge category, especially in department-store radio advertising and other local operations, stresses price.

Rule Number One: Read Out Loud What You've Written

The one most important rule is to learn about writing for radio, whether for commercials or continuity, is that every single word you set down on paper for use over the air *must be read aloud by you before you give it your personal approval.*

You may not have a private office in which to work. It makes no difference. Even if you have to adjourn to the coatroom for privacy, find yourself an unoccupied corner and play announcer. You see, every writer always relies on seeing in print the words that are written. What looks readable may not sound the least bit so.

Embarrassing fluffs by announcers rarely will occur if commercials have been given an advance "out-loud" test. Such a test would have prevented the following tongue twisters that appeared in two commercials. In both instances, the announcer faltered, started again, faltered, and finally gave up, passing over the incident with a quip. The writer succeeded in making the announcer laugh, but advertisers have a very unsympathetic view of the kind of humor that may cost them product sales.

One of the phrases causing the most trouble was "... prepared for *welcoming me in as a* . ..." Try out that phrase on an unsuspecting friend to see what trouble it can cause when read out loud rapidly without rehearsal. The other phrase was "... fresh, flavorful, fragrant coffee." Alliteration, as you will read later, is a real troublemaker, yet a quick reading aloud in advance of broadcast could have resulted in a correction.

To go a step beyond reading your own commercials, you should listen to the announcer as he delivers them. The announcer is someone reading the commercials who has nothing to do with producing them. He is not acquainted with the thinking behind them. His reading of your commercials may reveal additional pitfalls not discovered in your own reading. Notice the announcer's mistakes and remember to avoid copy that prompts those mistakes in your next set of commercials.

CLIENT: MOTEL 6
JOB: :60 Radio
TITLE: "Aunt Josephine"

TOM: Hi. Tom Bodett for Motel 6 with good news for the traveler. Well it's time for the biannual trip to see Aunt Josephine. She's a wonderful lady, but the only problem is her cats. It never fails, the moment you step in the door, the big black one, Muffie, starts that curling thing around your leg and for the rest of your stay, you're doomed to be the object of Muffie's desire. It makes it hard to concentrate on Aunt Josephine's story about Mildred's cousin's husband's neighbor, who just had their goiter treated. But maybe I got a way to get you off the hook with Muffie. Call 1-800-4MOTEL 6 and reserve a clean, comfortable room for the lowest prices of any national chain. And at Motel 6, you'll never wake up to find Muffie flipping her tail in your face. And personally, that's worth the price of the room right there. I'm Tom Bodett for Motel 6 and we'll leave the light on for you.

CLIENT: MOTEL 6
JOB: :60 Radio
TITLE: "Sure Bet"

TOM: When you need a place to sleep, Motel 6 is a good bet. Hi, Tom Bodett here. You know getting a good night's rest when staying with relative is never a sure thing. Like when you have to play a friendly game of Go Fish just to see who gets the spare bed and who ends up on the floor. Between your shifty brother-in-law hiding cards up his sleeve and Aunt Lucy whose seniority allows her the privilege of just cheating openly, your chances of getting one of the beds are somewhere between slim and none. So why not just spend the night at Motel 6. You're sure to get a clean, comfortable room, free local calls and free in-room movies—all for the lowest prices of any national chain. So you'll have a little extra change in your pocket. Unlike your brother-in-law, who hasn't been around long enough to know that once the sleeping arrangements have been decided, Aunt Lucy likes to play for money. Well I'm Tom Bodett for Motel 6, and we'll leave the light on for you.

Figure 19–1a. Straight commercial. Radio listeners have become well acquainted with the announcer's voice heard for this campaign. Delivered at a comfortable pace (between 160–170 words) the commercials are personal and friendly—and very competitive. The announcer's voice, an easy drawl, makes the commercial entertaining. A good example that shows the worth of a straight commercial that is delivered well. Also, a bit of humor in each commercial entertains listeners. To demonstrate the application of the campaign technique in radio, several of the commercials in this series are included in this chapter, and elsewhere in the book. *Created by The Richards Group, Dallas, TX.*

Figure 19–1b. Straight commercial. See Figure 19–1a for explanation of this campaign. *Created by The Richards Group, Dallas, TX.*

By keeping a few rules in mind as you approach writing for radio, you can give yourself a head start on those who walk gaily into commercial writing with the attitude that it's no different from any other kind of writing.

As you read your commercials aloud, get into the spirit of things. *Be* an announcer in your inflections, pauses, and most importantly, your pace. Deliver your words at the pace you'll want an announcer to deliver them in order to get the timing right—not too short and not too long.

Whether or not you observe the various admonitions listed, keep in mind one point: *Read them aloud!*

How to Make Your Words Easy to Say and to Hear

In many respects, you'll throw away the rulebook when you write radio commercials. In the following section are suggestions that are, in general, aimed specifically at radio writing, although some may be applied to the audio portion of television commercials and some can be used in print writing. All of them are useful, however, when you write for reception by the ear.

Use Short Words, Short Sentences, and Contractions

Short words are usually the best radio words. Regardless of their pronunciation or ease of understanding, words that contain more than three or four syllables should be used only when absolutely necessary. Thus, "a great car" is better than "an exceptional car," "lovely" is preferable to "beautiful," "good" is a better choice than "outstanding," and so forth. Similarly, short sentences are usually easier for the announcer than longer ones.

Sometimes, however, awkward sentence structure can make even short sentences poor radio. Short sentences aren't always the final answer. A skillfully written sentence that is moderately long but well phrased can often make better listening than a poorly written short sentence.

When you make an effort to break up your radio copy into short, easy-to-read-aloud sentences, you will discover

CLIENT: MOTEL 6
JOB: :60 Radio
TITLE: "Phone By The Throne"

TOM: If you can't do without a phone by the
        toilet, Motel 6 may not be the place for you.
        Hi. Tom Bodett with the cold, hard facts.
        You know, I never understood why some of
        those big fancy places put a phone by the
        throne. After all, if you're talking to
        somebody form there, what do you tell'em
        when they ask you what you're doing?
        Think about it. It's a moral quandary you
        just don't need. Well, yet another of life's
        major dilemmas solved by Motel 6. See at
        Motel 6 instead of putting a phone by the
        toilet, we give you a clean, comfortable
        room and a good night's sleep for the
        lowest prices of any national chain. All your
        local phone calls are free and there's no
        motel service charge on the long distance
        ones. Of course, you'll have to make those
        calls while sitting on the bed or something,
        but it's still a small price to pay. Besides, if
        you're talking on the phone from the bed,
        your voice won't have that funny ceramic
        echo. I'm Tom Bodett for Motel 6, and we'll
        leave the light on for you.

Figure 19–1c. Straight commercial. See Figure 19–1a for explanation of this campaign. *Created by The Richards Group, Dallas, TX.*

CLIENT: MOTEL 6
JOB: :60 Radio
TITLE: "TV Tom"

TOM: Men who like to save money, and the
        women who love them. Next, on Bodett.
        Hi, Tom here, with a few words about talk
        shows. Well, it seems like they're sproutin'
        up everywhere you look. And from the
        looks of them, anybody can get one, so
        why not me. My guests could be people
        who've stayed at Motel 6. I can see it now.
        The American male. Obsessed with clean,
        comfortable rooms? Or do they secretly
        hunger for the low prices? True
        confessions from a woman whose passion
        for free in-room movies drove her husband
        away. And salesmen addicted to free local
        calls. An on-the-road epidemic that's
        sweeping the nation. It'd be pretty riveting
        television, if you ask me. Of course, all of
        our guests would stay at a fabulous Motel
        6. And maybe even get some free
        luggage...no. Well, I'm Tom "Weekday
        afternoons at 3" Bodett for Motel 6. And
        we'll leave the light on for you.

Figure 19–1d. Straight commercial. See Figure 19–1a for explanation of this campaign. *Created by The Richards Group, Dallas, TX.*

another fact about commercial writing—certain conventional writing practices do not apply. Well-written prose has few sentences starting with the words "And" or "But" yet these two words are standard openers in radio sentences because they preserve the flowing, conversational quality of the announcer's delivery. Likewise, they stop him enough to keep him from crowding his words and from going too fast or too breathlessly.

You will find that sentence fragments will sometimes serve better than full sentences in radio. Listen to a conversation between two or more persons. Count how many times sentences are not completed. Yet the conversationalists understand each other perfectly. Utilize this conversational tendency in commercials, but use it carefully or you may end up writing gibberish.

The frequent use of contractions is another characteristic of radio writing. In printed prose, contractions may make writing appear overly informal and undignified. In radio copy, they often enhance the sincere and conversational qualities of the commercial. If you read, "Do not miss this chance to ..." or "You have not tasted candy until ...," you wouldn't criticize the writer for faulty technique. The writing seems natural.

When these phrases are said aloud, however, they sound stilted. They are not phrases that you, the announcer, or the listener would use. You would say, "Don't miss the chance ..." and "You haven't tasted candy. ..."

Give conscious attention to contractions. They are a definite part of American speaking idiom, and that means they are particularly good for radio use. As one caution, however, remember that you will occasionally want to emphasize a point, and the use of a contraction might weaken your sentence. Suppose, for instance, you are writing copy for a nonskid tire with a claim of "You can*not* skid." Thus, where a negative element needs emphasis, you might prefer to avoid the contraction.

Punctuate Intelligently to Help the Announcer
Closely associated with sentence length in radio is the use of punctuation. Punctuation, if anything, is more important in radio writing than in writing for print because bad punctuation can mislead the announcer and cause him to make a disastrous mistake over the air. To the radio writer, all punctuation marks are important, but the underline, the double dash, and the hyphen are especially important.

Underline. The underline should be used sparingly and with purpose. Usually the announcer will know through experience what words to punch, but here and there you may have a word you wish to stress because of company policy or some other reason. In such cases, underline the word but—and this is important—just the *one* word. It is almost never advisable to underline two words or a whole phrase. It is nearly impossible for the announcer to put true stress on more than one word. Similarly, avoid scattering underlined words throughout a commercial because, by so doing, you overemphasize your message and you make the announcer's job more difficult.

Double dash. A useful punctuation device is the double dash (—), which gives a conversational flow to your writing. It gives a dramatic pause that is less abrupt than the full stop created by a period. Used correctly, the double dash gives a graceful ease to radio writing and aids the announcer in his delivery. An example from a commercial for a savings bank reads, "But a <u>savings</u> balance—that's something else again." Notice not only how the double dash contributes a natural pause in the delivery, but also that the underline gives vigor to the whole sentence. Note, too, that all that is needed here is one word underlined. It would have been a mistake to underline "savings balance," since this emphasis would be awkward for the announcer.

Many writers use the three-dot (…) punctuation device in radio and print copy. Once a writer has contracted the three-dot habit, he finds it difficult to write complete sentences. Avoid this habit. If you wish to make a pause for effect, use the double dash, but do not overdo that either.

MUSIC:	(TV news theme under)
LARRY:	Hi. I'm Larry Simpleton …
JUDY:	And I'm Judy Bimbo, with some quick facts about TV news. Larry, why is our reporting so superficial?
LARRY:	Well, Judy, we figure the audience is pretty stupid, and we're none too bright ourselves.
JUDY:	That's exactly right, Larry, and since we don't have much hard news, we have to spend a lot of time agreeing …
LARRY:	You bet we do!
JUDY:	… and congratulating each other on terrific reporting.
LARRY:	Terrific reporting, Judy. Maybe you could also explain why we have to look like models.
JUDY:	I'd be happy to, Larry. TV news isn't about ideas … it's about mascara and high cheekbones. That's why we get these huge salaries.
LARRY:	Hmm!
JUDY:	Back to you, Lare.
LARRY:	Well, I'd just like to add that we're smug and condescending because we have these jobs and you don't.
JUDY:	Too true. Thank you for joining us. I'm Judy Bimbo …
LARRY:	And I'm Larry Simpleton. Goodnight from all of us at TV news.
JUDY:	(Privately to Larry) Good newscast, Lare.
LARRY:	Nice dress, Jude.
ANNCR:	Tired of the inane babble of TV news? The *San Francisco Examiner* is a better way to spend your time. To get two months for the price of one, call 800-345-EXAM. That's 800-345-EXAM.

Hyphen. When you wish to join two words in order to modify a third word, you can use a hyphen (-). Sometimes your announcer must be guided by the hyphenated words or a mistake in the reading will result. In the bank commercial mentioned earlier, the writer used a hyphen in this manner. "Open a dividend-paying savings account. …" If the hyphen had not been used here, the announcer might have read the passage as "Open a dividend." In using hyphens, however, avoid the precious, cute, and artificial combining of words that have given advertising writing a bad name in many writing quarters. Phrases such as "bunny-soft," "cozy-warm," and "baby-cute" illustrate the point.

Use Easy-to-Say and Easy-to-Understand Words

Avoid words that are hard to pronounce, even if they are easily understood words. "Indisputable" is a word that everyone would understand, but it could be a stumbling block for a radio announcer. "Applicable," "particularly," "demonstrably," and "detectably" would be correctly defined by most high school students, yet any of them could cause an announcer to hesitate a split second, thus disturbing the natural flow of the words.

Very innocent-looking words that are simple to pronounce by themselves can sometimes become nightmares for the announcer when they are combined with certain other innocent-looking words. A good example is the following sentence which was actually used on the air and very effectively tied the announcer in knots: "A government order of twenty-two stainless steel twin-score cruisers." Also, if you put "in," "an," or "un" next to a word beginning with any of these three sounds, you will give almost any announcer a moment of pronunciation juggling. For example, say "in an unenviable position" fast, and notice the mumble that results. To attempt to memorize all such sound and word combinations that might cause you trouble would be pointless. Experience will teach you some of the troublemakers, and reading aloud should take care of the rest.

Beware of adverbs. The suffix "-ly" is a tough one for radio people to pronounce with consistent precision. If you can twist your sentence to gain the same thought without the "-ly," you will usually have a better commercial. It is not as good radio to say:

The shoes that men are increasingly favoring.

as it is to say:

The shoes that more men are favoring every day.

And you might wish to say of a cereal product:

Nutritionally, too, it's the buy for you.

But in radio, much better to say:

For nutrition, too, it's the buy for you.

In these examples, you maintain the swing and the rhyme—both attributes of good radio commercials—yet you have constructed sentences that will be easy for the announcers to read without much chance of stumbling.

One fault you must guard against is permitting words to creep into your commercials that are similar, in sound, to other words with different meanings. One of these, for instance, is the word "chief." If you are writing a commercial about air travel, you might wish to say, "It has many advantages over all other forms of travel, the *chief* one being. …"

Now *you* know that word is "chief." You might have used "main" or "outstanding" or some other synonym, but "chief" looks all right to you, and it sounds fine as you read it. Now consider your *listener*. First of all, he's not hanging on your announcer's every phrase. Second, he hears the word "chief" only one time as it slips past, and he doesn't know, as you do, what comes next. It would be very easy for him to think the announcer said "cheap." You'll admit that the difference in meaning between the two words is great enough to warrant care in their use, whether you're selling air travel or aspirin.

"Breath" and "breadth"; "smell," "swell," and "spell" and "prize" and "price" are other examples of words that might be misinterpreted by the listener. It's just as easy to use a synonym and take no chances.

Remember: Alliteration Alienates Announcers

The print writer's use of alliteration in radio can cause trouble. Visually, the phrase "Prize-winners in perfectly proportioned peach halves" *seems* harmless. If you saw it in an advertisement, even if you are one of those who reads everything with your lips, you might view it as a nicely turned phrase. Say, however, that you have been assigned to write some radio commercials for X peaches and you hit upon that sentence—which looks fine as it leaves the typewriter or word processor. Perhaps it also looks fine to those with whom you must clear your copy. It gets an okay and is released to the radio station. How do you think it is going to look to the radio announcer who is scanning the copy ten minutes before broadcast time? The way to find out how he'll like it is to stand up and read it just as you want him to read it. Do that to the peach halves atrocity right now. Read it aloud. How does it sound? Doesn't it sound a little bit like a person about to lose an upper plate?

A little bit of alliteration is certainly acceptable in radio writing. In fact, wisely used, it often helps to spark up copy. But alliteration is like dynamite—a little too much is going to blow your commercial apart. Use alliteration if you wish, but be very careful not to overdo it. Your own sense of hearing will be your safety valve. If it doesn't sound good to you when you read it aloud, change it.

Watch Out for "S" and "K" Sounds

Another thing you may discover, as you stand up and announce your first try-'em-out-loud commercials, is that you have given your copy too many hissing sounds. Radio announcers hate the "double-ess" endings; they dislike it even in the middle of words because it is hard to say clearly and with force. The word "sensational"—almost a routine part of many copywriters' daily vocabularies—causes announcers to wince. Your commercials would probably sound better if you could manage to write them without ever using the letter "s," "z," or the soft "c."

For example, while reading the last two sentences, you are not likely to have experienced a difficulty or an unpleasant reaction from the words used. Yet several times in those two sentences, you can find the soft "c" or the "s" sounds. They would not have been pleasant sounding on the air. If this page were to be read for radio, some rewriting would have to be done. Remember, too, that the particularly harsh sounds in the English language do not broadcast well. The sounds "ark," "ack," "eesh," "ash," "app," and "amm" should seldom be used.

As you enunciate your copy, listen to your voice and try to sift out the sounds that grate on your ear. Assume that the sounds that grate on your ear as you hear them in the solitude of an office or room will sound much worse with even the minimum distortion produced by modern transmission.

As in Print Copy, Make Your Writing Flow

You were strongly advised to write transitionally in print copy. "Bridging" words and phrases were suggested, some of which you'll find repeated here. That same use of transition and "bridges" should also be part of your radio writing. Transitional writing should be as natural as breathing, whether you're working in print or radio.

A radio commercial should be a unified presentation, whether it's 30 seconds or 60 seconds. Each sentence should connect with and flow from the preceding sentence. Your points should be bridged by connecting words and phrases. Inexperienced radio writers tend to run together a series of unrelated points. The result is a jerky, clumsy commercial that even a very good announcer will find difficult. "Difficult" here, means that the announcer cannot achieve the smoothness of presentation that a well-written commercial encourages.

To create a natural flow, incorporate conversational bridges. Sometimes, the bridge may be a single word that indicates continuity, a carrying over of a thought from one sentence to another. "And" and "but" are such words, as are "furthermore," "so," and "also."

Sometimes you'll use a phrase to achieve transition. Examples include:

But that's only the start.

Listen to this.

In addition,

Remember, ask for

Here's something else you'll like.

If you've been needing help, think of this.

The following is a commercial that demonstrates how you can achieve unity through transitional writing:

If you live in the Midland area, you can make sure you have a great Christmas next year and get a fine gift for doing it. Here's how. Just come in before Saturday to Midland Trust to open a Christmas Club for next year, a Club that pays interest, by the way. That's right. Unlike many Christmas Clubs, this one pays regular interest. And here's another plus. When you open your Club you get a handsome, decorative hurricane lamp that'll brighten whatever spot you put it in. Just think, a valuable gift simply for opening a money-making Christmas Club. Even without the gift it makes good sense to open a Christmas Club. Bet you'll think so next year at this time when you have plenty of cash to spend in the holiday season. Better make a note right now to open a Midland Trust Christmas Club and to get your hurricane lamp—a yuletide duo from Midland's leading bank.

Notice all the bridging words and phrases:

Here's how

Just come in

That's right

And here's another plus

Just think

Bet you'll think so

Better make a note right now

Notice two more important aspects of this commercial. One is the strong action ending. Two is the repetition of the offer at the end of the commercial. Repetition of the main selling point is one of the attributes of good radio-commercial writing.

Although the use of bridging words can help the flow of a commercial, don't overdo their use. Too many such words can make the writing seem artificial and contrived. Use them naturally; don't force them into your sentences.

Use Slang Sparingly and Cautiously

When you are urged to "be conversational" in radio commercials, you are being given good counsel. However, this is counsel that might possibly lead you astray, because the conversation of a large percentage of Americans would be unsuitable for radio usage. You will have to use your judg-

ment in deciding what is conversational and what slips into the area of poor taste.

The inclusion of a certain amount of slang, informal phraseology, and current jargon will often lend a naturalness and spontaneity that greatly increase the believability and selling power of commercials. Whether to use such devices in your writing, and how much to use them, will depend primarily on what you are trying to sell and, more than that, to whom you are selling.

For example, on a sports program assumed to interest a young male audience, the most logical types of products to be sold would be items such as men's clothing, beer, shaving products and automotive services. If you were assigned to write commercials for such a show, it would probably be perfectly good technique to use occasional phrases such as "a rock-solid deal," "lets 'em know who you are," "top-gun precision," and similar masculine phrasings. Such writing will help make your audience feel that the commercial is part of the show, written for them alone, and hence will be more likely to take effect. Needless to say, that kind of talk would not sound very appropriate to a person listening to a soap opera.

Similarly, a children's program can be liberally sprinkled with words currently being used by children. If you are asked to write the commercials for such a show, you would be wise to do some on-the-spot investigating to pick up the phrases and slang of the moment. When you do, be quite sure that you are not writing expressions that mean something only in one locality—one neighborhood—or, if your show is national or your spot announcements are for wide distribution, one section of the country.

Today, many television shows contain language filled with four-letter words and vulgarity. Similar language also fills modern novels, plays, and motion pictures.

Radio, however, has retained the kind of acceptable language that once characterized all media and the entertainment world. You should observe this decorum in your commercials and be cautious even in the use of words that seem wholly inoffensive.

Remember, your audience will contain listeners of sensitive tastes, many whose religious teachings cause them to shun even the mildest expressions. An example is the word "darn." Now you may have used that expression since you were two years old, and you may have heard your mother, sister, and even your minister say it often. To many people, however, the word "darn" is simply another way of saying "damn," and even though many listeners may use the word themselves, you might offend one of them by putting it in your commercial. There is no need to take chances with words or expressions that have the slightest chance of producing a negative effect on even a few people. Those few might otherwise be easily sold on your product.

"Scram," "blow," "nuts," "oh yeah," "so what," "screwy," "lousy," "stink," "jerk," "baloney," and other such words should not be included in your radio-writing vocabulary. They do not represent the slang that makes acceptable, picturesque American talk for radio.

If You Don't Command Attention at the Start of Your Commercial, You Probably Have a Loser

Mrs. Jones is stirring cream sauce while she eyes the roast in the oven and the cauliflower boiling in a pan on the stove. Little Freddy is noisily playing games with his friend Billy in an adjacent room.

Now, the magic moment. Your commercial sounds from the kitchen set. What will win? Your commercial, or Mrs. Jones's cooking and other distractions?

What is done in the opening seconds of the commercial determines the answer. What have you done to *force* listenership? Are you using music, sound effects, or an unusual opening statement by the announcer? Surely you have done *something* to jar Mrs. Jones into attention. If you haven't, check off another commercial that lost the attention battle.

What you must never forget is that with rare exceptions, no one looks forward to hearing commercials. Accordingly, the person by the set should be pictured as: (1) tuning the commercial out mentally as one tunes out any unpleasant sound or message; (2) making no attempt to listen to the commercial because it is too busy or too abstract; (3) listening idly at the start and then, after a few seconds, paying no attention; or (4) giving the commercial full and undivided attention from start to finish.

The undivided listener is that one-in-a-million listener, so your job is to see what you can do to get the other three listener types to pay immediate attention. Having accomplished this first vital objective, your next challenge is to be interesting or exciting enough to hold these listeners for your whole message.

At the end of this chapter, you'll find a number of suggestions for attracting and holding listeners. As there's no mute button for radio, you currently have one advantage over television advertisers. Unless the radio listener goes to the bother of walking over to turn off the set or turn down the sound, you have a chance to make your commercial heard.

ANNCR:	(In hushed voice as if he doesn't want to be overheard) It's the year 1520 in Florence, Italy, and we're listening to a conversation between Michelangelo, the famous painter and sculptor, and his friend Tony. Both speak in very Italian accents.
TONY:	Hi, Mike. What are ya working on?
MIKE:	Lessee. My next job's the Sistine Chapel. Gotta paint the ceiling.
TONY:	*Forget* it. Here's an *important* job—a new pizza-baker. Right down your alley.
ANNCR:	Michelangelo never got around to the new pizza-baker but Pizza-World *did* and it's ready for you right now. And you're gonna love it. Here's how it works.
SFX:	(Sitar)

WISE MAN:	A perplexing problem has puzzled young people since the beginning of time. How to get a job without experience? How to get experience without a job?
ANNCR:	The answer is co-operative education. A nation-wide program that helps college students get real jobs for real pay, while they're getting an education. Write Co-op Ed., Box 999, Boston, Massachusetts 02115.
WISE MAN:	I knew that.
ANNCR:	A public service from the National Commission for Cooperative Education.
WISE MAN:	And the Ad Council.

Types of Commercials

If you are to produce commercials for a radio program—either network or local—there are a number of different techniques upon which you may draw. These techniques are discussed in the sections that follow.

Straight Commercial

The straight commercial is a straight-selling message devoted to the merits of your product, service, or institutional story. It might be compared with a piece of straight-line body copy, and it is delivered by a commercial announcer with no outside means of attracting or holding attention.

Many advertisers now look critically at this type of commercial since they feel that inattentive, uninterested listeners will not listen to the announcer for the full period of the commercial. Still, on thousands of radio stations, the selling messages are delivered straight, and they are still selling goods and services, even though artistically they are not as satisfying to creative people as other commercial types.

Dialogue Commercial

By "dialogue" we mean a conversation between two or more persons. Such a conversation can be conducted by: (1) an announcer and others, or (2) two or more characters who deliver all of the commercial without any participation by an announcer.

In the first case, the announcer may talk with users of a product, with product experts such as dealers or the actual maker of the product, or with company personnel. Sales features of a product or service are worked into these commercials. Such commercials can be convincing if the announcer and the people with whom he speaks are natural. One danger is that participation by actual users or company personnel can result in an amateurish commercial because nonprofessional talent frequently sound unnatural and forced.

In the second case you have a real problem, even if your speaking characters *are* professional actors or actresses. Making the dialogue believable and natural is exceedingly difficult. This type of commercial generally reduces credibility of advertising because radio listeners dismiss it as phony. It simply isn't a part of a daily routine for two persons to spend 60 seconds talking about a product. Still, the two-voice commercial is used, so you'd better learn how to handle it for maximum believability.

Ways to Make Two-Voice Commercials Believable, or at Least Acceptable. If a commercial is being delivered by two supposedly real-life people such as two wives, two husbands, a husband and a wife, or two children, it is almost impossible to deliver a number of product points without making salespeople out of the characters. Generally, such commercials make a stooge out of one of the characters. Thus, one housewife will say to the other, "But Kleen-O must cost a lot." The other then replies, "Not at all, Jane. Due to a new manufacturing process, Kleen-O has been able to reduce its price to the low, low price of 78 cents. And that's not *all* they've done either. Listen to this. ..."

The easiest way out of the artificiality of such two-voice commercials is to let the characters set the stage by posing a mutual problem. After an exchange of two or three lines, the announcer comes in to do the selling. This is natural because announcers are supposed to be salespeople.

But suppose you want to use the real-life characters for the whole commercial. Can you do so successfully? "Successful" here means that you maintain naturalness and believability at the same time that you put across enough product selling points to sell the product to the listening audience.

Following are many ways to so "succeed."

- One character reads copy from the package to the other character. By reading the copy, the character avoids being a "salesperson."
- One character reads copy from a product advertisement to the other character.
- Character talks to a store salesperson. The character asks questions and the salesperson replies by giving a sales talk for the product.
- Character talks to a knowledgeable repair or serviceperson, such as a plumber, electrician, and so forth. The latter points out why the unit works so well, lasts so long, is so easy to repair, or needs repair so infrequently.
- Character reads directions on the item itself, especially when those directions indicate the ease of operation.
- Character phones someone qualified to talk about the product such as a factory employee, a dealer, or a serviceperson. (In television, the split-screen technique can be used for the two characters.)
- Two salespeople talk about the product, mentioning salesworthy points.
- Sales manager conducts session with novice salesperson, demonstrating the perfect sales talk. This could well be humorously exaggerated.

- Copywriter gets reactions from his wife about sales points he's putting in his advertisement. She makes pertinent suggestions that give the woman's viewpoint that he has overlooked.
- Earnest student type is telling teacher what she's found out about the product assigned as a class study.
- Same technique as in preceding example except that professor is telling class and answering questions. Again, possibility for exaggerated humor exists here.
- Two computers talk to each other. Each discusses product facts in mechanical sounding voices associated with computers or mechanical person.
- Someone presses button of computer, or of a mechanical person, and gets flood of information to each question asked.
- If product is intended for a dog, such as a dog food, two dogs talk to each other about it. Or it could be two cats, two birds, or some other creatures.

Of course, with the above points, "success" demands more than technique. The techniques must be implemented creatively and effectively.

Dramatized Commercial

The dramatized commercial is an often-used type that may be compared with the narrative-copy approach. A situation is dramatized in a brief playlet in which the product is introduced as the solution to a problem. Thus, in the first 15 seconds or so, a boy is horrified to learn that he has bad breath. Then, he hears about a new kind of toothpaste, and in a twinkling, you discover that he wins love and romance. Finally, in normal routine, the regular announcer closes with a straight product sell and a plea to buy. Dramatized commercials usually require the hiring of a professional cast and may range all the way from a few simple, uninvolved lines of script to a full-scale production with music, sound effects, and lengthy rehearsals.

Like the dialogue commercial, the dramatized commercial often becomes artificial and unbelievable. Frequently, the action is humorously exaggerated to the point where the advertiser spoofs his product and audience. It can be a very effective technique if enough episodes are presented to avoid boring the radio audience. The same story presented day after day, however, can soon increase the number of tune-outs.

ANNCR:	If your car's engine were to stop ...
SFX:	(Car engine. Not starting up. Continue under:)
ANNCR:	... you'd probably know what to do to get it started again. The sad fact is, more people know how to jump-start a car than know how to save a life.
SFX:	(Car starts. Heartbeat starts and continues under:)
ANNCR:	Learn how to jump-start a life. Learn Red Cross CPR.

Musical Commercial

The musical commercial has become a common form of radio technique. "Jingles," as they are so often called, are hated when they are bad, but they are among the best-liked commercials when done well. Two cautions for creators of musical commercials:

- Be sure the music is good. Try to use music that can be committed to memory—outstanding commercial music that will please listeners indefinitely.
- In singing commercials, make certain that the words can be understood. Otherwise, you provide the audience with a pleasant musical experience but no incentive to buy. Make the lyric as well as the music memorable; if you do, you will have a strong selling vehicle for your product or service.

Musical commercials take many forms. For example, such a commercial might have a musical introduction (intro) of 10 seconds and a musical close of the same length. The intro and the close may be furnished by a "jingle house," an organization that writes music and lyrics on order. As a creative person, you may be required to supply the jingle house with information about the product or service, marketing objectives, and just what you want this particular commercial to accomplish.

If the material submitted by the jingle house is satisfactory, then you write 40 seconds of script to complete the commercial. Local accounts may use musical intros and closes indefinitely. Thus, as a copywriter you'll learn to live with the writing of the 40-second inner portion of the commercial. Such use of music is one way to relieve the alleged tedium of the straight 60-second commercial.

Music will sometimes be heard in the background throughout the entire commercial, very often coming up louder at the end. Except for unusual circumstances, it is not desirable to have music under the entire commercial; it is distracting and may make the spoken words harder to hear.

Although you will not be expected, unless you're a musician, to write the music for music commercials, it is helpful if you have a wide-ranging knowledge of popular and classical music. This knowledge will allow you to more easily specify music that will be suitable for the audience, the product, and the station.

It is very important that you be able to judge whether the music will wear well. If it's pleasing, there is almost no limit to the time it can be used; it can be a sort of trademark for the advertiser. If it is *not* pleasing, you can turn off your audience after very few airings of the commercial.

Knowing the musical tastes of those who enjoy musical commercials is not easy given the bewildering variety of popular music today. At one time, a few musical styles predominated, such as Dixieland, swing, romantic ballads, and New Orleans jazz. Young and middle-aged listeners today break into sizable units that like pop, hard rock, country rock, punk rock, Southern rock, and mellow rock. Add to these rock choices funk, punk-funk, soul, gospel,

and country; currently, there are nearly two dozen different types of country music alone, including country western, country swing, bluegrass, and Tex-Mex.

If you are responsible for guiding the choice of music for musical commercials, you'll need to know your audience, the latest trends in popular music, and how much of a following each style commands. This is no easy task.

How to Get an Accurate Word Count

If you are writing 60-second announcements and you plan them to be straight announcements delivered by an announcer, be sure that each one can be completed within one minute. An average announcer takes about 60 seconds to read 160–170 words, but don't rely on that estimate. Some commercials are easy to read; others are hard. The hard ones move at a slower rate. Often you will want your message to be given slowly and with exaggerated emphasis. Other times, you'll want the announcer to read it fast. Do not rely upon a rule of thumb. Read your announcements to yourself; time yourself to be sure.

Most straight commercials can be delivered understandably and sincerely at a rate of 160–170 words per minute. Some announcers, however, may be comfortable with a slower or faster rate than this. If you know what announcer will deliver your commercial, pace it to the announcer's style.

Type of Commercial Affects Word Count

The character of the offer being made might affect your word count. For instance, an announcement for a sweepstakes is usually charged with excitement. To maintain the excitement, the announcer will speed up his delivery, and thus you may elect to put considerably more than 170 words in such a commercial. You do so knowing that the listeners' playback of the commercial message will suffer in terms of individual points registered. Still, if you have made the listeners aware of the sweepstakes and its prizes, you will have accomplished your objective. You have made them want to enter. They can get full details later from entry blanks in stores or from magazine or newspaper advertisements.

ANNCR:
(Music intro)
(In slow southern drawl) The other night, me and my two friends was watching the musketeers fry on the bug zapper, when clear out of the blue, Billy Ray asked me where I got my New York accent from. I said to him, you know, I love the South, and I do. But ever so often I like to go up North. So I hop on New York Air and fly to Philadelphia, Boston, Hartford (speeding up his speech), Cleveland, Rochester, Newark or any one of four New York airports. Why, I can talk real fast to people named Salvatore and Irving, instead of Jimmy Bob and Sally Sue. Or I can say things like, ask your mudder and I dunno. And instead of having New York style pizza, I can have pizza in New York. Then when I've had my fill of the North, I hop on New York Air and

fly (slows speech to southern drawl) right back down to the South, because I just love it here. Well, I do. New York Air.
(SFX of airplane)

A similar principle is at work in the frenetic two-voice commercials often heard for local firms, such as tire shops. The two-person announcer team announces the message at a tremendous clip without any hope that many points will be recalled, but with a very real expectation that listeners will realize that the company is offering something very special in the way of price, a variety of choice, or a dazzling new product.

Two-voice commercials may, on the other hand, be used for supposed real-life conversations between two friends, a husband and wife, a salesclerk and customer, or any number of other combinations. In such simulated situations, slow down the word count. Make the conversation natural. In real life, people don't bark out words with machine-gun speed, so write fewer than the 160–170 words employed in straight commercials and far fewer than the count used in two-voice commercials delivered by a team of station announcers.

Count Words and Use a Stopwatch

If you want to be sure of your timing, count your words *and* use a stopwatch. Most writers are content merely to use a stopwatch, but a person reading a commercial sometimes tends to speed up the reading pace to make the commercial fit the time. The practice of counting the words will help keep you honest. On the other hand, just counting words and not using a stopwatch may cause trouble, since a commercial with a fairly low word count may read long because of the use of many polysyllabic words. The stopwatch helps correct for this.

When you become adept in writing for broadcast, you may let the number of lines of copy help determine whether you're writing within your time limitations—but this is only a rough guide. You'll always be right if you double-check yourself with the stopwatch and by counting the words. For example, you might be fooled by a commercial that uses several numbers and, consequently, is short on lines. Each numeral, however, counts as one word. If you give a telephone number and repeat it, you may be devoting as many as twenty-five words just for this part of the commercial.

From an advertising standpoint, it is far better to limit your message to the words that can be read with sincerity and selling strength than to take liberties with the time and length of your announcement. If you force the announcer to race through your selling message, you lose effectiveness and power.

Sound Effects Can Cause Trouble If You're Not Careful

The use of sound effects is an effective way to break up the monotony of the spoken voice, and there is a limitless number of sound effects that you can utilize. That, unfor-

CLIENT:	Agway Products: $19.99 Package Deal
JOB:	:60 Radio
TITLE:	"Ma' Nature—Wake-up!"
SFX:	(MAN SNORING)
SFX:	(DOOR OPENS)
MA:	Hey, Hey you, wake up!
MAN:	What, who's there?
MA:	It's Mother Nature, (Angelic voices).
MAN:	Look, you've got the wrong house. I lost my baby teeth years ago.
MA:	That's the Tooth Fairy.
MAN:	Oh, yeah.
MA:	Listen, you should be ashamed of yourself!
MAN:	Why, I always sleep like this.
MA:	Not that. Your lawn! IT'S a disgrace letting it go like that!
MAN:	My lawn? Well, if you're Mother Nature, why don't <u>you</u> fix it?
MA:	I stopped doing residential work a long time ago—Besides it's your responsibility.
MAN:	So what do I do?
MA:	Go to the Agway experts and ask for the 19.99 Package Deal.
MAN:	Package Deal?
MA:	Is there an echo in here? Agway has <u>one</u> fertilizer to control your weed problems. And <u>another</u> to green up your lawn next spring. Buy them both for just 19.99, and you get a free bag of Agway limestone pellets, to neutralize your soil.
MAN:	Fine. I'll do it tomorrow. Can I go back to sleep now?
MA:	Sure, you get to sleep, I've got to work all night...AD LIB FADE.
ANNCR:	Just ask the Agway experts for the 19.99 Package Deal—and get a free bag of Pelletized Limestone. Each Package Deal covers 5,000 square feet, and it's available at the Agway store nearest you.

Figure 19–2a. Humorous radio campaign. In this commercial the writer has avoided a common problem of two-voice commercials—the tendency to have the selling done entirely by the two persons in the dialogue. It is artificial in many two-voice commercials to have two persons in a dialogue delivering sales points like a high-powered salesperson. In this campaign, Mother Nature does a modest amount of sales talk but the chief selling is done by the announcer who closes out the commercial.

tunately, sometimes leads to the incorporation of *too many* sounds in a commercial and the consequent garbling of the spoken message. Another problem is that, in some cases, the listener has no idea what the sound effect is supposed to represent. As for the writer, it should be remembered that the sound effect must be counted in the timing of the commercial.

If you call for sound effects (SFX) in your commercial, figure the number of seconds taken up by the effects and allow for that in your word count. For example, if you're writing at a rate of 160 words for a 60-second commercial, each second of a sound effect should be figured as two and two-thirds words in your word count. Naturally, the same observation will apply to music. When you call for sound effects, it's helpful to take two precautions:

1. Indicate the number of seconds to be consumed by the sound effects.
2. Don't ask for a sound effect that the audience will not understand or that is impossible to convey without explanation. To illustrate, suppose you call for the sound

CLIENT:	Agway Products: Fall & Winter Fertilizer, Tulips, Daffodils
JOB:	:60 Radio
TITLE:	"Ma' Nature–Bathtub"

SFX:	(SPLISH, SPLASH, WOMAN SINGING IN TUB.)
MA:	Helloooo!
WOMAN:	What? Who <u>are</u> you? Can't you <u>see</u> I'm taking a bath!
MA:	I can see everything. I'm...
WOMAN:	Wait, don't tell me–you're my Fairy Godmother.
MA:	Fairy nothin, it's me Mother Nature. (Angelic voices).
WOMAN:	Well, don't you believe in knocking?
SFX:	(KNOCK, KNOCK, KNOCK)
MA:	Is that better? Look, you've got a problem with your color.
WOMAN:	Well, I always wanted to be a brunette.
MA:	You need more red, yellow and green.
WOMAN:	In my hair?
MA:	Stop with the hair–I'm talking about your yard and garden! You need to talk to an Agway expert.
WOMAN:	What?
MA:	Agway knows yards and gardens. They've got an incredible selection of bulbs. Get some tulips and daffodils for fiery reds and vibrant yellows. And there's a special fertilizer for a thick, <u>greener</u> lawn next spring.
WOMAN:	Fine, I'll do it right away. Now what about my hair?
MA:	Hmm...have you considered a hat?...AD LIB FADE.
ANNCR:	For vivid colors next spring, Agway's advice is to start today. Agway Greenlawn Fall & Winter Fertilizer is just 7.99 and covers 5,000 square feet. A bag of 15 red or yellow tulip bulbs is just 3.99. And daffodils are just 6 for 1.99. Stop by Agway today.

Figure 19–2b. Humorous radio campaign. See Figure 19–2a in this chapter for discussion of this campaign.

CLIENT:	Agway Products: Fall & Winter Fert., Buy Fall Seeding Mix, Turf Starter, Bamboo Rakes
JOB:	:60 Radio
TITLE:	"Ma' Nature–Back Seat Driver"

SFX:	(ENGINE STARTING, MAN HUMMING, ETC.)
MAN:	Dum-de-dum-de-dum
MA:	Hey you!
MAN:	Yaaaa! How'd you get in the back seat?!
MA:	I'm here to warn you about something.
MAN:	What are you, my Guardian Angel...?
MA:	No, it's me, Mother Nature. (Angelic voices)
MAN:	Well don't you worry, Guardian Angel. I've got my seatbelt on...both hands on the wheel...
MA:	But you're not paying attention.
MAN:	I've got my eyes on the road!
MA:	I'm talking about your lawn. <u>That</u> needs attention.
MAN:	My lawn?
MA:	We're gonna talk to an Agway expert.
MAN:	O...kay.
MA:	Agway knows what your lawn needs, and it's on sale–like a Fall & Winter Fertilizer for a thicker, greener lawn next spring. And, y'save dollars on their Turf Starter Fertilizer when you buy Fall Seeding Mix. And poly-bamboo rakes are really cheap.
MAN:	Sounds great.
MA:	And remember what I always say...
MAN:	Don't cross the street between parked cars?
MA:	Uh, no...
MAN:	A stitch in time saves nine?
MA:	I don't say that...(AD LIB FADE)
ANNCR:	Right now, the Agway experts have Greenlawn Fall & Winter Fertilizer that covers 5,000 square feet on sale for just 7.99. Buy 10 pounds of Agway Fall Seeding Mix and get six dollars off Greenlawn Turf Starter Fertilizer. And 24 inch poly-bamboo rakes are just 3.99. Stop by Agway today.

Figure 19–2c. Humorous radio campaign. See Figure 19–2a in this chapter for discussion of this campaign.

of an eggbeater. Many sounds can resemble an eggbeater at work. Because, unlike in television, the radio audience cannot see the eggbeater, they will have trouble identifying what they are hearing. To get around this difficulty, explain in words what is causing the sound. In the case of the eggbeater, simply write: "When you're beating eggs, etc." In short, except for something very clear, like the ringing of a telephone, don't expect your audience to figure out the sound effect you've called for. Tell them what they're hearing.

Live or Taped Commercials?

Customarily, especially in writing radio commercials for broadcast in local markets, the writer will ask, "Live or taped?" The answer will influence how you write the commercial—whether you'll ask for music, sound effects, or a special style of announcing.

Announcements are broadcast in two ways. An example will illustrate these methods.

Assume you are the manufacturer of a product for general consumption, but being relatively new in the business, you do not yet enjoy complete national distribution of your product. You must proceed in your marketing strategy by opening up different markets individually until each market has good distribution.

You select a new city into which you wish to introduce

your product and you allocate money to advertise it there. You decide that newspaper advertisements plus a series of spot announcements make the best combination of local advertising media available for your purposes, and you buy a schedule of spot time on the local radio station. You purchase minute spots that are to be extended over a period of six weeks.

- You can simply have those commercials typed, along with instructions as to how and when they should be read, and send them to the radio station. Then, a local announcer will be assigned to your account and will deliver the spots as you have written them.[1]

- You can hire an announcer whose voice you like and whose delivery you can control through rehearsals, tape all the announcements, and send that tape to the radio station in your new market. Instead of having one of their own announcers read the material, they will then play the designated tape at the times you request.

Need a Change of Voice? Use Tape

This procedure may also be used if you have purely local accounts, such as a bank or an insurance company. In a

---

[1] Usually, however, the station tapes the commercials delivered by its announcers.

```
(sfx: heavy traffic)

TRAFFIC
   SIGNAL 1:    Well, here we go. Rush hour on the expressway.
TRAFFIC
   SIGNAL 2:    Yeah, you ready to go to work?
SIGNAL 1:       Let's do it.
BOTH:           Yellow! (SFX: BELL) Red! (SFX: BELL)
SFX:            (traffic stops)
SIGNAL 2:       You know, bein' a traffic light is OK and all. But
                I sure wish that...Heeeyyyy!!!
SIGNAL 1:       What? What? Whattaya see?
SIGNAL 2:       Look down there!
SIGNAL 1:       Where? Where?
SIGNAL 2:       Center lane. Third car from the intersection.
SIGNAL 1:       Hey, isn't that...
SIGNAL 2:       Yeah. A 1995 Acura Integra G-S-R Sports Coupe.
SIGNAL 1:       In Milano Red, I do believe.
SIGNAL 2:       Yep. And the v-Tech Valvetrain System. 170
                horses. Wow!!!
SIGNAL 1:       Can we keep it here a little longer?
SIGNAL 2:       Better let'em go. We don't want the guy to be
                late for work.
BOTH:           Green! (SFX: BELL)
SFX:            (heavy traffic)
SIGNAL 1:       Hey, look! Here comes a 95 Accord. Should we
                stop him?
BOTH:           (pause) Naahhhh!!!|
SIGNAL 2:       Heads up! Babe in a convertible comin' up.
BOTH:           (quickly) Yellow! (SFX: BELL) Red! (SFX: BELL)
SFX:            (car comes to screeching halt)
ANNCR:          Come see the full line of exciting new Acuras,
                including the NSX Legend Sedan and Coupe and
                Integra. And take advantage of financing as low
                as 2 point 9 percent at_____Acura, (address).
```

Figure 19–3. Humorous radio commercial. In writing this commercial the person doing this bit of whimsy, in having two traffic lights delivering the commercial, was wise enough to make this clear early in the commercial by having Signal 2 state the fact. Although the traffic lights deliver some sales points, the burden of the selling is saved, as it should be, for the announcer at the end. *Courtesy of the Radio Advertising Bureau.*

local market, the announcers' voices, names, and personalities become well known to listeners. If, as so often happens, the announcers are competent and trusted, this audience familiarity is desirable. Occasionally, however, you'll want a change, especially if you're starting a new campaign. You may, accordingly, go to another town to tape commercials with an announcer whose voice is not known to your local listeners.

This change of voice has another plus. Let's say that your bank commercials are delivered each morning by a well-known local announcer. Before the day is over, that same announcer may have delivered commercials for two other banks. The audience may understandably wonder how the announcer (who sounds very, very sincere in his delivery) can be so enthusiastic about all three banks. Inevitably, there is some loss of credibility for the announcer and for the message. The taping of commercials delivered by a nonlocal announcer would provide a good solution to this problem.

So, live or taped? Each has its advantages. If your messages are simple, straightforward, and do not require a highly dramatic or specialized type of voice, the first way

is generally preferred, since it is less expensive. If you wish to control the manner of delivery, in regard to emphasis and pace, the tape is your answer.

Of course, the first technique, that of sending the station the script for your announcements, is workable only when you have a straight commercial handled by an announcer only. When you wish your spots to be dramatic, or to contain music or gimmicks, they necessarily must be taped. The local radio station could hardly afford to charge you the little they do for a spot announcement of a few seconds and also stage a musical production for you.

Another situation that will become familiar to you is the writing of a commercial that will be taped for a 50-second segment (written by an advertising agency for a national advertiser). The last 10 seconds will be delivered live by a station announcer, but sometimes will be taped by the local announcer if it is going to be used frequently. You will write the 10-second tag. In the tag you will localize, giving the name, address, and possibly the phone number of the local outlet.

As mentioned previously in the section about musical commercials, you may be writing around a musical introduction and ending, both of which are taped before you begin writing the words to go between the music portions.

ANNCR:	Clint Eastwood is a little upset.
EASTWOOD:	It seems some misguided people out there have been abusing our public lands and that really bothers me. Vandalizing parks, robbing historic sites, or overrunning wild areas. These are ours and we have to save them. As I see it, these clowns can either clean up their act, or they can get out of town.
ANNCR:	A public service message from the U.S. Department of the Interior and the Ad Council.

LYRIC:	Anywhere farmers get together You'll learn a lot about crops and weather; And when they talk about corn, the name you'll hear, Will more than likely be Pioneer.
	(Music open—The opening SFX need to establish a grain elevator on a busy day. All noises and muffled conversations should be off mike and in the background, but we should definitely hear a phone ring and a man answer, "Co-op Elevator, Frank speaking.")
PETE:	(Still slightly off mike) I gotta get home. See you guys later.
	(SFX: Door opens)
PAUL:	(Right on mike) Hi, Pete. Selling your corn today?
PETE:	No, just talking corn.
PAUL:	Did you learn anything?
PETE:	(Really thinking about it) Well, yeah, I did.
PAUL:	You did?

ANNCR: How do you feel about your career?
VOICE: I spent years training to be a teacher, but I think I made a mistake. This just doesn't feel like a fit.
VOICE 2: I've been a nurse for five years and I'm really burned out. I can't remember the last morning I woke up and looked forward to going to work.
VOICE 3: I was laid off not too long ago. Maybe this is the time to find work that I really like.
ANNCR: Just how satisfied are you with your job? Are you considering changing to a more rewarding career...one that's right for you? Perhaps it's time to go into business for yourself. For over five years_____ helped hundreds of successful professional individuals find more satisfying work. They can help you, too. Take the first step by attending the upcoming_____ seminar. Discover how to find a job that allows you to feel "on track" with your career. Seating is limited, so act today by calling 555-5555 for more information and reservations. That's 555-5555.

Figure 19–4a. Multiple-voice commercial. Too often commercial writers have supposedly real-life people deliver lines that sell a product or service. This commercial does not do that. Voices 1-2-3 simply set the stage for the announcer who comes in at the end with a strong selling message. And, at the very end he gives the telephone number twice. It's always a good strategy to repeat the number, since it's the rare listener who will be fast enough, or alert enough, to catch a number given just once. *Courtesy of the Radio Advertising Bureau.*

ANNCR: When you're considering employment or a new career, what matters the most? Being on the job as quickly as possible? Finding a job ...a career...that really feels right for you? The people company, _____, understands your concern. That's how they've been so successful at placing people just like you for over seven years in jobs from the Northeast to California. With their local and national networks, _____ can help your career advance if you have the skills. Have you ever thought of becoming a production or maintenance supervisor? How about an office clerk? Or, are you seeking entry level employment as an on-line production worker? _____ can help you today! For employment throughout the United States...contact the people company... _____. Here's the phone number...it's not long and it's not long distance. Call 1-800-555-5555. Again, that's 1-800-555-5555. If you didn't write it down you can find it in the White Pages. _____ is an equal opportunity employer.

Figure 19–4b. Straight commercial. A sensible touch in this career-placement commercial is the advertiser's recognition that the average listener can't always respond fast enough when telephone numbers are given at the end of the commercial. In this case, the commercial gives the number twice. That's good. And even better, the listener is told to consult the White Pages if there wasn't time to write down the number. *Courtesy of the Radio Advertising Bureau.*

End with a Call to Action

Books, plays, and motion pictures come to a climax at the end. So should radio commercials. Your climax is when you ask your listener to do something, or when you make a suggestion. There is hardly a radio commercial that should not ask for action. Examples:

See this bargain today.

Drop in. Learn for yourself.

Find out why National Bank is called the "Friendly" bank.

Let our experienced investment counselors help you.

Remember, give your family *extra* nourishment on these chilly days—give them steaming, delicious Seaside Chowder.

Come in *today*. We'll show you how easily you can play a Tune-Time Organ.

Try this new corn-popper now. It's a family-pleaser.

Why delay? Enjoy your home now. Get a quickly arranged home improvement loan.

Think it over, and then see us about terms.

PETE: Um Hmm.

PAUL: What?

PETE: Well, a lot of the guys who came in here, when they're talking about their corn yields?

PAUL: Um Hmm.

PETE: They keep comparing the hybrids they planted to Pioneer hybrids.

PAUL: So ... what's that prove?

PETE: Well, I figure, if Pioneer hybrids are the ones to beat ...

PAUL: Yeah?

PETE: Well ... they must be the ones to plant. (Both men laugh)

LYRIC: Livin' and learnin' and plantin' Pioneer.

Calling for action doesn't mean that you actually expect instantaneous obedience from the listener. A request for action does, however, give vitality to the ending. Without the unmistakable call for action, your commercial ending lacks punch. Furthermore, people usually need prodding. Who knows how many tires have been bought because an announcer said, "Don't drive another mile on those worn-out tires. It's illegal and it's unsafe. See your tire dealer *today!*"

As any salesperson can tell you, it's easier for sales prospects *not* to act. Your action words at the end of the commercial provide a psychological boost—an extra nudge—to your listeners.

Fundamentals for Writing Radio Copy

Writing copy by formula is not a recommendation you'll find in this book, but there *are* useful guides you can follow. In this chapter on radio-commercial writing, a number of such guides have been suggested. They are included, along with some additional points, in this summary. Observe these fundamentals and review them periodically. They can help you write successful radio commercials if you add that extra spark of innate creative ability that no set of guides, and no book, can give you.

1. Keep copy points to a minimum in deference to:
   a. The human mind's inability to absorb very much solely through the ear.
   b. The fact that your average radio listener is usually only a half-listener and will have difficulty catching one idea, let alone two or three.
2. Identify your product or advertiser quickly. If you wait too long to do so, your listener may have left the room, turned the set off, or stopped listening.
3. Make pictures with words. You are not writing for television. If that package you're pushing has blue stripes, suggest to your listener that he look for the blue-striped package. If it's a round container, call it a "round container."
4. Repeat important benefits, words, elements, and names. Remember the inattentive listener. The first time he will barely hear you, but the second time he may have that pencil ready to take down what you're saying.

   Repetition is especially important if you're giving a telephone number. As a general principle, don't bother giving a telephone number unless you plan to repeat it. 99 out of 100 persons will not catch the number the first time the announcer gives it, but there's an outside chance that the number will be remembered, or jotted down, if it is repeated. The same advice applies to the giving of addresses.

   As for the repetition of product names or the advertiser's name, there is no fixed rule, but many writers automatically try to get a name in near the beginning, the middle, and the end.
5. Get attention at the very start. You don't have to

scream to get attention, but you should come over "big" in some way to distract listeners from what they are doing at the moment—whether washing dishes, polishing the family car, or putting furniture in order. How can you be "big"? Achieve bigness through music, unusual voices, the kinds of words you use, and the sound effects you achieve.
6. Persuade, don't scream. While a number of success stories—especially in local advertising—have been built by the "screamers," you'll do better in the long run to lead listeners to your way of thinking rather than to lash them with shrieking messages.
7. Avoid the overworked superlatives and the trite, insincere, glib radio patter. Any comedian working for a laugh can always get it by imitating radio commercials because so many sound ridiculous, even without parodying.
8. Make dialogue believable and unforced. Again, as in point 7, even mediocre comedians can slay audiences with takeoffs on TV or radio copy. The finest target is the two-voice commercial. It's almost impossible to deliver a believable, serious commercial with the entire message handled by two actors. Set your stage with the characters from "life," but leave them quickly and let the announcer do the selling. Exceptions to this rule are humorous commercials in which obvious spoofing occurs.
9. Never forget that you're writing for the ear. This point, of course, sums up everything previously said about short words, alliteration, and unpleasant sounds. Radio writing is neither print copy nor television copy. It borrows from both, but it has its own unique areas. Above all, radio copy is conversational because the ear is attuned to the sound, flow, and nuances of conversation.
10. Watch your word count. Pace your commercial for understandability and sincerity. To be certain that you're not too far above or below your time limitation, count your words and use a stopwatch. You look like an amateur each time your commercial runs over the time.
11. In almost all commercials, make your endings strong, positive, and action suggesting. Naturally, in institutional approaches and certain humorous commercials, the big push at the end is appropriate, but in the let's-move-merchandise-from-the-shelves type of commercial, ask fxor the order.

ANNCR: Think about this. If everyone of us gave just five hours a week to the causes we care about, it would be like mobilizing more than 20 million full-time volunteers. Think what we could do about drug abuse. Juvenile crime. Illiteracy. All those things we keep hoping will go away. Just five hours a week. It has to start with somebody. So give five. What you get back is immeasurable. A public service of Independent Sector and the Ad Council.

Following are two commercials that demonstrate much of what has been suggested throughout the chapter and in the foregoing summary. You will see how the guides can be used both in a straight commercial and in a multivoice commercial.

Straight Commercial for Electric Food Liquidizer

(SFX for 3 seconds of the liquidizer working at its highest speed) What you've just heard is a Liqui-Speed electric food liquidizer that performs so many food preparation jobs you can substitute it for a blender, a food processor, and an egg beater—not to mention a chopper, a shaver, and a grinder. It'll let you dispense with some other kitchen implements, too, thus saving cupboard space. More important, you can use your Liqui-Speed for an almost limitless range of tasks. For instance—to name a few—it purees baby foods, makes peanut butter, grates cheese, and chops nuts. Result? Tempting meals from soup to dessert, a gourmet touch you've wanted, and a handsome addition to your kitchen with its contemporary design in gleaming chrome and stainless steel. Furthermore, its Swedish steel blades will *last* and *last.* Another happy note—Liqui-Speed is self-cleaning. See a guaranteed, moderately priced Liqui-Speed today at your nearest hardware or department store for an introduction to exciting new ways to prepare meals.

Features of Foregoing Commercial

- Written within time frame: 155 words plus SFX amounting to seven words for total of 162.
- Opening immediately explains the SFX to the listener.
- Transitional writing throughout, with word bridges such as "too," "More important," "for instance," "Result?" "Furthermore," and "Another happy note."
- An action ending that suggests action by listener and tells where the item may be purchased.
- Use of contractions such as "you've" and "it'll."
- Personal writing with liberal use of "you" and references to points important to user, such as saving cupboard space, cutting down need for so many kitchen implements and product's contribution to better meals.
- Putting over of one big point—the versatility of the unit. This point is carried from the opening lines to the last lines.
- Brand name mentioned four times.

Dramatized, Multivoiced Commercial for Electric Food Liquidizer

(SFX for 3 seconds of background noises—many voices and miscellaneous sounds)

ANNCR:	Here we are at the National Retail Hardware Show. Let's hear what hardware retailers are saying about a hot new item—the Liqui-Speed electric food liquidizer.
MALE VOICE 1:	This thing's so versatile I can sell it as a substitute for blenders, food processors, and other types of mixers. Might give me more shelf space.
MALE VOICE 2:	I like the *price.* Ought to move *fast.*
MALE VOICE 3:	Good-looking unit, too. All that chrome and stainless steel. It'll display well.
ANNCR:	And there it is—the Liqui-Speed liquidizer—

	moderately priced, good-looking, and, above all, *versatile.*
MALE VOICE 1:	My customers'll go for an item that does so *many* things. According to this display card it chops, grates, purees, liquefies, grinds, and on and on.
ANNCR:	His customers—and that's *you*—will like some *other* features of Liqui-Speed, too. For instance, it's self-cleaning, it's guaranteed, and it has durable Swedish steel blades. For greater variety in meal preparation, start using a Liqui-Speed liquidizer. See one at your nearest hardware or department store *today.*

Features of Foregoing Commercial

- Written within time frame: 162 words plus SFX amounting to seven words for total of 169.
- Opening immediately explains the SFX to the listener.
- People, other than announcer, are qualified to deliver product sales points believably.
- Product is mentioned four times.
- Big point—versatility—mentioned in beginning, middle, and end.
- Voices other than announcer deliver their lines naturally.
- Action ending that tells prospect where to buy the unit.

There's Lots of Outside Help for You if You Write for Local Advertisers

If you're working with local advertisers, there are a number of helpful resources available to you. For one, there are the area radio stations. Many have extensive libraries of music and sound effects upon which you can draw. It's up to you to find out what's available. Keep a list in your desk and use every opportunity to draw upon the station resources to make your commercials lively and different. One trouble is that too many copywriters aren't diligent enough in researching the availability of these resources. Most stations don't volunteer the information. You must dig it out yourself. Once you get your music or sound effects list, however, it can be an immense help in creating commercials that are out of the ordinary.

When you need musical help, you also can call upon the "jingle" houses mentioned in the section on musical commercials. These organizations can whip up, with amazing speed, music and lyrics to be used by local advertisers. The companies have on-call gifted writers and musicians who provide music and lyrics for any type of product, often at a surprisingly low cost.

Just give them the necessary background help (product facts, advertising objectives, and possibly some past copy) and let them give you what you need, whether it's a complete singing commercial or simply supplemental music.

Utilize every such help you can find. Although the straight commercial is still a powerful sales agent, try for the variety of music and sound effects—whether you obtain them from your local stations or from an out-of-town jingle house.

Try These Suggestions for Attracting and Holding Your Listeners

1. **Symbolic character.** When advertising products associated with certain countries, such as pizza for Italy or tea for England, a distinctive voice presumably of a native of those countries can make your commercial hold attention. Be careful. Imitate the accent but don't burlesque it, or you'll run the risk of getting complaints from sensitive listeners.

2. **Music using a well-known tune.** Bank commercials are usually not high in interest, but the use of a good music introduction and close can do much to attract and hold your audience. Consider this for any product lacking in strong listener appeal.

3. **Strong, familiar voice.** News commentators heard daily bring authority to commercials and command immediate attention. A station farm director, for example, has a voice known and trusted by farmers. As a result, he's a sure bet to seize and hold attention for commercials he delivers.

4. **Interviews.** Persons interviewed about your product in real-life situations such as a couple drinking your coffee in a well-known restaurant can have listeners holding on to every word, but only if the interviews sound natural and believable. If not, avoid this technique.

5. **Alter the sound.** In television, the speeding-up of the movement of characters gets laughs and attention. You can do this in radio by speeding or slowing the sound. Use this approach only occasionally, however, and avoid it completely if words can't be understood.

6. **Use humor skillfully.** Some of the most dreadful radio commercials are those in which local talent are used to deliver purportedly humorous lines. Contrarily, some of radio's greatest success stories are connected with humorous commercials. Good humorous commercials will have your audience actually looking forward to commercials and listening devoutly, but bad ones will kill you in the marketplace.

7. **Use sound effects involving the product.** Sound effects such as bacon sizzling, coffee percolating, and a vacuum cleaner in action are efficient devices for getting attention. In any such use, unless a sound is *immediately* identifiable to listeners, use words in the commercial that tell listeners what they're hearing. For example, "That coffee percolating in the morning is a sound that starts your day off *right.*"

8. **Use different commercials throughout the week.** If your commercial is on five times a week and never changes, it's deadly. Even though you pursue a common theme, write a different commercial for each day. If you don't vary commercials, you invite immediate turnoff when listeners realize that the same commercial is being delivered without change over and over.

9. **Integrate commercials.** Tie in with weather reports, time checks, and other features popular with listeners. Tie-ins with current events featured by the station have strong listener appeal.

CHAPTER 20

Television Advertising
It Gives You Full Scope for Creativity (Part A)

T ed Fischer, chairman of his agency's plans board, was engaging in some after-hours musing with the agency CEO. "As you know, Dan, I'm strong for TV, but I view it as an untamed monster. It devours our creative talent and yells for more. What was fresh yesterday is ancient tomorrow. Change. Change. Change."

Sighing, he went on: "Interactive ideas pop up like weeds. And then there are infomercials, new government regulations, constant carping about commercial clutter, politicians slamming program content, and production costs going through the roof."

Looking out the window at the city lights below, the chairman said slowly, "TV's critics are right in so many ways, and yet TV remains a communicator's dream for advertising, news, and entertainment. But it's <u>so</u> hard to use it effectively, yet honestly, intelligently, and in good taste."

As the chairman said, television and television advertising have their problems, but both continue to be cosmic forces. If you're a television commercial writer, you're aware of all of the problems assailing the medium, but you're also aware of the mighty effect of those commercials you create. You know that they move goods, and you exult in the challenge of turning out selling messages combining all the elements of sight, sound, drama, and intriguing visual effects.

You're pleased when you hear viewers say, "I liked the commercials better than the show." But sometimes you hear, "I can't stand all of those boring commercials!" Your job is to satisfy both groups.

Television Lures Writers

If you're typical, you'd *like* to be a good writer of print copy, but you *yearn* to write television copy because the mere idea fascinates you. Its scope, influence, and sales power make television the exciting medium. "Here at

last," you may say, "is what advertising creativity is all about."

Because of television's demands, a new breed of writers has evolved since television's first commercial was telecast. Today's television-commercial writers have not only the selling instinct needed by all copywriters, but also a whole range of talents not required by other advertising writers.

To practice their craft intelligently, the writers of television commercials must understand the problems and techniques of the producers and cameramen. This is a whole complicated world in itself. Ideally, they should know staging, acting, and the theater. If they are involved in animated television commercials, these writers should also possess knowledge of the complicated art of putting such commercials together.

To work in animation, it is imperative that you possess an above-average imagination, often tinged with a touch of zaniness. Humdrum writers have no part in the humorous and sometimes mad world of animated creation. The copywriters may deal with the producers of animation, an enormously creative group. Copywriters that lack knowledge of this unique craft cannot command the producers' respect.

In print advertising, a copywriter has a fairly realistic idea of what the finished advertisement will be like when the copy and the rough layout have been made. In contrast, the television-commercial writer has made only the barest start when the script is done.

Television is a visual medium. Most TV writers team up with an art director in the conceptual stage of a commercial. Together they discuss the strategy and then create a commercial that communicates that strategy in a memorable and effective way.

The creative team presents their storyboarded idea through a chain of approvals at both the agency and the client. Once they get a "go," the team is augmented by a producer, and these three carry the project through to completion.

The responsibilities of each member of the team are roughly as follows:

- *Copywriter* is responsible for the audio portion of the commercial. This means auditioning and casting the voice talent or announcer and directing them in recording sessions. The writer also has primary responsibility in choosing a music production house and working with the music producer on jingles, postscoring, and sound effects.
- *Art director* is responsible for the look of the commercial.This includes art design, color coordination, package retouching, and prop selection.
- *Producer* is responsible for the logistics of the commercial production—bidding, directors, maintaining budgets, acting as liaison between the director and the agency, and overseeing every facet of the commercial production to make sure things run smoothly.

During the shoot, the areas of responsibility mesh. Each member relies on the other for thoughts and opinions in order to make their commercial everything they hoped it would be. After the shoot, they work closely with a film editor. Take after take is reviewed for pacing and performance to find those that enhance the clarity of the message.

Contrast all of this uncertainty and complication with the delightful simplicity of the average radio commercial or print advertisement. A print writer does the headline, body copy, and gets a rough layout from the artist; the finished advertisement is simply a refinement of what has already been done. At a similar stage in the television commercial script, the copywriter has only just begun, and by the end of the production process, the commercial could be a flop.

Big Payoff if Your Commercial Stands Out

Not all television commercials depend upon zany imagination. Many commercials of the demonstration type are clear-cut from the beginning and may be likened to the straight-line type of body copy. There are probably more routine television commercials than highly creative commercials, and writers can make a good living turning out adequate, if undistinguished, television commercials. If writers have the creative spark, however, that enables them to come up with the creative point of difference, the rewards for such writing can be enormous. One such idea that made a fantastic difference in the marketplace was the "Don't squeeze the Charmin" campaign of Procter & Gamble.

With various creative and technical production factors combining to make the television commercial more complex than any other current form of advertising, there is a critical need for trained, competent television personnel.

Words and Visuals Share Responsibility in Television Commercials

Television is a visual medium. Ideally, your television copy theme should be one that simply puts into words a piece of action seen on the screen. The best television copy does not call attention to itself. In writing it, you are less concerned with words than either the radio or print copywriter. You are after significant action and ways of bringing it about. You are on your way to achieving these ends if, after writing a final script, you can evaluate it in this manner; Block off the audio portion and read through the video to see if it makes an interesting, logical, fluid series of pictures. If you can grasp a basic, solid message from the video alone, you have fully utilized the visual power of television.

Print writers can use heads, subheads, and an illustration to convey the sales story. In television, you must sustain interest and sell with a series of quickly vanishing visual impressions. No one scene can dominate as is the case in a powerful print illustration. Also, because of the rapidly changing scenes and the brief time, you cannot deliver the number of sales points possible in a big-space print advertisement.

Even more difficult are the problems of radio writers moving into television because they bring with them the practice of writing for the ear exclusively. The ear is much slower than the eye. For radio, each thought transition must be gradual; word pictures must be drawn carefully with clear definition, and verbal overemphasis is often required to drive home a point.

Television neither needs nor wants these standard radio techniques. In radio, words have always done the job. To relinquish this to the camera is one of the hardest and most essential things for the radio writer to learn about television. As a television copywriter, you will do well to heed the admonition: "Don't tell me—show me."

This is not to say that words are wholly unimportant. In fact, as people have become more accustomed to television, they tend to turn sets on just to have sound in the house. Also, while the sets are on (somewhat as in radio

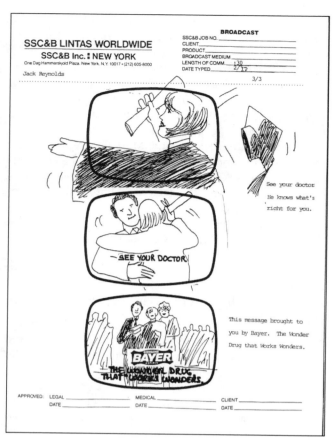

Figure 20–1. Television storyboard, the first step in the long process of going from the idea to the finished production.

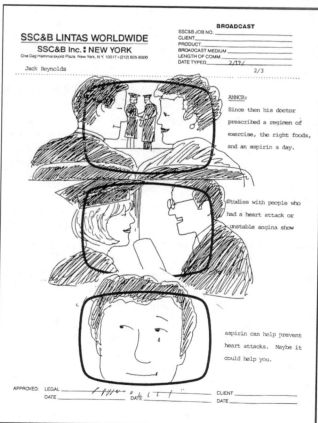

but to a lesser degree), people do more than simply watch the screen—they knit, cook, read, or even write. Thus, because viewers are not watching the screen every moment, the audio message becomes more important in that they can hear the sales message even while not watching the video action. Though it is possibly not quite as important as it was when viewers never lifted their eyes from television screens, the visual presentation remains the most important element.

An imaginative visual sense will be most helpful to you in creating effective television commercials. This ability will enable you to develop and exploit to its fullest the potential of television for imagery and product demonstration.

"Originality," however, can be dangerous, according to Rosser Reeves, once board chairman of Ted Bates & Co., a New York agency with a huge percentage of its billings in television. In his book *Reality in Advertising*, Reeves raised warning signals about the preoccupation with originality that can lead writers to absurd extremes.

In searching after the different, the clever, and the unusual, or in attempting to imitate some truly original approach, writers can forget that an advertising campaign is not designed to express their individual egos or talents for entertaining. Rather, it is a functional tool whose purpose is to fully bring the basic claim to life with ideas, information, and specific visual interpretations that speak convincingly about why your product is better.

Try for the Ideal—An Effective Commercial Written in Good Taste

A strength and yet a weakness of television advertising is its intrusiveness. It bulls its way into living rooms, bedrooms, and other rooms uninvited. Your message had better be worthwhile enough to partially overcome the resentment you have created.

Even more important is the ability to write commercials in good taste, because television advertising is so embarrassingly intimate in its presentation of our methods of dress and hygiene. Such poking about into our habits in the bathroom, bedroom, and closets causes emotions ranging from annoyance to downright revulsion and outrage. You'd better develop a considerate, sensitive touch in writing commercials in a period when viewers are assailed by messages for bras, pantyhose, feminine hygiene, deodorants, toilet-bowl cleaners, toilet papers, breath sweeteners, foot-smell remedies, dandruff removers, pimple cures, and nasal-drip relief.

Nothing seems too intimate for exploitation by television commercials, and great is the resulting outcry from a sizable portion of viewers. Are you going to contribute to the assault upon good taste, or will your commercials establish a proper tone while effectively selling your product?

In today's better educated, more cynical, and quick-to-resent society, the television commercial is too often viewed as *insulting* and demeaning. Unfortunately, the charge is true of many commercials, which portray men and women as mindless idiots who react to advertised products, or present silly little dramas that totally lack any semblance to real life.

Is your goal to perpetuate this attack on the good sense of the viewer or to lift the quality of television commercial writing to the point where it will be acceptable among people of intelligence, sensitivity, and good taste? It had better be the latter, because the voices are loud in the land against today's television commercials.

See That Your Commercial Has B.R.N.—Believability, Respect, and Naturalness

Above all else, your commercial must have *believability*.

This should be present both in claims for and demonstrations of products. There should be the honest promise of a believable benefit expressed in understandable language. Useful information should replace the extravagant, unsubstantiated claim. Change your captive audience to a captivated audience by giving them commercials they can believe, unlike so many of the paid—or so-called unrehearsed—testimonials that stretch credibility. Cynically, the audience has come to believe that anyone—stars or people on the street—will say what the advertiser wants said pro-

vided the money is sufficient. So, move away from "bombast, brag, and boast" to "simple, useful, and believable."

Your commercial must also show *respect*.

Women, the target of so many television commercials, are loud in their resentment of the women portrayed in commercials. You've seen them a thousand times exclaiming over products, discussing trivia as if their entire days were filled with vacuous pursuits and still more vacuous language. Slice-of-life commercials have been special offenders, depicting women whose chief concern in life seems to be ring-around-the-collar or ring-around-the-bathtub. Far too many commercials fail to give women respect for their significant contributions out of, as well as within, the home.

Finally your commercial must convey *naturalness*.

Television, more than any other medium, seems to eschew natural conversation and natural situations. It is not natural for two persons to talk for a full 30 seconds, or 60 seconds, about a product—especially in the high pitched, overly enthusiastic way of the supposedly real-life people shown on the screen. As a viewer, you know that this is so and you reject what is said as unnatural and, hence, as largely unbelievable.

Then, there are the wild gyrations of the youthful set, who seem to get high on soft drinks. A succession of quick shots showing youth in high gear driving beach buggies, skydiving, hang-gliding, dashing into the surf, racing down the beach, riding motorcycles, and turning somersaults on the ski slopes depicts an exhilaration no soft drink has ever been known to contribute.

All this is mood stuff, of course, but it is unnatural, like so much of television that substitutes mood for more solid material. In the case of soft drinks, there is some excuse because there is really very little to write about such products; however, the frantic pace of such commercials is part of the approach to selling in commercials that causes people to separate advertising talk from real talk and television life from real life. Lately, beer commercials have been guilty of the juvenile hyperactivity that we've become accustomed to seeing in the promotion of soft drinks.

What to Consider When Writing a Television Commercial

First, the Idea

The first step in writing a television commercial is the evolution of the idea. Your idea must strike at such basic motivations as love, ambition, self-preservation and economics. The idea should be developed with imagination and tempered with a knowledge of the medium, the advertiser's needs, and the consumer's desires. By applying simple reasoning, you will find that the product to be advertised contains within itself such sources of ideas as: what is new about the product; what benefits it offers to the user; the experience of consumers with the product; its advantages over competitive products; and its basic value.

LEO BURNETT COMPANY, INC.

AS FILMED AND RECORDED

"Pumpkin" :30

AD COUNCIL

CNTD7893

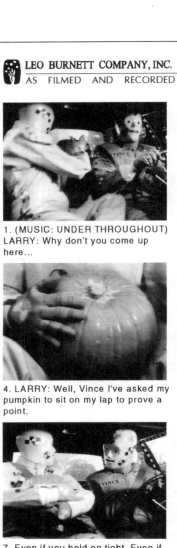

1. (MUSIC: UNDER THROUGHOUT)
LARRY: Why don't you come up here...

2. pumpkin.

3. VINCE: What are you doing Larry?

4. LARRY: Well, Vince I've asked my pumpkin to sit on my lap to prove a point.

5. VINCE: And what is that your Larryness?

6. LARRY: Even if we fasten our safety belts.

7. Even if you hold on tight. Even if you were watching the road.

8. VINCE & LARRY: Whoa!!

9. (SFX: CRASH)

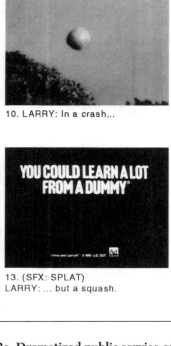

10. LARRY: In a crash...

11. your pumpkin will be nothing...

12. (SFX: WHISTLE)

YOU COULD LEARN A LOT FROM A DUMMY®

13. (SFX: SPLAT)
LARRY: ... but a squash.

YOU COULD LEARN A LOT FROM A DUMMY®

USE CHILD SAFETY SEATS.
1-800-424-9393

14. (AVO): You could learn a lot from a dummy.
(SFX: CLICK)
(AVO): Use child safety seats.

15. VINCE: We loved that little pumpkin to pieces.

Figure 20–2a. Dramatized public service commercial. This
is one of a series of such commercials.

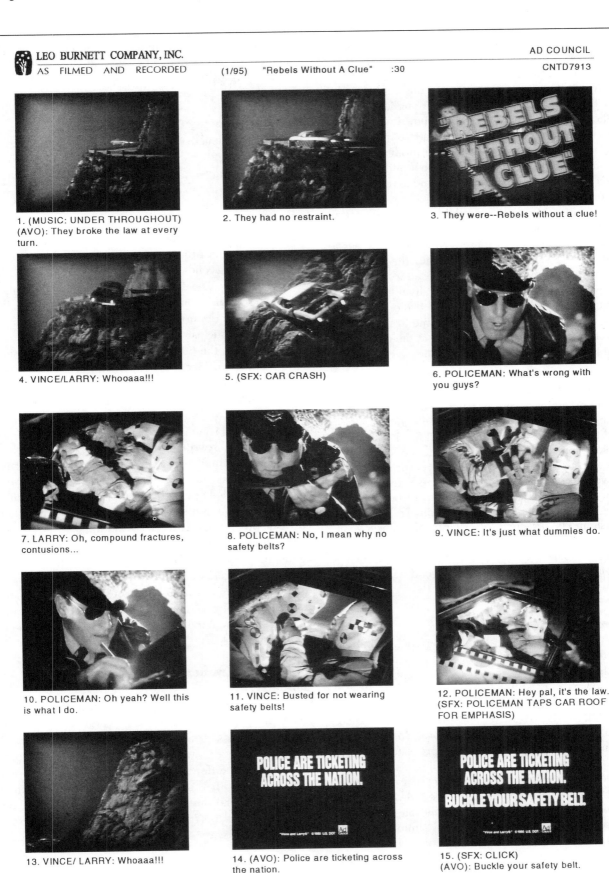

Figure 20–2b. Public service television commercial. The safety theme of this Advertising Council commercial is the theme of many of their productions.

In an effective presentation, you must touch the right motivational button and stimulate desire for the product and its benefits.

The greatest "strength of presentation" is in demonstration (or comparison). Demonstrate the new feature, the benefit, the advantage, and—where applicable—the price. Show the product: how it works, how it saves, how easy it is to use, how it makes one more attractive or more popular, and how it compares with rival products. When price is an important factor, superimpose it on the screen to make it seem even more of a bargain and to make it that much more memorable.

Another point is simplicity. While advantages of the product are important, don't try to make your television commercial a catalog of all these advantages. If it has a dozen or more advantages, that's great for the advertiser but not for the commercial. Time is needed to put across a point, which means the selling story should be boiled down to one principal point—or at most two or three. Be sure that the selling story has enough time to register on the viewer's mind and that there is time at the conclusion to sum it up with a convincing repetition.

Second, Definition of the Problem
Television commercials vary in length, cost, and production techniques, depending on the specific jobs they are intended to perform. Such variations call for definition of the problem, a matter that may or may not lie within your province as copywriter. The problem deals with such factors as overall sales objectives, location and identification of primary customers, and the limitations of budget. Are you going to hit targets singly or in number? Your commercials should be designed with a basic sales objective in mind: winning new customers, holding regular ones, increasing use per capita, forcing distribution, improving dealer relations, building prestige and good will, or even impressing stockholders.

Program or Spot Use?
Your commercials must also take into account whether they are to be used for program or spot presentation. To present the commercial in the presumed proper environment, an advertiser will often buy (through the advertising agency) a specific type of entertainment or information program. Often, the advertiser and the product become identified, for better or worse, with the program and/or its star. Commercials used within these programs can be "live" or on film or tape.

Spot television advertising is placed by advertisers on a market-by-market basis originating in the individual market where it is telecast. The advertisement may consist of a hard selling 10-second commercial announcement known as an "ID" (for station identification). It may also be a 15-second, 30-second, or 60-second announcement shown between programs, or within a local program or a network participating program in which a number of advertisers have bought spot time.

Spot commercials are almost always on film or tape. They come at the viewer from all angles and in all forms, and because many of them are irritating, they are the kind of advertising people usually complain about when they point an accusing finger at television commercials.

Factors Affecting Commercial Length
A commercial's length depends upon the theme, approach, and specific product advantages. Different sales stories may vary in their complexity. For example, a good demonstration commercial may require 60 seconds, every second of which will be useful and interesting to the viewer.

A product, in contrast, that has nothing to demonstrate and no high degree of product interest might be a bore as the subject matter of a 60-second commercial. Give it 30 seconds or 15 seconds if the idea of the product can be grasped easily by viewers. As the copywriter, you're usually going to be told how long the commercial will be. Thus, this is a subject that doesn't concern you much unless you are permitted to participate in precampaign planning sessions.

At one time, the 60-second commercial was the standard in television. Because of costs and because research showed that shorter commercials could be equally, if not more, effective, the 30-second commercial became the standard.

The standard commercial length in the future might be 15 seconds. Copywriters with any kind of message to deliver will find such a commercial frustrating. Demonstrations, product comparisons, and interviews cannot be handled efficiently in such a short time span.

"Clutter," the profusion of commercials within and between programs, has reduced the impact of commercials. Clutter became much worse when the 30-second commercial replaced the 60-second as the standard. If 15-second commercials dominate, clutter will be worse still. As a copywriter, you have an interest in clutter because attention for your commercial suffers when it is one of a number of commercials presented in rapid sequence between shows.[1]

Repeating Commercials: How Much Is Enough?
Having decided on program as opposed to the spot presentation of your commercial, it is wise to keep in mind certain principles about another factor: wear-out. Viewer knowledge increases with repetition up to a certain point; at that point, indifference or psychological deafness and blindness set in. It is difficult, if not impossible, to measure at what point this mental tuning out takes place, but there are four factors that seem to relate specifically to any commercial's life expectancy:

---

[1] As a possible ominous note for the future, 7-1/2-second commercials are being tried in France and Japan.

- Frequency of broadcast
- Content as it affects the viewer
- Variety of presentation in a given series
- Techniques used in commercial construction

Many advertisers have been successful with a minimum of well-constructed and oft-repeated messages. Skillfully built and judiciously scheduled, a spot can be used for many months or even years. Another can run its course in a few weeks in a heavy saturation campaign, yet still have been effective and economical. Kellogg's Rice Krispies ran a cartoon jingle fifty times in a row on a children's program and burned it out like a meteor. Yet it served its purpose well and it did so at a low cost per showing.

How acceptable a commercial is refers not to how much a viewer likes it but to its "what's-in-it-for-me" content and how well it entertains, informs, and holds forth a promised benefit. A film series should focus on a central theme for greatest impact throughout the series, but varied repetition is the key here, particularly in the manner in which the commercial begins.

Beer commercials are much the same in any given series, but the variety of ways in which they capture attention at the outset makes for interest. Singing jingles combined with animated cartoons are a combination with long life expectancy, especially if the commercial spot is used intermittently. You cannot, however, expect to repeat too often live action films in which memorable characters or settings are featured, since viewers tend to pick apart your commercial with each repetition.

Station Break Spots

Ten-second station break television spots can best be viewed as the rifle bullets of this medium. Here, you encounter the challenge of brevity plus the need for simple, clear-cut selling ideas expressed with visual impact. It may be simpler to write a 5- or 10-minute film script than a 10-second television spot.

In building spot commercials, you will be tempted to crowd too much material into both audio and video presentations, which will only result in a confused and meaningless jumble of words and scenes from which your viewer will derive little. Again, concentrate on the video or visual in your commercial, since this is what must remain with the viewer after your brief message. Remember, however, that the sound or audio plays an important role, too, enabling the viewer to hear you even from outside the room.

Ten-second station identification (ID) spots have the advantage over 60-second commercials in their ability to sustain a much stronger sales pitch and in the fact that they can be repeated more often than their longer cousin. They are also easier to schedule for more intensive coverage on a number of stations, and thus are effective in coping with local sales problems.

The ID spot, chiefly a "reminder" type of advertising, is on the television screen for a full 10 seconds. It gives you eight seconds of sound. As a commercial form, the ID must fight hard for identity and leaves small margin for error. Its brief moments of sound-and-picture glory are almost always preceded by the closing commercial of the preceding program and a chain break. It is immediately followed by the first commercial of the next program. In spite of its physical limitations, the ID can do a fine selling job as both a reminder for impulse type items and as a supporting element for concurrent campaigns for big-ticket advertisers in television and other media.

To detract attention from surrounding commercials, station break commercials often employ cartoons, which are particularly effective because they read well. Since this is primarily reminder advertising, the sponsor's name must be indelibly identified, probably along with a slogan or an important selling point.

It is better not to resort to camera tricks, such as dissolves or wipes, where action on the screen is involved. Stay with a basic setting and be content to move component parts in and out for the sake of fluidity. Hold to the premise, if possible, that the sponsor's signature or logotype should be on-camera for at least half, if not more, of the allotted 10 seconds.

Writing the 15-Second Commercial

Although there can be variations, the basic structure of the "15" calls for a headline or principal "reason why"; once this is set, it is a matter of using it in the audio and dramatizing it in the video. Such commercials are in contrast to those contrived and complicated by local advertisers who seek to make major products out of the precious seconds allotted. It is a challenge to succeed in registering one point strongly in even a 60-second commercial, let alone trying to do more in 15 seconds.

In constructing the 15-second commercial, select the dominant sales point and simply polish that point to its finest. Humor is often an effective ingredient for this type of commercial because it evokes the quick reaction needed for such a short presentation.

The success stories of advertisers who have used shorter commercials to advantage are numerous, and many of them have achieved this success with little or no other advertising. One of these, a watch company, used this formula:

> Buy five or six spots a week on a station and hold them for all-year use. Try to reach the entire family by buying spots in prime time (8:30 P.M. to 10:00 P.M.) with adjacencies to good shows, if possible. Buy a volume in spots commensurate with the company's sales in the particular market.

Another advertiser who had done a strong selling job with spots summed up the situation:

> Spots give us more coverage with the flexibility to handle sales problems peculiar to different areas. We can adjust our product commercials according to regional preferences in flavor, for instance.

3M Post-it Notes
"See This Thing/Olympics" :30

(SFX: WRITING AND POSTING SOUNDS THROUGHOUT)...

ANNCR (VO): When people count on you, count on Post-it Brand Notes.

Figure 20–3. Television commercial that sells in a clever and different way.

Storyboards

A storyboard, executed on a sheet of paper, presents a series of small sketches, with accompanying description of action, plus audio copy. The storyboard gives an advertiser an approximate conception of what the commercial will be upon completion. It is a sort of halfway point between the birth of the original idea and the finished film.

In large agencies, the copywriter teams up with an art director to come up with the concept. Once they have this germ of an idea, the art director maps out the action with sketches and the copywriter writes the script, indicating how it will fall in relation to the pictures.

Storyboards are preferable to written scripts for a number of reasons. Since the commercial will be presented through a medium in which the visual image is paramount in importance, it facilitates production to think in terms of pictures from the beginning. Furthermore, since a number of people may read and be called upon to approve a script, it is probable that each will have a personal visualization of how the story will appear on the screen.

If a storyboard is prepared, all concerned will think in terms of the pictures shown. Each can check the staging and action as the commercial is actually shot. Also, any errors in visualization from the standpoint of company policy or product value will be apparent and can be corrected before actual production begins.

A properly designed storyboard can also be utilized as a shooting script that suggests camera angle and staging, as a preliminary layout for set designs or backgrounds, and as a guide for the film editor when the film is cut. Closeups, camera moves, and optional effects can all be indicated. The director is also aided by the storyboard when planning the action and staging of the film to obtain the desired dramatic effect.

As in the case of print layouts, the first storyboards may be very rough, but the artwork becomes more refined as the storyboard goes through the various levels of persons who must inspect it.

Initially, the art director roughs up the sketches. But before the board goes to the client, an illustrator may tighten up the drawings. At the same time, the copywriter may try to find music and any visual aids which will enhance the client's understanding of the spot. Creative teams have been known to sing, dance, and pretend to be talking hamburgers in order to bring the commercial to life for a client.

As noted early in this chapter, the copywriter, account executives, client, and production people can tell from a print layout just about what the published advertisement will look like. In contrast, the filmed commercial that is finally produced from a storyboard is usually vastly different from the storyboard.

Thus, it takes a professional with plenty of experience and imagination to judge what is going to result from the incorporating of unusual voices, beguiling characters, superb music, dazzling color, energetic motion, and striking sound effects—none of which is truly conveyed by the storyboard.

Actually, the process works both ways. The storyboard idea may look good and the finished product poor. Or, the storyboard may convey little that gives a clue as to the outstanding commercial that will finally be developed from the idea.

One of the problems in doing a storyboard is that it is necessarily brief compared to the finished film, which is divided into frames that speed through the projector 24 to the second, or 1,440 to the minute.

Sometimes the problem isn't overwhelming, as in the case of a simple demonstration commercial that has only two to five scene changes involving two, or possibly one, performer. On the other hand, a commercial such as the typical Pepsi-Cola or Coca-Cola commercial is difficult to storyboard for full understanding. How can you convey in detail all of those quick shots, optical gimmicks, sound effects, numerous people, music, frantic action, and background scenes? You can't. You simply call for enough storyboard frames to serve as a rough guide. You're at the mercy of the production house to bring those few cold pictures to life.

It's especially difficult to plot in advance the exact time each of those frames will require in the finished film. Furthermore, some scenes need more accompanying copy to explain them, and, thus require more frames. The *exact* time they need is hard to tell in advance. Other scenes convey ideas in a fraction of a second, requiring only a glance of the viewer. They may need no accompanying copy.

Some Directors Need Detailed Storyboards; Others Don't

A word of caution is needed here to point out that the detailed and rigid storyboard is not always the best one. Much depends on who will take over from your storyboard to put the commercial on film. If directors are truly creative, you will be shortchanging your commercial by imposing exacting directions upon them. They may have ideas about enacting some of your scenes in a manner to make them much more forceful. Or they might have suggestions on how to cut costs by repeating the use of a certain setting or dropping a bit of action that lends only minor support to the story. Such directors can be a tremendous asset, so it is best to give these talented team members a green light with a storyboard that leaves them room for creative contributions.

Before a job is given to the director and production house, the copywriter, art director, and the agency producer usually sit down and compile production notes. These accompany the storyboard and describe the objective, the audience, the tone or mood, the plot, sets, props, casting considerations, and music. This gives the director an idea of what the creative team expects. As the project evolves, these treatments may be revised, but the production notes and storyboard offer a detailed blueprint from which to start.

ONE MINUTE MANAGERS NEED TEN SECOND MEMOS.

Post-it
Note Pad
Self-Stick Removable Notes

3M
Worldwide Sponsor
1988 Olympic Games

When People Count On You,
Count On Post-it Notes.

3M

Figure 20–4. Print version of the television commercial for the advertiser.

Balancing Audio and Video Is Tricky

A basic problem in writing your television commercial, regardless of its length, is the proper balance of video and audio. Be cautious about pacing the visual side of the commercial too fast and using too many scene changes.

The main trouble, however, lies not with scenes being too long or too short but with uneven pacing. Long scenes too often are followed by jet-speed, short ones.

This uneven pace stems from approaching the commercial's sales points with words rather than pictures. You may find one point easy to express in a few words and accord this point a correspondingly short visual. The more involved points get prolonged visuals.

This is working the wrong way. The brief copy point should either not be visualized at all or its audio should be extended sufficiently to cover a visual of comfortable length.

Remember: It is a mistake to pace your audio for television as fast as you would for the typical hard-sell radio commercial. In television, your audience has to follow video as well as audio, which makes it difficult to grasp a television sound track that is paced too fast. This pacing problem is particularly acute in film commercials where the announcer succeeds in getting in the full message only by racing through the script.

Video. Mr. Conant holds a football as he talks. In the background is a football field with players at practice. As in the first commercial, the video ends with the telephone number.

Audio. You know, football and retirement planning have two things in common. You need a good coach and a good game plan. In football you have a series of plays, some running and some passing. Retirement planning takes the same strategy. Several different investments to provide a good income. I'm Luther Conant, and over the years I've coached hundreds of people just like you to design a good retirement plan. Before you retire, before you select your retirement options, call me at 463-4040 and let's put a game plan together.

Video. Mr. Conant, head of the company, holds up a book as he talks. In the background are book shelves. Ends with closeup of book held up by Mr. Conant.

Audio. Hello, I'm Luther Conant and I specialize in helping people plan for their retirement, and now I've incorporated my ideas and advice in a new book written especially for people getting ready to retire. In layman's terms I explain goals, investments, retirement options, and how to design a retirement plan. *"It's Getting Late – Early"* was designed for those of you who have either waited too long or are retiring sooner than you expected. If you need help with your retirement decisions, give me a call.

Video. Once again, Mr. Conant talks against an athletic background, this time a basketball court with players shooting baskets and dribbling the ball.

Audio. Just like these kids are learning the fundamentals of basketball, we adults need to learn the fundamentals of proper investing. Not run and gun and random shooting and hoping your investment pays off. But instead, a deliberate plan with a definite plan of action to achieve guaranteed results. I'm Luther Conant of Conant Financial Services, and I believe in taking my retirees' money and investing in guarantees. Like going for the sure shoot. Guarantee of principal, guarantee of interest, guarantee of income.

Video. Now the scene shifts to a golf course. While Mr. Conant stands on the green holding the flag, his partner makes a chip shot that just misses the hole. As the action takes place, Mr. Conant delivers his message, and the video ends with the display of the telephone number.

Audio. Just like you need the right club for the right golf shot, you need the right investment for your retirement. Use the wrong club, you could ruin a good round of golf. Use the wrong investment, you could ruin your retirement. Whether you have twenty thousand dollars or two hundred thousand dollars, if you're doing a rollover this year, I can help you pick the investment for your retirement plan. I may not be able to improve your game of golf, but I can make your retirement a lot brighter. I'm Luther Conant.

Figure 20–5. Effective, inexpensive television commercials. Following are four low-cost commercials conceived and written by the head of a financial services company. Delivered by him against simple but interesting backgrounds, the commercials generated business at minimum expense. The audio portion was delivered with sincerity and avoided the pitchman tone. No attempt was made to tie the audio message directly to the video action. These were 30-second commercials with the audio portion running about 80 words.

These cautions do not apply to the mood commercials mentioned earlier in the chapter. In a soft drink commercial, to illustrate, you are not trying to register product points. Your aim may simply be to associate the drink with youth, good times, and activity. To accomplish this, you run scenes in rapid succession with no need to let any of them linger on the screen. Together with equally fast-paced music and offscreen announcing, you create whirlwind action and the mood you're seeking.

An airline might use this technique if it aims to emphasize all the interesting places to which it can take you rather than to stress any particular feature such as ontime arrivals, safety, the type of aircraft, or the service. Similarly, a hotel could run through a pool, the sauna, the dining rooms, the roof garden, and the nearby ocean beach.

For most commercials, however, don't race—*pace*. Be active but not frantic.

Common Sense Should Guide You in the Number of Words You Put in a Commercial

Most radio announcers read comfortably at 160 to 170 words a minute, but others can read considerably faster. A governor of Nebraska was once clocked at 487 words a minute in an election campaign speech. Obviously, such verbal speed is well beyond the television viewer's understanding. You will find that 135 words a minute (w.p.m.) will fit into many live-action commercials, although for the most part, you will need fewer than that. ecommendations range from 80 to more than 130 w.p.m., but experience has shown that a rule of thumb of two words per second usually works out consistently well.

Delivery rate is rather hard to define because of pauses and the fact that many commercials use more than one speaker. One study of 350 one-minute commercials compared word-count analysis data with effectiveness results for the same commercials. The most effective commercials ranged in word count from 101 to 140, demonstrating that a moderate speaking pace was desired over extremes of too many or too few words per minute.

Having a certain delivery rate, however, is no assurance of successful commercial writing. Some outstanding commercials have used no words; others have more than the usual word count. A sensible speaking pace can be a contributing factor, of course, but the important thing is the quality of your words, not their quantity. The advice around many big agencies is, "Say one thing and say it well." Some copywriters have the acronym K.I.S.S.—keep it simple, stupid—posted over their desks.

Quantity, as it applies to the shorter commercials, would be 20 words for the 10-second spot; 30 words for the 15-second spot; and 60 to 65 words for the 30-second spot. The one-minute commercial will usually work well with 120–135 words, but if the announcer is on camera, give him less to say, and if he must demonstrate, give him still less than that. The ground rules say that a 15-second sound track cannot run over 13 seconds and that a one-minute track should not exceed 58 seconds. You will be safer aiming for a shorter count, such as 11 or 12 seconds on the short spot, 25 or 26 on the 30, and 55 or 56 seconds in the one-minute version. This will permit an easier pace and more flexibility in your commercials. Remember, too, in production, it's much simpler to stretch than to tighten.

Scenes: How Many?

What has been said here about packing the audio holds true for the video portion of your television commercial. Don't confuse your viewers with too many scenes or with those that are too busy and distract from your sales story. You can avoid cutting scenes too short by allowing a minimum of three seconds for viewers to orient themselves to any new scene.

Scenes can also run too long, so keep in mind that after six seconds something had better move, or perhaps the viewer will. A different camera angle or some action within the scene can provide movement to prevent a scene from becoming static.

A single scene that is properly plotted out for action and camera angles can sustain interest for 20 or 30 seconds in a commercial. Ordinarily, however, you will want to think in terms of five or six seconds or more per scene. For more important visuals such as establishing a person, demonstrating, or a major copy point, you may want to use 10 to 20 seconds or more.

There is no firm rule about the number of scenes in a commercial, but here are a few general measures that will serve to guide you: No more than two to three scenes in a 10-second spot; three to five in a 15-second spot; and 10 in a 30-second spot. Keep in mind that a closeup from a previous shot is not considered a new scene to the viewer.

To show the futility of trying to set up firm guidelines, a study conducted during the writing of this book found that 30-second commercials were averaging 8 to 10 scenes; these were definite scene changes, not merely changes of camera angles or distance.

Customarily, a demonstration commercial will swallow up time and eliminate the need for constant scene changes. A woman demonstrating the use of a new, useful kitchen utensil may stay on camera for a full 30-second commercial without boring her audience. There is no need for scene changes here, although you might wish to change camera distances and angles. Such changes will give a feeling of added action and can improve the value of the demonstration.

Most of all, keep in mind that television is an *action* medium. You attain action in two ways: (1) by having action in the scenes themselves; and (2) by changing the scenes (and/or camera angles and distances) to create the feeling of action. Above all, avoid television commercials that are simply a succession of still-life photographs.

As You Write, Ask Yourself: "How Much Will This Cost?"

Before a project begins, the account people may inform you of your client's budget. While the agency producer is assigned the task of controlling production and costs, it does not give you license to turn out ideas without regard to this budget. You will learn by experience that it is wise to avoid costly scenes that will invite price-cutting surgery later, thereby endangering the continuity of the whole script.

The accomplished television copywriter is a many-faceted being—salesperson, psychologist, dramatist, film craftsman, producer, and lyricist. As such, you may take part in planning sessions, production briefings, and the various stages of actual production.

You can make all of these efforts more productive and efficient from the beginning with good writing—the best insurance against faulty interpretation and costly production. If your storyboard calls for five on-camera principal performers, do some rethinking. Could you rewrite and accomplish your goals with four, three, or even two performers? Remember, for videotape commercials, an on-camera session fee will run into hundreds of dollars for each person playing a major role, whether the person is called a "player" by SAG (Screen Actors Guild) or a "principal" by AFTRA (American Federation of Television and Radio Artists). This session fee pays for one use of the commercial on the network.

If the commercial is to be used in a major way over the networks, each player (or principal) must be given a reuse, or residual, payment every time the commercial is shown. Even off-camera announcers and singers are given such payments, although in lesser amounts.

When you call for a person in the commercial to speak, handle, or react to the product, that person becomes a player. Others, such as stunt people and specialty dancers, are also classified as players.

Extras are not entitled to residual payments and may be defined as those people seen as hands or backs of heads, for example. They may also be described as extras even if seen in total, but in this case they are well away from the product and they do not react to the product. In a sense, they are simply part of the background.

Because you've called for an unusual number of players (or principals), it may well be that the subsequent reuse payments can cost the client more than the charge for the commercial air time. Assess the value to be gained by the lavish use of players against the added cost. Sometimes you may judge that the use of the extra players will result in a more powerful commercial that will better achieve advertising objectives. If not, then cut down.

More Ways to Cut Costs

It's easy to call for *location* shooting when you're sitting at your typewriter, but it's not so simple to lug all the people, props, cameras, and other equipment to the location—and it can be frightfully expensive. Once again, ask yourself: Is it worth it? Sometimes, the answer must be "yes."

If you can't honestly say yes, there are ways around the problem. You could use a stock shot of the location as background; a special crew (without actors) could go to the spot to get such a shot; or you could use stills to establish the location. Actually, *one* shot may be all you need to fix the location in the viewer's mind and to provide the atmosphere you want.

You can also run up costs by asking for effects and shots that are more complicated than they need to be to put over your message. Do you need that view from the helicopter, that fisheye shot, the telephoto shot, or the extreme closeups? Some of the most effective television is simple television, and simple television can be less expensive. Think about it.

As example of cutting costs is illustrated by a local bank that couldn't afford to show seven on-camera bank employees demonstrating their various duties. Instead, only their hands were shown. These seven pairs of hands handled papers involved in a typical bank transaction. They were shown in closeup, always desirable, and the viewers could see what was happening to customers' money. It was easier to concentrate on the message than if seven persons had been shown. Also important, shooting time was cut from two days to less than one day.

Such economies are typical of low-cost local commercials in which you may call for public domain music or have the local station videotape material with their personnel. You may elect to shoot in 16mm film or use actual advertisements for artwork. You may lose some polish in the commercials using these techniques, but you can also help make television affordable for local advertisers.

One view of cost in your television commercial is that you may have written it in such a way that it is expensive to produce. Another view of cost is that you may have written it so poorly that it gets little or no attention, or is actually boring. In terms of viewers influenced to buy the advertised product, the advertiser may be spending a huge amount per viewer. It is costly to the advertiser when your commercial registers so poorly that viewers can't remember the product, its name, or its selling points.

Fighting for Attention

Writing for television drains some writers. Messages are so ephemeral. Today's idea is stale tomorrow. New, striking graphics are soon supplanted by even more striking graphics. A celebrity spokesperson of today is soon a has-been. The well-thought-out commercial often loses to a commercial that is inferior but, for some weird reason, catches on with the fickle public.

In big advertising agencies, the strain on writers is constant. The writer who can't come up with fresh, usable ideas may soon be leaving the agency.

At the bottom of all this is the fight to stand out in the midst of hundreds of commercials crying for attention. With the ability of viewers to remember the commercials they've seen at an all-time low, writers ask themselves: "Will this commercial I've written make even the slightest impression on viewers, let alone sell the product?"

All of these doubts and problems make television-commercial writing a job for the stouthearted.

Infomercials: When You Have a Lot to Say

What *is* an "infomercial" (also 'informercial')? Concisely, it is a television commercial in program form that features demonstrations or discussions of various products or services. In short form, infomercials may run for two minutes; in long form, they may last for 15 to 30 minutes. Sometimes, an infomercial may run even longer for especially interesting demonstrations and discussions.

Although infomercials have been around since 1982, they took off dramatically after Ross Perot, the Texas billionaire and politician, used them in his presidential cam-campaign in 1992. Simply produced with hand-held charts and delivered in Perot's southwestern twang, the infomercials entered a new era. Since that time, numerous corporations have tested infomercials. Ford, General Motors, McDonald's, Eastman Kodak, Apple, Microsoft, and Sony are just a few of the companies using program-length infomercials.

What kinds of products or services are shown on infomercials? A wide range of products are shown on infomercials. These products vary from costly, multiple-use exercise equipment to less costly (but not cheap) items such as Nordic-Trac and exercise bicycles. Infomercials are also used to promote cosmetics, herbals, health and beauty aids, exercise tapes, cookbooks, knife sets, and cooking items such as wok pans. Because some products simply aren't interesting enough to hold an audience for an extended time, not all products lend themselves to infomercial promotion.

When can you expect to see infomercials? Infomercials are not usually shown during prime time. Brokerage companies buy blocks of time from broadcasters and then sell it in 30-minute lengths to clients with infomercials to air. Sometimes, too, cable companies or stations accept an infomercial, run it as often as they wish, and are paid for each inquiry they generate.

Is the infomercial a direct-response tool? Infomercials are used almost exclusively as a direct-response tool. Infomercials look for orders and stress responding, usually through 800 numbers. Many use a casual, informational approach that employs users or experts as spokespersons. Enthusiastic discussion follows, often accompanied by a product demonstration. Of course, invitations to order appear usually more than once. Long-form infomercials tend to use a talk-show format with guests, dramatic revelations, before-and-after cosmetic applications, weight-loss examples, and personal endorsements by users or authorities. Short-form infomercials may use music, sound effects, and, to a limited degree, some of the elements of the long form.

Although the primary aim of most infomercials is to get orders through the use of 800 numbers, they also stir up sales leads and pick up names for a database. Infomercials are sometimes used to test the appeal of a new product or service.

These goals may be achieved through demonstrations, testimonials, panels, story-telling or talk shows. Of these, the demonstration is possibly the most effective approach, just as it is in traditional advertising.

How do you write an infomercial? If you're not looking for direct response (rare), you can be casual, friendly, conversational, and, of course, interesting. When you're writing to pick up orders or inquiries, you can still be friendly and conversational, but overall, you imbue your words with a sense of urgency. Because you're selling something, you must convey enthusiasm for your offer, and enthusiasm is, regrettably, sometimes carried to extremes in infomercials that reach a pitchman fervor. Most writers like infomercials because they provide an opportunity to tell a full story free from the constraints of 15-second or 30-second commercials.

When fashioning infomercials, you will do well to follow fairly standard advertising procedure in focusing on the product, delivering a strong sales message, and using reliable devices such as demonstrations, testimonials, believable endorsers, and problem-solution approaches.

Infomercial Case History

At the time this book is being written, an infomercial is appearing on television that incorporates many of the elements necessary for successful use of this technique.

First, it has an effective presenter, a former Miss America, whose delivery is low-key but persuasive and easily bearable over the 30-minute presentation.

Next, the product, a device called the Stimulator that is used to relieve pain somewhat in the fashion of acupressure, is interesting and lends itself admirably to demonstration.

Then, to back up what the likable presenter has to say about the product, a long list of Stimulator users who tell in natural, convincing words how successful the product has been for relieving their pain is presented. In describing their experiences, the endorsers bring in another vital element of successful infomercials—the demonstrations.

As they talk about the Stimulator, the persons in the commercials are shown using it on themselves or on others. To make these situations relevant to a broad spectrum of the audience, the endorsers are young, elderly, and middle aged, and they come in all shapes and sizes. Most important, none of them look like a professional model.

Leading the parade of endorsers is a famous stunt man whose impressive array of injuries has resulted in constant pain, which, he asserts, is relieved through the use of the Stimulator.

At $88.00, the Stimulator is not an inexpensive purchase, but reportedly, it has sold briskly. A product of this type arouses a certain skepticism. This is mentioned several times, but viewers are assured that there is a 60-day money-back guarantee if the product is not satisfactory. And then, as in all good direct response offers, there is a strong urge for action, made easy with the use of an 800 number and the acceptance of payment through all major credit cards.

Can radio utilize infomercials? Radio is an effective medium for infomercials, particularly those created in the short form. In fact, many television infomercials are written so that the audio, at least a portion of the audio, can be lifted and used on radio. A very prominent announcer for insurance delivers infomercials on television for two minutes, and later, radio listeners will hear that same two minutes when they turn on their radio sets. This is effective advertising because the radio version tends to recreate the video portion in the minds of the radio listeners.

CHAPTER 21

Television Advertising
It Gives You Full Scope for Creativity (Part B)

"You TV cretins give me a pain."
Kay Montross looked disdainfully at Sam Stapleton, a TV writer whose office adjoined hers. Sam smiled indulgently, "What now, Kay? Still grousing about that big boost in Ad Age for TV versus print?"
"No. What galls me is your smug assumption that print is dead and that the printed word and Gutenberg are relics of an irrelevant past."
So the argument goes on. Print advocates have a powerful story, but rather than rail at TV, they should work for a happy marriage of the two. TV results soar when print ads are combined with TV commercials. For some types of products and situations (demonstrations, for example), there's no denying that TV is supreme. But combine a 30-second commercial with a long, hard-selling print ad, and the result is a blockbuster sales combination.

Thinking visually is the first task of television writers, and it is an ability that print writers must learn. Once print writers have done so, their print-writing background becomes important because few television commercials can depend upon the visual alone to convey the message. Those scenes flashing on the screen frequently have little meaning without the accompanying words on the audio track.

Print experience versus television experience is the basis of a longtime argument that has no definitive answer. One point *is* certain. Sam will simply be one of a big team of experts in the task of producing television commercials just as you will be if you write television advertising. Counting all of the production people, account executives, client personnel, supervisors, and others, there may be more than fifty persons involved in carrying out *your* idea. *That* makes you important.

It would be nice to be able to tell you that, as a copywriter, you are going to decide just how your television commercials will be reproduced, but unfortunately, this isn't the case. Typically, you'll be told to write the commercials, and you'll also be told whether they'll be "live," "film," or "tape." You don't argue. Drawing upon your knowledge of each, you write your commercial to fit the requirements of the technique you've been told will be used.

Film, Tape, or Live?

Film commercials are those shot in a studio, on location outdoors, or wherever there is a suitable site for the desired action. Tape (videotape) is a system that records sound and pictures simultaneously on magnetic tape. Live refers to action seen on the television screen as it takes place right in the studio before the television camera.

Film commercial production is chosen by most national advertisers because it has many advantages over videotape production. Commercials on film have a higher quality look, giving the advertised product a higher quality image. Because film reveals subtle nuances of colors and shadows, it is more realistic than videotape. This can be particularly important when you are shooting food and want to evoke appetite appeal, or if you are looking for realism in outdoor scenes. Finally, film offers wider creative latitude.

Almost any approach is possible for the writer of film commercials, because production people have ingenious ways to execute the idea through special effects, sets, lighting, and careful editing. For all these reasons, and the fact that a national commercial can run for months or years, film is often a sound choice despite its higher cost.

Tape has been a great boon to local advertising because it makes possible the utilization of local talent and resources in a way not possible with live-studio production or with film.

At first, tape offered limited special effects. Now, as a writer, you can call for such effects and optical tricks—all at low cost. In fact, compared to film (not live studio), tape costs are lower for shooting and processing. Also, tape can record and store many commercials.

Advertiser:	UPS
Product:	Next Day Air Guaranteed
Length:	30 sec
Production:	"Nightlife"

Video

1. Open to bright starry night sky. Jet zooms through the sky toward us.
2. Cut to baggage men riding cargo carts out to plane to unload the mail.
3. Cut to TCU of UPS logo on tail fin.
4. MS of train of mail carts with UPS logo on side runs across screen.
5. Cut to baggage men loading another jet for take-off. They close the hatch.
6. Cut to plane slowly moving down runway. Takes off towards us into night sky.
7. Fade out. Fade in logo.

Audio

SFX:	lullaby chimes in background
SFX:	hum of jet approaching, getting louder as jet on screen gets closer
ANNCR:	Every night while you're sleeping, UPS is maintaining its status…
ANNCR:	… as the only company that delivers overnight to every address coast to coast.
ANNCR:	And now we guarantee it. Introducing UPS Next Day Air Guaranteed.
ANNCR:	And because we're so efficient, we'll still do it for up to half what other companies charge, which is guaranteed to cause our competition some sleepless nights.
SFX:	roar of jet taking off
ANNCR:	UPS. We run the tightest ship in the shipping business.

Advertiser:	UPS
Product:	Next Day Air Letter
Length:	30 sec
Production:	"Super Saver"

Video

1. Fade-in to closeup of large stack of mailing envelopes. Screen is dark, but a light from left of screen slowly falls on stack. Lights up screen.
2. Zoom to top envelope. Closeup on UPS logo on envelope.
3. MCU Envelopes slide off stack. One by one they glide through air across screen into next scene.
4. Cut to envelope gliding rapidly onto series of different desks. Each desk is typical of a different kind of person (i.e., very neat; messy).
5. Cut to last envelope landing on a desk in someone's casual office. "$8.50" flashes onto screen.
6. Cut to UPS logo on screen.

Audio

SFX:	abrupt screeching of airplane brakes as it's touching down
SFX:	Band strikes up in background playing a patriotic tune
ANNCR:	American businesses can now save millions …
ANNCR:	… of dollars every year with the UPS Next Day Air Letter.
SFX:	screeching of brakes each time a letter touches down on each desk
ANNCR:	Unlike other companies which frequently charge up to fourteen dollars … UPS, because we're so efficient …
ANNCR:	… charges only eight fifty. And we guarantee overnight delivery to every city coast to coast. The UPS Next Day Air Letter …
ANNCR:	… The "Super Saver" of overnight letters.

Live television production offers lower cost for the one-time commercial. It can also be produced, from the written script to the actual production on camera, in less time than film. Live commercials can, of course, be changed in wording or action at the very last minute, a significant advantage to an advertiser—especially in a keenly competitive situation.

On the other side, some of the most deadly commercials are done live in station studios for low-budget local advertisers. To supply some kind of interest, the writer calls for props to be supplied by the client, the station, or sometimes the advertising agency. These may be mixed in with slides. Also, the announcer may appear at the opening and close. Occasionally, if the station has a good film library, a writer may use stock shots effectively in a live commercial.

Since the development of videotape, live studio or live location shots have been used less and less. If you *must* write live commercials, use every bit of imagination you can in drawing upon the resources of the client and the station. Sometimes, however, if you have a personable announcer with a forceful delivery, it may be advisable to let your announcer make a straight, sincere presentation and to use few, if any, props.

Types of Commercials

Like all classifications, this one is arguable. Should you, for example, have a classification for hard sell or soft sell? Should there be an "image" classification? What about "emotional" or "reason-why" commercials? Can you really classify some commercials, such as the ones most commonly seen for soft drinks that feature young people cavorting madly about on beaches, ski slopes, or other locations? Should there be a humor classification?

As you look over the following list, you will see that most commercials will fall into these types. Some will be combinations of types. For those commercials not fitting into a type listed, just make up your own "other" list.

- Straight sell
- Stand-up celebrity presenter
- Dramatization
- Demonstration
- Testimonial (or endorsement)
- Copy put to music (the jingle)

Straight Sell

This is a very common type of commercial because it affords so much creative freedom. The script is delivered by an offscreen announcer, also referred to as an announcer voiceover. The visuals, focusing on the product or another type of action, are limited only by your imagination.

The announcer voiceover can be a man, a woman, a child, or a character voice (a cat, for example). The voiceover can give us straight copy points, employ humor, tell a story, affect an accent, or lend great drama to the reading. The treatment is decided and directed by the copywriter and/or producer.

Usually, the straight sales pitch will be delivered in a sincere manner at not too fast a pace. Exceptions are mail-order commercials that use an excited, rapid-fire delivery that comes to a climax with a strong urge to act immediately to take advantage of the offer.

Stand-up or Celebrity Presenter

The stand-up presenter is an announcer who is on-camera for part or all of the commercial explaining product features. Some of the most effective of these are delivered by well-known figures in the sports or entertainment worlds. They become spokespeople for a company's products or services. Such announcers must be believable, articulate, and forceful.

At times, performers may work not from a rigid, conventional script but, with a minimum of guidance, from a fact sheet that allows them to develop their video action and audio style in accordance with their entertainment personalities. There should be some guidance, however, for a celebrity presenter may well overshadow the product. The presenter must be at home with the product or service, such as one whose childlike sense of fun works perfectly with a children's treat, or the performer with an authoritative, no-nonsense air that lends credibility to selling points. Athletes who endorse athletic products achieve the same credibility, but they don't always succeed for products with which they would not naturally be associated.

Other good presenters are second-flight celebrities, such as cooking authorities who tout food products. Sometimes, through heavy exposure, a noncelebrity presenting a product becomes so well-known that he or she becomes a celebrity of sorts.

Your special task in celebrity commercials is to provide audio that is suited to the celebrity. In doing so, the celebrity will appear on the home screen as natural and likable, two qualities absolutely necessary for credibility. For your own peace of mind, you should ascertain whether the celebrity actually uses the product being advertised. The law says he or she should.

Finally, if the celebrity is a comedian and the commercial is humorous, let the humor be at the expense of the performer, not the product. Let the performer make a fool of himself or herself, but don't poke fun at the product.

Dramatizations

Akin to personality commercials, dramatizations are most often used on comedy, musical, and dramatic programs.

Slice-of-life commercials—those hated, yet effective, presentations—are a form of dramatized commercial. Dramatized commercials can be humorous, serious, complex, or simple. They are distinguished by the fact that participants in the commercial play roles—mothers, father, friends, athletes, neighbors. Their value is that they are so flexible that they give you limitless opportunities for promoting your product or service.

As you ponder the different types of commercials presented in this list, you'll soon realize that the dramatized commercial will often be a combination of all the types, with the possible exception of the straight sales pitch—and even that can at times be combined. In short, dramatization is the very essence of television commercials because, in a sense, most commercials are little playlets. That is another reason why some sort of acting or drama background is useful to television commercial writers.

It is easy in dramatized commercials to make characters phony, exaggerated, and wholly unbelievable, especially in the slice-of-life commercials seen on so many daytime serials. Danger lies in the fact that dialogue and facial expressions are artificial. Enthusiasm is *too* enthusiastic and the reactions and audio are too predictable. The world is about ready for conversations about products between two women, or between husbands and wives, that are not filled with bright, silly patter never heard in a normal household.

Demonstrations

There are several kinds of demonstrations that can be used as part or all of a given commercial:

- *Product versatility,* to acquaint viewers with new and interesting uses.
- *Product in use,* to show how it works or what it does.
- *Before-and-after,* to prove results in use.
- *Extreme example,* to dramatize proof of quality, as in the Timex watch commercials that subjected a watch to rugged treatment to prove it "takes a licking and keeps on ticking." Torture tests on proving grounds likewise aim to prove superiority of one make of automobile over another.
- *Competitive tests,* to show superiority over a competitor, as in various washing or sudsing tests that seek to show that one brand of soap or detergent produces whiter washes.

Demonstration commercials rely heavily on filmtape production in order to cover periods of time necessary to illustrate points of superiority in use. The full application of a home permanent can be filmed or taped and then simply edited to required length, showing key sales points. Film and tape also permit the use of split screens and other optical devices to lend additional impact and drama to before-and-after and competitive-test commercials.

In recent years, the Federal Trade Commission has insisted that product demonstrations be literally true. In the past, in contrast, glycerine was substituted for ice cream because the latter melted before scenes could be shot. Under the new rules, if the product being advertised is ice cream, then ice cream must be used in the scene, not a nonmelting substitute. This means that the ice cream must be kept cold until the last seconds before shooting and then rushed on to the set for a quick shot.

Such literalness has greatly increased the cost of shooting many commercials. Copywriters writing for television must keep in mind this requirement of literal honesty in every product demonstration they call for. This is in contrast to television's earlier days, when a maker of glass for auto windows demonstrated the clarity of the product by removing the windows. This supposedly gave the viewer a true idea of just what it was like to be looking through an auto window using the advertiser's glass. The courts, ruling against the advertiser, said that future commercials must use the window glass.

At one time, because of the difficulty of showing many products on television, production shortcuts were taken and given legal approval. Those days are gone, and you must write accordingly.

Testimonials (or Endorsements)

Commercials in which screen stars, sports heroes, and prominent figures from all walks of life are used as salespeople are a proven type of commercial. The main concern in this type of commercial is to avoid staginess and artificiality. A viewer is all too ready to disbelieve the words of your prominent personality unless you phrase the message in comfortable, conversational language that fits your star salesperson. Keep the testimony brief, natural, and believable, because even professional actors are not always capable of adjusting to selling roles.

Similar precautions must be observed in testimonials, reactions, or opinions featuring satisfied users or so-called passers-by in the interview type of testimonial commercial. Don't ask these obviously ordinary people to speak complicated and unreal-sounding advertising phrases in praise of your product. It simply will not be swallowed by your viewers.

Exercise care in the casting of these commercials, too, if you have a voice in the matter. Try to use people who are not too beautiful or handsome but who have faces with character that can quickly win over viewers. In television, there is not always time for viewers to take their eyes off the attractive face and get in step with your message. Use familiar, comfortable settings well within the experience of the viewers so that they do not have to reorient their minds to an unusual setting before grasping your message. If your commercial is filmed or taped, get enough footage on a particular interview to catch facets of personality and unexpected conversational phrases that no prepared script could ever conjure up for the nonprofessional performer. Subsequent editing can then cull the highlights of the interview for commercial use.

When you prepare a testimonial or endorsement commercial, keep a fearful eye on all the legal bodies ready to pounce if you stray from the legal restrictions—and there are many. Ways to stay out of trouble when writing such commercials are detailed in the legal chapter. Read the advice carefully, because no type of commercial causes more legal difficulty than the testimonial commercial.

Copy Put to Music

This type of commercial lends a new avenue of creativity to the copywriter. Here, copy points are written in a lyric, or rhyming, form and are set to music by a music production house. The accompanying visuals can build a story or be a series of quick vignettes. Rather than going for a harder sell, the latter type of commercial is usually fun and spirited and seeks to evoke an attractive image for the product. It's often used when there is no clear-cut product difference.

Copywriters who enjoy poetry and the rhythm of language are best suited to writing lyrics, but anyone can give it a try. To get started, write the words from a melodically memorable popular song. Then, use the rhyme scheme and meter as a guide to writing your jingle.

The music house will need an idea of the type of music you have in mind—country, rock, ballad, and so forth—along with information on the visuals and intended audience. These ideas help give the track the personality for which you are striving.

The most notable examples of jingles can be found in the breakfast cereal, automobile, and beverage categories.

CLIENT: Farm Bureau Insurance
JOB: :30 TV
TITLE: "I Promise"

VIDEO   **AUDIO**

Scene 1

Commercial opens on a high-wide shot of   **ANNCR:**
twenty-five to thirty cars lined up in a   All over Indiana teenage drivers are
horizontal line. The location is any space   making a promise they can live by.
large enough to accommodate such a line
of cars, probably a parking lot with a smooth,
freshly covered surface. A teenager
approaches each of the vehicles from behind.
He/she (half of the teenagers are boys and
half are girls) is carrying a set of car keys.
Each teenager appears to be ready to get
into the individual car he or she is
approaching and drive away. All twenty-five
or thirty teenagers speak in unison as they
approach their cars.

Scene 2

Cut to a tight shot of a teenager approaching
his car, speaking as he walks.

Scene 3

Cut to a tight shot of a teenager approaching
her car, speaking as she walks.

Scene 4

Cut to a tight shot of a teenager opening the   **Teenagers in Unison**
door on the driver's side of his car, speaking   "I promise to drive safely."
throughout the scene.

Scene 5

Cut to a tight shot of a teenager adjusting   **Teenagers in Unison**
the rear view mirror on her car, speaking   "I promise to not drink and drive."
throughout the scene.

Scene 6

Cut to a tight shot of a teenager buckling his   **Teenagers in Unison**
seat belt, speaking throughout the scene.   "I promise to drive defensively, especially
                                                 at night."

Scene 7

Cut to a tight shot of a teenager with   **Teenagers in Unison**
seatbelt on, beginning to a start car and   "I promise to buckle-up."
continuing to speak the pledge.

Scene 8

Cut to a medium shot of Clyde Turbeville or   **Spokesman**
Burt Taylor or George McGinnis or any   "Keep your promise and Farm Bureau
other suitable spokesman (including the   Insurance promises to give you a $1,000
possibility of a nondescript spokesman)   savings bond if you drive with us for
standing in front of the long line of cars. He   three consecutive years without a traffic
begins speaking as, one by one, the cars pull   ticket or an accident."
away from the line. Camera dollies into a
tight shot of the spokesman as he speaks.

Scene 9

Cut to a high-wide shot of the cars as they   **Spokesman**
continue to pull away from the line   "See your Farm Bureau Insurance agent
                                                 for details."

SUPER Farm Bureau Insurance logo and other information about the program.

Figure 21–1a. Thirty-second dramatization-dialogue commercial. Part of a campaign.

However, every type of product has used a jingle's warmth and memorability with success.

Animated Commercials

You'd be surprised how many times you'll have to answer "no" to animation as the best possible method for advertising your product.

If you're undecided about using animation as opposed to demonstration, use demonstration if your product has to be demonstrated for full sales effectiveness. Don't substitute cuteness for sales impact. If you decide that animation is the right method for the job, keep the following creative elements of the technique in mind.

Product character or trademark. Animation should fit the trademark or trade character naturally, without being forced. If your character is a Disney-type cartoon—full animation drawing with rounded lines, full shading, and natural features—it won't fit well with highly stylized, modern art treatment. Work with your producer to develop animation characters that will save you time and money and that are well suited to the story you want to sell.

Setting and staging. Setting and staging for animation are as important as for live-action films, so keep it simple and inexpensive, yet effective. Your message is on the screen only briefly, so give your cartoon characters and product full attention by eliminating distracting backgrounds. Use simple lines, for instance, to denote cabinets for a kitchen scene. Staging is as important as background, so if your action can take place in one location, don't have characters chasing through many different scenes. If you want special effects such as opticals that make products glow, sparkle, or change, write them into your original storyboards. Extra production charges are added if you want to work them in later.

Movement of characters. Try to keep the movements of animated characters similar to those of a human being in the same situation. Remember that movement in animation should be exaggerated to be appreciated by viewers. Be sure they see that your character's wink is a wink, that a look of surprise is *very* surprised, lest these pieces of action be missed. Allow sufficient time for the movement to be grasped by viewers. Try to plan your animated spots rather loosely so that there is time for little bits of side action that can give your commercial added interest and longer life.

Copy and narration. Consider the soundtrack of your commercial as consisting of two parts: the voice or narrative, and the music and sound effects. The best animated spots are written with a maximum of 40 to 50 words, rather

```
CLIENT:    Farm Bureau Insurance
JOB:       :30 TV
TITLE:     "Like Clockwork"


VIDEO                                           AUDIO

Scene 1

Commercial opens on a medium-wide shot of    Man:     You can always tell when
a nicely appointed country kitchen. A woman           it's 3:15 at the Monroe
is working in the middle of the kitchen. An           house.
oversized kitchen clock reads 4:15.

A screen door opens and slams shut. Coming   SFX:     Screen door opens and
through the door is a boy, perhaps eight or            slams shut. Running
nine years old. He makes a beeline for a               footsteps.
cookie jar sitting on the kitchen cabinet. He
sets his school books and lunch box down on
the kitchen table.


Scene 2

Cut to a tight shot of the boy as he comes    Kid  (Calling out): I'm home.
through the door.

Scene 3

Cut to a medium-tight shot of the woman       Mom:     Part of what makes a
who is working in the kitchen. She is about            house a home is being able
35 years old. She looks to the camera as if it         to count on certain things.
is one of her very best friends and speaks to
it.
```

```
Scene 4

Cut to a medium shot of the cookie jar. The   Kid:     What time's dinner?
boy enters frame and removes two cookies
from the jar. Then he leaves frame.           Mom:     Same time as always.

Scene 5                                        Kid:     Great!

Cut to a medium shot of the woman. The        SFX:     Running footsteps. Screen
camera dollies into a tight shot during her            door opening and
dialogue.                                              slamming shut.

                                               Mom:     That's why we have Farm
                                                        Bureau Insurance. It's an
                                                        Indiana company that's
                                                        been protecting families
                                                        like ours for nearly sixty
                                                        years. It's nice knowing
                                                        they'll always be right
                                                        here.
Scene 6

Cut to a medium shot of the kitchen as the    SFX:     Screen door opens and
boy runs back through the door and re-                 slams shut. Footsteps.
enters the frame. The woman gently teases
her son as she responds to her son.           Kid (relieved and apologetic): I almost
                                                        forgot.

                                               Mom:     So what else is new?
Scene 7

Cut to to a tight shot of the woman leaning   SFX:     Kiss. Running footsteps.
into frame as her son gives her a hug and a            Screen door opening and
big kiss on the cheek.                                 slamming shut.

Scene 8

Cut to a medium shot of the woman in the      Mom:     I like being able to count
kitchen. She continues to address camera in            on things. That's why I like
that same "best friend" attitude.                      Farm Bureau Insurance.

SUPER Farm Bureau Insurance logo over scene.
```

Figure 21–1b. Thirty-second dramatization-dialogue commercial. Part of a campaign.

than the 60 to 70 live-action count. This leaves room for the previously mentioned bits of action that can enhance your effort. Give your character time to speak effectively, and rather than trying to bend a character to fit copy, write copy to fit the character's intended voice.

Music and sound effects. These lend mood, action, tone, and emphasis that can "make" your animated commercial. If you are using offbeat or stylized art treatment, make the music suitable. Be sure the tempo of the music blends with your type of animation. Sound effects give impact and originality to your spot. If you want them, be sure to leave enough time for them in your script. They seldom fit when you try to squeeze them in later.

Timing the entire spot. It is difficult to time an animated commercial because of the need to consider copy, music, and action. There's no sure-fire solution, but one of the safest approaches is to act out the commercial in its entirety.

Product package and logotype. With simple handling, animation (and stop-action photography) can do great things for your package or product. If your package has illustrations that are not in character with your style of animation, use artwork representation rather than the real

package. You can use a matching dissolve from the artwork to the real package or logotype at the end of the spot. Emphasize important features of your package by bringing the elements off the box to full screen, as with a logotype that bounces off the package and then back on.

Animation and Live Action for Best Results

It is the consensus of almost all those who have worked with animation over a long period that the all-cartoon commercial should be approached with caution, because its promise generally outruns its performance. A danger of pure animation is its over-commitment to entertainment at the cost of sacrificing copy idea. Viewers are beguiled into enjoyment without being sold. Judicious use, however, of animation in conjunction with live action has much to recommend it.

There are two basic types of this hybrid commercial: (1) an opening animated segment (often comic or clever but containing the germ of the product story) followed with a live straight sell; and (2) a straightforward sales presentation that moves into animation after a live opening, usually to illustrate a product's "reason-why" story. The first type is best exemplified by commercials that use an animated character with a catchy jingle as an opening and then move into live-action scenes of the product in use. The second hybrid type is exemplified by those commercials for patent remedies that employ diagrammatic views of visceral plumbing to illustrate the nature of their internal action. In either case, the flexibility of the live-plus-animation commercial allows the advertiser to blend exaggerated hyperbole or humor with naturalistic demonstration, thus charming while also selling the viewer.

Combining live action and animation is effective, but it can be expensive. An economical method is to use animated characters over still-photo shots of your product, creating the depth of live action with the adaptability of animation. Another way of reducing expense is to use the same segment of animation to open or close an entire series of film spots. This lets you use your budget for animation of better quality or for more spots.

In trying to determine whether to use "live-on-film" or animated commercials for your particular product, there are some general considerations you'll recognize as helpful. Food products normally lend themselves better to television presentation with live action. Realism, which can be gained by showing real people preparing and enjoying meals, will almost always sell better than the cartoon characters with whom people cannot identify. Sales points of a new car, likewise, can best be demonstrated by actually showing a real person driving it rather than by showing drawings of the car. Cosmetic selling usually needs the realism of beautiful people whose hair, lips, complexion, and overall charm cannot possibly be captured in animation.

On the other hand, many times you will be selling a service instead of a branded product. When doing so, you can sometimes command more memorability and attention if you invent an animated character to tell your story. Insurance selling, gasoline advertising, and bank and loan association commercials all lend themselves to the use of animation.

Some relatively new offshoots of animation are pixillation and claymation. Pixillation uses stop-motion photographs; they are shot one frame at a time. The material can be combined with a nonverbal sound track, if desired. The result is an unusual look.

Claymation is clay figures photographed in progressive movements so that the figures appear lifelike when set to film. The most notable example of claymation is the "I heard it through the grapevine" commercial for the California Raisin Board.

Production Techniques

Following are some basic production techniques that may be used if your commercials are to be taped or filmed:

- Live action
- Cartoon
- Stop motion
- Photo animation

Live Action
Because it is similar to personal experience, live action is the most believable technique in television commercials.

Viewers can identify with the action on the screen and relate your commercial message to their own experience. While cartoons are figments of a fantasy world, and stop-motion and photo animation are products of camera trickery, live action has the quality of genuine reality.

There are two main types of live-action commercials: (1) narrative style with the voices off-screen; and (2) dialogue style with one or more persons speaking on screen to each other or to the audience.

Narrative style is less expensive, yet it has longer life expectancy because the speaker or speakers are not seen repeating the same story over and over, thereby suffering loss of credibility. Narrative live action lends itself best to *demonstration,* to display the product in use, with a voice presenting the sales story from off-screen; *exposition,* to set a scene quickly; *human interest,* to show family or other emotional settings; and *appetite appeal,* to exhibit tempting dishes, with the announcer's voice off-screen.

Dialogue has particular advantages for *personality commercials,* in which a name star or well-known announcer does the selling job; *testimonials* by actual users; and *key copylines* spoken by an actor as one part of a longer commercial.

The cost of live-action films, narrative or dialogue, varies a great deal because of the many factors involved: cast, settings, props, location trips, and so forth. Here again, the matter of the SAG code and residual fees to talent used in live-action commercials has tended to switch some advertisers to other techniques. To move away from live action is not always wise, for its basic reality and faculty for reaching out to meet the viewer on common ground makes live action the most useful technique in television commercials.

Cartoon
The cartoon is fun. It is high in viewer interest and it is probably lowest in cost per showing. While it wins interest quickly, it nonetheless lacks depth of penetration because it sacrifices credibility. Because viewers enjoy cartoons but may not be sold or persuaded by them, experienced advertisers will often follow the cartoon segment of their commercials with real people using the product and repeating its benefits.

Cartoons are most effective for *gaining interest* at the opening of a spot by presenting some whimsical situation or an unusual character; *trademark characters,* either the actual company or product trademark or one devised for purposes of a given campaign; *personalizing the product,* whereby a can of wax takes on life and personality with a cartoon face; *fantasy,* which enables just about any character or thing to do just about any type of action—an exercise in exaggeration to stimulate the imagination; *singing jingles,* because bouncy rhythms and cartoons are naturals that comprise one of television's longest-lived types of commercials.

There are three grades among cartoons: full animation, limited animation, and "grow" or "scratch-off" cartoon, in order of decreasing cost and effectiveness. Cost depends largely on what moves in your cartoon. Try to use no more characters than absolutely necessary in your commercial and to work closely with your animation director to make maximum use of cycles of the same sequence of pictures wherever possible, especially for backgrounds.

A limited animation, which costs about half as much as full, makes full use of cycles, often shows only extremes of facial expression, and relies heavily on camera movement and lens tricks.

The grow cartoon cuts costs in half again. It works with a single drawing, photographed from the rear as lines are scratched off on successive frames. When projected in the opposite direction, the cartoon seems to be drawn, or grow, on the screen.

Cartoons are honest fun and, as such, can do a selling job for impulse-purchase types of products. Where there is substantial reason for the purchaser to buy, cartoons need support from live action, as previously discussed.

Making the hundreds of drawings necessary to depict movement in animated commercials has always required expensive art time. Now, computers have stepped into the art and can be used to supply the detailed drawings for certain types of animation. Computers don't replace artists, but they relieve them of the tedious line-by-line renderings of animated movement.

Cartoon characters don't age as fast as live players. Thus, live-action film commercials are usually given a maximum life of twenty-six weeks, whereas an animated series can run three years or more. Furthermore, while these are used on television, the animated characters can be used in other media, such as transit advertising, window displays, and point of purchase.

Animated characters get no residuals, don't get old, don't demand more money, don't strike, don't switch jobs, and don't die. Little wonder that they have appeal to advertisers.

In addition, they can serve so many special purposes and appeal to such a wide range of ages and types. They are preeminent in achieving the light touch, humor, and sell—as in the following audio for a margarine.

FIRST COW: "Holy cow!"

SECOND COW: "Gracious sakes!"

THREE COWS: "Guess what comes from Land O'Lakes! Margarine! Butter folks at Land O'Lakes know the difference flavor makes. Taste Land O'Lakes margarine now! Land O'Lakes margarine on baked potatoes, on any dish … mooooo-ie!"

Sometimes cartoon animation solves a problem too difficult for live action, such as animation used by an advertiser to show how a hair groomer works on the hair—a visualization that was too complex for conventional photography.

Another advertiser, a baking soda manufacturer, resorted to animation to show how the product killed odors arising from kitty litter. Because kitty litter is not visually appealing in photographs, animation was selected over live film. Furthermore, the subject was handled in a light-hearted way by having two cats discuss this special use of baking soda. Consequently, a subject that could be distasteful in live-action film was presented without offense and in a memorable way.

Stop Motion

The ingenious technique that makes inanimate objects come to life is stop motion. This type of animation is accomplished by using a camera adjusted to move one or two frames at a time. The objects are moved slightly or changed between exposures. The result, when projected at normal speed, is continuous action.

Stop action should be confined to inanimate objects, since actors cannot remain in one position long enough for this type of shooting.

The technique provides an impressive way to introduce packaged products. For example, a number of packages shown unevenly spaced on a table suddenly assemble themselves into a neat display. The scene cuts to a close-up, then one package unwraps itself and out hops the product.

The advantages offered by stop motion relate to *personalizing the product,* as in the marching packages or other products that are made to fly, dance, walk, zoom, or take themselves apart; *mechanical action,* as in fitting parts of a motor or showing how attachments are used on appliances; and *demonstration,* without human hands, as in a commercial showing a wall oven that opens itself and a roast slides out. In the first of these advantages, stop motion shares with cartoons the ability to personalize a product, while in the last it vies with live action in its faculty for demonstration. It seems advisable here, too, to combine stop motion with a follow-up, live action, thus pairing the interest-rouser with the realistic demonstration.

Stop motion is expensive because each second of picture requires twenty-four shots. Furthermore, because of this minute movement, it is difficult to know how the footage will flow until a viewing takes place.

An outstanding example of stop-motion production is the television advertising for the Pillsbury Doughboy. This roly-poly character is used in all television commercials and print advertisements for Pillsbury brand refrigerated dough products and flour. So great has been his consumer appeal that he has become a symbol and company spokesman for Pillsbury in the United States, Canada, and Europe.

Photo Animation

The technique that sends bottles spinning and boxes zooming across the televiewer's screen is photo animation. It is the method that the low-budget advertiser can use to excellent advantage to achieve impressive effects, largely through the camera's movement and optical tricks.

Called "Fotan" by many producers, photo animation

```
CLIENT:    Farm Bureau Insurance
JOB:       :60 TV
TITLE:     "Bobby Knight"

Scene 1    Commercial opens on a medium-wide shot of the
           interior of Assembly Hall. It's dark, quiet, and void
           of people. Suddenly a soft whistle can be heard
           coming from one of the entrances to the basketball
           court. The song being whistled is the Indiana
           University Fight Song.
           A cleaning woman appears from one of the entrances
           to the court. She's wearing a white maid's dress, a
           red apron and a red scarf in her hair. She's pushing
           dust mop.
           The woman comes onto the floor, pushing her mop
           and whistling.
Scene 2    Cut to medium-tight shot of the woman, whistling as
           she mops the floor. The whistling gradually turns
           into singing.
Scene 3    Cut to a medium shot of the woman, mopping the
           Assembly Hall floor as she sings the I.U. fight song.
Scene 4    Cut to a tight shot of the dust mop as it moves
           across the floor.
Scene 5    Cut to a tight shot of a pair of men's shoes standing
           on the Assembly Hall floor.
Scene 6    Cut to a tight shot of the cleaning lady, looking up
           and being very surprised at who she sees.
Scene 7    Cut to a tight shot of Coach Bobby Knight.
Scene 8    Cut to medium shot of Coach Knight and the I.U.
           cleaning lady. The cleaning lady chuckles as Coach
           Knight smiles and steps aside. The cleaning lady
           resumes singing s she continues mopping the
           gymnasium floor.
Scene 9    Cut to a tight shot of Coach Knight. Freeze the
           frame.
SUPER Farm Bureau Insurance logo.
ANNCR:     Bobby Knight, another Indiana legend, brought to
           you with pride by Farm Bureau Insurance.
```

Figure 21–2. A campaign using a sixty-second dramatization commercial. In this commercial there is little action, but this is balanced by a high sentiment and the appearance of a popular coach. The "cleaning woman" in the commercial is actually an operatic star who played the role with gusto. This commercial demonstrates the fact that with some commercials words are not needed; visuals can tell the story when aided, in this instance, by some music.

lends itself best to *special announcements,* in which titles and tricks are the main elements, as in coming attractions for movies; *signatures* at the end of most commercials, in which the package, logotype, or slogan pops on the screen, often in synchronization with voice copy; *retouching products,* as in appliances of chrome and glass, using still photographs that are then reproduced on motion picture film with dissolves or other optical tricks to achieve a dramatic effect; and *catalog of products,* where an inclusive line of related items can be presented quickly, clearly, and, again, with startling effect.

Photo animation is not advisable for use with live action because it works only with separate still photographs or drawings. To move an inanimate object in a live-action scene involves costly optical treatment.

An example of Fotan at work was shown in the presentation of a liquidizer that made tomato juice out of tomatoes, coleslaw out of cabbage, and crushed ice out of ice cubes. Still photos of the original items were shown at top left of the screen. They moved in procession to the center,

were whirled downward in the appliance, and finally emerged at bottom right as completed dishes. Truly graphic!

Summary of Best Uses of Techniques

Live action (narrative) is best used for demonstration, human interest, and exposition.

Live action (dialogue) is best used for testimonials, personality commercials, dramatic spots, and key copylines.

Cartoon (full animation) is best used for developing trademark characters, personalizing products, exaggeration and fantasy, and singing jingles.

Stop motion is best used for demonstration, mechanical action, and personalizing product.

Photo animation is best used for titles and signatures, retouching products, and cataloging products.

Five Ways to Get Better Identification

A dismaying fact for the television advertiser is that a huge portion of the viewing audience cannot remember whose commercials they saw on a show they have watched night after night—this despite the millions poured into television advertising by the advertiser.

Only one viewer in five may be able to identify the sponsor of a show or the product advertised on it. Sometimes the figure goes even lower. Furthermore, in addition to lack of identification, there is *misidentification* wherein the viewer credits a competitor and names his product as the one advertised on a show. Thus, Post cereal may be identified as Kellog's, or Goodrich as Goodyear.

With television clutter offering a profusion of 15- and 30-second commercials, billboards, promos, local program break spots, and public service commercials, it's no surprise that the viewer is hazy about who is advertising what product.

As the writer, what can you do to improve the showing for your client? First, of course, you use a strong selling idea in the commercial. In addition, some devices and approaches that may help memorability and sponsor or product identification are listed below.

- **Avoid themes too much like your competitor's.** This is especially true if your product is not the leader in the field. Any confusion about the identity of the advertiser tends to result in the leader, not the runnerup, being remembered.

- **Establish a strong campaign theme.** When you know the theme is good, fight to keep it going. When advertisers change a campaign theme, they risk confusion and throw away the recognition they have built up. With confusion comes lack of identification or misidentification.

- **Use a strong presenter for the product.** A likeable, believable presenter can do wonders for product identification if used consistently over a long period of time, especially if the presenter puts on an interesting demonstration of the product.

After a while, the name of the presenter and your product are automatically linked—a link that becomes even stronger if you use the presenter in print copy, too. A possible danger in using a strong presenter is that the audience will remember the presenter and not the product, because of interest in the presenter. Careful creative work, however, can avoid the problem.

- **Use powerful demonstrations.** There's good memorability in a realistic demonstration, much more so than a mere relating of product facts. Watch out for comparative demonstrations, however, because if your product is being demonstrated against the leader's product, his product may be credited with your product's better performance.

  Comparative advertising is, in fact, a dangerous technique that can turn on you. If your demonstration has great strength in itself, you may not wish to risk a comparative demonstration.

- **Make the product-name registration strong.** Use techniques that enable you to bring in the name emphatically and frequently, not just in the opening and close. Likewise, the more you can keep your product on camera, the better for identification.

  Weaving the product and product name (and package) into commercials is a particular talent of Stan Freberg, whose humorous commercials have sold great quantities of his clients' products. Without diminishing interest or humor, he works in the name of the advertiser's product frequently—as in one commercial that showed a theater of people shouting the name of the product as it was flashed on the screen. No television viewer could fail to know what product was advertised in *that* commercial.

  As part of registering the name, try usually to end with an urge to action. Good planning can make the action ending a natural conclusion, but many writers seem to feel that the urge to do something is a jarring note that upsets the artistic balance of the commercial. Remember, however, from the *advertising* standpoint, the registration of your product name and/or package at the end of the commercial is the most powerful conclusion.

Other Techniques for Emphasis

- Call for closeups to be more vivid and personal—and do it quickly. If you start with an establishing shot, use it for only a few seconds.
- Develop your video first. If you write the audio before the video, you are simply writing a radio commercial with pictures and are chancing a loss of the inherent drama in a commercial that emphasizes the visual.
- Use superimposition when you want reinforcement. The "super" should be used sparingly, but when it is used, you'll increase the impact by saying in the audio the words flashed on the screen. Limit the number of words on the screen.

- Occasionally use the split screen to hold attention. A two-way split is easier for the viewer to follow, but the four-way split can be an attention-getter.

Questions to Ask about the Commercial You've Written

Before concluding this chapter, it may be profitable to imagine that you have a finished television commercial script in front of you. How can you size up its potential? Its creative worth? Its practicability from a production standpoint? Following are a few telegraphic queries on areas of your commercial that have been discussed in this chapter. You'll do well to remember these points while reading and evaluating the scripts that you may be writing.

You know that nobody can tell you *exactly* how to write a television commercial. Nobody can tell you exactly what to say or what to show. These are things that can come to you only with time and experience. In this chapter, you have been given an idea of what you will be expected to know about television-commercial writing and, to a lesser extent, production.

Remember, however, that as television improves technically and creatively, the scope of your activities in the field will broaden and the challenge to your resources will be greater. Only by increasing its effectiveness can the television commercial pay the ever increasing bill. This will increase your responsibility considerably.

Questions

- Does the video tell the story effectively without audio?
- Is the video fully graphic (specifying technique, describing staging and camera action)?
- Does the audio "listen" well (language, pacing)?
- Do the audio and video complement each other and are they correctly timed for each other (act it out)?
- Are there too many scenes (can some be omitted)? Do you need *more* scenes?
- Have you identified the product well?
- Does your script win attention quickly and promise an honest benefit?
- Have you "demonstrated"?
- Have you provided a strong visualization of the one major claim that will linger in the viewer's memory?
- Could a competitive brand be substituted easily and fit well (better not)?
- Is it believable? (*always* ask this)?
- Are you proud to say you wrote it?

Camera Shots

Sooner or later, if you work in television, you must learn to distinguish between the various distances represented by the terms "long shot," "closeup," and others. There's no precision in these terms in the sense that they are defined as a definite number of feet. The following guide makes particular reference to the package, which is so often the central object in television commercials.

- **Tight closeup (TCU).** The camera brings the viewer so close the detail is startling—perhaps a portion of a package, such as the product name or trademark; it is often used for this purpose. Depending upon where you work, it might also be called ECU (Extreme closeup) or VCU (very closeup).
- **Closeup (CU).** Here you zero in on an object or part of an object. Instead of just the product name, as in the TCU, you get the entire package in the camera's eye. Instead of just the lips of a person, you get the whole face or possibly the head and shoulders. Extraneous details are omitted in the closeup.
- **Medium closeup (MCU).** You draw back from the closeup. You still see the package, but you also see that it's on a table with a mixing bowl and other items. As the viewer, you sense that the package is important, but you see it in relation to other objects.
- **Medium shot (MS).** The package loses some of its importance in this shot. Some details are lost, as if the viewer had backed up a few feet from the MCU position. He sees the MCU objects, but now he may see them in relation to people in the spot.
- **Medium long shot (MLS).** You're close enough to recognize characters but far enough back to include items in the setting (such as the package) and to convey some of the background setting.
- **Long shot (LS).** Often this is called an "establishing" shot. It might include barely recognizable people, along with an entire room setting, but the package is now just one of many objects and may not even be noticed. The long shot, used outdoors, may be panoramic in its showing of trees, a portion of a lake, and people who may be discerned as individuals.
- **Extreme long shot (ELS).** As a panoramic shot, this can take in a vast expanse of desert, mountains, or a whole lake. People can be detected, but not as individuals. Again, like the long shot, this may be an establishing device to introduce dramatically what is to follow. Needless to say, we've lost our package entirely.

Glossary of Terms

Here are some of the terms used in preparing and producing a commercial. As you study them, keep in mind that this is a book about copywriting and not television production. For those interested, there are detailed texts on television production.

Across the board. A program scheduled three, five, or six days a week at the same time.

Ad lib. Impromptu action or speech not written into script; or, in music, to play parts not in the music.

Adjacencies. Shows (on same station) immediately preceding and following the program referred to.

ADR or **"looping."** Automatic dialogue replacement. An actor re-records his (or another actor's) dialogue while looking at a motion picture projected to match lip movements. It is usually done to replace the defective on-camera sound.

AFM. American Federation of Musicians.

AFTRA. American Federation of Television and Radio Artists.

Angle shot. Camera shot of the subject taken from any position except straight.

Animate. To arrange and film static drawings or objects so that when the photographs are shown cinematographically, they produce the illusion of movement.

Answer print. The first composite print of a commercial. Included are the picture, voice track, music, opticals, etc. Although changes can be made in an answer print, they are costly.

APO or **"action print only."** Used to assess the optical work. There is no sound track on this film at this stage. It is not color corrected.

ASCAP. American Society of Composers, Authors, and Publishers, which licenses public performances of music of its members and collects royalties.

AVID. One of the more popular digitized sound and picture editing systems used by editors today.

Background or **rear-view projection.** Special technique in which a wanted scene drawn from special photo or stock library is projected on a translucent screen that acts as a background for a studio set.

Back-time. To time a script backwards from end to beginning, with running time indicated every fifteen seconds or less in the margin of the script.

Billboard. Announcement at the beginning of show that lists people starred or featured.

Bit. Small appearance or few lines in show. One who plays it is called a "bit player."

Blimp. A soundproof enclosure for a camera. This makes possible the recording of voices without the camera noise intruding.

BMI. Broadcast Music, Inc., competitors of ASCAP.

Boom. Crane-like device for suspending microphone or camera in mid-air and moving it from one position to another.

Bridge. Slide, picture, sound effects, or music used to cover a jump in time or other break in continuity.

Camera or **cue light.** Red light on front of camera that is lit only when camera is on the air.

Camera right-left. Indication of direction in a setting as viewed from the point of view of the camera or televiewer.

Camera shots. (Referring to people) Head shot, only the head; shoulder shot, shoulders and head; full shot, entire person. (Referring to objects) CU, closeup or narrow-angle picture limited to object or part of it; no background; MCU, medium closeup; TCU, tight closeup; LS, long shot in which figures are smaller than frame and sensation of distance is achieved; FoS, follow shot in which camera follows talent; RevS, reverse shot in which same object already on one camera is picked up from an exactly opposite angle by another camera; DI-DU, dolly in and up; DO-DB, dolly out and back.

Cell. An animation term for a transparent film with the drawing of a single frame. Movement is achieved by running a series of cells.

Clear a number. To get legal permission to use specific musical selection.

Cover shot. Wide-angle television picture to alternate (for contrast) with closeup.

Crane. Camera mount that makes vertical and horizontal camera movements possible.

Cut. Switch directly from one camera picture to another and speed up action for dramatic effect.

Dailies or **rushes.** All printed takes of a shoot.

D.A.T. Digital audio tape, considered superior to the 7-1/2 or 15 IPS audio tape.

D.B. Delayed broadcast of a live show.

Dissolve. Fading out of one picture as another fades in; used to denote passage of time and present smooth sequence of shots.

Dolly. Movable fixture or carriage for carrying camera (and cameraman) about during taking of shots.

Double spotting. Also triple spotting. Station practice of placing a second or third commercial right after the first.

Down-and-under. Direction given to a musician or sound effects person to bring down playing level and sneak under dialogue lines that follow.

Dubbing. Mixing several sound tracks and recording them on a single film.

E.T. Electrical transcription, usually $33\frac{1}{3}$ rpm.

Fade. To diminish the brightness of the picture. Also can refer to diminishing of sound. A shot may fade into darkness, as in fade-out, or come from darkness into light, as in fade-in.

Fanfare. Few bars of music (usually trumpets) to herald start of show or commercial.

15 IPS. 1/4" audio tape recorded at 15 inches per sound (professional equipment).

Film mix. Blending of voice, music and sound effects on a single track.

Fluff. Any mistake, action, word, or phrase accidentally included, resulting in an imperfect sound or picture.

Frame count. Counting the specific frames for music cues and supers.

Freeze-frame. A single frame is printed over and over again. This creates an effect of a scene being stopped in motion.

Hiatus. Summer period, usually weeks, during which sponsor may discontinue his program, but thereafter resume his time period until the next hiatus.

Highlight. Emphasizing a subject or scene by special lighting or painting to make it stand out from the rest of the picture.

Hook. Program device used to attract tangible response from the audience; for example, an offer, a contest, etc.

ID. TV station identification or call letters (or 10-second commercial).

Inherited audience. Portion of a program's audience that watched preceding show on same station.

Interlock. Technique of achieving synchronous presentation of picture and matching sound from separate films.

Interpositives (IP). An intermediate film step between original camera negative and the optical negative.

Jump cut. Cutting to the same scene without a change of angle or framing.

KEM. The state-of-the-art editing equipment found at most commercial editorial services.

Kill. To strike out or remove part or all of a scene, set, action, or show.

Lead-in. Words spoken by announcer or narrator at beginning of show or commercial to set a scene or recapitulate some previous action.

Limbo shot. Used in closeups where background is not important. Pictures are taken against a nonrecognized background.

Lip sync. Direct recording of sound from scene that is being filmed; usually refers to film commercials in which actors can be seen with lips moving.

Live. "On-the-spot" television of events or people in contrast to transmission of film, videotape, or kinescope material.

Local. Show or commercial originating in local station as contrasted to network.

Mag track. The magnetic tape in 35mm form used in editing and interlocks.

Make good. An offer to a sponsor of comparable facilities as substitute for TV show or announcement cancelled because of emergency; or offer to repeat a commercial, without charge for time, because of some mistake or faulty transmission.

Matte. Imposing a scene or title over another scene. In such use, the background scene does not show through.

Monitoring. To check show or spot content and transmission with on-the-air picture.

Montage. Several separate pictures combined to make a composite picture. Sometimes passage-of-time effects created by running images in rapid succession.

Mortise. An optical effect that places an image on a specific part of a frame.

MOS or **"mit out sound."** A holdover term from decades ago meaning no sound is recorded.

Movieola. Older editing equipment used before the 1970s.

Optical. Trick effect done mechanically, permitting the combining of two or more pictures in one, creating wipes, montages, dissolves, fades, and other effects.

Overcrank. When the film camera shoots more than 24 frames per second, which slows the action (slow motion).

Package. Special show or series of shows bought by an advertiser, which includes all components ready to telecast.

Pad. To add action, sound, or any other material to fill the required on-the-air time.

Paintbox. Computerized post-production equipment used to alter and enhance video images. The paintbox could, for instance, replace an old package with a new one so a commercial could continue to be aired.

Pan. Gradual swinging of camera to left or right across a scene to see segments of it as camera moves.

Participating program. A single TV show sponsored by more than one advertiser.

Playback. Reproduction of a sound track in studio during film shooting to enable action or additional sound or both to be synchronized with action; also, playing or recording for audition or reference purposes immediately after spot is made.

Plug. Mention of a name, show, or advertised product; or, loosely speaking, the commercial announcement.

Process shot. Film combining real photography with projected backgrounds or model sets or drawings.

Projectors. Used in TV for still material. They include: Balop, which takes cards or opaques (no transparencies); balop card size is usually 3" x 4" or 6" x 8". Also, Projectall, which takes both opaque cards and transparencies or slides; card size is 3" x 4"; slides, 2" x 2".

Pull-up. Refers to the silence required at the beginning of a commercial. It is traditionally 1.5 seconds, although with the advent of videotape distribution of commercials, it is frequently .5 to 1.0 seconds.

Punch it. To accent or emphasize an action, sound effect, music, or line of dialogue.

Rating. Percentage of a statistical sample of TV viewers interviewed personally, checked by telephone, or noted in viewing diary, who reported viewing a specific TV show.

Residuals. Payments (required by the Screen Actors Guild) to talent for each broadcast of each film commercial on each network program per thirteen weeks' usage. If same commercial is used in spot markets, payment is additional per quarter.

Ripple dissolve. Optical effect in which scenes appear to ripple during a dissolve.

Rough cut. First assembly of film before completed editing.

SAG. Screen Actors Guild.

Scratch track. To obtain an audio timing guide for shooting or editing, a rough voice recording is made. This is the scratch track.

Segue. (Pronounced *seg*-way). Usually the transition from one musical number to another without any break or talk.

Sets-in-use. Percentage of all TV homes in a given locality whose sets are tuned in at a specific time, regardless of the station being viewed.

7-1/2 IPS. 1/4" audio tape recorded at 7¹/2 inches per sound (consumer equipment).

SFX. Abbreviation for sound effects.

Share-of-audience. Percentage of viewers watching a given show or station based on the total sets-in-use.

Slide. Usually refers to still artwork, titles, photographs, or film that are picked up or projected upon camera tube. Slides are of two types, transparent or opaque, their size varying according to station projection method used.

Split screen. Effect obtained when two or more cameras are used and thus two or more scenes are visible at the same time on different parts of the screen.

Sponsor identification. Percentage of viewers of a show or personality who can identify the name of the sponsor or are familiar with specific data about the product advertised on TV.

Spot. A spot is another name for a commercial.

Spot TV. Market-by-market buying of TV time (programs, announcements, participations, station breaks). It affords flexibility in adapting a TV ad campaign to time zone, seasonal variations, special merchandising plans, etc.

Station time. Portion of a station's schedule not normally available for network programs; totals three out of every six clock hours.

Stop motion. Film taken by exposing one frame instead of a number of frames at a time. Objects are usually moved by hand a fraction of an inch for each exposure according to a set pattern.

Super. Superimposing one scene over the other.

Sync sound. When sound is recorded synchronized with the camera. Used primarily with on-camera dialogue.

Take. Single shot picture or scene held by TV camera; also, command to switch directly from one picture or camera to another, as "ready one—take one."

Talent cost. Expense or cost (for music, talent, etc.) of a show or commercial aside from the time charge.

Telefex. Rear-view projection system for special effects, backgrounds, etc.

Teleprompter. Rolling script device for one-takes and celebrity talent. Lines are printed large enough to be read at distance on sheet that revolves, keeping pace with show's action.

Tracking shot. Shot in which camera moves to keep up with the action.

Transcription. Recording of highest quality, usually at 33¹/3 rpm, especially made for telecast or broadcast.

Truck. A camera move in which the camera and its mount move parallel to the scene being shot.

24 frames per second. The normal camera speed.

Under. Show that does not use all its allotted time; also, to sustain and subordinate one facet of the drama or situation under another.

Undercrank. Film camera shoots less than twenty-four frames per second, which speeds the action.

Video assist. In order to see what the film camera is recording, a video camera is positioned to enable what is being filmed to be seen on a television monitor.

Videotape. A system that records both sound and pictures simultaneously on magnetic tape; offers great advantage of immediate playback plus exceptionally fine picture fidelity. In one day, commercials can be completed on tape that previously took three weeks in running through film processing.

VO or voiceover. Narration-type recording as opposed to lip sync or live sound; also, voiceover narration where voice talent is not seen.

Wipe. Transition from one scene or image to another in which new scene replaces old one in some gradually increasing geometric pattern; that is, circle (circle in, circle out), square (expanding square), fan, roll, etc.

Word count. Number of words that will fit comfortably into a commercial of a specific length. Rule of thumb for television commercials is two words per second, although count will vary depending on type of commercial. Word count for radio is higher, at approximately 170 words per minute spot.

Zip-pan. Effect obtained by swinging camera so quickly around from one point of rest to another that the picture is blurred between the two.

Zoom lens. A lens of variable focal length. Its use achieves in-or-out motion without moving the camera or requiring a change of lens.

Who Does What on a Production

Television production involves a great many people. They all have titles and functions, and most of these people are "freelance"—that is, they are hired by the day or by the week and are not on permanent staff. It would be financially impossible for the production companies to employ all the crew members needed for a shoot on a full-time basis. The following is a list of important members of the production crew and what they do.

Assistant cameraman. This person sets up, loads, and unloads the camera for the camera operator. He or she deals with the technical aspects of the camera and also helps execute shots (by operating zoom and focusing).

Assistant director (A.D.). This person runs the set, coordinates the sequence of shooting, and is the "foreman" of the crew.

Best boy. The gaffer's assistant (the assistant to the head electrician).

Boom man. The person who operates the microphone on the boom.

Cameraman or **camera operator.** The person who operates the camera.

Director. The person in charge and responsible for the creative aspects of the shoot.

Director of photography. Designs and composes the lighting and camera moves with the director. This person sometimes operates the camera.

Gaffer. The head electrician on a shoot. The gaffer lights the scene under the direction of the director of photography (D.P.).

Generator man. The person who handles the genertion of power when conventional sources are unavailable.

Grip. Moves lighting equipment for the gaffer and handles the dolly.

Key grip. A specialist in designing and building rigging for camera mounts and lighting mounts.

Home economist. The person who prepares food on the shoot day.

Location scout. The person who presents various location choices to the agency and the director (usually Polaroids).

Producer. The person responsible for bringing together all elements.

Production assistant (P.A.). The assistant to the assistant director.

Production manager. The overseer of all production and related financial aspects of a job. Works closely with the director and hires key crew members.

Prop man. The person who secures props and is responsible for the product during a shoot.

Set designer. The person who works with the agency and the production company to design required sets. Also known as an art director.

Script supervisor. The person responsible for keeping track of what goes on during every take with comments from the director. This person also makes sure each scene is filmed in the correct time.

Sound man. The person who is responsible for recording all sound.

Stylist. The person who creates the aesthetic look of a production. He or she works under the director to obtain required sets, props, and wardrobe.

VTR man. The person who attaches video equipment to the film camera to allow video monitoring of what the film camera is shooting. Uses videotape to record each scene, too.

Wardrobe attendant. Responsible for the wardrobe before, during, and after a shoot. Supervised by the stylist.

Welfare worker. The required worker (in California) who supervises children on a shoot day.

The Internet, the World Wide Web, and You

Although, at least at present, the average copywriter is not likely to be deeply involved with preparing copy for cyberspace advertising, the growth in these areas is such that copywriters will undoubtedly be involved with it in the future.

Today, you are most likely to be concerned with the two main advertising media in the online market—*classified ads* and *billboards*. You can think of classifieds as brief messages that put what you have to say before people already shopping, just as consumers do when they browse the back of newspapers and magazines.

Billboards are electronic notices that come on the screen as one uses a commercial service, or surfs the Net. Usually, billboards offer longer messages than classifieds. Some practical tips you may follow in creating messages for classifieds and billboards:

- Write strong titles that build curiosity. Question titles are good here.
- Remember to talk to a specific person, not a mass audience. Your talk should be personal and should include strong attention-getting words such as "free," "save," "guarantee," "new," "now," "here's how," "at last," and "fast."
- In addition to a free offer, you can include such motivators as discounts or limited-time offers.
- Encourage responding and make doing so sound easy. If the online service offers an order or reply form, use it. If not, suggest e-mail.
- Be brief, especially in classifieds, where you'll use 32 or fewer characters.
- Don't use special formatting characters that may be unique to the computer system you're using.

What to Remember When Writing for an Advertiser Who Has Established a Site on the Web

With the rush of big-budget advertisers creating their own sites on the Web, a copywriter will be preparing advertising far beyond the simple classified ads. Advertising on the World Wide Web will involve motion, videos, sound, and color.

This advertising must have content that is credible, entertaining, and informative. The content must be appealing and relevant. Advertisers such as Federal Express, Best Western, Goodyear, IBM, MCI, and Sony will find acceptance only if they combine entertainment and information, frequently in an editorial-like context. A visit to the site should be interesting and fun. Graphics, sound, and video should be applied to hold audiences. As you can see from what has been said, there is more emphasis on entertainment and being interesting than in conventional advertising that you may be doing or have done in the past.

Graphics have an increased importance. These can be produced with specialized computer programs such as Corel Draw, Illustrator, or Freehand. You may also copy graphics (copyrights permitting) from photographs and artwork using a scanner. A scanner will view the graphic you want to copy, digitize it, and place it in a computer file.

As usual, you stress benefits and do so in a person-to-person style that is conversational. Incentives such as free offers and discounts will spur response. To make it easy to respond, you should include an e-mail address, phone or fax number, or postal address.

For readability, use good sized type which means that you avoid extraneous words.

Warning: Those you reach through the Internet can talk back if they don't like something about your approach, or the company or product you're promoting. Sometimes advertisers have been flooded by irate consumers who talked back through their computers to complain about shoddy products, rude treatment they've received, and even the presentation that has been made for the product. These complaints are painfully embarrassing to the advertisers, who are well aware that many others besides the complainers are being exposed to the complaints. As a creative person, you must be sure that nothing *you* do will bring out the complainers.

Terms That May Be Useful for You to Know

Browser. Software that enables people to maneuver through and explore the Web.

Cybermall. Shopping areas often included among the services offered by the consumer online services (such as Compuserve, Prodigy, America Online, and others).

Cyberspace. A general term for the universe of information sources such as the Internet.

E-mail. Electronic mail. A method of sending text messages from one e-mail address to another.

Gopher. A menu-driven software system that enables computers to interact with other computers using the same system.

Hypertext. Text that contains "links"—distinguished by an underlined or highlighted word—to other text or images.

Internet. A global network of networks connecting computers around the world. One component of the Internet is the World Wide Web.

Link. A site on the Web that can be accessed from another Web page.

Site. A pool of electronic information, including text, color photos and graphics, that individuals, groups, or businesses can readily put on the Web.

Surfing the Web. Sampling various Web sites to see what's there.

URLs. Uniform Resource Locators. An address for a site on the Web.

World Wide Web (WWW or Web). A part of the Internet that is hypertext based and comprised of sites that can be accessed either by browsing or using a URL.

CHAPTER 22

Research
It's the Copywriter's Friend

After finishing his talk to the group of copywriters, Jonathan Lingle, a Ph.D. from a renowned research firm, asked for questions. They came quickly. "Dr. Lingle," came a voice from the back row, "I've liked much of what I've heard, but truly hot ideas, it seems to me, can't come from number-crunching. They come from something in your heart or head—call it inspiration or a hunch—like a composer who produces music that bubbles up from who knows where."

"Good point. Admittedly, good ideas may not always be programmed, but all copywriters have those frustrating periods when inspiration is absent. In those moments, they should be glad to call upon research to remind them of what consistently does or does not work. Even that composer you mentioned doesn't work in a vacuum. Such a person, genius or otherwise, draws upon what has worked for other musicians. He reasons: 'If it worked for Mozart, maybe it will work for me.'"

So the meeting went on. There were questions from those who openly sought help; other questions displayed skepticism, sometimes tinged with hostility. In the main, however, Dr. Lingle convinced most of the group that research is a strong working partner of the copywriter.

What Consumers Say Often Varies from What They Believe or Do

To demonstrate the uncertainty surrounding certain types of consumer research, Andrew J. Byrne,[1] a specialist in direct response advertising and direct response marketing, warns that consumer research doesn't always provide truthful, usable answers to the marketer. For example, Mr. Byrne cites a survey of a large group who were asked, "Do you borrow money from a personal loan company?"

Every person in the group answered, "No."

Yet, the names of all of the interviewed people were taken from the records of a personal loan company. All had recently borrowed money.

In another survey, people were asked whether they had a library card. Nearly half the interviewees who said they had a library card did not have one.

A survey of beer drinking habits asked consumers whether they preferred to drink the "light" version of a particular beer or the "regular" type. At a ratio of 3 to 1, the respondents indicated a preference for "light." In fact, where both types were available, "regular" was outselling "light" by a 9 to 1 margin.

Speaking of effective research techniques for direct response advertising, Mr. Byrne sees positives and nega-

---

[1] Mr. Byrne furnished these examples and ideas specifically for this book.

tives for focus group research (described later in this chapter) but asserts that it is often impossible to show different advertisements to people and learn which ones will be more effective. He looks upon a focus group as a means of getting ideas and attitudes of people and as a way to gauge whether people understand what is being said to them in an advertisement. For testing effectiveness, he favors split run mailing tests, which are also described in this chapter.

Despite the shortcomings identified in the foregoing examples, copy people should gladly accept the help that research offers. Relying on intuition and inborn talent is fine for geniuses but not for most of us.

Use of Research Depends upon the Size and Kind of Business

Despite the heavy use of research, it is by no means universally used or highly regarded. Let's listen to what different workers in advertising have to say about their use of research:

A copywriter in a small advertising agency is talking: "No. We don't use research. Our clients can't afford it, and with our small profit margin, we can't afford to pay for it ourselves. We get along on experience and common sense."

We hear from a mail-order copywriter: "Research? Of course. There's no guesswork around here. We test by results, and that includes every element: headlines, body copy, illustrations, effect of color, coupons, timing, position, nature of the offer, etc., etc."

The big advertising agency copywriter says: "Yes. Our clients are sophisticated advertisers. They budget a healthy sum for research. Much of it is initiated and paid for by their market research division, which also gets into copy testing. A lesser amount is paid for out of our funds. As for techniques, we draw upon everything from the simplest types to motivational research and G&R's impact testing. It's a great help, but we still do many ads that simply reflect judgment."

Perhaps you will set up your own homemade research method. Many copywriters do. Retail copypeople, for example, have devised so many individual copychecking systems that it is impossible to list them all. Some are very good; others are very bad.

Research Results Vary Because People React Differently

From the start, it has been known that consumer reaction to advertisements is variable. An appeal that works during one year may fail badly the next year. The success of advertisements is uncertain, even on a day-to-day or week-to-week basis. There have been attempts to take the uncertainty out of advertising. "Foolproof" systems have been devised to eliminate guesswork in copy. Consumers and their reactions to copy appeals, headlines, and illustrations

have been studied as closely as scientists study the beetle and its activities.

It would be pleasant to relate that the research has been completely successful—but it hasn't. There are still uncertainties. As long as people themselves are so uncertain, there will always be a quantity of "by guess and by gosh" in copywriting. The weather, the political picture, the news, epidemics, and a thousand other variables can affect the success of a piece of copy. If any one of the variables is hard at work, the most scientifically conceived job of copywriting can fail.

Most copy researchers admit the variables. They admit that it is difficult to predict the exact degree of success or failure for any single piece of copy. They can merely predict that the copy should be successful or unsuccessful. Copy research is greatly concerned with development of techniques for measuring copy's effectiveness before its appearance in print or in broadcast—and then with analyzing why it failed or succeeded after its appearance.

Advertisers Have Different Approaches to Research

Some smart advertisers are high-readership advocates. They reason, "If they don't read it, they won't buy it because they don't know about it." Opponents say, "If a thousand persons read but only one buys, high readership means nothing. Advertisements pay off on conviction, not mere readership."

Many advertising people believe in checklists. Others ridicule their use. Some say that mail-order copy effectiveness can only be measured in returns from mail-order advertising. Many will refute the assertion by pointing out variables that will affect results even in this situation. There are, therefore, many measuring techniques for copy, but there is certainly no complete agreement on them.

As a copywriter, you should know what's going on. You should know the merits and faults of the different testing techniques, but you must be careful to avoid two dangerous traps.

- Don't let yourself become so sold on any one method of copy research that you are blinded by the merits of other types of research. Remember, there is no perfect research method, and no one set of measures is right for all communication strategies.
- Don't get so bogged down in the mazes of copy research that you forget to write copy that is vigorous, spontaneous, and alive. There is no substitute for the warm, human writing that digs down deep into the consumers' desires and makes them want to buy your product. You can be *too* scientific in your copy approach and tangle yourself in formulas.

Despite various problems, research has become an important part of advertiser/agency relationships. From the advertiser's perspective, research can be used to protect and to justify advertising investment to management. From the agency's perspective, research makes possible the testing of more ideas, thus increasing the chances of success for the copy. Obviously, much money and effort can be saved if you understand proper research techniques.

Pretest and Posttest Techniques

Although any research technique can be used in either a pretest or posttest situation, the nature of the interview and the data that is gathered will be influenced by whether the purpose of the research is primarily diagnostic or evaluative.

In a pretest environment, the researcher is more concerned with generating concepts and diagnosing alternatives than with evaluating the expected effectiveness of the actual advertisement.

In a posttest environment, the reverse is more often true, although a good posttest is often a good pretest for the subsequent campaign.

While each study project should be designed to satisfy particular research objectives, some of the more common techniques of copy evaluation are as follows:

Pretest:

- Focus group interviews
- Checklist
- Inquiry or direct response tests
- Split run tests
- Readability tests (Flesch formula)
- Physiological tests
- Motivational research

Posttest:

- Readership study (recognition, identification, recall)
- Impact method
- Communication and Reaction (C&R) tests (Actually, C & R testing is more of a pretest than a posttest, although it is used with both rough and finished executions.)
- PACT Principles[2]

Focus Group Interviewing

Sometime, if you haven't already done so, you will probably try out some copy on other students, your wife, your secretary, your mother, or strangers. "Just trying to get consumer reaction," you'll explain. The focus group interview is a more elaborate way to do the same thing.

Instead of arbitrarily selecting one person as your guinea pig, you will select a number of persons, perhaps eight or ten. Each person will be a typical potential buyer of the product for which you are testing the copy. In addition to being typical, group members must also be inter-

---

[2] Although PACT principles are listed here and elsewhere under posttesting, they are not, strictly speaking, a technique of copy evaluation.

ested—that is, "interested in the product." Copy for a product should not be submitted to group members who have not, and never will, use this type of product.

The group's rating of your advertising helps you determine possible reader reaction in advance of publication. If the group members can never be interested in your product, they are not competent to rate your advertisements, since what would appeal to them would not, in many cases, appeal to the regular or potential user.

Such group sessions are often watched by clients and agency personnel through a two-way mirror. Participants in the group know that they are being watched, but researchers maintain that this knowledge does not inhibit responses.

Groups, in addition to being used for opinions on advertising approaches and product testing, may also contribute usefully to concept development, product naming, packaging development, and campaign evaluation. For such participation, group members are usually paid a modest sum.

Specific Focus Group Techniques

Order-of-merit ranking. A focus group ranks different advertisements for the same product. Two or more advertisements are presented to the individual members who are asked to indicate, "Which of these advertisements do you like best?" or "Which of these advertisements would be most likely to make you want to buy the product?" All advertisements are thus rated until they are ranked in order of preference. This is sometimes called order-of-merit ranking.

Paired-comparison technique. Another method is the paired-comparison technique, in which advertisements are judged in pairs. The respondent picks what he thinks is the better advertisement in each pair. Then, through elimination, the best of all of the advertisements is selected. Usually, this system is used for choosing an approach, format, or theme rather than individual advertisements in one pattern.

Many times, different elements of the advertisements are rated. For instance, your advertisements might be identical except for the headlines, which will be rated in comparison with each other. The next rating will compare illustrations, the next copy appeal, and so on.

Focus group interviews do in a group what depth interviews do on an individual basis. By introducing stimuli (advertisements, parts of advertisements, products, packages), a group leader thus stirs an informal discussion among the eight or so persons in the group.

An interesting result of group interviews is the sometimes startling frankness with which group members will discuss subjects that could hardly be approached in the individual depth interview. Likewise, because group members usually try hard to contribute, it will often be found that the group will contribute more points and more talk than will be obtained from the individual interview.

Figure 22–1a. Advertisement A (Noxzema) tested with the impact method. Study this advertisement. Then study Advertisement B. Which advertisement do you think was more effective? See Addendum at the end of the chapter (page 296). *Courtesy of Gallup & Robinson.*

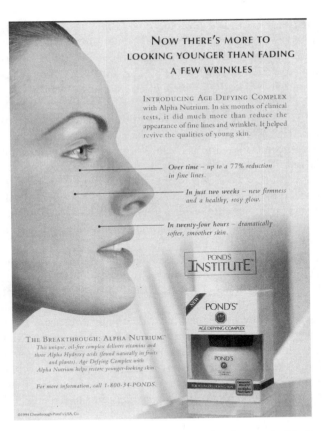

Figure 22–1b. Advertisement B (Pond's®) tested with the impact method. See Addendum at the end of chapter (page 296) to learn which advertisement was more effective. *Courtesy of Gallup & Robinson.*

Reasons for Using Focus Group Interviewing
Although the focus group method has been useful for indicating how an advertisement might fare in the final published form, it has faults mixed with its virtues. Some characteristics on the plus side of the focus group method are listed below.

Good results. In many instances, there has been a satisfactory correlation between group ratings and selling power of the advertisements rated. This correlation has been good enough, despite the faults of the method, to justify its continued use in pretesting copy.

Speed. Once the group has been selected, the job of rating the advertisements can ordinarily be done speedily and easily.

Moderate cost. A few interviewees equipped with copies of comprehensive layouts can do the whole job. A good many advertisements or separate advertising elements can be rated in one session, thus reducing the cost per unit tested.

Consumer viewpoint. You tend to overlook the consumer in some forms of copy research. You think of appeals, copy approach, or the market. The focus group makes you think of the market in terms of persons who view advertisements with like, dislike, or indifference. If you follow the ratings of a focus group, you are being guided by the preferences of a representative segment of your consumer target rather than by your personal, and possibly isolated, judgment. Also, your respondents are classified as to age, work, income, and other aspects.

Some Problems with Focus Group Testing
As in the case of most copy-research methods, it is easier to pick flaws in the group interview than to find virtues. The following list doesn't condemn the method but provides you with some reservations. It should also indicate to you some weaknesses to avoid if you attempt to set up a group.

Respondents. Finding the right person to serve on a consumer group is vital to the success of the method. Determining just what is "typical" and then finding persons who fit that description is likely to be a slow, tedious task. The requirement that such persons be "interested" in a particular product provides a double complication.

Difficult to make conclusions. The questions usually asked of a consumer group fail to obtain a final answer. Examine the two questions again: Which of these advertisements do you like better? Which of these two advertisements would be more likely to make you want to buy the product?

The first question has nothing to do with sales potential. The respondents may like the advertisement because the illustration features a beautiful person. The rest of the layout may please them; they might even read and like the copy. All this, however, might not have the slightest influence in making them buy the spark plugs being advertised. Their favorable answer for a particular advertisement was based upon subjective factors having nothing to do with influencing them to buy.

The second question, although it is aimed more at determining buying behavior, asks respondents to indicate how they might act. There is a great difference between a person's intentions and subsequent actions.

Some copy evaluators have combined the answers to the two questions. The combining is not practical. One question measures preference for an advertisement on a basis entirely removed from buying behavior. The other attempts to measure buying potential. Combining these two elements is tricky, and conclusions thus derived would be questionable.

Separating elements is dangerous. Although there is some value in dissecting advertising elements and letting the group judge headlines, illustration, and other items individually, the process is somewhat unrealistic. A person thumbing through a magazine is looking at advertisements, not headlines or illustrations. The general rating seems to be more accurate, according to the findings of the Advertising Research Foundation.

Probably the best procedure is to use both methods—individual element rating and general rating. Both should then be analyzed carefully before the findings are accepted. In any event, it seems dubious that final judgment of an advertisement should be based on a rating of the separate parts. Remember, some scenery taken feature by feature is not attractive. Assemble the features and you may have a charming vista. An advertisement taken by sections may not be noteworthy. Combine elements and the result is often a persuasive, compelling advertisement.

Group members become copy "experts." Almost everyone feels competent to criticize advertisements. Group members thus frequently forget their consumer function and begin to act like copy chiefs. This tendency causes real trouble, since the group members thus are no longer "typical" consumer prospects. Instead, they have become professional critics. When they no longer view the advertisements with a consumer's eyes, their usefulness as group members has ended.

Hard to compare more than two advertisements. Although many consumer groups are asked to compare more than two advertisements at a time, this is a questionable approach. The fewer the elements to be considered, the more reliable the judgment is likely to be. Thus, the paired-comparison method may be preferable to that which gives the respondent the task of ranking six different advertisements.

If he does his job conscientiously, the respondent will probably be confused as he considers all the elements found in six advertisements. It is difficult enough to obtain reliable opinions from consumer groups without complicating the task further by confusing them. The paired-comparison method at least eliminates some of the confusion.

Size of the sample. Although the trend has been toward small samples, the sample size may often have to be varied for different types of products or in order to clarify close voting situations.

Impractical for certain items. Some products of infrequent purchase, such as figure skates or shortwave transmitters, are not suitable for group interviews. Such products call for unusual promotions; ordinary testing procedures are not as suited to them as to ordinary items of everyday purchase like cereals, milk, or coffee.

Prestige factor is operative. Group interviewing, like any procedure requiring decision on the part of respondents, is often inaccurate because of the respondents' pride or vanity. Respondents not wanting to admit that a sexy illustration is appealing will vote against it; under actual reading conditions, however, the same illustration would win delighted attention. Intellectuals might be unwilling to admit that celebrity endorsements attract and convince them. As long as people are subject to vanity, the prestige factor will be at work in situations like those set up by the group copy testing procedure.

Test measures standings—not quality of advertisement. Respondents are asked to rate advertisements on a scale of 1 to 3. This system is followed whether advertisements are good or bad. In some tests, all the advertisements might be poor. The rating would simply indicate which was the least objectionable. The highest-rated advertisement might be used because the group voted for it, not because it had merit.

Campaigns are overlooked. Most national advertising is campaign advertising. One advertisement, by itself, might not have the push and appeal that it has as one of a series of advertisements. Yet the consumer group may be asked to judge an individual advertisement, ignoring the cumulative effect of the campaign.

Any one advertisement in the campaign might not have

sold this person. Yet the consumer group judges one advertisement in an attempt to answer the question "Which advertisement would be most likely to make you buy the product?" That one advertisement might fit in very poorly with the campaign, and with most national advertisers, the campaign is the important consideration. That is why, in many cases, national advertisers will continue to emphasize a campaign even though it is tempting to put all the emphasis on a current prize contest. Long-run considerations, however, are not necessarily a part of a consumer group's thinking.

Conditions are not natural. No matter how skilled the interviewer, or how well the questions are phrased, the conditions under which the consumer group operates are not normal home-reading conditions. The group member cannot help being less casual than in reading in the home. In this test, this person is on the alert for faults; the very act of comparing is unrealistic.

Certainly, the usual reader will not match advertisements against each other. Also, reading under group conditions allows undivided attention to the individual advertisements. Under more usual conditions, there would be the competition from surrounding advertisements. There would be unfavorable position. In finished printed form, one advertisement might gain over another through better type, use of color, and other mechanical factors.

Checklists

Before you engage in the use of checklists, you should clarify the meaning of the term. (See the appendix for examples of checklists.)

Almost everyone who has written copy has used a checklist at one time or another. Usually, the list will be a simple little affair—a casual reminder to put in certain important elements such as the slogan, price mention, and selling conditions. Other checklists bring in more elements to watch for. They keep the copywriter on the track without attempting to provide any scientific preevaluation as to the effectiveness of the advertisements.

The checklist, in its ultimate form, goes beyond reminding. It attempts, as in the case of the elaborate systems worked out a number of years ago, to serve as a yardstick for preevaluating the effectiveness of advertising. So confident were the proponents of checklist evaluations that they made wild assertions. One man claimed that through use of his system, you could tell a good advertisement from a bad advertisement before publication in nine minutes flat.

Some of the opponents, however, assert that:

1. Originators of checklist evaluation techniques are engaged in a meaningless battle of points with each such originator, simply trying to outdo the other in dreaming up new point lists.
2. Checklist preevaluation methods hamstring originality.
3. Copywriters use points by instinct.

4. Personal judgment is overemphasized in the checklist system.

Criticisms of Checklists

Since sooner or later you will probably be engaged in a discussion of checklists, the four arguments just given are examined here.

Checklists degenerate to a battle of points. This is true. If you use a formal checklist, devised by someone else, you can become a victim of the point battle as you compare the list with someone else's. The best procedure is to avoid long lists because the longer and more complicated the checklist, the less usable it is on a day-to-day basis.

Checklists hamstring originality. "Creative work cannot be written according to a cut-and-dried formula. The checklist provides a mechanical crutch for the copywriter, which, if followed, generally would tend to make all advertisements look the same." So go the comments of many copywriters. An illustration of how intensely some advertising people feel about this is provided by the example of one very large agency that threw one of its biggest accounts out of the "shop" when the account insisted on adoption of a checklist system by the agency copywriters working on the account's copy.

Checklist originators deny that their systems choke newness and sparkle in copy. Rather, they say, using a good checklist as a guide, the original writer can produce freely, confident that writing is channeled more effectively. The checklist merely systemizes a job that often has no system.

Copywriters use points by instinct, so checklists are useless. Most copywriters argue that they incorporate the necessary points in their writing without using any "system." They suspect that the checklist is an attempt by research people to invade the copywriter's field. "Possibly all right for beginners but not for the experienced person" is a frequent comment about checklists.

The comment is valid in the case of many copywriters, who, through long practice, automatically use attention-getting, selling points in everything they turn out. Other writers—beginners and some old hands—might be wise to adopt some system to keep them on the track in their thinking.

The best copywriters in the field might occasionally use a checklist to remind themselves of the fundamentals that sometimes slip away from them as they become more advanced in their jobs. Because checklists contain nothing new but simply present ever-constant, faithful sales points, they can be a great comfort to the beginner and an occasional aid to skilled copywriters.

Personal judgment is overemphasized. Any checklist, say the critics, is basically a personal judgment on what

Figure 22–2a. Advertisement A (Nuprin) tested with the impact method. Study this advertisement. Then study Advertisement B. Which advertisement do you think was more effective? See Addendum at the end of the chapter (page 296). *Courtesy of Gallup & Robinson.*

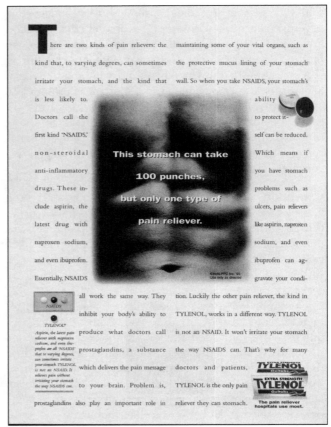

Figure 22–2b. Advertisement B (Tylenol) tested with the impact method. See Addendum at the end of the chapter (page 296) to learn which advertisement was more effective. *Courtesy of Gallup & Robinson.*

elements are needed to make an advertisement successful. Any copywriter can, they continue, evolve his own list. Even in using a checklist to evaluate an advertisement, the interpretation is a matter for individual judgment.

That this criticism has some truth is borne out by situations in which persons using the same checklist evaluating system arrive at radically different results in their ratings of the same advertisement. In short, one person may have more skill in applying the checklist than another, or both may be equally skilled but differ entirely in their use of the system. The method then becomes no better than the ability of the persons who use it.

About the most conclusive thing to say of the checklist is that it's up to you. It's a quick, inexpensive way to evaluate an advertisement. If you use a checklist, be sure that you don't let it make you write like an automaton and that you retain your good judgment.

Inquiry Testing

The idea behind inquiry testing is simple. You run advertisements and judge their relative effectiveness by the number of inquiries they generate. These inquiries may

result from a hidden offer buried in the copy or from a coupon offer, openly made, inviting purchases or inquiries.

The hidden offer rids the advertiser of professional coupon-clippers and inquiries from the curious. It also indicates extent of reading but results in fewer inquiries or sales than does the coupon offer.

In the usual inquiry test, different advertments are run at different times in the same publication, or at the same time in different publications. Results are then compared.

Split Run Testing

Another version of the inquiry test is the split run test. This test has some of the advantages or disadvantages of the usual inquiry test plus some advantages and disadvantages of its own.

"Split run" refers to the practice of testing advertisements by running two or more versions of the same advertisement on the same press run of a newspaper or magazine. Thus, Advertisement A may be exactly like Advertisement B except for the headline. In the case of a newspaper, each advertisement will go out on the same day and in the same position in the paper.

From the response to the advertisement, the advertiser can tell which of the two headlines was more effective. In the case of a magazine, as many as four versions of the same advertisement will go out, and each may be distributed in a different area. Response will be judged by the relative readership, by the coupon return, or by the replies to a hidden offer, any one of which may be employed in such tests. Any element of the advertisement may be checked—copy, illustration, or headline. In some instances, the advertiser will test four entirely different advertisements.

You may wonder why this form of testing is classified with the pretest copy testing techniques instead of the posttest techniques. Like inquiry, or direct response testing, it could be considered a posttest. It is placed in the pretest group simply because such testing usually precedes general use of the winning advertisement or advertisement elements.

Normally, the advertisements would not have been run before the split run test. In this sense, therefore, the test is a before-publication test. A fact you should realize, too, is that although several hundred newspapers offer split run service, only a few magazines offer split run, so much testing is quite limited in its scope for magazines.

Pluses for Split Run

Parallels running conditions. The trouble with so many copy-testing methods is that they are unrealistic. The researchers set up situations that are artificial despite all efforts to make them otherwise. The split run test, on the other hand, gives the advertiser an almost perfect simulation of the conditions under which the advertisements will be run.

There will be no tampering with actual reading conditions; there will be no dependence upon the skill of interviewers. Instead, the advertisement readers will read as they always do—right in their homes and unaware that they are taking part in a test. Their response to the advertisements will give an excellent, although not completely reliable, comparison of the effectiveness of the test advertisements.

Test itself produces business. An obvious advantage of split run testing is that the test pulls in business, unlike other tests, which produce nothing but information. A split run test may promote the product just as well and bring in just as much business as any other advertising used for the product.

Checks geographical differences. That sections of the country, or even sections of a city, vary in their response to different products, copy appeals, and so forth, is well known. Magazine-reading habits, for example, differ greatly in different cities. One tomato sauce manufacturer found that sales were very good in one city but very poor in another. A TV star who gets a good rating on the West Coast may fare poorly in the South and Midwest but get a good rating on the East Coast.

This is the sort of the thing that will vex you or any other advertising person. A split run test can help you, because it provides a means of checking the power of your appeals in four different sections covered by a magazine. Split run provides you with a method of making such a check. As one magazine executive, whose publication offers split run testing facilities, has explained it, split runs make possible:

> Pretesting before general release, eliminating ineffective advertisements; comparison of campaign theme and ideas; development of the presentation; evaluation of different headlines; measuring various illustrative treatments; comparing 4-color to black and white or to black and one color; exploring different layout techniques; comparison of the relative values of various hidden offers.

Problems in Split Run

The coupon or inquiry return from split run advertisements is not necessarily a true measure of the relative effectiveness of the advertisements. Here are some considerations:

- It is difficult to use split run for measuring effectiveness of general advertisements. The method is suited to mail-order advertisements. To make a mail-order advertisement out of a general advertisement for purposes of the test can distort the true picture of reader reaction to a general advertisement run under normal conditions.
- Since most of your readers won't reply to your test advertisements, respondents may not give a fair indication of your readership. Also, you learn nothing in the split run about people who don't send in the coupon.
- Mail returns may not give a true evaluation of potential store sales. People who reply to your coupon or hidden offer often are not typical of the kind of people who come into a store to buy the product. Children and professional "coupon clippers" make a business of replying to advertisements carrying offers, despite the fact that they have no real interest in the product. Split run using hidden offers can avoid this difficulty somewhat.
- Unlike some other copy testing methods, the split run test reveals nothing about the readers. You may know nothing about the way they read the advertisement, their economic or social status, or whether anything in the advertisement actually appealed to them.

Television Split Run

Split run television testing is offered on cable television. Cable stations make it possible to show different commercials in different households simultaneously. Any television commercial can be blanked out and another commercial substituted at any time. Later, surveys may be made by phone, mail, or personal interviews to get viewers' opinions. One of the most significant technological developments in the research industry is that actual *purchase* patterns can be tracked through panels of consumers who allow their buying habits to be monitored electronically through in-store scanners.

Other Pretests for Television

In addition to testing procedures that can be used for both print and broadcast, such as group discussion and split run, there are some that are used solely by television researchers. All of these cannot be described here, because researchers continue to find many new ways to ascertain viewers' reactions to commercials. One advertising agency, for example, put together a manual that described twenty-four leading methods of television copytesting. These were just the *leading* methods. There are many more. Included here, however, are four techniques: theater projections, on-the-air tests, masked recognition testing, and animatic testing.

Theater Projections

Many different techniques are used for a theater production type of testing in which as many as 400 persons may be invited to a theater for the private screening of some "new television material." Usually, the audience will see entertainment programs and television commercials. Later, the audience is asked for their reactions to the commercials, including comprehension, brand-name recall, likes/dislikes, interest, and believability. There might even be group discussions to obtain full information. Much television copy continues to be tested in these "laboratory" theaters.

On-the-Air Tests

Under the on-the-air testing method, the respondents do not know they are taking part in a test. A test commercial is aired in one, two, or a few cities. An advertiser's test commercial may be used on a regular program in one city, while the present commercial runs in other cities as usual. Sometimes, the advertiser may buy a new time period in selected cities for a local participation.

Following the airing, viewers who saw the new commercial are interviewed (usually by telephone) to find out their brand attitudes, their ability to play back the commercial message, and their brand knowledge. These interviews are compared with those of people who saw only the existing commercial.

Most such tests are conducted under an invited-viewing technique. The respondent is invited to view a familiar show into which a test commercial has been inserted.

A re-interview is conducted the next day that asks for commercial recall. In addition, the respondent is checked for attitude toward the advertised brand, ability to play back the commercial message, and knowledge of the brand.

The commercial's communication effectiveness is then evaluated in terms of its ability to command attention (intrusiveness) and its generation of a favorable buying attitude (persuasion).

These two factors are then usually compared to the norms of performance for similar products, and/or to control groups. The check of the control groups reveals the attitudes of respondents before they were exposed to the commercial (called pre-post design).

Masked Recognition Testing

This kind of post-test endeavors to register response to emotion-arousing commercials. The methodology requires that the respondent see a commercial one day and the same commercial on the following day. On the second showing, the product name is absent from audio and video. The respondent is then asked to recall the product name. It is thought that a commercial with strong emotional impact will result in the respondent's recalling the product name.

This same respondent may not, however, explain logically what in the commercial was appealing because the appeal of the commercial was largely emotional and hence less susceptible to explanation. As is evident, this type of test is more useful to determine product-name registration than to evaluate general content.

Animatics

This is less a technique of television pretesting as it is the form in which the commercials will appear when presented to the respondents. Rough or finished executions can be used in most testing techniques. Because it is too expensive for advertisers to produce a number of commercials for testing purposes, animatic testing fills in. This consists of the following steps:

1. An artist draws pictures—often line drawings—that visually depict the commercial in its various phases.
2. Still photographs are taken of each drawing.
3. A separate sound track is recorded.
4. A film is made of the many drawings.

From these steps, a limited amount of movement is captured on the film. Accompanying the visual is a voiceover sound track that uses the actual copy intended for the finished commercial.

When shown to a proper sample, such testing helps eliminate poor commercials and provides a basis for selecting the various components for the final commercial. Animatic-tested commercials that achieve a good response in the testing period have frequently shown up as satisfactory final commercials. Also, the animatic method can be used for research of consumer brand awareness and recall.

As is always the case, the method has its critics. Some say that it is best-suited to simpler techniques, but that it often is incapable of portraying the big or dazzlingly different idea. Also, the personal essence of an unusual spokesperson may not be conveyed, such as the glint in the eye, the subtle shadings of bodily and facial movements, or the eloquent use of the hands.

COMMERCIAL: SAAB 900 AUTOMOBILES, "Turning Over The Car"
LENGTH: 30 seconds   DATE: 10/28-30, 1994

1. M/ANNCR: The new Saab 900.

2. It won Automobile Magazine's

3. Design Of The Year.

4. Consumer's Digest rated it a best buy.

5. (Sound Effects in Background) Kiplinger's Personal Finance magazine . . .

6. called it the best new car . . .

7. in its class.

8. But with a 50% stiffer body, . . .

9. the new 900 . . .

10. is designed to survive . . .

11. much more than . . .

12. the scrutiny of the press.

– 1 –

Figure 22–3. Automobile commercial tested by Gallup & Robinson. Results of the test are shown in Figure 22–4 and Figure 22–5 that follow.

```
:30 SAAB 900 Automobiles
"Turning Over The Car"

PERFORMANCE SUMMARY

                                        Men & Women
Intrusiveness
    Unaided Recall, Correct Brand  . . . . . . . .35%
    Proved Unaided Recall . . . . . . . . . . . . .25%
    Proved Unaided and Brand Aided Recall  . .35%

Communication
    Lead Idea . . . . . . . . . . . . . . . . . . . . .51%
    Main Point  . . . . . . . . . . . . . . . . . . . .42%

Persuasion
    Favorable Buying Attitude (FBA) . . . . . . .51%
    Brand Rating (1) . . . . . . . . . . . . . . . . .58%

Commercial Reaction
    Commercial Liking (2) . . . . . . . . . . . . . .58%

(1) Excellent/Very Good (6-point scale)
(2) Liked Very Much/Liked (5-point scale)
```

Figure 22–4. Performance summary of the commercial shown in Figure 22–3. As the figures show, the Gallup & Robinson test produced high ratings for the Saab 30-second commercial.

As an alternative to this still-picture technique, critics suggest the use of real people, through videotape and sound, against a simulated background of drawings, photographs, or film footage. This technique, while not quite as inexpensive as animatics, is still moderately inexpensive and offers more realism as a testing device. Increasingly, advertisers are stringing together cuts from earlier executions to approximate the new story line.

Communication and Reaction (C & R) Testing

C & R testing is a generic term for several techniques commonly used by advertising agencies. In general, it directs a respondent's attention to a commercial or advertisement.

After the respondent has had an opportunity to look at the commercial or advertisement one or more times, he or she is asked a series of questions to determine what ideas were communicated and what reactions were spurred by the advertising and the ideas. Most larger advertising agencies have their own preferred version of the technique. It is used primarily as an early and economical system for screening advertising alternatives.

For example, tachistoscope testing, described later in this chapter, is one of the techniques used in C & R testing. C & R testing is one of the most common forms of pretesting in use today.

Readability Tests

There can be some question as to whether or not this discussion of readability properly fits into a chapter on testing. A person might ask, Isn't readability (and the Flesch formula) concerned primarily with writing style? Furthermore, isn't the Flesch formula, in particular, concerned more with postpublication analysis than pretesting?

To the first question, it may be said that if a writer examines copy in terms of readability principles—or has a researcher do it—before it is set in print in final form, it is possible to greatly increase the effectiveness of that copy. Thus, it seems proper to discuss readability in this research chapter even though there is no denying that readability principles *are* writing principles and can be used as such by the copywriter.

To the second question, it may be said that readability research *can* be used for pretesting or posttesting, but it seems more sensible to apply it in pretesting and thus avoid the use of writing that is less efficient than it should be.

Some years ago, United Press, worried that they were writing "over" their readers, made a thorough study of their wire stories. They found, among other things, that out of 100 United Press stories going out in a single day, the average sentence length was 29 words and the average length of lead sentences was 31 words. A sentence length of around 20 words is the most comfortable reading length for the mass of the population. UP found that although they were averaging around 30 words for their sentences, sentence length averages for other magazines ran as follows:

Magazine	Average Sentence Length
Time	16 words
Reader's Digest	18 words
Atlantic Monthly	24 words

United Press editors found that, in addition to writing long sentences, their writers were also using too many long, complex words. Alarmed by the trend, the wire service began a writing reform within the organization. Sentences were shortened, language was simplified, and readability, according to tests, increased noticeably and quickly.

What was true of United Press has been true of almost every organization writing to the public including magazines, newspapers, and advertisers. Sentences are too long, words are too long, and the writing is impersonal. The three factors, regrettably, make a good recipe for low readership.

Thanks to readership studies, you know that Advertisement A gets 55 percent readership and Advertisement B gets 20 percent. But why? It might have been the headline, illustration, or position in the publication. There are many ways to account for the difference.

One of the most important factors affecting readership is this matter of readability. Was the copy a chore to read

:30 SAAB 900 Automobiles
"Turning Over The Car"

6p. The commercial made me think I might consider a "Saab" the next time I'm in the market for a car.

Re-Exposure Respondents

COMMERCIAL REACTION		Total	Sex		Education		Income	
			Men	Women	Some College	No College	Under $50K	$50K+
		%	%	%	%	%	%	%
Agree completely	(6)	6.0	0.0	12.5	6.5	5.3	5.6	7.9
Agree strongly	(5)	22.9	29.3	15.0	22.6	21.1	22.2	23.7
Agree somewhat	(4)	26.5	22.0	30.0	30.6	10.5	25.0	23.7
Disagree somewhat	(3)	24.1	22.0	27.5	24.2	26.3	25.0	26.3
Disagree strongly	(2)	12.0	17.1	7.5	11.3	15.8	11.1	13.2
Disagree completely	(1)	7.2	9.8	5.0	4.8	15.8	8.3	5.3
DK/NA/Refused		1.2	0.0	2.5	0.0	5.3	2.8	0.0
Average Rating		3.6	3.4	3.8	3.7	3.2	3.6	3.7
Standard Error		0.1	0.2	0.2	0.2	0.4	0.2	0.2
(Base)		(83)	(41)	(40)	(62)	(19)	(36)	(38)

Figure 22–5. Reaction to test commercial shown in Figure 22–3. The figures shown here reveal how favorably the test groups might be disposed to buying the automobile shown in the television commercial. Notice the variations in the results.

or did it run off smoothly under your glance? What made the difference in readability between A and B? How do you actually measure readability? At least some of the answers to these questions have been supplied by a former Vienna lawyer, Dr. Rudolph Flesch, whose readability formula you can learn and apply quickly to your copy or anyone else's copy.

Flesch Formula

The degree to which the following four elements appear in 100-word writing samples is the basis for the Flesch formula. These elements are:

- Average sentence length
- Average number of syllables
- Percentage of personal words
- Percentage of personal sentences

These are not magic ingredients. Flesch has simply expressed mathematically what writers have always known: Short words and short sentences make for easier reading. In sentences, for example, the Flesch table points out that about 88 percent of the population can understand without difficulty sentences that fall in the "Fairly Easy" category. Such sentences average 14 words; their syllable count is 139 per 100 words. "Very Difficult" writing, in contrast, is suitable to only about 4.5 percent of the population. In this category, the average sentence runs 29 or more words and the syllable count soars to 192.

Personal words. An interesting facet of the Flesch formula is the stress on the use of personal words and personal sentences in order to achieve what is termed a high "interest" factor. Words such as "people" and "folks" (plus personal names and personal pronouns) are classified as "personal" words. Personal sentences include: spoken sentences set off by quotation marks; questions, commands, and other sentences addressed directly to the reader; exclamations; and incomplete sentences whose meaning must be inferred from the context. "Dull" writing has no personal sentences and contains only two percent or less personal words per 100 words. Typical users of such writing are scientific magazines, which, however absorbing to their limited audience, would be found dull by the mass audience. "Highly Interesting" in contrast, has 10 personal words and 43 percent of personal sentences.

For years, young writers have been told to "write simply—write on the level of your readers." It is not easy to decide what kind of writing is suited to the different levels. The fact that a folksy advertisement gets a good Flesch rating, and thus can be read by most of the adult readers, does not mean that all advertisements must be written in folksy style.

If you are selling a mass-appeal item, write in the way that will appeal to the biggest possible portion of that market. However, if you are writing *New Yorker* copy for a very expensive product, you will not be addressing a mass readership. The readers you want to reach will probably be affluent and appreciate precision instruments.

They probably will have an educational background that could support an advertisement with a "Difficult" Flesch rating.

Look upon Writing Formulas as Guides—Not Inflexible Rules

By no means should a copywriter write consciously to the Flesch or any other formula. The system is simply a device to tell you whether your writing is geared in readability to the various segments of your readership. That the method has some practicality is evident in its adoption by a number of advertising agencies and publications. The formula is applicable to any kind of writing and, as a matter of fact, has been used widely to determine readability of the editorial content of magazines and newspapers.

The principal danger in the use of the Flesch system is that writers might adopt it too literally. It would be oversimplification to believe that all you must do to write good copy is to write short words, short sentences, and throw in a personal reference now and then. Thought and writing skill must still be used by the copywriter. The Flesch formula does nothing but wave a warning when the copy begins to clank. Because copywriters can read their copy easily, they often forget that others won't have a similarly easy time reading it. The Flesch system acts as a warning that (1) These sentences are too long; (2) Only half your readers will understand this; and (3) Don't forget that your readers are human; they like personal references to themselves or other human beings.

Second, be cautioned that the Flesch formula cannot be applied literally to radio or television writing, since a good radio announcer can make material that looks difficult to the eye seem less complex when it is read out loud. Through skillful phrases and intonation, the announcer breaks long sentences into easily assimilated phrases. Even long, unusual words that would daunt the reader of a printed page will "sound easy" when delivered by a good announcer or actor.

In conclusion, don't use the Flesch system as a mold for your writing. Flesch doesn't measure literary excellence or selling effectiveness but how well you reach your audience. A formula should not be used constantly if you are to maintain elasticity in your writing. Use it occasionally as a sort of check on your writing. Employed in this manner, it can help your writing to be more consistently readable— especially if you are writing to a mass market.

Physiological Tests

Pupil dilation, skin moisture, heart rate, voice stress, and brain wave analysis are just some of the fascinating, even exotic, tests based on physiological reactions. Sometimes referred to as "autonomic nervous system measures," these tests have been entered into the list of almost desperate efforts to better understand consumers' attitudes toward, understanding of, and reactions to the advertising messages turned out by copywriters.

Although widely different, such physiological tests have one element in common. All of them measure involuntary response. They depend on not what respondents say (so often contradictory to the facts) but on how respondents react involuntarily to various stimuli.

One of these testing devices, the psychogalvanometer, has been around for some time. Operating on somewhat the same principle as the well-publicized "lie detector," the psychogalvanometer measures sweat gland activity of persons reading advertisements under controlled conditions.

Another more recent testing procedure measures brain wave activity. This testing is rooted in the science of psychobiology, the study of the brain and behavior. The researcher conducts a brain wave test in which the computer analyzes the extent to which the brain registers a piece of information. Proponents of this testing method have declared that they can tell which half of a subject's brain is reacting more strongly to a given stimulus. For example, the assertion is made that if "left-brain" activity dominates, the subject is reacting to words or logical reasoning, while "right-brain" activity indicates a subjective, emotional reaction.

After initial enthusiasm for brain wave testing, skeptics now say that there has been an oversimplification of the left-brain/right-brain theory and that brain wave testing for advertising shows promise, but much more study is needed to utilize this effectively. There was too much initial excitement for what has turned out to be a complicated type of research.

One of the initial problems was the difficulty in determining whether a brain reaction indicated a positive or negative impression on the subject's part. Now, most brain researchers believe they can separate positive from negative responses. This, however, is only one small step in the total process of utilizing brain wave activity for advertising research purposes.

Still another testing procedure is based on voice pitch changes. Judgments utilizing this method assess the degree of feeling behind a respondent's verbal expression of his or her attitude.

Pupil dilation observation, once considered a viable research technique, has now fallen into disuse. Changes in pupil dilation as subjects looked at advertising were supposed to indicate response to words and illustrations. Contraction of the pupil was interpreted as a negative response; dilation was considered a positive or favorable response.

Eyes are observed in another testing procedure, eye camera testing. This technique, around for many years, has been utilized more than the other techniques described. It is explained in more detail in the following section.

At the time of the writing of this book, another physiological test was being developed. This proposal, not yet tested by an advertiser, requires the wiring of a consumer's brain to a computer to get a readout on what the consumer thinks of a television commercial.

Eye Camera Tests

In these tests, a film record of the path of the eye over an advertisement is made by the eye camera. The eye camera indicates not only eye direction but also how long a reader's glance remains on any one section of the advertisement. Although the eye camera is probably more suited to long-range advertisements, it can be useful in the latter activity.

It can, for example, indicate the relative pulling power of the various advertisement elements. It can identify whether the subject is merely a headline reader or whether he also reads body copy. Also, the eye camera may reveal the extent of reading, although under the test conditions necessary for an eye camera test the subject is rather far away from home reading conditions.

Undoubtedly the eye camera can reveal the mechanics of eye flow. The greatest use for the eye camera is in determining the correct mechanical structure of the advertisement. It tells nothing of what the subject thinks about the advertisement or how he might react to it. It simply indicates how to arrange the advertising elements for the easiest reading.

In this sense, the eye camera text may be considered even more useful as a layout-testing device than as a means for testing copy. It can be argued, however, that interest in copy can be indicated by the length of time the eye rests upon it. As a counterargument, it may be that the subject had to spend more time on a particular section because it was so difficult to understand.

Motivational Research

Researchers know that the answer they can obtain from a respondent is often not the true answer to the question that was asked. Sometimes, the true answer is more complex than a set of questions can reveal. In some cases, the respondent masks what he or she truly thinks or feels. And sometimes the true answer is hidden in the subconscious, even the respondent is now aware of it. An advertising researcher, therefore, in probing for reactions about a product or campaign, may, if using ordinary research techniques, obtain a set of answers that will not reveal the true feelings of the respondents.

To dig under the surface, advertising may use a variety of techniques that developed out of what has been called motivational research. This form of investigation draws heavily upon psychology, a study of the processes and motivations underlying thinking, learning, and actions; and sociology, the study of mass behavior.

MR, as it is sometimes called by advertising people, has been used before or after campaigns have been run; thus it fits into both prepublication and postpublication copy research. Since its findings are used to establish a rationale for the whole marketing process, it should not merely be thought of as a copy research tool.

Motivational research practitioners usually proceed on the assumption that they do not know what their investigation may uncover, since irrational behavior, drives,

impulses, fears, and desires may cause people to act as they do toward the product or situation being studied. Out of a study may come reasons respondents could tell the ordinary researcher but probably will not.

Although there are many ways to obtain information, a good portion of motivational research depends upon depth interviewing and projective approaches.

Depth interviews

Depth interviews are not the exclusive province of motivational researchers; all types of researchers have conducted depth interviews for years.

Such interviews may last one or two hours, during which time questions are asked that seem, and often are, quite indirect but which actually center around the problems being investigated. Unsuspected motivations are often unearthed through these interviews.

Projective approaches

Most strongly identified with motivational research are projective approaches. These frequently use the following techniques:

- *Free association.* Typically, respondents are given lists of words, one at a time, and are asked to respond with the first word that comes to mind. Judgment is made on the basis of the frequency with which a word appears or how long it takes the respondent to say the words.
- *Sentence completion.* Respondents finish a series of incomplete sentences. A respondent will be guided along a certain direction but, if the test is correctly handled, will not know what data is being obtained.
- *Picture responses.* An illustration is shown to the respondent, who then interprets the illustration or tells its story.

When motivational research first appeared as a tool of advertising researchers, a sort of madness overcame portions of the advertising industry. People who had no knowledge of its meaning or techniques began to use motivational research. In many cases, ordinary consumer surveys might have obtained more information for these individuals and at considerably lower cost. Of late, however, the fever has subsided, as advertising people have become aware of the limitations of MR.

While much hitherto buried information has been obtained through motivational research, its use brings up questions among the companies, advertising agencies, and the media that employ it. For example, who is going to validate the results among the average businesspeople who pay for the research? How can these businesspeople judge the validity of the work conducted by psychologists?

Too, the businesspeople ask how they are to judge the accuracy of the techniques used when arguments persist among the motivational researchers themselves, not only about the techniques for getting the information, but also about the interpretation of the results obtained.

Regardless of the doubts and queries and the uneasiness of businesspeople suddenly wading in the esoteric terminology of the psychologist, motivational research, properly conducted, is here to stay. It will remain in some form because it helps reduce guesswork in advertising creation by giving copywriters answers to those eternal questions: "What do they *really* like or dislike?" "What do they *really* want?" "What do they *really* think?"

The absorption of creative advertising people with these questions is illustrated by the use of such techniques as psychogalvanometer testing and hypnosis during the past few years.

More Publication Pretest Techniques

The following methods are classed as pretests in the sense that they give advertisers reactions of respondents to advertisements that have been prepared for viewing but have not yet appeared in the whole publication run of newspapers or magazines.

This "preview" reaction saves the advertiser the cost of running ineffective advertisements by trying out new approaches in a limited way. As you will see, however, such testing can, in itself, be expensive. The three methods to be discussed briefly here are folio testing, dummy publications, and tip-ins.

Folio Testing

"Folio" here is an abbreviation for portfolio, or a folder of advertisements shown to a cross section of respondents, usually in their homes. A number of methods may be followed in this kind of testing. Advertisements may be shown and evaluated individually or the respondent may look over all of the advertisements before questions are asked.

Advertisements are either scored against one another or against averages. From this, the advertisements are positioned as higher or lower in performance according to each standard of measurement covered by the questionnaire. No more than eight advertisements are usually shown in one folio interview.

Dummy Publications

The "dummy" publication is a magazine or newspaper that has been prepared especially for test purposes. It contains editorial material and possibly 15 to 20 advertisements. Copies of the publication are given to a cross section of people who are directed to read the publication in a normal fashion.

An interviewer, they are informed, will visit them to question them about what they have read. The questions reveal advertising recall, advertising impact, and a possible increased interest in buying the products advertised. Although this is an expensive testing method, it has been useful in reproducing posttest scores using the same questions asked of those respondents who have read the dummy publications.

Tip-ins

A "tip-in" is a page that is glued to the gutter of a real magazine in such a way that a reader cannot tell it from the regular pages. In newspapers, an insert page may be used. On the page will be a pretest advertisement and another advertisement. The tip-in will be inserted in a specified number of copies of a publication—magazine or newspaper—before the publication's release date. These copies are then distributed to enough people to furnish the desired sample size.

Later, the persons who have read the publication with the tip-in page are questioned in a manner similar to that used for the dummy publications previously described. One possible advantage of the tip-in method over dummy publication testing is that the reading situation is more natural because a real publication is used. This may be offset somewhat by the fact that the tip-in copies are planted with readers instead of being bought as usual at newsstands or by subscription.

After-Publication Research through Readership Studies

The advertisement has been published. No advertiser can help wanting to know certain things about the advertisement. How many persons read it? How thoroughly did they read? How much advertiser and product identification was created? How well do the readers remember the advertisement? What features of the advertisement obtained the best readership? All of these questions and more are answered to a degree of readership studies undertaken after publication of the advertisement.

Arguments have been raised about readership techniques from the time they were first used. You may be sure of one thing, however. You will always have some form of readership study. Like them or not, you will need to know the various methods, and you should determine which one you believe in most firmly. You should learn readership terminology and the mechanical procedures for detecting misleading readership research.

The readership report, like radio and TV ratings, has become an obsession in some circles. The magic percentage figures of readership studies are hypnotic. They lull the advertiser into satisfaction with his advertising, or they goad him into anger. With many advertisers, a high percentage of readership is the final test of an advertisement's success. "The readership reports say we're on the right track," says the person who produced the advertisement. The advertiser leans back, satisfied.

Yet, there are so many variables to consider in readership reports that you would be wise never to accept a readership report at face value. Look behind the figures. Don't let the mesmerizing effect of good readership keep you from setting off on new copy trails. An evil of the reports is that they encourage status quo advertising. "We're going along fine," cries a cautious executive. "The readership reports are good. Why endanger our success with that new technique?" The hesitancy is understandable.

Yet, new ideas are the life of advertising. New ideas are responsible for increased sales and higher manufacturing output. If you rely on readership reports, you will find a good formula, and you will never leave it. Some advertisers have done well under that system. Most advertising, however, has been flexible. Most advertisers have been willing to try for the greater reward and have been willing to experiment.

Many good advertising ideas would have been lost had satisfied executives refused to experiment. Yet such refusals are frequent when readership figures for present campaigns are good. A gamble must be taken to desert the high-readership campaign for the bold, new idea.

Assume, as you read now about readership study techniques, that there is misinformation in the best of them and some good in most of them. What you find—good or bad—will depend upon your capacity for objective analysis.

Testing by Recognition

"What do you usually read?" "What advertisements did you see in yesterday's paper?" This type of recall questioning was used for years to determine advertisement reading. In this way, opinions but not actual behavior were obtained. As mentioned before, you will find a big area between what people say they do and what they actually do.

Recognition testing (which is based on presenting published material to find out what has actually been read) ignores opinion. Actual reading behavior is measured.

In magazine readership studies, Roper Starch Worldwide, Inc. is well known among research organizations using recognition testing. A quick glance at the technique used in a Starch study will show you how newspaper and magazine studies are conducted. Some of the essential differences in analyzing readership of the two media will be uncovered.

Advertisement Readership Service: Roper Starch Worldwide, Inc.

In the Roper Starch Worldwide, Inc. methodology, interviewers check respondents on their reading of advertisements one-half page or larger in a number of national publications. The responses of participants are then evaluated using a three part scale:

1. *Noted*—The percentage of issue readers who remember having previously seen the advertisements in the study issue.
2. *Associated*—The percentage of issue readers who not only noted the advertisement but also saw or read some part of it that clearly indicated the brand or advertiser.
3. *Read Some*—The percentage of issue readers who read any part of the advertisement's copy.
4. *Read Most*—The percentage of issue readers who read one-half or more of the written material in the advertisement.

In addition to determining the percentage of reading for advertisements, the Starch service also provides cost ratios of the advertisements and ranks them in terms of dollars spent to obtain readers. These figures are refined to the point that the studies tell the advertiser just how much it costs merely to get the advertisement seen, or seen and associated, or read most. You might get a high cost for the "seen" classification, but your copy may be read so well that a high percentage of those who read the advertisement read most of the copy. Your cost ratio for Read Most would then be low.

The real value of recognition studies is in cumulative studies. It would be unwise to let one study entirely influence an important decision. However, you can compare that one study with other studies.

Cumulative figures can show you whether your copy was "on" or "off." The principal strength of readership studies is in the long-trend aspect. As study piles on study, you see certain appeals pulling consistently. Certain ideas pull every time; others fail consistently. The studies attempt to explain why this is the case.

Readex Reader Interest Studies

Readex, an independent research firm, has been designing and implementing readership studies in print communications, with a specialization in business publications, since 1947. In one recent year, the firm conducted 225 studies for 107 different publications. It measures "interest" in all editorial and advertising items presented in each case.

"Interest" in advertising is considered by Readex to be a fundamental element of the selling process. The firm says that to sell a product or service, a prospective customer must first be made aware of the opportunity and then sufficient interest must be developed to motivate the prospect toward a sale.

When measurement is made of "Reader Interest" in all advertisements and editorial items, one score—the percentage of all respondents indicating interest—is reported for each. Advertisement scores are ranked and grouped by product category.

An additional service is "Reader Interest Plus," which measures both "Reader Interest" and "Remember Seeing" for all advertisements one-half page and larger and records "Reader Interest" in all editorial items. Advertisement scores are reported by product category.

Readex surveys go anywhere the mail goes, thus including hard-to-reach readers. Results are said to be geographically representative. Because readers complete the surveys at their convenience, Readex samples reflect most personal backgrounds.

A duplicate copy of the issue is sent to a random selection of the publication's primary domestic circulation. Respondents are asked to go through the issue from cover to cover and mark with a red pencil all items they "found of interest." Complete surveys are returned to Readex, with the results usually reported on a base of 100.

Methodology. Readex readership reports are developed by mailing duplicate copies of the study issue along with copyrighted instructions to a representative sample of regular readers.

Study kits are timed to arrive approximately midway between regular issues. The marked magazines are then returned to Readex by business reply mail. Reports are based on approximately 100 responses, and most are identified by name, address, title, and industry.

Results are usually available three to four weeks after the study closes.

Advantages of the Readex Methodology.

1. Mail surveys offer a cost-effective means of gathering data, allowing larger and more statistically sound samples.
2. Surveys go wherever the mail goes, thus reaching those respondents missed by personal or telephone interviews.
3. Respondents complete the surveys at their convenience; no appointments or second calls are needed.
4. There is no interviewer bias in the results.

Defects of Recognition Testing

Poor memory, dishonesty, and false pride, either in combination or singly, reduce the believability. Magazine researchers sometimes attempt to measure the effect of these three factors by setting up a "confusion control." Thus, they ask people to point out advertisements they have read in a certain magazine. The advertisements have not yet appeared in any publication but have been so cleverly inserted in the test issue that the respondents think they are already-run advertisements.

The researcher finds out how much the reading of such advertisements totals and makes a statistical allowance for this confusion factor in the final figures.

So many people become honestly confused in readership tests that an allowance must be made for this "honest" confusion. Marlboro advertisements, for example, have a strong family resemblance. It is easy to think that you have seen a specific Marlboro advertisement when actually you are remembering not that advertisement but the impression created by the series. Other persons, ashamed to admit they read certain items, skip by them when being interviewed. Thus, the accuracy of the readership percentage is reduced.

Not all reading is reported. Respondents may say "No, I didn't read that advertisement." In turn, the interviewer may accept the negative answer instead of making certain that the respondent has not actually read the advertisement. Much reading is not declared by the respondent. If respondents fail to tell you what they have read, you are helpless.

There is no way to correct for this factor or to validate your findings. The person conducting the test has nothing from which to work from. As one researcher has ruefully said, "If certain product advertising gets no more readers

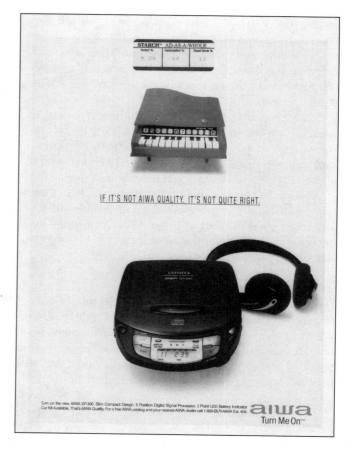

IF IT'S NOT AIWA QUALITY, IT'S NOT QUITE RIGHT.

Figure 22–6. Magazine page showing Starch readership scores. Notice how closely the Associated score is to the Noted score, a good sign because it means that almost everyone who saw the advertisement saw or read something relating to the brand or advertiser. *Courtesy of Roper Starch Worldwide Inc.*

than the surveys sometimes report, the products would have to be pulled off the market."

Recognition testing measures memory or observation; it does not indicate sales or conviction power. This is probably the strongest objection to readership studies as a whole. Proponents of recognition studies, such as Daniel Starch, have attempted to show that there is a relationship between high readership and high sales.

In *Factors in Readership Measurements*, Starch has said, "In general, the more readers an advertisement attracts and the more completely it is read, the more sales are produced by that advertisement—except that some types of copy treatment actually repel buyers. The more reading there is of such advertisements, the less buying there is."

Opponents point to many advertisements that obtained low readership but pulled big coupon returns—and vice versa. "You can't sell 'em if they don't see your advertisement" is the usual retort. The answer to that is, of course, that a thousand persons may see your advertisement and yet no one will buy the product.

Many times, too, short copy will rate higher in Starch's Read-Most figures than will long copy. Yet the lower-rated

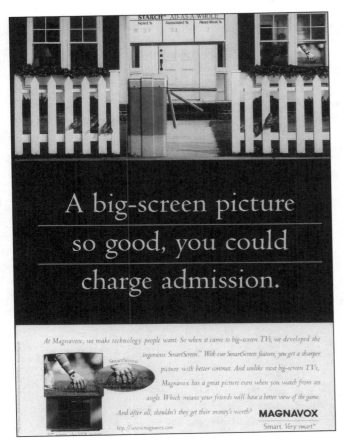

Figure 22–7. Magazine page showing Starch readership scores. The three important elements of a researched advertisement are shown at the top with a rating for each. *Courtesy of Roper Starch Worldwide Inc.*

and readership are the primary purposes of an advertisement, recognition tests are usually a cost-efficient research solution. Even hard-boiled mail-order people, the kind demanding "direct results," use a form of advertising that they didn't try generally until readership studies proved it effective: the editorial technique. Yet mail-order people scoff almost in unison at readership studies. "Sales, not readership" is their motto.

As already mentioned, the recognition study measures actual reading behavior—a more reliable measurement than that obtained through opinion or what the respondents say they have read.

The method is useful for comparing the readership of different campaign advertisements as well as that of competitors' advertisements. Unlike mail-order advertising, newspaper or magazine advertising may run a long time before sales results show that advertisements are not being read.

A readership survey gives the advertiser a reasonably quick and accurate method of checking advertising effectiveness. Poor format, for example, might discourage readership. One advertiser provides backing for this point. Readership was poor on an advertisement he felt certain contained effective copy. When he examined the advertisement critically, he discovered the trouble—the format was dull, conventional, and lifeless. Using the same copy but giving it a new dress, he tried again. This time, he inserted several lively illustrations instead of one drab one. Copy was broken into small doses. Captions were plentiful. The advertisement was a success.

A warning should be made here. When comparing readership results—from a Starch report, for example— you should compare products in the same group. Your most valid comparison in readership is made with your competitor's advertising. Comparing your leadership with that of a noncompetitor is meaningless.

Recognition Testing: Summing Up

Results from recognition studies have pointed the way to many techniques now used by copywriters. Recipes in food copy, for example, were shown from the first readership study to assure good attention from readers. Editorial techniques, shown by readership studies to get high readership, have been used more and more. Questions on layout and position have been settled through recognition studies. Such fundamental questions as "Will people read long copy?" and "Does small type stop reading?" have been answered by recognition studies. Although these studies have provided many answers, numerous questions are still being settled. As recognition studies pile up, a mass of evidence is becoming available. Admittedly the conclusions are averages; they cannot be projected to every individual case. Still, they point the way. The long-range value of the studies is obvious.

Consider vitamins, for instance. For years, advertisement copy that could squeeze vitamins in somewhere almost automatically had good readership. Then, through recognition studies, it was noticed that vitamins were not

long-copy advertisement will often far outsell the other because it "hooks" the readers it sells.

In a sense, high readership and sales might be in opposite corners of the ring. You may have devised your advertisement for high readership. Tricky, unusual features may get you your high figures, but you may have worked so hard for attention that you crowded out a powerful selling message. You may be full of pride when you see the Starch reports, but your sales manager may feel a different emotion when looking over falling sales.

The real readership of your sales story by people who may subsequently buy—not general, casual readership. You should ask, "How many prospects read our message?" A diamond advertisement, for instance, might get high readership among older readers sighing for romance. The diamond salesperson will trade a dozen older readers, however, for one young bride-to-be; she represents prospect readership.

Some Defects, Yes, But Recognition Testing Still Has Its Pluses

Regardless of weak spots, recognition testing can yield adequate measures of attention. Where gaining attention

SUMMARY REPORT

Sports Illustrated
Men Readers
Total of 41 1/2 Page or Larger Ads

ADVERTISER	RANK BY ASSOC.	INDEX			RATIOS			ADNORM INDEX		
		Noted	Read Some	Read Most	Assoc./ Noted	Read Some/ Noted	Read Most/ Noted	Noted	Assoc.	Read Most
Camera/Photo										
CANON/FIRST IN SPORTS (ADVERTORIAL)	133	156	180	333	100	98	63	112+	123+	211+
Cigarettes/Tobacco										
MARLBORO CIGARETTES	150	141	131	383	81	64	64	°°	°°	°°
MARLBORO CIGARETTES	113	124	°°	°°	94	°°	°°	°°	°°	°°
MARLBORO CIGARETTES/ UNLIMITED SWEEPSTAKES	119	127	123	133	91	75	28	°°	°°	°°
MARLBORO CIGARETTES/ UNLIMITED SWEEPSTAKES	71	80	°°	°°	97	°°	°°	°°	°°	°°
MARLBORO CIGARETTES	150	146	131-	383-	83	64	64	++	++	°°
MARLBORO CIGARETTES/ UNLIMITED SWEEPSTAKES SUMMARY	119	132	129	133	95	79	28	++	++	++
Elec. Entertainment Equip.										
AIWA COMPACT PLAYER	81	83	94	100	87	85	31	76	76	67
MAGNAVOX TELEVISIONS/ BIG SCREEN	77	76	77	58	84	73	19	°°	°°	°°
MAGNAVOX TELEVISIONS/ BIG SCREEN SUMMARY	77	76	77	58	84	73	19	69+	62+	47+
Elec. Entertainment Suppl.										
DIRECTV SATELLITE TELEVISION SYSTEM	100	95	114	125	81	83	31	100+	91+	107+
Food Beverages										
FOLGERS COFFEE/SINGLES	81	80	63-	100-	85	56	31	++	++	°°

(°) Less than 0.5%   (-) Fewer than 50 Words   (°°) Not Applicable   (=) Fewer than 4 Words   (#) Page/Copy Varies
(++) Not Available   (+) All Ads for Size/Color Used as Base

Roper Starch Worldwide Inc.

Figure 22–8. Summary report from a Starch study. A Starch study has a number of such summary reports giving the scores for advertisers whose advertisements were "Starched" in a specific issue. Notice the ratings for the Magnavox advertisement shown in Figure 22–7 and for the AIWA advertisement in Figure 22–6. *Courtesy of Roper Starch Worldwide Inc.*

catching as many readers. The vitamin honeymoon was over, and food advertisers began to think of other appeals.

Recognition studies are usually praised by those advertisers whose advertisements get high readership. They are often called unrealistic and silly by advertisers who happen to produce low-readership advertising.

Other Recognition Tests

Measurement of separate advertisements. Respondents are shown a number of advertisements clipped from a newspaper or magazine. They select advertisements that they think they have seen published. They are then asked detailed questions about each of the advertisements. An advantage of this method is that the interviewer can thus lessen the influence of nearby editorial matter on the reading of advertisements.

Often, in recognition tests, respondents will answer that they have seen an advertisement simply because they have read the editorial matter near it. Also, since the advertisement is taken out of the usual reading sequence of the magazine, there is no chance for this factor to inflate the claimed reading. The method, of course, still has the usual disadvantages found in recognition testing.

Controlled recognition testing. A number of techniques have been worked out to correct the interview error occasioned by respondents' dishonesty or faulty memory. Some of these techniques require control groups. In a typical situation, one group has seen the advertisements, but the other has not. Reading differences are then balanced.

Another technique, the system of "confusion control" already described, uses the standard procedure of showing some advertisements that have been run and others that have not. By applying a simple formula, the researchers can weed out the unreliable interviews and come out with a close estimate of actual readership. The formula for this type of testing runs like this:

1. One hundred persons are interviewed.
2. Three persons claimed readership of an advertisement that has not yet been published.
3. Thirty-three persons indicate readership of an advertisement that has run.
4. Subtract 3 from 100 (97).
5. Subtract 3 from 33 (30).
6. Readership is 30 persons out of 97, or 30.9 percent.

This method, used in magazine and newspaper studies, has also been used by the Traffic Audit Bureau (TAB) in analyzing poster reading.

Identification Test

In a typical identification test, a person is shown an advertisement in which all identifying features have been inked or pasted out. The person is then asked to identify the advertisement by indicating what company, product, or service is being advertised. The rest of the advertisements in the newspaper or magazine have been "masked."

Whether the results from identification testing are meaningful is debatable. Some advertisers feel, however, that high identification of their advertisements gives an important clue to the success of the advertising—especially in campaign advertising, where the advertiser wants assurance that the campaign idea and format are going over.

Recall Tests

A recall test tries to determine what you remember about an advertisement. Unlike the recognition test, no advertisement is usually shown. The recall test attempts to determine the positive, lasting impressions made by an advertisement some time after it has run.

Brand consciousness is probably measured better through recall testing than through any other method. Since no advertisement is shown, respondents must pull up facts about the advertising out of their minds without help from their visual sense. This form of testing is best administered by research experts, since the posing of the questions and interpretation of results are jobs for a specialist. Three forms of recall testing dominate:

> **When you first looked through this issue, did you...**
> *(please check only one)*
> ❑   see this item, but not read any of it?
> ❑   see and <u>read some or all</u> of this item?
> ❑   see, read any, and find the item <u>interesting</u>?
>
> ❑   did not see this item

Figure 22–9. Introductory page for Readex research study. Respondents' answers to these three questions provide the figures for the detailed studies furnished to advertisers by Readex, Inc. *Courtesy of Readex, Inc.*

- Unaided recall
- Aided recall
- Triple associates

Unaided recall. This form of recall testing is used very little. It consists of asking questions that provide no starting clue on which the respondent may base his answer. Information obtained from the vague questions that must be asked yield vague results. For instance, you might be asked, "What radio commercials do you remember hearing lately?" The same question might be asked about advertisements you have seen. Without any assistance from the interviewer, you are thus forced to pull out into the light some of the hundreds of advertisement impressions jostling around in your mind. Trying to attach some meaning to the answers is a nightmare for the researcher.

On an individual basis, it is almost impossible to isolate the factors that would cause you, as the respondent, to name some particular advertisement and not some other advertisement. On a mass basis, it would take a terrific number of interviews to bring out any usable facts. Suppose, for example, you were asked, "What recent advertising copy has impressed you most?" Picture the possible answers to this question. Think of the interviews needed to develop any worthwhile facts. Then think of the countless variables that might have brought the answers. For practical copy testing, you may forget the unaided recall.

Aided recall. Advertisers spend millions to create brand consciousness. This "burning" of the brand on the consumer is one of advertising's most important jobs. "How well is our advertising putting our brand across?" is a question of quivering interest. One purpose of aided recall is to indicate what brand a consumer thinks of when a certain type of product is mentioned, such as: toothpaste—Pepsodent; tires—Goodyear; and canned soup—Campbell's.

Perhaps you feel that testing brand consciousness is quite apart from copy testing. In a sense, your feeling is justified, since unlike readership tests and checklists, such testing doesn't delve deeply into the copy. Lack of brand recognition may, however, indicate that little association is being created between a type of product and a certain brand. Poor copy may be one of the reasons for lack of

Page 290 — Advertising Copywriting

identification. Other reasons might be faults in the position of advertisements, illustrations, media, timing, and campaign continuity.

What is the principal importance of the aided recall test? It indicates at least the beginning of an association between the brand and a product. Scientific illustrating, expert copy, and page advertisements are useless if such association isn't made.

If, when you want a blanket or chewing gum, you don't think of brands to fill your requirements, such as North Star or Wrigley's Spearmint, then the copywriter, artists, and other advertisement creators have wasted their time. If they have succeeded, the recall test will indicate not only the success of your advertising but also the relative failure of your competitors in obtaining brand consciousness.

The aided recall using a question, "Can you name a brand of shaving cream you have seen or heard advertised recently?" is virtually useless for single advertisements but can be useful for measuring campaign impact. From the answers, you learn whether the campaign is moving forward or is failing to impress consumers.

Impact testing. One of the more interesting forms of testing is impact testing, in which respondents "play back" for interviewers what they remember of advertising they have seen in magazines read in a recent period.

While a full impact report contains measures of recall, it also contains measures of idea communication, persuasion, and ad reaction. Each measure is important to the full appraisal of communication effectiveness. Recall is only one element of impact testing.

Gallup & Robinson, a well-known advertising research organization, has led the field in impact testing. The company has some of the biggest names in American advertising as clients.

These clients, who pay substantial fees for impact testing of each product they advertise, are informed by Gallup & Robinson what has been good and what has been bad about their advertising as revealed in each impact testing procedure that has been carried out. This information is given to clients on a regular basis in "clinics" that are usually conducted by Gallup & Robinson in the client's offices.

The test itself consists of an interview that usually lasts 25 minutes. Persons are approved as respondents after first proving that they have actually read the magazine being used for test purposes. They are then shown names of all products that have been advertised in 15 full-page or double-page advertisements in the test issue.

Respondents are then asked to tell what they remember of the advertisements that they think they remember seeing in the magazine issue. When they tell what they remember, the respondents are, in research parlance, "playing back" the advertiser's message. What the advertiser hopes will appear in the playback are:

- Sales points or arguments
- The advertiser's principal message
- Reasons for buying
- What ideas were obtained
- What went through respondents' minds as they read

It is obvious from a glance at these points that impact testing goes considerably beyond recognition testing in that its objective is to measure the effect of exposure to advertising rather than to determine mere reading of the copy message. Idea registration (called Proved Name Registration [PNR]) and buying urge may often be determined from impact testing.

Other measures that are typical are advertisement liking (whether or not people liked the advertisement) and brand rating (the influence that the advertisement had on their overall impression of the brand).

While the aims of impact testing, like those of motivational research, are to dig deeper than the surface to determine what to put into advertising or what makes advertising work, the method has its difficulties. Expense of such research is one factor, since costs of the method limit its use rather generally to the larger advertisers with big-budget campaigns. This limitation is unfortunate, because many smaller advertisers are thus frozen out, and as is very often the case, they are the ones who could profit most from using impact testing.

Another criticism, often expressed by researchers, is that the method is too difficult. The procedure is "understimulating," which means that the clues given for recall are so weak that an advertising impression has to be massive before it can be recalled.

Those who criticize impact testing in this manner, on the other hand, often call the recognition method, as used by Starch, "overstimulating." This means that exposure to advertisements during interviews is often more intense and longer than during normal reading of the magazine. Although there is some validity in the charge that the impact method is difficult, the fact remains that a great amount of copy guidance is obtained from impact interviews. Advertisers who employ impact research use it for long periods and seem satisfied.

Another Gallup & Robinson print-testing service is Rapid Ad Measurement. An offshoot of the magazine impact program, RAM, as it is called, permits quick reporting of results on advertisements that are tipped into stripped-down copies of *People* or *Time*.

In addition to speed, major advantages of the RAM approach include higher recall levels and greater number of verbatim responses for qualitative analysis. Other than for a reduced number of advertising cues, RAM interviews are identical to those used for magazine impact testing.

In addition to magazine print testing, Gallup & Robinson furnishes test results for radio, television, and newspapers.

Speaking of aided recall testing in general, it must be conceded that a single advertisement has so little chance to catch attention and sink the brand harpoon into the reader that you might well think of aided recall as a tool used mostly for campaign testing. Yet the very success of a campaign destroys, to some extent, the chance of using aided recall testing to measure the effect of the campaign copy.

advertiser	product/service category	page
Average for 37 ads this issue		
Based on SAW		
Ranger Boats	Boats/Motors	9
Zebco (Quantum)	Rods/Reels	C4
BASS PRO SHOPS Catalog	Miscellaneous	92
Plano	Accessories	3
Humminbird Wide	Electronics	50a-d (insert)
Based on Read		
TNN OUTDOORS	Miscellaneous	63
BASS PRO SHOPS Catalog	Miscellaneous	92
Humminbird Wide	Electronics	50 a-d (insert)
Fishing Tips Ad	Miscellaneous	41
The Tackle Shop	Miscellaneous	90-91
Based on Interest Rate		
BASS PRO SHOPS Catalog	Miscellaneous	92
TNN OUTDOORS	Miscellaneous	63
Eagle	Electronics	7
Fishing Tips Ad	Miscellaneous	41
ProCraft Boats	Boats/Motors	C3

Figure 22–10. Readex report on study of advertisers in outdoor magazine. Almost all the figures shown here exceed the averages for each category. *Courtesy of Readex, Inc.*

Take RCA, for instance. If you were asked what brand of television sets you had seen advertised recently, the answer "RCA" might pop out. Actually, you may have seen more advertising by Zenith, G.E., or Sony. Over the years, however, RCA had possibly built more impact than any other single brand in your mind. Your answer, then, was impelled not by recent observation but from impressions accumulated over the years.

To use aided recall testing for current advertising of a leading product such as RCA, you would need to refer to some unusual feature that had not been used in past years, such as a slogan, illustration, or headline. This kind of testing, although a form of aided recall, has been given a more impressive title: the "triple associates test."

Triple associates test.[3] Suppose someone came up to you and asked, "What automobile advertises 'Big car quality at lowest cost'?" If, at the time, Chevrolet were so advertising, and you answered, "Chevrolet," you would have made the three-way connection sought in the triple associates test. Here are the three factors:

- Product—low price automobile
- Brand—Chevrolet
- Copy theme—luxury car quality at lowest cost

As you can see, you are given two elements: the type of product and the theme. Then, you supply the brand, thus making the third association. You might not be given the theme exactly as it is used. The question might read, "What automobile advertises that it gives the value of a luxury car at a lower cost?"

Finding the extent of the association of brand with copy theme is the principal goal of the triple associates test. The information is used for determining campaign effectiveness only. Although advertisers want to develop high identification of the copy theme, they are even more hopeful that the triple associates test will connect brand and theme.

Consumer recognition of the theme for itself is of little value. In some campaigns, actual harm has been revealed when it was discovered that consumers associated the copy themes with the wrong products. Uncovering such misinformation is another value of the triple associates test. If the advertiser discovers that a high percentage of the consumers are identifying the company's copy theme with a competitor's product, then the advertisers should scan the advertising carefully—especially if the campaign has been running for some time.

Sales increases may be due to many factors other than the effectiveness of current advertising. A rising sales curve may be the final result of good advertising that appeared a number of months ago. It may also be due to

3 The triple associates test is included here for information purposes, but this approach is not as popular as in the past.

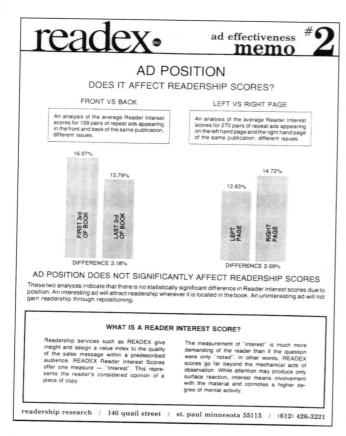

Figure 22–11. Readex research findings. Readex, Inc. memos such as this highlight findings that will guide advertisers. This memo shows graphically how the use of color and increasing the size of advertisements can result in higher readership. *Courtesy of Readex, Inc.*

improved selling methods, a change in the price levels, or a more favorable business climate.

Should your triple associates test show bad results, you might, in a view of the preceding, do some worrying about your advertising even though sales curves are going up. The upward trend might exist despite the advertising.

As in aided recall testing, you must be careful if you are the dominant advertiser. To illustrate, imagine that you are the first peanut advertiser to promote vacuum-packed peanuts. Imagine further that you are the only really big peanut advertiser. For your triple associates test, suppose you ask, "What peanuts are vacuum-packed?" How much reliability could you place in the findings when many persons could guess your brand?

To get around this difficulty, you can ask the consumers to indicate by brand which of several products are vacuum packed. In this list, you might name such products as coffee, soup, pickles, peanuts, and shoestring potatoes. If the respondents included peanuts among the several products that are vacuum packed, you would know that your advertising of the feature was making an impression. Similar testing conducted at regular intervals should tell you whether your campaign theme and brand recognition were becoming stronger or weaker.

To sum up, think of the following in connection with the triple associates test: (1) It is an excellent way to deter-

mine brand and theme association in campaign advertising; (2) Through this test, you can often obtain a more reliable indication of the success of your advertising than you will get from rising sales.

Moreover, many times, you will find a strong correlation between sales and high brand and theme awareness and vice versa.

On the negative side, don't forget that, as in so many tests of copy, the results don't necessarily measure conviction or selling power. You can establish superb recognition of theme and brand, but the consumers may buy your competitor's product. It's often easier to capture attention than conviction—especially if you depend on "irritating" consumers into becoming aware of you. In such cases, the triple associates test results may look good despite what consumers actually think of your product and your advertising.

Tachistoscope Testing[4]

The section on impact testing mentioned that critics have called the Starch technique "overstimulating" and the impact method "understimulating." Tachistoscope testing of advertising was begun because its originators believed neither recognition nor impact testing provided measurements sensitive enough to produce statistically significant differences among most printed advertisements.

A long-used testing device, the tachistoscope is a slide projector hooked to an electric timer. In the test situation, advertisements on slides are flashed rapidly before respondents, who then play back what they have seen.

Backers of the method assert that respondents will be stimulated enough to remember whether they have seen the advertisements and to recall certain elements about them, but they will not be overstimulated by having been given so much time to look that they "learned" the advertisement while the test was administered.

A criticism of such testing by those who favor recognition testing is that it is impossible to measure exposure to advertising and the influence of the advertising on those exposed to it at the same time. These critics add that the importance of memorability has been overstressed since it cannot be assumed that the reader who can play back the contents of an advertisement has necessarily been favorably influenced by the advertisement. Nor does failure to play the advertisement back prove that the advertisement has had no influence.

From the viewpoint of supporters of the impact method, tachistoscope testing fails to supply the interpretive data and analysis supplied by the former.

Sales Tests: Any Value for the Copywriter?

You will find sales tests mentioned in many books as a form of copy testing. It is true that the efficiency of different copy approaches is discovered in sales tests. Also, it is true that packaging, pricing, choice of media, labor conditions, income trends, salespeople, inventory controls, and other elements affect results of sales tests. The form of advertis-

---

4 Today, tachistoscope testing is used only infrequently.

ing—position, advertising size, and frequency—are tested as much as the copy itself.

Since copy is just one of the forces being examined in sales tests, it does not seem necessary for this book to delve very far into the subject. Copy has been the principal object of analysis in other copy testing procedures—and the copywriter is close to such tests.

Sales tests, on the contrary, are closer to the market research people, or the sales department. You will probably not have actual contact with such tests except to supply the original copy for the campaign. After that, you lose sight of the test, as the sales and marketing people move in.

A sales test, briefly explained, might be used if you decide to test the effect of your advertising in two markets. One of the market areas is considered a "control" area. The other is the "test" area. Three or more cities are usually found in each area. The new campaign will be used in the test section. In the control area, you will either (1) run no advertising or (2) continue to run your old campaign. Sales results in the two areas will then be compared by checking store inventories in selected stores before, during, and after the advertising is run. With the new scanner-based technologies in supermarkets, packaged-goods advertisers can track results to actual sales.

You might run a different campaign in each of the test cities. Then, the results will enable you to compare the campaigns against one another as well as against the control cities—or, through today's cable technology, different neighborhoods or even homes.

Some advertising people believe only in a sales test, because they look upon the test as operating under "actual" conditions as opposed to "artificial" conditions of other forms of copy research. Yet many factors make the sales tests extremely difficult to control. Results must be examined with great care to avoid erroneous conclusions. Some of the difficulties:

• Selection of appropriate control and test cities.
• Sales ability of salespeople in the different areas. Or salespeople in the test cities and good salespeople in the control cities might throw the whole test off, since the new campaign might thus show poor sales despite effective advertising.
• Dealer reaction. Unless dealers cooperate equally in all the test areas, sales variations will occur quite apart from the advertising.
• Competitive advertising and sales efforts may vary from city to city during the test period.
• Media differences are hard to control. Some newspapers and radio stations are much more aggressive than others in their merchandising promotions. They do a vigorous job of backing up the advertisers. Also, they may vary greatly in the amount of reader or listening interest they command.
• Unusual weather conditions during the test may affect sales results. A paralyzing snowstorm in one of the cities might affect its sales record negatively.

Think of the factors named. When you realize that there are many other variables and that, in addition, a sales test is expensive and time-consuming, you can see why, though it represents an important factor in research, it will not normally be a frequent part of your copywriting routines.

Surveys as a Source of Copy Claims

Surveys are among the favorite tools of marketers who wish to substantiate copy claims. "Let's do some research," is an often-heard preliminary to running a survey. It is hoped that the survey findings will supply support for sought-after claims.

Such surveys, based on an adequate and representative sample, are a legitimate means of furnishing material for a copywriter to use. While the copywriter's judgment and experience are respected, it is comforting to have the additional backing of survey research.

Unfortunately, too many surveys sponsored by advertisers are biased and do not, in other ways, meet the standards of good research. Most often the weakness is in the nature of the sample, and sometimes it is due to the interpretation of the findings. In the latter instance, the advertiser may conveniently pick out those facts that tie in with campaign objectives and ignore those that do not, or the advertiser may deliberately misrepresent or misinterpret the findings.

Comparative advertising often gives birth to such questionable surveys. An example is furnished in the case of a well-known manufacturer of microwave ovens. This company based comparative advertising claims on a survey conducted among its own authorized service agencies. The FTC, in an order against the advertiser, said that the limitations of the survey should have been made clear in the copy. This copy created an impression that the survey embraced *all* service technicians, not just the ones working for the company sponsoring the research.

What lesson is there for you in this situation? Simply that if you are furnished with such survey material, you should study it. If it has shortcomings, they should not be overlooked in your advertisement. A legitimate advertiser should welcome such intelligent and ethical judgment, which could well save the embarrassment of a legal judgment or FTC order.

There is no reason that you as a copywriter should accept such survey results unquestioningly even if they *are* supplied by the client. This is especially true in these days when the courts are holding agencies liable, along with the clients, for the truth of their advertising.

Copywriters and Researchers: An Uneasy Alliance

One of the factors in the frequent lack of harmony between researchers and copywriters is that the former live in a world of numbers and statistics. When they hand page after page of statistics to copywriters, the latter experience a profound unwillingness to plow their way through the figures in an attempt to unearth usable copy points, ideas, or phrases.

Such reluctance forms the basis of the possible resistance of creative departments to copy testing. Still, the copy people can be won over if the researchers try to get on the creative plane and work harder to help writers in understanding and applying research findings.

Some creative types think of copy testing as a crutch that encourages laziness on the part of copywriters who tend to rely so much on the researchers that the latter begin to control or unduly influence the creative process.

Researchers are trying to break down the gap between research and creative. They want to be viewed as helpers, not adversaries. Thus, we find such developments as VALS (Values and Lifestyles Systems), which originated at Stanford Research Institute. The program stresses helping advertisers apply information about consumers' habits and tastes to evolve more accurate advertising strategies.

Behind the research is an effort to find the "why" of purchases and to explain it in a form readily usable by creative people. Thus, a copyperson may know before the copy is written just what engages consumers in the buying process.

Although some creative people are opposed to being guided by copy testing, the trend in recent times has been toward more copy testing and more use of it, if for no other reason than that advertisers think it sensible for some form of testing to precede advertising expenditures.

Keep an Open Mind

Copy research is valuable even if it does nothing but reduce the margin of error in the guesses of advertising people. It can unkink the thumb in the famous "rule of thumb" measurement you've heard so much about. When you lose touch with the market and the consumer, copy testing may bring you back. If you were to be asked the principal values of copy testing, you might answer:

- To determine *before* publication what copy style, copy approach, or copy appeals are likely to obtain the greatest readership and/or sales conviction.
- To determine *after* publication the quantitative and qualitative aspects of readership and thus to indicate what copy techniques should be continued, discontinued, or modified for future use.
- To obtain through cumulative findings a body of information about copy that advertisers may use to produce advertising of the greatest efficiency—advertising that will cost the advertiser less in time, effort, and money because it avoids the mistakes of the past.

Do Not Let Testing Replace Good Sense.

Consider the Flesch formula, for example. Your copy will, according to the readability formula, receive an equally high rating if the copy is printed backwards or if the sentences are jumbled. Since the word count and personal references are the same in either case, the readability score will be the same. Good sense is the final determinant of copy effectiveness in this case—as it is in every copy testing method.

PACT Principles

In 1982, twenty-one major U.S. Agencies established copy-testing principles under a designation of PACT (Positioning Advertising Copy Testing). Nine principles were designated

as a foundation for the use of advertising research.

In the following, you will find the nine principles listed, with a brief explanation of each (the principles are provided in full by the contributing advertising agencies). The principles listed here will provide a useful guide in performing and understanding meaningful research.

- Principle I. A good copy testing system provides measurements that are relevant to the objectives of the advertising.
- Principle II. A good copy testing system is one that requires agreement about how the results will be used in advance of each specific test.
- Principle III. A good copy testing system provides multiple measurements. Single measurements are generally inadequate to assess the performance of an advertisement.
- Principle IV. A good copy testing system is based on a model of human response to communications—the reception of a stimulus, the comprehension of the stimulus, and the response to the stimulus.
- Principle V. A good copy testing system allows for consideration of whether the advertising stimulus should be exposed more than once.
- Principle VI. A good copy testing system recognizes that the more finished a piece of copy is, the more soundly it can be evaluated. Alternative executions are required and should be tested in the same degree of finish.
- Principle VII. A good copy testing system provides controls to avoid the biasing effects of exposure context.
- Principle VIII. A good copy testing system is one that takes into account basic considerations of sample definition.
- Principle IX. A good copy testing system is one that can demonstrate reliability and validity.

Addendum

Which—Noxzema or Pond's®—(see page 276) was more effective?

Ad A. It had more than twice the stopping power of Ad B. The product benefit is dramatically conveyed by the headline and illustration. Also, the copy reinforces the benefit and does so in simple, easy-to-read language. A convincing case history approach completes the powerful benefit story. Although Ad B has news value, its headline is less direct and the benefit is somewhat buried in the copy and "busy" layout.

Which—Nuprin or Tylenol—(see page 279) was more effective?

Ad A. It had almost twice the stopping power of Ad B. There is a strong linkage in this advertisement between the bold, attention-getting headline and the illustration and copy. It combines a clean, uncluttered layout with a concise to-the-point message. In Ad B, the layout shows a somewhat uninviting picture of the stomach instead of focusing on the product, and the benefit is buried in long, difficult-looking copy. Identification is subdued in contrast to Ad A.

CHAPTER 23

Legal and Ethical Aspects
You'd Better Know Them

As the new legal counsel to a large 4A's advertising agency, Glenn Trabert was musing to his wife about his first week on the job. "To answer your question, Dot, the toughest part of the job is saying No to highly aggressive, highly paid copywriters who take chances."

"What do you mean by 'take chances'?"

"Simply that, in order to beat out the competition, they make claims that can be inaccurate, misleading, confusing, or even dishonest. So I have to tell these jokers to cool it, or we'll be hit by the FTC, FDA, or some other government outfit. My job is to protect our clients, but you should hear some of these creative types yowl when I throw water on their dazzling, but questionable, claims."

In this litigious age, when class-action suits are in fashion and consumers are on the prowl to find fault with advertisers' claims, there is no place for copywriters whose copy is deliberately actionable.

It's Easy to Go Astray Legally

As a copywriter, you're paid to write copy that makes powerful claims. Sometimes, however, in your innocence of the law and regulations, you step over the boundary. If you stray into that shady area of untruthful or inaccurate copy, your client may end up before some government body, a situation that would prove both embarrassing for you and expensive for the client. For this reason, a study of marketing and advertising laws is called for. Continue to write strong copy but make it legal.

You may, particularly if you're writing copy for consumer products, feel you're working harder to please the lawyers than the clients. As you type, you have a haunted feeling. Just over your shoulder, you can sense stern-visaged representatives of the Federal Trade Commission, the Food and Drug Administration, the Better Business Bureau, and others whose job it is to protect the con-

sumer. In addition, your competitors may also be complaining about what you've written. Are they frowning as they read your copy? You fervently hope not, because your clients will be less than enchanted if your copy drags them into the press or the courts.

Before you worry unduly about legal trouble, however, remember that of the millions of words of copy produced each year, only a small percentage will get the advertiser or agency into any kind of legal trouble. Furthermore, if you find yourself assigned to products or services that *are* troublesome legally, you'll be given a set of appropriate legal "do's and don'ts" the first day on the job. By observing these cautions, using common sense, and being guided by your innate sense of honesty, you'll keep yourself, your client, and your agency out of trouble.

The single most important principle is to get the facts and make certain they are correct. Any attempt to write copy about a product or service without knowing in complete detail exactly what it is and does will invite legal difficulties.

It must be emphasized, though, that even telling the absolute truth is not enough. Each sentence in an advertisement, considered separately, may be literally true, and yet the entire advertisement as a whole may be misleading. This can come about because statements that ought to be made are omitted, or because the advertisement is composed or set up in such a way as to create a misleading impression. If the copy can be understood in different ways, the advertiser is not excused just because one of its meanings can be sustained as accurate.

Visuals create their own special problems for the copywriter. The visual portion of a commercial may be misleading even though the copy is truthful; or the audio may be misrepresenting the picture that appears on the screen. Product demonstrations, in particular, must be genuine, and the accompanying dialogue must be honest and accurate.

It's Silly to Use "Tricky" Copy

There is no point in being tricky when writing advertising copy. Short-term gains in sales might possibly result, but in the long run, such practice can only do harm to the advertiser. This can come about through loss of good will from disillusioned customers, even though no government agency or competitor brings a legal proceeding designed to force the discontinuance of the misleading copy.

Puffery

To this point, we have been dealing with what the law generally calls factual claims, but there is another recognized category, known as "puffery" or "puffing."[1]

American law has always recognized the difference between factual advertising claims and puffery. It requires substantiation for the former, but not the latter. Puffing is used to describe a statement that is so vague or hyperbolic that a reasonable person would take it neither literally nor seriously. As such, it is incapable of being deceptive, since buyers do not rely on advertising claims that are *obviously* exaggerated, hyperbolic, or even false.

One Federal Trial Court echoed the law's sentiment by acknowledging that advertisers "are expected to extol or even exaggerate the virtues of their products, or the advantages of buying from them." Over time, courts, regulatory agencies, and industry self-regulatory operations such as the National Advertising Division (NAD) of the Council of Better Business Bureaus and television network advertising standards departments have developed three criteria by which to distinguish puffery from factual claims.

General versus specific claims. General superiority claims constitute puffing, while claims about specific product attributes, benefits, or capabilities do not. Consequently, claims that a product is the best or better than a competitor's are puffery as long as they are not made in a context that allows them to be reasonably interpreted as specific in nature.

For example, a health insurer's claims that its plan was "Better than HMOs" and "so good, it's Blue Cross and Blue Shield" were characterized by a court as "the most innocuous kind of puffing." In other cases, a debt collection company's claim that its services were comparable to but cheaper than those provided by law firms was found to be too general to induce consumer reliance, and a "the best money can buy" claim was considered so general as to constitute puffery. Additionally, a shaving system's claim to a "major technological breakthrough" was ruled to be at worst mere puffing because, while not literally true, it was new.

Claims that are impossible to measure. Advertising claims that are not subject to measurement, quantification, verification, or other proof have routinely been treated as mere puffery. Such commonly used advertising words as "nice," "smooth," "popular," "aromatic," and "beautiful"—depending on their context—also qualify.

The three leading television networks all recognize the puffery/claim distinction. Capital Cities/ABC, for example, states that: "Objective claims are measurable and verifiable. They generally deal with performance, efficacy, sales, preference, mileage, taste, and other tangible attributes. These claims must be supported by adequate substantiation."

Its guidelines define puffery as "subjective claims which cannot be verified (e.g., "When you wear X, you'll look your best" and "Y is the most terrific game around"). If claims deal with subjective preferences that cannot be proved or disproved, they are acceptable without support "as long as the clear net impression that they are likely to make upon the viewing public is one of subjective personal preference or hyperbole."

Factual versus subjective claims. Another recognized form of puffing is when an advertiser expresses an opinion. Of course, as the ABC guidelines point out, an objective claim cannot be transformed into puffery merely by phrasing it in subjective terms. But genuine statements of opinion, such as a claim, that a movie will be a "blockbuster" and "the most want-to-see movie of the year," have been recognized as legitimate puffery. Likewise, a company's promise to build "relationships that last a lifetime," a photocopy manufacturer's claim that its product made "picture perfect copies," a seller's assurance that its car was in "excellent condition," and a claim that soap was gentle and left skin feeling "silky clean" have also been deemed puffery.

---

[1] This discussion of puffery was influenced by suggestions from Stephen R. Bergerson, of Fredrikson & Byron, P.A. Mr. Bergerson also contributed up-to-date material on copyright, right to publicity, privacy, and deceptive advertising as well as material on the FTC and the National Advertising Review Board (NARB) of which he is a member.

The FTC explicitly recognizes that, "There is a category of advertising themes, in the nature of puffing or other hyperbole, which do not amount to the type of affirmative product claims for which either the Commission or the consumer would expect documentation." That would include such well-known slogans as "Bayer Works Wonders," "It's The Real Thing," "If You Don't Have Blue Cross, You're Not Covered," "It's The Right Thing to Do," and "When You're Out of Schlitz, You're Out of Beer."

The importance of context: consumer perception. What is and is not puffing is decided on a case-by-case basis. What passes as acceptable puffery in one instance may be a factual claim in another; therefore, context is critical. Because advertising law's goal is to protect consumers from deception, the inquiry depends on what consumers believe the advertisement said.

Context includes the nature and sophistication of the advertisement's intended audience. An advertisement directed at a target audience that is sufficiently perceptive to recognize hyperbole is more likely to be considered harmless puffery than one aimed at a group of people who are less able to discern it.

The Importance of Context: An Advertisement Is the Sum of Its Parts

Advertising law has long recognized that when read together, words can mean something quite different than when read (or heard) separately.

In determining how an advertisement is interpreted by a reasonable consumer, the law views advertisements as aggregates rather than as collections of independent, isolated parts. The overall impact of an advertisement as a whole is always more determinative of its meaning than its individual words or phrases.

One court, in reviewing an FTC order, noted: "The Commission need not confine itself to the literal meaning of the words used, but may look to the overall impact of the entire commercial."

The NAD has also long recognized the importance of reviewing an advertisement in its context. In one typical decision, the NAD decided that the slogan "The Earth's Most Comfortable Shoes" was puffery because it was used within the context of an advertisement that focused on attitude and lifestyle rather than the comfort of the shoe itself.

In a 1995 decision, the NAD said: "In order to determine the communication of an advertising message, the advertisement must be viewed and assessed as a whole." A coffee manufacturer had challenged a competitor's television commercials, which said, "The coffee perking in this pot is America's best-loved coffee," arguing that it constituted a factual leading brand claim. The NAD concluded: "In the context of these nostalgic advertisements, no claim is being made about the current market position [of the advertiser]." Because the claim was made amid a juxtaposition of images from its old commercials, NAD said the claim was "not an objectively verifiable statement requiring substantiation but, rather, is simply subjective puffery."

Courts Are Becoming Less Tolerant toward Puffery as a Defense

The claim of puffery as a defense must be used with great care. An example is furnished in the judgment (for $40 million) against Jartran (*U-Haul International, Inc. v. Jartran, Inc.*, 601 F. Supp. 1140, 681 F.2d. 216 USPQ at 1078 [D. Ariz. 1984]). U-Haul, a competitor, objected to such advertising claims as:

Only Jartran can rent you trailers designed for the times.

No one can rent you a truck like Jartran can.

In finding against Jartran, the court said:

Over the spread of time, and with increased (or perceived) reluctance of courts to resolve such claims, the rule of puffery had become a privilege to lie.

In its opinion, the court held that since the claims were meant to be believed and relied upon, a reasonable prospective purchaser would take them seriously. Accordingly, they exceeded the scope of permissible puffery allowed by Section 43(a) of the Lanham Act. Section 43(a) is described later in this chapter. As is frequently the case, the agency was named as a defendant, settled out of court, and testified that they had advised Jartran against making many of the claims that were challenged.

Product claims and statements of opinion are not the only areas in which legal problems arise in advertising. Permission to use copyrighted material, trademarks, and people's names, pictures or likenesses; proper trademark usage; defamation; and idea piracy are just some of the other areas where an awareness in advance of the possible legal pitfalls may save a great deal of trouble and expense that otherwise might be encountered.

Federal Trade Commission (FTC)

The federal government agency most concerned with problems of advertising is the Federal Trade Commission. This agency, under the Federal Trade Commission Act, has broad authority to proceed against "unfair, deceptive acts or practices" in almost all kinds of commercial activity. The theory of the law is that both are unfair methods of competition. If a deceptive advertisement succeeds in its purposes, it will give the advertiser an unfair advantage over truthful competitors, but such advertising is illegal even when no competitors are hurt, because the Federal Trade Commission Act is also designed to protect consumers.

The FTC is an administrative agency of the United States that, like several others, combines the functions of legislator, prosecutor, and judge. It has a staff that looks for violations and also investigates complaints sent to it by consumers and competitors. If the FTC staff believes that a particular advertisement or campaign is in violation of the law, it needs the approval of the Commission itself (there are five commissioners) to prosecute the case. In recent years, the FTC and the courts have frequently filed charges against the advertising agency, in addition to the advertiser, when the agency knew or should have known that the advertisement was unfair or deceptive.

A formal FTC proceeding is similar to a court trial except that it tends to drag on much longer. An administrative law judge presides, FTC staff attorneys represent the Commission, and the accused parties, known as "respondents," are entitled to be represented by their lawyers. If the administrative law judge decides the case in favor of the FTC, the respondents will be required to "cease and desist" from their unlawful practices. The order can be appealed to the full five-member Commission. If affirmed there, a further review is available in a federal court of appeals and, eventually, in the United States Supreme Court.

Cease and Desist Orders

A cease and desist order may appear to be a mere slap on the wrist. Indeed, many FTC false advertising cases take so long to reach a conclusion that the challenged campaign has run its course and has been discontinued. But a violation of the FTC Act also can be punished with a civil penalty of up to $10,000 for each time the advertisement runs, so substantial sums can be involved, in addition to the expense of defending the proceeding from the beginning. Furthermore, the FTC has the authority to seek a preliminary injunction against an advertisement that is the subject of its regulatory proceedings and, in cases where the advertising has been especially effective, to require corrective advertising (discussed later in this chapter).

Advertising cases are often settled at an early stage by a consent decree agreed to between the FTC staff and the respondents. Should the advertiser later violate a consent order, it is subject to the same $10,000 penalty (or some sum up to that amount) per violation. As an example, a hearing aid manufacturer was required to pay a 2.75 million dollar fine for violating a 1976 consent degree to which it had agreed. At about the same time, the maker of STP oil additive was fined $888,000 for violating the terms of a consent decree to which it had agreed almost 30 years earlier.

Consent decrees are often accompanied by an agreement requiring the advertiser to pay civil damages. For example, in 1994, the Dannon Company agreed to pay the FTC $150,000 to settle charges that its advertising implied falsely that its frozen yogurt was low in fat, low in calories, and lower in fat than ice cream.

Other Functions of the FTC

In addition to the numerous cease and desist proceedings it is constantly bringing, the FTC also functions in several other ways. For instance, it issues Advertising Guides and Trade Regulation Rules. In addition to the Federal Trade Commission Act itself, which is phrased in general terms, the FTC administers several special statutes dealing with particular fields of commerce, including margarine, wool, fur, and textile products.

Two basic premises that the FTC stresses are especially helpful guides in the writing of advertising copy. Both deal with the importance of context, which was already discussed in the puffery section of this chapter. One premise is that deceptiveness is determined in light of the advertisement's intended audience. The other is that the advertisement's net impression, not its individual parts or liberal truthfulness, is what is important when determining whether the advertising is lawful.

Advertising Agency Liability

Many who work at advertising agencies mistakenly believe that if a government regulatory agency or competitor successfully challenges an advertisement, it's the advertiser that's liable. That's only half right, because agencies are often held liable along with the clients.

For example, in 1952, the FTC sued Colgate-Palmolive and its agency for its now infamous "sandpaper test" television product "demonstration." The advertisement was designed to show that Rapid Shave was so moist that it could allow a razor to shave sandpaper. But the agency used clear plexiglass sprinkled with sand instead of sandpaper—and it didn't disclose the mock-up. The Court rejected the agency's argument that it shouldn't be liable because it was only acting as Colgate's agent, and held that agencies could escape liability only if they (1) lack actual knowledge of the advertisement falsity or (2) had no reason to question its truthfulness.

In 1967, the FTC decided its most important in this line of cases. Sucrets and its agency were charged with deceptively claiming that its active ingredient killed germs that caused sore throats. The agency argued that since it had relied on technical information provided by the client, it shouldn't be accountable. In its decision, the FTC articulated what remains today's legal standard: If an agency either knows or has reason to know of the advertisement's deceptive nature, it is jointly and severely liable with its client. Courts usually find that agencies, given their communications expertise, had reason to know that an advertisement was deceptive.

In 1994, a federal court extended the FTC's thinking to private civil cases, holding both Wilkinson Sword and its agency jointly liable for $953,000 in damages awarded to Gillette for a deceptive advertisement claim.

The lesson of the law is clear. While agencies aren't responsible for conducting their own independent tests or becoming their client's adversary, they must exercise reasonable diligence and some independent judgment and cannot turn a blind eye to their client's proposals or demands without legal consequence.

Other Regulatory Considerations

During the 1980's, the FTC became relatively inactive, which created a regulatory vacuum, as it became unproductive to turn to the FTC with a complaint about an advertisement. Consumers and advertisers were forced to find new ways to deal with such problems. The result has been an increase in private litigation between advertisers. Also, there has been a strong trend for advertisers to turn to self-regulatory bodies for help.

Along with the foregoing, another major development has occurred—the National Association of Attorneys General has coordinated the efforts of individual state attorneys general in regulating advertising at the state level. State regulation of advertising has serious implications for national and local advertising, since each state can interpret its deceptive advertising laws differently. What one state considers perfectly legal another may challenge as unlawful.

Section 43(a) of the Lanham Act. Once limited to trademark disputes, the Lanham Act, through its Section 43(a), is now utilized heavily by advertisers to challenge competitors' advertising claims. Section 43(a) reads:

> Any person who shall use in connection with any goods or services … any false description or representation … and shall cause such goods and services to enter into (interstate) commerce … shall be liable to a civil action by any person … likely to be damaged.

Application of 43(a) has resulted in an increase in private litigation because advertisers may now sue competitors for other than product disparagement or trade libel. For example, one advertiser may enjoin another's advertising when the other makes a "false representation" about its *own* product, even if the defendant advertiser has *not* made any reference to the plaintiff or its product. Court decisions have extended the reach of Section 43(a) to sales materials and articles placed in trade publications to publicize products. Courts around the country draw upon previous decisions of the FTC in settling many 43(a) cases.

Also of increased importance in settling disputes between advertisers is the use of the National Advertising Division (NAD) of the Council of Better Business Bureaus and of the local Better Business Bureaus. The work of the NAD is described in detail later in the chapter.

Four Advertising Practices That Might Prompt Challenges

Advertising law is so pervasive that it is impossible to categorize all possible applications. There are, however, certain specific areas of difficulty that constantly recur in advertising cases. Some of those of particular interest to advertising copywriters are discussed in the following sections.

Premiums. When an article of merchandise is offered as a premium, it is essential for copywriters to learn as much as possible about the premium, just as they must learn about the product of the advertiser itself. A misdescribed premium is the responsibility of the advertiser, not of the manufacturer of the premium merchandise.

Your ad.

The lawyer.

In the hands of the wrong lawyer, your ad is an endangered species. Unlike most lawyers, Steve Bergerson doesn't instinctively go for the kill. Because in his twenty-five years as an agency AE and one of the nation's leading ad and promotion attorneys, he's learned how to keep great creative alive.

Fredrikson & Byron, P.A.

1100 International Centre • 900 Second Avenue South • Minneapolis, MN 55402
612-347-7043 • Internet: http://www.fredlaw.com

Figure 23–1. Legal advertisement. The theme here is that a sympathetic lawyer and good copywriter can work well together.

The most common problem arising out of the use of premiums is a misrepresentation of their value. Sometimes advertisers who are extremely careful when making claims about their own products are somewhat less careful in describing the premiums that they offer. If an advertisement states that a premium is worth a certain amount or has a value of a stated sum, that amount should be the price at which the premium merchandise actually is sold when offered for sale on its own.

Coupons also raise a multitude of problems under separate state laws. In order to make it practical to use coupons in national distribution, it is common to take two precautions. First, coupons should have a cash value assigned to them. This ordinarily is a nominal sum like 1/10 of a cent, but the manufacturer must be prepared to redeem the coupons in cash at that rate on demand. Second, the coupon traditionally carries what is called a "nullification clause," reading somewhat along the following lines: Void where prohibited and subject to all laws.

Sweepstakes, Contests and Lotteries. A sweepstakes is a game of chance. A contest is a game of skill. In each, the winner gets a prize. Sweepstakes and contests are lawful advertising methods. Legal difficulties arise in two principal ways. The first difficulty results when the sponsor fails to comply with the myriad of detailed requirements that all of the states impose. This includes providing all required information in the rules and advertising copy and, in some cases, registering the promotion. The second difficulty arises when the promotion constitutes an illegal lottery. This not only violates the Federal Trade Commission Act as an unfair method of competition, but it is also a criminal offense under the laws of every state and several federal agencies, including the U.S. Postal Service and the Federal Communications Commission.

A lottery exists when a payment (or other legal consideration) must be given in exchange for the chance to win a prize. All three elements—chance, consideration, and prize—must be present for the promotion to be considered a lottery.

Since there must be a prize in order for the promotion to be effective, marketers need to eliminate one of the other elements.

Chance means that the participant has no way of controlling the result. It may be understood as the opposite of skill. An essay contest in which awards are given by impartial judges for merit is not chance, but a promotion that requires listing the standings of teams in both the American and National leagues at the end of a particular month is something completely outside the control of the participant. It is guesswork, or chance, and not skill.

Consideration generally means having to give something of value in order to enter a sweepstakes. For example, buying some breakfast cereal in order to get the entry form on the back of the box constitutes consideration. It does not matter that the price of the cereal was not increased for the sweepstakes. The consumer bought that particular box of cereal when he otherwise might have purchased a different brand or no cereal at all. The familiar provision for using a free "reasonable facsimile" of the entry blank is included in order to avoid a violation of the lottery laws by eliminating the element of consideration. It is important to note that states often define consideration in terms other than money. A *prize* may lawfully be awarded by chance if there is no consideration of any kind. Conversely, if a prize is given for true skill, as distinguished from chance, then it is permissible to charge consideration to enter the contest, because one of the elements of a lottery has been eliminated.

"Good purpose," incidentally, does not excuse a lottery. Although enforcement officials rarely crack down on fundraising drawings for charities, enterprises of this sort are technically lotteries, just as if they were operated for advertising purposes or for private gain.

Testimonials and Endorsements. The law treats testimonials and endorsements just the same as other advertisements, and an advertiser cannot escape responsibility for a false or misleading product claim by putting it in the mouth of an endorser. Testimonials and endorsements, which are statements of a person's own experience or opinions, must be true and free from misleading statements. Simply because someone is willing to write a letter saying that a particular drug performed in a certain way does not mean that the claim is necessarily true, even though the author of the letter believes that it is true.

The Federal Trade Commission will take action against advertisements containing testimonials given by people who are not competent to pass judgment upon the accuracy of the statements of opinion that they are making. There is a great deal of difference between a baseball player saying that he eats a particular brand of bread and likes it, and the same baseball player saying that eating a particular brand of bread has a beneficial effect upon his health.

There is nothing wrong with an advertiser paying for the use of a testimonial, but an advertiser who pays an endorser to say something in particular must disclose that in the advertisement unless it is clear that the person is acting as a spokesperson and is not expressing his own views.

It is improper to take an endorser's words or sentences out of context. A testimonial should be given in its entirety; or if it is not, the portion that is used should not create a different impression from what the complete text would have implied if given in full.

When testimonials are used in advertising, they must be genuine. The natural tendency of any reader of an advertisement containing a testimonial or endorsement is to believe that a real person gave it. A fictitious endorsement, therefore, is an unfair trade practice.

The use of a testimonial also implies automatically that it is reasonably current. If the endorser no longer uses the product or if the product has been so changed since the date of the testimonial that the endorsement no longer fairly applies to the product that is advertised, then the testimonial should be discontinued.

A public opinion poll or market survey is the equivalent of a testimonial on a mass scale, and its design, execution, and results must be used with corresponding care. In addition, reference to a poll or survey in advertising copy will be construed as a representation that proper sample techniques were used and that the sample was of meaningful size and was representative of the advertisement's intended audience.

Warranties. A special law on warranties for consumer products went into effect in 1975. It requires a designation of whether the warranty is full or limited in some way. A full warranty must include a statement of the period of time it will remain operative. A limited warranty must set forth clearly what limitations are included.

These restrictions have teeth in them. For example, the law requires that the remedy (generally repair or replacement) must be provided to the consumer without charge and within a reasonable time after notice of a defect or malfunction. A warrantor cannot refund the purchase price as an alternative to repair or replacement unless the consumer agrees to accept a refund, or the warrantor can demonstrate that a replacement is not available and that repair is not commercially practicable.

In 1985, the FTC published its Guides for the Advertising of Warranties. (The subject of FTC Advertising Guides is taken up in the following section.) It is clear from the many pages of the Guides that any copywriter using the term "warranty," or its equivalent, must exercise special care and must be certain that the use of the term fits in with the FTC's policies.

There are so many pitfalls and complexities attached to the use of a warranty that the copywriter writing a warranty advertisement should study carefully the FTC's Guides for the Advertising of Warranties. It must be stated, however, that the FTC has the power to challenge warranty advertising that complies with the Guides but is deceptive in some manner not addressed by the Guides. Thus, while adhering to the requirements listed by the Guides will probably help a copywriter stay out of trouble, there is *still* a possibility for legal problems.

Advertising Guides

The Federal Trade Commission issues Advertising Guides, detailed statements that constitute basic policy developed by the Commission for specific industries, products, and advertising practices. The Advertising Guides are released to the public in the interest of obtaining voluntary cooperation and avoiding legal proceedings. Some of the issues covered in the Advertising Guides are discussed in the following sections.

Deceptive pricing. Claims of special savings, extra discounts, less than the usual price, and reductions from ticketed prices have been among the most troublesome problems faced by the Federal Trade Commission enforcement and Better Business Bureau officials. The Deceptive Pricing Advertising Guides go into these problems in explicit detail. Examples of both approved and disapproved types of statements are given, along with the basic principles that will satisfy Federal Trade Commission requirements.

A statement, for instance, that there is a reduction or saving from a specified retail price, or from the advertiser's usual or customary retail price, is improper if an artificial markup has been used to provide the basis for the claim of a saving. The claim is equally improper if it is based on infrequent or isolated sales or on a price that was charged some time in the past, unless, of course, these facts are stated clearly and adequately.

The saving or reduction must be from the usual and customary retail price of the article in the particular trading area where the statement is made, and the saving or reduction must be from the advertiser's usual and customary retail price charged for the article in the regular course of business.

Certain words and phrases are recognized as representations when an article is being offered for sale to the consuming public at a saving from the usual or customary retail price. Obviously, these should not be used unless the claim is true. Examples of words or phrases of this type are: "special purchase," "clearance," "marked down from stock," "exceptional purchase," "manufacturer's close-out" and "advance sale."

Preticketing with fictitiously high prices comes in for special attention in these advertising guides. No article should be preticketed with any figure that exceeds the price at which it is sold usually and customarily in the trading area where it is offered for sale. In this connection, the Federal Trade Commission points out that those who distribute preticketed price figures are chargeable with knowledge of the ordinary business facts of life concerning what happens to articles for which they furnish the preticketed prices.

The same basic principle applies to the use of the preticketed price in advertising copy. The manufacturer may be held responsible for exaggerated prices in national advertising even though it is the retailer who misuses the figures; and the retailer will not be excused merely because it was the manufacturer who first advertised the fictitious price.

The key point to remember is that the word "price" itself constitutes an implication that the figure given is the usual and customary price charged by the advertiser in the recent regular course of his business in the trading area reached by the advertisement. This rule must be the starting point for all price advertising.

"Free" guide. The FTC's "Use of Word 'Free' and Similar Representations" guide requires that all offers of "free" merchandise or services be made with special care to avoid any possibility that consumers will be misled or deceived. This includes similar promotions in which the word "free" may not be used, such as the "2-for-1 sale," "50% off with purchase of two," "1¢ sale," or "Buy 1—Get 1 Free."

The word "free" or its equivalent, such as "gift" or "bonus," indicates that the consumer is paying nothing for that article and no more than the regular price for the other. "Regular price" means the price, in the same quantity, quality, and with the same service, at which the advertiser has openly sold the product in the geographical area where the "free" offer is being made, in the most recent and regular course of business, for at least a 30-day period. In other words, the "regular price" may not be inflated in order to get back part of the cost of the "free" goods.

If there are any conditions or obligations attached to the receipt of the "free" merchandise, they must be stated clearly and conspicuously so as to leave no reasonable probability that the terms of the offer might be misunderstood. Disclosure of the terms in a footnote of an advertisement to which reference is made by an asterisk or other symbol is not considered adequate disclosure by the FTC.

In order to make certain that a "free" offer is meaningful, it should not be advertised in a given trading area for more than 6 months in any 12-month period. At least 30 days should elapse before another such offer is made in the same trading area. And no more than three such offers should be made in the same area in any 12-month period.

Tires and tubes. The Federal Trade Commission Advertising Guides for tires and tubes grew out of a long series of proceedings involving misleading terminology and various types of exaggerated product claims in this industry. One of the guides, for example, states that manufacturers should not use deceptive designations for the different grades of their products.

If the first-line tire of a particular manufacturer is designated "standard," then the same manufacturer's tires of a lower quality should not be designated as "super standard." If discontinued models or obsolete designs are offered, those facts must be stated clearly. Used products must be described adequately, so that it is clear they are not new. Terms such as "nutread" and "snow tread" do not constitute sufficient disclosure of this fact.

The unqualified use of absolute terms such as "skid-proof," "blowout-proof," and "puncture-proof" is improper unless the product really affords complete and absolute protection under any and all driving conditions.

The term "ply" is defined in technical detail. Tire advertising should contain an adequate statement of the identity of the fabric or other material used in the construction of the ply. Statements implying that tires possess a specified number of plies are not to be used unless this is the fact. The term "ply rating" is an index of tire strength and does not necessarily represent the number of cord plies in a particular tire. If a term such as "eight-ply rating" is used to describe a tire containing fewer than eight plies, then the statement must be accompanied by a conspicuous disclosure of the actual number of plies in the tire.

These technical provisions are included here as an illustration of the degree of detail into which the FTC goes on appropriate occasions. Obviously, it would be foolhardy to write copy for automobile tires without studying the Federal Trade Commission's Tire Advertising Guides carefully.

Trade Regulation Rules and Guides

Still another function of the Federal Trade Commission is the promulgation of Trade Regulation Rules and Trade Regulation Guides. The former is merely the Commission's interpretation of the law; the latter *is* the law. Typically, these are quite complex and detailed sets of regulations worked out by members of the FTC staff in conference with representatives of a broad segment of the industry affected. They put the requirements of Federal Trade Commission Act as applied to that particular industry into concrete form.

Over the years, such regulations have been initiated by the FTC for dozens of different products, industries, and practices, including ready-to-eat cereals, household furniture, consumer credit, home insulation, use of 800 numbers, and the mail-order rule, to name a few. A few others will be referred to here, largely to indicate by example the fact that it is important for copywriters to be aware that such rules exist and that they are often very exacting.

Watches. A watch either is waterproof or it is not. In order to describe it as waterproof, the case must be of such composition and construction as to be impervious to moisture through immersion for the life of the watch.

The Federal Trade Commission trade practice rules include details of a specific test that requires complete immersion for at least five minutes in water under atmospheric pressure of 15 pounds per square inch and for at least an additional five minutes in water under atmospheric pressure of at least 35 pounds per square inch without admitting any water. If a watch does not pass this test, it may not be described as waterproof, although, possibly, it may be described correctly as "water-resistant" or "water-repellent." Here, too, a specific test has been promulgated by the Federal Trade Commission.

Similarly, the terms "shockproof," "jar-proof," "magnetic," and "regulated" are defined carefully. Improper use of any of these terms will be considered a violation of the principles of the Federal Trade Commission Act.

Products made of "gold." The use of the word "gold" creates a number of problems in the industry. The unqualified word "gold," or its abbreviation, cannot be used alone unless the part of the product so described is composed throughout of gold of 24 karat fineness. The word "gold" cannot be used at all to describe an alloy of less than 10 karat fineness. When the gold is more than 10 karat but less than 24 karat, the karat fineness must be shown in immediate conjunction with the word "gold."

Terms such as "duragold" or "goldene" may not be used unless the article is made of pure gold or of an alloy of at least 10 karat fineness. No phrase or representation indicating the substance, charm, quality, or beauty of gold may be used properly unless the article is of at least 10 karat fineness.

"Gold-filled," "rolled-gold plate," and similar terms are also described in terms of their technical definitions. It is an unfair trade practice to use any of these terms under circumstances where they do not meet the requirements laid down in the trade practice rules.

Luggage. The correct name of the material from which the luggage is manufactured must be stated. Luggage not made of leather, of course, must not be misdescribed. It is also an unfair trade practice to use trade names that are misleading because they suggest the presence of genuine leather in a product made from imitation leather, or the presence of one variety of leather in a product made from a different variety.

Even genuine leather frequently is processed in such a way as to indicate that it is leather of a different type. The words "genuine," "real," "natural," and the like may not be used to describe leather that has been embossed or processed to simulate a different kind, grade, type, or quality.

The facts must be disclosed in detail when the product is advertised. For example, "top-grain cowhide," "simulated pigskin grain," or "split cowhide, backed with simulated leather" are appropriate terms that explain what the leather is and what finish has been applied to it.

Top-grain leather is the best grade. The trade practice rules provide specifically that leather from which either a layer of the top surface or a so-called buffing has been removed shall not be considered top-grain leather. In addition, terms such as "waterproof," "scratchproof," "dustproof," and "warp-proof" should not be used unless they are literally true of the product.

Special Statutes

As indicated, the Federal Trade Commission is charged with the duty of enforcing a group of special statutes dealing with specific products or industries, in addition to its general powers under the Federal Trade Commission Act. During the past few years, it has become increasingly common to find specific statutes of this sort introduced into Congress, and there may be more of them from time to time. Some of the principal ones now in effect will be discussed briefly.

Wool products. The Wool Products Labeling Act defines "wool," "reprocessed wool," and "reused wool." It requires a clear and explicit statement of the true composition of any wool product and also a statement of other fibers in addition to wool, if there are any, that are contained in the product. Although this law deals specifically with labeling, the same principles are applied as a matter of policy to the advertising of wool products, and the rules and regulations under the Wool Products Labeling Act should be consulted in preparing advertising copy for any product containing wool.

"Wool" means the fiber from the fleece of the sheep or lamb or the hair of the angora or cashmere goat. It may also include the so-called specialty fibers, which derive from the hair of the camel, alpaca, llama, or vicuna. Accordingly, it is proper to use just the word "wool" or terms such as "alpaca," "camel hair," "llama," "vicuna," "cashmere," or "mohair" if in fact the fiber is that type of wool. If, however, the fiber is reprocessed or reused, those words also must be included in order to avoid misleading the public.

The key facts that must be shown are the kind of wool involved and its percentage by weight. In addition, if 5 percent or more of any other fiber is included in the total fabric, the presence of this fiber also must be disclosed. And the weight of any nonfiber that is used as loading or filling must be disclosed with its proper percentage stated prominently.

Fur products. Since there are so many different types of fur and they come from so many different parts of the world, the principal objective of the Fur Products Labeling Act is to make certain that the true type of fur is named and that the country of origin is given in all instances. A Fur Products Name Guide has been issued by the Federal Trade Commission in which the name of the animal can be looked up and checked according to its sci-entific designation. The country of origin, of course, must be determined and disclosed.

Disclosure is required also if the product contains used fur; bleached, dyed, or otherwise artificially colored fur; or paws, tails, bellies, or waste fur.

Trade names or trademarks may not be used if they might create a misleading impression concerning the character of the product, the name of the animal producing the fur, or its geographical or zoological origin. The Fur Act specifically applies to advertising as well as labeling.

Textile fiber products. Another special statute in the series assigned to the Federal Trade Commission for administration is the Textile Fiber Products Identification Act. Like the Fur Act, this statute specifically applies to advertising as well as labeling.

If any fibers are mentioned at all, the correct generic name of each fiber present in the amount of more than 5 percent of the total fiber weight of the product must appear. Detailed regulations have been issued by the Federal Trade Commission, including a list of definitions of generic names for manufactured fibers.

In advertising any textile fiber product, all parts of the required information must be stated in immediate conjunction with each other, in legible and conspicuous type or lettering of equal size and prominence. The generic names of the fibers that are present in amounts of more than 5 percent must be listed in the order of their predominance by weight. If any fiber is present in an amount of 5 percent or less, then the list of ingredients must be followed by the designation "other fiber" or "other fibers" to make this fact clear.

Specific examples of various types of approved expressions are given in the regulations. The following statements, for instance, would be appropriate for use in advertising: 60 percent cotton, 40 percent rayon, exclusive of ornamentation; all nylon, exclusive of elastic; and all cotton except 1 percent nylon added to neck band.

An imported textile fiber product must be marked with the name of the country where it was processed or manufactured. This requirement applies in cases where the form of an imported textile fiber product is not basically changed even though it is processed in the United States, such as by finishing and dyeing. However, a textile fiber product manufactured in the United States from imported materials need not disclose the name of the country where the textile was originally made or processed.

Other statutes enforced by the Commission deal with fabric care labels, fuel economy advertising, vocational and home study programs, door-to-door sales, and used car marketing.

Red Flag Words

The eyes of the regulators (and your competitors) are especially sensitive to certain "red flag" words. For this reason, the copywriter must learn to recognize the danger signals. This does not mean that these words can never be used; it

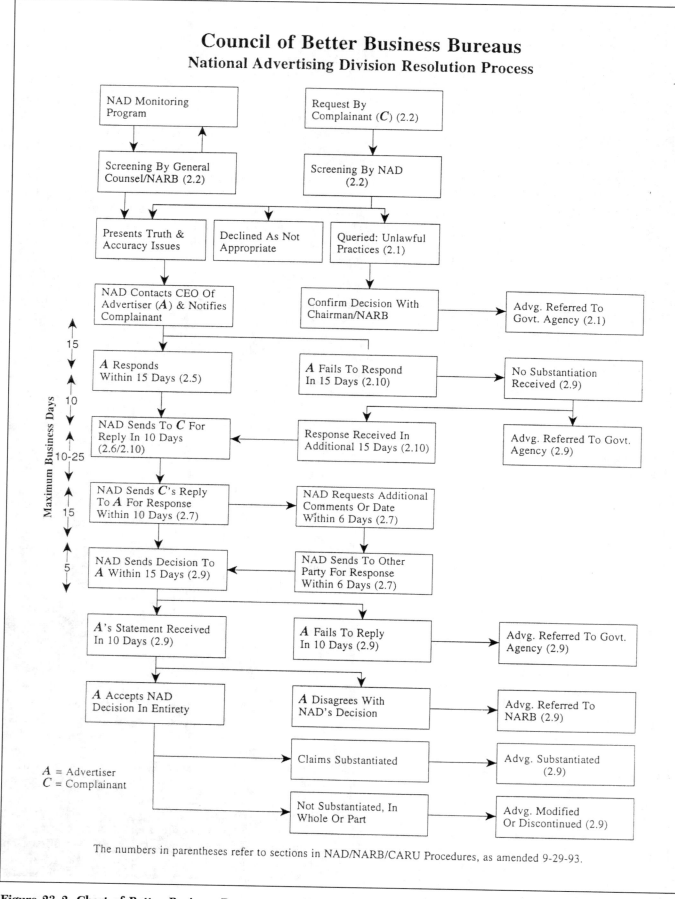

Council of Better Business Bureaus
National Advertising Division Resolution Process

The numbers in parentheses refer to sections in NAD/NARB/CARU Procedures, as amended 9-29-93.

Figure 23–2. Chart of Better Business Bureau operation. Better Business Bureaus—National and Local—aid advertisers in keeping them out of legal trouble.

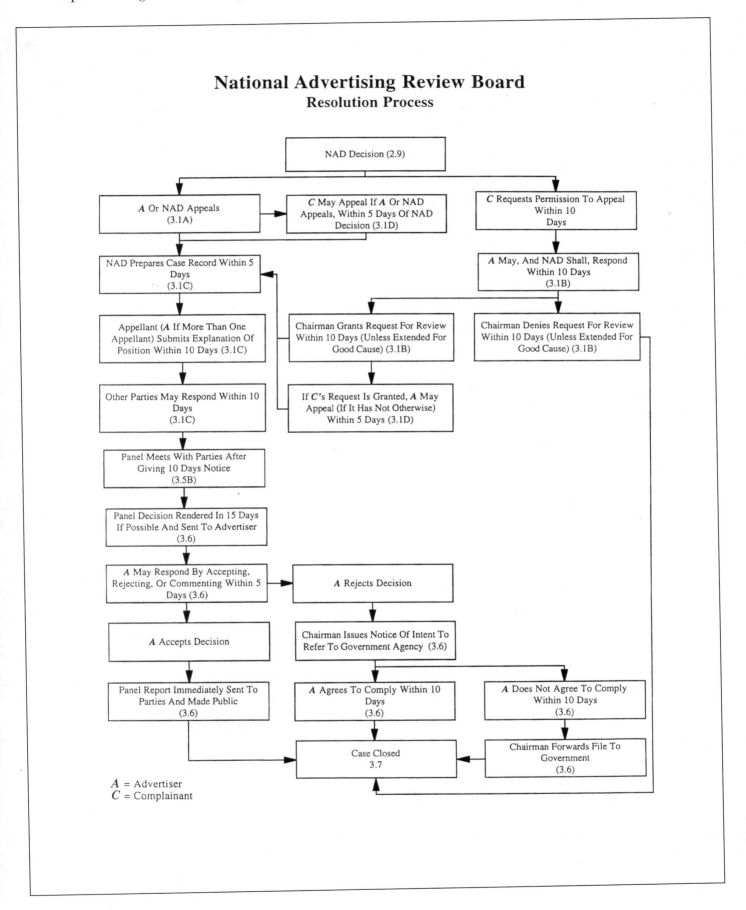

National Advertising Review Board
Resolution Process

NAD Decision (2.9)

A Or NAD Appeals (3.1A)

C May Appeal If *A* Or NAD Appeals, Within 5 Days Of NAD Decision (3.1D)

C Requests Permission To Appeal Within 10 Days

NAD Prepares Case Record Within 5 Days (3.1C)

A May, And NAD Shall, Respond Within 10 Days (3.1B)

Appellant (*A* If More Than One Appellant) Submits Explanation Of Position Within 10 Days (3.1C)

Chairman Grants Request For Review Within 10 Days (Unless Extended For Good Cause) (3.1B)

Chairman Denies Request For Review Within 10 Days (Unless Extended For Good Cause) (3.1B)

Other Parties May Respond Within 10 Days (3.1C)

If *C*'s Request Is Granted, *A* May Appeal (If It Has Not Otherwise) Within 5 Days (3.1D)

Panel Meets With Parties After Giving 10 Days Notice (3.5B)

Panel Decision Rendered In 15 Days If Possible And Sent To Advertiser (3.6)

A May Respond By Accepting, Rejecting, Or Commenting Within 5 Days (3.6)

A Rejects Decision

A Accepts Decision

Chairman Issues Notice Of Intent To Refer To Government Agency (3.6)

Panel Report Immediately Sent To Parties And Made Public (3.6)

A Agrees To Comply Within 10 Days (3.6)

A Does Not Agree To Comply Within 10 Days (3.6)

Chairman Forwards File To Government (3.6)

Case Closed 3.7

A = Advertiser
C = Complainant

Figure 23–3. Legal chart. Here we are shown the workings of one of the most important bodies reviewing advertising for honesty and accuracy—the National Advertising Review Board (NARB).

only means that special care is required because they are so easy to misuse. The presence of a red flag word frequently is an indication that the entire premise of an advertisement is wrong from the legal viewpoint. Of course, it is possible to violate the Federal Trade Commission Act without using a single word on this list, but experience has shown that these are likely to create legal difficulties.

It would be futile to compile a complete list of red flag words; the passage of time would eliminate some old ones and add others. A few important examples will be discussed to illustrate the general principles involved in avoiding trouble. The fundamental idea is to make sure that you know just what your target audience thinks the words mean and to ask whether your product can fulfill the promises contained in these words.

Two such words have been discussed already: "free" and "guarantee" (or "warranty"). They are such trouble-makers that they have been treated separately. The following are some additional sources of difficulty. Notice that a good many of these red flag words apply particularly to drug and cosmetic copy. Advertising for such products is watched with special zeal because these products affect physical and mental welfare. At one time, the Federal Trade Commission analyzed 915 of its cases and found that from all the different classifications of commodities, 65 percent of the questioned advertising copy related to drug products and 14.4 percent related to cosmetics. In other words, almost 80 percent of all questioned copy fell into these two classes.

Banish, rid, stop, correct, end. Each of these five words says to the consumer, "This is the last of your trouble—it's all over now—permanently and forever." There may be times when you can use these words in their literal meaning. Too often, however, the Federal Trade Commission finds them used inaccurately—if not dishonestly.

Words in this group probably have been more used and abused in drug copy than in any other type of advertising. See if the following examples don't look familiar: Banish sleepless nights; Rid yourself of constipation; Stop psoriasis; Correct sluggish liver conditions; and End headaches. Each of these statements promises permanent relief to sufferers. It is the permanency feature that makes the Federal Trade Commission balk. Permanent relief means cure, and drugs seldom cure.

Cosmetics copy also often uses these words carelessly. It is too easy to write: "Acne sufferers—rid yourself of unsightly pimples" or "Ashamed of your hands? Banish roughness."

Think before you use these words. Consider whether your claims are truthful. Ask yourself "Can my product cure, fix, or remedy *permanently* the condition under discussion?" If you can't answer that it does, you'd better use a different word, or qualify your statement with "may help rid you of. …"

Cure, remedy, therapeutic, curative. Millions of people suffer chronically from innumerable ailments, such as ulcers, varicose veins, eye trouble, headaches, and arthritis. Each of these afflicted persons is anxious for relief. Some of them swallow gallons of patent medicines led on by unthinking or untruthful copywriters who promise "cure" or "remedy."

Unfortunately, real cures are rare. The proper procedure for the copywriter is to find out what the product actually has accomplished and to claim only that it will relieve specific symptoms—not cure the disease (unless the manufacturer is certain that it really will).

"Remedy" is put in the same class as "cure" by the Federal Trade Commission. "Therapeutic" and "curative" are eyed suspiciously also.

Drug copy isn't the only type using these red flag words. Cosmetics, soaps, toothpastes, and foods are only a few of the other products that slip one of these words into their copy on occasion. All four of them are alarm signals.

Blemish-free, clear, smooth. There are few forms of mental suffering as acute as that felt by people who have bad complexions. Since they are so extremely susceptible to advertising promising them skin that is blemish-free, clear, or smooth, the Federal Trade Commission has been especially critical of such copy. Here are some points to remember in writing copy for a product used for skin care. If the product is applied externally and you promise that it will rid the skin of blemishes, you must:

1. Establish the fact that the skin is blemished because of external factors and not because of a systemic condition.
2. Indicate that the product can be effective only if the cause of the blemishes is external.
3. Be sure your statements are based on proven facts. If the product is taken internally, then reverse the procedure of Steps 1 and 2.

"Clear," as applied to skin, is interpreted as blemish-free. Think of this definition when you use the word. Then set up conditions as you do when you use the expression "blemish-free" itself.

A "smooth" skin normally is difficult to promise unless you establish the fact that: (1) The skin is already rough because of some specified treatment or condition; and (2) The regular use of your product will bring a change. Be sure that the manufacturer has support for your claim. It is better, incidentally, to stick to the comparative in this case. An outright promise of smooth skin through use of a product is easy to make but very difficult to fulfill. Many complexions will never become smooth through use of any product, but they may get smoother than they were. Be satisfied with that.

Safe, harmless. When you say unqualifiedly that a product is "safe" or "harmless," you are asking for trouble. Humans have a fiendish capacity for proving you wrong, whether you're writing about drugs, electrical apparatus, machinery, or even baby products. To say that a product is safe or harmless under all conditions is like saying a gun is unloaded. Too often, you're mistaken.

Suppose a drug product is advertised as "safe" or "harmless." Regulators immediately want to know: (1) Isn't it possible that certain persons may be allergic to one or more of its ingredients? and (2) Can all persons reading the statement rely on the fact that the preparation will not harm them?

Improper use of these red flag words in copy is more than just false advertising. Suppose a person does suffer from using the product because it turned out not to be safe or harmless. There is the basis for a possible damage claim.

As far as the law is concerned, when you say your product is safe, you don't mean safe to a certain degree, you mean completely safe. The same thing goes for "harmless." If you're not sure, don't use either of the words.

Science, scientific, test, evidence, proof, research. Use these words, singly or in combination, and the credulous public conjures up visions of test tubes, microscopes, and long hours spent in the laboratory by white-coated technicians. If what you are writing is a television commercial, the picture may be right there on the tube to reinforce the impression created by the words. Yet this group of red flag words probably has been the most abused of all.

Scientists themselves use these words with great restraint because they imply a careful, systematic investigation conducted under unbiased conditions by experts who are trying to find the truth, not to prove that their employer's brand has a slight edge over its competitors in some particular respect. Perhaps your company's laboratory discovers something about a product that you can translate into a copy claim. Do the findings of a couple of chemists become "science"? Because an informal poll of ordinary practicing physicians shows a slight favoring of your product, does this constitute "overwhelming scientific proof" that your product is superior? When you stop to think about the fact that even eminent scientists often honestly disagree, you can realize how an extremely inaccurate and misleading impression can be created by the careless use of these red flag words.

Approach "science" with humility and use "proof" and "evidence" sparingly. If you have substantial evidence to back you and if your use of the terms is literally true, then, of course, you would be foolish *not* to employ this very strong copy approach. Otherwise be careful.

Doctor, laboratory. These red flag words have much the same kind of built-in trouble potential as the group last discussed. A doctor's recommendation is considered a precious asset for any kind of product that can either help you or hurt you. "Laboratory" goes right along with it, because that is where doctors frequently get their inspiration. But beware of the temptation to be anything but scrupulously accurate in your use of these terms. The Federal Trade Commission, knowing how gullible the public is about doctors' recommendations, is hypersensitive to copy of that type.

If you want to keep your "doctor" copy out of legal turmoil, here are a few points to bear in mind:

- Make sure the "doctors" to whom you refer are genuine physicians, licensed to practice medicine by a recognized governmental authority.
- If they are not such doctors, then make it very clear just what kind of "doctors" they are; for instance, doctors of philosophy, naturopathy, or chiropractic medicine.
- Avoid the unqualified representation that a preparation is "a doctor's prescription." If true, the statement "formulated in accordance with" a doctor's prescription is acceptable. But be sure of your facts.
- Don't make a blanket statement of medical approval for your product based upon an informal survey that asked doctors for their personal preference or for a "less harmful than Product X" type of statement; these and similar limited expressions of opinions do not constitute sufficiently reliable recommendations.
- If an analysis by doctors reveals an insignificant advantage for your product over your competitor's product, don't blast forth with a claim of superiority. In the past, cigarette advertising sometimes was characterized by this kind of magnification of infinitesimal differences, failing to reveal to the public the fact that all tested brands contained substantial quantities of the substance involved in the analysis and that the differences were insignificant.

Often the word "laboratory" is used simultaneously with "doctor." The principal caution to observe with this word is that you must not refer to "our laboratory" when the client does not operate a control or research laboratory in connection with its organization.

At the same time, don't mention laboratory and doctors together unless the doctors actually did their research in the laboratory from which you assert they obtained their facts. Otherwise, you may have them approving research that they would not have endorsed according to their own ideas of research methods.

The word "laboratory" is viewed suspiciously whether or not doctors are mentioned in the same advertising copy. The strict attitude of the FTC is shown in a number of cases in which manufacturers were forbidden to use "laboratories" as part of a trade or corporate name because they did not actually operate any laboratory.

Free, low, reduced/less, light, good source of, high, more, lean/extra lean. These words, when used on food labels or in food advertising, are strictly regulated by the federal Nutrition Labeling and Education Act of 1990, which was effective in May 1994. Also, strictly regulated, are words that have the same meaning, such as "zero," "no," "without," "little," "few," "fewer," "contains/provides," and "fortified and enriched," all of which must meet specific and complex statutory requirements.

The act also specifies seven "health claims" regarding relationships between certain diseases or health conditions (such as calcium and osteoporosis, sodium and hypertension, and fat and cancer) that advertisers can make if the nutrient meets rigid statutory specifications. Nutrient content claims relating to other diseases or health conditions not included on the statutory list are prohibited. The act's provisions are far too complex and detailed to review here, but a copywriter working on food products would need to be very familiar with its terms.

To resolve FTC charges that it engaged in deception through its development of Häagen Dazs® frozen yogurt product ads, BBDO Worldwide, Inc., agreed to a 1994 consent order to not misrepresent the amount of fat, calories, or cholesterol in any frozen yogurt, frozen sorbet, and most ice cream products. The FTC alleged that the advertisements represented that the entire yogurt product line was low in fat and 98 percent fat-free and that each frozen yogurt bar contained only 100 calories and only 1 gram of fat per serving by stating:

> Why is Häagen-Dazs frozen yogurt better than your first love? Häagen Dazs is still 98% fat free

A fine print disclosure in the bottom corner of two of the challenged advertisements stated: "frozen yogurt and sorbet combination." According to the FTC, many flavors of the frozen yogurt and frozen yogurt bars contained far more calories and fat than claimed in the advertisements. BBDO was considered independently liable for the deceptive claims because it knew or should have known that they were false and misleading. The settlement required BBDO to meet the Food and Drug Administration's qualifying amount for any nutrient-content claim. For example, if it claims that a frozen food product is "low fat," the product will have to meet the specific qualifying amount for fat established by FDA's labeling regulations for "low fat" claims.

Recycled, recyclable, biodegradable, compostable, ozone friendly, landfill safe, eliminates pollution, environmentally friendly/safe. Each of these words will be closely scrutinized by the Federal Trade Commission and state Attorneys General. The FTC issued Environmental Marketing Guidelines in 1992, and in 1991, the Attorneys General of 11 states issued The Green Report II: Recommendations for Responsible Environmental Marketing. Both documents demonstrate the importance of carefully substantiating such claims with competent and reliable scientific evidence, and they emphasize the need to appropriately qualify them in light of any differences between the impression they would create with consumers and a broad body of scientific knowledge.

Again, any copywriter using these or similar terms needs to be very familiar with the legal requirements and restrictions spelled out in the FTC's Guide and the Attorneys General Report. For example, ARCO (a major petroleum company) agreed in 1995 to settle an FTC challenge to its claims about the environmental benefits of Sierra antifreeze, which stated that Sierra was "environmentally safer," "biodegradable," and "The Ultimate In … Environmental Safety."

Figure 23–4. Legal advertisement. Lawyers have always played a prominent role in fashioning the structure of sweepstakes in order to keep advertisers out of legal trouble.

The consent agreement barred the company from making safety claims about any antifreeze, coolant, or deicer unless they are based on reliable scientific evidence, and it required a cautionary statement on ARCO's packaging.

New. The Federal Trade Commission usually won't believe that if product has been used for a time, it can be restored entirely to its original state through the use or application of your product. Whenever your copy asserts that the product says "just like new" despite age, use, and abuse, get ready to defend your statements. "New" to the Federal Trade Commission means fresh—no different from the day you bought it. Remember that picture when you write "looks like new." Also keep in mind that the phrases "works like new" or "lasts like new" are subject to cynical legal scrutiny.

The scrutiny becomes especially watchful when the advertiser says that a process will make something old work like new. A "better performance" claim may very well be accurate and do a good selling job without ever getting attention from the Federal Trade Commission, while the little word "new" in the copy waves the red flag and asks for trouble, which frequently comes.

Another facet to the use of the word "new" affects those advertisers who use "new" interminably in their advertising and on packages, thus giving the impression that the product is actually a new product or a newly improved product. Generally, the Federal Trade Commission has taken the position that "new" should not be used to describe a product that has been in use for more than six months. Furthermore, it may be used properly only when the product is truly new or has been changed in a substantial respect. Moreover, this claim does not apply to mere changes in packaging.

Although no more red flag words will be discussed, there are, of course, many more than have been presented here. The purpose in providing this partial list is twofold: (1) to make you cautious in the use of these specific words; and (2) to alert you to the necessity for honesty and accuracy in all copywriting.

One of the dangers of running afoul of the Federal Trade Commission is that once they have discovered one product of a company to be advertised untruthfully, the Commission may then require that the company's other products live up to the regulations.

This point is illustrated by a giant retailing firm whose advertising for a dishwasher was cited as being untruthful. As a consequence, not only was the company enjoined to cease and desist making certain claims for the dishwasher, but the company was also told not to make claims for any of its major home appliances unless they were true and were backed up by reliable tests or strong substantiating evidence. Thus, if your copy brings the FTC down on you for one product, you can almost assume that your client's other products will be given a closer scrutiny in the future.

Food and Drug Administration (FDA)

Because of the constant jockeying for competitive advantage among advertisers of brand name merchandise, the FDA is vigilant in matters affecting labeling. In 1987, for instance, new FDA guidelines were issued that recognized the growing interest of the public in health and diet. As previously discussed, Congress gave the FDA far-reaching new authority when it passed the Nutrition Education and Labeling Act. The Act established standards for health claims relating to foods. Under the guidelines, a manufacturer of high-fiber bran cereal that was promoted as an aid to a cancer-prevention diet can now make such a claim, which heretofore had little chance of approval. The change reflects not only increased responsibility on the part of advertisers to back up their claims but also a flexibility on the FDA's part to recognize changes in the marketplace. At the same time, the new standards are very strict.

The Food and Drug Administration exercises control over a tremendously wide area of the entire American economy. Food is our country's single largest industry. Drugs are among the most widely advertised of all items. In addition, the Food and Drug Administration has jurisdiction over "devices," which are defined as instruments or apparatus for use in the diagnosis, cure, or treatment of disease or to affect the structure or function of the body of humans or animals. This definition includes everything

from a fever thermometer to a massage machine to BreatheRight® nasal strips.

And last, but by no means least, come cosmetics, which the law defines to include articles intended to be "rubbed, poured, sprinkled, or sprayed on, introduced into or otherwise applied to the human body or any part thereof for cleansing, beautifying, promoting attractiveness, or altering the appearance," with the single exception of soap.

Labeling Is the FDA's Chief Concern

The Food and Drug Administration is concerned primarily with the false or misleading labeling of products under its control. From the standpoint of the advertising copywriter, the principal problem, therefore, is package copy. In addition, any literature that accompanies a product is considered part of its "labeling"; and leaflets, brochures, or the like also come under the jurisdiction of the Food and Drug Administration when they are designed to accompany the product at the time and place of sale.

Advertising for products controlled by the Food and Drug Administration is supervised by the Federal Trade Commission under its general powers over false and misleading advertising. Obviously, it would be inviting trouble to make a statement in advertising copy that would go against the prohibitions of the Food and Drug Administration if it happened to appear on a label.

The statute under which the Food and Drug Administration operates deals specifically with the question of labeling that becomes misleading by failure to state what should have been included. The law provides that, in determining whether labeling is misleading, there shall be taken into account not only representations made or suggested, but also the extent to which there is a failure to disclose facts in the light of any representations that are made.

There also is a specific provision that any information required to be on a label must be placed prominently with such conspicuousness and in such terms as to make it likely to be read and understood by the ordinary individual, under customary conditions of purchase and use, for the particular product involved.

FDA Issues Helpful Definitions for Copywriters

Numerous detailed provisions are made for a great variety of specific products, some in the law itself and others in the voluminous regulations that have been issued from time to time by the Food and Drug Administration. Particularly worthy of mention is the fact that the statute provides for the Food and Drug Administration to issue definitions and standards of identity for foods, and many such have been published for a great variety of edible products. These definitions and standards of identity typically prescribe minimum quality standards that a product must meet in order to be entitled to bear that name. If the product for which you are writing copy fails to satisfy these standards, then it is not proper to use what you might think is its ordinary name. For example, if cocoa contains less than 10 percent of cacao fat, it must be sold as "low-fat cocoa"; and only if the product contains more than 22 percent cacao fat can it be called "breakfast cocoa." Obviously, this is the kind of factual detail that must be checked before copy is prepared.

Another example of the FDA's close scrutiny to detail in labeling was afforded in its notification to Procter & Gamble in 1991 that it might need to change the name of its Citrus Hill Fresh Choice orange juice because it considered the word "fresh" to be false or misleading and inappropriate on the label of an orange juice made from concentrate. In a similar ruling, the FDA told Citrus World, marketers of Fresh 'N Natural orange juice, that the use of fresh on a pasteurized product is inappropriate and would tend to confuse consumers.

Procter & Gamble replied that research showed that consumers were not misled by the use of the word. The label had also been questioned by the Texas State Attorney's Office.

If no standard of identity has been established for any particular food, then it must be labeled to disclose each ingredient by name—except for spices, colorings, and flavorings, which may be declared simply as such. There are provisions also for exemptions from these requirements, and the Food and Drug Administration has exempted various foods for various reasons. In a number of instances, the indications are that these exemptions are only temporary, and definitions and standards of identity may be issued at a later date.

Drugs and Cosmetics Are Watched with Special Care by the FDA

Drugs and devices must be labeled with adequate directions for use. Special mention must be made if a drug is likely to deteriorate. New drugs may not be offered for sale at all unless they have been tested adequately and approved. Drugs listed in standard formularies such as the United States Pharmacopoeia must be labeled with their official names, and any differences of strength, quality, or purity from the official standards must be stated conspicuously on the label.

Cosmetics are subject to misbranding and false labeling restrictions similar to those affecting foods, except that there is no provision for definitions and standards of identity with respect to cosmetics. Note that a product may be both a drug and cosmetic. The claim on the label made by the manufacturer concerning its function will determine which set of legal requirements the product must fulfill. It is possible that the identical product can be sold under two different labels for two different purposes, in one case as a drug and in the other as a cosmetic.

Postal Service

The United States Postal Service exercises control over advertising in two main areas. The first of these affects advertising that uses the mail. This includes both direct-mail advertising and mail-order advertising. For example, a lottery or any fraudulent scheme—that is, a plan for obtaining money or property through the mails by means of false pretenses— is a violation of the postal laws. The Postal Service need not even take the offender to court. It can conduct an administrative proceeding, and if it finds a violation has been committed, the Postmaster at the local office is directed to stamp the word "Fraudulent" on all mail addressed to the offending party and return it to the sender. Postmasters also are instructed not to pay any money orders drawn in favor of such a party.

Second, in addition to this direct method of control, the Postal Service exercises indirect control over advertising carried in any publication that goes through the mails. This comes about because of the very valuable second-class mailing privilege, which amounts to a government subsidy in favor of periodicals that have what is called a "public character"; that is, those that contain news, literature, scientific information, or the like and have a legitimate list of subscribers.

Second-Class Mailing Privileges Can Be Revoked

The Postal Service has the power to revoke second-class mailing privileges if the periodical fails to maintain its so-called public character. Advertising misrepresentations might be sufficient to warrant this type of extreme action, although there seems to be no record of its ever having been done.

The particular concern of the copywriter with the second-class mailing privilege is that, while any periodical which has this privilege may contain advertising, the advertising must be clearly indicated as such. If an advertisement is written and set up so that it gives the appearance of being editorial matter, then the word "advertisement" itself must appear as an identifying symbol in sufficiently conspicuous type and placement so that it will be readily noticeable to the reader. Failure to comply may lead to revocation of the periodical's second-class mailing privilege.

Mail-fraud cases prosecuted by the Postal Service run into the hundreds of thousands and involve an estimated hundreds of millions of dollars in losses, possibly as high as between 60 and 100 billion dollars. Such fraud cases are an embarrassment to the media that run the advertisements in good faith only to find out through the Postal Service that the advertisers are dishonest.

These cases may be involved with misrepresented merchandise, false solicitations for charities, and telemarketing schemes. Another area for widespread dishonesty is in coupon redemption schemes operating through coupon clearinghouses. Millions of coupons have been fraudulently redeemed through legitimate clearinghouses, but the Postal Service is working to stamp out these fraudulent operators.

With the explosion in recent years of direct response advertising, the rulings of the Postal Service have touched many more advertisers than formerly and will continue to do so if advertisers are careless or dishonest.

Federal Communications Commission (FCC)

The Federal Communications Commission also exercises an indirect type of control over advertising. Radio and television advertising is subject to the general supervision of the Federal Trade Commission, just like advertising in print and other media. The FCC, however, licenses every radio and television station, and it is one of the overall conditions of such a license that the station must operate in what the law calls the "public interest, convenience, and necessity."

If the Federal Communications Commission should find that, because of advertising misrepresentations or any other reason, a station has not been operating within this quoted statutory purpose, then it has the power to revoke or refuse to renew the station's license. This power obviously can be a potent one.

While the Federal Communications Commission has criticized false and misleading advertising, it is the Federal Communications Commission's general policy not to take any specific action with respect to this type of offense, but rather to bring the matter to the attention of the Federal Trade Commission. But the Federal Communications Commission has indicated its disapproval of advertising of lotteries and hard liquor. All such advertising practices jeopardize the licensee's chances of securing a license renewal, which ordinarily must be done yearly.

The Commission has been known to bring to the attention of a station (informally) what it considers objectionable advertising. This method of procedure can be extremely effective, since few stations would care to risk the loss of their broadcasting franchises and some would be unwilling even to risk the publicity of a public hearing in connection with a renewal application.

Bureau of Alcohol, Tobacco and Firearms

The Bureau of Alcohol, Tobacco, and Firearms is charged with the responsibility, among other things, of administering the Federal Alcohol Administration Act. On this basis, the Bureau of Alcohol, Tobacco and Firearms imposes on the liquor industry what is almost without doubt the most detailed and severe set of controls that any industry in the country must face in its advertising practices.

The Bureau of Alcohol, Tobacco and Firearms exercises supervision over distilled spirits, wine, and malt beverages. Its control starts basically with the labels to be used on the products. There are detailed regulations setting forth what must appear on the labels, and no label can be used on an alcoholic product unless it has been approved by the Bureau of Alcohol, Tobacco, and Firearms in advance.

The next step is direct control over the advertising of the products. The class and type of the beverage must appear in every advertisement. These must be stated conspicuously, and the designation in the advertising copy must be the same as that on the approved label for the product. Detailed information about alcoholic content is required for distilled spirits, but statements of alcoholic content are prohibited in advertisements of malt beverages and wine. The name and address of the company responsible for the advertisement always must be included; it may be the distiller, the distributor, or the importer in proper cases. The name and address of the advertiser, the class and type of the product, and the alcoholic content (in the case of distilled spirits) are the so-called mandatories in liquor advertising.

The Bureau of Alcohol, Tobacco and Firearms regulations also specifically prohibit certain types of advertising statements. These include false or misleading statements; disparagement of competing products; obscene or indecent statements; misleading representations relating to analysis, standards, or tests; and guarantees that irrespective of their truth or falsity, are likely to mislead the consumer. Other prohibited types of advertising include statements indicating authorization by any municipal, state, or federal government; the use of certain words such as "bonded" (unless the product in fact is bottled in bond), "pure," and "double-distilled"; claims of curative or therapeutic value; misleading statements as to place of origin; and many others. In particular, no statement concerning an alcoholic beverage may be used in advertising if it is inconsistent with any statement on the labeling of the product itself.

Other Federal Laws

There are certain specialized industries in which still other federal agencies exercise specific control over advertising. For example, the Securities and Exchange Commission has the power to stop the sale of a security if its advertising contains an untrue statement of a material fact or if it fails to state a material fact necessary to make the advertising not misleading in the light of all the circumstances. Another example is the Federal Aviation Agency, which has control over advertising by airlines of their passenger and freight services.

There are other federal statutes that apply to particular products, and some of them contain labeling and advertising controls. Among these are the Economic Poisons Act, which governs insecticides, fungicides, and similar products; and the Federal Seed Act.

Another group of statutes deals specifically with the use in advertising of particular symbols or representations, including the laws which prohibit or restrict the use of the American flag, the Red Cross symbol, the 4-H Club emblem, Smokey the Bear as originated by the U.S.

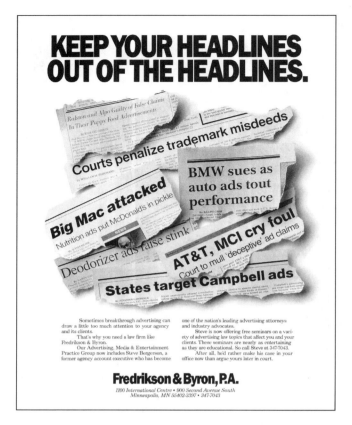

Figure 23–5. Legal advertisement. As the headlines in this advertisement testify, legal pitfalls beset advertisers through lawsuits brought on by competitors, state governments, and federal agencies.

Forestry Service, postage stamps, U.S. Olympic names and symbols, and a number of others. A leading advertising agency once had to scrap a filmed television commercial because the letters "FBI" were mentioned in a flippant manner; the Federal Bureau of Investigation called the agency's attention to a law that makes the use of those initials in advertising a misdemeanor.

These statutes are so specialized in nature that it would be impractical to discuss all of them in detail. They are mentioned primarily to indicate the necessity for checking with legal counsel in each instance to find out, before preparing copy, whether or not some special law deals with the subject.

Obscenity

There are legal as well as moral objections to obscenity. The problem here is one of definition. Standards of taste vary from community to community and, even more noticeably, from time to time. Nevertheless, a writer should have no difficulty in drawing the line between obscenity and acceptable copy. Although poor taste is not in itself unlawful, it certainly is disapproved by most advertisers. A copywriter who avoids poor taste almost automatically will avoid any question of violation of the obscenity laws.

Copyright

We are not concerned here with protecting an advertisement under copyright laws; rather, we are concerned with the problem of using somebody else's copyright material as part of your advertising. There are many misconceptions about the right to use such material.

A copyright does not protect the basic idea of the creator. Advertising copywriters therefore may use the basic ideas upon which any copyrighted work is based. But copying or closely paraphrasing the way in which the original author's idea is expressed does constitute an infringement. The same rule applies to art, music, lyrics, illustrations, designs, and all other creative work.

It is sometimes thought that copyright infringement occurs only when the fact of copying is concealed; that is, when the copier attempts to pass off the work as his own. This is not so. The mere fact that the source is acknowledged does not prevent the use from being an infringement of copyright. Actual consent of the copyright owner must be obtained. A fee frequently is charged for this privilege, but that is something that must be arranged in advance, because the copyright owner may decide to withhold permission altogether.

To obtain a copyright for a work, all that is needed is to create the work. Protection is automatic. And while no filing is necessary, filing does substantially increase the protection and the remedies for infringement. A copyright notice need not be placed on the work, but it is usually advisable.

An issue that has become important recently is the "work for hire" doctrine of the Copyright Act. In the case of work made for hire, the employer or other person for whom the work was prepared is considered the copyright owner. Unless the parties have agreed otherwise in a written instrument signed by them, a commissioning party or employer owns the copyright. This doctrine is of obvious interest and concern to creative people.

Fair Use

The one basic exception to a copyright owner's right to control his work is the Copyright Act's "fair use" doctrine. It is this exception that makes it possible, for example, for reviewers to quote passages from books that they are reviewing and for a scientist to copy from the works of others in the same field in order to be able to comment on scientific developments. The fair use doctrine requires that the use pass a four-part test, one part of which is the purpose for which the copyrighted material is to be used. For instance, it must be clear whether the material is to be used for commercial or noncommercial purposes. Thus, the fair use exception has limited application to advertising.

Specifically, to take even a small extract from a copyrighted work and use it in a commercial advertisement is hardly fair use.

This point was made unmistakably in a case involving the Liggett & Myers Tobacco Company, which copied, although not in exactly the same words, just three sentences from a doctor's book about the human voice that made some favorable comments about the use of tobacco. Specific credit was given for the source of the quotation, but no permission had been obtained to use it.

When the case went to court, the decision was in favor of the copyright proprietor, because while there must be a "substantial" similarity to constitute infringement, this does not necessarily mean a large quantity. In this case, the court decided that even three sentences amounted to substantial copying because of the relative importance of the material that was taken. It was decided also that the use wasn't a "fair use" because it was for a purely commercial purpose.

Copyrighted Music

Another popular misconception has to do with music that is protected by copyright. There is a widespread impression that as long as no more than eight bars of a popular song are borrowed, there can be no infringement of copyright. This is wrong. The same basic standards apply to the infringement of a musical copyright as to a literary copyright.

In other words, was the part taken from the copyrighted work "substantial" and was the use a "fair" one? The distinctive characteristics of the melody or the lyrics of a popular song can be expressed in fewer than eight bars. It is, therefore, not safe to use the words or music of a song unless permission has been granted or it has been checked and found to be in the public domain.

Copyright does not protect the title of a work. But this does not mean that everyone necessarily is free to use the title. The practice of commercial tie-ins of all types is so common today that titles of books, plays, motion pictures, songs, and even comic strips have become highly important commercial properties and are often protected by trademark or unfair competition laws. The legal test is whether the public is likely to infer that there is some connection between the title as used in advertising and the work on which the title originally appeared. If so, the title may not be used without permission.

Summary of Copyright Law Aspects

Copyright law protects the *creative expression* of ideas, but as previously discussed, it does *not* protect the ideas themselves (patents do that). Known as "works of authorship" the types of materials covered by copyright law include:

1. Literary works
2. Musical works, including any accompanying words
3. Dramatic works, including any accompanying music
4. Pantomimes and choreographic works
5. Pictorial, graphic, and sculptural works
6. Motion pictures and other audiovisual works
7. Sound recordings

Copyright law gives the copyright owner the exclusive right to do and/or authorize any of the following:

- To reproduce the work in copies or phonorecords.
- To prepare derivative works based on the work.
- To distribute copies of phonorecords of the work to the public by sales or other transfer of ownership, or by rental, lease, or lending.
- To *perform* the work publicly (in the case of literary, musical, dramatic, and choreographic works; pantomimes; and motion pictures and other audiovisual works).
- To *display* the work publicly (in the case of literary, musical, dramatic, and choreographic works; pantomimes; and pictorial, graphic or sculptural works, including individual images of a motion picture or other audiovisual works).

Libel

To libel somebody means to injure the person's or product's reputation by making a false statement that will subject it to ridicule or contempt in the community, particularly if it would tend to cause damage to the "victim."

The penalties for libel can be severe. If the defamatory statement can be proved true, it is a complete defense to a charge of libel, but the possibility of such a situation developing out of advertising copy is remote. Most of the litigated cases in which individuals have been libeled by means of advertising involved false testimonials.

Libel can be committed by a radio or television advertisement as well as by a printed advertisement. Libel also can be committed by pictures. The use of a professional model is no assurance against a suit for libel. The usual form of model release, which will be discussed in the succeeding section, does not waive any rights under libel laws.

One particularly well-known case involved an advertising photograph. The angle at which the picture was taken and the way in which the light fell created an obscene impression that was not noticed by the people who prepared the advertisement. The model sued on the theory that this was damaging to his reputation, and the court agreed that the photograph was libelous. Protection against this unfortunate kind of result can be obtained by having the model approve the finished layout, or sign a release waiving the right to do so.

It is possible to defame a business or product as well as a person. Disparagement of competitors and their products constitutes an unfair method of competition and may bring on a private suit.

Rights of Privacy and Publicity

The use of the name, picture, or likeness of a person in advertising without consent constitutes a violation of the person's right of privacy. In most states, this right is created by specific legislation that requires that the consent be in writing. Privacy statutes are limited to living persons, but about 25 states go further and give the heirs of a deceased person a "right of publicity," which gives heirs of deceased celebrities the right to complain about the unauthorized use of the deceased's name or picture. Obviously, the most restrictive of these laws must be taken into account when preparing copy for national advertising.

The right of privacy and publicity makes it necessary to obtain a release from every person (or the person's representative) who appears in an advertisement. Similarly, an endorsement or testimonial cannot be used without a release from the person whose name is to appear in connection with it. Anyone who is legally a minor must have his or her parent or legal guardian sign the release in order for it to be valid.

Releases frequently are limited in their scope. A model release, for example, may permit only the use of the picture of the person and not his or her true name. Furthermore, the right to use a picture does not always carry with it the right to use words in connection with the picture indicating that the model endorses a product or service. Even a release permitting a person's name to be used as an endorser does not necessarily include the right to create a statement praising the product and attribute it to the person as though it were the person's own words.

In addition, as indicated in the preceding section, the possession of a model release in the customary form does not excuse libel; thus, a photograph covered by a release might be used in conjunction with libelous words in such a way as to violate the legal rights of the model.

Courts used to rule that figures in the entertainment and sports world had no desire for privacy in the same way that an ordinary citizen did; they sought publicity actively. As a result, the privacy of such persons had been limited on the theory that the person had given up his right of privacy by making himself into a public figure. This thinking has been reversed and no longer applies to strict commercial uses such as advertising. While a magazine or newspaper can use a publicity still of a motion picture star for editorial purposes, the picture cannot be used as part of an advertisement without a release. Celebrities now have the same right as private citizens to control use of their names and likenesses for commercial purposes.

In recent years, the courts have considered the right of publicity as something distinct from the right of privacy. Only a public figure possesses this right of publicity. It is the law's recognition of the fact that the name and picture of a personality in the entertainment or sports world have a definite commercial value for endorsements, testimonials, and the like. Accordingly, the use of the name or picture of such a person for advertising purposes without written consent may give rise to a claim for substantial damages.

The right to publicity may be defined as the right to control the commercial exploitation of the publicity value of a celebrity's name or likeness and to prevent others from unfairly appropriating its value for their commercial benefit.

Unlike the right to privacy, the right to publicity is a *property* right. Thus, it survives the death of its owner and descends to the owner's heirs.

As a copywriter, accordingly, you must realize that in a growing number of states, you can no longer use the name, voice, or likeness of a deceased celebrity without the con-

sent of the heir(s). For example, as of 1 January 1985, the California Civil Code defines the deceased personality as anyone who has died within 50 years prior to that date.

It will be desirable, occasionally, to use a personal name in advertising, and the copywriter may devise a fictitious name for that purpose. This always creates the risk that, unknowingly, the fictitious name will turn out to be borne by some real person, who will then make a complaint. It then becomes a difficult, if not impossible, task to prove that the name in the advertisement did not refer to the actual living person.

In order to avoid such problems, some agencies maintain files of cleared names—usually persons on their own staffs or working for their clients who have consented to the use of their names in advertising. Even if a duplicate of such a name should turn up in the form of another person, the advertiser or agency always can go to the release file to establish that the cleared name is the one that was used in the copy. However, this will not excuse the use of a celebrity's name, even if, by coincidence, the agency has an employee bearing the same name who is willing to sign a release.

Proper Trademark Usage

Basic trademark principles were discussed in Chapter 10. The purpose of this section is to describe the proper ways of using trademarks in advertising in order to avoid the possible loss of the valuable legal rights that a trademark represents.

Some trademarks have become associated so completely with the products to which they are attached that they are treated by the public as merely a name for the product rather than an identification of one particular brand of that product. When a trademark literally becomes a household word in this way, it has ceased to be a trademark. As a result, no single manufacturer can possess the exclusive right to use it on his product, and the tremendous investment that may have gone into establishing the trademark and creating a brand image through extensive advertising has been lost to the advertiser.

The question is an important one for advertising copywriters, because the improper use of a trademark in advertising can give the public the impression that it is a generic term instead of a brand name, and that is what it will become very quickly under such circumstances.

Another indication of the seriousness of the problem is to list a few well-known products whose commonly accepted names today once were the valued trademarks of particular manufacturers. These include aspirin, lanolin, milk of magnesia, celluloid, kerosene, shredded wheat, thermos, linoleum, cellophane, and escalator. In order to preserve a trademark, keep in mind that it indicates only one particular brand of the product and is not the name of the product itself.

Proper trademark usage would become almost automatic if the copywriter recognized that, grammatically, a

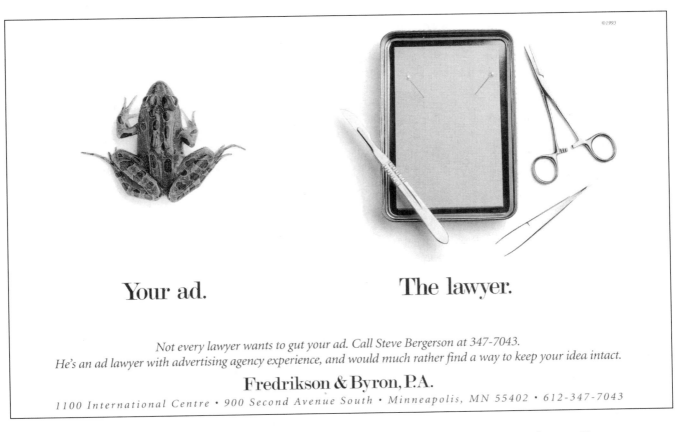

©1993

Your ad.   The lawyer.

Not every lawyer wants to gut your ad. Call Steve Bergerson at 347-7043.
He's an ad lawyer with advertising agency experience, and would much rather find a way to keep your idea intact.

Fredrikson & Byron, P.A.
1100 International Centre • 900 Second Avenue South • Minneapolis, MN 55402 • 612-347-7043

Figure 23–6. Legal advertisement. Sometimes copywriters see their copy squashed by overprotective lawyers. Here the copywriter is assured that the lawyer will try to preserve the copywriter's idea while, at the same time, making sure that the copy is legal.

trademark is a proper adjective. A trademark tells the consumer little about the product itself; it modifies the name of the product, and therefore, it is an adjective. On the other side, because the trademark is an adjective, there must be noun for it to modify, and that noun—such as pickles, ice cream, or potato chips—is the generic name of the product. Also, remember that because the trademark is a *proper* adjective, it is entitled grammatically to an initial capital letter.

The key principle in using a trademark properly is to make certain that it is always identified as a trademark and is not used as the name of a product. The following five rules will help you make that point and, therefore, preserve the trademark.

1. *Use the generic product name with the trademark.* To avoid stepping on anyone's toes, let us imagine an Empire Manufacturing Company that produces washing machines under the trademark Gremlin. In its advertising, Empire should not talk simply about a Gremlin; it should advertise a Gremlin washing machine or a Gremlin automatic washer.

A simple way to test your copy for this purpose is to omit the trademark from the sentence in which it appears. A complete thought still should be expressed, as in the sentence, "Get your clothes cleaner with a Gremlin washing machine." "Get your clothes cleaner with a Gremlin" is not satisfactory.

When you use the generic name of the product every time you refer to the trademark, you help avoid a situation in which the public will begin to use the term loosely, and you thus prevent loss of its trademark significance. If aspirin had been sold as Aspirin pain-relieving tablets instead of just as aspirin, it might still be the exclusive trademark of the Bayer Company.

2. *Use a trademark notice.* Designate the trademark with an appropriate notice at least on its first or most conspicuous appearance in any advertisement. If the trademark has been registered in the U.S. Patent and Trademark Office (and this requires a legal check), use the official circle-R notice,®, the abbreviation Reg. U.S. Pat. & Tm. Off., or the full-length statutory version Registered U.S. Patent and Trademark Office. If it has not been registered, then use the abbreviation TM or the word "Trademark" (or SM and "Service Mark" if being used to advertise a service). The longer forms of

notice obviously do not fit in body copy. Instead, put them in a footnote referred to by an asterisk. If you prefer, the note can appear at the top of the page or run along either side. Also, you may want to skip the asterisk, particularly if two or more trademarks are used in the same advertisement, and tell the whole story in a note; for example, "Empire and Gremlin are trademarks of Empire Manufacturing Co. Reg. U.S. Pat. & Tm. Off."

Another way to indicate clearly that a trademark is not merely the name of the product is to use the word "brand" after it. Some well-known examples of marks treated this way by their owners are Scotch brand tape and Pyrex brand glassware. When the copy talks about the "Gremlin brand" of a certain product, there is no doubt that Gremlin is the brand name or trademark and not the generic name of the product itself.

3. *Use special typography for the trademark.* At a bare minimum, the mark should be capitalized. When a mark appears in lowercase letters, indistinguishable from the rest of the copy, it creates the impression that it is a generic name and not a brand name.

There are many other typographical methods that can be used to give distinctive treatment to a trademark so that there will be no doubt of what it is. It may appear in all caps, in quotation marks, in handlettered form, in a frame, in italics, in boldface, underscored, set large than body copy, in a different typeface, or in a different color form the balance of the text; or the manufacturer's logo may be scaled down and included in body copy.

There should be a special form of display for the trademark, and it is important to stick to it. Many companies issue style sheets and specifications giving the exact proportions of the letters and the proper size relationships among all parts of the mark. The reason for establishing a standard form of trademark display is to avoid blurring the image of the trademark in the consumer's mind.

4. *Avoid incorrect grammatical forms.* Do not use the trademark as a noun. Specifically, do not pluralize it, because that suggests it is a noun. Say, "a full line of Gremlin products," not "a full line of Gremlins." Some trademarks themselves end with the letter "s." Do not create a false singular form by dropping the "s."

Never use the trademark as a verb. Do not say "Gremlin your clothes."

Also, do not use a trademark in the possessive. It is wrong to say something like "the Gremlin's remarkable service record." Instead, invert the order of the sentence and introduce the generic term; for example, "the remarkable service record of Gremlin washers."

5. *Do not vary the trademark.* Don't change the spelling, insert or delete hyphens, make one word into two, or combine two words into one. Don't abbreviate the trademark or use it as the root for coined words.

Going back to our imaginary clothes washer, an advertising campaign developed around the idea of "gremlinating" the household wash would quickly break down the distinctiveness of the Gremlin trademark. Changes in the form of the trademark detract from its status because they suggest to the consumer that it is just another word that is subject to variation or grammatical manipulation, and not a brand name.[2]

Many companies publish manuals giving specific directions on how their trademarks are to be used. These manuals are prepared largely for the use of advertising copywriters, and it goes without saying that you should follow such a manual if one has been issued by the advertiser on whose product you are working.

Additional Advice on the Proper Use of Trademarks

Writing in the December 10, 1994, issue of the magazine *Editor & Publisher,* in an article entitled, "Keeping Out of the Graveyard," Stephen R. Bergerson, an authority on the legal aspects of advertising, outlined some basic principles of trademark use. Mr. Bergerson pointed out that trademarks never die a natural death; they die because of someone's carelessness. To avoid such premature death, Mr. Bergerson has these suggestions:

- Never use a trademark as a noun ("introducing the new 1994 Rollerblades")
- Never use a trademark as a verb ("Xeroxing is easier than ever")
- Never use a trademark in the possessive ("Crockpot's wonderful new colors")
- Never add an "s" to pluralize a trademark ("two Sankas")
- Never use a trademark as a descriptive adjective ("Please make a Xerox copy")

Finally, remember to:

- Use the word "brand" in connection with trademarks ("Weedeater brand")
- Use product names with trademarks ("Rollerblade in-line skates")
- Use all three together ("Weedeater brand weed trimmer")
- Use appropriate trademark symbols (® if the brand has been federally registered; ™ if it hasn't been registered)
- Capitalize the trademarked word either initially or completely

All of these practices are designed to encourage everyone to recognize and use a trademarked word not as a name but as a way to distinguish a product from its competitors. Consider these words: Rolodex, Frisbee, TV Guide, Realtor, Styrofoam, Kitty Litter, Hush Puppies, Naugahyde, Vice grip, Astroturf, Laundromat, and Walkman. Are they trademarks or names? They aren't in the dictionary, but they are in trouble.

---

[2] Adapted from Sidney A. Diamond, *Trademark Problems and How to Avoid Them* (Chicago, Ill.: Crain Books, rev. ed., 1981), pp. 248–255.

Figure 23–7. Legal advertisement. Trademark law is one of the most complex areas for advertisers. As this advertisement points out, trademark infringement can be expensive.

Comparative Advertising

Direct reference to competitive products or services in advertising once was a rarity that people considered in bad taste or even morally reprehensible. Since the early 1970s, following a period when veiled references to "Brand X" were in vogue, a substantial amount of advertising has appeared in which competitors are mentioned specifically. No longer is a product or service simply "the best on the market"; instead, many advertisers do not hesitate to identify the competition and make direct comparisons. Philosophical questions of morals or ethics are outside the scope of this chapter, but does comparative advertising raise any legal questions? Yes!

In order to identify a competitor in advertising, it almost invariably is necessary to use the competitor's trademark so that the public will understand the comparison. For that reason, the legality of comparative advertising is often tested in the framework of lawsuits claiming trademark infringement. In one case, a manufacturer of low-priced domestic perfume advertised that his product duplicated the exact scent of "Chanel No. 5," a famous and expensive brand of French perfume. When this use of the Chanel trademark was attacked, the court responded by ruling that there was nothing wrong with referring to a competitive product by its trademark, provided that the comparative advertising was accurate.

This ruling came at a preliminary stage of the lawsuit. During the trial, however, Chanel proved that its competi-

tor's statements were untrue. Scientific tests established that the chemical composition of the imitation was not identical to that of Chanel No. 5. The experts testified that it, therefore, could not possibly smell precisely the same. The false statements were stopped by court order. Nevertheless, the decision confirmed the right of the imitator to use the trademark Chanel No. 5 in its advertising as long as it does not confuse the public into thinking that its product is manufactured or sponsored by Chanel.

More often, comparative advertising prompts a challenge to the comparative claim itself. Another comparative advertising case was the legal battle between the makers of Tylenol and Anacin. The pain-relieving ingredient in Anacin is aspirin, while Tylenol contains acetaminophen, an aspirin substitute.

American Home Products, the maker of Anacin, advertised that "Anacin can reduce inflammation that comes with most pain. Tylenol cannot." With the help of some consumer surveys, the court concluded that this and similar statements created the impression that Anacin was claiming to be a superior pain reliever to Tylenol. Scientific evidence, however, established the fact that acetaminophen is just as effective as aspirin in reducing pain.

While actually claiming greater effectiveness against inflammation, which was true, the advertisements nonetheless gave the impression to the consumer that Anacin was more effective against pain, which was not true. American Home Products was ordered to stop all advertising that represented Anacin as providing better pain relief than Tylenol. Again, there was no restriction on American Home Product's use of the trademark Tylenol in its advertising of Anacin, as long as the use did not create the likelihood that consumers would believe the products were associated with one another, an unlikely event in comparative advertising.

Comparative advertising is legally permissible as long as there is not misrepresentation. But if inaccurate or untrue statements are made, the advertisement can be attacked by a competitor as disparagement of its product or service, which is a violation of the provisions of Section 43(a) of the Lanham Act regarding deceptive advertising claims and trademark infringement, and substantial damages might be awarded. Strict accuracy is the basic legal requirement that a copywriter must bear in mind; this requirement must be observed with special care when the advertisement makes a direct reference to competitive products or services. Remember that comparative claims tend to function as legal lightning rods. They often draw sharp, heated responses.

Unsolicited Ideas Cause Trouble

It has been explained that a copyright does not protect the basic idea of any literary or artistic work. Nevertheless, many ideas are treated as property by law, and like other areas of intellectual property, they can be stolen.

SUBJECTS AND TITLES:

1. _____
2. _____
3. _____

_____
(date)

NAME AND ADDRESS OF ADVERTISING AGENCY

Attention: Mr._____

Dear Sirs:

I am asking you to let me present an idea, suggestion, or uncopyrighted work which I think may be of interest to you or to some of your clients. This presentation is being made on my own initiative and not at your request.

I understand that the established policy of your company is to refuse to entertain or receive ideas, suggestions, or uncopyrighted works except on the distinct understanding that they may be used by you or your clients without any obligation whatever to the person submitting them. Anything I submit to you or your company will be on that basis; disclosure by me of any idea, suggestion, or uncopyrighted work is gratuitous, unsolicited, without restrictions and involves no confidential relationship between us.

Use by you and your clients of any ideas, suggestions, or uncopyrighted works submitted by me, and the compensation, if any, that I may receive therefore, are matters resting solely in your discretion.

Very truly yours,

_____
(Signature)

_____
(Print or Typewrite your name)

_____
(Address)

_____

One of the constant problems that plagues advertising agencies and advertisers alike is the unsolicited idea. An astonishing member of people are constantly engaged in attempting to present what they consider novel merchandising ideas, catchy advertising slogans, and similar helpful thoughts, which they confidently expect will bring them substantial remuneration.

The fact is that professionals are much better at thinking up advertising ideas than amateurs. Even if the unsolicited idea has merit, it frequently turns out to be simply a duplication of an idea that is already in the public domain or in the company's files as the result of studies by its own staff or the staff of its advertising agency. Yet it is sometimes an impossible task to persuade the member of the public who submitted the unsolicited idea that it was not his or her brainchild that was stolen.

Generally speaking, there is no legal liability for using someone else's idea unless it was submitted and received in confidence or in accordance with a contract that spells out the relationship between the parties. An unsolicited disclosure by itself cannot create a confidential relationship. Also, there is no liability if the idea is an old one, not originated by the person submitting it. Nevertheless, lawsuits claiming idea piracy—most of them unsuccessful—are constantly being brought against manufacturers, broadcasters, advertising agencies, and even universities.

Idea piracy suits are a nuisance and can be extremely expensive. Many large advertisers and advertising agencies have set up standard procedures by which they attempt to protect themselves from receiving unsolicited ideas in the first place or to ensure that they will receive these ideas only after the submitter has signed a written release in advance that will protect the agency and the advertiser from the risk of litigation. It is important for a copywriter to learn just what system his employer follows for dealing with situations of this kind.

The copywriter may also be exposed to friends or acquaintances from outside the profession who are sure they have a "wonderful idea" to submit. When faced with such a situation, the copywriter would be well advised to refuse to listen to the idea and to explain as politely as possible that the employer has a standard policy either not to consider ideas from the outside at all or to consider them only when submitted in writing and accompanied by an appropriate standard form of signed release, whatever the case may be. Considerable difficulty, expense, and eventual hard feelings can be avoided through this precautionary technique.

State Laws on Advertising

Federal laws apply to all national advertising and much regional and local advertising because either the advertising itself or the product crosses state lines, thus involving interstate commerce under control of the federal government.

In addition, almost all of the states have their own individual laws dealing with advertising. Writing copy for strictly local advertising, such as that for a retail store to run in a local newspaper, obviously involves the law of the particular state. But the situation is even more complicated than this, because states have the right to pass judgment on national and regional advertising that affects their local interests, even though the same advertising may be simultaneously subject to federal controls.

In one specific example, a number of states have their own advertising requirements for liquor. Advertising copy that appears in one of these states must comply with the regulations of the Federal Bureau of Alcohol, Tobacco, and Firearms, and also with the requirements of the local authorities.

Most of the states have also enacted laws, based on the model statute recommended by *Printers' Ink,* prohibiting untrue, deceptive, or misleading advertising. There are often criminal statutes that provide for a fine and imprisonment, as distinguished from laws such as the Federal Trade Commission Act, under which the typical penalty is to pay civil damages and to cease and desist. Local authorities seem reluctant to proceed criminally in such cases, but the state statutes also always provide for civil prosecution.

States are even stricter than the federal government in their legal approach to enforcing the lottery laws. Typically, a state also has a collection of other statutes covering specific areas of commerce that deal with advertising. Among the industries regulated in this manner are small loan companies, employment agencies, optometrists and opticians, barbers, hairdressers, and real estate brokers.

In addition, many states have their own Pure Food and Drug Laws, and almost all states prohibit obscene or indecent advertising. Intoxicating beverages are a special case, as already indicated, and the specific law of each state must be checked if liquor advertising is involved. All of these laws are enforced by the State Attorney General, although some are enforced by county or city attorney offices.

Keep an Eye on the Consumer Movement When Writing Copy

Laments are sometimes heard from creative people about the maze of legal regulations that have grown out of the consumerism movement. Fear is expressed that creativity will suffer as copywriters attempt to work within the limitations of the ever increasing rules, guidelines, and prohibitions.

Allen Rosenshine, president of Batten, Barton, Durstine & Osborne, had these words of comfort for creative people:

Maybe the legal restrictions have become so stringent that we just can't do product demonstrations anymore.

Well, I don't believe that.

What I DO believe is that we are tending to shy away from the legal problems rather than trying to meet them head on. If we look long enough and hard enough, we will find something meaningful about the product that is worth saying, and can be said legally.

If we can't, then we have a basis for a client recommendation to the effect that a product improvement is necessary. And even if it isn't the big breakthrough product improvement that will bring competition to its knees, as long as it makes sense conceptually, there is no reason why the creative department can't advertise it dramatically, but within the bounds of legal propriety.

That's exactly the kind of creative imagination that clients have been paying for in the first place.

And even if we can't make open-ended comparisons anymore, even if we CAN'T say a product is "better" without saying "better than what," that is not the end of advertising.

Even if we CAN'T say "our product is the best you can buy," that's not the end of advertising either …

I suggest we spend our time more productively if we work out our own set of guidelines that would enable us to work within the current—or even projected—legal restrictions.[3]

---

[3] Speech delivered to the Eastern Regional Conference of the American Association of Advertising Agencies, June 5, 1972, New York City.

Corrective Advertising

Orders requiring corrective advertising are based on the theory that false and deceptive claims have a residual effect on the consumer; as a result, conventional orders to discontinue the misrepresentations are insufficient to protect the public. In those instances, the FTC requires (and some advertisers have agreed to supply as part of the settlement of FTC complaints against them) ongoing statements that will dissipate the misleading claims.

A typical order requires that 24 percent of advertising expenditures for the product in question must, for a year, be devoted to advertisements, approved in advance by the FTC, stating that previous claims were erroneous or subject to misinterpretation. These corrective advertisements give the true facts; for example, the marketers of "Jogging in a Jug" agreed to pay the FTC $480,000 to settle charges that they made many false health claims, including claims that the drink cured or alleviated heart disease, arthritis, lethargy, dysentery, lowered serum cholesterol, and stabilized blood sugar levels.

This settlement also required the respondents to have competent and reliable scientific evidence to support any future claims regarding the performance, safety, benefits, or efficacy of its products and to use corrective advertising that stated "there is no scientific evidence that Jogging In A Jug provides any health benefits."

A Company's Reputation Can Suffer If Corrective Advertising Is Run

That advertisers view corrective advertising seriously is illustrated by a giant pharmaceutical firm that threatened to stop all its advertising for one of America's best-known remedies if it were required to run corrective advertising. The company declared that compliance would ruin them in the hotly competitive market for this remedy. The reason for this statement becomes clear in light of the court decision, which required that $24,000,000 of future advertisements contain a statement refuting an important and long-made claim for the product.

As a copywriter, you may do your client real harm if *you're* the one directly responsible for such offending claims. Evidence of this is research that shows that the reputation of the affected company is hurt when corrective advertising is run. Attitude scores tend to drop on the variables of honesty and sincerity when corrective advertising appears.

Deceptive advertisements seemingly are perceived as a result of dishonesty and insincerity rather than a mistake due to lack of experience.

One interesting sidelight, however, is that corrective advertising does not seem to reduce the credibility of all advertising in general.

Doctrine of Substantiation

The FTC's advertising substantiation program began with a resolution adopted in 1971. Orders were sent calling for the submission of documents, including test reports and testimonials, to support advertising claims concerning safety, performance, quality, and competitive prices. These orders went to various manufacturers of such products as television sets, air conditioners, pet food, electric razors, toothpaste, and detergents.

Such orders referred to specific product claims for which substantiation had to be furnished; for instance, "Sani Flush kills common household germs in 15 seconds"; "Tabby Canned meets 100% of a cat's daily nutritional needs"; and "Ajax Liquid contains more ammonia than any competing product."

The Doctrine has since become the bedrock of advertising law, and it is the basis of many advertising challenges.

The Federal Trade Commission adopted a "Policy Statement Regarding Advertising Substantiation" in 1984. The Policy Statement articulated the Commission's position that Section 5 of the FTC Act requires that advertisers and ad agencies have a *reasonable basis* for their objective claims *before* their initial dissemination. It reads, in part, as follows:

> First, we reaffirm our commitment to the underlying legal requirements of advertising substantiation—that advertisers and advertising agencies have a reasonable basis for advertising claims before they are disseminated.
>
> The Commission intends to continue vigorous enforcement of this existing legal requirement that advertisers substantiate express and implied claims, however conveyed, that make *objective* assertions about the item or service advertised. Objective claims for products or services represent explicitly or by implication that the advertiser *has* a reasonable basis supporting these claims. These representations of substantiation are material to consumers. That is, consumers would be less likely to rely on claims for products and services if they knew the advertisers did not have a reasonable basis for believing them to be true. Therefore, a firm's failure to possess and rely upon a reasonable basis for objective claims constitutes an *unfair* and *deceptive* act or practice in violation of Section 5 of the Federal Trade Commission Act.

Many ads contain express or implied statements regarding the amount of support the advertiser has for the product claim. When the substantiation claim is *express* (such as "tests prove," "doctors recommend," and "studies show"), the Commission expects an advertiser to have *at least the advertised level* of substantiation. Of course, an advertisement may *imply* more substantiation than it expressly claims or may imply to consumers that an advertiser has a certain type of support; in such cases, it must possess the amount and type of substantiation that the advertisement actually *communicates* to consumers.

Absent an expressed or implied reference to a certain level of support (as is the case here), and absent other evidence indicating what consumer expectations would be, the Commission assumes that consumers expect a *"reasonable basis"* for claims. The Commission's determination of what constitutes a reasonable basis depends, as it does in an unfairness analysis, on a number of factors relevant to the benefits and costs of substantiating a particular claim. These factors include: the *type of claim,* the *product,* the *consequences of a false claim,* the *benefits of a truthful claim,* the *cost of developing substantiation* for the claim, and the amount of substantiation *experts in the field believe is reasonable.*

If a copy claim is based on test results, the test must have been a "competent and reliable" one. "Competent and reliable" means that the test has been conducted and evaluated in an *objective manner,* by *qualified persons,* using *generally accepted procedures* that produce *accurate* and *reliable* results.

Much Legal Help Is Available for a Copywriter

It may very well seem that the task of keeping up with this enormous array of legal requirements is beyond the capacity of any single individual. Fortunately, the basic responsibility ordinarily is not the copywriter's alone. This is true particularly in a large advertising agency, which either will have its own staff of lawyers or will use the services of an outside law firm to check copy for compliance with legal requirements.

It is, nevertheless, of great importance for the copywriter to have at least a minimal familiarity with the kinds of legal problems that do exist. A conscientious copywriter will acquire as much information as possible, not only about the product or service on which he is working, but also about the kinds of legal restrictions that may apply to the particular industry involved.

The fundamental source of information about the product or service, of course, is the advertiser itself. The details may come directly, or more likely indirectly—through the account executive or supervisor in the place of employment. Information about legal requirements can come from the agency's own staff or from the client, but it is important to remember that both the advertiser and its agency can be named as defendants in a claim of deceptive advertising.

In addition, many industries have trade associations that provide quantities of helpful information. Better Business Bureaus are also valuable sources of assistance.

A number of industries have their own self-imposed codes of regulations. As a practical matter, although these do not have the force of law, it is essential that they be followed. Some well-known examples are the codes of The National Association of Broadcasters, The Distilled Spirits Institute, and The Motion Picture Association of America.

Another useful aid to advertisers, and thus to copywriters, is the AAF *Washington Report* that informs the industry of impending legislation. Often, the American Advertising Federation (AAF) files comments opposing new bills restricting advertising. In doing so, the AAF will work with such bodies as the FTC, the FDA, the Congress, and state legislatures in presenting the industry's views. Located as it is in Washington, D.C., the AAF is quickly aware of any proposed regulations of advertising.

Figure 23–8. Legal advertisement stressing importance of talent contracts.

The NARC: Self-Regulation on the National Level

Reasoning that it is better that an industry keep its own house in order than to have the government issuing edicts, advertising people have long, and effectively, advocated self-regulation.

Most conspicuous and effective of the self-regulating bodies is the National Advertising Review Council (NARC). It is composed of representatives of the Association of National Advertisers, American Association of Advertising Agencies, American Advertising Federation, and the Council of Better Business Bureaus.

On the operational level, the National Advertising Division (NAD) of the Council of Better Business Bureaus reviews or initiates complaints about advertisements. Advertisers may then be asked to substantiate their claims. If they cannot, they are asked to drop or modify an offending claim.

Occasionally, the NAD process is unable to settle a case with an advertiser. If so, the matter goes before a five-member panel of the National Advertising Review Board (NARB), which is made up of 10 advertising agency representatives, 30 national advertisers, and 10 persons not connected with advertising.

If, by some chance, the panel's decision were to be ignored, the case would then be sent to a government agency for investigation. To this time, only one advertiser has ignored a panel's decision, and that company was subsequently fined and ordered to engage in corrective advertising by the FTC.

Only a tiny percentage of NAD cases are referred to the NARB. NAD findings are reported regularly in the business press, including the magazine *Advertising Age*. Generous space is given to such news. In some cases, the advertiser's claim is substantiated and thus reported. In other instances, advertisers either discontinue or modify claims. One example of this is a House of Fabrics advertisement for a direct-mail promotion that stressed a reduced price but did not make clear other charges. The company agreed to modify future advertisements with a disclaimer that listed all additional charges. Another example is an Avis television commercial in which listeners were told they could rent a Cadillac for $45 a day. The NAD felt that a qualifying statement included in the commercial changed the meaning, especially for viewers who might have missed the qualifier. Avis disagreed but clarified the modifier in future advertising.

So it goes. In the cases given in the foregoing, and in most of the other NAD cases, there is no dishonesty involved, but simply a lack of clarity or lack of sufficient explanation.

Better Business Bureaus: Self-Regulation on the Local Level

All local Better Business Bureaus have advertising review programs designed to preserve advertising's credibility and to protect consumers by seeking voluntary compliance with legal and ethical standards from local advertisers. Many have systems, called Local Advertising Review programs, modeled after NAD and NARB, that have been approved by the American Advertising Federation and Council of Better Business Bureaus. If a Bureau and advertiser cannot agree on an advertisement's appropriateness, the matter is referred to an advisory panel that acts much like the NARB panels.

Appendix

The Appendix contains helps and suggestions as follows:

- Copyfitting guide
- Type specimen sheet
- Proofreading marks
- Nine checklists, rating systems, and evaluation methods.
- Layout suggestions
- Commonly misspelled or misused words

What you find in this section should be useful on many occasions. It is material for the working copywriter or for the student who is working at learning copywriting. Too often, material in a book appendix is never read. In this case, such neglect would be a pity, since every item in *this* appendix should be useful to you at one time or another.

Copyfitting Guide[1]

Even experienced copywriters can write too much copy for the space. Beginning writers consistently do so. Seldom does anyone write too little copy for the space, but this can happen, too.

There are complicated copyfitting systems requiring mathematics that will help you. Then, there are crude word-count systems in which the total is based on an average number of words per line multiplied by the number of lines.

The first system is too time-consuming for the impatient copywriter, and the second is too inaccurate. On the latter point, for example, "honorificabilituditadibus" is counted as one word. So is the article "a."

Figure A-1 is a page from a type specimen book. In this page, you are given type sizes from tiny 5-point type all the way to 36-point. Body type size usually does not exceed 12 points. For newspaper copy, 10- to 11-point type is desirable, with 11-point type being especially good for easy reading.

If you use this type specimen page as a guide, you must remember that 10- or 11-point type in one face may take more or less room than 10- or 11-point type in another face. Still, if you're careful enough to be guided by the pages reproduced here, your chances of being markedly wrong in your copyfitting for the usual advertisement are remote.

For a quick idea of how much copy you should write, find out the length of lines in your body text. Let's say that the line is four inches long. Assume, too, that you've decided upon 11-point size. Since you discover that 11-point type fits 15 characters to the inch, four inches will take 60 characters. Set your typewriter for 60 characters and then type away.

Naturally, you'll have to determine how many lines deep your copy is to go. Multiply 60 by the determined number of lines to get the total number of characters. Usually, however, all you need to know is the character count per line, and then you simply type the number of lines needed. You normally don't worry about the total number of characters, although sometimes you may be given a specific character count for your copy.

Remember these type specimen pages if you're in doubt about how much copy to write. They can save you much reworking of copy, not to mention the embarrassment of having your copy returned for pruning.

---

[1] These instructions for copyfitting and proofing apply if you are not using a computer for these procedures. See Chapter 5 to see how the use of a computer has changed these instructions.

5 pt.
Printing has performed a role of achievement unparalleled in the revelation of new horizons, and in emphasizing t he potentials of social and cultural development. The invention of printing stands at the peak of man's broad civiliz
PRINTING HAS PERFORMED A ROLE OF ACHIEVEMENT UNPARALLELED IN THE REVELATION OF NEW HORIZONS   1234567890
PRINTING HAS PERFORMED A ROLE OF ACHIEVEMENT UNPARALLELED IN THE REVELATION OF NEW HORIZONS   123
Printing has performed a role of achievement unparalleled in the revelation of new horizons, and in emphasizing in th
PRINTING HAS PERFORMED A ROLE OF ACHIEVEMENT UNPARALLELED IN THE REVELATION OF   123

5½ pt.
Printing has performed a role of achievement unparalleled in the revelation of new horizons, and in emph asizing the potentials of social and cultural development. The invention of printing stands at the peak of m
PRINTING HAS PERFORMED A ROLE OF ACHIEVEMENT UNPARALLELED IN THE REVELATION   1234567890
PRINTING HAS PERFORMED A ROLE OF ACHIEVEMENT UNPARALLELED IN THE REVELATION OF NEW   456
Printing has performed a role of achievement unparalleled in the revelation of new horizons, and in emphas
PRINTING HAS PERFORMED A ROLE OF ACHIEVEMENT UNPARALLELED IN THE REVEL   456

6 pt.
Printing has performed a role of achievement unparalleled in the revelation of new horizons, and in emphasizing the potentials of social and cultural development. The invention of printing stand
PRINTING HAS PERFORMED A ROLE OF ACHIEVEMENT UNPARALLELED IN THE REVEL.
PRINTING HAS PERFORMED A ROLE OF ACHIEVEMENT UNPARALLELED IN THE REVELATION o 1234567890
Printing has performed a role of achievement unparalleled in the revelation of new horizons, and
PRINTING HAS PERFORMED A ROLE OF ACHIEVEMENT UNPARALLELED IN THE R   789

6½ pt.
Printing has performed a role of achievement unparalleled in the revelation of new horizo ns, and in emphasizing the potentials of social and cultural development. The invention of
PRINTING HAS PERFORMED A ROLE OF ACHIEVEMENT UNPARALLELED IN THE
PRINTING HAS PERFORMED A ROLE OF ACHIEVEMENT UNPARALLELED IN THE REV   1234567890
Printing has performed a role of achievement unparalleled in the revelation of new horizon
PRINTING HAS PERFORMED A ROLE OF ACHIEVEMENT UNPARALLELED IN   123

7 pt.
Printing has performed a role of achievement unparalleled in the revelation of new horizons, and in emphasizing the potentials of social and cultural development. Th
PRINTING HAS PERFORMED A ROLE OF ACHIEVEMENT UNPARALLELED IN
PRINTING HAS PERFORMED A ROLE OF ACHIEVEMENT UNPARALLELED IN T   1234567890
Printing has performed a role of achievement unparalleled in the revelation of new
PRINTING HAS PERFORMED A ROLE OF ACHIEVEMENT UNPARALLE   456

7½ pt.
Printing has performed a role of achievement unparalleled in the revelation o f new horizons, and in emphasizing the potentials of social and cultural develo
PRINTING HAS PERFORMED A ROLE OF ACHIEVEMENT UNPARALLE
PRINTING HAS PERFORMED A ROLE OF ACHIEVEMENT UNPARALLE   1234567890
Printing has performed a role of achievement unparalleled in the revelation of
PRINTING HAS PERFORMED A ROLE OF ACHIEVEMENT UNPARA   789

8 pt.
Printing has performed a role of achievement unparalleled in the revelat ion of new horizons, and in emphasizing the potentials of social and cultural development. The invention of printing stands at the peak of m
PRINTING HAS PERFORMED A ROLE OF ACHIEVEMENT UNPARAL
PRINTING HAS PERFORMED A ROLE OF ACHIEVEMENT UNPARALLE   1234567890
Printing has performed a role of achievement unparalleled in the revelatio
PRINTING HAS PERFORMED A ROLE OF ACHIEVEMENT UNP   123

8½ pt.
Printing has performed a role of achievement unparalleled in the re
PRINTING HAS PERFORMED A ROLE OF ACHIEVEMENT UNPA   1234567890
PRINTING HAS PERFORMED A ROLE OF ACHIEVEMENT UNPA
Printing has performed a role of achievement unparalleled in the rev
PRINTING HAS PERFORMED A ROLE OF ACHIEVEMENT U   456

9 pt.
Printing has performed a role of achievement unparalleled in th
PRINTING HAS PERFORMED A ROLE OF ACHIEVEMENT U   1234567890
PRINTING HAS PERFORMED A ROLE OF ACHIEVEMENT U
Printing has performed a role of achievement unparalleled in the
PRINTING HAS PERFORMED A ROLE OF ACHIEVEME   789

10 pt.
Printing has performed a role of achievement unparalleled
PRINTING HAS PERFORMED A ROLE OF ACHIEVEME   1234567890
PRINTING HAS PERFORMED A ROLE OF ACHIEVEM
Printing has performed a role of achievement unparaleled
PRINTING HAS PERFORMED A ROLE OF ACHIE   123

11 pt.
Printing has performed a role of achievement unpara
PRINTING HAS PERFORMED A ROLE OF ACHIEV   1234567890
PRINTING HAS PERFORMED A ROLE OF AC
Printing has performed a role of achievement unparal
PRINTING HAS PERFORMED A ROLE OF AC   456

12 pt.
Printing has performed a role of achievement un
PRINTING HAS PERFORMED A ROLE OF AC   1234567890
PRINTING HAS PERFORMED A ROLE OF
Printing has performed a role of achievement unp
PRINTING HAS PERFORMED A ROLE OF   789

14 pt.
Printing has performed a role of achieve
PRINTING HAS PERFORMED A ROLE   1234567890
PRINTING HAS PERFORMED A RO
Printing has performed a role of achievem
PRINTING HAS PERFORMED A RO   123

Characters per pica: 5 pt—4.5; 5½ pt—4.1; 6 pt—3.8; 6½ pt—3.5; 7 pt—3.2; 7½ pt—3.0; 8 pt—2.8; 8½ pt—2.7; 9 pt—2.5; 10 pt—2.3; 11 pt—2.1; 12 pt—1.9; 14 pt—1.6; 16 pt—1.4

Figure A–1. Type specimen sheet. *Courtesy of Rochester Monotype Composition Co.*

Figure A–2. Proofreaders' marks. *Courtesy of University of Chicago Press, The Chicago Manual of Style, 13th edition (1982).*

Proofreading

You'll be asked to proof your own work and, sometimes, that of others. Likewise, someone may be proofing yours. When you use the standard proofreading symbols and methods, you're using a common language of the writer, editor, and printer.

Figure A-2 is a simple listing of proofreading marks. For most copywriters, this listing is sufficient.

An incidental piece of information that might be useful to you is that there is no proofreading symbol for the underline. When you underline a word, a printer automatically will set it in italics. To make sure that he understands that you want an underline, put a line under the word or phrase and then on the side of the sheet use these words: "Printer: Underscore, not italics."

Checklists, Rating Systems, and Evaluation Methods

In the chapter on advertising research, you read about checklists. For most copywriters, a checklist is merely a simple list of product points. For instance, if you were writing about a flashlight, you might list:

- Floats
- Casts beam one-half mile
- Waterproof
- Shatterproof plastic
- Three long-life batteries
- Lightweight
- Can be focused
- One-year guarantee

For the conscientious copywriter ever anxious to improve performance, there are many other useful methods. Many copywriters pay little attention to these. This is unfortunate, because much is to be gained by using these suggestions either before, or after, writing copy.

Ad scoring systems

Some years ago, David Ogilvy, noted advertising man and author, offered the following scoring system for rating the mechanical or physical aspects of an advertisement. His suggestions are still valid today.

To use this system, assume that the advertisement begins with a score of 100. Then, deduct points according to whatever transgression has been committed. It is doubtful that any advertisement will obtain 100 points when you rate it in this manner. The scoring system has much merit, however, in making the copywriter and artist aware of some important principles.

On the content side, Mr. Ogilvy decries (1) any advertisement that is obviously dishonest, (2) an advertisement that would obviously be considered indecent or blasphemous by more than five percent of the readers of the publication in which it appears; and (3) any advertisement that is an obvious imitation of another advertiser's advertisement.

Layout and Printing Factors	Points Deducted
1. Graphic technique obtrudes itself between the copywriter and the reader.	17
2. Illustration is lazy—it does not work hard at selling the product.	11
3. It requires more than a split second for the reader to identify the kind of product being advertised.	10
4. Brand name is not visible at a glance.	9
5. Layout looks more like an advertisement than an editorial page.	7
6. Illustration lacks "story appeal," something interesting happening.	6
7. A drawing is used instead of a photograph.	6
8. Layout is cluttered or complicated.	5
9. There is more than one place to begin reading.	4

10.	Type is used self-consciously for purpose of design.	4
11.	Body copy is set in reverse or in a tint.	4
12.	Any illustration appears without a caption.	3
13.	Illustration is defaced in any way; for example, by having the headline run into it.	2
14.	Illustration is any shape other than rectangular.	2
15.	Headline is set in more than one typeface.	2
16.	Body copy is set in a sans serif face.	2
17.	Measure is wider than 40 characters.	2
18.	Long copy is not broken with crossheads.	2
19.	First paragraph is more than 12 words.	1
20.	Paragraphs are squared up.	1

Two-part copywriting system

You will find the following suggestions in two parts. In the first part, you'll find major considerations to think about in your advertisement. The majority of this material applies to newspaper or magazine advertisements, but the suggestion about including telephone numbers and hours in item 5 would apply specifically to newspaper advertisements.

In the second part, the scoring sheet enables you to determine how well the six major considerations have been applied.

Warning: Don't apply this too literally to all advertisements. In fact, you can't apply it to all advertisements. For example, there are splendid corporate, or institutional, advertisements that would rate poorly if judged by this system. There are image-building advertisements that would also fare badly. In short, before you use this copywriting system, be sure that your subject matter, technique, or objective is suitable.

1. **Theme.** Can the sales message in the ad be stated in a simple declarative sentence?
2. **Headline.** A good headline includes the company name and a reader benefit. It should also be selective so the reader knows that the ad is directed at him or her. And, of course, the headline should be simple enough to be clearly understood.
3. **Illustration.** The illustration should attract readers and help tell the story or reinforce the main sales point of the ad. If possible, it should show the product in use.
4. **Text or body copy.** The text should follow the headline, amplifying user benefits and explaining and offering proof that the product or service being advertised is a good one. And the text should end with an action

close. It should tell the reader what to do next and it should make it easy for him or her to do it.
5. **Signature.** The ad should end with a clear and visible presentation of the company name. Address (complete with zip code), phone number, and hours open for business should be included.
6. **Ad layout.** The ad layout is nothing more than the arrangement of items two, three, four, and five. It should be planned to draw readers into the ad, guide them through it, and visually present the image the advertiser wants to present.

Communications checkpoints

One major corporation established the following "communications checkpoints" criteria for its review-rating program. The objective was to determine whether an advertisement was above average, below average, or average in qualitative terms. Many company advertising departments establish such guidelines to judge their own output and that of their advertising agencies.

1. Does the advertisement offer a reward for the reader's time and attention? A benefit to the user? News? Service? Does it entertain or amuse?
2. Does the advertisement avoid the necessity for mental work by the reader? Is the headline specific, clear, and direct? Does the illustration work hard to support the sales message? Is the layout simple and orderly, avoiding clutter?
3. Does it provide validation and support for the sales claim? By demonstrations? By tests? By case history or testimonial? By guarantee?
4. Does it exploit the principle of repetition? Is the story told in the headline? Again in the illustration? Again in the copy?
5. Does the treatment avoid the stereotype? Is it arresting? Fresh?
6. Is the total effect modern and advanced?

Essentials of good advertising

In Figure A-3 you will find material aimed specifically at the copywriter who is creating newspaper advertising, especially advertising for retail stores. The basic ideas and the copy came from the Bureau of Advertising of the American Newspaper Publishers Association. The material had been published in the Bureau's *Annual Retail Advertising Plan Book*. It was also used as a mailer sent out by one newspaper to help local merchants and others prepare better advertisements. It is reproduced as it appeared in an International Newspaper Promotion Association Copy Service Newsletter, edited by James B. McGrew, of the Lancaster Newspapers, Inc., Lancaster, Pennsylvania.

Ad evaluation checklist

In Figure A-4, you will find an elaborate advertising evaluation checklist that can be used: (1) to check your own

Dear Advertiser,

The increasing complexity of retailing — such as the rapid growth and diversity of competition, changing customer shopping habits and the continuing squeeze on profits — has made it vitally important that merchants get full value from their advertising dollars.

The newspaper ad is the retailer's best store window and salesman. Nearly everyone reads a daily newspaper, and readers shop the newspaper for good values. Yet, the effectiveness of advertising varies widely. In terms of readership and sales results, some ads are far more successful than others.

The most important single factor determining how many people will read any newspaper ad is the skill and technique used in preparing the ad.

The following suggestions for copy and layout are drawn from several studies. When effectively used, these techniques and rules generally increase readership

LANCASTER NEWSPAPERS, INC.
8 W. King St., Lancaster, Penna. 17604

essentials of a good ad

1 make your ads easily recognizable

Advertisements which are distinctive in their use of art, layout techniques and type faces usually enjoy higher readership than run-of-the-mill advertising. Make your ads distinctively different in appearance from the advertising of your competitors. Then keep your ads appearance consistent. This way, readers will recognize your ads even before they read them.

2 use a simple layout

The layout should carry the reader's eye through the message easily and in proper sequence from headline to illustration to explanatory copy to price to your store's name. Avoid the use of too many different type faces, overly decorative borders and reverses. These devices are distracting and reduce the number of readers who receive your entire message

3 use a dominant element

— a large picture or headline — to insure quick visibility. Photographs and realistic drawings have about equal attention-getting value, but photographs of real people win more readership So do action pictures Photographs of local people or places also have high attention value. Use good art work. It will pay off in extra readership

4 use a prominent benefit headline

The first question a reader asks of an ad is "What's in it for me?" Select the main benefit which your merchandise offers and feature it in a compelling message "How to" headlines encourage full copy readership, as do headlines which include specific information or helpful suggestions. Your headline will be easier to read if it is printed over part of an illustration.

5 let your white space work for you

Don't overcrowd your ad. White space is an important layout element in newspaper advertising. White space focuses the reader's attention on your ad and will make your headline and illustration stand out. When a "crowded" ad is necessary, such as for a sale, departmentalize your items so that the reader can find his way through them easily

6 make your copy complete

Sizes and colors available are important, pertinent information. Your copy should be enthusiastic, sincere. A block of copy written in complete sentences is easier to read than one composed of phrases and random words. In designing the layout of a copy block, use a boldface lead-in. Small pictures in sequence will often help readership Don't be too clever, or use unusual or difficult words.

7 state price or range of prices

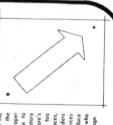

Don't be afraid to quote your price. Readers often overestimate omitted prices. If the advertised price is high, explain why the item represents a good value — perhaps because of superior materials or workmanship, or extra features. If the price is low, support it with factual statements which create belief, such as information on your close-out sale, special purchase or clearance.

8 specify branded merchandise

If the item is a known brand, say so in your advertising Manufacturers spend large sums to sell their goods, and you can capitalize on their advertising while enhancing the reputation of your store by featuring branded items. Using the brand name may also qualify the ad for co-operative advertising allowances from the manufacturer.

9 include related items

Make two sales instead of one by offering related items along with a featured one. For instance, when a dishwasher is advertised, also show a disposal, or if you're advertising a dress or suit you can increase potential sales by also including shoes, hats or handbag in the same ad.

10 urge your readers to buy now

Ask for the sale. You can stimulate prompt action by using such phrases as "limited supply" or "this week only." If mail-order coupons are included in your ads, provide spaces large enough for customers to fill them in easily. Don't generalize, be specific at all times.

Figure A–3. The ten essentials of good advertising.

Headline

Overall, is the headline:	10-8 Strong	7-5 Average	4-0 Weak	POINTS
	____	____	____	____
1. Does the headline relate to the product?	Closely	Fairly	Poorly	
	____	____	____	____
	_____			
	_____			
	_____			
2. Does the headline contain a benefit?	Strong	Fair	Weak	
	____	____	____	____
	_____			
	_____			
	_____			
3. Is head lively and full of action?	Lively	Fairly lively	Static	
	____	____	____	____
	_____			
	_____			
	_____			
4. Is headline tied in well with opening copy?	Very	Slightly	Not at all	
	____	____	____	____
	_____			
	_____			
	_____			

Figure A–4. Advertising evaluation checklist.

5. Is headline tied in well with illustration?

Very	Slightly	Not at all all	
____	____	____	____

_____

_____

_____

6. Is headline aimed directly at prospect-reader of publication?

Very directly	Fairly well	Not at all	
____	____	____	____

_____

_____

_____

Miscellaneous Comments

_____

_____

_____

Body Copy

Overall, is the body copy strong, average, weak?

10-8 Strong	7-5 Average	4-0 Weak	
____	____	____	____

_____

_____

1. Is copy well organized in progressing logically from beginning to end?

Very well organized	Fairly well organized	Poorly organized	
____	____	____	____

_____

_____

_____

2. Does copy start out fast and interestingly?

Very well	Fairly well	Starts slow, uninteresting
———	———	———

———————————————————————————————

———————————————————————————————

———————————————————————————————

3. Copy identifies company and/or product?

Strongly	Fairly well	Not at all
———	———	———

———————————————————————————————

———————————————————————————————

———————————————————————————————

4. Copy stresses main benefit?

Strongly	Moderately	Poorly
———	———	———

———————————————————————————————

———————————————————————————————

———————————————————————————————

5. Copy stresses subsidiary benefits?

Strongly	Fairly well	Poorly
———	———	———

———————————————————————————————

———————————————————————————————

———————————————————————————————

6. Copy written in language of prospect-reader?

Very much so	Fairly well	Not at all
———	———	———

———————————————————————————————

———————————————————————————————

———————————————————————————————

7. Can copy be called helpful?　　　　Very　　　Fairly　　　Not
　　　　　　　　　　　　　　　　　　helpful　　helpful　　helpful

　　　　　　　　　　　　　　　　　 ——　　　——　　　——　　　　　　——

_____

_____

_____

8. Are copy claims believable?　　　Quite　　　Fairly　　　Not
　　　　　　　　　　　　　　　　　believable　believable　believable

　　　　　　　　　　　　　　　　　 ——　　　——　　　——　　　　　　——

_____

_____

_____

9. Copy ending urge to action or some　Strong　　Average　　Weak
　　other positive manner?

　　　　　　　　　　　　　　　　　 ——　　　——　　　——　　　　　　——

_____

_____

_____

Miscellaneous Comments

_____

_____

_____

_____

Layout, Illustration, Typography

	10-8 Very	7-5 Fairly so	4-0 Not at all

Overall, is the total physical effect of the
ad effective in achieving sales objectives,
campaign objectives, or other objectives?

　　　　　　　　　　　　　　　　　 ——　　　——　　　——　　　　　　——

_____

_____

_____

1. Is headline strong enough physically
   to achieve impact?

   Strong impact   Fair impact   Little impact

   _____   _____   _____   _____

   _____

   _____

   _____

2. Is main illustration strong enough
   physically to achieve impact?

   Strong impact   Fair impact   Little impact

   _____   _____   _____   _____

   _____

   _____

   _____

3. Is main illustration interesting to
   prospect-reader?

   Very interesting   Fairly interesting   Not interesting

   _____   _____   _____   _____

   _____

   _____

   _____

4. Is copy typographically easy to read?

   Very easy   Fairly easy   Hard to read

   _____   _____   _____   _____

   _____

   _____

   _____

5. Is size of ad space suitable to accomplish
   ad objectives?

   Very suitable   Fairly suitable   Not suitable

   _____   _____   _____   _____

   _____

   _____

   _____

6. Is layout technique (drawing or photo) suitable for purposes of ad?

Very suitable	Fairly suitable	Not suitable	
———	———	———	———

_____

_____

_____

7. Does logo stand out?

Very well	Fairly well	Poorly	
———	———	———	———

_____

_____

_____

8. Does layout "track" well in leading the reader logically through the ad?

Very well	Fairly well	Poorly	
———	———	———	———

_____

_____

_____

Miscellaneous Comments

_____

_____

work; and (2) to check the work of others and thus provide a valuable critique. Used in this way, it eliminates the infuriatingly vague type of comment expressed in the words "I don't like it, but I can't tell you exactly why."

Thus, this checklist can be used by the copywriter or by the copy chief. It is not, as you can see, a casual, once-over-lightly evaluation, because it embraces headlines, body copy, layout, illustration, and typography.

The person using this evaluation system on a regular basis might wish to work out a point scoring system and evolve a total for the "perfect" advertisement. Thus, advertisements could be judged in terms of how far or how close they are to a perfect rating.

Copywriting marketing code

Figure A–5 provides a detailed code useful for the teacher grading classroom copy assignments. By using the code designations, the teacher can eliminate writing the same criticisms over and over again. As any teacher knows, a classroom of students will make the same mistakes. Just about every mistake that can be made in the layout, copy, headlines, and grammar is reflected in the code.

VALS

For many years, copywriters have thought in terms of *demographics* when writing copy. As you read in Chapter 3, it is valuable for writers to know such demographics as

Values and Lifestyles Systems (VALS)

Groups and types	Approximate % of population	Lifestyle	Buying style
Need-driven			
1. Survivors	4	Struggling for survival. Distrustful.	Price dominant. Focused on basics.
2. Sustainers	7	Hopeful for improvement over time. Concerned with security.	Price important. Want warranty.
Outer-directed			
3. Belongers	35	Preservers of status quo. Seek to be part of group.	Do not want to try something new. Heritage brand buyers.
4. Emulators	10	Upwardly mobile. Emulate rich and successful.	Conspicuous consumption. Sacrifice comfort and utility for show.
5. Achievers	23	Materialistic, comfort-loving. Oriented to fame and success.	Luxury and gift items. Like "new and improved" products but not radically changed products.
Inner-directed			
6. I-Am-Me	5	Transition between outer- and inner-directed. Very individualistic.	Impulsive. Trendy products.
7. Experiential	7	Seek direct experience. Intense personal relationships.	Process over product. Interested in what product does for them, not what it says about them.
8. Societally conscious	9	Simple, natural living. Socially responsible.	Discriminating. Want true value and environmentally sound products.
Integrated	2	Meld outer-directedness with inner-directedness. Mature, tolerant, assured, self-actualizing, often have world perspective.	Little importance to marketers from numerical standpoint but heavily represented in corporate and national leadership.

Layout and typography

L-1 sloppy lettering
L-2 poor balance
L-3 coupon badly designed (crowded, too little room to write, no sell)
L-4 headline and/or logo too small to get attention
L-5 headline is jammed against top
L-6 illustration idea dull or not appropriate
L-7 too empty looking
L-8 just generally amateurish
L-9 use some small illustrations to liven up your ad or to better explain the product
L-10 your layout has no focal point
L-11 your illustration is too small
L-12 your layout is sloppy
L-13 copy lines are set in too wide a measure
L-14 copy blocks are too small
L-15 layout (or certain sections of it) looks crowded
L-16 too much solid, unbroken type
L-17 too much material run together; don't obscure points by running them together. List for easy reading.
L-18 layout cut up into too many elements

Copy

C-1 poor writing
C-2 skimpy copy treatment
C-3 illogical writing; doesn't fit in well, or doesn't make sense
C-4 writing is confusing
C-5 take too long to get started
C-6 writing is awkward
C-7 trite, worn-out, or cliche-ridden language
C-8 too fancy or literary for audience
C-9 needlessly negative
C-10 language is artificial, unnatural, or stilted—or all three
C-11 you don't make clear just what you're selling
C-12 your writing is too impersonal
C-13 you don't get excited enough
C-14 don't jam too many ideas in one sentence or paragraph
C-15 dull, lifeless slogan
C-16 poor product name
C-17 you don't stress the U.S.P. or point of difference
C-18 copy isn't geared well to the medium you're using
C-19 you fail to stress the most important point
C-20 too sweeping a claim
C-21 statement is misleading
C-22 unbelievable
C-23 exaggerated

Technical and Grammatical Faults

C-24 unsupported comparative
C-25 grammar is incorrect
C-26 antecedent is not clear
C-27 bad punctuation
C-28 use paragraphs
C-29 your writing lacks transition
C-30 use active tense
C-31 avoid this backward "newspaperese"
C-32 write complete sentences
C-33 I'd prefer more cohesive writing rather than a mere listing of points a la catalog copy
C-34 wrong spelling

Headlines

C-35 weak headline~doesn't interest or doesn't sell
C-36 head (or copy) lacks benefit or direct personal appeal to reader
C-37 not a good tie-in of headline and opening body copy
C-38 you should use some subheads
C-39 headline isn't specific enough
C-40 headline doesn't involve the reader

General Faults

C-41 you fail to use basic principles (in writing, merchandising techniques, in physical form, copy style, etc.)
C-42 wrong form
C-43 too much copy for space (or paragraph, or point being made)
C-44 too much "we" or company viewpoint
C-45 company's promotional backing not sold hard enough, or specifically enough
C-46 you're emphasizing the weaker appeal
C-47 not enough difference between your various ads
C-48 need more product details
C-49 need fewer product details
C-50 should use product name here
C-51 weak ending
C-52 doesn't end with urge to act.

Figure A–5. Code for evaluating copy and layouts submitted by students. If each student is given the code, the instructor can simply put down the numbers, thus saving much writing of comments.

age, sex, income, and education in order to direct their messages intelligently.

Later, *psychographics* offered another useful tool, with the emphasis centering on lifestyle and personality traits. A number of groupings were involved (see Chapter 3) that enabled copywriters to focus their copy on people they could visualize through psychographic descriptions.

Still later, VALS, a product of the Stanford Research Institute was developed. VALS, while reminiscent of psychographics, makes some departures that have caused it to be widely used by advertisers and their agencies. In the following, you will find a skeleton of the system. This merely shows the groupings under VALS and the buying style of each.

Client fact sheets

Most advertising agencies have worked up client fact sheets that are filled out by the account executives to serve as a guide to copywriters assigned to the account. Usually, the account executive will obtain the information in consultation with the client.

Such guides can be very elaborate. The following example (Figure A-6) is relatively simple but nonetheless useful to the copywriter.

Copy Strategy

In Chapter 3, you read a brief discussion of copy platforms and copy strategy. The following is a much fuller discussion used by a marketing consultant with years of experience in marketing and advertising with leading advertising agencies and corporations.[2]

This, as you can see, is no mere checklist. It is a searching analysis of the reasoning and procedures involved in creative planning.

What Is a Copy Strategy?

- A copy strategy is a document that identifies the basis upon which you expect consumers to purchase your brand in preference to competition.
- It is that portion of the marketing strategy that deals with advertising copy. The fundamental content of a copy strategy emerges directly from the product and the basic consumer need that the product was designed to fulfill.
- A copy strategy should state clearly the basic benefit that the brand promises and that constitutes the principal basis for purchase.
- Although not mandatory, the strategy may also include:

  —A statement of the production characteristic that makes this basic benefit possible.
  —A statement of the character you want to build for the brand over time.

Characteristics of a Good Copy Strategy

Here are some of the things that characterize a good strategy statement:

- It's clear. The basis upon which the consumer is being asked to buy your brand in preference to others should be quite clear to everyone involved.
- It's simple. Key here is that the number of ideas in the strategy be kept to a minimum.
- It's devoid of executional considerations. The copy strategy identifies *what* benefits you are presenting to consumers, avoiding executional issues that deal with *how* these benefits are to be presented.
- It's inherently competitive. The copy strategy should provide the answer to the question, "Why should I buy this product rather than some other?"

Purpose of a Copy Strategy

- The copy strategy provides basic continuity for a brand's advertising. The copy strategy should be considered a long-term document, not subject to judgment changes.
- The copy strategy provides guidance and direction for the creative people. It prescribes the limits within which they can exercise their creative imagination, while being sufficiently flexible to allow latitude for fresh and varied executions.

Creative Fact Sheet for Advertising Development

1. What major problem does the consumer have that the product/service can solve? Or, what major opportunity exists?
2. Advertising objectives? (Measured in changes in awareness, preference, conviction, etc.)
3. Creative Strategy/Considerations?
   A. Define our target demographic (age, income, etc.).
   B. Is there a current customer profile that differs from A? If so, explain.
   C. Who are the principal competitors?
   D. Explain the product or service:
   1. What is it?
2. What will it do for the consumer? (Primary & secondary benefits)
3. How does it differ clearly from others?
   E. Now, give the reason why you can offer the consumer benefit stated in (D-2) by adding "because" to the statement. If evidence or research supports this claim, please note.
   F. Explain (or attach samples of) efforts made by competitors for a similar product/service. What executions by the competition do you feel are worth considering?
4. Mandatories & Policy Limitations (federal, regional, etc.).
5. In one sentence, what message are we trying to make to the consumer? (What should their perception be?)
6. Additional comments/ information.

Figure A–6. Sample client fact sheet.

---

[2] Supplied by Larry Atseff, Alert Marketing, and Ogilvy & Mather Sales Promotion Services.

- The copy strategy provides the client and agency a common basis upon which to evaluate and discuss the merits of an advertising submission in terms of intent and idea content.
- A clear copy strategy can save a great deal of creative time and energy because it identifies those basic copy decisions that you do not intend to review and rethink each time you look at a new piece of advertising.

Questions to Ask When Evaluating a Copy Strategy

A copy strategy is a basic document designed to provide direction for a brand's advertising over a long period of time. It is the translation of the marketing strategy into the area of copy. Because a copy strategy identifies those aspects of a brand's copy that are not subject to judgment changes, it should be developed with great care.

The precise intent of a copy strategy should be clear to everyone who reads it. This requires *focus*—the simplest possible statement of why you expect the consumer, long-term, to select your brand in preference to competition. A properly focused copy strategy means precisely the same thing to everyone who must work with it.

To evaluate the focus in your strategy, first conduct a realistic inventory of the benefit ideas to be found within it (or that you believe to be necessary to your sale). Then, ask yourself these questions:

1. *Are you prepared to accept the commitment to execute each benefit in every advertisement?* If your strategy contains more than one major benefit idea, is a *prioritization* indicated by the strategy?
2. *Examine each element in your strategy to make absolutely certain that it is truly strategic rather than executional in nature.* Does each idea in your strategy represent the "what" you are selling rather than the "how" you will make that sale?
3. *If you have a strategic "reason-why" is it stated simply and precisely?* If you don't have a reason-why, don't invent one.
4. *Can you define a character for your brand that will provide long-term strategic direction for your advertising?* If you can't, don't invent one. If you can, state it simply and clearly. Avoid generalities and platitudes.
5. *Does the tone/mood reflect the brand character you are trying to create?*
6. *Is your strategy expressed as simply and succinctly as possible?* Do you really mean precisely what the words in your strategy say? Are there any excess words that could be omitted without changing the meaning of your strategy?
7. *In net, will it be instantly apparent to everyone who must work with your strategy precisely why the consumer is being asked to purchase your brand rather than any competitor's?* This is the *focus* of your strategy.

Suggestions—Major and Minor—for Preparing a Layout[3]

No artist or professional copywriter will need these instructions. They are supplied here for beginning copywriters who prepare rough layouts. They are reminders of fundamentals.

1. Layout must be in actual size in which it will appear in the publication. Thus, if you are asked to do a 2-column by 10-inch ad for a newspaper, you will make a layout that is in that size. If you're asked to do a 1/3-page ad for a magazine, make the layout the size shown for 1/3-page in the magazine.
2. If your layout is less than a page, you may want to put a border around it.
3. For all parts of a layout, use a heavy, black pencil, or india ink with a speedball pen. This includes all lettering, your illustration, the lines you rule for your copy blocks, and your border.
4. In all retail ads, include price of product or service as a layout element.
5. *All* of the following must appear on your layout: headlines, subheads, overlines, price figures (in retail ads *always,* and in national ads when suggested), logotypes, and slogans (if any).
6. Headlines, price figures, logo, and illustrations should be big enough to be competitive with other ads and/or to stand out on the page.
7. If you use guidelines for your lettering, rule the guidelines lightly in pencil and then erase them when you've finished the lettering.
8. When lettering, don't try to letter in a type style such as bodoni, cheltenham, etc. Don't do script lettering, and don't letter in handwriting. Print in block letters.
9. For heads, capitalize the first letter of the first word. Other words should be lowercase. But product name can be all caps.
10. Everything on the layout should be in the size you want it to be in the published ad.
11. When you use subheads, and thus have separate copy blocks, mark the copy blocks neatly. Use a small, encircled letter: Ⓐ Ⓑ Ⓒ. Put the letter in the middle of the copy block.
12. Avoid the use of several small copy blocks. These chop up the ad too much. The ideal length of a line is 21 picas (3-1/2 inches).
13. Don't box copy by running a line down each side of your lines.
14. When you rule your lines for copy blocks, remember that the copy must fit within the space occupied by the lines. Also, remember that the number of lines you

---

[3] These suggestions can be used in their entirety by anyone preparing a layout without a computer. For those using a computer, eliminate points 3, 7, 8, 11, and 14.

draw for the copy block may differ widely from the number of printed lines that appear in the finished ad.

15. Avoid running copy to the edge of the layout. Leave room on the side.

16. There should be a dominant element somewhere in the layout. Usually, this will be the illustration. Sometimes, it might be a very big, bold headline.

Spelling

Poor spelling is a national disgrace. If, by the time you reach the point where you are writing copy, you are a poor speller, there is probably not much chance that you will improve suddenly. The following collection of commonly misspelled or misused words (Figure A–7) might help you avoid mistakes that will embarrass you and your employers. If you consult the list regularly, you may be surprised at your improvement.

able—capable
accommodate
accept—except
achievement
acquire
affect—effect
all ready—already
all right
all together—altogether
allusion—delusion—illusion
among
amount—number
anxious—eager
apparent
apt—liable—likely
arguing—argument
aware—conscious
balance—remainder
beginning
belief—believe
between—among
bring—take
business
can—may
category
choose—chosen
coming
clothes—cloths
complement—compliment
comparative
conscience—conscientious
continual—continuous
controversial—controversy
council—counsel
criticism—criticize
define—definitely—definition
describe—description
disastrous
each other—one another
embarrass
environment
existence
experience

explanation
familiar
farther—further
fascinate
fewer—less
formally—formerly
grammar
guarantee
hear—here
height
imaginary
immediately
imply—infer
Indian
interest—interesting
irrelevant
its—it's[4]
lay—lie
learn—teach
led
lend—loan
loath—loathe
loneliness
loose—lose—losing
majority—plurality
marriage
may—might
mere
moral—morale
necessary
noticeable
occasion
occurred—occurring—occurrence
opinion
opportunity
paid
particular
party—person
performance
personal—personnel
possession
possible
practical—practicable
precede—procedure—proceed

prejudice
probably
professor
profession
prominent
proved—proven
pursue
quit—quiet—quite
raise—rise
receive—receiving
recommend
referred—referring
relevant
repetition
respectfully—respectively
rhythm
sense—sensitive—sensitivity
separate—separation
shall—will
shining
should—would
similar
sit—set
studying
succeed—succession
surprise
technique
than—then
their—there—they're
thorough
to—too—two
transferred
prepare
prevalent
principal—principle
privilege
unnecessary
villain
whether
will—shall
women
writing—written
your—you're

Figure A–7. frequently misspelled or misused words.

[4] In the classroom, these are the two most commonly misspelled words.

Index

About The Author

Philip Ward Burton is the author of over 150 books and articles on the subject of advertising. A distinguished educator, he is professor of Journalism at Indiana University and former Chairman of the Advertising Department at Syracuse University.

Before pursuing a teaching career, Mr. Burton worked as a creative director, a copy chief, a copywriter, and a market and research director for a number of advertising agencies. He has also done consulting for General Electric, National Cash Register, and International Paper Products, among others.

Between semesters at Indiana University, Professor Burton continues to write on advertising-related subjects. An eighth edition of his Which Ad Pulls Best? (along with co-author Scott Purvis) was published by NTC in the spring of 1996.